The Economics of Change in East and Central Europe

The Economics of Change in East and Central Europe

Its impact on International Business

Edited by

Peter J. Buckley
Professor of Managerial Economics,
University of Bradford, UK

Pervez N. Ghauri
Professor of Marketing,
University of Groningen, The Netherlands

ACADEMIC PRESS
Harcourt Brace & Company, Publishers
London   San Diego   New York   Boston
Sydney   Tokyo   Toronto

This book is printed on acid-free paper

ACADEMIC PRESS LIMITED
24–28 Oval Road
LONDON NW1 7DX

United States Edition published by
ACADEMIC PRESS INC.
San Diego, CA 92101

A catalogue record for this book is available from the British Library

ISBN 0–12–139165–5

Typeset by Fakenham Photosetting Limited, Fakenham, Norfolk
Printed and bound in Great Britain by
Hartnolls Ltd, Bodmin, Cornwall

Contents

Contributors

GABRIEL BENITO, *Ostfold Distrikt Hogskola, O.S. Allé 9, 1750 Holden, Norway*

PETER J. BUCKLEY, *Management Centre, University of Bradford, Bradford, West Yorkshire, UK*

GUILLERMO A. CALVO, *Research Department, IMF, Washington DC, USA*

WILLEM B. CARIS, *University of Limburg, 6200 MD Maastricht, The Netherlands*

MARK CASSON, *Department of Economics, University of Reading, Whiteknights, Reading RG6 2AA, UK*

REFIK CULPAN, *Pennstate University, School of Business Administration, 777 W. Harrisburg Pike, Middletown, Pennsylvania, USA*

JOHN H. DUNNING, *Department of Economics, University of Reading, Whiteknights, Reading RG6 2AA, UK*

JACOB A. FRENKEL, *Research Department, IMF, Washington DC, USA*

PERVEZ N. GHAURI, *Department of Marketing, Faculty of Management, University of Groningen, The Netherlands*

ANNE-GRETHE HENRIKSEN, *The Norwegian School of Management, Sandvika, Norway*

JOHN HIDEN, *Department of European Studies, University of Bradford, Bradford, West Yorkshire, UK*

NEIL HOOD, *Department of Marketing, Strathclyde Business School, University of Strathclyde, Glasgow, Scotland*

SUBHASH C. JAIN, *The University of Connecticut, School of Business Administration, Marketing Department, 368 Fairfield Road, Storrs, Connecticut, USA*

MARTIN JOHANSON, *Swedish Consulate General, 10th Line, dom 11 v.o., 199 178 St Petersburg, Russia and Department for Business Studies at Uppsala University, Sweden*

B. NINO KUMAR, *University of Hamburg, Fachbereich Wow, Holsetenhofweg 85, D-2000 Hamburg 10, Germany*

THOMAS LANE, *Department of European Studies, University of Bradford, Bradford, West Yorkshire, UK*

KRISTIAN MÖLLER, *Helsinki School of Economics, Runeberginkato 14-16, 00100 Helsinki, Finland*

ERIC MONAMI, *Université Libre de Bruxelles, CP 145, Avenue F. D. Roosevelt 19, B-1050 Brussels, Belgium*

CHARLES DE MORTANGES, *University of Limburg, P.O. Box 616, 6200 MD Maastricht, The Netherlands*

JACOB NAOR, *University of Maine at Orono, School of Business Administration, South Stevens Hall, Orono, Maine, USA*

BILL NEALE, *University of Bradford, Management Centre, Bradford, West Yorkshire, UK*

TERUTOMO OZAWA, *Professor of Economics, Colorado State University, Department of Economics, Fort Collins, Colorado 80523, USA*

C. L. PASS, *Management Centre, University of Bradford, Bradford, West Yorkshire, UK*

ASTA SALMI, *Korppaantie IB 18, 00300 Helsinki, Finland*

D. D. SHIPLEY, *Department of Business Studies, Trinity College, Dublin, Republic of Ireland*

PIROSKA SOMOGYI, *Polifoam Plastic Processing Co Ltd, Budapest, Hungary*

BRUNO TIETZ, *Handelsinstitut, Universität des Saarlandes, 6600 Saarbrücken 11, Germany*

ALFRED TOVIAS, *Department of International Relations, Hebrew University, Jerusalem, Israel*

LEWIS R. TUCKER, *University of Hartford, Barney School of Business and Public Administration, Department of Marketing, West Hartford, Connecticut 06117, USA*

LAWRENCE WELCH, *Monash University, Graduate School of Management, Clayton, Victoria 3168, Australia and Norwegian School of Management, Sandvika, Norway*

ALEXANDER DE WIT, *Université Libre de Bruxelles, CP 145, B-1050 Brussels, Belgium*

ARCH G. WOODSIDE, *Freeman School of Business, Tulane University, New Orleans, Louisiana 70118, USA*

STEPHEN YOUNG, *Department of Marketing, Strathclyde Business School, University of Strathclyde, Glasgow, Scotland*

ILIANA ZLOCH-CHRISTY, *Auhofstrasse 164/1/4, 1130 Vienna, Austria*

Preface

This book is written, and edited, with the conviction that it covers a subject of immense importance for the future of the world of economy. The collapse of the 'iron curtain' across Europe was greeted with euphoria. Its consequences in terms of economic cooperation and development are only now beginning to be understood. Generally, the chapters in this book are concerned with the consequences of liberalization of East and Central Europe for international business. The concerns are very much for the impact on trade, technology and investment flows. Underlying this is a concern that the former socialist economies should develop democratic, open and participative structures that allow enterprise to flourish without corruption. This agenda is difficult to achieve but it is vital that it should succeed if turmoil and depravation are to be avoided.

The editors would like to thank all the contributing authors for their dedication and cooperation. In addition, we gratefully acknowledge editorial support from Academic Press, Mrs Chris Barkby for her efficient wordprocessing and Jennifer Pegg for constant encouragement.

Peter J. Buckley
Bradford
Pervez N. Ghauri
Groningen

To Saad

1

Statement of the Issues

Peter J. Buckley and Pervez N. Ghauri

Geopolitical Factors

The years 1989 and 1990 were perhaps the most dramatic and exciting in the history of post-war Europe, witnessing the end of the cold war and the liberalization of Central and Eastern Europe. In a way, there has been a return to the circumstances of the immediate post-war years, when Europe needed to be restructured and stabilized. There are great opportunities for the world economy and for Western firms and businesses; there are also risks of disillusionment, frustration, social and political unrest, civil war (as we have already experienced in the former Yugoslavia) and other unpredictable consequences especially in the transition period. However, it is not appropriate to compare the present-day rebuilding of Eastern Europe with the rehabilitation of Europe after the Second World War. At that time, European countries were all in the same situation – the legal and social infrastructure was in place, while the industrial infrastructure had suffered and needed rebuilding. It was relatively easy to set up or restore democratic institutions, and within a decade the Western countries were on their feet again.

In Eastern Europe, after more than forty years of communism, however, the task is much more difficult. These countries do not have the social and political structure necessary to establish democratic institutions. Moreover, they have to establish links with the rest of the world as well as internally. The telecommunication and transport sectors are almost non-existant (Lindsay 1992). Nevertheless, in some cases we can find examples of lessons that can be learned for reforms in Eastern Europe – for example, the post-war European experience with monetary overhang and monetary reforms. Additionally, a number of stabilizing anti-inflationary measures, taken in certain Latin American countries, e.g., in Chile and Mexico, also provide some lessons (Edwards 1991).

This volume deals with the economic changes which have taken place in Europe during the last five years and their impact on international business activities. We do not need to stress the importance of Europe for the world economy. Taking the definition of Europe to be all the countries between the Atlantic in the West and the Ural Mountains, running down the middle of the Russian Republic, in the East, there is a total population of more than 720 million. Here Turkey is included as a

European country, but the southern republics of the former Soviet Union are excluded.

Europe, until now has been split into three economic blocs: the European Community (EC), the European Free Trade Area (EFTA) and the Council for Mutual Economic Assistance (Comecon), as shown in Fig. 1.1.

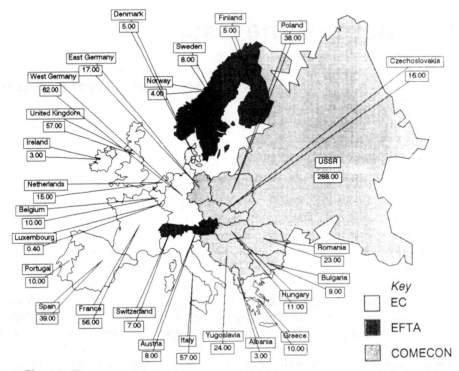

Fig. 1.1. Europe: population by nation and bloc (1989). *Source:* Lynch (1992: 14).

As we know, the Comecon bloc no longer exists, but even when it did, it was difficult to get accurate information and statistics on its performance, even from the World Bank and other international sources. We also know that EFTA is facing radical changes, with Denmark already having full membership of the EC and Austria, Finland, Sweden and Norway having applications pending for EC membership.

The importance of Europe as a market and as a political bloc is stronger now than ever. European countries account for 50 per cent of world trade; the EC is dominant, accounting for about 37 per cent, Eastern Europe is far behind with 7 per cent, and EFTA has 6 per cent of world trade (Lynch 1992: 21). Much of the trade taking place within Eastern Europe (the former Comecon nations), however, is not included in these statistics.

The Eastern European countries have varied assets and liabilities, but these countries still rely largely upon raw material production, including metal ores, coal, oil, gas, and agricultural products. In the 1990s post-communist era they are striving hard to industrialize their societies along Western-style economic lines. Although some industrial sectors are highly developed, such as the defence industries and shipping, most of their industrial sectors have suffered from under-investment, resulting in outdated technologies and production processes. As mentioned earlier, economic statistics on Eastern and Central Europe are deficient. However, some statistics on GDP per head of population are available, as shown in Fig. 1.2.

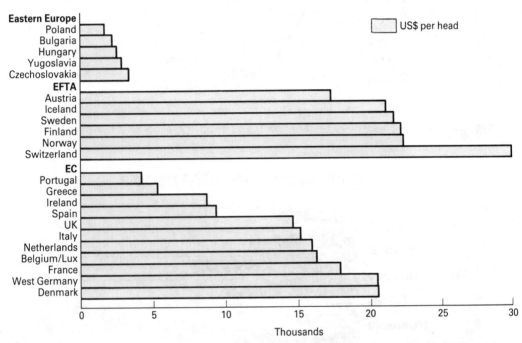

Fig. 1.2. European wealth: GDP per head of population (1989). *Source:* Lynch (1992: 34).

Progress of Liberalization and Marketization

According to OECD and World Bank estimates, the Eastern European economies are likely to deteriorate before they improve, as illustrated in Fig 1.3.

The main problem is that there are too many interrelated blockages to growth to be dealt with at once. Issues such as the reduction of trade barriers, reform of the banking and loan systems, the pricing mechanism and control, property and contract law are all interrelated; it is not possible to make judgements on which should be tackled first. According to one estimate (*The Economist*, September 21, 1991), the Eastern European countries would need a total of US$420 billion annual investment for the next ten years to bring their economies up to equivalence with Western Europe. There has been no real evaluation of their resources or assets, and figures on past levels of annual growth are not trustworthy (Lynch 1992). As far as living standards in Eastern Europe are concerned, Figs 1.4 and 1.5 illustrate the comparison with some other countries.

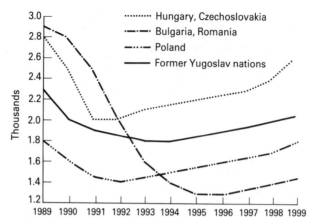

Fig. 1.3. Wealth per person in Eastern Economies in US$ (1989). *Source:* Lynch (1992: 60).

Comparison per 1000 people

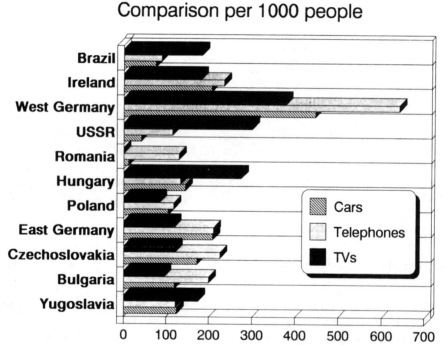

Fig. 1.4. Living standards in Eastern Europe as compared with some other countries.

One major problem is the enthusiasm with which the people of Eastern and Central Europe have embraced the political changes and have discarded communism, in the hope of a dramatic and rapid improvement in their standards of living. Now that people have started to realize that this transition will not be rapid, and that it is in fact rather questionable whether they will be able to achieve Western-type democracies, economies and living standards, they are becoming frustrated and disillusioned.

In the transition to free markets, the Eastern European countries face three main

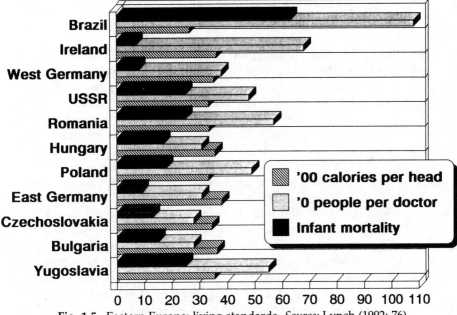

Fig. 1.5. Eastern Europe: living standards. *Source:* Lynch (1992: 76).

problems (Edwards 1991: 1): first, how to stabilize their economies, achieving internal and external macroeconomic balance; second, how to implement the structural and market-oriented reforms in an effective and orderly way, and third, how to proceed with the privatization process. These three issues together, with pressure for speedy reforms, are the major concerns of the political leaders and their advisors (see e.g. Hinds 1990, Lipton and Sachs 1990, Nordhaus 1990 and Covicelli and Rocha 1990). However, there are very few solutions: the questions are posed and discussed but no one can suggest answers to these questions or the right way to proceed. It is certain, however, that trying to establish Western-style democracy needs development of social, political and economic infrastructure, and that the changes must come quickly to establish stability in the region. Privatization is considered a solution, but there is no easy way to privatize Eastern Europe. Over-optimistic estimates are now being revised, and people now believe that it might take twenty years before the privatization of all or most sectors in these countries can be achieved (Lindsay 1992).

The Future

During the last five years enormous changes have been experienced in all of the countries of the former Eastern bloc. These changes have involved the collapse of centrally planned communist systems and have changed the map of total post-war Europe. Today, in most countries of Eastern Europe, there are democratically elected governments which are committed to establishing market economies based on pluralist property forms and free competition. Most of these countries have the transfer of technology and improved trading links with Western economies at the top of their priority lists. All are desperately trying to establish economic relations with Western Europe in particular and with other economies of the world in general (Havlik 1991).

A general opinion is that, although it is quite unlikely that these economies will revert to communism, their progress towards a market economy is not going to be as smooth as they originally expected. The situation in the former Soviet Union is uncertain, especially in certain republics, which may go in different directions. The changes and uncertainties in the former Soviet Union are very complex and hard to predict. As expressed by Peter Bijur, President of Texaco, the uncertain economic outlook in the Soviet Union is the single biggest challenge facing investors (*Petroleum Intelligence Weekly*, 1991). Many experts believe that the economies of the former Soviet republics, after having been planned centrally for about forty years, are likely to get worse before getting better (Kase 1992).

Hungary, Poland, Czechoslovakia, Romania and Bulgaria embraced the free market and political pluralism (although the process has been quite slow in the case of Romania and Bulgaria) at an early stage. The three leading reformers, Poland, Hungary and Czechoslovakia, have freed most prices, made their currencies con- vertible for most businesses, have opened their doors for foreign investors and have demolished several other trade barriers; the results are quite visible. Count- less small entrepreneurs have started small businesses and Western firms have set up offices in these countries. These five countries, however, like much of the rest of Europe, have been facing a severe recession. In the five, GDP dropped by 8 per cent in the period 1989–91, and industrial output dropped by 17 per cent and then a further 11 per cent during the course of the two years. This is illustrated in Fig. 1.6. Although great caution is required before interpreting these statistics, it is clear

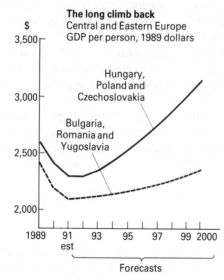

Fig. 1.6. Central and Eastern Europe GDP per person. *Source:* The Economist (September 21, 1991: 4).

that these economies have considerable problems. Inflation rates and unemployment are enormously high and rising (*The Economist*, September 21, 1991). According to World Bank predictions, output per head in Eastern Europe may not recover to 1989's levels until 1996.

The three most dynamic countries, Poland, Hungary and Czechoslovakia, have taken rigorous measures to move towards a market economy. In many other countries and former Soviet republics, however, newly emergent nationalism, combined with a vacuum of functioning political institutions, poses formidable obstacles. In spite of all this, most of these countries have clearly defined their goal and objectives as the establishment of a Western-style market economy (Havlik 1991).

Following the overthrow of communism, economists from the former Eastern bloc, who had long studied and admired the Western economies, advocated immediate adoption of Western-style market economies without giving any consideration to a 'middle way' or a gradual step-by-step transition, as suggested by Gorbachev's Perestroika. Unfortunately, it takes decades to develop the system and infrastructure for a market economy to function effectively. The market economy is based on laws regarding property and contracts, with judicial systems, banking and financial systems, taxes, social security systems and labour laws. There is a difference between studying market economy systems and managing their implementation. The experience of some developing countries which have tried to copy Western systems is not entirely relevant, because in those countries the infrastructure mentioned above, the ownership system and the rules were already in place.

The experts thus conclude that even on the basis of a very optimistic assessment, it is likely to take two or more decades for the Eastern European economies to come close to those of Western Europe. Economic indicators for five Eastern European countries are presented in Table 1.1.

The weaker East European countries are facing great problems. Albania is facing a high level of social instability and at the end of 1991 the economy was near to collapse, with almost universal shortages, while the government was desperately trying to bring about reform. In Bulgaria, the electoral victory of the opposition party in autumn 1991 created great expectations, but they realized very soon that their mandate was not strong enough to implement and enforce the necessary reforms. Romania looked quite stable and promising after the new government took over from Ceauşescu, but the disturbances by the miners in 1991 upset this stability and resulted in further social and political unrest. In the case of the former Soviet Union, the dramatic break-up of the union, disastrous economic performance, the political turmoil, and impatience of the people with the speed and effects of economic reform are leading to rather pessimistic future prospects. The three Baltic states, Estonia, Latvia and Lithuania, are working independently on their reforms with some foreign help, especially from the Scandinavian countries (Lindsay 1992).

The perceived economic leaders of Eastern Europe – Poland, Hungary and Czechoslovakia – are indeed ahead of the others, especially the Commonwealth of Independent States (CIS), but even in their countries political stability is elusive. Czechoslovakia has been the most unstable and has now undergone division into two separate republics. Hungary's apparent political stability has masked deep

Table 1.1: Economic indicators for five Eastern European countries.

	Poland			Czechoslovakia			Romania			Hungary			Bulgaria		
	1989	1990	1991*	1989	1990	1991*	1989	1990	1991*	1989	1990	1991*	1989	1990	1991*
Real GDP % change over previous year	-0.2	-12.0	-3.7	1.4	-3.1	-9.8	-9.9	-10.2	-10.0	-0.2	-3.5	-6.0	-0.4	-11.8	-19.8
Industrial output, % change over previous year	-2.5	-28.8	-5.7	1.0	-3.7	-4.5	-2.1	-22.0	-20.0	-1.0	-10.0	-12.0	1.1	-10.7	-12.0
Exports, $bn	15.6	18.6	18.6	14.3	13.5	13.7	6.1	3.5	3.2	10.9	10.8	11.4	7.9	6.4	6.1
Imports, $bn	17.4	14.7	18.8	17.1	19.0	16.5	3.8	5.2	3.9	12.4	12.6	11.3	10.0	8.9	6.5
Inflation rates, %	251	684	80	1.4	15.0	40.0	1.1	27.0	130.0	17.5	28.2	36.0	6.4	26.3	200.0
Unemployment rates, %	0.3	6.1	7.3	0.0	1.0	2.8	0.0	0.0	3.6	0.5	1.6	2.9	0.0	1.6	2.7
Trade balance, $bn	-1.8	3.9	-0.2	-2.8	-5.5	-2.8	2.3	-1.7	0.7	-1.5	-1.8	-0.1	-2.1	-2.5	-0.4
Exchange rate per $	1,439	9,500	11.392†	15.0	18.2	29.0†	14.5	34.7	60.0†	59.1	63.2	75.0†	0.86	2.15	18.0†

*Forecast †August, 1991.
Source: The Economist (September 21, 1991: 5)

resistance against economic change, while in Poland, people are unsatisfied with the political changes and the speed of these changes, feeling they have failed to achieve what had been anticipated (Lindsay 1992). Comparative progress in these three countries is illustrated in Table 1.2.

Table 1.2: Comparative progress in Czechoslovakia, Hungary and Poland.

	Czechoslovakia	*Hungary*	*Poland*
Economy	Gap between Czech and Slovak republics widening as they split. Czech industrial production is up, but Slovaks, stuck with obsolete defence plants, may pump economy	After fall of 3.5% in 1992, GDP expected to grow 1.3% in 1993. Tight money has slowed inflation to 22%, from 35% in 1991, but unemployment is 11% and rising	GDP was expected to contract 3% in 1992 after 10% fall in 1991. Government still struggling to control budget deficit. Doing so would permit IMF to release $2.5 billion
Privatization	Some $11 billion in shares to be issued by year-end [1992]. Will leave 40% of economy in private hands. Second round expected in 1993	Nearly half of GDP already being produced by private sector. But sales of big state companies proceeding very slowly	Politics slowing privatization plans, but Prime Minister Hanna Suchocka trying to set up mutual funds to buy stakes in companies
Finance	Bourses to open in Prague and Bratislava in January. Using privatization proceeds, government has injected $2 billion into banks, which have also shed $3 billion in bad debts	Stock market growing, with volume up 30% since 1991. Value of 21 listed companies reaches $1 billion. But massive bad loans and thousands of bankruptcies dogging banks	Parliament due to vote in October on $2 billion restructuring of nine ailing state banks. Government angling to renegotiate country's $45 billion foreign debt by 1993.

Source: Based on *Business Week*, September 28, 1992: 30–1

As regards the former Soviet Union, many believe that although uncertainty over the economic outlook is its single biggest liability, if and when the economy recovers, domestic demand for commodities and products such as oil and gas will increase. On the other hand, if the economic recovery is slow, the commodities and products can be sold in foreign markets, as there is always a market for oil and gas. This would provide foreign exchange, which is badly needed for investment.

Unfortunately, analysts have been successful in convincing the world that the former Soviet Union is far behind the West. It is said that a citizen of the CIS makes one quarter of an average US citizen's income, where the average GNP per person is $22,000 as against $5,000 for the former Soviet Union (*The Economist*, January 28, 1991). This comparison, and the wealth of the former Soviet republics in oil, gas and other commodities, highlights the need for foreign capital.

Post-war Europe experienced a surge in the inflow of foreign capital, especially from the USA. A similar kind of need has now emerged in the former Soviet and other Eastern European countries. The US Department of Commerce estimated direct US investments in Eastern Europe to have increased between 1988 and 1989 by 16 per cent, reaching a level of $176.1 billion (*Business Weekly*, March 26, 1990, p. 48).

Some Country-Specific Issues

Albania

Albania is a country which is still struggling to construct a coherent economic reform programme. Although the Albanian communist party has revised and reformed itself, it is still the party, or former party members, who hold power. The country is thus still quite unstable. With three million people and the poorest economy among the Eastern European countries, Albania has a long way to go to achieve a Western-style economy. Few Western countries or firms have been interested in investing in the country, except for a few oil and gas exploration projects. The crumbling industrial infrastructure seems stuck in a 1950's time-warp (Lindsay 1992; Luxner 1992). To develop this sector, Albania will need to scrap existing industries and develop new ones.

Since 1990, farmers have been encouraged to sell their products on the open market, and private enterprises are emerging. But the new businesses are mainly snack bars and other services; the necessary legal and political infrastructure for large-scale private business to operate in the country is missing.

The country became a member of the IMF and World Bank in October 1991 and is trying to attract funds from the European Bank for Reconstruction and Development (EBRD). Other than that, Albania has not announced any concrete programmes for changes. A decree has been passed to allow private enterprises, mainly in services, trade and retailing, and some reforms in banking are under way – a joint-venture Albania-Swiss bank named Iliria has been set up. The EBRD has provided $2 million to upgrade the tourism industry and Albturist has signed a $36 million contract with CBC (France) to renovate the Dajti Hotel, one of the only two tourist hotels in Tirana (Luxner 1992).

Trade, imports and exports, were set free from controls in October 1991 (with some exceptions), and a foreign investment agency was set up. The Tirana branch of the savings bank has been allowed to deal in foreign exchange, the rate of exchange being fixed at new Lek 30 = 1 ECU, the currency having been attached to the ECU. In spite of all this, Albania remains the poorest country in Europe and is considered to be last among the Eastern European countries in the race towards a market economy.

After the meeting between President Bush and Albanian president Barisha in June 1992, an Albanian-American Trade Association (Aata) was formed to encourage trade between the two countries. According to the US Commerce Department, US exports to Albania during 1991 came to $18 million, while imports totalled less than $3.2 million. It was also estimated that Albanian GDP would fall by 20 per cent during 1992, following a 40 per cent fall in the previous year. Food shortages are acute and experts fear that the civil war in nearby Yugoslavia might spread into Albania (*Business Eastern Europe*, June 29, 1992).

Bulgaria

In the elections held in 1990, the reformed communist party in Bulgaria, now known as the Bulgarian Socialist Party (BSP), won a remarkable victory. However, the opposition, the Union of Democratic Forces (UDF), complained about the communist leadership remaining and throughout 1990 Bulgaria was hit by strikes and demonstrations. As a result the BSP had to resign from power and a coalition government was formed at the end of 1990. In October 1991, parliamentary elections were held at which the UDF won and formed the government.

Although some reforms of the banking sector, macroeconomic stabilization and price liberalization were introduced during 1990, little progress was made because of the unrest. In June 1992, there was a major government reshuffle. From the standpoint of Western executives, the most important change was the appointment of Ilko Eskenazi as a member of the cabinet, a convinced free marketer and enthusiast for foreign investments. His intention was to negotiate with the EC for concessions and to develop a trade relationship with the EC (Lindsay 1992; *Business Eastern Europe*, June 22, 1992).

Shortage of hard currency has been a major obstacle for Western firms wishing to enter Bulgaria. OECD imports to the country in 1992 were less than $1.7 billion, and this was not expected to grow in 1993. Western companies have been facing long payment delays. With a foreign debt of $11 billion by 1991, Bulgaria has been practically blacklisted by foreign banks. Letters of credit and counter-trade are considered the only safe way of doing business with Bulgaria. Buy-back is normally reserved for sales of machinery and equipment, and a normal period of compensation for a foreign supplier is up to two to three years from the installation of the equipment (*Business Eastern Europe*, June 22, 1992).

Table 1.3: Some facts and forecasts on Bulgaria.

	1990	1991	1992[a]	1993[b]
Industrial output (%)	−16.3	−27.5	−15.0	−7.0
Consumer prices (%)	19.3	334.0	100.0	75.0
Unemployment rate (% of total workforce)	1.5	10.5	12.5	15.0
Total exports ($ bn)	2.5	3.7	3.8	4.0
Total imports ($ bn)	3.3	3.8	4.5	4.8
Balance of trade ($ bn)	−0.8	0.0	−0.7	−0.8
Current account balance ($ bn)	−1.1	−0.9	−1.7	−2.2
Exchange rate				
Lv per 5 (average)	2.2	19.0	26.6	37.0

[a]EIU estimate. [b]EIU forecast.
Source: Business Eastern Europe (March 8, 1993)

In conclusion, although a number of major items of legislation were passed starting from early 1991, little has been done to develop an effective market economy or to attract foreign investment in Bulgaria. Banking reforms have been half-hearted, creating a deteriorating financial and liquidity situation in many commercial banks. The country is badly in need of training for staff and executives in the development of market institutions, especially in accounting, banking, insurance and entrepreneurship. Inefficiency and low productivity are considered to be the main structural deficiencies of the Bulgarian economy – per capita labour productivity is reported to be barely 15–20 per cent that of most developed countries. Most of the production facilities are virtually obsolete, and agriculture is in crisis due to over-centralization, neglect and drought (Grosser 1991).

Czechoslovakia

As mentioned earlier, Czechoslovakia, along with Hungary and Poland, have made the greatest progress towards Western-style market economies. Czechoslovakia traditionally has had an advanced industrial base and its technology and products are comparable with those of the West.

When the Czechoslovakian reform movement first started, during the second half of the 1960s, its aim was the introduction of some free market elements. These reforms were stopped, however, by the invasion of Soviet-led Warsaw Pact forces in 1968, and the reformists were eliminated. From that point onwards, the idea of reform became a taboo in public life, and the Czechoslovakian leadership showed no enthusiasm in 1985 when Gorbachev introduced his Perestroika. The student demonstration in Prague on November 17, 1989, which marked the outbreak of the so-called 'velvet revolution', was supported by artists and the 'Charter 77' opposition movement (led by Vaclav Havel), forced the government to consider reforms. Free elections were held as a result of these demonstrations, and on December 29, 1989 Havel was elected President (Levcik and Lukas 1991).

The country is now struggling in the aftermath of the separation of the Czech and Slovak republics. President Havel had to step down from power over this issue in early 1992, and in October 1992 Czech and Slovak premiers Vaclav Klaus and Vladimir Mecier announced a formal agreement to split Czechoslovakia in two countries on January 1, 1993. A comparison of the two republics is presented in Table 1.4.

Before the Second World War Czechoslovakia ranked as one of the most highly industrialized nations in Europe. Until about the mid-1960s it was at par with Austria as regards GDP per capita, while today its per capita income is about 30 per cent lower than that of Austria. Nevertheless this level may be considered very high as compared to other Eastern European countries. A realistic assessment shows that in the next ten to fifteen years, Czechoslovakia could regain its position as one of the most industrialized countries in Europe (Levcik and Lukas 1991). GNP has been constantly increasing since 1989, inflation has been well within the limits of acceptability (2 per cent according to government estimates, 4–5 per cent according to international experts). Investment and agricultural output have also been on the increase.

Most of the investment has been made in production (energy and metallurgy), and retail trade turnover as well as income are on the increase. Exports have been increasing (they were 16.1 per cent in 1989, as compared to 10.5 per cent in 1988) and there is a trade surplus with the West. A number of reforms and measures have been initiated as regards price structure, tax system, opening the economy to the world, liberalization of foreign trade and a radical programme for banking (Havlik 1991: 176).

Table 1.4: A comparison of the Czech and Slovak economies, 1990.

	Czech Republic	Slovak Republic	Ratio Czech/Slovak
Population (mn)	10,354	5,310	1.95
GNP (K mn)	438,135	185,657	2.36
Republics' total expenditures (K mn)	238,398	129,499	1.84
Production of electricity (kwn mn)	62,558	24,068	2.6
Black coal output (000 t)	22,406	–	–
Brown coal output (000 t)	78,588	3,456	22.74
Iron output (000 t)	6,106	3,561	1.71
Steel output (000 t)	10,094	4,779	2.11
Zinc output (t)	–	1,246	–
Tin output (t)	613	–	–
Lead output (t)	23,665	–	–
Oil refining (000 t)	7,297	6,503	1.12
Cement output (000 t)	6,434	3,781	1.7
Cotton fabrics (000 sq m)	487,091	93,338	5.22
Clothing (000 pcs)	24,173	21,086	1.15
Automobiles (units)	187,780	3,453	54.34
Colour TV sets (units)	6,025	379,775	0.01
Refrigerators & freezers (units)	–	448,992	–
Grain output (000 t)	8,947	3,617	2.47
Potato output (000 t)	1,755	779	2.25
Meat: total (000 t)	676	288	2.35

Business Eastern Europe (June 29, 1992: 310)

Table 1.5 Some facts and forecasts on the Czech Republic.

	1990	1991	1992[a]	1993[b]
GDP (Kcs bn)	na	432.1	403.2	400.0
GDP at current prices (Kcs bn)	na	705.6	738.3	860.0
Real GDP growth (%)	−3.5[c]	−15.0[c]	−6.7	−1.0[d]
Personal consumption (% change)	1.1[c]	−19.4[c]	5.9[d]	1.7[d]
Gross fixed investment (% change)	−12.9[c]	−13.1[c]	−0.8	2.5[d]
Merchandise exports (% change)	na	8.3[c]	0.3	4.7[d]
Merchandise imports (% change)	na	−8.8[c]	−0.1	8.0[d]

[a]EIU estimate. [b]EIU forecast. [c]Figure for CSFT. [d]January 1, 1984 prices.
Source: Business Eastern Europe (February 15, 1993: 5)

In January 1990, the commercial exchange rate was further devalued by 18.6 per cent to 17 Kcs = $1, and by 50 per cent for non-commercial exchange, to 38 Kcs = $1. These two different rates are maintained and it is hoped to achieve full convertibility gradually. A large-scale privatization bill was in place effective from 1 April 1991. Under the law, each enterprise would determine its own plan for privatization, which would have to be approved by the Ministries of the Czech and Slovak republics. In the Czech republic, by the end of September 1991, over 19,760 businesses had been approved for privatization. Over 1,110 businesses had been leased out and eighty-six businesses had been returned to their original owners (Lindsay 1992).

It is a general opinion that Czechoslovakia has been quite successful in its progress towards a free market economy. Experts fear that the division of the country into the two republics might delay or disturb this process, but it is a positive sign that the division took place without any armed struggle like that in Yugoslavia.

Table 1.6: Some facts and forecasts on Slovakia.

	1990	1991	1992[b]	1993[c]
GDP at current prices (Kcs bn)	241.7	275.1	270.0	260.0
Real GDP growth (%)	−3.5[a]	−16.3	−8.3	−5.0
Personal consumption (% change)	1.1[a]	−25.2	12.0	2.0
Gross fixed investment (% change)	−12.9[d]	−32.3	−20.0	3.0
Merchandise exports (% change)	na	13.9	1.9	2.0
Merchandise imports (% change)	na	10.8	−6.0	−2.0

[a]Figure for CSFR, [b]estimate, [c]forecast.
Source: Business Eastern Europe (February 22, 1993: 5)

Hungary

In the early years of liberalization and reform, Hungary seemed to be in an imposs-ible situation. By early 1990 it had accumulated a debt of $20 billion and it had a foreign exchange reserve of only $700 million. The government had failed to meet the conditions of the last stand-by credit which was held by the IMF in 1989 and was unable to stop the outflow of foreign exchange arising from private imports. At that time Hungary had a huge trade surplus with the former Soviet Union. How-ever, a continuing interest on the part of foreign companies and improvements in the balance of trade in 1990 and 1991 have been helpful in bringing Hungary's performance up to the level of the economic leaders of Eastern Europe (Friedländer 1991).

Hungarian experience of monetary policy, and its ineffectiveness in the earlier years of reforms due to the non-existence of a Hungarian capital market, show that for money and monetary policies to become an integrating factor in the economy, the establishment of real markets is necessary (Havlik 1991). In Hungary, spon-taneous privatization has led to a contraction of the public sector of the economy, while the small-scale private sector has expanded. Although Hungary has been implementing economic reforms since 1968, the present reforms aim more at re-placing the system of central allocation of resources by market allocation, and at the creation of equal legal conditions for local as well as foreign capital and enterprises. Increasing the share of foreign enterprises in the economy as a whole, thus attract-ing foreign capital, is one of the prime objectives of Hungarian reforms. As an incentive, Hungarian enterprises with a foreign partner pay 20 per cent less tax on profit than a local owned company, if the foreign capital represents more than 20 per cent of the total capital of at least 5 million Forints. Figure 1.7(a) and (b) show

(a) **FOREIGN CAPITAL INVESTMENTS**
($ billion)

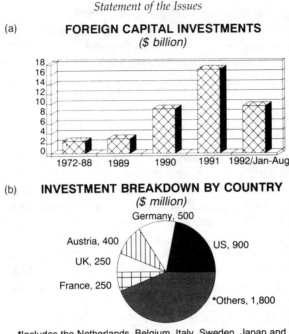

(b) **INVESTMENT BREAKDOWN BY COUNTRY**
($ million)

*Includes the Netherlands, Belgium, Italy, Sweden, Japan and
South Korea.

Fig. 1.7. Foreign investments in Hungary. *Source: Business Eastern Europe* (October 5, 1992: 485).

foreign capital investment in Hungary. As we can see, the US and Germany are the biggest foreign investors in Hungary.

Table 1.7: Some facts and forecasts on Hungary.

	1990	*1991*	*1992**	*1993***
Unemployment (%)	1.8	7.5	13	16
Industrial production (%)	−10	−21.5	−14	0.5
Current account balance ($ bn)	0.3	0.4	1.0	0.9
Gross external debt ($ bn)	21.3	23.5	24.0	23.4
Debt-service ratio (as a % of exports)	47	41.6	29	25
Trade balance ($ bn)	0.3	0.4	1.0	1.0
Gross fixed investment (%)	−9.8	−25.6	−14.9	1.5
Private consumption (%)	−3.6	−9.5	−5.4	1.8

*EIU estimate. **EIU forecast.
Source: Business Eastern Europe (February 8, 1993: 5)

Foreigners are allowed free transfer of funds in foreign exchange, whether the enterprise is in profit or not. Hungary is in advance of several other Eastern European countries, in so far as its legal and institutional framework for foreign investment is developed, adequate and most of all functioning (Friedländer 1991). The large investments by Hunslet (UK), General Electric, General Motors, Ford and Suzuki are some examples. The first half of 1992 showed a trade surplus of

$483 million. Exports were expected to increase by 20 per cent in 1992, while imports would grow only by 5 per cent. By the end of April 1992, Hungary had a current account surplus of $600 million and a hard currency reserve of $5 billion, which represented enormous progress since 1990 (*Business Eastern Europe*, June 15, 1992).

Poland

In Poland, the reforms and transition towards a more liberal economic system started quite early with solidarity movement. On January 1, 1989, restrictions on private business activities were eased and thousands of people left the state sector to start small businesses, which were often one-man firms. In total, 294,304 new firms were registered, 95 per cent of which were one-man firms. There was severe economic turbulence in 1989 and the gap between income and expenditure of the population rose, both nominally (by 364 per cent) and in real terms (35 per cent). Prices of consumer goods increased by 244 per cent and there was a monthly average inflation of 8.5 per cent; as a result there were heavy wage increases. The trade surplus in convertible currency decreased by $267 million to $742 million, as imports exceeded exports. In trade with the West, the estimated fall in the surplus was from $459 million to $270 million (Laski and Gabrisch 1991).

A more concrete programme of transition to a market economy was started in 1990. The ministry for privatization expressed hopes that within three years starting from 1991, 50 per cent of the state property would be in private hands, and that within five years, 80 per cent of the state-run economy would have been privatized. However, the country faced a slump in output and trade, mainly because of the disturbances in trade with the former Soviet Union and Comecon countries. The lack of capital in the country has also meant that other methods are required to privatize the 500 largest enterprises, such as the sale of preferential shares to the employees, and the distribution of free privatization bonds.

The Warsaw Stock Exchange was reopened in April 1991 after having been closed for almost fifty years, but so far its significance has been purely symbolic. A new foreign investment law was introduced in June 1991 to make investment conditions more attractive; however, some restrictions still remain and permission for foreign investment has to be obtained from the ministry for privatization; applications must be made in Polish. There are no tax holidays, but the finance ministry may exempt a company from income tax if the foreign partners' contribution exceeds ECU 2 million and if the company is based in a high unemployment area or ensures the introduction of new technology. This exemption was to be available until 31 December 1993 (Lindsay 1992). Figure 1.8 shows the countries that are investing in Poland. Here we can see that Germany is the biggest investor.

At present, the World Bank is supporting a programme for privatization of Polish commercial banks and has provided a $200 million credit for this purpose. Due to the lack of competition, the profitability in banking is extremely high and the country is attracting a number of foreign banks which have established local offices. Remittance of profit in foreign currency is permitted, up to 30 per cent of profits, while a larger percentage is negotiable. Private land or property can be purchased after permission from the Interior Minister, and property can be leased for a long period, up to 99 years.

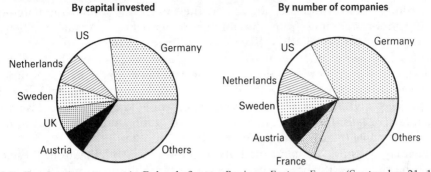

Fig. 1.8. Foreign investment in Poland. *Source: Business Eastern Europe* (September 21, 1992: 460).

The Western banks and experts believed that the return of Jan Lewandowski as Minister of Privatization would jump-start the privatization process in the country. It was intended that some thirty companies would be sold to Western interests by the end of 1992. Fiat recently announced a $2 billion investment in FSM Bielsko, and other deals were expected in ball-bearings, paper and pulp, tyres, glass and motor vehicle components. A $3–5 billion investment was expected in the petroleum sector (Lindsay 1992; Reed 1992).

According to recent statistics released by Poland's central statistical office, industrial production rose by 5 per cent in June 1992 and foreign trade results for the first half of 1992 showed a surplus of nearly $1 billion. The revenues from export for this period were 12.5 per cent higher than for the same period in 1991 and the overall trade surplus for 1992 was estimated at $2.2 billion (Reed 1992: 374). These figures would seem to suggest a relatively quick transition towards a market economy for Poland.

Table 1.8: Some facts and forecasts on Poland.

	1990	1991	1992*	1993**
Industrial production (% change yr/yr)	−24.2	−11.9	3.5	9.0
Budget balance (% of GDP)	3.5	−3.5	−5.0	−5.5
Unemployment (% of workforce, year-end)	6.3	11.8	13.6	15.5
Registered joint ventures at year-end	1,645	4,796	8,860	11,500
Private-sector employment (% of total)	45.8	50.6	56.0	61.0
Private-sector share of GDP (%)	35	42	45	52
Exchange rate (Zl per $, year-end)	9,500	10,957	15,800	19,000

*EIU estimate. **EIU forecast.
Source: Business Eastern Europe (February 1, 1993: 5)

The Baltic States

Estonia, Latvia and Lithuania gained complete independence from the former Soviet Union in 1991. However, their economies remained highly dependent on

Comecon, 95 per cent of their trade and their most important raw material and energy imports coming from the former Soviet Union. As far as their own resources are concerned, they have some primary sources such as forests and fisheries, but their technological base is outdated and needs rehabilitation. According to the European Commission, the investment needs of the Baltic countries, for two years only, amount to $3,500 million. The Nordic Investment Bank has identified projects worth $2,000 million which are essential to build the necessary infrastructure. There is, however, an acute shortage of foreign exchange and financial stability is fragile (Nordic Investment Bank 1991).

Potential investors are concerned about the investment climate in these countries. The reform of the banking system is just beginning, and questions concerning property ownership, investment protection and trade agreements have still not been fully resolved. Relative to some other former Eastern bloc countries, however, progress has been quite rapid and many laws, e.g. on tax holidays, foreign investors, repatriation of profits, and exemption from work and residence permits are already in place.

Breaking away totally from the other former Soviet republics and focusing more on Western markets is of the utmost importance for all three countries, but the necessary experience and knowledge of marketing required to penetrate Western markets is missing. As a result, these countries will have to continue to depend, to a large extent, on trade with the former Soviet republics. How and on what terms this trade should continue, is therefore a big question.

The Baltic states have been active in establishing relationships with Western and especially Nordic countries, from which they have received a lot of support. They became members of the United Nations at the 1991 General Assembly and thereby can benefit from access to UN organizations. They were also invited as special guests to the IMF/World Bank annual meeting in Bangkok in 1991, and have applied for membership to these organizations. There is strong support in Western Europe, and especially in the Nordic countries, for help to be given to the Baltic states, and a number of bilateral and multilateral assistance programmes are taking place.

In each of the three Baltic countries, plans are in hand to privatize state-owned industries and other enterprises, selling them off to domestic and foreign investors. Lithuania has concentrated mainly on industrial enterprises. Latvia has focused more on the agricultural sector and on the creation of private co-operative enterprises.

Special priority is given to small and medium-scale enterprises in each of the three countries. For example, in a recent list of eighty Lithuanian enterprises announced as being available for privatization for hard currency, 72 per cent of them required investments of less than $5 million. Many of them were in the manufacturing sector, but there were also a number of enterprises related to food and fish production and to tourism.

Nearly 300 potential investment projects have been reviewed in *Baltic News* (1992: 6); of those for which hard currency investment requirements had been estimated, 66 per cent needed investments of less than $5 million, while a further 11 per cent of investments were in the range of $5–10 million.

Estimates of the requirements of the Baltic countries for investment in agricultural inputs, such as fertilizers, pesticides and animal feed from abroad for the coming years, together with the investment requirements for machinery and other equipment imports, are set out in Table 1.9.

Table 1.9: Investment in agricultural inputs and machinery ($ millions).

	Agricultural inputs	*Machinery and equipment*
Estonia	260	n.a.
Latvia	600–800	1,000
Lithuania	55	240

Source: Baltic News (June 1992: 8)

According to a survey undertaken by the Nordic Investment Bank in November 1991, of 200 project proposals studied, 116 were for the small and medium-scale enterprises (Nordic Investment Bank 1991: 24).

Table 1.10: Some facts and forecasts for the Baltic states.

	Lithuania		*Latvia*		*Estonia*	
	1991	*1992*	*1991*	*1992*	*1991*	*1992*
NMP produced (% change)	−21.0	−15.0	−7.9	−25.0	−13.1	−20.0
Gross industrial production (% change)	−18.0	−45.0	2.3	−32.0	−7.0	−40.0
Consumer price inflation (%)	224.7	900.0	172.2	900.0	105.8	500.0

Source: Business Eastern Europe (September 7, 1992: 440)

Estonia

The smallest of the Baltic states, with 1.6 million people, Estonia has a similar historical background to those of Latvia and Lithuania, although its cultural background is quite different. Estonia was under Danish and then Swedish rule until 1710, when the Russian empire took it over. It became independent in 1919, but was again annexed by the Soviet Union in 1940. The language is totally different from Latvian and Lithuanian and is closer to Finnish.

The country is very active internationally and has asked for international economic assistance to be directed to nine main policy areas (Nordic Investment Bank 1991):

1. To avoid economic and social catastrophe.
2. Restoration of democratic institutions.
3. Education, social welfare, planning, training and technology transfer.
4. Infrastructure development.
5. Energy.
6. Environmental protection.
7. Restructuring and privatization of agriculture.
8. Science, scientific research and development.
9. Regional projects.

There are five priority projects at this time, in the following industries: chemical and thermomechanical plant ($80 million), paper mills ($120 million), pulp plant ($520 million), fibreboard plant ($50 million) and packing plant ($30 million). Other priority industries are cotton textiles, cement, glass, food and other small-scale industries (Nordic Investment Bank 1991).

The industries in the northern part of the country are advantaged because of the location of mineral resources. A number of companies, in particular from Nordic countries, are especially active and have already established projects (see e.g. Chapter 12 in this volume).

The Estonian government re-established the kroon as the unit of Estonian currency in July 1992. The kroon was last used in Estonia before the Soviet annexation. Since July 1992 the kroon has been convertible to the major hard currencies in this world at an exchange rate which is fixed to the German mark, 8:1. That gives Estonia an advantage over the other former Soviet republics, which are using the unstable rouble that is not convertible. In September 1992 the World Bank supported the Estonian kroon (EEK) with additional funds, on the condition of implementing certain changes in the Estonian monetary system.

Latvia

During the period before the Soviet occupation, Latvia was an active European country in the League of Nations and had Germany and Great Britain as its main trading partners. It declared its independence on May 4, 1990 together with the other Baltic states. Independence was fully achieved in August 1991 following the dramatic changes in the former Soviet Union. Since then, the government has been striving to achieve a smooth transition to a democratic state and market economy. The constitution has been changed to effect the necessary property rights and to develop a free market economy. A programme for privatization is on its way and a number of measures are being taken to attract foreign capital. The country has signed protocols of co-operation with the Netherlands, Poland, Czechoslovakia and with Denmark and other Scandinavian countries. The Nordic Council has opened an information office in Riga to speed up this co-operation.

Among the priority industries, energy, forests, construction, flax and wool, agriculture and food, pharmaceuticals, port development and medical equipment are worth mentioning. Latvia has been trying to present itself as a gateway to Eastern European markets, especially Russia, and claims to provide terms and conditions to foreign investors which are comparable to those in Western countries. The registration of foreign companies and repatriation of profit have been facilitated and will be subject to further reform. Several currency exchange points have been opened, with a combination of a fixed exchange rate set centrally and market rates of exchange. Foreign investors' interest in Latvia is apparent from Table 1.11.

Lithuania

Strategically located as a neighbour to Poland, Germany and Russia, and with a population of 3.7 million in 1990, Lithuania is the biggest of the Baltic states.

The government of Lithuania has spelled out its priorities for investment and areas where foreign investment is required and welcome, with health and environ-

Table 1.11: Foreign investment in Latvia.

The following companies have invested more than $100,000 in Latvia:

Company	Country	Investment ($ '000)
Wodlinger Broadcasting	US	70,000.0
C American Enterprises	US	10,012.5
UB	India	10,000.0
Semaiteks	Germany	2,570.0
Lathaag Corp	US	1,800.0
Wolf Sisnambau	Austria	1,500.0
Saule Inc.	US	1,300.0
Farmocean	Sweden	1,000.0
Baltic Partners	Denmark	500.0
Ortorutticola Lombardidia	Italy	488.2
Di Fomasan L. Eastern Holding	UK	360.0
Orto Fruiticola Srl	Italy	300.0
Post & Tele Agency	Finland	269.5
Swedish Telecom Int.	Sweden	269.5
Anderson Mikael	Sweden	255.0
Vigorous C.H. Enterprises	Taiwan	230.0
Sovmedia E.U.R.L.	France	172.4
Hakon	Czechoslovakia	170.0
Neukurcher Anton	Austria	160.0
Riga Overseas Investment	Canada	130.1
H. H. Hanna & Associates	India	120.0
Baltica Administration	Denmark	104.5
Magna Gross Export	Denmark	100.0
Zegermaher Jurij	US	100.0

Source: Business Eastern Europe (August 10, 1992: 392)

ment, energy, transport and communication, paper and pulp, furniture and food industries at the top of the list. The Kaunas biological water treatment plant, for which a Swedish company has carried out a feasibility study, is expected to require $30 million, and similar projects are needed in all the larger towns. In the energy sector, it is estimated that modernization of the Mazeikiai oil refinery will require an investment of $400 million and another $128 million for the establishment of an industrial polymeric polypropylene plant. In transport and communication, $140 million has been proposed to be spent on the construction of the Via Baltica (in Lithuanian territory), with five hotels and restaurants on the highway. Upgrading of the cellular and national telephone system is badly needed, as is the case with the air traffic and postal systems.

There are about 600 industrial enterprises in the country, all of which the government is reviewing to determine the timing and procedure for their privatization. The privatization process has been quite effective and quick: already by April 1991, in the agricultural sector alone, there were 7,518 private farms and over 5,000 co-operatives. The country has released a list of its investment requirements in the food and agricultural industries for the years 1992–5, which is available to potential investors and is set out in Table 1.12.

Table 1.12: Lithuanian state enterprises chosen for hard currency privatization.

Industry	Name	Address	Location	Telephone	Main line of business	Number of employees
Manufacturing	Vilnius polymer products Plant	Kirtimu 45	Vilnius	640,943	Linoleum, rubber products, glue	320
Manufacturing	Panevezys 'Metalistas' Plant	Sermuksniu 19	Panevezys	61,717	Metal accessories, constr. buildings, locks	851
Manufacturing	'Elektrotechnika' Panevezys	Kranto 36	Panevezys	61,423	Household lighting equipment	353
Manufacturing	Utena Laboratory Electric Furnace Plant	Basanaviclaus 114	Utena	51,985	Furnace for laboratories	750
Manufacturing	Mazelkial Electrical Engineering Plant	Laisves 216	Mazelkial	32,448	Household electrical appliances	1,632
Manufacturing	Panevezys 'Ekranas' Plant	Elektronikos 1	Panevezys	63,188	TV tubes and devices	6,975
Manufacturing	Kaunas 'Metalas' Factory	Juozapaviclaus 82	Kaunas	741,675	Household heating, sanitary engineering	1,026
Food processing	Pavencial Sugar Refinery	Kursenal Ventos 79	Siaullal	71,642	Sugar	770
Food processing	Marijampole Sugar Refinery	P.Armino 65	Marijampole	50,675	Sugar	592
Food processing	Kedainial Sugar Refinery	Pramones 6	Kedainial	50,342	Sugar	590
Food processing	Panevezys Sugar Refinery	Imonlu 22	Panevezys	62,007	Sugar	563
Food processing	Klalpeda Dairy Plant	Silutes pl. 33	Klalpeda	70,827	Milk	697
Food processing	Vilnius Dairy Plant	Saltoniskiu 9	Vilnius	751,131	Milk	995
Food processing	Vilnius Oil & Fat products Plant	Paneriu 62/1	Vilnius	630,788	Oil, fat & soap	210
Food processing	Marijampole canned milk products Plant	Kauno 114	Marijampole	71,420	Tinned Milk	1,968
Food processing	Mazelkial Milk processing Plant	Skuodo 4	Mazelkial	65,341	Milk	484
Food processing	Utena Dairy Plant	Pramones 8	Utena	51,570	Milk	712
Food processing	Alytus Butter Plant	Putinas 4	Alytus	35,458	Milk	500

Source: Baltic News (June 1992: 6)

Russia and the Commonwealth of Independent States (CIS)

One of the more unexpected of the recent changes in Eastern Europe was that the communist parties should have given up power in almost all the countries, including the former Soviet Union. Since Gorbachev's policies of Perestroika and reform, the former Soviet economy has been suffering increasing difficulties and the country as a whole has been torn by deep national and ideological conflicts. These conflicting national and ideological interests have made the adoption of reforms extremely difficult. Formal declaration of independence by most of the constituent republics of the USSR, including Russia, Byelorussia and the Ukraine were the first steps towards the break-up of the Soviet Union. Perestroika and glasnost, as well as promises of radical reform, raised the expectations of the people but failed to deliver economic improvement (Havlik 1991). At the end of 1991 the Soviet Union disintegrated, to be replaced by the Commonwealth of Independent States (CIS).

In 1987, the Soviet regime passed a decree to allow joint ventures and since December 1988 foreign partners have been permitted to take majority shares. As a consequence of legislation introduced in January 1991, foreign persons may now set up joint ventures. Foreign companies are also allowed to set up wholly owned subsidiaries and to repatriate profits. At present, most of the former Soviet republics have adopted their own foreign investment and privatization rules and regulations. These include the right to purchase foreign exchange at market rates for the transfer of funds abroad. Companies in which the foreign share exceeds 30 per cent are allowed to export their own products and to retain the convertible currency proceeds. In Russia, foreign investors can also apply for concessions for the extraction of mineral resources and are even protected from subsequent contractural revisions (Adjubei 1992).

Interest on the part of foreign investors in the former Soviet Union is evident from the fact that, as of July 1991, some 4,200 foreign investment projects were registered in the former USSR territories. This figure compares with 1,274 projects registered by early 1990, and only 191 by early 1989. However, Russia and other former Soviet republics are considered as laggards in the process of privatization and transition towards a market economy, especially in comparison to Hungary, Poland and Czechoslovakia, and even as compared to the Baltic states.

The aggregate share of foreign direct investment (registered) for joint ventures in former Soviet republics has dropped from 40 per cent in 1989 to 17 per cent in mid-1991. There has been, however, a tremendous increase in registered joint ventures; by January 1991 the amount of statutory capital involved in registered joint ventures was $3,151.7 million. By the third quarter of 1991 there were 1,570 operating joint ventures, of which 1,278 had already started production; there were 163,800 employees working in these joint ventures, as compared to 18,000 in January 1989 (Adjubei 1992).

These figures show that, in spite of the slow progress towards economic liberalization in the republics of the former Soviet Union, there are nevertheless good prospects for foreign firms. There is an enormous domestic demand for certain raw materials and goods such as telecommunication equipment, personal computers, chemicals, copying machines and equipment, drugs, high-quality paper and other consumer products, as well as services. Some of the problems, besides that of a very protracted transition period, include: unpredictable changes in the rules and regulations, bureaucratic obstacles and delays, lack of suitable accommodation for foreign employees, non-availability of skilled labour in marketing, management and accounting, poor labour motivation and non-convertibility as well as unpredictable variations in the market exchange rates of local currencies.

The investment needs are beyond our perception. For example, the UK-based Telecommunication Research Centre estimated that the modernization of telecommunication networks in Eastern Europe would cost $350 billion over the next fifteen years (*The Financial Times*, June 18, 1990). Another estimate reveals that upgrading and modernization of the railway network in the former Soviet Union would need an investment of more than $158 billion (*Moniteur du Commerce International* (MOCI), May 28, 1990: 14).

The situation in CIS and Russia is unstable. On December 5, 1991, Uneshekonombank of the former Soviet Union froze payments from all accounts; as a result, many foreign companies were unable to obtain payment for goods supplied against letters of credit opened through the above bank. The total amount of frozen letters of credit is currently estimated at $700–800 million. The Foreign Exchange and Economic Council compile a list of companies to be allotted foreign exchange on a monthly basis, depending upon the country's foreign exchange receipts.

On July 1, 1992 the Council was replaced by the Foreign Exchange and Economic Commission. It was planned that the Commission would make decisions on a case-by-case basis. It is, however, still difficult to assess the criteria which determine the selection of cases or companies. According to the new foreign exchange rules, the government is obliged to buy foreign exchange from the Central Bank at a 'unified' market exchange rate. However, insufficient funds were allocated in the budget to maintain even the current level of payments from frozen Uneshekonombank accounts (*Business Eastern Europe*, September 7, 1992).

It was estimated that Western sales from Russia would decline in 1992 from $19.8 billion to $18 billion for the year. The figures for export receipts in the first half of 1992 were 20 per cent down on the same period in 1991. Moreover, real GNP was expected to decline by 20 per cent in 1992. Agricultural and industrial production are in continuous decline because of supply problems, resistance to reform and the slowness of the privatization process. Although the legal framework for privatization is in place and the auctioning off of retail stores and other enterprises has begun, there has been no real momentum. The government is encouraging foreign investors to take part in this privatization process but this has been rather difficult, because no exchange rate has been fixed for the acquisition of property and the law regarding private ownership of land is inadequate.

During the first half of 1992, between sixty and seventy foreign joint ventures and wholly owned subsidiaries were registered every month. These were mostly small investments with a very small statutory capital. By the end of June of that year, the total number of foreign joint ventures and wholly owned subsidiaries was 4,000. A drastic import cut was enforced in the first half of 1992, saving some $490 million. In spite of this, a trade deficit of $4 billion was predicted by the end of 1992, as total exports fell by 30 per cent in the first half of 1992 and continued to fall. As of June 1992, Russia's total foreign debt amounted to $74,3 billion; it was expected to increase to around $80 billion by the end of 1992. The rouble has also continued to weaken: it had been expected that by the end of 1992 it would end up at rouble 200 = $1, but the reality was much worse, as shown by Table 1.13. By March 1993 the rouble exchange rate against the dollar had fallen to 600 roubles to the dollar. Inflation was also expected to remain high, price liberalization in January 1992 having led to inflation of 600 per cent (in January); although it has slowed down somewhat, it will remain within the range of 10–20 per cent. According to the same estimate, unemployment was expected to rise to 6 million by the end of 1992. It was thus concluded that there would be no economic stability or improvement in Russia and CIS before 1993 (*Business Eastern Europe*, September 7, 1992)

Table 1.13: Rouble exchange rate against the dollar, 1989–93.

1989	0.6*
1990	1.6**
Oct 1990	1.7
Jan 1991	37.6
Dec 1991	60.0
Jan 1992	110.0
June 1992	146.0
Sept 1992	210.0
Nov 1992	368.0
Dec 1992	398.0
Jan 1993	417.0
mid-Jan 1993	493.0
end-Jan 1993	568.0

*Official. **Commercial.
Source: Business Eastern Europe
(February 8, 1993: 9.8)

It was estimated that during 1993 things would stabilize – unemployment and inflation rate would decrease while GNP and the balance of payments would improve because of stabilization in the legal environment and the process of privatization (*Business Eastern Europe*, August 31, 1992).

Romania

Following the fall of the communist regime, the National Salvation Front formed the government in Romania; it failed to convince the West that substantive changes had been made to dismantle the centrally planned economy and replace it with a more democratic and market-oriented structure. Western financial and economic institutions were correspondingly reluctant to consider Romania for investment or other support projects. However, riots in Bucharest in autumn 1991 led to the fall of Petre Roman's government, and by the end of 1991 a law for privatization had been passed and had come into effect. Economic reforms instituted included liberalization of prices and foreign trade, and by November 1991 the government had introduced internal convertibility (Lindsay 1992).

The privatization laws are now considered to be among the more liberal in the former Eastern bloc and the country is opening up its 6,000 state industrial enterprises to investors from all over the world. Foreigners are allowed to own up to 100 per cent of the equity in these companies. The ambition was that by June 1992, 30 per cent of the entire state industrial sector would be in private hands (Neher 1992). Total foreign investment in the country is illustrated in Figure 1.9.

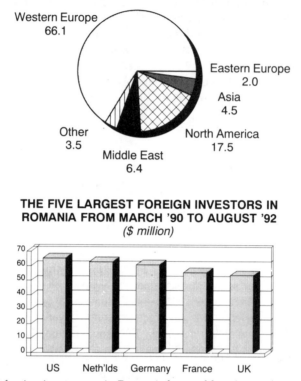

THE FIVE LARGEST FOREIGN INVESTORS IN ROMANIA FROM MARCH '90 TO AUGUST '92
($ million)

Fig. 1.9. Total foreign investment in Romania by world region to August 7, 1992 (%).
Source: Business Eastern Europe (September 7, 1992: 436).

Since December 1, 1990 the former banking system has been dismantled; National Bank has been given the role of central bank and all the commercial and deposit operations have been transferred to the newly established Romanian Commercial Bank. Three new commercial banks have also been established as share-holding companies free to operate anywhere in the country. The Romanian Savings Bank is an old state-owned bank, and is the only savings bank in the country, with branches in every town and village. The Romanian Bank of Foreign Trade was established in 1968 and now has an international network of 3,000 correspondent banks as well as subsidiaries in London, New York, Paris, Frankfurt, Milan and Cairo. All international transactions over the years have been handled by this bank. Part of its capital, $110 million, is held in dollars. The ambition is to privatize this bank with the state as a minority owner, retaining a 20–30 per cent holding. There are plans to set up an export credit guarantee bank and at least one more private bank with foreign participation (Lindsay 1992).

The Romanian privatization programme was planned to take place in two phases. The first phase was to include the auction of 100 per cent of the capital of thirty companies. A list of twenty candidate companies was published in December 1991, consisting of companies with a turnover of between $0.56 million and \$27.8 million during the first half of 1991. Most of these companies were successful exporting companies (Neher 1992).

Romania also opened up its ailing oil and gas industry for bidding in mid-1992, since when four Western companies have concluded exploration contracts with Rompetrol. Romanian oil production fell to 6.79 million tonnes in 1991 and gas to 24.4 billion cu.m., which were the country's lowest levels in twenty-five years. The oil and gas fields require up-to-date equipment and technology to raise production, and special tax incentives, for example twenty-year tax holidays and production licences for twenty-five years, are being offered. Table 1.14 sets out the companies to which licences have been granted.

Table 1.14: Western involvement in Romania's oil and gas industry.

Company	Country	Initial investment
Shell	Netherlands/UK	\$44 million
Amoco	US	\$18.5 million
Enterprise Oil	UK	\$26 million
&		
Canadian Occidental	Canada	

Source: Based on Neher 1992.

Investment Opportunities in East and Central Europe

It has been established that most of the East and Central European countries have gone through a change in government and have announced their ambitions to create Western-style free market economies. It is now appropriate to examine whether there has been any change in the inflow of foreign direct investment (FDI) into these countries. Most of these countries have removed their trade barriers, have launched ambitious privatization programmes and are explicitly welcoming foreign investors. In spite of all this, reactions from Western companies have been rather cautious. A potential market bigger in size than the EC and in desperate need of technological development, consumer and industrial goods, represents enormous opportunities for Western companies and businesses. It is difficult to obtain a true picture of the extent of participation by foreign firms in Eastern European countries, or on the flow of investment into these countries, as reliable data are hard to come by. Moreover, the data which are available are hardly comparable with other countries or industrial sectors (Dunning 1992).

Direct investment in East and Central Europe is becoming a major factor in global resource flows. Most multinationals, although rather reluctant at this stage, have expressed ambitions of entering these markets. Companies such as McDonalds, Pepsi Cola, Coca Cola, Statoil, Ericsson, Fiat, Nokia, Volkswagen, Estée Lauder, Philip Morris and a number of pharmaceutical firms have already established operations in a number of these countries. It is therefore quite important that the flow of FDI to these countries and how it is likely to influence the flow of FDI to other parts of the world should be analysed. In East and Central European countries a number of incentives are being provided to Western multinationals and other investors, in the hope that these linkages at the firm and business levels will help in the reintegration of these economies into the world economy (Gutman 1992).

For decades, opportunities for Western firms to penetrate Eastern European economies were rather poor, and most investments were made by other socialist countries. These countries have thus been highly dependent on each other, and especially on the former Soviet Union. In some sectors, for example energy, this dependence was extremely high.

After 1991, this situation changed drastically, partly because of the decline in production by the former Soviet Union, and partly because the independent republics now want to do business on their own and prefer to sell their raw materials to the West to earn hard currency. Most of the former trading partners are thus in acute need of energy.

Whether these countries will be able to attract foreign investment or not depends upon a number of issues such as the speed and smoothness of the transition from a centrally planned to a market economy, communications, residential and commercial infrastructure for foreign firms and investors, economic and political stability as regards to banking and currency issues, the legal system, particularly property and privatization rights and rules, and the incentives provided to foreign firms and investors, such as tax holidays, facilities for expatriates, remittance of profits, and efficiency in official approvals and permissions.

One very important factor is that while developing new rules and regulations regarding the above variables, policy makers in these countries must consider the compatibility of their policies and rules with those of other countries from which they wish to attract investments. This would reduce uncertainty for foreign investors. These countries not only have to provide new rules and incentives relating to foreign investment, but also have to assure investors that these rules will be there to stay for a long time and will not be changed. It is, therefore, an extremely important and sensitive issue for the countries of East and Central Europe, that they should establish a credibility for their policies and rules.

One of the biggest problems in attracting FDI to these countries has been the uncertainty and scepticism associated with East and Central Europe in the minds of Western investors. Another factor behind the rather slow development and inflow of FDI has been uncertainty of the economic environment in Western Europe, which has been rather volatile due to the implementation of the 1992 Single Market, uncertainties about the Maastricht agreement, and crises in financial markets. National and multinational companies in Europe are busy restructuring themselves and their industries.

The psychological barriers towards investment in East and Central Europe have yet to be overcome. Nevertheless, most experts and commentators agree that the countries of East and Central Europe represent some tremendous opportunities for foreign investors, although as of 1990, the total FDI inflow to these countries had been less than $200 billion – much less than that of other, less developed countries. Table 1.15 illustrates the number of joint ventures registered in East and Central

Table 1.15: Number of joint ventures registered in Central and Eastern Europe, as of April 15, 1990, December 4, 1990 and July 1, 1991.

Country	Total number of joint ventures			Joint ventures with US partners			Population (in millions)	Number of joint ventures per million of population		
	April 1990	Dec. 1990	July 1991	April 1990	Dec. 1990	July 1991		April 1990	Dec. 1990	July 1991
Soviet Union	1,400	2,900	3,700	140	230	–	289	4.8	10.3	12.8
Poland	866	1,903	2,500	60	149	177	38.2	22.7	49.8	65.4
Hungary	600	2,800	4,500	14	200	200	10.6	56.6	264.1	424.5
Bulgaria	60	60	75	10	10	13	9.0	6.6	6.6	8.3
Czechoslovakia	32	600	1,000	1	35	40	15.6	2.0	38.5	64.1
Romania	5	587	1,000	1	53	55	23.2	0.2	25.3	43.1

Cited in: Jermakowicz and Drazek (1992: 2).

Europe as of July 1991. For more statistics on FDI, see other chapters in this volume, for example Chapter 20 by Dunning.

By the second half of 1992, the East and Central European countries, with a combined population of more than 400 million, had attracted FDI stocks comparable with those of Ireland, Norway and Austria, each with a population of less than 5 million. Western economies have attracted fifty times as much foreign direct investment per head of population. Nevertheless, the presence of foreign capital has increased significantly from the previous years. By October 1, 1991 the total number of foreign investment projects registered in these countries was estimated to have grown to 29,902 from 8,441 one year earlier, and 2,231 two years earlier. The total amount of FDI had increased to $9,421 million, from $4,761 million a year before (Artisien, Rojec and Svetlicic 1992).

It should be noted that many foreign direct investments are small projects, with an average value of $500,000, the average size varying from $125,000 in Poland to $1.25 million in the CIS. The countries with greater natural resources tend to attract more foreign capital, and investments aimed at import substitution predominate. Although wholly-owned subsidiaries are allowed in a number of countries, foreign companies are reluctant to make such investments. East Europeans residing abroad have been the major investors, at least at this stage. There is an inclination towards the service sector, which needs smaller amounts of capital and in this sector, most investments have come from Western Europe – for example, 80–85 per cent of the inflow of FDI in Czechoslovakia, Hungary and Poland, and 60 per cent of FDI in the CIS, has been from Western Europe (Jermakowicz and Drazek 1992).

The task of the governments of these countries is to establish export-oriented enterprises, which in the past have been neglected. The policies of earlier regimes were defensive, and industrialization strategies were focused on import substitution, together with heavy protection from imported goods. There has now been a shift in favour of more export-oriented industrialization strategies. These efforts, although undermined by the problems mentioned earlier, are yielding some positive results and there are now a number of East and Central European multinationals which are active in other countries. Although most of these companies are operating in the less-developed countries of Africa and Latin America, there are also a number of operations in Western countries, including Germany, the UK, Italy and Greece. In the period between 1987 and mid-1990, the seven East European CMEA countries established nearly a hundred new companies in the West alone which are fully operational (Gutman 1992).

A number of publications have appeared on investment opportunities in East and Central Europe, and on the political and economic uncertainties in this market. Yet there has been little work concerning the possibility of an uncontrolled flow of goods and services from Eastern Europe to the markets of the West. The EC represents the natural export market for firms from Eastern Europe, but can impose duties, rules against subsidies and anti-dumping rules on such products and services, effectively creating barriers against exports from these countries. It seems likely that the three leading economies, Czechoslovakia, Hungary and Poland, will eventually sign bilateral association agreements with the EC and start playing by its rules (Oliver and Eichmann 1992). As a part of these 'association agreements', the EC can demand that these countries implement competition and state subsidy rules which are compatible with EC rules.

It is, however, apparent that it might be difficult for the EC to impose such rules on the countries of Eastern Europe. No Eastern European country has signed the GATT subsidies code, but it is to be expected that a number of these countries are ready to do so, in anticipation that the subsidy code will contain special and beneficial waivers for economies which are in the process of transition to a free market.

In conclusion, we can see that the dramatic changes in East and Central Europe over the last five years have changed the rules of the game in international business. The chapters presented in this volume also illustrate that we are dealing with new dimensions of international business which have never been studied before. We are therefore at the edge of an evolving area which is characterized by new variables. We have to modify our models to include the emerging dimensions such as the improvement of skills of customers, patience, ethical issues such as corruption or undue compensation, helping policy makers to help you, working with greater levels of uncertainty, collaboration with other foreign companies including competitors, accepting unskilled non-contributory partners in joint ventures, the merits of wholly-owned subsidiaries in comparison to joint ventures, and the importance of networking and lobbying. All the above new dimensions of international business are examined in the chapters in this volume, which we believe brings forward a number of issues which merit consideration in future theories and models of international business.

References

Adjubei, Y. (1992) 'Foreign Investment in the Commonwealth of Independent States: Growth, Operations and Problems', in Artisien *et al.* (eds) *Foreign Direct Investment in Central and Eastern Europe*, London: Macmillan.

Angelis, I. (1991) 'The Role of Money and Monetary Policy in Hungary', in Havlik, P. (ed.) *Dismantling the Command Economy in Eastern Europe*, Boulder, Col.: Westview Press.

Artisien, P., Matija, R. and Svetlicic, M. (eds) (1992) *Foreign Investment in Central and Eastern Europe*, London: Macmillan.

Arzeni, S. (1992) 'Encouraging the Entrepreneur', *OECD Observer* 174, Feb./March: 19–22.

Balabanov, T. and Raimund, D. (1992) 'Eastern and East-West Energy Prospects', in Havlik, P. (ed.) *Dismantling the Command Economy in Eastern Europe*, Boulder, Col.: Westview Press.

Belov, A. (1992) 'Foreign Investment Protection Treaties in Russia', *Business Eastern Europe*, May 25: 254.

Bernard, B. (1992) 'Going to Market', *Europe* 314, March: 6–7.

Brimelow, J. (1992) 'An Economy in Trauma', *Forbes* 149(4): 181.

Business Eastern Europe (1992) May 25, London: The Economist Publisher.

Business Eastern Europe (1992) June 15–29, London: The Economist Publisher.

Business Eastern Europe (1992) August 3, London: The Economist Publisher.

Business Eastern Europe (1992) September 21–8, London: The Economist Publisher.

Business Eastern Europe (1992) October 5, London: The Economist Publisher.

Business Eastern Europe (1993) February 1–22, London: The Economist Publisher.

Business Week (1990) March 26.

Caselli, G. P. and Pastrello, G. (1991) 'Poland: From Plan to Market through Crash', in Havlik, P. (ed.), *Dismantling the Command Economy in Eastern Europe*, Boulder, Col.: Westview Press.

Chambers, F. and Hyland, D. (1992) 'Building a Banking System from Scratch – Advice for the Emerging Market Economies', *Banking World* 10(3): 22–4.

Covicelli, F. and Rocha, R. (1990) 'Stabilization Programs in Eastern Europe: Poland and Yugoslavia', *World Bank*.

Dietz, R. (1992) 'From Command to Exchange Economies', in Havlik, P. (ed.) *Dismantling the Command Economy in Eastern Europe*, Boulder, Col.: Westview Press.

Dunning, J. H. (1992) 'The Prospects for Foreign Direct Investment in Eastern Europe', in Artisien *et al.* (eds) *Foreign Direct Investment in Central and Eastern Europe*, London: Macmillan.

The Economist September 21 (1991), 'A Survey of Business in Eastern Europe: Don't give up now': 1–30.

The Economist December 21 (1991), 'Life After Gorbachov': 33–5.

The Economist April 11 (1992), 'The Least Likely Agricultural Miracle': 85–6.

Edwards, S. (1991) 'Stabilization and Liberalization Policies in Central and Eastern Europe: Lessons from Latin America', NBER Working Paper Series, National Bureau of Economic Research, USA, working paper no. 3816.

Eronen, J. and Simula, M. (1992) 'Foreign Trade Strategies of East European Countries – Case: Pulp and Paper Trade', *Soviet & Eastern European Foreign Trade* 27(3): 66–82.

Feer, J. (1992) 'Pole to Pole', *World Trade* 5(2): 106–10.

Flint, A. (1992) 'Countertrade in EE & CIS Dances to two Tunes', *Business Eastern Europe* June 1: 261–3.

Friedländer, M. (1991) 'Hungary: Slow but Determined Reform Policies', in Havlik, P. (ed.), *Dismantling the Command Economy in Eastern Europe*, Boulder, Col.: Westview Press.

Gabrisch, H. and Laski, K. (1991) 'Transition from Command to Market Economies', in Havlik, P. (ed.) *Dismantling the Command Economy in Eastern Europe*, Boulder, Col.: Westview Press.

Grosser, I. (1991) 'Bulgaria: Delayed Transition Exacerbates Economic Crisis', in Havlik, P. (ed.) *Dismantling the Command Economy in Eastern Europe*, Boulder, Col.: Westview Press.

Gutman, P. (1992) 'Joint Ventures in Eastern Europe and the Dynamics of Reciprocal Flows in East–West Direct Investments: Some New Perspectives', in Artisien *et al.* (eds) *Foreign Direct Investments in Central and Eastern Europe*, London: Macmillan.

Haslach, R. (1992) 'The Bright Lights of Eastern Europe', *Europe* 314, March: 8–9.

Havlik, P. (ed.) (1991) *Dismantling the Command Economy in Eastern Europe*, Boulder, Col.: Westview Press.

Hinds, M. (1990) 'Issues in Introduction of Market Forces in Eastern European Socialist Economies', *World Bank*.

Howard, C. (1992) 'Perestroika from Pleasantville: Lessons Learned Launching Readers Digest in the Soviet Union and Hungary', *Public Relations Quarterly* 36(4): 15–21.

Jermakowicz, W. and Drazek, C. (1992) 'Joint Venture Laws in Eastern Europe: A comparative Assessment', in Artisien *et al.* (eds) *Foreign Direct Investment in Central and Eastern Europe*, London: Macmillan.

Johnson, R., Fabrizio, L., Toohney, B. and Mowrey, M. (1992) 'Baltics; Romania; Hungary; Czechoslovakia', *Business America* 113(7): 19–20.

Kase, R. (1992) 'Petrolium Perestroika', *Colombia Journal of World Business* 26(4): 16–28.

Kiser, J. (1992) 'R&D Management: Looking to the East', *R&D* 34(2): 58–60.

Laski, K. and Gabrisch, H. (1991) 'Transition by Shock in Poland', in Havlik, P. (ed.) *Dismantling the Command Economy in Eastern Europe*, Boulder, Col.: Westview Press.

Layman, P. (1992) 'Meeting Targets Eastern Europe Investment Fears', *Chemical and Engineering News* 70(12): 11–12.

Levcik, F. and Lukas, Z. (1992) 'Czechoslovakia; Changes in Economics Practice lay Behind Rhetoric' in Havlik, P. (ed.) *Dismantling the Command Economy in Eastern Europe*, Boulder, Col.: Westview Press.

Lindsay, M. (1992) *Developing Capital Markets in Eastern Europe, a Business Reference*, London: Pinter Publishers.

Lipton, D. and Sachs, J. (1990) 'Creating a Market Economy in Eastern Europe: The Case of Poland', *Brookings Papers on Economic Activity*, January.

Luxner, L. (1992) 'Albanian–US Association to Promote Bilateral Trade', *Business Eastern Europe*, June 29: 313.

Lynch, R. (1992) *European Marketing – A Guide to New Opportunities*, London: Kogan Page.

McClenahen, J. (1992) 'Light in the East', *Industry Week* 241(5): 14–19.

Melcher, R. and Brady, R. (1992) 'Soviet Breakup? Coup That's Minor Turbulence', *Business Week* 3252, Feb. 17: 70–2.

Mérö, K. (1991) 'The Role of Money and Monetary Policy in Hungary', in Havlik, P. (ed.) *Dismantling the Command Economy in Eastern Europe*, Boulder, Col.: Westview Press.

Nash, T. (1992) 'Chips Off the Old Block', *Director* 45(8): 42–6.

Neher, J. (1992) 'Privatization: A Program of Unprecedented Scope', *Institutional Investor* 26(3): S14–S17.

Nordhaus, W. D. (1990) 'Soviet Economic Reform: The Longest Road', *Brookings Papers*.

OECD Economic Outlook (1991) 'Economic Developments Outside OECD: Central and Eastern Europe' 50, December: 53–7.

Oliver, G. and Eichmann, E. (1992) 'European Community Restrictions on Imports from Central and Eastern Europe: The Impact on Western Investors', *Law & Policy in International Business* 22(4): 721–86.

Papp, B. (1992) 'Will Hungary's Privatization Process Accelerate?' *Business Eastern Europe* May 25: 252.

Petroleum Intelligence Weekly (1991), February 18: 8.

Reed, J. (1992) 'Polish Privatization Back on Track', *Business Eastern Europe* August 3: 373–4.

Smith, T. (1992) 'Special Report: Independent States – Collapse of Soviet Union Opens Opportunities in Independent States', *Business America* 113(7): 16–18.

Sorensen, T. (1992) 'Crack in the Ice for US Business', *International Business* 5(3): 88–9.

Studemann, F. (1992a) 'Serious about Skoda', *International Management* (European Edition) 47(3): 46–9.

Studemann, F. (1992b) 'Baltic Renaissance', *International Management* (European Edition) 47(2): 42–3.

Thoniley, D. and Papp, B. (1992) 'Western Firms Organising Business with Ex-USSR', *Business Eastern Europe* June 22: 297–9.

Wood, B. (1992) 'The Eastern Bloc Two Years Later', *Europe* 314, March: 12–13.

2

Enterprise Culture and Institutional Change in Eastern Europe

Mark Casson

Introduction

Western experts advising East European countries on their transition to market economies face an embarrassing problem: namely, that there is no adequate economic theory of institutions on which to base their policy recommendations. As a result, the advice given by Western economic experts tends to stress those aspects of the economic system which can be understood using the limited range of concepts employed by conventional economic theory.

One manifestation of this is the extraordinary emphasis given to adjusting real wages down to the low level of productivity in industry (Kolodko and Rutkowski 1991). The idea is sound, but its significance has been exaggerated to distract attention from the fact that so little can be said about other equally important issues.

Many East European enterprises have suffered from the collapse of the Soviet market; since their products are ill-adapted to Western requirements, the value productivity of East European enterprises is very low (Wyplosz 1992). Measured in terms of imported consumer goods, the equilibrium real wage is so low that many families would sink even further below the poverty line if short-run adjustments were to be made in full.

Because most major enterprises are state-owned, wages can be subsidized using the 'soft' budget constraints within which these enterprises work (Sachs 1991). But this means that a large amount of government expenditure has to be allocated to subsidizing loss-making industries. Although defence expenditure has been cut back, resource savings have been limited because many workers are still employed in the state-owned defence supply industries, even though there is little for them to do. Expenditure on subsidies to state-owned enterprises diverts resources from schools, hospitals, social services, and so on, so that the 'social wage', which includes unpriced services, falls even if the real wage does not.

Tightening up these budget constraints has now become an objective in its own right. But if the real wage is maintained while enterprise budgets are cut, the number of people employed must fall. This should, in theory, eliminate overmanning and help to improve productivity, thereby restoring some of the balance between productivity and the real wage. In practice, however, it has proved difficult to raise productivity without new investment. Thus unemployment has risen and, in the absence of adequate social security provision, widespread prostitution, theft and even violent crime has resulted.

Budgetary imbalance leads East European governments into either printing more money or borrowing from abroad. These are the obvious ways for them to try and finance new investment. They could, in principle, borrow from or tax their own citizens, but the margin of taxable surplus, and the willingness to lend, are both too low. Inflation caused by increases in the money supply is the obvious result (Hansson 1991). This is, of course, just yet another way in which the real wage is reduced to its equilibrium level. For with nominal wage stickiness, inflation simply erodes real purchasing power.

Faced with these difficulties, East European governments have been obliged to turn to the International Monetary Fund (IMF) and the European Bank for Reconstruction and Development. The IMF perceives East European issues in the context of its experience in lending to less developed countries. It believes that correct domestic pricing is necessary to guide the structural adjustment process, and that this is possible only if tradeable goods are priced at international levels. In extreme cases, domestic price distortion can sustain industries which have negative value added at international prices. The IMF therefore favours the dismantling of protection, the abolition of exchange controls, and the maintenance of monetary discipline through currency boards. The correct pricing of capital requires financial markets, and these in turn require a modern banking system. Efficient pricing of labour means not only short-run 'cold turkey' while real wages are reduced, but the elimination of long-run distortions caused by high marginal rates of taxation on wage and salary income.

Bitter experience of lending to irresponsible governments has created considerable cynicism within the IMF towards public sector investment projects. This has led to a series of related targets: to encourage privatization; to promote transparency of government finances, in order to discourage corruption and reveal the true opportunity costs of prestige projects; and to achieve 'coherence' between the policies of debtor governments and the IMF – for example, to reduce high-pressure selling of arms and conspicuous high-technology equipment by Western firms.

There is general consensus that in the long run, the key prerequisite for raising living standards is to raise productivity. It is here that the limitations of Western advice became apparent. While Western advisers are quite convincing on the question of how to reduce the real wage to match a given level of productivity, they are much less convincing on the subject of how to raise productivity to sustain a given real wage.

Raising productivity is not just a matter of increasing the aggregate capital stock, as a simplistic application of neoclassical economics might suggest. If this were the case, previous investments would have yielded a much higher rate of return. The problem is not so much the aggregate capital stock but its composition. It is also the effectiveness with which labour utilizes the capital, the quality of the raw materials used, and the suitability of the product. In other words, it is a micro-level problem.

Micro-level analysis of new investment can be carried out using project appraisal techniques – private net present value calculation, or social cost-benefit analysis, to capture external effects. But for separate micro-level decisions to be properly co-ordinated, accurate prices are needed. When markets are not in place, such prices are difficult to obtain. Moreover, since the absence of some markets distorts prices in other markets, it is a complete system of markets that is required. An incomplete system of markets could, in principle, generate such distorted prices that it would be worse than no system of markets at all.

A market system is thus, to some extent, an indivisible asset. The creation of a market system requires an institutional revolution, to put as many markets in place as quickly as possible. Once the system is in place, micro problems can be solved using a bottom-up approach, because the market incentive system will support an efficient delegation of decisions.

But the creation of a market system requires a top-down approach. Markets require property rights, and property rights normally benefit from being centrally enforced. The framework within which rights are created and modified is usually centralized as well. The key problem is how to design this system to meet the needs of the East European economies. At the moment there is no generally accepted set of principles for the institutional design of a market system.

A market system is not a purely technical artefact. It is also a social organism. The information flows of the market system are embedded in language and culture, and in networks of trust which assure the reliability and intelligibility of the information. As such, a system needs to be adapted to local customs and traditions, if it is to be used effectively. The implementation of general principles must therefore take account of local factors of this kind. But without an understanding of these principles, appropriate forms of institutional adaptation may not occur.

Enterprise and organizational design

Western economic advice to East European enterprises tends to be practical rather than conceptual, and specific rather than general. Western experts can advise on how to set up an accounting system for cost control, how to carry out technological appraisal and market research, and so on. But the methods are usually based just on standard industry practice, rather than on any explicit comparison with alternative systems.

It is difficult for the experts to articulate general principles of organizational design because, once again, these are not well understood. This is not really surprising, because markets and organizations are alternative co-ordinating mechanisms, and so many of the general principles apply to both. Internalization theory (Coase 1937) indicates in general terms where the boundaries of the firm and market should lie, but it does not fully analyse the choice between alternative market structures, on the one hand, and alternative organizational structures on the other. Industrial organization theory explains the importance of avoiding monopoly, a point which is usually made in the context of markets but which applies equally well within the firm, where selfish individuals or groups can use monopoly power to block necessary change. But the problem of reconciling the gains from scale economies with the costs of monopoly is still not fully resolved, as current Western controversy about natural monopoly regulation makes clear.

It is issues that require a fully dynamic analysis where the limitations of conventional theory are most acute (see, for example, Husain and Sahay 1992). Even fundamental issues such as how to grow small enterprises to a significant level remain opaque, because they involve questions of evolution, uncertainty and change. Similar problems make it difficult to advise on the reorganization of large, state-owned enterprises too (Bös 1992). While there is general agreement that East European economies need more medium-size enterprises, there is no consensus on how this apparently desirable state of affairs is to be brought about.

The fundamental problem, it is suggested here, is that the nature of entrepreneurship is not fully understood. A better understanding of entrepreneurship would provide several of the missing principles which the appraisal of alternative economic institutions requires. While it may be obvious at a practical level that entrepreneurship is the key to economic development within a market system, entrepreneurship has never been accorded the central place in Western social science that it deserves. Thus while specific techniques can be taught by Western experts, these experts have little advice to offer on the general principles governing the growth of enterprise.

Part of the problem is the naive Western view that everyone is potentially entrepreneurial and that failures of entrepreneurship are simply the consequence of rigidity and repression. The repression of entrepreneurship is typically blamed on the State. Deregulate and privatize, it is argued, and you can rely on people to do the rest.

The alternative view is that entrepreneurship is a very scarce attribute. Most people wish to conform rather than to stand out, and are accustomed to following other people's opinions rather than thinking for themselves. According to this view, a society needs to make the most of its limited supply of entrepreneurial talent, selectively recruiting able individuals to an entrepreneurial elite which takes strategic decisions on behalf of other people. If entrepreneurship is extremely scarce then it may be more important, in fact, to concentrate entrepreneurs in the government service and political life, where there are many big decisions to be made, rather than, say, to disperse them across medium-sized enterprises in the private sector.

These contrasting views have important practical implications. The scarcity view tends to support an 'industrial policy' approach to the restructuring of state-owned enterprises. It suggests that entrepreneurial public officials, acting with the benefit of Western advice, could usefully develop an integrated restructuring programme for the mature heavy industries and negotiate a comprehensive financial package underwritten by Western governments. The populist view of entrepreneurship, on the other hand, suggests that such policy-formulation is premature. Only when the diverse views of individual owners of newly privatized enterprises have been sought can sound policies be devised. It is not the intellectual sophistication of the judgement that matters on this view, but rather that the judgement is informed by the calculated self-interest of the private owners of the firm. Current privatization practice based on the distribution of vouchers to the electorate clearly reflects this second view.

In practice, both views have something to commend them. Where small-scale entrepreneurial activity, such as petty trading, is concerned, the assumption that many (though certainly not all) people possess entrepreneurial potential may have some validity. But when it comes to large-scale activities, where some familiarity with scientific and managerial techniques is called for, scarcity seems to be the rule. This is, of course, the kind of entrepreneurial activity that Schumpeter (1934) had in mind when he articulated his distinctively elitist view of economic development. If this assessment is correct, then more weight clearly needs to be given to the industrial policy approach outlined above.

Another implication of the naive Western view is that the emergence of appropriate institutions is a sufficient condition for entrepreneurship to flourish. Such institutions will emerge from a competitive process which selects the best-adapted institution for each niche of the economy. The alleged justification for this view is that Western capitalism evolved over centuries as a result of numerous small and localized experiments in organization. The most successful of these experiments have led to the emergence of certain common organizational forms, as diverse as parliamentary democracy, the limited liability company, the stock market, and so on. In almost every country, it is stressed, these forms have emerged with local variation which is crucial to their effective performance. Thus in Britain, government is centralized, companies have a single board to represent the interests of the owner as dominant stakeholder, and the stock market involves extensive participation by small investors. In Germany, on the other hand, government is decentralized on federal lines, large companies have two-tier boards to represent a diversity of stakeholder interests, and the stock market is less important than the banks in financing new investment by industry.

This theory suggests that the reasons underlying the success of these firms and the rationale of their local adaptation is too complex to be understood. There can be no grand design for an economic system (Hayek 1960). The demise of the socialist central planning system is held to be the obvious demonstration of this. But there is no design for the market system either. The bad news, therefore, is that Eastern Europe must just wait for its own institutional structures to evolve. The main precondition for this is simply freedom – freedom for anyone to experiment pragmatically with a new organizational form, and the freedom of others to imitate a successful experiment if they wish.

Since this theory offers no 'quick fix', however, it leaves a gap in the market. Surely there must be Western models which can be taken down 'off the shelf' and used as a basis from which local adaptations can emerge? It surely cannot be reasonable to expect Eastern Europe to replay Western European history, simply to ensure that institutions are well adapted to their needs.

Sixty years ago most East European countries shared much of the Western culture of the time, and this suggests that it might be possible to reinvent the institutions of the pre-socialist era. Such reinvented institutions would presumably resonate with cultural traditions, and so stand a good chance of working effectively. Apart from the serious problem that sixty years implies a gap of two generations, during which the West and the East have grown apart, there is also the difficulty that – with one or two exceptions, such as Hungary and the Czech republic – the early twentieth century was not a particularly successful period for East European economies, partly because of the unresolved political tensions stemming from the partitioning of territory after the First World War. Thus it might be necessary to turn the clock back much further in order to reinvent a country's golden age.

This paper argues for an intermediate position, which neither uncritically imposes contemporary Western European institutions on Eastern European econ-omies, nor simply liberalizes as much as possible as quickly as possible and then waits for order to emerge slowly from the ensuing anarchy. The key to the pro-posed policy is that entrepreneurship and the institutions that support it are, in fact, susceptible to analysis, and that it is possible to use this analysis to design institutions that will be well adapted to local conditions. It is a medium-run strat-egy to be pursued over a five to ten-year period. The important thing is to be able to identify the principles governing the efficiency of entrepreneurial institutions. These principles can then be applied using the local knowledge of businessmen and politicians who are familiar with local conditions. The Western experts' contri-bution will comprise, first, the elucidation of these principles and, second, the development of a partnership with East European practitioners in framing the constitutions and formulating the precise organizational structures involved. These principles are outlined in the following section, following which the main argu-ment is resumed.

The influence of institutions on economic performance

Entrepreneurship is popularly understood as involving the founding of small firms and their subsequent growth, first to medium-size enterprises and, ultimately, to large-scale ones. The founding of a firm is usually visualized in terms of the discovery of an opportunity that the founder decides to exploit.

Discovery

Discoveries can be imbued with very different degrees of significance. Most dis-coveries by small-firm entrepreneurs relate to localized changes in the economic environment. Economies are in a continual state of flux, and those who are the first to discover the latest change acquire a temporary monopoly of this information which they can exploit for profit (Kirzner 1973). Such entrepreneurship is essen-tially responsive. When circumstances change again, the opportunity disappears and a new one appears elsewhere.

A trivial instance is where a craftsman who has been made redundant by a large firm 'discovers' that he can still make a modest living by practising his craft out of his garden shed, doing odd jobs for neighbours and bartering payment through the local 'black' economy. Businesses of this kind typically have no potential for growth.

This does not mean that small informal businesses cannot grow. It is not unknown for door-to-door commission salesmen, reflecting on their successes and failures, to evolve a marketing concept with considerable potential. The difference between the craftsman and the salesman in this respect is that the former is typically oriented to the emotional satisfaction derived from indulging the instinct of workmanship, rather than to the income derived from providing satisfaction to other people instead. The marketer is geared to helping other people solve their problems, while the craftsman's effort goes into solving his own problem of how to derive interest and enjoyment from his work (Smith 1967).

Sometimes major discoveries can be made, however. The chance of making a major discovery enhances entrepreneurial prestige – it implies that the entrepreneur can 'make his mark' by leaving the world in a very different state from that in which he found it. These chances seemed high for the merchant adventurers of fifteenth- and sixteenth-century Europe, and for the mineral prospectors in nineteenth-century Africa, Australasia and Western America. There were uncharted territories to be explored and an open geographical frontier. Most of these frontiers are now closed in the physical sense. It is nowadays in the world of ideas that the most important frontiers remain open, and in the application of these ideas to solve practical problems and improve the material standards of everyday life.

Yet in intellectual terms the frontier is far more open in some societies than in others. There are prominent systems of thought which maintain that all the really important ideas have already been discovered. Marxism is, to some extent, in this category: it is amazing to realize, for example, that in the former Soviet Union, historical materialism was considered so definitive that two of the major breakthroughs of twentieth-century physics – relativity and the uncertainty principle – were considered unsound because of their conflict with Marxist views of causality and determinism.

Religious revelations that are taken as definitive can sometimes exert a similar constraining influence. Interestingly, though, Western Christianity has embraced a Cartesian dualism, in which scientific inquiry into material creation can coexist alongside moral and metaphysical speculation about the mind and soul. Occasional conflicts, as between Darwinism and Biblical fundamentalism, should not obscure the fact that religion has done little in the West to curb scientific optimism. It has, indeed, actively promoted certain lines of inquiry – for example, by providing a moral impetus to fund expensive medical research.

Appropriation

Optimism about scientific discoveries, and the possibility of their social application, is only one of several entrepreneurial stimuli. Another concerns the possibility of appropriating ideas for private profit. Western societies take an ambiguous view on this. On the one hand, there is the attitude that what is uncharted is not yet appropriated, and so is 'up for grabs'. When allied to the view that discovery is normally a consequence not of luck, but of dedicated effort, this view suggests that the private appropriation of a discovery is a natural reward for the expenditure involved.

On the other hand, there is the Christian view that everything is ultimately God's creation and that man is not the owner but only the steward of it. This suggests that everything is, in some sense, already appropriated, and so can only be held under licence. A similar conclusion follows from the socialist view that everything is owned by society, whether or not some individual has yet discovered it.

There is an important difference between them, however, in that society usually expresses its rights through the representatives who govern it, and these representatives therefore acquire considerable power over the disposal of such rights. In practice, this means that the discoverer must negotiate with central government in order to obtain a licence to exploit a discovery – a licence which in many cases may well be denied. The religious concept of stewardship does not have to be expressed through a powerful earthly representative – though medieval popes, for instance, were not slow to exploit some possibilities of this kind. The exercise of stewardship can be decentralized through the conscience of the discoverer, and the voluntary self-restraint he shows in the exercise of his rights. Central regulation is then invoked only if negative externalities emerge which call for the rights acquired as a result of the discovery to be more precisely defined.

It is evident that in the Western system, the right to appropriate discoveries is much stronger than in a socialist or theocratic state, and that the pecuniary incentive to innovate is much greater as a result. The existence of a wide range of undiscovered and unappropriated ideas is taken for granted. An optimistic view of the consequences of discovery is generally taken, and this is reflected in the desire to encourage the discoverer by giving him the 'natural' reward for his effort. It is recognized that the exploitation of a new discovery may have unintended consequences. Political institutions are designed to be responsive to popular concerns about their indirect effects, and if necessary, legislation can be passed to protect existing rights.

Private ownership

Ideas themselves are notoriously difficult to appropriate. Patent infringements are difficult to detect, the litigation is costly, and the scope of patent systems is limited in any case. Often the most effective way to appropriate rewards from an idea is to focus on its application. The typical entrepreneurial idea is exploited by putting existing resources to a novel use. The entrepreneur integrates forward by buying up the resources required by the application. If these resources are in fixed supply, and he can keep his idea secret until negotiations are complete, then a pure rent can be obtained which reflects the value of the idea.

This mechanism requires that ownership of these resources can be traded freely between individuals. It also requires that ownership is a quite general right which allows the owner to deploy his resources in any way he likes, provided that it does not infringe the rights of other parties. This highlights the basic point that in an entrepreneurial economy, individuals as well as corporate entities can hold rights and that, with certain minor limitations, they can acquire or dispose of them as they wish (Putterman 1990). What is more, because the rights are quite general, the redeployment of an asset to a novel use does not require the creation of a novel right to authorize this specific use. All potential as well as actual uses are included in the ownership right (Casson 1982).

A strength can easily become a weakness, however, and the very generality of the ownership right means that unanticipated conflicts can readily emerge. Two parties may coexist happily without co-ordination, so long as they do not make choices that directly impinge on each other. When by chance one decides to make a different choice, the other party is disturbed and an inconsistency in the initial distribution of rights is revealed which had hitherto been hidden by a fortuitous combination of choices. The rights of one of the parties must now be modified, and the question of whether the party whose rights are restricted should be compensated must also be addressed. The private ownership system generates many instances of this kind, and its success depends crucially on the efficiency with which such conflicts can be resolved.

It is unfortunate that the political and legal systems of East European countries are currently ill-equipped to deal with a regular stream of cases of this kind. It is even more unfortunate that they are preoccupied with more fundamental problems relating not so much to inconsistencies between rights relating to different resources, as to inconsistencies relating to the *same* resources – conflicts between rival claimants to the same resources stemming from controversy over whether previous transfers of ownership were legitimate or not. Until such issues have been resolved, markets in these resources are effectively blighted, because no one can afford to acquire a resource if they are unsure who holds the legal title to it. Since the acquisition of resources is one of the basic ways in which entrepreneurial ideas are exploited, this is a fundamental problem which must urgently be resolved.

Screening

While small discoveries can often be exploited using the personal wealth of the entrepreneur and his immediate circle – taking a second mortgage on the house, borrowing from family and friends, etc. – it is difficult to exploit a really major discovery in this way. If an employer will not back the idea, then the discoverer must become self-employed and seek support from financial institutions. Such backers are likely to take a view of the opportunity the entrepreneur believes he has discovered which is very different from that of the entrepreneur himself. The entrepreneur's very limited experience may make him unaware of the many practical difficulties that face a small business – difficulties that are only too familiar to the financial institutions he approaches.

While the entrepreneur has made an initial judgement that an opportunity exists, the financial institution must independently validate that assessment by making a judgement of its own. It is only natural that those who make 'discoveries' tend to be more confident about them than are those to whom the discovery is reported. The success of an economic system depends crucially on the quality of judgement exercised by financial institutions of this kind. Since financial institutions are normally in competition with each other, it is not the quality of any one institution that is crucial, but the quality of the institutions as a whole. It is possible that all the financial institutions in a given country may share a particular cultural bias which influences the kind of project to which they prefer to lend. In one country there may be a bias to large high-technology projects, for example, and in another to small-scale retail projects, or to property development. There may also be cultural differences between the institutions and their borrowers, caused by differences in education, social background, urban *versus* rural residence, and so on. Such differences may impair communication, leading the institutions to overestimate certain risks involved, so denying funds to viable projects. A relatively homogeneous society sharing a culture that embraces a diversity of perspectives is likely to be most successful in screening entrepreneur's ideas.

Liquidity

Financial intermediaries such as banks are not just in the business of lending to entrepreneurs – they are also in the business of supplying liquidity to their depositors. If pressed, banks may wish to liquidate their investments, and so they are interested in how much of their investment can be recovered at short notice, should circumstances require it. They therefore tend to require collateral of a highly liquid form, such as land, or inventory ready for sale. In some cases these very specific collateral requirements, coupled with the short-term nature of bank lending, may be a serious constraint on the entrepreneur's ability to take a long-term view of his business.

The obvious way for a firm to mitigate this liquidity problem is to borrow funds through a stock market instead. A stock market provides the individual investor with an opportunity to liquidate his investment by selling his shares to another individual. It does not require him to physically withdraw funds from the firm, since what he withdraws is immediately replaced. The entrepreneur is still under some external pressure, however, because if the equity shares carry votes, then a significant sell-out by existing shareholders could place control of the firm in hostile hands.

The efficiency implications of this are not so adverse as they may seem, however. Entrepreneurs can always make mistakes – no one's judgement is perfect – and so it is advantageous for a firm to make as few irreversible commitments as possible until its plans have clearly survived the 'market test'. A firm which requires a large injection of outside capital to make an irreversible lumpy investment – in a large customized piece of durable equipment with no second-hand value, for example – is a less attractive economic proposition, other things being equal, than a firm which plans to make only a small trial investment in standard equipment which can be scaled up through replication if experience shows that it is successful.

It is interesting to note, in this connection, that many of the most successful individual entrepreneurs of the twentieth century have been the founders of retail chains, who have developed and refined their marketing concept by experimenting in one location before standardizing it and repeating the formula many times over elsewhere. Although their businesses rapidly grew to be very large, they were financed to a significant extent by reinvested profits – a strategy made possible by replicating small reversible investments, rather than committing to a single large irreversible one. The industrial mega-projects of the East European socialist regimes illustrate the converse case, in which large irreversible commitments have been made on the basis of a largely hypothetical analysis of needs and resources because the owner – the State – has attached no weight to the liquidity aspects of the investment.

Confidence

When the assets of a business are illiquid, the owners of equity are underwriting its commitments by providing insurance. The owners accept a large payment under good conditions as a compensation for low payments under poor conditions. Their 'premium' is reflected in the average rate of return.

If everyone has confidence in the firm, then insurance will be forthcoming cheaply – the share price will be high and it will be easy for the firm to raise funds through new issues. But when confidence is low it may be difficult to get anyone at all to subscribe to new issues. If the degree of confidence in an enterprise reflects well-informed opinion, then there is no problem, but if confidence is volatile and led by rumour and fashion, then a considerable degree of distortion may be introduced into the growth of industry – fashionable industries expand at the expense of unfashionable ones, and investment proceeds in intermittent spurts as general confidence fluctuates over time. One of the dangers of 'popular' capitalism is that ill-informed investors may be attracted into the market as a boom is reaching its peak, encouraging even greater excesses of investment which defer recovery from the ensuing slump.

Conflict resolution

When equity markets are poorly developed, as they are in many countries, then confidence becomes important in a different way. Large-scale projects normally require several shareholders to finance them, and these shareholders become locked into the firm by the difficulty of disposing of their stock. While they may have perceived a common interest in backing the firm at the outset, unanticipated managerial issues may emerge which create conflict between them. While all were initially optimistic, for example, one or two may become pessimistic and try to urge caution when others still want to expand.

Disagreements between shareholders are not the only cause of problems, moreover. There may be other stakeholders – such as employees and even major customers and suppliers – who may feel (particularly if they are creditors) that their opinion should be considered, too. Western capitalism generally regards the interests of shareholders as dominant, but this is not universally accepted in capitalist countries and there is still a popular view – advocated by trade union leaders and socialist politicians – that natural justice requires that workers, whose effort is embodied in the product of the enterprise, should be considered as having equivalent rights. Although the capitalist employer would typically argue that these rights were voluntarily surrendered when the wage bargain was struck, the advocate of workers' rights will reply that this concession was only extracted through negotiation under duress, or that it is so fundamental as to be inalienable anyway.

These are not the sort of disagreements that any of the parties can easily walk away from. On the other hand, it is difficult to achieve consensus. Some political process is required which will allow each party to compromise without appearing to undermine their ideological position. If the process is perceived to be fair then it will be taken as legitimate by the loser. But it is difficult for a process to appear fair if its outcome is a foregone conclusion. There needs to be an element of chance in the process – a chance mechanism which could equally likely favour any of the parties. Voting is the preferred mechanism in democratic nations, but at the enterprise level independent arbitration is popular too. The absence of a recent democratic tradition in East Europe is a potential source of weakness in this respect. Resort to coercion is obviously an imperfect method of conflict resolution; democratic methods are required not only at the national level, but at the enterprise level too.

There is a sense, of course, in which resort to a political mechanism is itself a symptom of failure. It indicates that conflicts of economic interest are being magnified, if anything, rather than reduced, by ideological factors. If there were a single unified ideology then everyone would agree on who the stakeholders were, and on the nature of their responsibilities to other parties. From an efficiency point of view this would be preferable to the ideological conflict which is perpetuated from generation to generation even in advanced Western countries. It is true that ideological differences are a manifestation of the same intellectual vitality that sustains innovation. Serious danger arises only when the ideological positions grow so far apart that there is little common ground. Toleration of diversity is desirable, but only within the limits of a reasonably homogeneous culture. Societies with a strong cultural tradition (such as Japan) tend to have quick and peaceful mechanisms of internal conflict resolution, and perform efficiently as a result.

Networks

Conflict resolution is important not only within the firm, but between firms as well. Competition is the classic conflict-resolution mechanism in inter-firm relations. Each firm plays off its trading partners against their rivals. The scope for bilateral bargaining is dramatically reduced by the threat to switch to another partner.

This threat is only credible, however, if the firm is not heavily dependent on a particular customer or supplier. If the firm has invested heavily in adapting its plant to a particular source of supply or demand, then its bargaining power is undermined (Klein, Crawford and Alchian 1978). It needs to trust in the integrity of its partner instead. Trust is also important in constraining the incentive to default on transactions. However satisfactory the outcome of a bargain may be, it is quite useless if the other party has no intention of honouring the contract. While blatant default – such as short supplies or non-payment – can be punished in law, covert default on quality is more difficult to detect. It is also more difficult to prove in court, given the way that the law of evidence normally works.

Networks of trust have proved very important in the textile and garment industry, for example. This industry is particularly interesting because it is historically important as an engine of economic development. It is labour intensive, uses a standardized technology, and uses relatively small amounts of inexpensive equipment, for which a good second-hand markets exists. It is therefore well suited to small owner-managed firms which can grow under constant returns to scale by reinvesting profits, as described earlier.

But each small firm requires an independent source of textile inputs and an independent buyer of its output too. To reduce transport costs and inventory levels in a highly competitive industry, the supplier and customer must be close by. Hence textile firms at adjacent stages of production tend to agglomerate into industrial districts. Within a district there is an elaborate network of inter-firm linkages in which, if the district as a whole is to be internationally competitive, the costs of transactions must be very low.

Building networks of trust between independent businesses can be very time-consuming unless there has been some preliminary socialization between the owners concerned. In many countries ethnic connections based on extended families play an important role in this. In some urban areas in less-developed countries, having ancestors from the same village may prove an effective bond between recent immigrants. In established urban communities, churches, local political parties and clubs can play an important role, both in facilitating introductions and in creating an atmosphere of trust. It is interesting to note that some of the most conspicuous examples of networks of trust are found outside the Western countries from which East European policy-makers typically take their lead. Powerful networks are common in the Chinese communities of South East Asia and in Islamic societies as well. Their positive influence on the competitiveness of Japanese industries, too, is well known. Eastern Europe needs to borrow its institutional models eclectically if it is to reform itself along best-practice institutional lines.

The institutions which engineer trust generally operate, it should be noted, on a non-profit basis. This highlights an important point not usually recognized by advocates of market liberalization – namely that the enforcement of many market contracts hinges ultimately on the efficacy of non-market institutions. An entrepreneurial society is not, therefore, necessarily a profit-centred one. Indeed, too much emphasis on the selfish pursuit of profit will tend to undermine affiliation to these non-profit institutions. In the long run this will impair efficiency, as contracts become more difficult to enforce and a sophisticated division of labour between firms becomes more difficult to sustain.

Law and government

If a costless system of law were available to the business community then, of course, trust would not be a problem. Every conceivable contingency affecting the rewards to contracting parties would be itemized and any disagreement referred to an impartial judge. The judge's decision would reflect a perfect comprehension of all the relevant facts of the case – facts which in everyday life are sometimes quite impossible to ascertain. The absurdity of the scenario confirms that the law is not a sufficient answer to the problem of trust in the business community.

It is equally utopian to suppose, however, that even with a rich variety of non-profit organizations, the web of mutual obligation would embrace every conceivable pair of contracting parties. Ultimately, therefore, there needs to be some coercive sanction against persistent offenders against the moral code of the business community. While a system of law may not be sufficient for contractual enforcement, it is necessary in dealing with persistent offenders.

The practical difficulty lies not so much in creating an institution, such as the State, with sufficient coercive power, for even very primitive communities have a military defence force which can be deployed for civilian use. The problem lies in a constraining abuse of state power. A good legal system requires the exercise of self-restraint by judges (in refusing bribes, resisting intimidation, etc.) and a good political system requires similar self-restraint by leaders (in not suspending the democratic constitution once they have been elected, for example). Even where individual members of society cannot trust each other, they need to be able to trust the judges and politicians who intermediate between them.

This highlights the point that successful economic transition in East Europe requires an efficient judicial system and reputable government (Siebert 1992). While it may be true that a democratic system offers the best guarantee of this, democracy *per se* may not be essential. The important point is that whoever rules is widely trusted to respect rights and enforce contracts. This is important not only internally, but externally too. The integrity of government is an important issue for foreign lenders: while they may be prepared to tolerate a non-democratic system (for if it is stable, it offers the prospect of long-term consistency of policy), they will not tolerate a government which repeatedly reneges on its commitments. One of the key issues for East European transition is therefore a political rather than an economic one, namely, to find the best way of maintaining a stable and honest government that will respect individual rights.

Cultural influences on performance

The preceding discussion has emphasized that entrepreneurial activity is very much embedded in the social and political system. This raises the question of whether certain attitudes towards social and political life are more conducive to entrepreneurship than others. It has already been suggested, for example, that a confident, scientifically optimistic attitude is required for successful innovation.

It has been suggested too that a high-trust atmosphere promotes effective co-operation, both within and between firms. The importance of co-operation in entrepreneurship demonstrates that the typical Western view of the successful entrepreneur as a highly competitive and assertive individualist is very misleading. It is particularly unfortunate that the low-trust attitude of contemporary Western culture reinforces the low trust that is already apparent in many East European countries as a legacy of the Stalinist era. Not only did Stalinist thinking itself involve a suspicious attitude to others, but the increasing absurdities of over-centralized planning led to a general distrust of promises made by anyone working within the economic system. This atmosphere of distrust was exacerbated by the widespread use of informers reporting to the secret police. A low-trust attitude is, in general, a source of weakness rather than strength, and it must be hoped that the recovery of 'traditional values' in some East European countries may help to build up the kind of high-trust culture that the West is currently in a poor position to supply.

An entrepreneurial culture must combine high trust with some degree of indi-vidualism. A successful entrepreneur is usually an individualist in the sense that his views do not always conform to the general opinion of those around him – indeed, if they did, he would have little value, since anyone else in the group could arrive at the same decisions he did. But as an individualist, he must not be moti-vated by entirely selfish means (Casson 1991). It is certainly useful for him to experience the tension of striving for something that it is difficult to attain, for such an attitude reduces the subjective cost of hard work. But the striving should not be for material success alone. Many successful entrepreneurs of the past have held very naive views about the intrinsic value of the goods they produced. This naivety was a considerable source of strength in giving conviction to their personal efforts to promote their product and enabling them to motivate their employees to take their work very seriously. These naive views were in turn often a manifestation of religious or philosophical convictions. Many successful entrepreneurs in both the US and the UK have belonged to sects which demanded high levels of personal commitment from their members. The tensions of business life were reflected in the tensions these religious groups experienced between their own value systems and those of the establishment of their day. Although material success often led these entrepreneurs (or their descendents) to compromise with established values in order to win respectability, this does not detract from the fact that success was in large part attributable to the high moral value that they accorded to their early business activities. East European enterprises need to rediscover a sense of mission too. This is important in convincing customers of management's commitment to product quality and motivating employees by giving them pride in their job. Cultural factors will be important in determining whether the new business leaders emerging in East Europe have these qualities or not. First impressions suggest that, unfortunately, many of them do not.

Culture can contribute not only to enhanced co-operation: it can improve the quality of decision-making too. Given all the imponderables in the typical business situation, and the need for a quick decision, good judgement is extremely important. Judgement typically requires a combination of theoretical perspective and practical knowledge. This combination is found in relatively few cultures. Marxism is essentially a theoretical construct, and in countries previously dominated by Marxist ideology, theory is likely to be valued much more highly than practical experience. Although this may not apply to industrial craftsmen, it certainly applies to the political and business elites.

The West can offer examples of businesses which have been run on the basis of theories too, however, and the results have generally been poor. Most theories oversimplify and suggest that just one or two factors dominate where business performance is concerned. In large Western firms, concepts of 'divisionalization', 'globalization' or 'diversification' are often applied uncritically, without reference to the firm's industrial and institutional environment. Where day-to-day decision-making, rather than long-term strategy formulation, is concerned, theory manifests itself in the belief that one set of indicators – sales, market share, mark-up, or whatever – is more important than all others. Power within the organization is given to the managers who collect the relevant figures and plan the relevant responses, while managers who deal with other issues which are, in reality, no less important, do not get a chance to make their views known. It is their role to implement policies handed down from the more powerful managers, and not to question these decisions on the basis of their own set of data.

A theoretical orientation also encourages a preference for radical rather than incremental change. Theory not only throws up new ideas, but provides a framework within which the practical application of those ideas can be legitimated. It gives an unwarranted sense of confidence to those who overlook the very restrictive assumptions on which the theory is based. This preference for radicalism rather than incrementalism is likely to be another instance of the Marxist legacy. It is already apparent in the very doctrinaire way in which market principles have been applied in liberalizing East European countries. One theoretical system – based on an abstract notion of a market – has been substituted for another theoretical system based on surplus value. The dilution of theory with practical experience has yet to come. One reason, of course, is that practical experience of markets is singularly lacking in East Europe, for historical reasons. The speed at which it can be accumulated, and the willingness to use it, will be a major factor in the success of the transition to a market economy.

Overall, it seems that the cultural legacy of Marxism may prove a major handicap in the newly liberalizing economies (Etzioni 1991). The need for interpersonal trust in the development of business partnerships and business networks is underestimated, as a result of the cynical low-trust culture promoted by the Stalinist style of management (Attali 1992). Even in countries such as Hungary and Poland, where intermittent attempts at decentralization have been made, this legacy still seems to remain. While there is little problem in most of the countries with people being ambitious to improve their quality of life, the extent to which moral as well as material objectives are important remains unclear. In several countries the churches are still a powerful influence, but traditionally the Catholic Church, which is dominant, has tended, unlike the Protestant tradition, to promote organic solidarity rather than individualistic values.

Foreign direct investment and the transfer of cultural values

The macroeconomic perspective set out at the beginning of this paper makes it clear that much of the new investment required for industrial restructuring must come from foreign sources. Pure capital – in the form of fixed-interest loans – is relatively homogeneous, and can be obtained from private, governmental or intergovernmental sources. Where indigenous technology and management are weak, however, and access to foreign markets is poor, foreign expertise is required as well. Much of the expertise at the enterprise level resides in foreign firms.

It is quite possible, in principle, to obtain these different inputs from different sources using arm's-length contracts: to issue bonds to obtain capital and then invest the capital in the purchase of licences, brands and consultants' expertise (Casson 1979). It is often advantageous to link such procurements, however. To encourage the supply of good quality expertise it is useful to introduce an element of payment by results, and one way of doing this is to persuade the supplier to take an equity stake. This may also be advantageous from the supplier's point of view, too. For example, it allows a licensor to monitor the resale of technology to third parties, to control exports to markets already serviced by other licensees, and so on.

Similarly, capital investors may wish to acquire an equity stake so that they can influence the way their funds are used. This is particularly important when collateral is illiquid and intangible, and where the limited liability of equity holders makes it difficult to recover funds from an insolvent firm. It is for reasons of this kind that policies for industrial reconstruction tend to focus on the selective encouragement of foreign direct investment.

Every foreign investor is going to be concerned about the security of their property rights, and so the stability and integrity of the government is crucial to them (Samuelsson 1992). Since foreign investment is needed urgently, governments have an imperative to acquire reputation as quickly as possible. One way of doing this is to bind themselves through treaties with other governments, giving these other governments a legitimate excuse for intervention should the rights of their private foreign investors be infringed. The current policy of making treaties with the European Community is one such example of this political strategy.

Historically, of course, many countries have achieved political credibility with foreign investors by submitting to colonization or occupation. The post-war recovery of both West Germany and Japan involved periods of foreign occupation, during which a good deal of US technology and management practice was transferred to those countries. It might not be too fanciful to suggest that under the veneer of reunification, something similar is happening in former East German territories now. One reason that West German technology and management practice is rapidly advancing in eastern Germany is that the political risks of private investment are now so low.

From a strictly economic point of view, other East European countries might benefit from political subordination of this kind. There is no reason, in principle, why there should not be a market in government, in which one government could contract with another government to assume some of its powers for a limited period of time. The moral hazard is, of course, potentially acute, because the foreign government might be reluctant to relinquish its powers at the end of its term, particularly if it had in the mean time managed to acquire a monopoly of force.

Another objection is that government is a culture-specific activity, so that political structures do not transfer readily between countries. This is certainly supported by the nineteenth-century British experience, where an optimistic belief in the universal superiority of a very specific package of democratic institutions was belied by the very mixed results which were obtained in different parts of the world.

It is not only government that is culturally specific, though: enterprise management is culturally specific as well. Foreign direct investment transfers not only technology and management skills, but cultural values too. What is more, the cultural values are very much bound up with attitudes to technology and preferences for particular management forms, so that the cultural content cannot easily be separated out to leave a culture-free residue.

The transfer of culture may, to some extent, be a bonus so far as economic efficiency is concerned. In a social context, however, it is understandably perceived as a negative factor by those committed to the traditional values of the host country. From the perspective of this paper, the crucial issue is whether the foreign culture that is transferred is more conducive to entrepreneurship than the indigenous one.

Taking the culture as a whole, the answer must be an affirmative one. Foreign investors are typically firms that have already proved successful in their home countries, and are therefore presumably imbued with a culture that supports competitive advantage. Even if their home country culture is not particularly entrepreneurial, the corporate culture of the foreign investor will be.

This is not to say that each individual aspect of the foreign culture is to be recommended, though. It was noted earlier that contemporary Western culture has a number of negative aspects, so far as entrepreneurship is concerned. The decline of traditional religious and moral systems, and the weakening sense of community caused by rising geographical mobility, mean that Western values are becoming low-trust, with increasing emphasis being placed on the law as a co-ordinating mechanism. The law does not seem to be meeting this challenge very well in Western countries. At the social level, crime statistics show an upward trend, while at the corporate level costly investments have to be made in auditing systems to detect employee fraud, and in legal services to recover debts, prevent patent infringement and the like.

However, to compensate for this deteriorating environment, many of the most successful Western firms have invested heavily in training schemes designed to inculcate values of loyalty and stewardship. These reduce the costs of supervising employees, although because they focus loyalty exclusively on the firm, they do not afford the same social externalities that traditional moral education did. It has been emphasized that the Stalinist legacy of cynicism is a major threat to effective management in East European enterprise, and so corporate cultures which can address this problem should prove particularly valuable. There is a reasonable chance that major foreign investors will be free of some of the worst excesses of contemporary Western culture, so that the values transmitted through foreign investment will, on the whole, be beneficial ones. There is, however, a case for vigilant monitoring of major foreign investments, to ensure that this is indeed the case.

It is often claimed that co-operative enterprises in Eastern Europe already enjoy a high trust culture and that this culture may in fact be undermined by the import of Western values. This claim seems a rather dubious one, however. Worker participation through owner-management may well be an outward symbol of an internal state of harmony, but it is not necessarily so. In so far as harmony exists, internal efficiency gains should allow the co-operative enterprises to compete with foreign investors – at least in those sectors where access to foreign markets or technology is not essential to success. On balance, therefore, it seems reasonable to require that claims about the efficiency of co-operative enterprise should be put to the market test.

The conclusion is that foreign direct investment should be encouraged as much because it transmits cultural values than in spite of that fact. There is a danger that inappropriate values may be transmitted, but the danger is not so great as might be feared, because foreign direct investment is a selective process in which only the more successful firms tend to participate. These firms will tend to have corporate cultures that are conducive to enterprise. The criteria that such cultures must satisfy have been set out in this paper. It is therefore perfectly feasible to screen foreign direct investments in order to eliminate those with negative cultural externalities, although skilful judgement will be required to do this effectively.

Conclusions

The problems of economic transition in Eastern Europe have created an atmosphere of crisis. Sensing political instability, reformers in East European countries have pushed through radical measures designed to raise the costs of returning to communism to a prohibitive level. The political trade-off between changing too slowly and allowing the communist elite to regroup, and changing too quickly but losing popular electoral support, has dominated economic trade-offs between different institutional arrangements. Economic liberalism has provided a simple powerful ideology for the reformers. For citizens accustomed to a simplistic Marxist ideology, an equally simplistic ideology that puts everything into reverse has a natural appeal as an explanation of what went wrong under the previous regime. So far as foreign creditors are concerned, pro-market rhetoric on the lips of local politicians sounds very reassuring. The obvious danger is that the politicians may come to believe their own rhetoric and underestimate the subtlety of the problems involved.

This paper has emphasized the importance of increasing the reputation of government in order to allow the reform process to be undertaken at a less hectic pace. More weight should be given to industrial policy in the restructuring of heavy industry, as a complement to, rather than a substitute for, popular privatization. While it is true that the institutions of a market economy constitute an indivisible system, it is also true that the design of the system requires careful thought. Imitating existing Western institutions may be an adequate short-run response, but it should be regarded as a provisional solution, to be used only until a more sophisticated one can be found. The principles that should guide the design of these institutions have been set out in this paper.

The fact that East European economies have an opportunity to create institutions from scratch should not be wasted by acting as though the only way to develop an adequate set of institutions is copy them from other countries and then adapt them to local conditions, using evolutionary processes that may take hundreds of years. Sufficient is known about the conditions conducive to entrepreneurship to make it evident that many existing Western institutions perform very imperfectly. It should not be difficult for East European countries to do better than some of their Western counterparts if they simply avoid making the same mistakes, the biggest of which would be to regard the low-trust legalistic culture of the West as a source of strength rather than as a serious weakness. In this respect, the institutions and value systems of Japan, or the South East Asian 'tigers', are models that might be considered as alternatives to Western ones – at least so far as short-term imitation is concerned.

In this paper the design of institutions has been analysed under eight headings: discovery, appropriation, screening, liquidity, confidence-building, conflict resolution, networking and legislation. A number of important principles have been identified, although there are many more which could not be covered but which are also relevant. A distinction has been drawn between the small-scale skills of the petty trader, such as a former black marketeer, and the large-scale skills of the technological innovator and system-builder, and the difficulties of upgrading the skills of the former to those of the latter have been stressed. The need to create an intellectual climate which rewards large-scale private innovation as well as petty trading has been noted. The role of financial institutions in screening complex and sophisticated projects has been discussed, with special reference to reconciling the technical need for large-scale investment with the investor's need for liquidity. A variety of issues relating to conflict resolution have been considered, and the vital importance of combining a strict business morality with a legal system which is well adapted to resolving minor cases has been highlighted. The design of systems that embody principles of this kind provides a full agenda for economic reform in the medium run.

For the long run, it is reasonable to expect that each East European country will choose its own individual path of social and political development. The consequences of these choices can also be analysed using the general principles set out in this paper. Some paths may emphasize a return to the values of some previous 'golden age' – even if these hinder economic success in the modern environment. Such a choice may be perfectly reasonable, provided it reflects popular preferences and is based on a well-informed analysis of the consequences. Other countries may embrace Western cultural values more fully. They would be well advised to consider, however, whether such values really are as conducive to long-run economic success as contemporary political rhetoric claims.

References

Attali, J. (1992) 'The Collapse of Communism and the International Response', Speech delivered at the London Business School, 30 March.

Bös, D. (1992) 'Privatization in East Germany: A Survey of Current Issues' *IMF Working Paper*, 92/8, Washington DC: International Monetary Fund.

Casson, M. C. (1979) *Alternatives to the Multinational Enterprise*, London: Macmillan.

Casson, M. C. (1982) *The Entrepreneur: An Economic Theory*, Oxford: Martin Robertson.

Casson, M. C. (1991) *Economics of Business Culture: Game Theory, Transaction Costs and Economic Performance*, Oxford: Clarendon Press.

Coase, R. H. (1937) 'The Nature of the Firm', *Economica* (New Series) 4: 386–405.

Etzioni, A. (1991) *Eastern Europe: the Wealth of Lessons*, Washington DC: George Washington University; The Socio-Economic Project.

Hansson, A. H. (1991) 'The Emergence and Stabilization of Extreme Inflationary Pressures in the Soviet Union' *Wider Working Paper* 93, Helsinki: World Institute for Development Economics Research, United Nations University.

Hayek, F. A. von (1960) *The Constitution of Liberty*, Chicago: University of Chicago Press.

Husain, A. M. and Sahay, R. (1992) 'Does Sequencing of Privatization Matter in Reforming Planned Economies?' *IMF Working Paper* 92/13, Washington DC: International Monetary Fund.

Kirzner, I. M. (1973) *Competition and Entrepreneurship*, Chicago: University of Chicago Press.

Klein, B., Crawford, R. G. and Alchian, A. A. (1978) 'Vertical Integration, Appropriable Rents and the Competitive Contracting Process', *Journal of Law and Economics* 21: 297–320.

Kolodko, G. W. and Rutkowski, M. (1991) 'The Problem of Transition from a Socialist to a Free-market Economy: The Case of Poland', *Journal of Social, Political and Economic Studies* 16(2): 159–79.

Putterman, L. (1990) *Division of Labour and Welfare*, Oxford: Oxford University Press.

Sachs, J. D. (1991) 'Accelerating Privatization in Eastern Europe: The Case of Poland' *WIDER Working Paper*, 92, World Institute for Development Economics Research, United Nations University.

Samuelsson, H-F. (1992) 'Foreign Direct Investments in Eastern Europe: Current Situation and Potential', Geneva: United Nations Economic Commission for Europe and United Nations Centre on Transnational Corporations, GE. 92–20047.

Schumpeter, J. A. (1934) *The Theory of Economic Development* (trans. R. Opie) Cambridge, Mass.: Harvard University Press.

Siebert, H. (1992) 'Transforming a Socialist Economy: the Case of Eastern Germany', mimeo, Kiel: Kiel Institute of World Economics.

Smith, N. R. (1967) *The Entrepreneur and His Firm: The Relationship between Type of Man and Type of Company*, East Lansing, MI.: Bureau of Business and Economic Research, Graduate School of Business Administration, Michigan State University.

UNIDO (1991) 'Industrial Restructuring in Central and Eastern Europe: Critical Areas of International Cooperation', Vienna: United Nations Industrial Development Organization, PPD/1PP/REG.

UNIDO (1992) 'Foreign Direct Investment in Central and Eastern European Countries: Recent Developments and Determinants', Vienna: United Nations Industrial Development Organization V.92–55129.

Wyplosz, C. (1992) 'After the Honeymoon: On the Economics and the Politics of Economic Transformation', *INSEAD Working Paper* 92/52/EP, Fontainebleau.

3

The Opening Up of Eastern Europe: the Implications for West European Business

Bruno Tietz

Background – The Initial Scenario

Never before in history has there been anything remotely comparable to the complexity of variables with which companies must now contend. These include:

- The completion of the Single European Market;
- the creation of a market economy in the new German federal states;
- the economic and political opening up of Eastern Europe;[1]
- the increasingly global dimension of trade;
- the North–South problem and, with it, the problems of developing countries.

Two main events have put their stamp on action for the 1990s; first, the quantum leap precipitated by the signing of the Single European Act on July 1, 1987, which paved the way for the Single European Market and the elimination of barriers within Western Europe; second, the ideas of Perestroika introduced by the USSR in 1985 which, in principle, were the catalyst for the opening up of Eastern Europe in the first place and for such innovations as the right of residents of the former USSR to travel abroad – although the initial draft legislation to implement this freedom was rejected.

What are the implications for the business community?

1. Companies must re-examine their vision and strategy of their own future.
2. Companies must identify the markets in which they would like to be active in the future.

Companies may decide to restrict their activities to a national or a regional level.

A study prepared for the Coca-Cola Retailing Research Group Europe.

They may equally decide to be active in several or many countries in Western Europe. However, they may decide to look towards Eastern Europe. The opportunities for trade are particularly good in what was East Germany and in Czechoslovakia. West German companies have moved very quickly into the former East Germany.

In the immediate future, the Czech Republic and Slovakia are likely to be the most attractive countries for retailing, more so than Hungary or Poland. This is so because the quality of products stemming from former Czechoslovakia is above average. In view of its industrial tradition and earlier experiences with democracy and the principles of a free-market economy, the former CSFR will have fewer adaptation problems than other countries, In addition, it has the attraction of being a low-wage country.

The principles of a planned economy and a market economy

The differences between a socialist society and one based on democratic pluralism stem from a different conception of the fundamental rights which the State considers important and therefore worth protecting, and from the influence which the State exerts on its citizens.

In Marxist-Leninist ideology, basic attitudes to human interaction are predetermined and irrevocable. They form an integral part of the system, although no attempt has been made to assess whether these attitudes have any link with reality. There is a universal assumption that in a socialist society the individual is prepared to do something for the common good, without the need for tangible motivation. It is expected that the individual will subjugate himself/herself willingly to the dictates of the State. The opportunities for choice in all walks of life are either reduced or eliminated completely.

In contrast, in a society based on democratic pluralism, there is general freedom for the individual to think and act as he/she wishes, within a framework of basic constraints. Political parties are in competition. They vie with each other for the political support of the electorate. Press freedom facilitates availability of information on diverse subjects, thus contributing towards the development of public opinion. To restrain egotistical traits and to ensure an acceptance of social responsibility and commitment, the State will fix parameters. In addition human interaction, which is in a permanent state of friction, means that compromise solutions, which are compatible with the requirements of society, will have to be found for any problem.

In a centrally planned economy citizens and consumers are treated rather like children – it is Utopian to think that the individual will act for the common good. Man is not altruistic; on the contrary he is strictly egotistical. The pressure exerted by bureaucracy on its citizens alters the inherent strength of individuals and numbs their ability to achieve. A market economy established within a democracy respects decisions made by the individual. In terms of politics, however, this respect will only apply to decisions which enjoy the support of the majority.

In the centrally planned economy, decentralized bodies are primarily agencies to enforce the authority of the State. Individual initiative can only move within narrow bounds between preset political and economic parameters.

The Dynamics of East European Social and Economic Systems

The reform process in all Eastern bloc countries started in the 1960s. However, until the end of the 1980s the following inalienable principles existed in all of the countries:

1. the automatic leadership right of the communist party;
2. the retention of basic elements of centralized planning, despite greater participation, greater freedom of action for individual companies and a certain
   market orientation.

In particular, the entrenched power structures were strongly resistant to fundamental changes. The unwillingness of the authorities to adapt was significant.
  Problems common to all Eastern European countries include:

1. the major lack of a sound infrastructure;
2. serious environmental pollution;
3. serious supply problems, in the main;
4. major currency problems;
5. in most cases high inflation rates;
6. high – and increasing – budget deficits;
7. in most cases significant pent-up demand which cannot be met;
8. generally high rates of subsidies (e.g. in 1980 subsidies accounted for 60.7 per
   cent of the Polish national budget and in 1988 41.9 per cent);
9. high budget-financed investments;
10. recession brought on by restructuring.

Eliminating fears

Those living in Eastern Europe have wide-ranging fears about the reform process.
These include:

- the fear of job losses;
- for those on low incomes, the fear of a reduction in the necessities they can
  afford following the elimination of subsidies and the resultant price increases;
- the fear of losing their savings;
- the fear of reduced state welfare benefits.

These fears go hand-in-hand with the dismantling of unsuitable, though sensible,
structures. The perceptions of a market economy are imprecise. People find it
difficult to sort out problems which, in a market economy, would be clearly defined
(e.g. the question of ownership). There is a general belief that viable alternatives
can be established reasonably quickly, but this actually encourages chaos. On top
of this there are the issues of political uncertainty and mutual insecurity.

The problem of excessive demands

Western Europe must be clear as to what can be expected from Eastern Europe in
the medium term. It must be able to recognize if the economy or society of a

country is being subjected to excessive demands. Environmental and energy problems are examples of this. Despite the catastrophic conditions which exist, economic development cannot be stimulated if, in the short term, the demands on Eastern European countries in terms of, for example, anti-pollution measures are equal or greater than those which would be considered reasonable in EC states such as Portugal or Greece.

Any attempt to establish priorities and achieve a consensus in Eastern Europe will remain influenced by efforts to safeguard the supposed achievements of the welfare state. In contrast to a more open and more ruthless market orientation these influences will inhibit development to a greater or lesser extent. In such circumstances the price mechanism will not be effective, because of the subsidies that are available.

The major difficulties between East and West European societies are highlighted in Table 3.1.

Differences in reform policies

It is a mistake to assume that all East European countries are at an identical stage of development. Differences in social and economic structures within individual East European countries (for example, between Czechoslovakia and Romania) are greater, at least in psychological terms, than those within Western Europe. Similarly, there are significant differences in the reform policies adopted by the various countries within Eastern Europe.

Take, for example, the differences in privatization policies set out below.

Czechoslovakia

There is a great fear of foreign domination. For this reason, price reform and restructuring have taken priority over privatization and the encouragement of foreign companies.

In 1991 Czechoslovakia started to privatize the retail sector, which had previously been under state control, together with thousands of small companies such as taxi firms and restaurants. Privatized companies cannot be resold for a specified period – currently two years. The first auction was held in Prague in January 1991, at which seventeen food and electronics shops went under the hammer. About 100,000 retail outlets, previously under state control, were scheduled to be privatized in Czechoslovakia on a gradual basis.[2] Larger companies have been offered for sale since April 1991 for which foreign companies have been able to bid.

Hungary

In Hungary an attempt has been made to counter the dangers inherent in a sell-off of national assets by the creation of a Commission which will monitor the privatization of state property (the State Assets Agency). This Commission is answerable to Parliament and not to the government.

Hungary has passed legislation providing compensation for earlier expropriations. This has created the framework for an acceleration in the rate of privatization and should increase the interest of foreign investors.

In September 1990 the State Assets Agency drew up an initial privatization

Table 3.1: Selected differences in East and West European societies.

Western Europe	GDR (1990)	Eastern Europe
Market and democracy		
Well-established understanding of the synthesis between democracy and a market economy.	Growing understanding of the relationship between democracy and a market economy.	Start of the democratization process with a move away from the one-party system including, by necessity, the end of the primacy of the communist party, the practice of plurality of offices, and the end of patronage and nepotism.
Market versus plan		
Ever-increasing importance of marketing, even if the proportion of marketing value and product value of any market output varies depending upon the development stage of the economy.	Rapid change from a planned to a market economy. Inadequate knowledge of marketing and management.	Difficult process and resistance to the ideological rejection of a third way which would combine elements of collectivism and market principles and a movement towards the market economy.
Clear ownership structures.	Still serious difficulties on the question of ownership; no clear understanding of central issues; *Treuhandanstalt* (trustee body) badly structured.	Trend towards several forms of ownership: • state • collective • co-operative • private.
Companies have wide discretion in decision making.	Attempts to protect domestic companies.	As before, more (USSR, Bulgaria) or less (Czechoslovakia, Hungary) in the way of Guidelines and Central Directives
Price formation		
Despite considerable price regulation in many sectors, internal and external price freedom, with prices playing a market role.	Laborious elimination of subsidies and price levies with a trend towards market prices in the absence of pricing principles, pegged to West German price levels (advantage and disadvantage).	Repeated postponement of price liberalization, gradual approach often with a half-hearted linkage to the freedom of factor prices i.e. wage support for social reasons, continuing lack of understanding between pricing, decentralized decisions and ownership structures.

programme covering twenty large Hungarian state-owned organizations. These privatizations – which include the Centrum chain of department stores, with thirty-six shops and turnover of 18.6 billion Forints, and the Danubius hotel chain – were scheduled to be implemented after June 1991.

As a further step, about 600 smaller Hungarian companies are to be transferred to private ownership.[3]

Poland

The radical economic policy introduced in Poland is bearing fruit. In 1990 more than 500,000 companies were established, exports increased by 34 per cent to about DM 9 billion, and the trade surplus was $4.7 billion. However, unemployment has increased to 17 per cent of the working population.

The Future Social and Economic Systems of Eastern Europe

The current transition period in Eastern Europe is characterized by a series of fundamental weaknesses – social, economic and above all psychological.

In Eastern Europe, unlike Western Europe, industrial leaders have often also been political leaders. Many of these individuals are unable or unwilling to come to terms with the facts that for their entire lives they have identified with and supported a system which was not tenable in the long term. It is extremely difficult for them to accept the superiority of a system adopted by their former ideological 'enemy'. Struggles for both self-affirmation and a substantiation of their own professional position are perceived as difficult by many managers involved in the process of converting to a market economy. Changes to the economic system generated from within remain limited. Half-measures adopted for economic reforms remain the major problem in the process to transform Eastern Europe.

Thus, there is a so-called 'as well as' economy to be found in the former USSR, which is still trying to combine communism and a free-market economy, despite the events surrounding the coup of August 19, 1991.

Despite the new processes of democratization and decentralization leading to the regaining of sovereignty and in some cases, independence of the former Soviet republics, the democratic forces are still being confronted by a powerful 'Nomenklatura' trying to jeopardize reforms. Further development in Russia will depend most of all on the outcome of Yeltsin's struggle to assert himself.

There are two possible scenarios for developments in Eastern Europe: an abrupt switch to a market economy, or an attempt to find a new social order within the market economy incorporating democratic features with strong collectivist elements.

It is still not absolutely clear which countries will opt in the long run for either of these scenarios. As far as can be ascertained at present, Poland, former Czechoslovakia and Hungary have opted for the first scenario. If a country seeks to pursue an option on a long term basis for the second scenario, further delays in the process of social and economic restructuring are inevitable. The recession brought on by structural changes will be extended and an economic resurgence prevented.

In the search for a new, third path, the lack of a clear understanding of the functions of the market will result in objectives which are both contradictory and incompatible:

1.   The attempt will be being made to combine a better supply of goods and services at cheap prices with measures to protect existing jobs and to pay high wages – to live as under capitalism and work as under socialism.
2.   Despite a hesitant and vague approach, the establishment of independent companies will have to be implemented through the ownership mechanism.
3.   Because of the desire to remain independent, which in some cases is deeply entrenched, countries may reject co-operation with Western companies, although they lack the ability to operate their own market-based economy.

A realistic interpretation of the future in Eastern Europe is that an attempt will be made to follow the second of the two scenarios outlined above for several more years, until it becomes apparent that the various constituent parts of the system which they have adopted are incompatible. There is incontrovertible evidence that countries will gradually be forced to go over to the first scenario, i.e. the abrupt switch to a market economy.

The overall conclusion has to be that the countries of Eastern Europe will experience extreme difficulty in finding their new social, political and economic identities.

The new fragmentation of Eastern Europe should strengthen market forces, since smaller independent states are probably more capable of adapting to changed conditions. The pre-existing economic structure will, however, make sure that the former republics of the Soviet Union continue to depend on each other. The deterioration of foreign trade which followed the collapse of Comecon inflicted damage on all parties concerned.

Replacement of the planned economy by the market and marketing

The switch in Eastern Europe from a planned economy to a market economy has confirmed the realization that the market, which by definition includes the process of marketing, is more than just an element in economic control. The process of Perestroika has been characterized by a growing acceptance of the principles of freedom and democracy, and a greater understanding of the principles of a market economy. The following are said to be the major features of a market economy:

*   personal freedom;
*   supremacy of the rule of law;
*   acceptance of private ownership;
*   a realistic perception of human nature, with its strong ambivalence between egoism and altruism;
*   opportunities for choice and variety in all walks of life;
*   management conducted by decentralized companies;
*   trade conducted by decentralized institutions.

Restructuring the economies of Eastern Europe from the bottom upwards will require a rapid and intensive development of marketing expertise, together with the development of management practices based on market economy principles.

One of the main challenges in this process is the need to awaken the instincts, required for a market economy. This will necessitate immediate changes to the educational system in Eastern Europe. An important part of the learning process in Eastern Europe must be the realization that the means of production must undergo a fundamental rationalization, so that production costs can be reduced. In addition it must be accepted that the switch to a market economy will almost inevitably result in rapidly increasing transactional and marketing costs. Accompanying this will be a willingness to attach far greater importance to the trading function.

Chaotic developments

The possibility that developments in some East European countries may not follow the course anticipated, delaying the returns anticipated by Western investors, cannot be excluded. Inevitably managers in the East are unlikely to have much basic trust in the market – it is difficult for economists formerly schooled in the ideology of the planned economy to change their behaviour to accord with the principles of the market economy while at the same time retaining their authority to make decisions.

The dynamics of the social and economic systems in Eastern Europe are summarized in Table 3.2.

The following trends in East European countries are now apparent:

1. Privatization by the sale of state companies and agricultural units, and by the leasing of state companies and agricultural units.
2. Creation of an independent banking and monetary system, with a central bank and commercial banks competing with each other.
3. Encouragement of competition by allowing new companies to enter the market.
4. Foreign capital admitted and Western external trade encouraged.

Diverse problems have been encountered:

1. All countries have a sizeable black or parallel economy which in some cases – as in the former USSR – is run by permanent criminal organizations, closely linked to the official economic system.
2. The principles of a market economy have been adopted either half-heartedly or not at all. This has led to major problems, particularly high inflation rates and unstable markets.
3. The time before any upturn in the economy can be expected has been seriously under-estimated.
4. The effects of inadequate infrastructure have been underestimated.
5. It is difficult to dismantle existing power structures.
6. The question of the division of power between politicians, civil servants and industrialists has not yet been resolved.
7. The question of how to safeguard the democratic framework remains outstanding.
8. The serious structural problems will take several decades to solve. Solutions will require priorities to be agreed by those in power and for a consensus to be

Table 3.2: The dynamics of social and economic systems in Eastern Europe.

Initial position 1985	Current situation	Future Scenario A	Future Scenario B
Basic elements of the social order			
Strict or very strict centralized economy.	Switch to a market economy but with major efforts to retain elements of the planned economy.	Development of a clearly identifiable market economy, despite major friction during the 5–10 year conversion period.	Attempt to 'plan' the conversion to the market economy with an attempt – probably unsuccessful – to avoid friction.
Rather slow and leisurely changes.	In some cases contradictory policies and measures.	Rapid awakening and a new beginning.	Serious delays to the process of economic development.
One-party system dominating social policy.	Several parties allowed to operate; communist party renounces its monopolistic right to govern.	Switch to a parliamentary democracy.	Attempts to anchor fundamental elements of the communist system within a multi-party system.
State and co-operative ownership, hardly any private ownership. Suppression of private companies continued in some cases well into the 1980s.	Conditions for domestic private ownership increasingly based on legal principles. Serious administrative problems remain.	Extensive privatization of companies and combines, including the basic privatization or de-collectivization of land. Co-operatives maintained.	Limited privatization of productive assets, collective farming retained but with variations in the level of collectivization.
Foreigners only allowed minority participation in joint ventures.	Foreigners allowed to hold majority shareholdings in commercial companies.	General acceptance of foreign ownership and entrepreneurs.	Foreign ownership and entrepreneurs only allowed on a controlled basis.
Basic features of the economic system			
Weak economic growth.	Economy fluctuates between negative and slow growth, high inflation.	After an initial transitional period marked by continuing negative growth, GNP grows rapidly in real terms.	The new system will mean major transitional problems, with little economic growth.
Productivity ranging from very poor to average.	Productivity ranging from very poor to average; unemployment high.	Rapid increase in productivity; gradual reduction in unemployment.	Only limited increases in productivity because of the superimposed social network.

Table 3.2: The dynamics of social and economic systems in Eastern Europe (*continued*).

Initial position 1985	Current situation	Future Scenario A	Future Scenario B
Planned production with fixed prices, control of price characteristics and increasingly volume characteristics.	Reduction in the planned element; in some cases completely (Poland) but sometimes retaining considerable elements of planning, subsidies and price adjustments.	Switch to price control, with management decisions decentralized.	Mixture of planning and price mechanisms; however, no historical model, and effects difficult to gauge.

Role of market mechanisms

Initial position 1985	Current situation	Future Scenario A	Future Scenario B
Markets not based on consumer requirements.	Beginnings of a deliberate orientation to customer/ consumer requirements.	Adoption of the marketing philosophy of Western industrial countries.	An attempt to follow path of socialist market principles.
Distribution and rationing.	Intense awareness of undersupply, compared with Western industrial countries.	After a transitional period, convergence of supply and demand.	Attempt to organize demand; in some cases, demand controlled by non-market mechanisms.
Pent-up purchasing power.	Reduction in pent-up purchasing power by cross-border shopping forays and imports.	Shortages overcome by market mechanisms and the beginnings of an affluent society; development of new marketing and transaction companies.	Market orientation slow to develop, with supply bottlenecks.
No knowledge of the workings of the market.	Gradual build-up of knowledge on the workings of the market; black market operates.	Rapid development of a market philosophy and marketing knowledge.	Protracted search for a separate market/ marketing ideology.
Apart from a few Western export companies, foreign trade run on a monopolistic basis.	More decentralization in foreign trade as an important core process in the acquisition of marketing expertise.	Foreign trade unrestricted; desire for a freely convertible currency and membership of international institutions.	Obligation to control currency and foreign trade policy because policies of liberalization incomplete.

found. In the initial stages it will be impossible to achieve this through the mechanism of the market.

9. Even if Western institutions are copied (e.g. the creation of a two-tier banking system and separation of party and government), the actual results will differ from those in Western democracies and market economies, because Eastern Europe has been locked into a completely different social structure for many decades.

Future problems for Eastern Europe

It can be assumed that for the foreseeable future it is unlikely that many of those in positions of authority in Eastern Europe within the ranks of the civil service, industry and other institutions will be discriminating or subjected to fundamental changes. There will be no radical breaking down of the existing informal network of decision makers in government and industry. The strength of personal relationships will be crucial in determining which aspects of the market economy succeed. The previous situation of complex alliances between decision makers in industry, politics and the civil service will still prevail.

New decentralized solutions in connection with private property will have to be developed by managers of public authorities and private enterprises. The development of a new kind of interaction between democratic partners, parliament, administrators, and private enterprise and other institutions must be broadly supported by the public. There is a high risk of social unrest if the economic development remains unstable.

Implications for companies from Western Europe

The Western investor in Eastern Europe is confronted with numerous barriers, in particular:

- the continued unsuitability of the legislative framework for foreign investment;
- at the local level, authorities lack experience; diplomatic representatives abroad lack experience; communication networks are inadequate; telephone links are particularly poor.

Enormous reconstruction work remains to be done in Eastern Europe to bring it up to West European levels of affluence. Co-operation between politicians, civil servants and industrialists, in both East and West, will be required if this is to be achieved.

When the eventual economic upturn occurs and the satisfaction level of the population has improved, the possibility of discriminatory measures being taken against foreign organizations, including those which were instrumental in bringing this very improvement about, cannot be excluded. It is possible that the only way to counter the expected debate in Eastern Europe on foreign domination will be for the local integration of expatriate Western managers. Ultimately this may have to include the adoption of the nationality of the host country. In addition joint undertakings or joint ventures may act as an antidote to hostility towards foreigners.

If companies from Western Europe are to succeed in Eastern Europe, it is essential that they should integrate into the strong informal network of transaction control.

Country-by-Country Analysis of Eastern Europe

The gross national product of the entire East European economy is only 40 per cent that of the EC, despite the fact that its population of some 410 million inhabitants (1990) is about 30 per cent higher than that of the EC. At present, the Western business profile in Eastern Europe is minimal: Western countries account for only about 1.4 per cent of Soviet foreign trade and 3 per cent of Poland's foreign trade.

In 1990, population figures for selected countries and economic regions were as follows:

EC	342 mn
USA	250 mn
Eastern Europe	120 mn
Japan	124 mn
USSR	290 mn

Using the parameters of population, economic strength, degree of economic liberalization and acceptance of foreigners, the countries of Eastern Europe can be divided into three groups:

Top group	*Middle Group*	*Bottom group*
Czech Republic	Poland	Romania
Slovakia	Bulgaria	Albania
Hungary	Former USSR	

The civil war in Yugoslavia and its fragmentation into various republics mean that it must be considered separately. It was previously in the top group, but has fallen back.

Basic statistical data on the East European countries are set out in Tables 3.3 and 3.4.

Recession in Eastern Europe

In 1991 the WIIW, the Vienna-based Institute for International Comparative Economic Studies, published a research report which contained estimates of the industrial production and gross domestic product of Eastern Europe and the USSR in 1990. According to this report, industrial production in East European countries, including the Eastern part of Germany but excluding the Soviet Union, had dropped by 20 per cent. The drop in GDP was estimated at 14 per cent. Compared with the situation in Eastern Europe the recession in the Soviet Union was more

Table 3.3: Statistical data 1988.

	Albania	Bulgaria	Czech	GDR	Yugoslavia	Poland	Romania	USSR	Hungary
Area (000 sq m)	29	111	128	108	226	313	238	22,400	93
Population (mn)	3	9	16	16	24	38	23	285	11
National product ($bn)[a]		14	92	154	61	68	28	685	28
National product per capita ($)[a]		1,500	5,900	9,200	2,600	1,800	1,200	2,400	2,600
Exports ($bn)		17.2	24.9	31.1	12.6	14.0	12.9	110.6	10.0
Imports ($bn)		16.6	24.3	32.2	13.1	12.2	9.5	107.2	9.4
Exports to OECD countries ($bn)		0.7	3.8	2.7	5.7	5.7	4.0	23.7	4.1
Imports from OECD countries ($bn)		2.4	3.6	3.0	7.3	5.0	1.2	24.8	4.0
Debt/exports (%)[b]		45	21	62	63	279	21	36	173
Industrial production ($bn)[c]				3.5	2.0	-4.0	–	3.5	-1.0
Inflation rate (%)[b]		11	10	10–15	1,256	270	–	>10	18
Per capita income (EC average = 100)[d]		45	65	–	45	30	20	35	55
Econ. growth in %[e]		-11	-3	–	-3	-12	-12	-4	-5

Notes:
[a] In some cases estimates.
[b] Gross, less credits with Western banks.
[c] 1989, % change compared with previous year, in some cases estimates.
[d] Estimates based on comparisons of purchasing power.
[e] 1990.

Source: Dresdner Bank; quoted in Grassau, G. (1990), 'Full steam ahead to the East' published in *Industriemagazin*, 1990, 9: 101; see also unattributed article 'I am an eternal optimist', *Der Spiegel*, 1991, 17: 149–58.

B. Tietz

Table 3.4: Changes to selected external trade indicators in the seven European Comecon countries, 1986–9.

	1986	1987	1988	1989
	($)	($)	($)	($)
Balance of trade with:				
OECD countries	−1,082	+1,491	−2,502	−2,816[a]
Current account balance	+0.449	+5,251	+3,885	−1,900[b]
Gross debt	113,249	129,603	133,335	148,200[b]
Net debt	83,886	97,899	98,910	114,574[b]
Net interest payments	5,466	6,385	7,255	8,153[b]
	(%)	(%)	(%)	(%)
Net debt/exports	152	158	153	169[b]
Net interest payments/exports	10	10	11	12[b]
Debt service quota[c]	33	33	35	35[b]
Reserves/imports	58	62	59	53[b]

Notes:
[a] January to September.
[b] Forecast or estimate.
[c] All interest and amortization payments to service the medium and long-term debt as a proportion of annual exports.
Source: OECD Financial Market Trends 45; quoted in unattributed article: 'Germany feels the Upheaval in Eastern Europe', Neue Zurcher 211 (50), 2.3.90: 16

modest, industrial production having fallen by 5 per cent and GDP by 3 per cent. For the entire region including Yugoslavia, the WIIW estimated that in 1990 industrial production had dropped by 9 per cent and GDP by 6 per cent.

It is probable that the recession was brought on by the need to adapt, as currently being experienced by East Germany and other East European countries, and is a necessary element of the process of conversion from a planned to a market economy. The recession will create the new economic basis from which the upturn will emerge.

For most countries in Eastern Europe, the recession was expected to continue in 1991 and in some cases into 1992 as well; in Czechoslovakia it was likely to get worse and in Hungary, the former Soviet Union, Romania and Bulgaria it would probably remain the same. In addition, all countries have had to cope with deteriorating world economic conditions. The collapse of Comecon, high energy costs, recession in the West and rising interest rates on the world financial markets have put a burden on their current account balances and have reduced growth potential. Table 3.5 shows the magnitude of the downturn in production and in GDP during 1990, across Eastern Europe as a whole. Attempts since then to stabilize economies, particularly in the former Soviet Union and Yugoslavia, and to a somewhat lesser extent in the remaining East European countries, have had little chance of success because of political, social and ethnic tensions.

In March 1991 Jacques Attali, President of the European Bank for Reconstruction and Development, stated that 2,000 billion ECU would be required to bring East European living standards, including those in the USSR, up to levels in Western Europe.

Table 3.5 Eastern bloc economies, 1990.

	Industrial production	*GDP*
Bulgaria	−13.0	−12.0
Czechoslovakia	−3.5	−3.0
Hungary	−10.0	−5.0
GDR	−29.0	−22.0
Poland	−25.0	−17.0
Romania	−21.0	−15.0
Eastern Europe	−19.5	−13.8
Soviet Union	−5.0	−3.0
Yugoslavia	−10.6	−10.0
Region as a whole	−9.3	−6.3

Source: Institute for International Comparative
Economic Studies, Vienna; quoted in unattributed
article, 'Dramatic Recession in Eastern Europe –
Production shortfall in the Soviet Union still moderate',
Saarbrucker Zeitung, February 6, 1991: 7

Debt figures for Eastern Europe

According to an OECD survey, debt levels in the seven European countries of Comecon increased rapidly between 1986 and 1989, to the point at which there was a negative current account balance. In Poland, the ratio between net indebtedness and annual exports is similar to that in the worst countries of Latin America. Similarly the debt limit is considered to have been reached in both Bulgaria and Hungary. Inflation has accelerated and the net national product has scarcely risen. Trade with OECD countries was weaker in 1989 than in 1988.

In 1990 the external indebtedness of the USSR exceeded $54 billion; the foreign trade deficit was $4.7 billion.

By 1990 (Table 3.6) the combined indebtedness of Czechoslovakia, the Soviet Union, Hungary, Poland, Bulgaria and Romania had reached a total of $123 billion, an 85 per cent increase on 1985's figure. The hard currency debts of the above countries amounted to 211 per cent of their export revenue.

Generally speaking, private banks in the West adopt cautious credit policy towards these countries because they are unable to gauge the inherent risks. This means that the conditions required for growth are impaired because of lack of investment resources. Several countries such as Bulgaria and the former USSR have reneged on debt repayment, or have asked for a moratorium. The position is similar to that in developing countries; lenders are being forced to make value adjustments. This problem reduces the inflow of money, whereas it needs to be increased. The World Bank, the International Monetary Fund, the European Bank for Reconstruction and Development and other institutions have been under pressure for some time to tackle the worsening recession by taking appropriate countermeasures.

In some cases the conditions imposed on loans to Eastern bloc countries have been unrealistic. For example, the International Monetary Fund makes funds conditional upon the introduction of a free market economy and the elimination of

Table 3.6: Net hard currency debts of East European countries, 1990.

Country	Debt figure ($ bn)	Interest paid as % of export revenue
Bulgaria	9.8	43
Czechoslovakia	6.3	10
Poland	41.8	41
Romania	1.3	1
Hungary	20.3	35
USSR	43.4	14
Total	122.9	–

Source: OECD; German Economic Institute, Cologne, quoted in unattributed article, 'Chronic shortage of foreign exchange', *Handelsblatt* 46 (81), April 26/27, 1991: 12

import restrictions, despite the poor state of the balance of payments. This policy cannot succeed. Because of this, credit is being reduced and interest increased.

This highlights the dilemma confronting the growth policy adopted in Eastern Europe. Despite the validity of demanding a process of trade liberalization, Eastern bloc countries will be obliged to maintain policies of import restriction for many years. It will be very difficult for them to buy capital goods from the West, and correspondingly difficult to develop conventional industrial locations producing goods of a standard comparable to those in the West.

Balance of payments problems are forcing Hungary and the other small countries in Eastern Europe to adopt a stop-go policy as part of their reform process.[4]

The situation in Hungary is an example of the balance of payments dilemma which has confronted the East European countries following the liberalization of their economies. By 1988 the gross debt in convertible currencies had grown to $17 billion from an annual debt service of only $3 billion. This level represented more than 50 per cent of the country's export income. The expected trade surplus of about $500 million for 1989 would only cover about one-third of its interest liabilities of $1.5 billion.

Future prospects

The economic outlook for the countries of Eastern Europe remains adverse. The efforts to convert their economies will take longer than was originally anticipated, although the speed of the transition to a market economy varies. The switch to market principles in Eastern Europe was first evident in the export of goods and services for Western currency, and in the development of wage and salary differentials. For example, wages paid by Hungarian companies which have entered into joint ventures with the West are about 50 per cent higher than the average for that country.

Incoherent reform policies are creating difficulties for all foreign investors, but Western companies remain well advised to be prepared for co-operation in the future. Reliable and topical information on the changing legal and economic structures in all those countries of interest to Western enterprises is essential.

Differing Market Conditions in Eastern and Western Europe

In the early stages, the transition from a scarcity/supply economy in Eastern Europe to an affluent society will be achieved by established products and services and by using established marketing methods. The risks of markets becoming saturated are likely to remain remote for several decades.

Established products will be required to bring Eastern Europe up to a Western standard of living. Known and well-practised marketing strategies will be required, once these countries have overcome their inherent ideological and psychological resistance to change.

By contrast, in the Single European Market the existing range of marketing tactics used by suppliers and retailers will continue to develop; innovations will be needed to meet the steadily increasing demands made by increasingly affluent customers. High living standards and low population growth, combined with high standards of education in Western Europe, will increase the international potential for both products and for retail operators.

There is a clear polarization between the situation in Western Europe and that in Eastern Europe, where economies are less well developed and population growth is comparatively buoyant. The main requirements in Eastern Europe are for basic, mass-produced products and for clearly defined niche products for a small elite. There will be no mass market for quality goods, with the import of products sold internationally, until a middle class has become established and middle income levels achieved.

The dynamics of consumption and demand

In Eastern Europe the dynamics of consumption and demand are likely to follow a specific wave-like pattern. On the crest of this wave will be communication products – for example, consumer electronics and modern photographic equipment and related products such as books. Rising demand for records, tapes and CD discs will follow the acquisition of basic equipment. The quality of that basic equipment will be determined by how fast incomes grow.

Another important factor will be mobility, with a strong demand for cars. An international study of car ownership in 1986 revealed the following number of cars per 1,000 head of population.[5]

USA	570	Hungary	145
West Germany	446	Yugoslavia	125
France	388	Bulgaria	120
Japan	235	Poland	105
East Germany	204	USSR	42
Czechoslovakia	173	Romania	11

Donald Peterson, the former Ford boss, has forecast that 60 per cent of growth in the motor industry over the next 20 years will be accounted for by Eastern Europe.

At the same time, demand for housing and household goods will be stimulated, resulting in opportunities for the construction and furniture sectors. The increase in demand for clothing and foodstuffs will be more tentative. As consumers will be unable to afford everything at the same time, economies will be made in these areas. It is likely that in the short term, demand will be for high-quality products, at least in the new German federal states, former Czechoslovakia and Hungary. This will arise, not just because of environmental factors, but because of the desire for things which will retain their value.

The polarization of demand will be much more evident in Eastern Europe than in Western Europe.

Brand awareness

Because the quality of their own products leaves much to be desired, Western goods, despite their limited availability, are already well known: brand and quality awareness already exist in Eastern European countries – international brands such as Coca-Cola, Levi jeans and Canon cameras, for example, are already well known in Eastern Europe. In addition, and for historical reasons, former brand leaders such as Meinl coffee and Bata shoes are also very popular.

Brands known in the West and introduced to the East quickly become well known and accepted. As symbols, they soon gain acceptance in Eastern Europe. Branding is a vital way of building up market share.

Experience in Eastern Europe shows that the demand for high-quality products very quickly follows Western trends.

Trade in Eastern Europe

The neglect of consumer demand and the failure to produce consumer goods, prevalent in East European economic systems is, for all practical purposes, associated with a disregard of trade. It is important to understand the historical doctrines which brought about the development of these attitudes towards trade and its role in a centrally planned economy.

In Marxist-Leninist theory, trade has its roots in:

1. The mercantile system, which was the prevalent economic policy in European countries in the age of absolutism after 1500 and which at its extreme manifested itself in bullionism (attempts to maximize the difference between exports and imports).
2. The physiocratic system and the theory of an inherent natural order developed by Francois Quesnay in 1758, in which the trading class and dealers were seen as a sterile class.

Marxist ideology is based on a separation of production and distribution. As the trading class is unable to provide any added value, it is seen as unproductive.

The administrative and control structures imposed on the trading sector are still having an effect. The trading function in Eastern Europe was fully integrated into the system of parameters, guidelines and controls operated by the state planning system, and was based on the principle that the role of the trading sector was to sell whatever agriculture can produce, mining can extract and industry can manufacture. Industry was organized primarily on the basis of monopolies; insufficient attention was paid to market conditions.

International comparison of employment in the trading sector

The neglect of trade in East European countries is evident from a comparison of employment levels (Table 3.7). In 1985 about 15.4 per cent of the working population in EC countries was employed in the distribution sector. The equivalent percentage in East Germany was 10.2 per cent, while in the USSR it was only 6.9 per cent.

Table 3.7: Changes in employment levels in the retail/wholesale trade in selected economic regions, 1985–8.

Economic Area	Number employed in trade (mn)		% of working population employed in trade (%)	
	1985	1988	1985	1988
EC	19.01	–	15.4	–
USA	24.19	–	21.1[a]	–
Japan	10.89	–	17.7	–
USSR	8.12	8.43	6.9[b]	7.2[b]
East Germany	0.87	0.88	10.2[c]	10.3[c]

Notes:
[a] *Wirtschaftswoche*, No. 33/1989: 56–7.
[b] Economy of the USSR in 1988, officially authorized statistics: 34–5.
[c] 1989 East German Statistical Yearbook: 19.
Source: Kamp, K. (1990), 'Major gaps in Trading Network', *Dynamik im Handel* 34 (10): 10

The structure of retail trade

In Eastern Europe the retail sector is split into three main groups:

1. food retailers;
2. retailers of industrial goods;
3. general retailers.

These in turn are divided into retailers with their own sales space, and those without their own sales space, e.g. kiosks, petrol stations, outlets selling fuels and cars.

B. Tietz

In contrast to Western Europe, the number of sales outlets in Eastern Europe continues to increase, partly because numbers were previously very low and partly – as in Hungary – because privatization has resulted in a sharp increase in the number of outlets.

Table 3.8: Retail outlets in East European countries, 1988.

Country	Outlets 1980 ('000)	Outlets 1988 ('000)	Outlets 1988 with sales space ('000)	Outlets 1988 without sales space ('000)	Population 1988 (mn)	Outlets per 1,000 inhab. with sales space	Outlets per 1,000 inhab. without sales space
East Germany	103.5	94.8	73.3	21.5	16,675	4.4	1.3
Bulgaria	40.0	44.0	34.4	9.5	8,987	3.8	1.1
Czechoslovakia	64.8	62.8	55.9	6.9	15,624	3.6	0.4
Poland	203.7	227.0	160.7	66.4	37,775	4.3	1.8
Romania	58.1	58.8	52.1	6.7	23,112	2.3	0.3
Hungary	46.9	63.7	53.2	10.5	10,590	5.0	1.0
USSR	695.2	736.0	565.3	170.7	286,717	2.0	0.6

Source: 1989 Comecon Statistical Yearbook, Moscow 1990, based on internal statistics

Major importance of state ownership and co-operatives

The ownership of retail outlets in Eastern Europe is split between state ownership, co-operative ownership, and private ownership. The relative importance of each of these ownership forms is illustrated on a country-by-country basis in Table 3.9. As can be seen, in Eastern Europe, distribution has predominantly been in the hands of the State and of co-operatives.

Table 3.9: Changes in ownership of retail outlets in Eastern Europe, 1980–8 (%)[a].

Country	State Ownership 1980	State Ownership 1988	Co-operative Ownership 1980	Co-operative Ownership 1988	Private Ownership 1980	Private Ownership 1988
Bulgaria	42.5	52.0	42.5	43.0	15.0	5.0
Czechoslovakia	57.5	60.0	42.5	40.0	–	–
East Germany	47.5	37.5	30.0	31.3	22.5	31.2
Poland	15.0	17.5	75.0	65.0	10.0	17.5
Romania	55.0	52.5[b]	45.0	47.5[b]	–	–[b]
Hungary	35.0	27.5	42.5	32.5	22.5	40.0
USSR	47.5	45.0	52.5	55.0	–	–

Notes:
[a] Rounded up.
[b] 1987.
Source: 1989 Comecon Statistical Yearbook, quoted by Seitz, H. (1990). 'The new order in the Soviet Union – Trading Options', lecture given at the 1st European Trade Forum, *New Opportunities in East Germany and Eastern Europe*, June 28/29, Berlin

In some countries, as recently as the 1980s, private ownership, which in some cases had been allowed to supply certain very local needs, was seriously restricted and curtailed. Bulgaria and East Germany provide examples of this.

Furthermore, state-owned outlets are even more important in terms of the proportion of total retail sales that they handle than they are in terms of actual proportion of outlets.

Table 3.10 The importance of state and co-operative retail outlets in selected East European countries, 1986.

Country	Retail trade state		Retail trade co-operatives	
	% of outlets	*% of turnover*	*% of outlets*	*% of turnover*
Bulgaria	52.0	71.4	45.2	28.5
Czechoslovakia	59.2	74.7	40.7	25.3
East Germany	35.1	54.3	29.8	31.7
Romania	28.9	69.1	33.8	36.2
USSR	46.8	71.0	53.2	26.4

Source: Leipzig, *Handelshochschule* (commercial university), quoted by Seitz, H. (1990). 'The new order in the Soviet Union – Trading Options', lecture given at the 1st European Trading Forum, *New Opportunities in East Germany and Eastern Europe*, June 28/29, Berlin

Small shops and few large outlets

In Eastern Europe, retail sales space per head of population is only 20–30 per cent of that in Western Europe. In Western Europe, the sales space per 1,000 head of population is about 1,000 sq.m.; in West Germany it is even higher, at 1,200 sq.m.

Table 3.11: Size of retail outlets in Eastern Europe.

Country	Sales space ('000 sq.m.)	Population in 1988 (mn)	Sales space per 1,000 population	Department stores (absolute)
Bulgaria	2,012 (1985)	8,987	224	348 (1984)
Czechoslovakia	4,769 (1986)	15,624	306	172 (1983)
Poland	13,610 (1986)	37,775	362	367 (1984)
Romania	–	23,112	–	–
Hungary	2,413 (1986)	10,590	226	1,342 (1986)
USSR	52,292 (1985)	280,717	189	800 (1984)

Source: Handelshochschule Leipzig, 1989 Comecon Statistical Yearbook, Moscow 1990

In the 1980s the average shop size in the majority of East European countries changed very little. This is true of both food and non-food outlets. In 1986, retail outlets varied in size between 50 sq.m. (Hungary) and 95 sq.m. (USSR).

Food outlets dominate the retail scene in Eastern Europe. Leading the field in Eastern Europe is Hungary, where 70 per cent of the turnover in the retail sector

Table 3.12: Changes in the average size of a retail outlet in selected East European countries, 1980–6 (sq m).

Country	1980	1986
Bulgaria	56	60
Czechoslovakia	71	85
East Germany	64	66
Poland	66	70
Hungary	52	50
USSR	87	95

Source: Handelshochschule Leipzig, quoted by Seitz, H. (1990). 'The new order in the Soviet Union – Trading Opportunities', lecture given at the 1st European Trading Forum, *New Opportunities in East Germany and Eastern Europe*, June 28/29, Berlin

comes from food and drinks (excluding the restaurant trade): Romania has the lowest percentage, with food accounting for 55 per cent of retail turnover.

Table 3.13: Structure of retail sales in selected East European Countries, 1988 (%).

Country	Specialist retailer[a]	Restaurant trade[a]	Food total[b]	Non-food
Bulgaria	81.1	18.9	68.75	31.25
Czechoslovakia	87.3	12.7	60.00	40.00
East Germany	89.9	10.1	60.00	40.00
Poland	94.1	5.9	62.50	37.50
Romania[a]	–	–	55.00	45.00
Hungary	90.3	9.7	70.00	30.00
USSR	91.5	8.5	57.50	42.50

Notes:
[a] 1987.
[b] Turnover from food and drinks retailers excluding restaurant sales.
Source: 1989 Comecon Statistical Yearbook, Moscow quoted by Seitz, H. (1990): 'The new order in the Soviet Union – Trading Options', lecture given to the 1st European Trading Forum, *New Opportunities in East Germany and Eastern Europe*, June 28/29, Berlin; Comecon Statistical Yearbook, quoted by Stutzer, D. (1990): 'Unlimited demand but limited capacity', *Lebensmittel* 42 (41), October 12: 82.

Poor Infrastructure

Poor transport infrastructure and the small number of private households with access to a vehicle has meant that most people have to walk to the shops. This has favoured retail outlets in town centre locations or near residential areas and has made it difficult to establish retail outlets on greenfield sites.

Profit margins

Profit margins in Eastern Europe are much lower than in Western Europe. For example, gross profit margins in Czechoslovakia in 1990 for the combined whole-sale and retail sector (as a percentage of retail turnover) were as follows:[6]

Basic foodstuffs	20%	Shoes	15%
Confectionery	14%	Glass and china	20%
Outer clothing	21%	Sports equipment and toys	17%

In 1991, however, margins in the retail sector increased from these levels to a rate of 35–40 per cent. This was meant to alleviate the effects of the doubling of interest rates and wages increases.

Declining turnover in recent years

In recent years the actual turnover of the East European retail trade has been tumbling. Between 1980 and 1990 it fell by 50 per cent in Yugoslavia. In Czechoslovakia, in the first seven months of 1991 alone, turnover in retail trade fell by 44 per cent, while the inflation rate at the same time was 60 per cent. In Bulgaria, Romania, Poland and the USSR, it is known that consumption levels have decreased considerably, with no immediate prospects of improvement.

Rents in Eastern Europe

Considerable interest has been shown by potential investors in East European towns, particularly in their capital cities. This has been generated by the increasing demand for office space. In Budapest and Prague, for example, monthly rents have increased by an equivalent of DM 50 per sq.m.; in Warsaw the increase has been even higher. Experts reckon that the return on office space in these cities is between 12 and 15 per cent.[7]

Retail trade in the USSR

According to Soviet statistics, in 1988 turnover in the retail sector in the USSR was 366.4 billion roubles, which represents 1,200 roubles per head of population. At this time, the annual per capital income was only 2,500 roubles; it was unlikely that the figures for 1990 would be as high. The reforms in the USSR introduced in 1985 have not solved any supply problems, and have favoured the development of the black market there.

Since 1988 companies have been free to sell on the free market anything which they produce beyond the level prescribed by the central government. This has led to extremely high prices, fuelled even further by speculation.

In 1990 about 23,000 retail shops were privatized and offered under lease in the USSR. In addition to these small outlets, the Moscow department store GUM, with a turnover of 2.5 million roubles, making it the biggest department store in the USSR, was also leased. The total turnover of the retail trade in 1989–90 has been estimated at some 340 billion roubles. In 1990 the turnover of the privatized sector accounted for 8 per cent of this total. In the mean time, a number of wholesale establishments and restaurants have also been set up.

In late 1990 a further privatization programme for the retail sector was presented, under which about 75,000 food stores of less than 100 sq.m. and 80,000 non-food stores of less than 160 sq.m. sales area were to be privatized. It was also proposed that at some time in the future larger stores should be turned into public limited companies. The monopolies in the Soviet wholesale trade sector are to be broken up in various ways:

1. National inspectors will be dismissed.
2. Warehousing businesses will be let on lease.
3. Existing companies will be turned into public limited companies.
4. A co-operative wholesale trade will be set up.

Privatization in Czechoslovakia

The fall in turnover has had an adverse impact on privatization. The intended privatization of 13 per cent of all shops was scaled down to 8 per cent by the Ministry of Trade. Most privatized shops have a sales area of less than 60–100 sq.m.

The privatization also extends to real estate. Food shops have to be run for a minimum of two years after privatization, but this restriction does not apply to the non-food sector.

Privatization is being implemented through auctions. In the first round, only Czech citizens may make bids. Only those shops that are offered a second time may be purchased by foreigners.

Black and grey markets

All the Eastern European countries have experienced the development of 'black' and 'grey' markets. In some, especially in the former USSR, there has been the development of a strong shadow economy. All producing companies are obliged to make contributions to the supply of consumer goods and to take care of their staff, and a supply cycle operating outside the formal retail sector has been created.

Experience has shown that black markets cease to operate as soon as goods are no longer scarce and currencies function properly; hence black and grey markets tend to be of a transitional nature.

A General Business Strategy for Western Companies Trading in Eastern Europe

The philosophy in Eastern Europe

Any consideration of the strategic options resulting from the opening up of the Eastern countries must start with the philosophy prevalent in Eastern Europe. The problems of infrastructure and distribution which exist in Eastern Europe mean that a somewhat more comprehensive view of trade is required.

An important criterion for successful involvement in Eastern Europe is 'increasing convergence'; i.e. the creation of production facilities and trading outlets which can offer services capable of being marketed throughout Europe. A fundamental requirement for any trading venture in Eastern Europe is, therefore, the immediate creation of a well-rounded policy in which there are no fundamental differences between activity in East and West, as travel and cross-border shopping forays will bring about a rapid increase in the awareness of Western products and practices.

Languages

Some knowledge of the national language is almost essential. Russian has to be spoken by people interested in the former USSR, where the older generation tends to speak German, while the younger people are more familiar with English.

In all other Eastern European countries German is the first and English the second foreign language. In Poland, French is rather more important than English.

The axiom of complete commitment

The central principle fundamental to success is the commitment of top management to Eastern Europe. Unless the level of identification is extremely high, the risks of an involvement in the East will be under-estimated and its opportunities over-estimated. As a rule the time span required in Eastern Europe tends to be under-estimated.

Aspects of authority – the dominance principle

The dominance principle is crucial in Eastern Europe; for decades there was a belief in the strength and importance of institutions. In the early stages, capitalism in East Europe will have to orientate itself accordingly. The most realistic market structure will be a narrow oligopoly, with the concept of decentralization only gradually gaining acceptance.

Individual strands of an East European strategy for commercial companies

A strategy involving entry into Eastern Europe must be based upon:

- analysis of the market;
- analysis of potential locations;
- analysis of potential partners;
- selection of partners;
- agreement with partners;
- training and transfer of expertise.

Factors that will promote the development of trade are:

- the existence of the right contacts with administrative authorities;
- the ability to find the right partners;
- the training of local management in the country of the Western partner;
- the willingness to be involved in offset trading;
- the ability to adopt a long-term approach;
- the ability to develop production in Eastern Europe with components supplied from Western Europe;
- the ability to develop local production or production through joint ventures;
- the ability to develop language skills;

- the willingness to employ former East European residents who have completed an appropriate business training.

The development of trade will be impeded by:

- a lack of foreign exchange;
- the fact that few of the consumer goods presently produced in Eastern Europe at present will survive in the long term;
- the need for good staying power;
- the lack of language skills.

Product restrictions in Eastern Europe

If equipment and products are developed abroad, they must fit in with the servicing potential within individual countries. There are several service constraints at both the local and the regional/national levels that must not be overlooked.

Product quality must adjust to servicing capabilities. The greater the division of labour and sophistication of skills within the service infrastructure of any country, the fewer the constraints imposed by servicing factors. The opposite will also apply; if division of labour and trade skills are less well developed, the constraints imposed by servicing requirements will increase accordingly.

Eastern Europe is weak in this respect and this will impose considerable constraints on product complexity for some considerable time; this is certainly true of such products as electrical equipment and electronic components in motor vehicles. Product complexity will gradually increase in line with infrastructure developments, but in the initial stages this will mean, for example, less electronics in products ranging from household equipment to cars.

The lesson to be learnt is that if the servicing infrastructure is weak, the complexity of products must not exceed either the local technical skills or the logistical structures.

The constraints of complementary products should also be borne in mind. For example, tractors with powerful engines cannot be coupled to agricultural machinery designed for tractors with a low engine capacity.

Integrated strategies

From the outset, any company wishing to trade in Eastern Europe must develop an integrated strategy which takes account of all purchase and sales conditions.

Management strategies for Western companies in Eastern Europe

In terms of management structures there are significant differences between developments in Eastern and Western Europe. In Western Europe, there is increasing centralization of market-oriented decision-taking, with divisional structures having control over regional structures. In Eastern Europe, orientation is primarily on a national basis, with regional structures having supremacy over divisionalization.

This variation is explained by the differing operation of the markets.

One word of caution, however: unless there are mass markets or niche

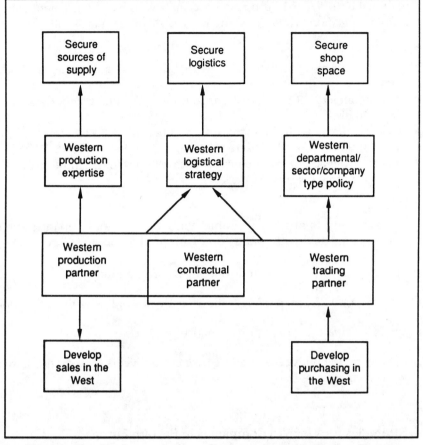

Fig. 3.1. The development of a trading organization in Eastern Europe.

dominance, the principles of divisionalization should not be followed slavishly. Excessive divisionalization can represent self-inflicted wounds.

Project management for Eastern Europe

Standardization in Western Europe has resulted in a logical shift from a country-based philosophy to one based on country groups, or on Western Europe as a whole. However, in Eastern Europe there will be differences in the way individual countries develop and in the way they cast off their former Comecon links and develop their own national structures. This means that any strategy should be country-based, at least for the next decade.

Admittedly the products to be sold in all East European markets can be very similar. However, the way the market is approached and the marketing strategy adopted should vary from country to country. In all cases it will make sense to assign separate project/working groups to each of the countries in Eastern Europe where a company is already present or intends to be present in the future.

Because of the speed with which change occurs, it cannot be assessed from abroad. A qualified management team must be developed in each country. Every company must employ East European specialists who have permanent contacts in the country in question. The role of any management team is as follows:

1. *Contacts*:
    - foster contacts with national, regional and local authorities and administration;
    - foster contacts with trading organizations with potential for co-operation or integration;
    - foster contacts with the increasing number of specialists released by state institutions as a result of deregulation;
    - rigorous development of contacts with all scientific institutions in Eastern Europe with a bearing on trade.

2. *Structural activities*:
    - prepare development programmes with the relevant companies and enterprises concerned with trading and with production, to support the trading activities;
    - prepare contracts for such development programmes.

3. *Operational activities*: prepare operational activities in line with agreed policies.

4. *Financial activities*: secure required finance.

5. *Budgeting*: rolling budgets extending over several years to cover the activities in any given country.

Retail Strategies for Western Companies in Eastern Europe

The most sensible policy for retailers will probably be to start with city and urban outlets and gradually extend to rural areas. There is much to be said for coming to an arrangement with existing state trading organizations and co-operatives, so that existing capacity can be utilized for both food and non-food retailing.

Because of limited product ranges and the existing level of supply, it is unlikely that the establishment of large food outlets will be an overriding priority.

Even during the initial phase, the development of specialist markets can be successful, particularly in locations where a specialist market can be linked to a non-food self-service department store acting as an anchor store. Discount stores will be particularly welcome.

Most active Western countries in Eastern Europe

Precise information on which West European retailers have moved into Eastern Europe is hard to find and, moreover, quickly becomes out of date. The Corporate Intelligence Group in London, however, published a report in September 1991 on 'Cross-Border Retailing in Europe', which identified seventy-seven Western retail operations that had moved into Eastern Europe. German retailers had been by far the most active, accounting for twenty-five of these operations, followed by Italian and Austrian retailers (fourteen and thirteen operations respectively). No other Western country came near to these levels of activity.

Most attractive retail sectors

The retail sector that has attracted the most attention from Western retailers is clothing. The report from The Corporate Intelligence Group showed that the fashion/clothing sector in fact accounted for one-third of all the moves into Eastern Europe (twenty-three of the seventy-seven moves identified to date). Next in order of importance came mail order or catalogue selling (eleven moves), food and groceries (nine moves) plus supermarkets and discount groups (six moves) and department stores (eight moves).

Franchising

One suitable approach for Eastern Europe may well be to invest in efficient franchise systems. This strategy could offer rapid expansion prospects, even within the framework of existing state trading organizations and co-operatives.

The concept of franchising includes many features which are not unknown in a centrally-planned economy. The concept will, therefore, be more easily understood. The customary commission element included in franchising schemes will, for example, be acceptable.

As an example of such a development, Leclerc has started to train Polish entrepreneurs to open their own shops in Poland. In addition, the Italian clothing group Stefanel has signed an agreement with Universal, a Romanian retail group company, to establish a chain of franchised clothing stores. Stefanel already had one shop in Bucharest and planned to have seven franchised units at the end of the first year and a chain of sixty shops within three years.

Direct selling by West European manufacturers

Manufacturers from Western Europe are already active in Eastern Europe, either on their own or through join ventures.

For example, BSHG, the Munich-based Bosch/Siemens household equipment company, has opened shops in Belgrade, Split and Zagreb in Yugoslavia in a joint venture with Genex; Schöller-Mövenpick is seeking to pull the rug from under the feet of competitors like Langnese (Unilever) by selling direct from stalls in East Germany and Eastern Europe.

Another example would be Yves Rocher, which for ten years has had eight employees working in a central department responsible for trade relations with the state-trading countries. This department has been taking care of the entire Eastern market, from the People's Republic of China to Cuba and from the USSR to Yugoslavia. Business was quite monotonous until the Berlin Wall collapsed. The goods went to trade centres which dominated the distributive channels, had foreign currencies at their disposal and sold Rocher cosmetics in exchange for convertible currencies to customers. Yves Rocher, however, also used barter deals in order to stimulate sales in the socialist countries.

Whenever possible, Rocher also made use of any domestic production capacity that was available. This was based on co-operation or joint ventures. By selling for domestic currencies, a broader circle of female customers was able to buy the products, at reasonable prices. The range of products was deliberately extended to

Table 3.14: Foreign retailers in Eastern Europe by country of origin, 1991.

Country of operation	Host country							
	Bulgaria	Czechoslovakia	Hungary	Poland	Romania	USSR	Yugoslavia	Total
Austria	–	3	5	1	–	1	3	13
Belgium	–	–	2	–	–	1	–	3
Denmark	–	–	–	1	–	–	–	1
Finland	–	–	–	–	–	1	–	1
France	–	–	–	3	–	3	–	6
Germany	3	2	8	4	–	6	2	25
Italy	1	2	2	2	2	3	2	14
Netherlands	–	2	–	–	–	–	–	2
Spain	–	–	–	–	–	–	1	1
Sweden	–	1	1	1	–	1	1	5
Switzerland	–	–	1	–	–	–	–	1
UK	–	–	1	1	–	1	1	4
USA	–	1	–	–	–	–	–	1
Total	4	11	20	13	2	17	10	77

Source: 'Cross-Border Retailing in Europe', The Corporate Intelligence Group

Table 3.15: Foreign retailers in Eastern Europe, analysed by Retail Sector, 1991.

				Country				
Retail Sector	*Bulgaria*	*Czechoslovakia*	*Hungary*	*Poland*	*Romania*	*USSR*	*Yugoslavia*	*Total*
Clothing/fashion	1	4	6	3	1	6	2	23
Grocery:	–	1	4	–	–	3	1	9
Supermarkets/Discount stores	–	2	–	2	–	–	2	6
Total food	–	3	4	2	–	3	3	15
Mail Order/catalogues	1	2	2	1	–	3	2	11
Department stores	2	1	2	1	–	2	–	8
Furniture/household	–	1	1	2	–	1	1	6
Footwear	–	–	2	2	1	1	–	6
Health & beauty	–	–	–	1	–	1	–	2
DIY	–	–	–	1	–	–	–	1
Miscellaneous	–	–	3	–	–	–	2	5
Total	4	11	20	13	2	17	10	77

Source: 'Cross-Border Retailing in Europe', The Corporate Intelligence Group

include essential goods such as soaps and shampoos, in order to avoid the image of a luxury goods supplier.

In Czechoslovakia the goods were sold via a national organization and paid for mostly with the domestic currency. Much of the Polish market has been conquered by Rocher. Most payments are made in foreign currencies. In Bulgaria, Rocher is extending its popularity by sponsoring sporting events. The former USSR represents 80 per cent of the company's activities in the East, primarily on the basis of barter and clearing contracts. In Romania, the first steps have been taken since the 'revolution'. Rocher admits, however, that the Hungarian market has been neglected because of all the activities elsewhere.

Organic growth by retailers

Retailers can of course opt for a policy of organic growth. In Poland, for example, Spar has started a test market operation in the Krakau area; Otto is supplying non-food products to 12 Sezam department stores; Hertie is opening a small department store in Posen in co-operation with Bovis; and Quelle is setting up a joint venture to sell a range of products in Southern Poland.

Acquiring Eastern firms

The Austrian group Julius Meinl has acquired a 51 per cent share of the Hungarian food chain, Csemege Trading Company of Budapest, a consequence of the privatization policy of the Hungarian government. Csemege is the largest food retailer in Hungary, with 119 shops, sales of 15 billion forints ($190 mn) and 4,300 employees. In addition, the company has ninety-five Intourist shops offering Hungarian specialities aimed mainly at tourists.

Julius Meinl was prominent in Hungary before the Second World War. Market research has shown that the name is recognized by 53 per cent of the Budapest population as being synonymous with coffee and quality foodstuffs.

Servicing policy

For technical equipment it may well be appropriate to develop service networks which are largely independent of the supplying company. The former repair stations are available as a starting point. This offers the possibility of extending the concept of franchising to technical skills.

Consignment depots and shop-in-a-shop units

The large multiple retailers in Eastern Europe have now established wholesale departments linking with supply depots; for example, the Centrum department stores in Hungary have linked with Moulinex in France and Media Markt in Germany. In addition, franchised departments and shops-in-shops have been introduced in some stores, e.g. Ardek EG, Germany, selling clothes for children and teenagers.

Through its subsidiary Eduscho Österreich GmbH of Vienna, the Bremen-based company Eduscho has set up a joint venture coffee retailing company in Budapest – Eduscho Budapest GmbH. Alfa Mozaik AFESZ, the Hungarian food production and distribution company, has a 50 per cent stake in the joint venture. Initially three sorts of coffee are to be sold through food and restaurant outlets. In addition a separate distribution network consisting of Eduscho branches and Eduscho depots will be developed using the West German structure as its model. Eduscho reckons that coffee consumption, currently running at 4 kg per head, could double in Hungary in just a few years.[8]

Tchibo decided to go East by producing coffee jointly with government-owned enterprises. Thus Tchibo Praha is producing a brand of coffee in the Czech Republic. Similar methods are being applied in Hungary, Poland and in the former Yugoslavia.

Direct marketing in Eastern Europe

Mail order and direct marketing operations should be able to achieve a good market share within a very short time, either with or without facilities locally, particularly if customers are also offered instalment terms.

Avon, the cosmetics company, which is already represented in over one hundred countries and which employs some 1.5 million consultants, entered the Hungarian market in 1990. Its policy is similar to that adopted in other countries, i.e. products can be obtained exclusively from an Avon consultant who sells direct. About 220 products are offered at reasonable prices, with payment in Hungarian Forints. Orders are processed and dispatched from the head office and production plant of Avon Cosmetics GmbH Deutschland at Neufahrn near Munich. In addition a separate sales organization has been set up in Budapest. Market research has estimated that personal spending on cosmetics in Hungary is about DM 200 billion. Avon is reckoning on a market share of between 5 and 10 per cent.[9]

Suppliers with a fixed base are also involved, at least in the catalogue/campaign business; an example of this would be the campaign launched by Konsum/Interbuy in co-operation with the Association of Consumer Co-operatives (VdK) in East Germany to sell TV sets.

Financial services

The 'unleashing of consumer credit in Eastern Europe' correctly predicted by Helmut Wagner of ASKO (i.e. the widespread willingness of the individual to incur personal debt), also implies a need for suitable financial services and banking products in Eastern Europe, offered in co-operation with Eastern and Western banks.

Mail order

Neckermann Versand AG has been active in Hungary since 1987, where it co-operates with the trading organization Skala Coop/Skala World Trade. In 1990 it launched a new brochure for the Hungarian market, 500,000 copies of which were distributed. This contained a range of eighty hardware products, which can be ordered in writing or by telephone from the Neckermann sales office in Budapest. The goods are delivered direct to customers, irrespective of where they live.

Conclusions: the Development of Business in Eastern Europe

The instability and non-convertibility of many Eastern European currencies, combined with the chronic shortage of foreign exchange associated with indebtedness, have made it difficult to assess the economic potential of any involvement in Eastern Europe. However, the attractiveness of markets in Eastern Europe is determined less by the current economic structure and more by the speed and intensity of the liberalization process.

There is overwhelming evidence that the first major upturn in Eastern Europe will be in the wholesale trade, which may well exert a dominant influence over both the supply industry and retailing, in the initial phase. At the same time it should be possible to develop the retail trade by using existing companies or by developing land already in use. The opening up of Eastern Europe by trading organizations will be characterized by a twin dynamism:

1. the wholesale trade as joint developers with industry and promoters of domestic and foreign markets;
2. the retail trade, ensuring that the consumer is supplied with products commensurate with market demand.

Important developments in this respect are:

1. The considerable head-start enjoyed by companies already active internationally in Western Europe.
2. The trend towards reciprocity between partners in the West and East, through the medium of joint ventures.
3. Close strategic alliances between West European banks, insurers and other service providers and production and trading companies in Eastern Europe.

Several countries, in particular the former Soviet Union, previously neglected the import of consumer goods despite the weaknesses of their own consumer goods industries. It is, therefore, important to use trade to encourage the development of an independent, viable consumer goods industry in Eastern Europe. The implication is that West European trading companies must seek to overcome the one-sidedness and over-specialization associated with both industry and the distributive trades.

Every company must concentrate on achieving a maximum level of self-sufficiency fairly quickly. This means that trading organizations from Western Europe must also establish contact with industrial companies from Western Europe and encourage them to grant licences in Eastern Europe or to pass on expertise to East European partners. This will ensure that goods acceptable and exportable to the West can be offered as quickly as possible on the domestic market and then made available for export as well.

Such considerations as these show that successful involvement in Eastern Europe will require major networking; i.e. there will be companies which will manufacture westernized goods in one production shift or within the production department of an existing company. These goods will be sold partly at home and partly abroad. As the components for such goods, for example in the textile and shoe industry, cannot always be produced in Eastern Europe, they will have to be imported from Western Europe during the initial phase.

The involvement of Western companies in solving logistical problems will be far greater than might have been assumed at the outset; poor logistics are a root cause of bottlenecks in Eastern Europe.

A major emphasis must be placed on the training of local managers. Several

West European companies have started training programmes running for several months, in which managers from the East are trained in the West.

West European companies must be wary of under-estimating the cost of an involvement in Eastern Europe. Any company that decides to trade in one or more countries should set up a firm budget covering a period of several years. It must assume that the return on both market investment and the investment in the trading infrastructure will take several years to materialize.

Despite these enormous problems, entrepreneurial initiative is the only way to make a contribution towards increasing the pace of economic development in Eastern Europe, the only way to secure peace in the Northern hemisphere and to create a framework in which the problems of developing countries and the threatening North–South conflict can be solved.

Notes

1. For the purposes of this paper, Eastern Europe also includes the former USSR.
2. See unattributed article, 'Czechoslovakia – 100,000 shops under the hammer', *Textil Wirtschaft*, 1991, 46(6): 51.
3. See unattributed article, 'Budapest adopts a step-by-step approach to the stony path of privatization', *Handelsblatt*, 1991, 46(83), April 30: 8.
4. See also Schenk, K-E. (1989) 'Perestroika: Opportunities for the World Economy?', *Volkswirtschaftliche Korrespondenz*, the Albert-Weber Foundation 28(9).
5. CIA (publisher) (1988) *Handbook of Economic Statistics*.
6. Statistics from the Internal Trade Research Institute, Prague.
7. See also unattributed article, 1990, 'Continuing increase in rents in East European cities', *Blick durch die Wirtschaft*, 33(222), November 15: 1.
8. See unattributed article (1990) 'Eduscho goes to Hungary', *Lebensmittel* 42(27), July 6: 18.
9. See unattributed article (1990) 'Avon – now in Hungary', *Direct Selling Bulletin* 3: 14.

4

Economic Reforms, External Imbalances and Assessment of Risk in Eastern Europe

Iliana Zloch-Christy

The economic transformation and the external debt problems of the countries of Eastern Europe* have been accompanied by greatly increased interest on the part of the Western business community in evaluating country risk. The former Soviet Union and its satellites in Central and Eastern Europe are regarded as a region with an unstable political structure and serious macroeconomic imbalances. Within a period of less than two years, the totalitarian communist regimes across Central and Eastern Europe were shaken up by a strong democratic movement and have now been largely replaced by non-communist governments. The development of a democratic movement in the former Soviet Union has paralleled the onset of serious economic crises and nationality problems. In August 1991, after the unsuccessful coup attempt against Gorbachev, the Soviet communist party was banned.

Although the future political landscape in Romania is still unclear, all the indications are that Eastern Europe in the mid-1990s will be radically different from the same region in the mid-1980s, when it was dominated by Soviet influence, communist rule and centrally planned economies. The process of economic and political transformation is likely to be irreversible.

The changes in Eastern Europe raise the issue of evaluating political risk in the region. Even though these countries are gradually developing as market economies, political risk is still the major issue. The need for political risk assessment should not be underestimated in Western business and financial circles, and should be an integral part of any international portfolio management process. This

---

* 'Eastern Europe' up to October 2, 1990 denotes Bulgaria, the former Czechoslovakia, the German Democratic Republic (GDR), Hungary, Poland, Romania and the former Soviet Union. More recently, Eastern Europe as a distinct geographical area with its own political and reformist identity, of course, omits the former GDR.

This chapter was initially written during the author's visiting scholarship at the Hoover Institution on War, Revolution and Peace, at Stanford University, California, in May 1991. The author would like to acknowledge the stimulating intellectual atmosphere of this institute.

chapter attempts to provide a preliminary basis for a future research towards an analytical framework for a discussion of approaches for evaluating political and social risk in doing business with Eastern Europe and to reconsider methodologies for country risk assessment.

The structure of the chapter is as follows. First there is a brief exploration of the basic changes in Eastern Europe envisaged by the recent reforms. There is then an examination of the external imbalances (external debt situation) of the region, followed by an exploration of the methodologies of country risk assessment to be applied to Eastern Europe. This focuses on the liquidity and structural indices, and on some indicators of the debt burden and creditworthiness. Following on from this there is an examination of the approach to the question of how to assess the effects of the market-oriented reforms changes in Eastern Europe and then an analysis of the political and social risk assessment, which asks four main questions: how to define political and social risk assessment in Eastern Europe; what the key aspects of political risk assessment are; what the fundamental questions in political risk analysis are; and what the main aspects of the assessment of the social conditions are. The main findings are presented in the conclusion.

Transformation and Liberalization in Eastern Europe

The present transformation occurring in the countries of Eastern Europe aims not only at changing priorities and changing policies, as the previous attempts did, but also at changing the economic and political system. The reforms in Central and Eastern Europe in 1990–1 and the revolutionary events in the Soviet Union in August and September 1991 show clearly the three main pillars of the reform process:

1. Privatization (to a certain point) of the means of the production and diversification of the forms of economic activity.
2. Decentralization of management decision making in the economy.
3. Reducing and eliminating the political monopoly of the single party and creating political liberalization, with openness (glasnost), more democratic rights, and multiparty systems.

The terms 'self-dependence', 'self-financing' and 'self-management' characterize the main directions of the decentralization of decision making in Eastern Europe. There are two major differences between the present reforms and all of the previous so-called 'reforms'. It has been stressed by the policy makers themselves that in the first place, economic reform will not succeed without political reform and therefore the two reforms must be simultaneously carried out; and second, there is an intention that the Eastern European command economies should be restructured, from top to bottom.

The Eastern European countries and their economies are a delicately balanced web of interest and social stratas. Economic reform requires fundamental changes in the general management and macroeconomic system, and considerable shifts are required in resource allocation at the sectoral, branch and regional levels, as well as in income policy, a long and difficult process. The economic and political developments undertaken so far allow for the (probably premature) conclusion that the Eastern European economies are in a state of mixed economy at present – capitalism without profit, and socialism without planning. Further discussion on this issue is beyond the scope of the present paper.

Economic Reform and the External Debt Situation

The external debt situation of the Eastern European countries deteriorated rapidly in the late 1980s. Such large external imbalances represent serious macroeconomic constraints on the process of economic and political transformation. The total gross debt of the region reached some $142 billion ($123 billion net) at the beginning of 1991, the most heavily indebted countries being the then Soviet Union, Poland and Hungary. Bulgaria experienced serious debt servicing difficulties in early 1990, and debt rescheduling proved unavoidable. Debt-service ratios reached alarming levels in Bulgaria, Poland and Hungary in 1990: 77 per cent, 71 per cent and 65 per cent respectively (a level of 25 per cent being considered critical, in business circles). The Soviet Union began to accumulate large arrears to banks and suppliers in 1990, but did not request formal debt rescheduling, although a further increase in its debt levels, as well as refinancing of some of the debt repayments due, appeared inevitable.

The policy strategies of the creditors and debtors so far have included measures by the Western creditors (and particularly the private institutions) aimed at reducing their exposure to the region, together with increases in direct and equity investment. The Eastern European countries continue to seek debt relief measures (Poland, Bulgaria), borrowing from international financial organizations and official credit agencies (particularly for the former Soviet Union, Bulgaria and Poland) and debt rescheduling (Bulgaria). This indicates that clearly defined strategies on dealing with the present external debt situation in Eastern Europe are a necessity for both creditors and debtors.

An interesting question related to assessment of the creditworthiness of the region arises: would the process of economic liberalization in Central and Eastern Europe lead to an abatement of the pressure on the external balance of these countries in the short- and medium-term?

External financial problems cannot be solved without trade. Thus foreign borrowing should be considered as a trade across time. On the other hand, debt-servicing capacity must be judged with regard to long-term economic growth prospects, rather than on gross and net debt levels – in other words, on the efficiency of the macro and microeconomic organization, or the system, which determines the principal questions with respect to economic life regarding 'what', 'how' and 'for whom'. The Eastern European countries cannot solve their transfer problem with the Western nations without a long and difficult adjustment in economic policy towards development strategy which increases the efficiency of production and the creation of a production base that is competitive by world market standards. However, recent experience in the 1970s and 1980s in Eastern Europe and in many developing countries shows that the road to economic inefficiency is paved with good intentions (Poland, Hungary, Latin America, Africa).

What can be expected in the first half of the 1990s, the period of the economic transformation in Eastern Europe? Will the self-regulating natural order of the market mechanism be achieved quickly? What are the prospects for an economic order where 'government governs best which governs least'?

It goes beyond the scope of the present paper to go into detail in addressing these questions; the following brief answers can be suggested. The economic reforms are in their embryonic period at present. The reform programmes in all of the Eastern European countries lack entirely logical structures. The reformers are on the road of endlessly searching for better ways in which the government can help (or stop hindering) economic progress. But it is obvious that there will be no magic formula with which the Eastern European governments may find the best policies for implementing a mixed market economy, or perhaps a mixed socialist economy. There is no doubt that it will take time – associated with stability and continuity of policies – for the governments in Eastern Europe to establish the legal framework of the economy, to determine the macroeconomic stabilization policy, to effect the allocation of resources needed to improve economic efficiency, and to establish programmes for the distribution of income. In other words, the economic reforms will not change *de facto* the logic of the economic system and remove all centrally planned controls and restrictions in Eastern Europe in the medium term. And we should not forget that removing old constraints usually leads to new ones. Another problem concerns the creation of new policy-making and managerial groups in Eastern Europe, who have adjusted to the new economic order – the reform process at present and in the future requires not only radical new laws, 'dekreti' and good rules for economic management, but people – decision makers, officials and managers – who have adjusted to these new rules. For more than four decades the Eastern European countries have spoken a different economic language to that of the Western (European) nations. It takes time to learn a new language, or to eliminate old 'dialects' and 'accents'.

All that indicates that it would be over-optimistic to expect an abatement of the debt-servicing difficulties in the region in the short- and medium-term.

Methodologies of Country Risk Assessment in Lending to Eastern Europe

From a bank's point of view, risk is exposure to a loss. Lending across national borders involves both economic risk (balance of payments difficulties, general problems in economic management, etc.) and political risks (sociopolitical upheavals, willingness of the authorities to meet foreign debt obligations, etc.). These risks are not easy to assess. Even if the risks of any given economic policy or political decision could be judged accurately, there would still be uncertainty over which policies should be adopted. Avramovic's (1964) appraisal of the uncertainty of creditworthiness and country risk evaluations is still valid today:

> The appraisal of creditworthiness of anybody – be it an individual, a business firm, or country – is a mixture of facts and judgements. Even if we had the theory of debt servicing capacity and could satisfactorily explain the likely behaviour of major variables and their time path, we would still be facing uncertainties arising from current economic

and financial policies which the decision makers in the borrowing countries may choose to adopt, be it at their own initiative or in response to all sorts of pressures.

(Avramovic 1964: 7–8)

Analysis of an Eastern European country's creditworthiness requires an answer to two fundamental questions: First, is the country's liquidity sufficient to cover its immediate needs (i.e. can debt service interruptions be avoided)?; second, is the economy sound, well managed, and capable of generating adequate external revenue for future debt servicing?

The first question relates to the country's immediate liquidity (foreign exchange) position, and the second to its ability to continue to solve its structural problems.

Potential short-term debt service difficulties can be analysed by a liquidity index. A typical index is a weighted average of scores (varying on a scale of, say, 0 to 100 of specific indicators; some of them are discussed below). Usually an index value of 30–50 points is considered a grey area; a value of 50 points and above suggests liquidity difficulties may occur. The index might be based on developments in some, many, or all of the following basic indicators of the hard-currency debt burden:

- total debt service relative to exports of goods and all services (debt service ratio);
- international reserves (or Western bank assets) relative to imports of goods and all services;
- short-term trade-related debt relative to three months of hard-currency imports (debt trade ratio);
- the country's net compressible import capacity (imports other than raw materials, fuel, capital equipment and food);
- current account deficit relative to exports of goods and all services;
- interest payments relative to exports of goods and all services;
- interest earned on international assets as a percentage of interest due on external debt;
- international reserves relative to short-term debt;
- large reserve losses;
- gross or net debt relative to exports of goods and all services;
- access to the international capital markets and ability to roll over debts;
- delayed payments and arrears;
- implementation of IMF stabilization programme and/or use of IMF/BIS credit lines for balance of payments adjustment;
- implementation of (short-term) programmes for introducing convertibility on the current account and associated with that, terms (fixed or floating exchange rate policy) and the probability of their sustainability over a six-month period;
- spread over LIBOR.

In the case of the Eastern European countries, supplementing an evaluation of a country's liquidity position with an analysis of its structural problems, indicating the likelihood of future payments problems as well as the ability to solve existing ones, is essential.

The soundness of the Eastern European economies could be analysed by a structural index. A typical index is a weighted average of scores of individual indicators (some of which are discussed below). On a scale similar to that of the liquidity index, 50 points and above is the area indicating that repayment difficulties may occur. The structural index could include the following indicators:

- rate of growth of GNP/GDP;
- hard-currency exports relative to GNP/GDP;
- growth of real per capita GNP or GDP (recent two years' average);
- the ratio of percentage change of exports relative to the percentage change in GNP or GDP;
- hard-currency exports relative to GNP/GDP;
- net debt relative to exports of goods and all services;
- net debt relative to GNP/GDP;
- growth of total exports and of hard-currency exports (most recent year and two-year average);
- percentage change in consumer prices (most recent year and three-year average);
- lending by the World Bank and the European Bank for Reconstruction and Development for structural adjustment purposes and for encouraging the private sector;
- composition of inter-regional trade (in convertible currencies);
- trade agreements (clearing or convertible currency settlements) with the former Soviet Union and with other Eastern European countries:
- implementation of programmes for multilateral payments union in the Eastern European countries (indicating the potential for transferability, trade multilateralism and currency convertibility in the medium-term);
- programmes for privatization of the domestic economy (sectors and their potential competitiveness by world market standards);
- programmes for encouraging foreign direct and equity investments.

The liquidity and structural indices described above are useful for comparative country risk analysis. The indicators they include (by no means an exhaustive list) show different aspects of a country's debt situation, but no single indicator is sufficient. Careful analysis will review developments of many indicators, before coming to conclusion. The debt servicing problems of the Eastern European countries in the late 1980s and in 1990–1 (particularly in the former Soviet Union, Bulgaria and Hungary) and the changes in their economic management and economic structures, suggest the following list of indicators as having a strong appeal for analysis of Eastern European borrowers:

- debt service ratio;
- access to the international financial markets;
- stand-by programmes with the IMF, and BIS lines of credit;
- multilateral clearing agreements in Eastern Europe;
- programmes in implementation for introducing currency convertibility;
- ratio of gross or net debt relative to exports of goods and all services.

It is not a goal of the analysis presented in this paper to discuss in detail the importance of individual indicators. However, it should be stressed here that a change in the perceptions about the creditworthiness of the Eastern European countries should be reflected in the assessment, for example, of the intra-regional trade in clearing accounts and in convertible currencies. This indicator is very important, particularly for the smaller Eastern European countries, which are more vulnerable than the Soviet Union to external shocks and which have less flexibility and fewer alternatives to shift from Eastern European to Western markets at present. All of these countries are very dependent on energy imports. Those countries which could continue to rely to a large extent on Russian imports settled on clearing basis (not a probable scenario, given the debt problems of the former Soviet Union, its internal economic and political difficulties and its new political strategy towards its former allies) would experience less severe convertible currency balance of payments difficulties than countries importing a greater part of their energy requirements from the world market.

How to Assess the Effects of the Economic Transformation

Assessing the opportunities and risks in Eastern Europe at present requires an answer to the difficult question of how to measure the effects of changes, in the sense of how successful the introduction and the implementation of the reform changes is. Providing a specific answer to this question would obviously be no more than an intellectual exercise. This section seeks to establish a basis for a better understanding of the direction in which the reform process and the economic development in Eastern European countries can be expected to move.

The central measures by which macroeconomic performance in every country (market economy, centrally planned economy, mixed economy) is judged are GNP, employment, inflation, and net exports. The main objectives of macroeconomic policy are a high level and rapid growth rate of output, a high level of employment, price stability, export and import equilibrium, and exchange rate stability. The instruments used in implementing macroeconomic policy in market economies usually include fiscal, monetary, income, trade and exchange rate policies. But the above mentioned policies and instruments have different economic effects in the (centrally) planned economies. As a starting point for assessing changes in macroeconomic policies in the reform-oriented Eastern European countries, obviously it is necessary to analyse in Western economic terms what instruments these countries apply for achieving the above-mentioned main objectives of economic policies – in other words, the impact of domestic fiscal, monetary, income, trade and exchange rate policies on the macroeconomic performance, the allocation of resources and the adjustment to external disturbances. Do the Eastern European countries continue to rely on policies of 'direct control', or on market-oriented policies and instruments? Some interesting questions in this regard are:

- How does the system for allocation of capital work?
- What is the role of interest rates?
- How does the allocation of foreign exchange in the economy occur?
- What is the role of the banking system in the economy?
- What are the changes in the price system?
- How many new enterprises have been created?
- What is the role of the bureaucracy in economic decision making?
- What targets are they pursuing and how are they trying to achieve them?; and many others.

The transformation from centrally planned to market oriented or market economies in Eastern Europe will obviously take a long time. It is difficult to make an assessment of precisely how long it will take, but it seems reasonable to assume that at least the first half of the 1990s will be a transition period. In the author's view the following basic changes are required in the transition period:

1. Market clearing prices.
2. Elimination of direct and indirect state subsidies.
3. Import liberalization.
4. (Last but not least) unified exchange rates and convertibility on the current account.

The analysis of the effects of the economic reforms should carefully assess also the nature of any changes in the performance of the governments in Eastern Europe, in so far as there are any radical (market oriented) changes in the exercise of their four basic executive functions related to the economy:

1. Establishing the legal framework of the economy.
2. Determining the macroeconomic stabilization policy.
3. Altering the allocation of resources to improve economic efficiency.
4. Establishing programmes that affect the distribution of income.

Associated with these basic changes is, of course, the expectation that the market-oriented economic reforms will be linked closely with political liberalization and a diminution of the role of the communist party and communist bureaucracy in the management of the economy. In other words, using the definition of the Hungarian economist and Harvard professor Janos Kornai (1986), the reform process should be associated with 'any change in the economic system, provided that it diminishes the role of bureaucratic coordination and increases the role of the market'. The successful introduction and implementation of the economic reforms could be analysed by assessing how close practice is moving towards radical changes in ownership, incentives, correcting informal 'rules of the game' (which complement, hinder, or enforce government resolution and legal regulation), etc.

On the microeconomic level, the analysis should concentrate on the following objectives:

*   autonomy of the enterprise;
*   accountability of the enterprise for profit and loss;
*   personal profit interest of the enterprise's employees;
*   enterprise efficiency (as compared to that of the pre-reform period).

It should be stressed here that these microeconomic objectives are associated, of course, with the existence of capital market in the individual countries. The factor for the accountability of the enterprises for profit and loss is one of the most important indicators of the successful implementation of a market-oriented economic reform in the bureaucratic Eastern European economic systems, since it gives an answer to the following two fundamental questions: first, do the enterprises operate on the basis of 'hard' or 'soft' budgetary constraints, and second, to what extent do firms' profits depend on bureaucratic intervention (direct setting of prices, taxes, subsidies, etc.)?

This brief discussion of the approaches to assessing the effects of the market-oriented reform process in Eastern Europe as regards changes at the macro- and microeconomic level, and the role of the government, undoubtedly raises as many questions as it answers. But I hope that it establishes a basis for an analysis of the present and future economic performance in the region, and its fundamental problem: that of market versus central planning.

Political and Social Risk Assessment

The conventional wisdom in lending to Eastern Europe has been that the risk to lenders is always a country-risk problem, rather than a project-risk problem. This concept of country-risk analysis requires certain reconsideration today. The present economic reform in the former Soviet Union and in the other countries of the region have increased the autonomy of domestic enterprises, creating the possibility for them to have direct access to Western markets. These changes increase the importance of evaluating political and social risks in lending to Eastern Europe.

Political risks in lending across national borders are those generated by political entities beyond one's national jurisdiction. The political risks in doing business with Eastern Europe concern the national and international political processes that can influence the level of risk involved in the undertaking of a Western entity operating in an environment susceptible to significant influence by political factors. The political risks are associated with sociopolitical upheaval, willingness of the authorities to meet foreign debt obligations, and many others. These risks are essentially dynamic and uncertain, and are not easy to assess.

There are two key aspects of political risk in relation to country risk analysis in lending to Eastern Europe:

1. Interactions between domestic economic policy and political developments.
2. Interactions between political developments, foreign confidence and capital inflows.

Starting from these issues, the analysis of political risk in lending to Eastern Europe requires an answer to four fundamental questions:

1. What is the country's leadership and its determination in carrying out economic and political reforms?
2. What are the social conditions in the country; does social support exist for government policies?
3. What is the influence of the former Soviet Union on the country's domestic and political developments, and can Russian assistance be expected in case of economic difficulties?
4. What is the state of East-West political relations?

A key starting point of political risk assessment is an evaluation of a country's leadership. This evaluation may illuminate the prospects for the success and continuity of the country's political developments (democratization, multi-party system), as well as its economic and borrowing policies and its economic management. Any Western businessman considering setting up a joint venture in, for example, the Baltic republics, or in Ukraine, or Georgia, will be keenly interested in the prospects for the Russian reform policies in the medium and long term. Any

Western banker considering provision of credit to a Soviet enterprise is also confronted with this basic question. The coup attempt of August 1991, the new Union treaty, the declaration of independence by most of the Soviet republics in August and September 1991, and recognition by the Western nations of the independence of the Baltic states in September 1991, makes clear the importance of careful analysis of both the short- and medium-term policies (sustainability and prospects) of the country's leadership.

The first question to be asked by Western businessmen providing loans to an entity in the Baltic states or in the Ukraine obviously would be how sure one could be that a particular enterprise or bank in these states would repay debt in the medium term, and who will provide guarantees – Soviet banks, or national institutions in the individual independent republics. A similar question arises in lending to Polish, Hungarian and Bulgarian entities (although the nationality context is basically different). Although each of the above-mentioned Eastern European countries belonged for more than four decades to the Soviet bloc, with central planning and totalitarian communist regimes, there are in practice many country-specific differences between them. No two Eastern European countries are alike. What is important for the analyst is to understand the key developments in a particular country and to know which questions to ask.

The most important question to be asked, and particularly in the case of the former Soviet Union, is what are the chances that a particular country's leadership will succeed in implementing the plans for liberalization of the economy and the associated plans for the political democratization of these formerly totalitarian Eastern European societies? If the economic reforms fail, the result would obviously be economic and political instability, and continued relative economic decline.

Interesting questions in the evaluation of a country's leadership are: Does the leadership consist of reformers, or of rather conservative (former) party bureaucrats and *apparatchiks*? What are the professional skills of the leadership? Does it support technocrats or not? Does it understand economics? What is the managerial background of the leadership?

Associated with these questions are other questions related to the political support of the leadership. Which groups support the party and government leadership? What is the basis of its control, e.g. popular support? How strong are the opposition parties? The next question to ask concerns whether the leadership consists of the old conservative guard or of radical reformers.

In individual Eastern European countries there will be specific issues or problems which need to be examined and then watched for future developments. Some of the questions to be asked may concern who will be the successor of a particular political leader, and whether the transition will be smooth? For example, who will be the successor of the leaderships which replaced the former dictators of Bulgaria and Romania? In the case of Romania, a further interesting question arises – will the new leadership continue its predecessor's unsophisticated economic and debt management (a centralized planning system and ban on foreign borrowing), or will it follow a path of economic and political transformation? In the case of the former Soviet Union, many questions arise concerning the outcome of the current political turmoil in Russia.

Another country-specific question which needs to be highlighted and examined is whether there are any ethnic or religious disturbances. Almost all of the East European countries face a risk of unrest due to such disturbances, which could have a major impact on the domestic politics and the economy. Without going into detail, note must be taken of the ethnic disturbances and nationality movements in the Baltic states, Georgia, Azerbaijan and elsewhere in the former Soviet Union, as well as in Romania, Hungary and the former Czechoslovakia, not to mention Yugoslavia.

Another interesting question concerns the degree of foreign confidence in the economic and political developments in individual Eastern European countries. Foreign confidence in a country's development and its leadership greatly affects the state of trade and credit relations between East and West. For example, the confidence of the Western countries in the policy of Hungary in the early 1980s gave this country access to the IMF and the World Bank and to new capital inflows, which allowed debt reschedulings to be avoided. The political liberalization which occurred in Poland in 1989 (legalizing Solidarity, and the election of a Solidarity-led government) were the main factors which affected the change of Western attitudes towards Poland and the fact that Poland received the first credits from the IMF and the World Bank in early 1990, as well as preferential export tariff treatment from the USA, more favourable conditions on rescheduling of Paris Club and commercial credits, and others. The confidence shown by the Western countries in the leadership of Gorbachev and Yeltsin during and after August 1991 will be important for the provision of technical assistance and new credits to the former Soviet Union, as well as for the establishment of joint ventures in the near future. Foreign confidence will be crucial for the inflow of funds also in the other Eastern European countries such as Bulgaria.

Economic and political developments in individual Eastern European countries can rarely be considered in isolation from regional and world events. Main trends in intra-regional economic developments (pricing policy, clearing and co-operation agreements, and others) should be examined. Some of the interesting questions to be asked concern changes in the intra-regional pricing policy and how they will affect intra-regional relations and relations with the developed Western nations and the developing countries? What are the prospects for creating a multilateral payments union in the region?

Political risk analysis requires an assessment of the relations between the individual Eastern European countries and the former Soviet Union. The notion of 'Soviet umbrella' against future economic difficulties in the individual Eastern European countries belongs definitely to the past. However, there are country-specific differences in the relations between the former Soviet Union and individual Eastern European countries, which an analyst should follow. It seems also that the former Soviet Union still has no clear strategy on how to deal with the former Warsaw Pact countries on a political and economic level. In early 1991 the (former) Central Committee of the (now banned) communist party and its Department for Foreign Relations argued that the Soviet Union should have a greater influence on the countries in the region, while the Soviet government (and its Ministry of Foreign Affairs) argued for the 'political freedom' of the latter.

It has to be stressed here that economic instability might arise in the Eastern European countries because of policies in the former Soviet Union. All of these countries have had strong economic and trade links with the former Soviet Union, and there is still the potential for their economies to be influenced by the economic situation there. An interesting question to be asked concerns what will be the policy of the Soviet Union as regards the rouble debts of its former allies?

Lastly (but not least), the state of East–West political relations should be one of the most important parts of a political risk assessment for Eastern Europe. The East–West political dialogue determines economic, trade and credit policies in the individual Eastern European countries towards the West. Some of the (many) questions to be asked at present are: what are the prospects for economic relations between Eastern Europe and the European Community in the light of the Single European Market? Can one anticipate that some of the Eastern European countries will apply (and be accepted) for full membership with the European Community, and what will be the effects of the present association agreements (1991–1992) on their domestic and political developments and on their relationship with the former Soviet Union? What are the prospects that the former Soviet Union will receive significant Western assistance in the process of reforming its economy, in the form of financial credit and direct and equity investments?

Political risk assessment also requires an analysis of the social conditions in the individual Eastern European countries. Social tensions are less immediate, in the sense that they are unlikely to apply, for example, to export payments. However, they are particularly likely to apply to long-term investment projects (joint ventures, co-operation agreements, and others). The analysis of social conditions is a critical part of a country risk evaluation, particularly for countries like the former Soviet Union, Poland and Hungary. The main question to be asked concerns whether there is social support for government policies. The events in Poland in the 1970s and in the 1980s, as well as the implementation of the present economic stabilization programme of the non-communist government, suggest that an accurate assessment of such social tensions may be a matter of urgent consideration for Western bankers and businessmen. Social tensions can precipitate political crisis, change the government priorities and policies, and even change the leadership. In the case of the former Soviet Union, a careful analysis of the social conditions in this country is essential, since improvement of the social conditions and living standards will be of crucial importance to any social support for Yeltsin's policies. The protest and social unrest in connection with the price increases which took place in the Soviet Union in May 1990 indicate clearly that radical economic changes could lead to a change of government policies and to general political tensions. Social support was a crucial element in the failure of the 1991 coup attempt.

This section has presented a set of issues the analyst should investigate when exploring political and social risk in Eastern Europe. Some tentative answers have briefly been indicated as well, at least to some of the questions. Even if the analyst arrives at answers different to these, it is hoped that the questions would nevertheless prove helpful.

Conclusion

This article has presented a basis for an analytical framework for an assessment of opportunities and risks in Eastern Europe, centring on creditworthiness assessment and political and social risk assessment. Recent developments in Eastern Europe strongly suggest that the creditworthiness assessment will prove misleading to some extent unless it is accompanied by a political risk assessment, indicating potential changes in the transforming Eastern European societies and economies in the medium and long term. Most of the Eastern European economies have embarked on a road which has not been travelled before: the attempt to liberalize, or marketize a command planned economy. Theory, and the experience of previous reforms, do not suggest clearly what should be the optimal strategy for achieving these goals, or what are the best answers to questions concerning the right proportion between public and market goods, between state administration and market, or between achieving capital profitability and welfare goals. There is also a strong correlation between political liberalization and economic transformation in this region. All this indicates that a new approach to the analysis of the economic reforms, external imbalances and country risk in the Eastern European countries is now a necessity.

References

Avramovic, D. (1964) *Economic Growth and External Debt*, Baltimore: Johns Hopkins University Press.

Kornai, J. (1986) 'The Hungarian Reform Process: Visions, Hopes and Reality', *Journal of Economic Literature*, December: 1687–1737.

Zloch-Christy, I. (1988) *Debt Problems of Eastern Europe*, Cambridge: Cambridge University Press.

— (1989) 'Programmes for Economic Liberalization and the External Balance of Eastern Europe' mimeo, International Monetary Fund, September.

— (1991) *East–West Financial Relations: Current Problems and Future Prospects*, Cambridge: Cambridge University Press.

5

Business Strategy During Dramatic Environmental Change: a Network Approach for Analysing Firm-Level Adaptation to the Soviet Economic Reform

Asta Salmi and Kristian Möller

Background and Objectives

This chapter describes how radical environmental change and its impact on the business strategy of a firm can be captured and analysed through a focal net concept. It focuses on the strategic behaviour of a Finnish computer-exporting company, Nokia Data, in the context of the Soviet economic reform, and covers the period 1983 to early 1991.

We argue that the years of economic transformation of the former Soviet Union provide very useful laboratory conditions for analysing how firms adapt to radical economic change. An understanding of the dynamics of the economic reform period also forms a necessary platform for understanding the emerging mixed market economy of present-day Russia. Moreover, the centralized economic system of the Soviet Union in the late 1980s provides a network analogy for those current markets which are characterized by a combination of a high level of central control and partial market competition.

Change and uncertainty affect all business markets, and especially the international business arena. Traditionally environmental uncertainty has been emphasized in the context of entering new markets which are different in geographical and more especially cultural aspects. In these circumstances, firms are 'prewarned' – they anticipate and are prepared for a different environment.

Here we focus on another, probably more radical aspect of change: on changes in

This chapter is based on a more extensive study, 'Institutional Changes in International Networks. Case study of a Finnish exporting firm's adaptation to the Soviet economic reform', carried out by Asta Salmi at the Helsinki School of Economics in 1991.

established markets where the firms have known their business partners and developed long-term relationships with them. The economic reform which took place in the Soviet economy, and its consequences for the country's foreign trade, has produced changes that are fundamental and long-term by nature. The reform has not only changed the identity of the economic institutions carrying out the foreign trade, it is also changing the norms guiding the economic behaviour of these institutions. Through profit-oriented incentive schemes it has also altered the value system and behaviour of the managers. As such, the Soviet economic reform and its ensuing change processes represent a unique situation for studying the nature and impact of radical change on the behaviour of firms and their business relationships which developed originally in a stable and very hierarchical economic system. The traditional Soviet trading system forms the necessary template against which the adaptations in business strategy can be examined (Van de Ven 1987).

As an example of East–West trade, the former trading arrangements between Finland and the Soviet Union offer an especially promising research context for analysing change, since the bilateral trade between the countries made the traditional trading system very stable. Finnish firms have long traditions of doing business with the Soviet Union and are consequently able to report the relative changes during the reform period, unlike the many Western newcomers in the market.

East–West trade has been investigated predominantly at the macro level. This level of analysis does not allow for a deeper understanding of the adaptations taking place at a firm level. It is these changes at the firm level which, in aggregate, produce the macro transformation and define its nature.

The purpose of this study is to increase our understanding of the behaviour and strategic adaptation of firms doing international business in a context of rapid and fundamental changes. More specifically we have attempted to:

1.   Identify and describe the major changes in the competitive environment of the Soviet market as they have been seen by a Finnish exporting firm.
2.   Identify and describe the strategic responses of the focal firm.

It is essential that firm behaviour should be analysed in its competitive context. An interpretative approach is followed by mapping the environmental changes as perceived and interpreted by the management of the focal firm. A historical and holistic case analysis approach is adopted as the basic research method in our attempt to understand change. The network approach to business markets/environment forms the dominant cognitive background for the study.

The Finnish computer exporting company, Nokia Data, was chosen for the object of study. Computers represent industrial high technology products, and their export to the Soviet Union was for some time strictly controlled by the Soviet side, as well as by the embargo regulations initiated by the United States. The setting aside of these regulations as well as the liberalization of economic life in the Soviet Union has produced great changes in the markets for computers and information technology in general.

The time-frame focused on is 1983 to early 1991. The first part of the 1980s provides a comparative template still dominated by the pre-reform structure – very stable, strictly controlled and regulated. The Soviet economic reform started in

1985/86, following which Soviet foreign trade and the competitive environment of information technology products started to change.

In the next section the conceptual framework – the focal net – is developed and discussed in the context of the Soviet foreign trade environment. There then follows a description of the empirical study, followed by presentation of the results. The chapter is concluded by a discussion of the theoretical and managerial implications.

Network Approach and Change in the Soviet Foreign Trade System

First, industrial networks are briefly described and a justification is given for using a network approach in the Soviet trade context. Attention is given to the issue of different levels of change (and levels of analysis), and to the concept of focal net.

The network approach

The network approach (see e.g. Ford 1990, Axelsson and Easton 1992) postulates that any firm operating in an industrial and social context can be described as acting in a network with a certain structure. To paraphrase Johanson and Mattsson (1991: 265):

> The network structure, that is the way in which the firms are linked to each other, develops as a consequence of the firms doing business with each other. At the same time, the network structure constitutes the framework within which business is done.

Key concepts in understanding networks are relationships and positions. Networks are formed by actors having relationships with each other, and the relationships an actor has with other organizations define its position in the network.

Relationships are generally described through bonds – economic, legal, technical, cognitive, social, and procedural bonds have been discerned (Hammarkvist, Håkansson and Mattsson 1982). The relationships can vary both in their structure or composition, described through the profile of bonds, and in their intensity or strength, as well as duration.

In addition to the direct relationships, each organization also has indirect relationships. These are linkages between organizations which are not directly related but which are still influenced by each other's actions through a third firm or actor with which they both have a relationship (Easton 1989).

At each moment in time, each individual firm occupies a certain position in the network. This position characterizes the role that the firm plays in the network. A distinction between micro-position and macro-position has been made, in which the former refers to a firm's relationships with a specific counterpart and the latter to its relations to a network as a whole. Positions are defined by the functions performed by the firm for other firm(s), the importance of the firm in a network, the strength of the relationships with other firms, and the identity of the other firms with which the firm has direct relationships (Mattsson 1985, Mattsson 1987, Johanson and Mattsson 1988). A firm's position in the network reflects its strategic identity – see Håkansson and Johanson (1988). The strategic identity is formed and developed through the interaction with other firms.

A network which is characterized by strongly bonded organizations having well-established positions can be regarded as highly structured. The level of structuration is related to the ease of entry and exit of organizations in the network, and also of changing one's position.

In contrast to traditional network research, which analyses total networks, this study analyses the network from the focal company's viewpoint. The concept of the focal net of the company is the main unit of analysis. Focal net is defined here as including all those direct and indirect inter-organizational relationships with different partners that the company perceives as affecting its Soviet business. This suggestion is in line with the notion of the inter-organizational resource dependence theory that the company itself defines its boundaries (Pfeffer and Salancik 1978). Focal net also provides an answer to the network delimitation problem which is always present while studying networks.

Network and the Soviet international trade system: a perfect match?

A network is argued to be a valid construct for describing the Soviet industrial 'markets' for a number of reasons. The Soviet foreign trade system was never based on operating markets, but on a system of hierarchical economic institutions which were centrally controlled. The success of a foreign exporter depended heavily on the relationships it was able to establish with the key Soviet trading institutions.

The traditional Soviet trade network used to be tightly structured; there was high interdependence between organizations, positions were well-defined, and the bonds between organizations were strong. Different organizations had clearly defined and unchanging roles. In particular, the division of work between Soviet organizations was evident: special units (foreign trade organizations – FTOs) were responsible for the operative and commercial aspects of foreign trade; industrial enterprises took care of the technical aspects and production; whereas the overall co-ordination and planning of trade was the responsibility of the Foreign Trade Ministry and Industrial Ministries, together with different planning organizations and state committees.

Entry and exit of firms in the network were infrequent. This is typical of tightly structured networks, where it is difficult for outsiders to break existing bonds. For newcomers, it was difficult to enter the Soviet network; the FTOs acted as gate-keepers, demanding clear indications of trustworthiness and commitment.

In doing business with the Soviet Union the strongest, most important, and often the sole relationship was the one between the Western seller and the corresponding FTO (Soviet buyer). Consequently, the few studies on relations in East–West trade have focused on this dyad. Such issues as negotiation practices (Wass von Czege 1983) and selection of contracts (Kogut 1986) have been analysed.

In spite of the 'monopoly position' of the FTO, Western sellers quite actively tried to contact also the Soviet end-users, industrial enterprises, in order to influence the FTO's decisions (cf. the strategy of indirect influence via other actors, Håkansson and Johanson 1988). The difficulties in contacting end-users have often been expressed. Vientiprojekti (1981) revealed, however, that almost half of all Finnish exporting companies had contacts with the final Soviet end-user.

In sum, the network approach has a high face validity as a descriptive system of the former Soviet foreign trade system. Seldom do the metafora and the substantive field in focus match so well.

Levels of change and the focal net

Analysing change involves a problem of the level of analysis. Within a network approach this is related to the issue of defining or delimiting the network boundaries. This issue is discussed with the help of Fig. 5.1, which depicts one solution to the level of analysis issue.

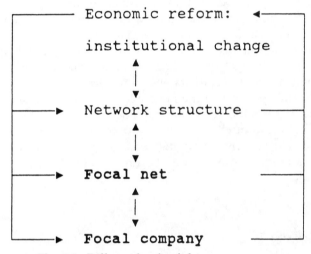

Fig. 5.1. Different levels of change processes.

The Soviet economic reform was a change process which affected the entire Soviet economy and which also had an extensive social impact. Its effects are still going on in Russia. In Fig. 5.1 this is depicted as institutional change influencing the political, legal, economic, social, and scientific dimensions as well as norms and current business practices in the Soviet society. These dimensions form the environment of firms operating in the Soviet/Russian markets.

Institutional change is manifested and reflected in the changes of the network structure of various industrial sectors, as well as in the structure of the trading system. The loss of the trade monopoly by the FTOs and the granting of trade rights to hundreds of 'industrial enterprises' exemplify structural changes. Changes in the values and goals of Soviet institutions also bring changes in the behaviour of these institutions and their representatives.

Changes in the network mean changes to the focal nets of firms in the networks, and further to the individual companies.

The focal net construct offers a solution for trying to capture the changes in the competitive context of any focal firm as well as in its position in that context. The focal net forms a 'bridging construct' between a firm and its environment. It mediates the impact of changes in the larger network or institutional environment on the focal firm.

The perceptual nature of the focal net emphasizes the role of managers as the key agents of interpreting the environmental change, as well as planning and carrying out the firm's responses. This enactment view of environment (Weick 1969, Håkansson and Snehota 1989) suggests that the firm's orientation towards a market or competitive environment is a function of its experience and knowledge of the market. The collective exposure and experience of the firm depends on its current and historical relationships in the network which are related to the way the company has organized its marketing and relationships; see Håkansson (1986).

So far, the 'top down' part of the change processes has been discussed, cf. Fig. 5.1. Economic and social change are by no means linear, 'one-way' effects, but complex reciprocal, heuristic and iterative systems. Each company may affect its focal net; and changing the focal net, in turn, changes the larger network where it is embedded. Also, the network changes may affect the economic reform process and the more general institutional and social change.

This brief discussion has argued that a network perspective is a valid theoretical approach for analysing the impact of the Soviet economic reform on the firm-level strategic adaptations. Focal net, direct and indirect relationships within the focal net, and a focal firm's position in the net are key constructs. It should be remembered that the focal net is a perceptual phenomenon, constructed by the management of the target firm through an enactment process.

Focal net is argued to form a bridging construct between focusing entirely on firm level or on a more extended, and often more 'objectively' defined, network level.

Research Methodology

Historical single-case analysis was chosen as the research approach. Longitudinal approach is necessary when processes and changing structures are investigated, especially if there is little guiding theory about the focal phenomena. Firms' positions in the Soviet foreign trade network cannot be understood without any access to the history of their positions. Past positions and experience influence the current and future actions of the organizations.

Comparison, between different periods or phases, within the single case is the main analytical approach used. The managers of the case firm were interviewed about the major changes they perceived in the Soviet competitive environment, as well as to uncover the dominant strategic steps taken by the target company. The focal net construct is used to operationalize the managerial narratives and descriptions. It also facilitates the comparison of the various change periods identified by the management.

Several criteria were used in selecting the case company. First, a firm that had had long experience in the Soviet market and was expected to stay in the market, was looked for. Also, a main export product(s) was selected which would have constant or increasing demand in the Soviet Union. Second, a complex case was looked for, which would offer fruitful and revealing insights into the focal phenomena – a company which was known to have experienced changes in its focal net. In this respect, this single case is revelatory (Yin 1989).

A computer manufacturing and marketing unit, Nokia Data, of a multi-divisional Finnish corporation was chosen. The Soviet trade department of the company, which was responsible for selling the unit's computers to the Soviet Union, was chosen as the focal company in this study. Here this department is referred to as 'Nokia Data', and the Nokia corporation to which it belonged as the 'Group'. Nokia Data fulfilled the necessary conditions in case selection. However, its activities included only marketing of the unit's existing product range; consequently, this study concentrates on marketing operations.

Information was collected mainly by personal interviews at the company's Soviet trade department. In total, nine people were interviewed (one to three times each). A semi-structured questionnaire was used in the interviews, indicating the themes of discussion. The interviews were tape-recorded and transcribed. Typically they lasted for two to three hours each.

Key informants had been employed by the Nokia Data from the very beginning of the analysis period; thus in principle, the information was reachable. It turned out that respondents had no major difficulties in recalling the situation even in the beginning of the 1980s.

In addition to oral information, written data material was gathered. The sources included confidential strategic planning documents and other internal material, as well as information bulletins and annual reports of the company. Also, journal articles regarding the company, computer industry and the Soviet market were analysed.

The case study report was reviewed by the key informants in the company.

Soviet Economic Reform and Strategic Adaptation: Business Strategy of a Finnish Computer Exporter, 1983–91

First, the Soviet economic reform is briefly outlined. Then the results of the case analysis are presented through comparative descriptions of the changes in the focal net of the case company and in its business strategy.

Economic reform in the Soviet Union: major changes in the trading environment

Basically the Soviet Union has been changing from a planned communist economy towards a market economy. As far as the country's foreign trade is concerned, the reform was in practice carried out by breaking down the state monopoly. Consequently, new Soviet organizations were allowed to enter into the trading network.

Table 5.1 lists the main stages of the Soviet economic reform, especially as far as foreign trade is concerned.

In summary, the Soviet economic reforms have the following macro implications for Finnish firms:

1. The partner (previously the state) is changing the way it has organized the trade. Some partners disappear, new ones replace them, etc. Thus this leads to

Table 5.1: Main stages of the Soviet economic reform.

Early 1980s	Present reform wave started in the smaller socialist countries
March 1985	Gorbachev's accession to power
August 1986	Decree of the CPSU (Communist Party) Central Committee and the Council of Ministers on measures to improve the management of foreign economic relations:
	• organizational changes, foreign currency funds etc.
	• January 1, 1987: 21 ministries and 70 large enterprises obtained the right to perform foreign trade operations, in addition to the traditional foreign trade organizations
January 1987	Decree on the establishment of joint ventures on the territory of the USSR
September 1987	An additional decree on foreign trade:
	• refinement of the earlier legislation
December 1988	Decree on further improvement of the foreign trade activities of state organizations, co-operatives and other organizations:
	• the right to enter into foreign trade for all companies that are registered for it
	• licensing of imports and exports, etc.
March 1989	Decree on state control of foreign trade operations:
	• refinement of the 2.12.1988 decree
January 1991	Abolition of the bilateral trade and clearing payment system in Finnish–Soviet trade
August 1991	Failed coup, and subsequent rapid reorganization of Soviet system.

the question of how a Finnish company should react to this major organizational change of the partner.

2. The basis for trade changes from long-term contracts to more market-oriented trade. This principally means more competition and increasing risks for the Finnish firms, but may involve new opportunities as well. Related changes include changes in earlier power positions, degrees of political influence, so-called 'right relations', etc., prevalent in traditional Finnish–Soviet trade.

3. Consequently, the business atmosphere changes: rituals, the ways of thinking and of doing things change as the business becomes more market-based. Thus, both partners must adapt to the new situation and must learn new business practices.

This brief discussion can provide only an outline of the major planned changes in the Soviet trade environment. It can be used as a kind of street map when evaluating the experiences of the focal firm.

The results of the case analysis are presented in chronological order. The first, traditional phase includes a brief description of the case firm, as well as the basics of computer exporting to the Soviet Union.

1983–4: traditional trade in minicomputers

In the 1970s, trade in computers between Eastern and Western Europe consisted mostly of deliveries of large systems. The largest Western suppliers were active in the Soviet market. ICL was the first Western supplier to establish a representative office in Moscow, in 1968; the Nokia Corporation opened its representative office in 1971.

Nokia Data's first sales to the Soviet Union took place in 1975. Nokia Data tried to focus, so far as possible, on their niche area, banking systems. By the mid-1980s, however, it was concluded that this product range could not bring enough volume of business, since the Soviet banking system was not developed enough to require special banking systems. Consequently Nokia Data's Soviet exports have largely consisted of standard products and related software.

The traditional Finnish–Soviet bilateral trade system provided the framework for the company's Soviet business. The trade was bilateral until 1991, which meant that over a certain time period the value of exports and imports between the countries had to be in balance. According to the system, annual protocols on the exchange of goods defined the yearly export volumes. These protocols were negotiated at national government and ministerial level. The protocols defined a quota for electronics, which more or less set the limits for Finnish deliveries of electronics to the Soviet Union.

The export quota in the annual protocol as such did not guarantee any final deals, but offered guidelines for entering into actual business negotiations with Soviet buyers and customers. At this stage, competition took place between Finnish producers who wanted to have a share in the electronics quota. In practice, Nokia Data was the only Finnish producer of minicomputers, so it did not compete with computer producers but instead with suppliers of other electronics products.

Of course, in the Soviet market, there was competition from other foreign suppliers as well. However, in the early 1980s the embargo regulations enforced by the multilateral Cocom (Co-ordinating Committee for Multilateral Export Controls) became stricter, which made the Soviet market less attractive, and some Western companies withdrew from the market. As long as the bilateral clearing system prevailed fully, the company considered other Finnish exporters to be its main competitors.

The Soviet buying situation during this traditional period was extremely well structured. There were about seventy specialized foreign trade organizations (FTOs, or 'buyers'), which had the right to carry out foreign business. In addition, there was the involvement of the end-user, or customer, to whom the product was delivered.

During the first half of the 1980s Nokia Data exported minicomputers to the Soviet Union, and for quite a long time the main buyer there was Elektronorgtehnika, EOT. EOT was subordinate to the Foreign Trade Ministry, and its responsibility was to import computers to the country. EOT's share of Nokia Data's Soviet trade was over 90 per cent.

EOT was a very large organization, and rather rigid in its approach. To some extent it was more bureaucratic than other FTOs. It was not fully able to take the end-user's viewpoint, but instead emphasized price factors when making the buying decision.

The export contract was signed between Nokia Data and EOT, and the minicomputers were delivered (during different years) to ten main customers, the end-users. These included banks, ministries, other governmental organizations (like Soviet Supreme, State committee Gossnab, the atomic commission GKAE, and the Estonian Academy of Science), together with industrial enterprises.

Business negotiations were carried out with both the FTO and the end-user. This dualistic negotiation process was retained until about 1986. Technical negotiations were usually conducted first with the representatives of the end-user. After these Nokia Data prepared the official quotation, on which discussion on the commercial terms with the FTO was started. FTO's negotiators were professionally highly skilled, so agreement on terms of deliveries, warranties etc. was reached quite rapidly. Price, in turn, was subject to longer discussions. The representatives of the FTO were essentially businessmen, not necessarily well-informed or interested in the technical details of the deal, so contacts with the end-user were essential. Actually two contracts were concluded: one between the end-user and the EOT, and another between Nokia Data and EOT.

It should be emphasized that Nokia Data delivered hardware, the data-processing equipment. Customers made application software and also took care of the maintenance on the basis of training and support from Nokia Data. Up until 1986, all the customers were so large that they had their own internal organizations for maintenance.

Typically, each Soviet end-user had the right to conclude only one foreign trans-action per year. Therefore, each business deal was usually very large and required many negotiations and a long decision-making process. This imposed extra re-quirements on the supplier; each contract involved a package, which had to cover equipment, programs, spare parts, together with training, installing, possible rep-arations during the warranty period, service and support activities.

The situation during the years 1983–4 is depicted in the simplified focal net shown in Fig. 5.2.

Nokia Data's focal net was very highly structured during the early 1980s. The company knew all its competitors well – basically they were other Finnish firms competing for the annual electronics quota – as well as the formal buyer, Elektro-norgtehnika. Nokia Data's marketing personnel were familiar with their counter-parts in the EOT and were well versed in the stable system of Soviet trade nego-tiations. The FTO was the key organization in the net, as it was responsible for the final decision to buy the product and signed the contract, and it also represented all of Nokia Data's customers.

Nokia Data's explicit customer strategy was to concentrate on certain sectors and large customers, and to maintain long-term customer relationships. An important focus group were large banks. This was in accordance with the company's produc-tion line, which had started with banking systems.

The highly structured competitive situation favoured Nokia Data in several respects. As the only Finnish producer of minicomputers it had in fact a monopoly position concerning the export of computers from Finland. The tightening of the Cocom embargo to some extent kept other Western companies out of the Soviet market.

Figure 5.2 also includes the relationships of the Nokia corporation ('the Group'). The Group and its CEO had contacts with all the major institutions in the Soviet Union, including high-level officials. However, Nokia Data did not attach undue importance to these relationships.

It seems that Nokia Data's strategy was well adapted to both the competitive situation and to its resources and capabilities. Focusing on a limited number of end-user sectors and on large potential customers in general was necessary

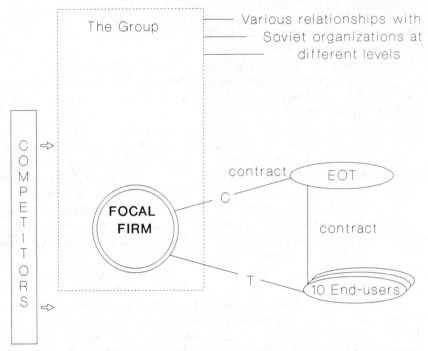

Fig. 5.2. Focal net, 1983–84. Where —— C —— denotes commercial negotiations, —— T —— denotes technical negotiations.

because of the limited marketing personnel of Nokia Data – the Soviet Department consisted of only four to six persons. By maintaining long-term relationships with complex and demanding customers it was able to both utilize its system producer know-how and employ effectively its scarce but competent personnel. A further benefit was the indirect influence with the EOT which the end-users were able to exert on Nokia Data's behalf.

The fact that the customers were able to organize their own maintenance as well as software was an additional plus factor, as it saved Nokia Data's resources.

In sum, these results support the network theoretical proposition that well-structured and centrally co-ordinated networks tend to favour experienced players with long-standing positions and well-developed relationships.

1985–87: new export products

At the beginning of the 1980s, microcomputers appeared on the world market. For a two-year period (1985–86) Nokia Data exported both mini and microcomputers to the Soviet market. Since 1986, its exports have consisted mainly of microcomputers, and deliveries of minicomputers have been only occasional. Nokia Data admits that it was slower than its competitors in reacting to the change in Soviet demand from minis to micros and not surprisingly, a sharp decline in sales was experienced in 1987.

With the new export product, relationships to new FTOs were established. After 1986 business with the earlier main partner EOT rapidly came to an end. One of the main reasons for ending the relationship was that the partners could not agree on the prices of microcomputers. Within the EOT, the department which was responsible for trade in computers was taken to be a 'difficult' and bureaucratic partner.

The main buyers of microcomputers were two other FTOs: Vneshtehnika, which gained the right to import computers to the Soviet Union, and Lenfintorg, which was involved solely in Finnish–Soviet border trade. They represented about equal shares of Nokia Data's sales.

Vneshtehnika was subordinate to the State Committee of Computer Technology. It bought computers from Nokia Data for three important end-users: the Ministry of Black Metallurgy, the GKAE Atomic Commission, and the Ministry of Energy. Previously, opinions had been guarded about Vneshtehnika, it being a difficult and very bureaucratic FTO. In Nokia Data's case, however, the business started quickly and the partner proved unexpectedly flexible. The main explanation for this can be found at the level of personal relationships: the two contact persons, responsible for business with Nokia Data, turned out to be very co-operative; they were young, willing, and eager to do business.

The other new FTO partner, Lenfintorg, was an organization responsible for the border trade between Finland and the Soviet Union. Border trade took place outside of the annual trade protocol quotas. Lenfintorg had the right to trade in different kinds of products, the only limitation being that exports and imports must be in balance in each deal. Therefore, in order to export to the Soviet Union through Lenfintorg, the exporter had to find another Finnish company which was importing from the country.

Through Lenfintorg Nokia Data sold principally to four end-users: a steel factory, the Ministry of Gas Industry, and two subordinates to the Ministry of Black Metallurgy: an ADP-central and a mining combinate. The most important of these customers was and has been since the Ministry of Gas Industry. Also in Lenfintorg's case business was conducted quite smoothly because of the good personal relationships.

The GKAE Atomic Commission was the only old customer which followed Nokia Data from EOT to the new buying organization. All the other customers with Vneshtehnika and Lenfintorg, were new to Nokia Data. Each of them, when making the first contacts, agreed with Nokia Data that it was better to arrange the business through other FTOs than EOT.

During the period 1985–87, Nokia Data's business negotiations with the FTOs and the end-users followed the same lines as during the earlier years. After 1986 the Soviet customers gained some latitude in their buying from abroad: the option of buying several times and from several suppliers each year. Therefore, any particular deal did not need to cover the whole year's need, and it became easier and quicker to conclude the deals. As Nokia Data had a competitive advantage in selling systems, offering a total package and wide product range, it lost some of its edge as a result of this liberalization.

Nokia Data (Soviet sales department) also started making sales to Finnish companies. These were system sellers, who bought Nokia Data's products to use in their own Soviet projects (e.g. industry automation projects).

Throughout 1985–7 embargo restrictions remained very strict, limiting to some extent the number of Western competitors in the market. Although the main competitors were other Finnish companies, doing business within the clearing-system, the change from exporting minicomputers to microcomputers increased immediately the number of potential competitors. About half a dozen competitors were active in the market. However, competition was not seen as being very keen, and Nokia Data was still putting its main effort in selling minicomputers.

Microcomputers very quickly became increasingly standardized, and foreign components became more important in Nokia Data's computers, while the share of labour costs in production costs decreased. Correspondingly, it became more difficult for Nokia Data to comply with the bilateral trade agreement's requirement concerning Finnish origin. The Finnish Licence Bureau began taking a greater interest, resulting in more paper work and liaison. The Licence Bureau was responsible for the granting of export licences and had an involvement in domestic share requirements.

One of the first changes in the Soviet foreign trade legislation arising from the economic reform was to devolve the right to enter into foreign trade to twenty-one ministries and seventy large enterprises (in addition to the seventy 'old' FTOs). This change had no concrete effect on Nokia Data's Soviet trade or focal net, however.

The decree, passed at the beginning of 1987 allowing the formation of joint ventures between Western and Soviet partners on Soviet territory had a much greater impact on Western companies. There was considerable enthusiasm over joint ventures in the Soviet Union, and propositions poured in. Nokia Data's partners showed interest in the joint venture issue, but Nokia Data took a more cautious approach to these propositions.

During the period of the bilateral trade and clearing payment system in Finnish–Soviet trade, it was possible to transact business in convertible currencies without regard to the annual protocols, if the customer was in a position of having extra currencies to be used for imports. Nokia Data started selling against convertible currencies in 1987. Currency sales were first occasional, but by the end of 1980s they accounted for one-quarter of total sales.

Figure 5.3 illustrates Nokia Data's focal net in the Soviet Union in 1985–86.

The net had extended considerably. In addition to the earlier FTO (EOT), there were two new FTOs. Through these three FTOs, seventeen major end-users were reached. Some of them did not necessarily buy each year, but contacts to them were made on a regular basis and long-term relationships were maintained. The focal net also included Finnish system suppliers, with whom business negotiations were not divided into two separate technical/commercial phases as was still the case with the Soviet organizations.

Reference to the Licence Bureau is included in order to emphasize its control over Finnish–Soviet business. It had already previously been responsible for controlling the trade (export volumes and domestic share requirements), but its role became more important for the focal company when exports of more standardized microcomputers with foreign components began.

The Cocom embargo regulations were still restricting the exports. Thus the number of competitors was limited. The company was mainly exporting minicomputers, but gradually also increasing the sales of microcomputers.

In 1987, the focal net structure remained largely the same, except that the EOT was no longer buying and had disappeared from the net. Customers which had been served through the EOT were lost too, except for the GKAE Atomic

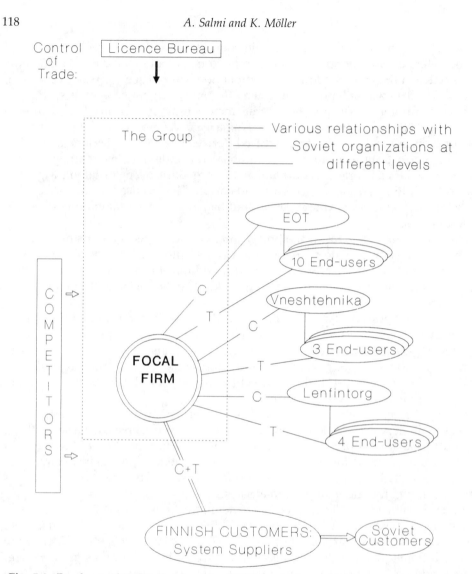

Fig. 5.3. Focal net, 1985–86. Focal net for 1987 was similar, with the exception that EOT and its customers were excluded. Where —— C —— denotes commercial negotiations, —— T —— denotes technical negotiations, –> denotes control.

Commission, which started to buy through Vneshtehnica. The company's main customers in 1987 were banks and the Ministry of Black Metallurgy.

A sharp drop in sales was experienced because of Nokia Data's outmoded orientation to minicomputers, which coincided with the disagreement with the EOT over microcomputer prices leading to the loss of this major buyer.

The emergence of microcomputers had a large impact on the focal net, increasing the number of buyers (FTOs) and end-users, as well as competitors. Its strategic profile helped Nokia Data to establish relationships with some of the newcomers. Its relationship with the EOT could not withstand the competitive pressure of lower-priced micros. This, together with the mistake in evaluating buyers' movement from minis into micros, led to a sharp decline in Soviet sales. The growth of indirect demand through Finnish customers indicated the impact of extending Soviet economic activity.

1988: first effects of the economic reform

The first joint ventures between Western and Soviet partners were established in autumn 1987. Even though Nokia Data was not interested in establishing its own joint venture, some of the newly established joint ventures became its customers in 1988. The joint venture customers included both re-sellers and end-users of Nokia Data's products. The FTOs were not involved in joint-venture business; therefore the total negotiation process could be carried out with one and the same partner.

As Nokia Data started to export microcomputers in volume, it had to deal with new customers, which were smaller than its traditional trade partners. Generally these did not have a separate department or resources specialized in computers. At first, Nokia Data arranged the maintenance service for these customers from Finland, but it was realized after a couple of years that this arrangement was not efficient in the longer run. After looking for a suitable Soviet partner, a co-operation agreement was signed with the VNIINS technical institute in the Soviet Union. Since 1988 Nokia Data's maintenance service has mainly been carried out by this institute.

In 1988–90 a new quota was included in the annual protocols on the exchange of goods between Finland and the Soviet Union: the quota for direct trade. This quota could be used for exporting different kinds of products to Soviet organizations which were exporting to Finland. Nokia Data started to use this direct trade quota in addition to the electronics quota. The direct trade quota, and selling against convertible currencies were new aspects which gave more freedom for companies in Finnish–Soviet trade, and gradually started to break down the traditional bilateral trade system.

In December 1988 a decree was passed in the Soviet Union which gave foreign trade rights to all Soviet organizations which registered for foreign trade. This produced an explosive growth in the number of potential contacts: by the beginning of 1990 the number of Soviet organizations with foreign trade rights already amounted to some 14,000.

The 1988 decree created a burst of activity in the Soviet Union, as many organizations became interested in the new opportunity to do foreign business. However, only a few people in a few Soviet organizations were familiar with foreign trade practices in general, and the bilateral trade system in particular. Consequently many of Nokia Data's Soviet customers were lacking in foreign trade competence and preferred using the traditional trade channels and FTOs' services.

Essentially, after the 1988 foreign trade change, the buyer and customer could be one and the same Soviet organization. The dualistic negotiation practices gradually disappeared, so that both commercial and technical issues came to be discussed simultaneously.

Figure 5.4 maps out Nokia Data's focal net in the Soviet Union in 1988. EOT was no longer a partner, but the two other FTO partners and the related end-users engaged during 1985–7 remained the same. This is worth emphasizing, since many

Western companies encountered more changes in their FTO partners; in some cases, whole organizations disappeared or merged with others.

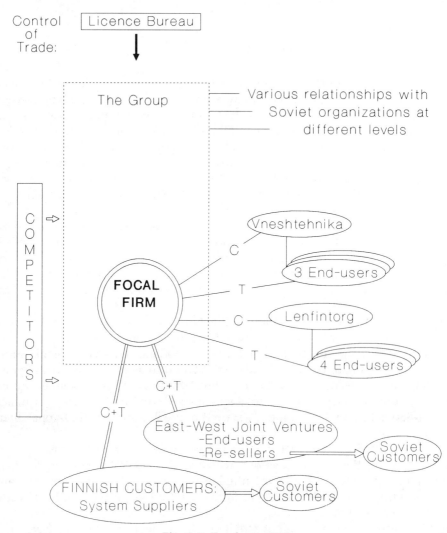

Fig. 5.4. Focal net, 1988.

In addition to Finnish system suppliers, joint venture customers in the Soviet Union emerge within the focal net as the first major result of the economic reform. Business negotiations with these resembled more closely Western practices. The focal company's joint-venture relationships were not as long-term by nature as the relationships with earlier partners.

During this period, the trade can be summarized as follows: the company's sales of microcomputers had taken off; this meant to some extent smaller customers, but the emphasis was on large traditional customers; and embargo restrictions continued to keep many competitors out of the market. From a strategic perspective, Nokia Data was starting to adapt its former policy of large, complex and enduring relationships only to the increasing number of smaller customers. This is reflected in the new co-operative maintenance contract for catering more efficiently for the needs of smaller and more varied Soviet customers.

1989–90: changes in trade environment

Extension of foreign trade rights in the Soviet Union turned out to be only a temporary phase of commercial freedom. At the beginning of March 1989, new Soviet legislation restored some control to the Ministry of Foreign Economic Relations. Henceforth an import licence, which was usually granted by the ministry's subordinate firm, Informves, would be needed for international trade.

At this stage, problems were caused by the rapid changes in the Soviet legislation and uncertainty over different organizations' rights and responsibilities. The precise date when certain contracts were concluded had a decisive effect on their implications.

In 1989, the USA relaxed the embargo regulations, and the so-called 286-level microcomputers were exempted from the export ban. This led immediately to an invasion by Western competitors of the Soviet market, and by the end of 1989 the prices of microcomputers had fallen by half.

Along with the economic reform, there was an overall liberalization of the Soviet economy which was reflected in freer information flows. Freer use of such information dissemination devices as computers and copying machines became possible. This increased the possibilities for exporting computers.

A new type of customer appearing in the Soviet Union was the so-called 'middle-man'. Within the information technology field, some of the intermediaries had previously been ADP units of larger organizations, but had become independent and started buying computers from abroad; while others were small consultant companies, developing software for foreign computers and selling it on. Often several Soviet organizations had shareholdings in middle-men. For instance, in 1988 the Soviet Finance and Trade Company (Sovfintrade) was established. It was subordinate to the Soviet government, but its shareholders included, for instance, banks and FTOs. All in all, the middle-men are a very heterogeneous group of customers, which have been established during the economic reform in order to enhance the foreign trade. They are a rapidly growing customer type in the Soviet Union, and have also been very active in making contacts with Western companies. Nokia Data at first was cautious in its approach, but since then has entered into this area of business.

During this period the Group and its head office started to play a smaller and smaller role in Nokia Data's Soviet trade. The business now involved working more with bodies other than the traditional FTOs; the role of state planning organizations in the trade diminished, and direct selling relationships to the end-users started to become common.

This development is reflected in the 1989 focal net depicted in Fig. 5.5. The customer types include newcomers: the middle-men. The number of competitors had increased in the market as a result of liberalizing the embargo regulations. The Soviet licence organization Informves is included, to show its control dimension. In a similar fashion, the Finnish licence bureau was still controlling the trade. The more 'market-like' nature of the competitive situation was immediately reflected in the price level of microcomputers. Rapid changes in legislation created increased uncertainty about the institutional environment.

Fig. 5.5. Focal net, 1989.

By the end of the 1980s the need for Western exporters to the Soviet Union to find suitable business partners had become a competitive issue. The Soviet market was starting to resemble Western conditions, with the striking difference that much less information was available on potential customers and the market situation.

While there were no problems in getting information about the economic reforms as such, it proved almost impossible to get reliable company-specific information about new partners – for instance, company business mission, organizational chart, number of personnel, share capital, company history, solvency, etc. Lack of this type of information makes it in practice impossible to carry out any company analysis.

In this situation Nokia Data based its business on old acquaintances and earlier personal relationships. Nokia Data was also contacted by quite a few people, who had earlier been in its partner organizations, changed place and proposed new business.

In 1990 Nokia Data still defined its main customers in the Soviet Union as banks and the official administration (ministries). According to this strategy, activities with small companies, co-operatives and joint ventures were avoided, on the basis of needing to employ its scarce but very competent personal resources as profitably as possible. By the end of the year, however, the changing market forces led to a change in this old strategy.

In summer 1990 the 386-level microcomputers were removed from the Cocom embargo list. Restrictions now affected only exports of the most advanced technology. Softening of embargo regulations attracted new competitors to the Soviet market, and by the end of 1990 the price of microcomputers had come down by half again. Since that time, the lowest price level of standard microcomputers has been in the Soviet Union!

In 1990 Nokia Data's Finnish customers included not only system suppliers, but also companies acting as intermediaries, buying products from Nokia Data to be sold to the Soviet Union. Their purchasing volume grew quite rapidly.

The dramatically changing situation is reflected in the 1990 focal net, where the FTOs have disappeared due to their very small role – see Fig. 5.6. There were now about thirty Soviet end-user customers, and some quite small deliveries were being carried out. The size of orders varied between two and 1,000 microcomputers.

The focal net includes an enhanced 'frontier of competitors', to emphasize the very tough competition in the Soviet computer market. Relationships with the Soviet middle-men were maintained, but no deals were concluded in 1990.

Towards the end of 1990 Nokia Data laid down a goal for the development of project sales, use of agents and trade in convertible currencies. The ever increasing number of potential customers and their difficult tractability shifted the traditional emphasis from the successful 'large customers only' policy. Lack of currency, lack of market information, economic uncertainty and general institutional uncertainty characterized the market. At the same time, the intensified competition lowered the price level considerably. Nokia Data's product was strongest in situations where very reliable computers were needed. An example is a delivery in autumn 1990, which included much equipment for the Supreme Soviet.

1991: a period of increasing uncertainty

The dramatic socioeconomic events of 1991 can be considered only in respect of the main characteristics, as the case analysis was concluded by July 1991. The focal net of 1990, depicted in Fig. 5.6, provides the starting point. The trading partners included Soviet end-users, East–West joint ventures, and Finnish companies, as well as different kinds of middle-men. Essentially, the controlling organizations Informves and the Finnish Licensing Bureau lost their role.

Business was carried out with other organizations than the FTOs, usually directly with the end-users. Only one FTO (Lenfintorg) was occasionally buying from Nokia Data.

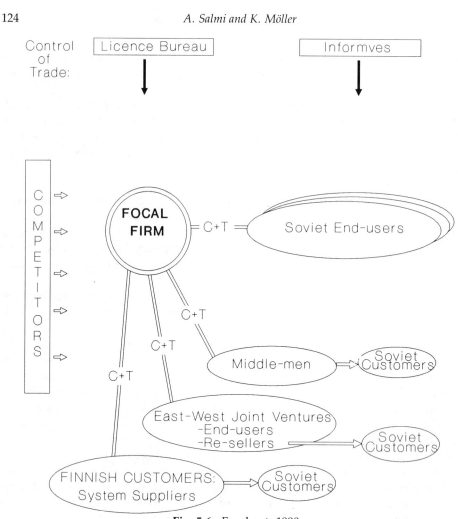

Fig. 5.6. Focal net, 1990.

As of the beginning of 1991, the system of bilateral trade and clearing payments in Finnish–Soviet trade was abolished. Ending this system unavoidably led to a drop in Soviet exports, both in the Group, and among other Finnish firms. It also hastened Nokia Data's new strategic plans for developing Soviet trade.

The number of contacts increased tremendously and it became necessary to develop new ways of business. Nokia Data decided to look for suitable intermediaries, thus entering into indirect exports. It was the company's goal to increase the number of intermediaries considerably during 1991. These were mainly responsible for sales to smaller customers.

There was a distinct change in the number of competitors in 1991, when all business changed over to convertible currency trade. Earlier the company had categorized its competitors as primary (sellers of electronics in Finland) or secondary (competitors from other countries). In 1991 the company saw perhaps more clearly than before that its competitors included others than just Finnish electronics sellers; so the number of Nokia Data's main competitors multiplied.

In principle, the Soviet Union offered a very large potential market, and in 1991 practically all computer sellers were there; competition came from the Far East (Taiwan, Korea, Malaysia, etc.) as well as from Western countries. More suppliers meant more variety in the supply, but also greater variation in quality. Soviet buyers were eager to make use of their right to buy from many suppliers. This led to difficulties in gaining total service and staying in touch with the supplier, and after a number of unsuccessful trials, some customers started to prefer buying the whole package from one dealer. This has increased Nokia Data's export potential, and the company was optimistic about re-establishing relations with many of its former customers.

Nokia Data's success factors were good knowledge of many large customer enterprises in the Soviet Union and good support service. References from earlier customers have proved to be especially important with the escalating number of new contacts. After the steep decline in computer prices, the price level has become an essential problem for the company. Sales features which are used in the West – quality, ergonomics, security, proximity of supplier, total package – were less relevant to Soviet exports. In Soviet decision making, the main criteria were still price and quantity, not quality.

The most important factor affecting the trade in 1991 was the general shortage of currency in the Soviet Union. This problem was made worse by the decentralization of funds between numerous organizations, compared to the earlier central co-ordination.

Conclusions

It is useful to distinguish the discussion of the results into focal net issues and business strategy issues, although obviously these are deeply intertwined.

This study has set out to map and evaluate the impact of the Soviet economic reform activities on the focal net and strategy of a Finnish computer exporter. It is important to note that besides the actual reform, other important forces influencing the computer market were identified: technological change leading to the emergence of microcomputers, changes in the international political climate influencing the embargo regulations on electronic products, and changes in the Finnish–Soviet bilateral trade system. Together, these forces radically changed the focal net of Nokia Data.

Changes in the focal net

During the traditional period, up until around 1984, the focal net was structured extremely tightly. Roughly, the focal company encountered only three types of organization: the buyer (FTO); end-users (customers); and (a few) competitors. The role of each of these organization types was clearly defined and stable. In other words, the focal net was neatly delineated, it was not extensive, and it was well structured.

The exchange processes carried out within the net remained stable over many years. The control mechanisms were well known; the rituals of the social exchange, though somewhat different from those of Western markets, were predictable; and even the persons involved remained basically the same. So the negotiations, although sometimes difficult, were quite predictable in respect of style, arguments employed, and persons participating in them.

Competition, as perceived by the focal firm, was quite stable and predictable as well. The Cocom embargo regulations made the Soviet market rather unattractive for many Western companies emphasizing volume or lacking the knowledge of the Soviet trading system. The Soviet emphasis on long-term commitment also stabilized the net – a show of enduring commitment was presumed from the Western exporters, rendering entry into the network time- and resource-consuming. This stability was enhanced by the bilateral trade system between Finland and the Soviet Union, which provided annual quotas for the Finnish electronics exporters.

The first force influencing this placid state of affairs was the emergence of microcomputers. The change from minicomputer-dominated exports, to almost entirely micros, took place during 1985–7. This change was related to increasing demand for computing capacity in the Soviet Union. The number of potential end-users started to increase rapidly, and new FTOs became engaged in computer importing. This technological development was also the background factor influencing the emergence of Finnish systems suppliers as a new relevant customer group – micros started to be included in most industrial processes and machinery.

The introduction of microcomputers not only extended the number of end-users but led also to the emergence of qualitatively different customer groups. The increase of smaller customers who did not have the resources for maintaining and servicing their computers compelled the focal firm to establish a service system through a Soviet partner.

The introduction of micros also resulted in an increase in the number of competitors. The impact on competition, however, was limited; exports of high technology products were still restricted by the embargo regulations. Altogether, the focal net was becoming more complex, but the roles of the participating institutions were the same and the exchange processes maintained their traditional character.

During the period 1988–90, Soviet economic reform rapidly started to change the whole foreign trading network. First, joint ventures became another notable customer group, including both end-users and re-sellers. A quota for direct trade was added to the Finnish–Soviet annual quota system, allowing trading with those Soviet organizations which had exported to Finland. As selling against convertible currencies was also possible, the strict quota system of the bilateral trade agreement started to break down.

The extending of foreign trade rights to all Soviet organizations registering for foreign trade increased the potential number of contacts enormously. The impact of this fundamental change on the focal net of Nokia Data was relatively slow, however. This is due to the fact that the company as well as many of its old customers preferred to maintain the established relationships.

By 1990 the liberalization forces had transformed the focal net considerably. FTOs had almost disappeared and among the customer groups both Finnish and Soviet re-sellers or middle-men, representing a developing distributor network for computers and software, had gained importance. This development coincided with the lifting of most of the embargo restrictions, leading to rapidly increasing international competition in the Soviet markets.

When comparing the end-situation of this study with the traditional focal net, the changes which have taken place can be highlighted.

1. The net structure has become more complex through the inclusion of different end-user types, middle-men, and competitors.
2. In addition to the increasing extensiveness, the control and co-ordination forces within the net have changed from being clear and directional, though bureaucratic and cumbersome, to ambiguous and unpredictable. The centrally controlled system was dismantled and some characteristics of the market mechanism have started to emerge. Indistinct legislation, lack of information, and great institutional uncertainty related to the rapid stagnation of economic organizations have led to a net characterized by high perceived uncertainty.
3. Competition has emerged as one of the dominant forces in the net, due to both the Soviet reform and the removal of the embargo regulations. Together with the emphasis on price, the competitive rules of the net have completely changed.
4. Throughout all the changes, relationships – often at a personal level, and also manifested in the strategic profile of the firms – established through trading history, provide a cohesive force in the turbulent net. These elements of continuity are relied on while attempting to reduce the risks brought on by the radical change.

Changes in business strategy

The previous section has synthesized the changing nature of computer exports to the Soviet Union between the early 1980s and 1990–1. We conclude by analysing the strategic behaviour of the focal firm. Three phases are contrasted with each other: the business strategy attuned to the traditional trading situation, the attempt to maintain the traditional strategy with adaptation, and the qualitative strategic change faced by the company at the end of the examination period.

Nokia Data's traditional business strategy was well suited to the centrally controlled, well-structured trading environment which prevailed during the first part of 1980s. The company's character as a high-quality, full-service system producer matched well the needs of many Soviet organizations. It had a small but adequate marketing force, many of them speaking Russian and familiar with both the formalities of the Soviet trading system and its ritualistic side.

The firm entered the 1980s with an established position in the trading network and was able to utilize established personal and organizational relationships with the all important FTOs as well as with its major end-users. By focusing principally on the Soviet banking sector and administrative organizations such as ministries, the Supreme Soviet, and the Atomic Commission, rather than industrial enterprises, the company had developed an impressive list of reference customers in the Soviet Union. This strengthened its position in the network and supported its strategic image as a dependable, high-quality system producer and seller.

The restricted net was well matched to the limited but high-quality resources and managerial capabilities of Nokia Data. It was able to focus on customers whose demands recalled its capabilities. The complexity and formalities created an advantage for it as its personnel had the necessary qualities and established relationships to conduct bilateral trade within the Soviet administrative establishment. Nokia Data had a small but suitable niche and its strategy matched it efficiently.

During the transitory change of its focal net, Nokia Data tried to maintain its established business strategy. The primary focus remained on the large and complex Soviet end-users, preferring to work through the FTOs. This made obvious sense from the organizational learning perspective: Nokia Data tried to prolong its successful strategic behaviour as long as possible. Only when the microcomputer revolution changed the potential end-user structure considerably did Nokia Data make any adjustment towards catering for these other customers, by establishing the maintenance services through a Soviet partner. This solution was a workable one; it both saved Nokia Data's own resources and relied on relationships which kept close to the smaller end-user customers.

During these transitory years, 1985–8, Nokia Data tried to work against the forces which were changing the network. This strategy was unworkable in the longer run, but it bought some time in which to adjust to the changing network and the new competitive forces.

The inertia shown by Nokia Data in adapting both to the change from minis to micros and to the parallel change in the market and customer structures has several reasons. The small, well-structured focal net with established relationships favoured the resource and capability base of a small but knowledgeable operator like Nokia Data. Its management and personnel had learned to master the 'business recipe' (Spender 1989) of the Soviet computer market. There was also an element of Soviet customers which preferred the established way of doing computer business; their learning processes and accrued capabilities supported the buyer-side inertia. So both the economic and cognitive factors worked together for the continuation of the old business strategy within Nokia Data.

By the end of 1980s the management of Nokia Data realized that its core marketing strategy, focusing on the large system-buying customers, had to be complemented with another distribution channel. This was the only way to try to increase the sales volume for varied and dispersed medium- and small-sized Soviet end-user organizations. Steps for developing a network of agents were underway when the research period ended. Nokia Data planned, however, to rely consistently on its established strategic profile as a high-quality, dependable but also rather expensive producer. This continued to match its resource base and capabilities, as well as the position it maintained in the network of Soviet administrators, managers and experts with whom the company had carried out exchange processes during the 1980s. A high value was attached to this network, as personal relationships were used to offset the uncertainty dominating the network atmosphere at the beginning of the 1990s.

The broadening of the customer base shows the importance of considering the nature of the customer relationships when planning what kind of customers to include in a small firm's customer portfolio. The costs of serving and revenues received from various types of customers, the level of technical advice and service needed formed the basis for Nokia Data's solution for starting to build a network of agents. The company tries consistently to maintain its strategic posture and image in the market by handling the key accounts itself. The more uncertain 'mass market' was intended to be handled through agents who would themselves be closer to various larger user segments.

Nokia Data's ability to rely on the personal networks established through a decade of interaction emphasizes the investment character of the establishment of relationships. The resulting connections are enduring assets which are valuable even in periods of dramatic environmental change.

This brief discussion has attempted to provide an analysis not only of the changing Soviet computer trading network and the focal net of the case company, as well as its strategic adaptation, but also of the usefulness of the network approach and especially the focal net concept in analysing dynamic environmental change from the perspective of a focal company.

Since the summer of 1991, even more drastic institutional change has taken place in the former Soviet Union and this change process is still going on in present-day Russia. In this paper we have emphasized the need to consider different levels of changes (and analysis) in order to understand firm-level adaptation in a socioeconomic context. We argue that the analysis given here provides a useful starting point, as well as a conceptual system for future studies trying to penetrate the emerging economic system of the present-day Russia.

References

Axelsson, B. and Easton, G. (eds) (1992) *Industrial Networks: A New View of Reality*, London: Routledge.

Easton, G. (1989) 'Industrial Networks – A Review', *Proceedings of the 5th IMP Conference*, Pennsylvania.

Ford, D. (ed.) (1990) *Understanding business markets. Interaction, relationships, networks*, London: Academic Press.

Hammarkvist, K-O., Håkansson, H. and Mattsson, L-G. (1982) *Marknadsföring för konkurrenskraft*, Malmö: Liber Förlag.

Håkansson, H. (1986) 'The Swedish Approach to Europe', in Turnbull and Valla (eds), *Strategies for International Industrial Marketing*, London: Croom Helm.

Håkansson, H. and Johanson, J. (1988) 'Formal and Informal cooperation strategies in international industrial networks', in Contractor, F. J. and Lorange, P. (eds), *Cooperative Strategies in International Business*, Mass.: Lexington Books.

Håkansson, H. and Snehota, I. (1989) 'No Business is an Island: the Network Concept of Business Strategy', *Scandinavian Journal of Management* 5(3): 187–200.

Johanson, J. and Mattsson, L-G. (1988) 'Internationalization in industrial systems – a network approach', in Hood, N. and Vahlne, J-E. (eds), *Strategies in Global Competition*, New York: Croom Helm.

Johanson, J. and Mattsson, L-G. (1991) 'Strategic Adaptation of Firms to the European Single Market – A Networks Approach', in Mattsson, L-G and Stymne, B. (eds), *Corporate and Industry Strategies for Europe*, Amsterdam: North-Holland.

Kogut, B. (1986) 'On Designing Contracts to Guarantee Enforceability: Theory and Evidence from East–West Trade', *Journal of International Business Studies* 17(1): 47–61.

Mattsson, L-G. (1985) 'An Application of Network Approach to Marketing: Defending and Changing Market Positions', in Dholakia, N. D. and Arndt, J. (eds), *Changing the Course of Marketing: Alternative Paradigms for Widening Marketing Theory, Research in Marketing*, Supplement 2, 263–88. Greenwich: JAI Press.

Mattsson, L-G. (1987) 'Management of Strategic Change in a 'Markets-as-Networks' Perspective', in Pettigrew (ed.), *The Management of Strategic Change*, Oxford: Basil Blackwell.

Pfeffer J. and Salancik, G. R. (1978) *The external control of organizations. A resource dependence perspective*, New York: Harper & Row.

Salmi, A. (1991) 'Institutional Changes in International Networks. Case study of a Finnish exporting firm's adaptation to the Soviet economic reform', unpublished licentiate thesis, Helsinki School of Economics.

Spender, J-C. (1989) 'Industry Recipes. The Nature and Sources of Managerial Judgement', Oxford: Basil Blackwell.

Van de Ven, A. H. (1987) 'Review Essay: Four Requirements for Processual Analysis', in Pettigrew (ed.), *The Management of Strategic Change*, Oxford: Basil Blackwell.

Vientiprojekti (1981) *Yritysten kilpailukeinojen käyttö: Vertaileva analyysi Neuvostoliittoon ja markkinatalousmaihin suuntautuvasta viennistä*, Helsinki.

Wass von Czege, A. (1983) 'Soviet Negotiating Tactics in Trade with the West', *Soviet and Eastern European Foreign Trade*, Spring: 32–54.

Weick, K. E. (1969) *The Social Psychology of Organizing*, Reading, MA: Addison Wesley.

Yin, R. K. (1989) *Case Study Research. Design and Methods*, Revised Edition, Newbury Park: Sage Publications.

6

Modernizing Hungary's Industrial Structure: The Contribution of the EC

Alfred Tovias

Introduction

It is the contention of this chapter that by signing an Association Agreement with Hungary in December 1991, while at the same time being engaged in the completion of the Single European Market, the European Community is contributing both directly and indirectly to the economic transformation of Hungary's industrial structure. The first contribution is in terms of imposing external discipline.

After briefly reviewing the contents of the Association Agreement related to industrial structure, the paper then proceeds to show how the EC's import penetration into the Hungarian market will help in terms of modernizing its economic infrastructure. This impact will go well beyond one deriving from the selective import of Western machinery and technology, an industrialization strategy adopted by the previous Hungarian regime in the early 1970s and which proved to be a partial failure, there being little point in modernizing when the markets served by Hungarian firms were unsophisticated and stagnant. Given the total absence of ideological motivation on the part of Hungarian managers, there were neither the alternative incentives nor the external pressures to modernize in depth. This contrasts radically with the present situation, which is characterized by the will manifested constantly by government officials and managers of 'returning to Europe'. What this implies in terms of quality control, upgrading and imposition of new, higher standards, is apparent to everyone.

Last but not least, the third contribution of the European Community to Hungary's economic transformation will derive from improved market access and reduced transaction costs in trade with the EC. These will facilitate Hungary's incorporation in the Western European system of intra-industry trade, allowing for exploitation of scale economies. Given Hungary's present endowment in highly

The author is deeply indebted to Peter Balasz, Andras Inotai, Gabor Oblath, Tibor Palankai and Adam Torok for their stimulating comments on the subject of this chapter.

skilled manpower, increasing specialization can only lead to future modernization. This is pretty revolutionary.

At first sight, 'returning to Europe' may seem a rather conservative slogan. For most of the Hungarian establishment it means becoming a 'normal' European country, leaving aside social innovations and economic experiments. It means having confidence in Europe, copying the European model and accepting more or less what the EC dictates. It is like putting the country on automatic pilot. The paradox is that in fact the process of catching-up, harmonization and integration with Western Europe puts Hungary on a renewed industrial development path.

Industry-related items in the Association Agreement, and in the EC-92 Programme, of Relevance to Hungary

The transmission belt of the EC's modernizing influence on Hungary's industry should be primarily the EC-Hungary Association Agreement concluded in December 1991 (also known as Europe Agreement). The president of the Commission, Jacques Delors, declared openly at the occasion of the signature of the new agreements with Poland, Czechoslovakia and Hungary: 'Association expresses the Community's determination to help these three countries in their double goal which involves tremendous efforts towards greater democracy and the modernization of the economy'.[1] Of course, the completion of the EC's Internal Market since January 1 1993 should have an indirect positive influence as well.

It must be stated from the outset that the new Association Agreement goes not only much beyond what is to be found in any of the 1972 EC agreements with individual EFTA countries, not to mention the agreements with non-member Mediterranean countries, but also beyond what was contemplated in the Commission's own guidelines of August 1990. In the preamble of the Agreement, the EC states its 'willingness to provide decisive support for the completion of the process towards a market economy in Hungary'. Moreover, both sides express their belief 'that the Association Agreement will create a new climate for their economic relations and in particular for the development of trade and investment, instruments which are indispensable for economic restructuring and technological modernization'. It is interesting to note that there is nothing of the sort in the EC agreements with Mediterranean countries. Article 1 refers, among other things, to the intention of gradually establishing a free trade area between the two sides. As far as industrial products is concerned, there will be a transitory period of ten years, divided into two equal stages (Article 6).

On the entry into force of the Agreement (in practice on January 1 1992) it was agreed that the EC would abolish all tariffs on imports, except for a series of sensitive products for which the total abolition of duties would take place between one year and four years after the date of entry into force of the Agreement, depending on the product. For other goods the EC would introduce tariff quotas, although more generally QRs would be abandoned totally at the date of entry into force of the Agreement (Article 9). Special protocols regulate trade in textiles and steel products. The EC must eliminate any remaining restriction on exports to Hungary (related to Comecon) by 1997 (Article 13).

Hungary will have to reduce its duties on EC-originating imports by stages. There are three lists: one setting as the final date of abolition January 1 1994; a second one January 1 1997 and a third one January 1 2001. QRs must be abolished by the end of the year 2000 (Article 10). However, exceptional measures of limited duration may be taken by Hungary, in the form of increased customs duties not exceeding 25 per cent (Article 29). During the first stage (in principle, of a duration of five years) Hungary may introduce for at most two years measures which derogate to the very liberal establishment rules accorded to EC firms in Articles 45 to 50, in the case of newly emerging industries which are being locally created. Hungary has accepted to approximate its laws on protection of health and life of humans, food legislation, consumer protection, technical rules and standards and the environment to the *acquis communautaire* (Article 69), all points extremely relevant for industry.

National treatment is applied by the EC to Hungary on contract award procedures as from entry into force of the Agreement, whereas Hungary does the same with respect to the Community only after the first stage of the transitional period (Article 67). Article 72 is devoted to industrial co-operation, although it has little operational content. It is worth while mentioning here the declaration whereby the EC will participate 'in Hungary's efforts in both public and private sectors to modernize and restructure its industry under conditions which ensure that the environment is protected'. As we will see later in this chapter, provisions relating to conformity of industrial standards have much more teeth.

Turning now to the EC-92 programme, there are within it a few positive aspects for Hungary's industry, such as a reduction in the number of norms and standards (from twelve to one) with which producers will have to comply once minimum Europe-wide standards have been adopted allowing for free circulation in the Community of approved products. This is very important for Hungary's food and machinery sectors, which may be able to achieve some economies of scale, thanks to the dismantling of the EC's internal technical barriers. There will be also a reduction in the number of tests and inspections to be overcome for some types of products in order to sell in different EC member countries;[2] obtaining a certificate from one of the EC-approved laboratories will be enough. The main beneficiaries in Hungary will be the food, chemical, pharmaceutical and equipment industries.

Import penetration, FDI and modernization

Hungary's import liberalization *vis-à-vis* the EC has the advantage of being based on an international contract. It cannot be renounced by any future government, as was the case of previous unilateral trade liberalization exercises by the Hungarian government, the last one consisting in reducing tariffs *erga omnes* from 16 per cent to 13 per cent (on average) as from February 1991.[3] In fact the Agreement is as solid as the EC wants it to be, imposing an external discipline on Hungary and providing a term of reference for local policy planners and firm managers. The latter know from now on what is expected of them at different dates in the next decade. This holds both for local producers of capital goods competing with imports *and* for local potential users of machinery and equipment.

In this respect, it appears that Hungary, which has now switched almost entirely to trade for which convertible currencies are used in settlement, did not actually apply tariffs to imports settled in non-convertible currencies, mainly from the former Comecon countries. In fact, for balance of payments reasons, imports from non-convertible currencies sources appear to have been favoured in the past, and much of the machinery and equipment tended to be acquired in the East. With the imposition of most-favoured-nation tariffs on imports from former Comecon suppliers, the situation is going to be reversed – the dissolution of Comecon and the conclusion of the Association Agreement mean that Hungary is switching the trading block with which it is associated. This implies the progressive substituting of equipment from the East by newer machinery from the EC.

It is important in this context, to note that Hungary's m.f.n. tariffs are at present particularly high for electrical machinery, investment goods and transport equipment. The simple average tariff for non-electrical machinery was 18.7 per cent in 1988, but ranged from 32 per cent for metal-working machinery and 31.6 per cent for printing, to 13.6 per cent and 12.4 per cent for power-generating and agricultural machinery respectively. The simple average tariff for electrical machinery was even higher: 26.2 per cent. Imports of a number of items, such as electric furnaces, incurred 50 per cent m.f.n. tariff rates. The reason for these high rates has not always been to protect local production (which was non-existent in many cases), but rather to protect other Comecon producers exporting to Hungary. Since these investment goods are no longer covered by import licensing (with the exception of telecommunications equipment) and they are included in the first of the three lists which Hungary has agreed upon for very rapid tariff elimination vis-à-vis the EC, one can expect a tremendous growth of trade in a matter of years in favour of EC machinery producers, at the expense of Comecon suppliers, which (with the exception of ex-GDR suppliers) will be knocked out of the Hungarian market.

As far back as the early 1970s, it was clear to many Hungarians that technology was lagging and that the Soviet Union had failed to contribute to Hungary's economic modernization since the late 1940s. To overcome the problem, the 'reformist' regime of Kadar thought of allowing imports of equipment from the West (e.g. for food processing), if necessary by borrowing, something which incidentally contributed to Hungary's present debt problems. The main supplier would be West Germany. The idea was that exports to the West of goods using the new technology would pay for imports of capital goods from there. Other Eastern European countries (such as Poland) also tried the same route, failing miserably. The record of Hungary was slightly better, although not convincing.[4] Ironically, the result is that much machinery imported from the West then is now old – not to speak of the Comecon-originated machinery. For instance, East German textile and printing machinery conformed to international technological standards, but for the little detail that they were not automated. Thus in government priority sectors (chemicals, machine-building, pharmaceuticals, food, printing, textiles), machinery has been imported mainly from the West for two decades. Whereas existing capacity was based on old machinery bought in the 1950s and 1960s either locally or in Comecon countries, capacity development was based on Western machinery.[5]

With respect to existing capacity, the record for obsolescence is to be found in the capital goods sector, where more than a third of the equipment is at least twenty years old and almost half of the machinery is more than a decade behind that of industrial countries. But there is a substantial technological gap in the textile and clothing sectors as well, where experts perceive much of Hungary's potential comparative advantage to exist. The average machine is ten to fifteen years old, but there are also some fifty-year-old machines, with zero book value.[6]

There has been little capacity development in recent years, due to a lack of convertible currency. Modernization of the production structure cannot be achieved without a massive inflow of foreign capital. This is where foreign direct investment enters the picture. The direct investor brings along not only capital goods, which are mostly new, but also new technology. Although there has been some FDI in Hungary since at least 1972,[7] there has been a considerable increase since 1988, when Act VI on the Economic Associations and Act XXIV on Foreign Investment were approved. FDI figures for 1988, 1989 and 1990 were respectively $200 million, $500 million and $1 billion.[8] By mid-1991, FDI inflows were expected

Table 6.1: New joint ventures in Hungary in the first half of 1991.

Currency	Number	Capital invested in conv. currency (mn. forint)
$	671	4,655.4
Pound sterling	116	2,202.7
DM	1,052	2,209.2
SF	190	438.5
Austrian sch	669	7,675.5
Italian lira	176	1,696.0
Swedish krone	62	204.8
Soviet rouble	8	6.3
Other currencies	133	6,948.3
Total	3,077	26,036.7

Source: Ministry for International Economic Relations

to reach the $1.5 billion mark,[9] although much of it was in the service sector and not all was used to buy foreign equipment. Not infrequently, much of the equipment brought in by TNCs is second-generation technology, although some of it is up-to-date, as in the important cases of Suzuki, Electrolux, General Electric, General Motors and Ford. The latter firms, mostly from non-EC countries, have had the EC markets in mind for their products without any doubt, speculating rightly that an Association Agreement with the EC was going to be concluded sooner or later.[10] Thus one of the present paradoxes is that technical modernization originates in embodied and non-embodied technology coming from OECD countries which are not members of the EC.[11] Clearly this is going to change in the years to come, when EC suppliers of equipment will be favoured as a result of the Association Agreement.

Most observers agree that at an earlier stage, some FDI in the industrial sector was motivated by the will to be positioned in a key Eastern European country functioning as a springboard to penetrate the former Soviet Union and other former Comecon markets.[12] This strategy appears for the moment to have no future, given the recessionary tendencies of these economies and their increasing pauperization.

Trends in quality control and technical standards

Over a century ago, early Hungarian industrialists looked for inspiration to Austria and Britain. After the First World War, however, and until the early 1950s, Hungary was inspired by German technological culture, which contributed to the vitality and modernity of certain sectors of the capital goods industry up until 1945. The exclusive German orientation, and a corresponding lack of knowledge of English, isolated Hungary from American industry, which was then taking the technological lead in key sectors of potential interest to Hungarian industrialists. One of the paradoxes of the imposition of Soviet standards, norms and modes of operation on Hungary after the Second World War was some exposure to US technology, since the Soviets in turn had been drawing inspiration from the US since the 1930s. The Soviet Union also took into account German industrial norms in many cases. Thus until the early 1950s industrial technology was based on Western standards, but then the Cold War took its toll. Comecon created its own standards, differing widely from international trends and geared mainly to the requirements of the Soviet market. Thus standards of quality required from Hungarian firms were down-graded. Importing machinery, components and technology from the West in the 1970s was wasteful, insofar as they ended up being used to supply markets with very low requirements, besides contributing heavily to foreign debt, since firms were using convertible currency imports to generate transferable rouble exports.

According to most experts, however, although isolation has had some retarding effects, catching-up with Western technical standards should not be a problem, provided there is motivation for engaging in the effort. Out of 19,000 industry standards, there are 'only' 2,100 former Comecon-based standards, although these are concentrated in the engineering and machinery sector. Hungary announced in 1990 its decision no longer to take part in Comecon standardization activities. According to some sources, Hungary has already suspended the application of legislation relating to former Comecon standards, but other sources state that during a transition period, Comecon standards will remain in use. Other standards to a great extent follow German DIN standards.[13] Quality control, however, is much worse than in the West.

This is where the EC enters in the equation – more specifically, the combination of EC-92 and the Association Agreement. On the one hand, equipment imported by Hungary will increasingly originate in the EC and will be based on EC-unified standards in many cases. Moreover EFTA-based producers of capital goods will use EC-wide standards. All these suppliers of intermediary products, machinery and equipment will have a large influence in shaping the future industrial structure of Hungary by bringing along their standards, patterns, models, norms, customs, and procedures. The effect will certainly be all-pervading, and penetrating the EC market after 1992 will require even greater marketing efforts by Hungary's exporters, in view of the increased competition but also higher standards imposed by the 1992 Programme. Hungarian exporters hoping to gain access to European markets will have to upgrade product quality, so as to conform with environmental and safety requirements in the EC. Thus, the main EC-92-linked problem for Hungarian industrial firms is that they must succeed not only in making Hungarian products competitive with those produced in the EC before 1993, but with those to be produced after 1992. The challenge of EC-92 for Hungarian exporters will be reflected in more competition not only in EC markets, but world-wide. All this has led the Hungarian government to base Hungarian standards and certification procedures on European ones as from the beginning of 1991. In practice this means that the Hungarian consumer will benefit indirectly from higher European standards. From another perspective, the change in standards comes with ideal timing: Hungary is switching standards at a time when there is tremendous simplification and harmonization work in Western Europe itself on norms, standards and certification.

Some key ingredients facilitating the economic transformation of Hungary

So far, according to most experts, there has been no substantial modernization behind the recent export expansion by Hungary to convertible currency countries, and particularly to the EC. New exports are not yet the result of expanded investment capacity, but rather a result of more entrepreneurship and some opportunism. Much of what is being exported is low quality and very labour-intensive, making capital of the fact that non-qualified labour costs in Hungary are still much lower than in Western Europe. In other words, the impact of the modernization process described in the preceding sections is yet to come. In fact the relative abundance of skilled people has not yet translated into increased exports.[14]

For this to happen, the necessary precondition is of course improved market access into the EC, much beyond what was contemplated in the non-preferential agreement concluded in September 1988. The Association Agreement of December 1991 improves the situation remarkably in this respect, adding predictability and stability to EC–Hungarian trade relations.

This seems vital for TNCs wishing to invest in Hungarian industries producing parts and components to be used by other European subsidiaries based in the European Economic Area. In other words, the Association Agreement contributes greatly to the incorporation of Hungary in the European system of intra-industry trade. This could be a critical factor for the partial salvation of Hungary's capital goods industry, which is in the doldrums as a result of its traditional orientation to the East.

There is no doubt whatsoever that the Cocom restrictions had a retarding effect on the modernization of Hungary's industrial structure in the 1980s, particularly in the areas of software and telecommunications. A second contribution of the Association Agreement is that it forces EC countries to do away with the remaining Cocom-related export controls in the next five years.[15] Without such a measure, it would be inconceivable that Hungary could succeed in its industrial integration in the Western world.

Subcontracting activities will also be enhanced by the conclusion of the Association Agreement. It is well known that the success of subcontracting is a function of the physical and cultural distance between the two producing partners. In that respect Hungary is better placed than, say, Malta or Mauritius, which have been competing with Hungary in this kind of activity in the textile sector. Hungarian experience with subcontracting in this field dates back to the 1970s. Western companies delivered high-quality materials which, combined with the low Hungarian wages for skill levels comparable to those in Austria and Germany, gave the producer a lead in certain clothing markets. However QRs and other trade restrictions limited the extent of 'safe' subcontracting.[16] This will change now. The contribution of subcontracting in terms of modernization comes in the form of technical advice and assistance received by the supplier for the training of workers in the developing country. This is considered by the customer to be part and parcel of the deal, since production is supposed to comply with the norms and standards of his country. For the supplier, this is of course not as good as transferring the whole technology to the developing country would be, but it improves enormously the awareness of the importance of quality control there.

Until now, reference has been made here to the qualitative contribution of the Association Agreement in the realm of market access. Turning now to the quantitative importance of the barriers which the EC is going to eliminate largely as a result of the Agreement, some indications are given below.

Tariffs

Table 6.2 shows the average tariffs applied by the EC-10 (Belgium, Denmark, the Federal Republic of Germany, France, Great Britain, Greece, Ireland, Italy, Luxembourg, and the Netherlands) under the common customs tariff (CCT) in 1983 on imports from Hungary, OECD countries, the socialist (or former socialist) countries (excluding China), developing countries (including China), Mediterranean countries, EFTA countries and the rest of the world. There have been only minor changes in tariffs since 1983. This was the mid-point of implementation of the Tokyo Round agreement, which still prevails, but the EC had also introduced some of those tariffs ahead of schedule. The overall pattern has changed somewhat since then, with Spain and Portugal now being progressively brought within the CET. There have also been minor changes in the GSP and in the arrangements under the Lomé Convention. More importantly, as from 1989 the EC-12 started to grant improved treatment to Hungary. However, these data give a reasonably accurate picture of the situation as of December 1991, i.e. prior to the *de facto* application of the Association Agreement.

From Table 6.2 it appears that the overall average rate of 6.8 per cent applied against imports from Hungary until January 1992 was much higher than the corresponding rates for the world as a whole or for other groups of countries (such as EFTA, ACP or Mediterranean countries), which are part and parcel of what in EC jargon is known as the pyramid of privilege. Thus, until recently GATT m.f.n. treatment was basically the treatment reserved for non-European industrial countries and the socialist countries. Apart from the tariff preferences, Hungary also happens to export many goods which attract relative high protection in the EC market, including many labour-intensive goods. This high-protection composition of trade is also why the average rate against Hungary was more than double the average rate against other socialist countries, although item-for-item, the rates are mostly the same. Clearly, the Association Agreement should markedly improve Hungary's export prospects to the EC because the former was lagging behind in terms of tariff barriers in relation to countries with overlapping production features (both within the EC and on its periphery).[17]

Non-tariff barriers

In Table 6.3, information is given for each SITC division (excluding SITC 9) on the EC's NTB treatment of Hungary and other broad groups of countries in 1988 (the same groups as shown in Table 6.2). The table shows a significantly higher incidence in the application of NTBs against Hungary's trade than against other groups of countries (even other socialist countries) and against the world in general.

In respect of individual SITC divisions, there are only a few in which the share of trade from Hungary affected by some kind of NTB is lower than that for other groups of countries. The breakdown by different types of broad categories of NTBs is given in Table 6.4. The types of NTBs have been classified into the following broad categories: price-increasing NTBs (e.g. variable levies, anti-dumping duties, tariff quotas, etc.), threats (e.g. monitoring systems, automatic licensing, anti-dumping or countervailing investigations, etc.), and quantitative restrictions (e.g. quotas, voluntary export restraints, restraints under the MFA, etc.). As is evident from the table, Hungary's export sectors significantly affected by NTBs in the EC include textiles and clothing, petroleum and petroleum products, animals oils and fats, leather goods, paper and paperboard manufactures, iron and steel, sanitary and plumbing equipment and footwear. Given this list of 'sensitive' products, it is obvious that the Association Agreement which touches upon some of the NTBs mentioned above, like quotas, will enhance particularly subcontracting activities in labour-intensive sectors, with a corresponding impact in terms of quality control and further integration of Hungary in the European system of intra-industry trade.

Some final remarks on modernization by contagion

According to a poll made in 1991,[18] 76 per cent of Hungarians want to join the EC within five years. What lies behind this overwhelming support of membership of the EC? Beyond the political restatement of the widely shared wish of 'returning to Europe' after an absence of several decades, the Hungarian people see the European challenge as a historical opportunity for changing gear and rapidly promoting economic and technological change. In some sense, they are following the lead of Spain, Portugal and Greece, whose citizens understood long ago that, given the choice, being the last of a first-rate group of countries in terms of creativity and technological progress was better than occupying the first place of a second- or third-rate club. In fact, the relative position of Hungary in relation to the former Comecon, on one hand, and the EC on the other, is currently akin to that of

Table 6.2: EC Tariffs applied in 1983 against groups of exporters (%).

SITC	Description	World	OECD	SOC	LDC	MED	EFTA	Hungary
All	Total Trade	2.6	3.2	2.7	2.1	1.9	0.3	6.8
00	Live Animals	2.2	0.6	4.6	5.6	5.4	1.8	4.8
01	Meat & Preparations	13.2	13.2	9.5	14.3	14.2	9.1	9.6
02	Dairy Products & Eggs	10.8	11.1	3.3	1.9	12.0	11.4	12.0
03	Fish & Preparations	8.2	6.8	12.7	11.5	10.2	3.4	3.3
04	Cereals and Preparations	0.0	0.0	0.0	0.0	0.0	0.0	0.0
05	Fruit & Vegetables	8.3	7.1	13.0	9.7	5.7	16.6	14.2
06	Sugar, Preparations & Honey	25.9	27.0	26.6	25.9	15.2	26.3	27.0
07	Coffee, Tea, Cocoa, Spices	2.5	1.9	2.8	2.5	3.5	8.0	11.6
08	Animal Feeding Stuff	1.7	0.1	0.3	2.3	0.6	1.6	0.2
09	Misc Food Preparations	12.6	10.7	7.3	14.2	1.5	7.1	4.6
11	Beverages	12.4	7.1	21.3	22.4	16.7	9.0	20.1
12	Tobacco & Manufactures Thereof	61.8	66.1	48.7	45.5	70.0	88.2	.
21	Hides, Skins, Inc Fur, Undressed	0.0	0.0	0.0	0.0	0.0	0.0	0.0
22	Oil Seeds, Nuts, Kernels	0.0	0.0	0.0	0.0	0.0	0.0	0.0
23	Rubber Crude, Synthetic	0.0	0.0	0.1	0.0	0.1	0.0	1.2
24	Wood, Lumber & Cork	0.1	0.1	0.0	0.1	0.0	0.0	0.1
25	Pulp and Waste Paper	0.0	0.0	0.0	0.0	0.0	0.0	0.0
26	Textile Fibres (not Yarn, Thread)	0.6	0.6	1.6	0.6	0.1	0.0	2.6
27	Crude Fertilizers & Minerals	0.0	0.0	0.2	0.0	0.0	0.0	0.0
28	Metalliferous Ores, Metal Scrap	0.0	0.0	0.0	0.0	0.0	0.0	0.0
29	Crude Animal Veg Materials Nes	3.6	3.8	0.8	2.7	7.9	1.7	0.7
32	Coal, Coke, Briquettes	2.9	3.0	2.8	2.7	1.8	0.0	0.9
33	Petroleum & Petroleum Products	0.2	0.4	0.6	0.2	0.4	0.0	3.5
34	Gas Natural and Manufactured	0.1	0.6	0.1	0.1	0.1	0.0	1.0
35	Electric Energy	0.0	0.0	0.0	0.0	0.0	0.0	
41	Animal Oils & Fats	0.5	0.6	2.4	0.2	0.7	0.5	2.2
42	Fixed Vegetable Oils & Fats	6.7	9.9	7.4	6.5	8.4	8.8	8.9
43	Processed Animal, Veg Oil & Fats	9.2	9.3	0.7	9.5	0.1	13.8	0.5
51	Chemical Elements & Compounds	3.3	3.2	4.1	4.0	3.6	0.2	3.0

Code	Description							
52	Mineral Tar & Crude Chemicals	0.3	0.1	0.8	0.3	0.1	0.0	1.1
53	Dyeing, Tanning & Colouring Materials	2.7	2.5	8.8	3.9	3.4	0.0	10.0
54	Medicinal & Pharm Products	2.7	2.5	5.7	5.0	3.6	0.1	6.8
55	Essential Oils & Perfume Materials	2.3	2.5	0.7	1.6	1.1	0.0	3.2
56	Fertilizers Manufactured	2.5	2.4	3.6	4.1	3.0	0.0	7.5
57	Explosives, Pyrotech Products	3.9	3.1	5.7	5.4	2.3	0.0	8.9
58	Plastic Materials, etc.	5.7	5.6	12.5	8.7	3.6	0.0	13.4
59	Chemical Nes	3.4	3.3	5.2	4.0	0.9	0.0	6.8
61	Leather/Furs Inc Manufs	2.1	1.2	3.7	2.8	3.2	0.0	5.1
62	Rubber Manufactures	2.9	2.3	6.6	4.3	2.9	0.0	6.8
63	Wood & Cork Manufactures	4.1	2.8	8.3	5.9	4.2	0.0	6.4
64	Paper/Board & Manufactures	2.7	2.6	8.9	6.7	6.3	1.4	10.5
65	Textile Yarn, Fabrics & Articles	5.3	3.2	10.1	7.6	3.0	0.1	12.0
66	Non-Metallic Mineral Manufactures	2.0	2.0	4.2	1.1	0.7	0.0	8.6
67	Iron & Steel	2.3	1.7	5.8	3.3	3.8	0.0	6.0
68	Non-Ferrous Metals	0.6	0.8	0.5	0.5	3.1	0.0	4.1
69	Metal Manufactures Nes	3.0	2.5	5.3	4.9	2.5	0.0	6.1
71	Machines Non-Electric	3.3	3.3	5.5	3.9	2.4	0.0	5.3
72	Machinery Electric	6.0	5.7	6.2	7.0	3.5	0.0	6.3
73	Transport Equipment	4.7	4.8	8.9	3.4	6.0	0.0	16.9
81	Sanitary, Plumbing, Heating, Lighting Equ	2.2	0.9	6.8	4.7	4.3	0.0	8.5
82	Furniture	3.2	0.9	6.6	5.4	4.2	0.0	6.7
83	Travel Goods, Handbags	4.9	3.3	5.1	4.3	4.2	0.0	6.1
84	Clothing	7.3	2.1	10.5	9.3	5.4	0.0	13.2
85	Footwear	6.5	0.7	9.6	9.1	5.9	0.0	11.7
86	Prof Scientific etc. Instruments	6.1	6.2	6.9	4.4	1.5	0.0	6.9
89	Misc Manufactures Nes	5.1	4.9	6.0	5.0	2.4	0.2	5.5

Notes: Missing values implies no imports in these categories.

SOC – Socialist countries of Asia and Eastern Europe plus the USSR and Cuba, excluding China and Hungary.

MED – Mediterranean countries, not elsewhere included.

LDC – Developing countries, not elsewhere included, including China.

OECD – OECD countries, including Spain and Portugal, excluding Turkey.

EFTA – Austria, Finland, Norway, Sweden, Switzerland and Iceland.

Source: Calculations by the author using GATT data. To the extent possible, account has been taken of preferential rates and their usage

Table 6.3: EC Imports from partner groups affected by NTBS in 1988 (%).

SITC	Description	World	OECD	SOC	LDCS	MED	EFTA	Hungary
All	Total Trade	13.8	16.0	21.4	20.7	7.5	6.7	35.2
00	Live Animals	59.9	11.3	80.3	55.7	9.8	87.4	88.3
01	Meat & Preparations	83.1	89.0	85.3	74.6	47.6	95.7	39.7
02	Dairy Products & Eggs	83.0	85.0	75.7	60.8	38.4	69.7	89.8
03	Fish & Preparations	3.0	34.8	40.9	60.3	48.7	63.6	7.9
04	Cereals and Preps	100.0	100.0	100.0	100.0	100.0	100.0	100.0
05	Fruit & Vegetables	53.3	68.4	56.7	38.0	61.7	46.4	61.5
06	Sugar, Honey	98.1	78.1	87.7	99.3	94.8	74.2	58.1
07	Coffee, Tea, Cocoa	27.2	37.2	37.5	22.1	9.7	59.9	65.5
08	Animal Feeding Stuff	29.2	43.7	24.2	23.0	63.7	4.6	39.8
09	Misc Food Preparations	49.9	50.1	61.1	14.0	62.4	81.3	85.4
11	Beverages	2.1	3.5	0.8	0.2	0.2	0.5	0.3
12	Tobacco & Manufactures	0.0	0.0	0.0	0.0	0.0	0.0	0.0
21	Hides, Skins, Fur	0.0	0.0	0.0	0.0	0.0	0.0	0.0
22	Oil Seeds, Nuts, Kernels	1.2	2.7	0.8	0.1	0.0	2.7	9.6
23	Rubber Crude, Synthetic	0.4	0.0	7.4	0.1	0.0	0.0	6.8
24	Wood, Lumber & Cork	0.0	0.0	0.0	0.0	0.0	0.0	0.1
25	Pulp and Waste Paper	0.0	0.0	0.0	0.0	0.0	0.0	0.0
26	Textile Fibres	12.8	8.7	18.3	12.8	45.5	7.0	18.9
27	Crude Fertilizers	18.3	3.1	17.1	16.4	3.5	17.7	40.0
28	Metalliferous Ores	7.4	12.2	1.9	3.7	0.9	2.5	5.2
29	Crude Animal Veg Mats	18.0	14.0	30.2	19.4	14.7	16.1	21.9
32	Coal, Coke, Briquettes	0.0	0.0	0.0	0.0	0.0	0.0	0.0
33	Petroleum & Products	12.3	17.2	28.1	10.5	14.0	4.3	32.6
34	Gas Natural and Mnfd	1.2	0.0	11.1	0.0	0.0	0.0	0.5
35	Electric Energy	1.5	0.0	11.1	0.0	.	0.0	.
41	Animal Oils & Fats	6.6	10.3	2.2	0.2	0.0	1.2	34.4
42	Fixed Veg Oils & Fats	6.4	2.2	0.2	0.1	98.7	0.2	0.0

43	Procesd Oils & Fats	0.0	0.0	0.1	0.0	0.0	0.0	4.2
51	Chemical Elmnts & Cmpds	1.8	2.6	4.0	0.9	0.0	2.6	1.2
52	Mineral Tar	0.8	0.1	3.0	1.0	0.0	0.0	2.9
53	Dyeing, Tanning Matrls	0.9	0.7	15.1	5.1	0.0	0.0	7.3
54	Med & Pharm Products	5.3	5.4	4.9	2.7	4.4	6.8	7.1
55	Essential Oils S	0.8	0.5	0.1	2.0	0.0	0.0	0.0
56	Fertilizers Manufactured	1.7	6.6	11.6	0.0	0.0	0.0	11.5
57	Explosives	0.4	0.0	21.7	5.6	0.0	0.0	24.8
58	Plastic Materials, etc.	1.5	1.1	20.2	1.9	0.0	0.0	9.1
59	Chemicals Nes	8.2	14.3	6.6	19.4	8.7	1.7	5.5
61	Leather/Furs Inc Manufs	16.4	11.2	32.1	12.1	92.7	3.5	43.1
62	Rubber Manufactures	6.2	0.9	26.4	14.9	0.0	0.0	16.6
63	Wood & Cork Mnfs	33.5	23.8	52.1	46.3	4.6	23.2	16.7
64	Paper/Board & Mnfs	35.4	42.2	27.0	12.7	0.0	12.7	78.6
65	Txtl Yarn, Fibrcs, Artcls	29.6	1.4	77.6	69.7	0.1	0.6	96.9
66	Non-Metallic Min Mnfs	7.3	5.0	36.4	4.6	11.0	0.1	32.7
67	Iron & Steel	32.7	19.2	57.9	28.7	8.9	44.5	61.4
68	Non-Ferrous Metals	2.0	4.4	0.4	0.5	0.1	1.5	5.8
69	Metal Manufactures Nes	2.5	1.5	7.6	3.5	5.7	2.1	4.3
71	Machines Non-Electric	4.2	6.6	7.5	0.8	0.1	0.5	11.2
72	Machinery Electric	6.8	9.9	18.9	7.1	5.4	3.7	7.0
73	Transport Equipment	11.0	34.3	11.0	3.3	3.4	3.1	7.4
81	Sanitary, etc. Equip	3.1	1.1	1.6	5.3	0.2	0.3	62.5
82	Furniture	13.1	8.0	21.6	11.5	10.6	9.8	19.6
83	Travel Goods, Handbags	0.2	0.0	2.7	0.0	0.0	0.0	4.2
84	Clothing	52.9	0.2	93.7	77.3	0.3	0.3	90.2
85	Footwear	40.5	22.7	69.0	45.4	21.3	25.9	66.7
86	Prof Scientific Insts	5.4	7.5	24.1	1.5	0.9	1.6	3.9
89	Misc Manufactures Nes	3.4	5.5	8.5	3.1	0.1	0.5	3.2

Source: UNCTAD Computerized files on NTBs

Table 6.4: EC Imports from Hungary affected by broad categories of NTBS applied in 1988.

SITC	Description	Imports '84 $ '000	Price	NTB Types Threats	QRS	All
All	Total Trade	3,861,468	27.7	7.0	26.3	35.2
00	Live Animals	364,167	87.3	0.9	84.9	88.3
01	Meat & Preparations	320,130	40.3	1.9	11.5	39.7
02	Dairy Products & Eggs	5,661	99.5	0.0	26.2	89.8
03	Fish & Preparations	12,303	7.9	0.0	0.0	7.9
04	Cereals and Preparations	42,912	100.0	4.2	98.8	100.0
05	Fruit & Vegetables	122,643	44.0	8.1	21.1	61.5
06	Sugar, Preparations & Honey	4,563	46.2	0.0	20.9	58.1
07	Coffee, Tea, Cocoa, Spices	9,621	65.5	0.0	12.7	65.5
08	Animal Feeding Stuff	63,378	19.7	0.0	39.8	39.8
09	Misc Food Preparations	87,246	98.3	0.1	0.0	85.4
11	Beverages	65,259	98.5	0.0	98.8	0.3
12	Tobacco & Manufactures Thereof	3,618	0.0	0.0	0.0	0.0
21	Hides, Skins, Inc Fur, Undressed	8,361	0.0	0.0	0.0	0.0
22	Oil Seeds, Nuts, Kernels	6,660	0.0	1.1	9.6	9.6
23	Rubber Crude, Synthetic	2,763	0.0	0.0	6.8	6.8
24	Wood, Lumber & Cork	137,358	0.0	0.0	0.1	0.1
25	Pulp and Waste Paper	306	0.0	0.0	0.0	0.0
26	Textile Fibres (not Yarn, Thread)	51,669	0.4	8.8	10.2	18.9
27	Crude Fertilizers & Minerals	92,610	3.7	19.9	37.3	40.0
28	Metalliferous Ores, Metal Scrap	135,675	0.0	4.5	0.6	5.2
29	Crude Animal Veg Materials Nes	37,332	0.2	2.5	21.6	21.9
32	Coal, Coke, Briquettes	423	0.0	0.0	0.0	0.0
33	Petroleum & Petroleum Products	321,309	0.0	21.6	11.1	32.6
34	Gas Natural and Manufactured	75,366	0.0	0.0	0.5	0.5
41	Animal Oils & Fats	11,691	34.4	0.0	3.2	34.4
42	Fixed Vegetable Oils & Fats	2,637	0.0	0.0	0.0	0.0
43	Procesd Animal, Veg Oil & Fats	621	0.0	0.0	4.2	4.2
51	Chemical Elements & Compounds	387,792	0.1	0.0	1.1	1.2
52	Mineral Tar & Crude Chemicals	99,108	0.0	0.0	2.9	2.9
53	Dyeing, Tanning & Colouring Matrls	2,160	0.0	0.0	7.3	7.3
54	Medicinal & Pharm Products	19,323	0.0	0.5	6.6	7.1
55	Essential Oils & Perfume Matrls	2,286	0.0	0.0	0.0	0.0
56	Fertilizers Manufactured	30,384	0.0	0.0	11.5	11.5
57	Explosives, Pyrotech Products	2,331	0.0	0.0	24.8	24.8
58	Plastic Materials etc.	20,799	0.0	0.0	9.1	9.1
59	Chemicals Nes	19,080	3.3	0.0	5.3	5.5
61	Leather/Furs Inc Manufs	20,574	0.0	37.3	5.8	43.1
62	Rubber Manufactures	22,887	0.0	0.0	16.6	16.6
63	Wood & Cork Manufactures	26,847	10.5	0.0	7.4	16.7
64	Paper/Board & Manufactures	10,386	76.9	0.0	10.1	78.6
65	Textile Yarn, Fabrics & Articles	97,056	85.2	2.0	81.0	96.9
66	Non-Metallic Mineral Manufactures	58,986	10.8	1.2	24.2	32.7
67	Iron & Steel	161,280	37.3	54.3	60.7	61.4
68	Non-Ferrous Metals	61,407	0.0	0.1	5.7	5.8
69	Metal Manufactures Nes	44,838	0.0	0.7	3.6	4.3
71	Machines Non-Electric	204,147	7.7	2.5	2.2	11.2

Table 6.4: EC Imports from Hungary affected by broad categories of NTBS applied in 1988 (*continued*).

		Imports '84		NTB Types		
SITC	Description	$ '000	Price	Threats	QRS	All
72	Machinery Electric	167,283	0.5	3.2	3.8	7.0
73	Transport Equipment	52,497	0.0	3.4	4.0	7.4
81	Sanitary, Plumbing, Heating, Lighting Eq	11,961	62.4	7.0	7.0	62.5
82	Furniture	39,870	0.0	10.1	9.5	19.6
83	Travel Goods, Handbags	3,042	0.0	0.0	4.2	4.2
84	Clothing	181,944	85.9	0.5	90.0	90.2
85	Footwear	36,810	0.0	88.9	51.2	66.7
86	Prof Scientific etc. Instruments	29,835	0.0	1.6	2.3	3.9
89	Misc Manufactures Nes	59,157	0.0	0.9	2.3	3.2

Source: UNCTAD Computerized file on NTBs

Portugal in the 1970s in relation to its African colonies and the EC respectively. Before the April 1974 Revolution, the main export market for Portuguese industry had been its colonies in Africa, from where Portugal's energy and raw materials came. Industry was quite inward-looking and there was not much foreign investment. Customers overseas were passive. As a result, equipment was antiquated and there was not much need for quality control. Once the colonial system came to an end, many understood that the era of captive markets and easy life was over, but that simultaneously there was a golden opportunity to modernize by switching trade blocs.

The Association Agreement with the EC and the need to adjust to EC-92 will contribute to Hungary's industrial restructuring because they are taken both by its government and by its industrialists as an integral part of Hungary's strategy of modernization by catching-up with the *acquis communautaire*.

Notes

1. Agence Europe, December 16/17, 1991.
2. Note, however, that this rule will not be systematically applied on Hungarian exports unless Hungary becomes at some stage a member of the European Economic Area providing for the mutual recognition of tests.
3. See EIU (1991), no. 2 and GATT (1991), vol. II. This has affected mainly industrial production equipment and accessories; e.g. duties on car parts were reduced from 60 per cent to 10 per cent and on sewing machines from 50 per cent to 8.5 per cent.
4. See Hanson (1982).
5. Reference is made here to co-operation agreements with OECD countries, which were in fact a kind of buy-back agreements whereby the seller of equipment or technology agreed to buy back from the buying country products derived from the production of the plant (the so-called 'related products') – see UNCTAD, January 25, 1991. According to GATT (1991), vol. II, p. 133, in 1990 the turnover realized in the framework of industrial co-operation agreements among companies amounted to about 5 per cent of Hungary's exports to industrial countries. In 1988, 1,952 such agreements were in

force; among them 1,265 with companies from market economies. Most are with German, Austrian, Swiss, French, US and Swedish companies.

6. Much of the information reported here is based on unpublished research directed by A. Torok of the Research Institute of Industrial Economics of the Hungarian Academy of Sciences.

7. See Hungarian Chamber of Commerce (1991). One or two joint ventures were established every year during the early 1970s ($1.5–2 million). In the mid-1980s this process became more intensive: in 1985, thirteen economic associations with foreign participation invested $17 million. By 1988 more than 100 such firms were registered, with prime capital of more than $160 million, of which foreign participation was $70 million. The number of joint ventures had jumped to more than 5,000 by the end of 1990 and as shown in Table 6.1, an additional 3,000 were created in the first half of 1991 alone.

8. See GATT (1991), vol. II: 36.

9. See EIU (1991), No. 2.

10. A typical example: US Senator Tom Lantos, a businessman of Hungarian extraction has invested in a brand-new float glass factory which will export 90 per cent of its production to Western Europe.

11. The exception seems to be German firms, which have been investing in Hungary to produce there and export back to Germany (rather than to the EC as a whole). As reported by Inotai (1989), it has occurred with relative frequency, particularly in Western Hungary, that in return for German capital small and medium-sized firms have served as parts suppliers to Bavarian finished products manufacturers. The almost total absence of French, British and Italian investors in industrial sectors is particularly striking.

12. See *The Economist*, September 21, 1991. Foreign investors in the service sector (such as retailing) obviously have the Hungarian local market in mind.

13. See GATT (1991), Vol. II: 36.

14. Probably some retraining is required in many cases; the EC is also helping in this respect (e.g. through implementation of the TEMPUS programme).

15. According to the EIU (1991) No. 4, the Cocom list of prohibitive items which were not allowed to be sold in former socialist countries has been substantially liberalized. But licensing for software programmes, though less of an obstacle, will still operate for a while.

16. In that respect, Mediterranean and ACP countries had until now a clear advantage over Hungary.

17. For an estimation of the quantitative impact of the EC's tariff elimination on Hungary's exports, using high-powered simulation programmes, see Tovias and Laird (1991).

18. See Eurobarometer, *European Affairs*, February–March 1991: 68.

Bibliography

Asian Productivity Organization (1978) *International Sub-contracting: A Tool of Technology Transfer*, Tokyo.

Commission of the European Communities (1988) 'The Economics of 1992' ('The Checchini Report'), Directorate General for Economic and Financial Affairs, *European Economy*, 35, March.

Commission of the European Communities (1990) *Fifth Report of the Commission to the Council and the European Parliament concerning the Implementation of the White Paper on the Completion of the Internal Market*, COM(90)90 final, Brussels, March 28, 1990.

Commission of the European Communities (1990) *Communication from the Commission to the Council and the Parliament, Association Agreements with the Countries of Central and Eastern Europe: A General Outline*, COM(90) 398 final, Brussels, August 27, 1990.

Commission of the European Communities, *Europe Agreement, EC/Hungary*, November 22, 1991, preliminary draft.

Economist Intelligence Unit (1991), *Hungary*, Country Reports, various issues.

GATT (1991) *Trade Policy Review: Hungary*, Geneva, vol. I and II.

Germidis, D. (ed.) (1980) *International Sub-contracting*, Paris: OECD.

Hanson, P. (1982) 'The End of Import-Led Growth? Some Observations on Soviet, Polish and Hungarian Experience in the 1970s', *Journal of Comparative Economics* 6(2), June: 130–47.

Hungarian Chamber of Commerce (1991) *Investors' Guide to Hungary 1991*, Budapest: The Foreign Investment Promotion Service of the Hungarian Chamber of Commerce.

Hungarian Scientific Council for World Economy (1989) 'The Single European Market 1992: Chances and Tasks for Hungary', *Trends in World Economy* 62.

Inotai, A. (1990) 'Foreign Direct Investment in the Hungarian Economy', paper presented at the conference *Les Nouvelles Opportunités des Marchés de l'Est*, Paris: Institute for International Research, May 30 and 31.

Marer, P. (1991) 'Foreign Economic Liberalization in Hungary and Poland', *American Economic Review* 81(2), May: 329–33.

Palankai, T. (1991) *The European Community and Central European Integration: The Hungarian Case*, New York: Institute for East–West Security Studies, Occasional Paper Series, No. 21.

Sinkovics, A. and Angresano, J. (1991) 'Hungary and the European Community: Problems and Prospects', paper presented at the ECSA meeting, Washington, George Mason University, May 22–4.

Tovias, A. and Laird, S. (1991) *Whither Hungary and the European Communities?*, Washington, D.C.: The World Bank, Policy, Research and External Affairs Working Papers, WPS 584.

UNCTAD (1991) *Transfer and Development of Technology in a Changing World Environment in the 1990s*, TD/B/C.6/153, January 25.

7

Viking Raps – a case study of joint venture negotiation in the former Soviet Union

Martin Johanson

Introduction

In view of the limited opportunities for establishing subsidiaries in the former Soviet Union, entering into a joint venture with a Soviet partner can be viewed as the principal mode of entry into the Soviet market. Given the turbulent situation in the Soviet market and the difficulty for outsiders in perceiving how the Soviet economy works, knowledge about this area is a crucial factor for the firm entering the Soviet market.

This chapter focuses on Swedish–Soviet joint venture negotiations. The focus of the study has been placed on knowledge development in connection with the negotiations. Taking the network perspective as its theoretical background, the chapter develops a negotiation model which is used in the description and analysis of negotiations between the Swedish vegetable and fat producer Karlshamns and their counterpart in the formation of the joint venture Viking Raps.

Developments in the former Soviet Union provide a unique opportunity to follow and study joint projects in a market that is undergoing a drastic structural reorganization. According to Yin (1989) the case study approach is preferred when the aim is to examine contemporary events and the main questions are 'why' and 'how'. The aim of this paper has been to ask why and how. Consequently, in order to examine the joint venture negotiations, an inductive method has been used. An open questionnaire was used to give the respondents the opportunity to freely give their views about the negotiations.

The study is limited to Swedish and Soviet firms, the Swedish firm previously having had no experience of the Soviet market, and attempting to become established in the Soviet market. It is from this firm's perspective the model is developed.

What are Negotiations?

Many different models are used for studying negotiations between parties from different cultures. Fayerweather and Kapoor's (1976) model is suitable, since it has its origin in studies of joint venture and other kinds of extensive engagement negotiations between governments in developing countries and firms from industrialized countries. The model has two advantages. On one hand its four 'C' variables – common interest, conflicting interest, criteria and compromise, giving an explanation of what characterizes negotiations and why negotiations take place. On the other hand it emphasizes that the negotiations have to be seen in a wider context. The cultural, social, economic and political environments that surround the negotiation must be taken into consideration.

McCall and Warrington (1989) have been inspired by the IMP project (Håkansson 1982). This model stresses the interaction between firms. Concerning negotiations, they assume that the interaction is affected by two special dimensions, the cross-cultural and the capabilities of the negotiating people. Assessing these dimensions they derive four factors, which alternately influence each other and thereby the negotiations and the interaction. The four factors are the negotiator's behaviour, the negotiation situation, the negotiation strategies and skills, and the environment.

These two models have their strengths and their limitations. Although the four Cs in Fayerweather and Kapoor's model are changing over time, the process that McCall and Warrington describe takes place over time: different skills dominate under different phases, and their perspectives give too static a picture of the negotiations. The purpose seems to be to give advice and an outline of how negotiators should handle certain situations, rather than to understand how and why negotiations develop over time, and what happens within the parties during the negotiations.

Ghauri's model (1983) also seems to have been influenced by the interaction approach. He developed a model of package deal negotiations in order to study how the parties' different backgrounds influenced the negotiations through the variable atmosphere, and its four subvariables – co-operation/conflict, distance, power/dependence and expectations. Compared to the other two models it has a considerable advantage in that it has a feedback from the process to the background factors. The negotiators and their goals change over time; recognition of this increases the understanding of what happens, when parties from different cultures negotiate – i.e. that negotiation is a learning process.

Point of Departure

Snehota (1990) discusses what he calls the economic problem. He claims that knowledge about utilization of resources is imperfect, being scattered among individuals, none of whom has complete knowledge. Knowledge is always limited in scope and specific to the individual. But as conditions related to knowledge change, knowledge is modified and takes on new forms. Snehota goes on to argue that 'economic activity is not limited to the framework of finding means to given ends, but is connected to the identification of ends and goals for which resources can be used' (Snehota 1990: 29).

For that reason the economic problem is a matter of resource utilization, rather than of finding the means by which given ends can be achieved. Among the individuals concerned there is a parallel and continuous interaction between knowledge on the one hand, and ends and means on the other hand. Consequently, the actors enter the market with bounded frames of ends and means, limited knowledge about which resources are available and for which purposes they can be used. The actors' heterogeneous and bounded knowledge gives them an incentive to begin various kinds of exchange with other actors. 'The flow of exchange thus reflects the dispersion and distribution of knowledge of resource utilization and existence rather than distribution and allocation of resources' (Snehota 1990: 32).

So, if we accept that individuals at each moment of time have bounded knowledge, we understand the importance of time for ends and means. As knowledge and experience through exchange are acquired and created, so the individuals concerned can identify new and more specific ends and means.

Network Perspective and the Joint Venture

Markets seem to organize themselves into networks. The smallest part of the network is the firm, but one firm does not make a network. It is the relationship between the firms which is the foundation of the network. These relationships develop over time, as the firms exchange resources. By establishing and developing exchange relationships in a market, an actor can gain access to other actors' resources and knowledge. 'While the two parties are interacting, their problems are confronted with solutions, their abilities with needs, etc. Reciprocal knowledge and capabilities are revealed and developed jointly and in mutual dependence by the two parties' (Håkansson and Snehota 1990: 191).

Consequently, a joint venture can be viewed as a relationship between two or more firms, and the purpose is to study how such relationships are born, i.e. negotiated and formed in the chaotic Soviet market. A joint venture, as distinct from other kinds of relationships in different networks, is characterized by a certain formal structure, made possible by legislation. The parties to the joint venture transfer, according to the contract negotiated, certain resources to the joint venture.

Establishment in Foreign Markets

Since the model in this chapter deals purely with firms establishing themselves in a new foreign market through joint ventures, Johansons and Vahlne's model (1977), which describes the knowledge development of the firm and its importance for engagement in foreign markets, is of interest. Their model focuses on the internationalization of the firm, which consists of gradually increasing commitment in foreign markets. The basic assumption of the model is that lack of market knowledge is a major obstacle for development of the firm's international operation. This knowledge can only be acquired by operating abroad. Becoming established is something that happens over time.

According to the network approach, networks are stable structures, within which relationships have been developed and established for a long time, since stable relationships demand acceptance and trust between the firms. Evidently, an established firm without contacts with other firms is an impossibility. Over time, the establishing firm interacts with other firms in the network, an interaction which in some cases is developed into relationships. When these relationships have developed to the point that the establishing firm is considered as a trustworthy supplier or purchaser – i.e. the firm has a position which does not demand additional investment – the firm can be considered as established in the network (Hammarkvist, Håkansson and Mattsson 1982). This means that establishment has a time dimension. It takes time to build up relationships of the required quality and quantity. This implies that an establishing firm, in possession of a recently formed joint venture, can never be considered as established in the market, except from the perspective of the other owners. The future operations of the joint venture determine when the firm will become established in the eyes of the other actors in the network. The sum of the other actors' perceptions determines whether a firm is established or not – it must have an identity. The conclusion of this discussion is that establishment in a foreign market is a process which takes time, where the establishing firm through its operation acquires knowledge and builds up relationships to other firms in the network, which gradually leads to a deeper engagement in the market. An ownership in a joint venture is the first relationship, the first step in an establishment process – but nevertheless an important step.

A Model of Negotiation for the Formation of Joint Ventures

The aim is to develop a model which encapsulates the critical features of joint venture formation in the former Soviet market. The model is based on the belief that, even in the short-term, we deal with unpredictable processes; you never know what you will know, but what you will know will certainly influence your behaviour – especially when you are new and operate in an unstable and turbulent market. The negotiations always have a history, which is the point of departure for new activities.

Negotiating joint ventures is something which goes on over a period of time; it is not just a certain event or decision. Over time, when firms negotiate, they engage in various exchange activities, something happens in the minds of the negotiators and firms participating in the negotiations. The activities lead to different events and decisions, and the consequences of the activities change the participating firms and the individuals concerned. This is even more true of firms with different technologies, from different cultures, countries and with different economic systems, since there is a greater disparity in levels of these firms' knowledge than in those of firms from the same country, with the same technology and from the same economic system. Through the activities the knowledge grows, which gives the negotiators more and more – or in some cases less – reason to take part in the new relationship, in this case a joint venture in the former Soviet Union.

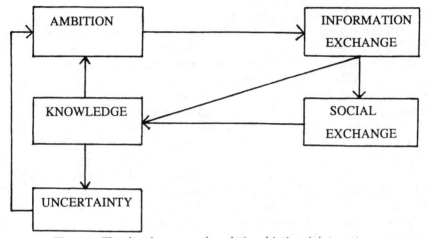

THE ESTABLISHING FIRM   THE ACTIVITIES

Fig. 7.1. The development of a relationship in a joint venture.

Ambition

Actors in the market act on the basis of their imperfect and bounded knowledge. Accepting the discussion above, that knowledge grows through various exchange activities, it is also rather easy to accept that the goals, demands, tactics, strategies, purposes, assumptions, plans or whatever we prefer to call it, which the actors in the market formulate, change also, as a result of the growing knowledge. What the actors participating in the different kinds of exchange want to receive from these exchanges may vary between firms and over time, which leads to dynamism in both the market as in the specific exchange. These goals, demands, purposes or objectives are viewed as something quite loosely defined, and as being changeable; a term which catches some of the character of this concept is ambition. It is not argued that people and organizations do not work against certain targets, but the concept of ambition is preferred since it better catches the character of the changing goals, aims or purposes. Ambition is very closely related to the level of knowledge and the perceived uncertainty.

The activities—information exchange and social exchange

What happens under the negotiations? What is going on between and within the firms? What do firms want to carry out? In accordance with the discussion above, the firms and individuals have heterogeneous levels of knowledge, which is the reason why exchange takes place and relationships are developed. When firms try to become established in new markets and when they develop relationships with other firms they lack knowledge, and knowledge is something which information can give them.

Consequently, information is a resource which has to be exchanged within the negotiation. The information exchange can take different forms. To receive information, the firms' negotiators have to meet, although it is theoretically possible to just exchange information remotely, by telephone for instance. The need to meet increases the more complex the engagement and the greater the differences in culture and language between the negotiators.

Information exchange is not the only kind of exchange that takes place. The information exchange in itself gives rise to another kind of exchange, the social exchange. The ambition to exchange information forces the negotiators to meet, socialize, solve problems together and so forth. This also forces people to exchange other resources, themselves, their abilities and capabilities. For this reason we argue that resources are not just tangible. The social exchange is a natural consequence of the information exchange, i.e. it does not fulfil an isolated function.

Before leaving the exchange, some comments are required on how information is exchanged and how it affects the social exchange. Some questions can illustrate this problem: 1. Does the firm have information? 2. Is the firm willing to give information? 3. Is it capable of acquiring information which it does not have? The answers to these questions provide much information about the firm's abilities. But a fourth question is also important: Is the information which the firm possesses or can acquire relevant and still valid? This question is important, because it concerns the firm's position in a changing market and its negotiators' abilities. There is no point in exchanging information which is useless.

Knowledge

Throughout this chapter it has been repeated that knowledge is bounded and heterogeneous. But assume that the firms' knowledge was homogeneous. What would they then have to negotiate about? Of course, some problems and questions would have to be resolved, but two firms with a long relationship will presumably be able to reach an agreement quickly, since their relationship has given them so much time and opportunity to acquire knowledge about each other's technology, organization, personnel, goods and so forth.

In accordance with Johanson and Vahlne's (1977) model, we distinguish between two types of knowledge; the objective, which can be taught, and the experiential, which can only be learned by experience. They view the experiential knowledge as the critical factor, because it is harder to acquire than objective knowledge.

Snehota (1990), inspired by Polanyi, writes about tacit knowledge. Tacit knowledge is hard to define or to touch, but nevertheless, it is an important aspect of understanding human behaviour. Tacit knowledge is usually referred to as skills, abilities and capabilities. As with experience, this type of knowledge can only be acquired through human activities. Snehota underlines the difficulty of acquiring and transferring tacit knowledge to other actors. Tacit knowledge is closely connected to certain situations. In this case, on the one hand related to negotiations with firms, and individuals, and on the other hand with a certain country, culture, economic system and/or language. Tacit knowledge is a by-product of the obvious will to acquire objective knowledge, and can only be acquired by confrontation with the new market.

The former Soviet Union has for a long time been a stable but closed country, providing little information about itself. And the information that has been given has been doubtful. During recent years, however, circumstances have changed rapidly. Nevertheless, the fact that the old information has been doubtful and that the situation today is so unstable means that the establishing firm needs a lot of fundamental information, that only the Soviet parties can give.

We want to make a distinction between how to use the two concepts. Johanson and Vahlne (1977) use the term 'acquire' for both types of knowledge, but we prefer to use 'acquire' for objective knowledge and 'create' for experiential knowledge. Negotiators have an obvious will to acquire information from their counterpart, but there is no such desire to acquire experiential knowledge. Experiential knowledge is a by-product, which is created when individuals act, through their common activities. Every situation creates new experiential knowledge, which is especially valid when structures are changing fast. Furthermore we see that the created experiential knowledge in one loop can affect both the information exchange and the social exchange in the next loop, since it is in the first place connected to the negotiations. The parties do not just act on the basis of their knowledge – their knowledge is generated from their acting.

Discussing knowledge, we have to introduce the concept of context. 'The context is enacted, it is created by the organization itself and in a sense it even constitutes the organization itself. . . . The organization exists and performs in a context rather than in an environment, in as much as it has a meaning and a role only in relation to a number of interrelated actors' (Håkansson and Snehota 1990: 192).

The context is distinguished from environment. Environment can be seen as the context, where the actors do not have an identity. Snehota (1990) writes that context is the part of the network which is relevant to the firm. The relevant part of the network is the firms which affect the focal firm. They belong to the focal firm's context: 'Other actors apart from these with whom direct exchange relationships are maintained, affect the behaviour of the business enterprise in relationships it maintains with others and on which depends the results' (Snehota 1990: 145).

The critical feature in the definition above is the effect of the focal firm. But on the other side of the coin is the identity of the actors in the network. The two factors are of course closely related. Context is the relevant part of the network, i.e. those actors which have an identity and/or affect the focal firm. The resources give an actor an identity. Actors without resources do not have an identity.

According to the way in which knowledge evolves, in our case study, negotiations can be considered as a process by which some part of the former Soviet environment becomes the Swedish firm's context, as more and more of the Soviet network, its actors and resources, get an identity in the eyes of the Swedish firm. New possibilities, problems, suppliers, customers and so forth are identified, so the parties' contexts and knowledge become increasingly similar. The parties join each other in various activities leading to events, experiences and knowledge shared by the parties. Through information and social exchange the Swedish firm acquires knowledge about the joint venture context. The Swedish firm has little knowledge about the new market; its personnel will seek to acquire knowledge in three specific fields:

- the counterparts and its resources;
- the scope of future co-operation;

- the market, i.e. the other actors and their resources.

Even if the negotiations do not achieve concrete results, the establishing firm and its negotiators will have increased their knowledge. This could be useful in negotiations with other firms in the Soviet market.

Uncertainty

Johanson and Vahlne (1977) argue that the incremental approach to internationaliz-ation decisions is mainly due to lack of market information and the uncertainty occasioned thereby. We have already argued that negotiations have to be seen in a longer perspective and as a step in an establishment process. The models discussed underline the parties' different backgrounds and cultures, but the point is that studies of negotiations have to have a future dimension. Where will the nego-tiations lead? The firms are, or become, conscious about where the negotiations will lead, which probably influences their behaviour. An establishment means a certain degree of seriousness and long-term perspective, which would characterize the first step, the establishing firm's first relationship with another firm in the network. This means that during the negotiations conditions have to be created which ensure that the owner can keep the relationship alive. The recently initiated relationship will not just continue, it will be reinforced and developed, demanding an increasing commitment of resources.

To negotiate joint ventures is to reduce uncertainty. This can be done with legal instruments, but it is hard to define the legal structure without any knowledge about the kind of problems that can occur. Without homogeneous knowledge and context, legal arrangement alone are not enough. It can be anticipated that it will be necessary for the establishing firm to reduce uncertainty to an acceptable level in which the different firms together can run a joint venture which in the longer run will achieve the firms' ambitions. Uncertainty is closely connected to the gradual acquisition and creation of knowledge, and is reduced due to increasing know-ledge. In some cases, for instance in a highly turbulent setting, the uncertainty may arise as a consequence of increased knowledge. To simplify matters, acquired knowledge about technology or the price of a certain good influences both the perceived uncertainty and the firm's ambition. But increased knowledge does not necessarily reduce uncertainty – it can also increase the uncertainty. Without knowledge, the firm does not have any problems. When firms acquire that know-ledge, they are at the same time identifying new problems – the uncertainty grows.

The Case

Viking Raps was formed in July 1989 by the Swedish firm Karlshamns and two Soviet firms, Lipetskpicheprom and Agroprombank. At that time Viking Raps was concerned with equity and the planned production of the biggest joint venture in the Soviet Union. The case study is based on five interviews with Karlshamns' three negotiators; the person responsible for the technical issues (1), the person responsible for the legal and economic issues (2), and the firm's vice-CEO (3).

Karlshamns is Sweden's largest producer of oil and fats for the food industry. The firm also produces margarine, ice-cream, food ingredients, foodstuff and special products for the technical industry. Karlshamns is one of only a few such firms in the world to possess a fractionation plant.

From 1985 to 1989 Karlshamns' turnover increased from 2,042 Mkr to 3,388 Mkr per year, while the number of employees increased from 966 to 1,688. In the mid-1980s it was decided that the firm should give priority to its international operations. The most interesting markets for Karlshamns were USA and the European market. Since then, Karlshamns has made acquisitions and greenfield investments in new firms to strengthen its position in these markets. The strategy for international operations did not take in the Soviet Union, although Karlshamns was aware that conditions there and in the other countries in Eastern Europe were changing. There was therefore no external pressure for Karlshamns to formulate a strategy for these parts of the world:

> It was the other way around. We were strong in Eastern Europe, but saw this as a weakness, since they had a weakly developed food industry, which could mean that in the long run we would not be at the forefront of quality and development of new products. (3)

The aim was instead to transfer resources from Eastern Europe to the USA and the EC – something which Karlshamns went on to do during the second half of the 1980s. Karlshamns' experience of different kinds of co-operation was hitherto limited to an agreement in 1976 about management assistance in Saudi Arabia up to 1995.

Karlshamns had been exporting fats to the Soviet Union – principally cocoa-fat substitutes. The yearly sales on average amounted to the some percentage of total turnover. The size and the organization of the foreign trade system in the Soviet Union had been such as to scare Karlshamns from trying to achieve a dominant position in the market.

The firm has been careful to retain control over production capacity and has tried to avoid becoming dependent on any single large customer. Karlshamns' marketing efforts have consisted of developing and maintaining contacts with the Ministry for Foreign Trade and its foreign trade organizations. Over the years, Karlshamns has organized various kinds of meetings and seminars for Soviet delegations. A few salesmen have been responsible for the Soviet market over the last fifteen to twenty years, but they did not take part in the negotiations.

> The only thing in common was that it happened in the Soviet Union, and there were different people who were responsible for the Viking Raps project and the import. (1)

> But still, the salesmen have been there. They were the background, which meant that we dared to enter into this. (3)

In the Soviet Union, most vegetable oil was produced from sunflower, but it was decided to move these plantations for production of vegetable oils to the north, which would require hardier plants. They searched for new alternatives and chose rape, but they did not have the knowledge or technology to exploit rape for production of oil, margarine or foodstuff for animals. The 1987 five-year plan for the oil- and fat-producing industry included an imported fractionation plant. One of the persons who had produced this plan was Kharitonov, who became the leader for the Soviet negotiators. The plant was intended to come into operation in 1989. Since Viking Raps was formed, Karlshamns has learned about the plan, but during the negotiations they did not know anything. It was the Soviet agriculture attaché in Sweden, who found Karlshamns. He knew that Karlshamns converted huge quantities of rape – in fact, the main part of the Swedish rape harvest. In the summer of 1987, the Soviet ambassador Boris Pankin visited the municipality of Karlshamn and the firm. In November the same year the Minister of Agriculture, Murachovski, was in Sweden and visited other Swedish firms that might be interesting to the Soviet food industry. Karlshamns did not have any great expectations – over the years, many Soviet delegations had visited the firm, without any results, but the Minister was impressed and invited Karlshamns to the Soviet Union. During the following months a lot of strange contacts arose, initiated from the Soviet side. They came direct from Moscow, from the Trade representation and from the Embassy in Stockholm. Karlshamns perceived these contacts as being without any structure or logic, something which irritated the management.

Between Christmas and New Year's Eve 1987 a small group, one engineer and one salesman, responsible for the Soviet market, went to Leningrad in order to market the cocoa-fat substitute and present the firm at a one-day seminar. After Karlshamns' presentation, three men remained in the room. They came from a research and development institute and from the Ministry for agriculture (Gosagroprom) and asked for a minutes of presentation protocol, which Karlshamns gave them. Shortly after, Karlshamns received a request for a fractionation plant, complete with an oil factory plant, which in principle was what the parties later on started to negotiate about.

> The inquiry was pathetic and illogical. The fractionation plant was the diamond in the crown, so we did nothing. (2)

Shortly after this Karlshamns received an angry letter from a Foreign Trade Organization, which had helped to design the request and now demanded an answer. In these first months of 1988, despite these contacts being totally against Karlshamns' internationalization strategy, it was decided to keep the doors open to negotiations. The contacts, still without any structure, went on in the spring of 1988, so Karlshamns decided to invite a delegation directed by the agriculture attaché from the Soviet Embassy to find out what all these contacts meant and what the Soviets were really looking for. They could not give an answer, so Karlshamns asked them to send a new delegation. A delegation of specialists, under the direction of the Deputy Minister of Agriculture, Sjerbak, arrived. From this point on he maintained an interest in the project, occasionally also taking an active part. Besides him, the delegation consisted of three persons, who thereafter took part in the negotiations. Karlshamns presented the firm and its knowledge and the Soviet negotiators became enthusiastic, although they could not understand why Karlshamns was only an oil and fat producer, and not an equipment and machine producer.

Since an establishment in the Soviet Union would not have fitted in with the firm's strategy, the project was discussed intensively at Karlshamns during the first months of 1988. Karlshamns saw a licensing agreement as a possible way of cooperation, but when Karlshamns' negotiators met Murachovski for a one-hour meeting in Moscow in March 1988 he mentioned, for the first time, the idea of forming a joint venture. At this meeting the parties wrote and signed a letter of intent.

> We tried to convince them to do it in another way, but it was clear from their first paper that only a joint venture was of interest to them. It was as important for them as it was for us not to engage ourselves financially. (3)

Besides this requirement, the Soviet party's needs were enormous: they needed knowledge about management, marketing, etc. Karlshamns' technology could also give them a way to produce substitutes for cocoa fats, which was a considerable import expenditure. Karlshamns saw the formation of a joint venture as a possible way of establishing the firm in a new market, which they thought in the long run had enormous potential.

> We had a couple of months to discuss how we should handle this. We saw it as a possibility, but as a possibility with an unusually high risk. We spoke about it as the lottery ticket and how much we were prepared to pay for the lottery ticket. We were conscious that everything can go wrong, but we saw, when we were positive, that the political transformation process had its end, and that it would be replaced by a phase with more or less some kind of market economy. And in that phase ... we saw a huge and very interesting market. (3)

Through Viking Raps, Karlshamns could gain access to raw material, cheap manpower and sites reserved for Viking Raps. Karlshamns determined two needs that should be fulfilled if Karlshamns was to participate in Viking Raps. These concerned the financial risk and how Karlshamns could receive a cash flow in hard currency for its expenditure. In order to minimize the financial risk Karlshamns declared that they should not provide any hard currency for Viking Raps' equity. Karlshamns' contribution should be human capital, i.e. know-how, which would be expressed in terms of hard currency. The parties had very big problems in defining and valuing Karlshamns' know-how. Kharitonov knew very well the value of Karlshamns' know-how, but insisted throughout the negotiations that Karlshamns would have to provide hard currency. This question was discussed for a very long time until the Soviet party agreed to accept that Karlshamns' contribution should be in the form of human capital. Besides these two needs, Karlshamns tried to be open and avoid locking themselves up with certain demands.

When the negotiations in March 1988 entered a new phase, Karlshamns formed a new project group with three members; one responsible for technological matters, one for economic questions, and the firm's vice-CEO. The latter worked with the project mainly when they visited the Soviet Union and reported to the board of directors. The member who was responsible for economic questions had participated in the group earlier in Leningrad just after Christmas 1987, but then as an engineer. He had previously worked in other complicated projects, for instance to help with the plant in Saudi Arabia. He followed the Viking Raps project from the first unstructured contacts. The technology manager was former head of the maintenance division, which had given an insight in most of the firm's different production sides. He had expressed a wish to do something else, so after a short period with the know-how selling department he joined the Viking Raps project. None of these three had any experience connected with the Soviet Union. When certain details concerning technology or production were discussed, relevant specialists occasionally turned up. The members of the project group saw

Karlshamns as a complete firm, which had a lot to offer the Soviet party; the know-how was mainly on the process side but the firm also had a broad product line, well organized R&D and a strong position on environmental issues. The project was closely followed by the firm's board of directors, who became involved during negotiations concerning important issues. No conflicts or disputes occurred about the general outlines.

Three weeks after the letter of intent was signed, two big groups, from both sides, met to confirm details and to decide the direction for the further work. For the first time a lawyer joined the group. Like the others, he had no former experience of work in the Soviet Union, but following this meeting he actively took part in the project. During the meeting Karlshamns undertook to prepare a pre-feasibility study. This became a base document, to which both parties continuously referred during the negotiations. Preparing the document also gave Karlshamns the initiative, which they wanted in order to be able to control the progress of negotiations. Karlshamns understood that it was necessary to have some structure for the work and one of their negotiators found a publication from UNIDO which contained a description of how a feasibility study is prepared. It was available in Russian, which the Soviet negotiators appreciated. They accepted to use it.

At this point the place for and the capacity of the future Viking Raps were still unknown to Karlshamns, but since the plant was planned to use rape, the parties started to find out how much rape would be placed at Viking Rap's disposal. Thereafter the parties planned a plant with all the different processes on a yearly supply of 300,000 tonnes of rape. When this was done the parties once again studied the supply of rape in Lipetsk and other areas. And then after half a year of negotiations the Soviets suddenly mentioned that they had to plan for the use of alternative sources of vegetable oil too. First they did not want to explain why, but after some time they explained that the harvest had not gone to plan and probably would not. Thus the quantities on which the parties had done their calculations could not be expected to be placed at Viking Raps' disposal. To keep the capacity of Viking Raps' plant they even planned for the use of sunflower oil, something which Karlshamns did not appreciate at all, since they saw themselves mainly as a user of rape. But Karlshamns had to adapt and accept.

> Probably we will be talking about 150,000 tonnes of sunflower and 210,000 tonnes of rape, but I have a definite, unpleasant feeling, with the information I have today, that it will be 200,000 tonnes of sunflower and maybe 100,000 tonnes of rape, at best, during the first years. (1)

During all the negotiations, issues concerning raw materials and supplementary materials were intensively discussed. The parties had different opinions about the detail of the contract. The Soviet negotiators wanted to have a flexible contract, since everything was available and should be supplied in the agreed quantities and satisfactory qualities. Guarantees would not be necessary. But to Karlshamns it was important that the contract should include guarantees, so that it would be possible to liquidate Viking Raps if certain conditions were not fulfilled. Even the raw material pricing system used in the Soviet Union was discussed. The system would not be advantageous at all for Viking Raps. Karlshamns spent much time trying to convince the Soviet party that the system had to be changed, but the Soviet party defended the system. In the end they agreed to fix the prices of raw materials at certain levels.

Their system meant that Viking Raps would pay more for the rape it buys from the kolchoz or farmer than it would get for its output. This was due to the Soviet system of farm subsidies. This system would not give Viking Raps any profit at all. (1)

Karlshamns received samples of raw materials, which to some extent were of satisfactory quality, and quality guarantees were included in the contract, giving Viking Raps the right to send back raw materials which fell below the agreed quality. Karlshamns also demanded and got prices on various supplemental material. Karlshamns also got samples of certain key chemicals, which were tested in the laboratory. Based on these tests, contract quantities and qualities could be determined. All resources supplied from the Soviet market should be paid for in roubles at the world market price. To keep the hard currency expenses as low as possible, the parties agreed on a common ambition to become independent of imports within five years. A lot of products, necessary for quality of the production, would have to be imported in the beginning.

When the first contacts were established with Karlshamns, it was the Soviet Ministry of Agriculture, Gosagroprom, which was responsible for the project, but on May 1, 1988 there was a reorganization of agriculture: the Ministry closed down and responsibility for the negotiations was decentralized to the Russian Republic's Ministry of Agriculture. The leader of the Soviet negotiation group, Kharitonov, came from the Allunion Ministry and was responsible for the vegetable oil industry. After the reorganization he was left in the air for a while, but eventually was given the task of finalizing the negotiations; later he became Viking Raps' first CEO. The reorganization did not mean so much to Karlshamns. No negotiators were replaced; they came from the Ministries but also from Lipetskpicheprom, Agroprombank and from GIP-3, the institute for constructions for the food industry. In all, twenty to twenty-five Soviet negotiators took part, of whom seven or eight formed the core group.

It quickly became clear that the Russian Republic's Ministry for Agriculture would not be owner of Viking Raps, but Lipetskpicheprom and Agroprombank. Lipetskpicheprom ran factories for the production of sugar, chocolate and bread, butcheries and industries for refining of berries and fruit. It was also owner in a joint venture producing apple and carrot juice and packing citrus juices. At that time, Lipetskpicheprom produced no vegetable fats or oils. The firm's turnover for 1988 was 400 million roubles. When Karlshamns heard about the Soviet plans for Viking Raps they immediately expressed a wish to anchor the project locally, so the vice-chairman in Lipetskpicheprom, Assarenko, began to take part in the negotiations. After Viking Raps was formed he became the joint venture's first chairman of the board. Agroprombank became the second Soviet owner in Viking Raps. It was the bank for the agriculture branch and had previously served mainly kolchozes and sovchozes. Gradually the bank had began to engage itself in the Soviet food industry. An economist, Tjimanski, represented Agroprombank, taking part from time to time in the negotiations, but moved to other work some months before Viking Raps was formed. He had worked in the West and Karlshamns' negotiators believed that he had quite a good economics knowledge. Apart from Tjimanski, the Soviets and Karlshamns' negotiators had two different ways of looking at the economic issues. The parties used different concepts, so the negotiations had more the character of education than of discussion:

We have given so many lectures in economics, it is incredible. It is not correct to call it negotiations in Moscow. Half of them were deliberation and discussion and the other half lectures – pure education. We were sitting and making our first calculation. I brought my pocket calculator. '-Ahh, kampjuuter!', Kharitonov exclaims when he saw it. Then we had to simplify the calculation to just five products, so it comprised ten lines. We worked for two days until he understood its function – he was a former director of a huge factory. But none of them had any knowledge in economics and accounting. They looked upon the means for investment as something you get from daddy and then just let disappear. In short, they did not care about economy. (2)

Besides their problems in understanding a market economy they had great problems in producing or acquiring any information. Karlshamns asked for economic information about the Soviet organizations, but they could not give any.

> They were open to the extent that they had knowledge and concepts. I did not meet any hush-hush, but I met an inability to get information, which was extremely irritating. (2)

> It was difficult to get information – information that was important for driving this project forward. (1)

The Soviet Union's increasingly severe economic problems, which could have meant that Viking Raps would have had to pay for the supply in hard currency, even though this should not have been necessary according to the agreement, were not discussed during the negotiations.

> It was a problem which we were conscious of, but it was not considered in the agreement. If the expenses in hard currency had increased 20 per cent, we would not have had any guarantees. (2)

Another important problem to solve for Karlshamns was how to receive hard currency. Export became a necessary condition for Viking Raps' survival. The Soviet party had no special wishes about the export destination and export quantities. During the negotiations Karlshamns conducted market research about oil price development during recent years and a prediction for the coming years. This study formed the basis for the calculations in the feasibility study. The export would consist of raw sunflower and rape oil and would be managed by Karlshamns' trading division. In order to avoid competition with itself, Karlshamns excluded export of final products, which the Soviet party accepted. The exports would not be confined to special markets, and were planned to be at a level of 30,000 tonnes of oil.

> Viking Raps would just export raw oil, which was only extracted from the seed. There existed so many millions of tonnes in the world market that these tonnes would not matter. (3)

One related problem was the Soviets' lack of will to motivate and argue for their decisions, which made it difficult for Karlshamns to take measures. The Soviet negotiators' deficient ability to acquire information meant that a lot of questions were never resolved. Karlshamns tried, together with the Soviet party, to solve problems concerning logistics, distribution and different kinds of supply, but without any success. According to the agreement the Soviet party had the responsibility to guarantee provision of telex, telefax and telephone communications, making it possible for Viking Raps to communicate with the world around. Karlshamns would not have to involve itself in the distribution of raw materials or equipment in the Soviet Union.

We knew exactly how everything should be designed. The Russians accepted it by signing the contract, but unfortunately they did not understand. (1)

Probably, we will have to engage ourselves in logistic and distribution. There are thousands of problems which we have not sorted out yet. We have bad basic information about everything that surrounds Viking Raps and which we cannot control, such as infrastructure and different kinds of supply. (2)

In the beginning the parties negotiated at the Soviet Gosagroprom's office in Moscow, which Karlshamns considered very inefficient. Karlshamns took the initiative of moving the negotiations to KF Procordia's office in Moscow. KF Procordia markets among other things KF's products in the former Soviet Union. In the office all modern aids were available and it was possible to order food and have it served in the office. Karlshamns soon understood that the structure of the work would have to be changed. Karlshamns' negotiators wanted to work in small groups with different problems, while the Soviets worked in a more hierarchical way, which meant that all problems and questions had to pass Kharitonov. He wanted to have control of everything and did not delegate tasks to the other negotiators, so they were passive and had no authority to make decisions. Karlshamns tried to change the Soviet way of negotiations, they tried to break down the work and allocate it to different groups, so that lawyers could speak with lawyers and engineers with engineers. Not until having negotiated half a year did they meet some sympathy but Kharitonov continued to dominate the Soviet negotiators.

Few of the Soviet negotiators had any experience of other countries than the Soviet Union. Only some of the seven, who had been in Sweden in April 1989, had been abroad. This lack of experience meant that they behaved rather clumsily in Karlshamns' eyes. Their knowledge of foreign languages was poor – only one of the negotiators spoke English, making the parties dependent on using an interpreter.

This was definitely most difficult, always having to use an interpreter. It is impossible to exaggerate the problem of using an interpreter. (3)

The lack of a common language could be the reason why the parties seldom communicated between the meetings. Another reason was the poor infrastructure in the Soviet Union, which made it impossible to communicate with Lipetsk. After a while the Soviet negotiators started to use KF Procordia's office as their centre for communication.

It was very frustrating, we could not use the phone without problems. The Ministry for agriculture did not have telex, so we could not communicate directly with them. (2)

In the beginning of the summer of 1988, (1) and (2) visited Lipetsk for the first time. They were well received and the picture of Lipetsk and the conditions for Viking Raps corresponded to what the Soviet negotiators had promised, although they did not check out the rape plantation.

For me it was interesting just to look around in the town, the environment and the landscape. They showed us four alternative sites which were planned for Viking Raps. The reception was more open and efficient than what we were used to from Moscow. (1)

The Soviet negotiators had a generally good knowledge of technology, although

Karlshamns thought that they had had few opportunities to convert their theoretical knowledge into practice. Even so, the negotiations over technology took a long time. Although there were no big disputes or differences of opinion, for (2) it was the most problematic issue. The parties had different ways of working these problems through. Karlshamns' negotiators understood after some time that the Soviet negotiators had problems in working with large issues and details at the same time and in the end counting the money. Instead they dived into matters of detail, without an overall perspective.

From the beginning of autumn 1988 the parties began to negotiate the contract. The Soviet party expressed a wish that a substantial part of Viking Raps' equipment should be Soviet, so Karlshamns asked the Soviet party if it would be possible to visit Soviet plants for production of oils and fats. The purpose was to study the level of the technology and the kind of equipment they used. Late in autumn 1988 Karlshamns made a study tour and visited a handful of plants. They went to Armavir and Krasnodar, which was the Soviet centre for production of vegetable oils. As in Lipetsk, Karlshamns was received with considerable openness when they visited institutes and firms. In Krasnodar they went to a research institute, where they met theoretically very competent personnel.

> It was a very important trip for me and for the feasibility study. During this trip we could see with our own eyes and decide which equipment could be Soviet. (1)

Equipment which was not critical for the quality of the future output, could be of Soviet origin, but if the plant was to produce to the same quality as in Sweden, the equipment would have to be imported. If this could not be the case, Karlshamns would leave Viking Raps. Later on the parties agreed that the quality of the output should be the same as in Sweden.

In Krasnodar, Kharitonov mentioned for the first time that they were conducting parallel negotiations with competitors to Karlshamns. Subsequently the Soviet party sometimes mentioned the competitor's proposals in order to put pressure on Karlshamns. On the whole this occurred when the parties negotiated costs; on one occasion they even showed one of the competitor's calculations. The Soviet negotiators used the competitors without mentioning them by name, but Karlshamns never felt threatened. Instead they thought it was interesting to see the presented calculations as alternative ways to go.

During the winter of 1988–9 and the spring of 1989 the parties continued to meet in Moscow. The work proceeded slowly, bit by bit; problems were solved, while an agreement became more and more structured and the feasibility study began to take more definite shape.

In April 1989 a Soviet delegation visited Karlshamns. The negotiations had then reached a point at which the last parts of the agreement and the production volumes could be discussed. On home ground, Karlshamns could press the Soviet party and have the initiative. The parties had an intensive week, when a lot of questions were addressed; the week was much appreciated by the Soviet party, and they were confirmed in their choice of collaborator. Around two months before the contract was signed, the first version of the feasibility study was finished. It was slightly revised, before it was attached as an appendix to the contract, which was closed in the beginning of July 1989.

> We do not stand or fall with the Soviet Union. This is totally beside budgets and plans.

We do not build our company's future on success in this project – it is a qualified market research. We will be pleased if this project in cash flow can pay back in ten years. During the nineties we will have to fight to make debit and credit meet. (2)

Analysis

How the negotiations began

Karlshamns' ambitions in the former Soviet market were initially modest. However, the Soviet organizations succeeded in their efforts to interest Karlshamns, although Karlshamns' knowledge about the future activities and about the market were limited. Over a long period Karlshamns' main activity was to try to acquire information about the Soviet organizations' purposes, which proved difficult. Karlshamns were quite frustrated and perceived a high degree of uncertainty about what was going on.

When Karlshamns learned that the Soviets' ambition was to form a joint venture, they had to discuss the idea very carefully. It was against Karlshamns' policy, since it should take place in a new and non-priority market and should consist of operations and the transfer of know-how, of which Karlshamns had no experience. However, they adapted their ambitions – they found they could consider taking part in a joint venture in the former Soviet Union. But, since the situation there was unstable, and Karlshamns' knowledge and experience of the market were so limited, Karlshamns perceived a high degree of uncertainty. They thought they could reduce this by satisfying two particular needs during the negotiations, which they defined as minimizing the financial risk, by contributing to the joint venture human capital only and no hard currency, and by creating conditions that could guarantee Karlshamns compensation for their expenditure under certain circumstances.

Karlshamns tries to acquire information

When Karlshamns had defined their two needs, they realized that they had to work out a feasibility study together with the Soviet party. In order to work out a feasibility study Karlshamns had to acquire information about the Soviet party and the Soviet market; they had to give information about themselves as well. The result of the work, the feasibility study, would provide knowledge about the future co-operation, the joint venture's organization and operations.

In general, the Soviet negotiators were used to working in another way to Karlshamns. They looked upon and used information differently. Karlshamns had big problems in acquiring economic information about conditions in the Soviet market. Karlshamns never acquired information about the rape suppliers, about logistics or about the Soviet distribution system.

The parties exchanged samples of different goods, giving Karlshamns an opportunity to learn what it would be possible to purchase in the Soviet market. First Karlshamns' negotiators did not know where the Soviet negotiators intended to site Viking Raps, but after some months of negotiations the Soviets declared that

Lipetsk would be the place. In the beginning of the summer of 1988 Karlshamns visited Lipetsk, where they were well received. Karlshamns' negotiators also visited some other plants in the former Soviet Union, giving them a good picture of the Soviet oil and fat industry.

The value of the feasibility study

Early on, the parties understood that they could not just negotiate by telephone or telex. They had to meet. The Soviets lacked experience of working and socializing with foreigners. The negotiators had no common language. This made negotiations difficult.

During the work on the feasibility study, Karlshamns learned that the Soviets' level of economic knowledge was poor. Or to put it another way, their knowledge differed from Karlshamns' way of thinking about economic matters. To a large extent it was because of the Soviets' poor knowledge that it was so difficult to discuss all the economic questions. For example, the Soviets were unable to understand why Karlshamns did not want to provide any hard currency.

Probably the most essential thing Karlshamns learned about the Soviets during the negotiations was their inability to deal with all kinds of information. The Soviets had no access to economic information about their own organizations, even though this was important for the feasibility study and the project. But Karlshamns did not have the impression that the Soviets tried to hide anything from Karlshamns. This inability irritated Karlshamns, since it meant that they could get no answers to a lot of questions concerning the project.

The Soviets worked more hierarchically than Karlshamns – their chief negotiator, Kharitonov, tried to control every step, which disturbed Karlshamns' negotiators. Furthermore, the Soviets had a tendency to concentrate on matters of detail, lacking a holistic view and returning to issues that the parties had solved long ago. Also, the Soviets were poor in terms of explaining their decisions and the information they gave, as when they told Karlshamns that the planned quantity of rape oil would never be available, without saying why or how.

All these points taken together gave Karlshamns knowledge about the Soviets' ways of working and their abilities. To some extent it also gave Karlshamns knowledge about the Soviet market and what a foreign firm can encounter.

The growth of knowledge – and uncertainty

The Soviet negotiators' lack of information and their inability to acquire information meant that many questions were never answered. Karlshamns were left in a position of poor knowledge about how the logistic and distribution would function. According to the contract, the Soviet parties are responsible for these questions, but that does not mean that Karlshamns' perceived sense of uncertainty is reduced.

Suddenly, during the negotiations, the Soviet negotiators told Karlshamns that the production of rape had failed to follow the plans – something that increased the perceived degree of uncertainty. The parties had to make plans to use alternative sources of vegetable oil. This event illustrated to Karlshamns that similar events could be expected to happen in the future. The price system used for rape in the former Soviet Union created a high level of uncertainty as well, since there was the potential for it to be impossible for Viking Raps to make a profit. But Karlshamns managed to modify the system, and by achieving two principal needs, Karlshamns were able to reduce the uncertainty to a level that they considered acceptable.

References

Aslund, A. (1989) *Gorbachev's Struggle for Economic Reforms*, London: Pinter Publishers.

Fayerweather, J. (1976) *Strategy and Negotiation for International Corporation*, Cambridge, Mass.: Ballinger Publishing Company.

Ghauri, P. (1983) 'Negotiating international package deals', *Acta Universitatis Studia Oeconomiae Negotiorum*, Uppsala.

Hammarkvist, K-O., Håkansson, H. and Mattsson, L-G. (1982) *Marknadsföring för konkurrenskraft*, Malmö: Liber.

Håkansson, H. (ed.) (1982) *International Marketing and Purchasing of Industrial Goods – An Interaction Approach*, Chichester: John Wiley.

Håkansson, H. and Snehota, I. (1989) 'No Business is an Island', *Scandinavian Journal of Management* 5(3): 187–200.

Johanson, J. and Vahlne, J-E. (1977) 'The Internationalization Process of the Firm – A Model of Knowledge Development and Increasing Foreign Market Commitment', *Journal of International Business Studies* 8, Spring/Summer: 23–32.

Molnàr, J., Nilsson Molnàr, M. and Alvstam, C. G. (1984) *Handla med öststaterna*, Stockholm: P. A. Norstedt & Söners förlag.

McCall, J. B. and Warrington, M. B. (1989) *Marketing by Agreement. A Cross-Cultural Approach to Business Negotiations*, Chichester: John Wiley.

Nieminen, J. (1990) 'The route of Finnish Firms to joint venture in the Soviet Union', paper presented at the conference for East European Studies in Uppsala, November 23–5.

Snehota, I. (1990) *Notes on a Theory of Business Enterprise*, Uppsala University.

Yin, R. K. (1989) *Case Study research: Design and Methods*, Newsbury Park, Cal.: Sage Publishers.

8

Creating International Joint Ventures: Strategic Insights from Case Research on a Successful Hungarian–Japanese Industrial Enterprise

Arch G. Woodside and Piroska Somogyi

Introduction

The primary concern in this paper is to report on why and how the most successful existing Hungarian–Japanese joint venture was initiated, designed and implemented, and to suggest several tentative strategic management implications from the analysis.

Several theoretical propositions are examined for exploring joint venture behaviour and motivations, based on in-depth observations of real-life decision processes. The propositions are based on the works of Kogut (1988), Ohmae (1989), Bjorkman (1989), and Woodside and Kandiko (1990).

Theoretical Perspectives

The study is focused on the 'realized strategies' (Mintzberg 1979) of joint venture idea generation, design, and implementation – that is, the strategies that actually occur in the streams of decisions, interactions and behaviour of persons when committing organizations to an action. For the project, a decision is defined as a 'specific commitment to action' (cf. Mintzberg, Raisighani and Theoret 1976).

Initiating the need or opportunity for a decision, acquiring relevant information for making a commitment, processing the information, evaluating alternatives, and

The funding support provided by Tulane University, USA, and the International Management Centre, Hungary, for the research reported in this chapter is acknowledged with appreciation.

making a commitment have been identified as phases in decision processes (Howard, Hulbert and Farley 1972; Mintzberg, Raisighani and Theoret 1976; Mintzberg 1979).

Two key empirical findings on decision process phases are particularly useful for theory development and for planning research on IJV designs. First, specific phases in decision processes can be identified and described, although these phases rarely follow a planned sequence (from problem formulation, a search for alternative solutions, evaluation, choice, and implementation). Second, organizational decision processes are complex and dynamic, with iterative steps permitting all phases to be observed in every time unit occurring during the process. Related to these two points, Mintzberg, Raisighani and Theoret (1976) concluded: 'we find logic in delineating distinct phases of the strategic decision process, but not in postulating a simple sequential relationship between them.'

Mintzberg, Raisighani and Theoret (1976)
These authors suggest that decisions may be categorized by the stimuli that evoked them, along a continuum. At one extreme are opportunity decisions, initiated on a purely voluntary basis to improve an already secure situation, such as the introduction of a new product to enlarge an already secure market share. At the other extreme are crisis decisions, where organizations respond to intense pressures. Here a severe situation demands immediate action – for instance, seeking a merger to stave off bankruptcy. Thus, opportunity and crisis decisions may be considered as forming the two ends of the continuum. Problem decisions may be defined as those that fall in between, being evoked by milder pressures than crisis. Crisis decisions are typically triggered by single stimuli. They present themselves suddenly and unequivocally, and require immediate attention, as in the cases, for example, of a fire or a bankruptcy. Problem decisions typically require multiple stimuli. Decision-makers, presumably, wish to learn as much as possible about the situation before taking action.

Kogut (1988)
Kogut proposes three theories on the motivation of joint ventures, from the perspectives of transaction costs, strategic behaviour and organizational learning. The transaction cost approach suggests that the firm chooses to transact according to the criterion of minimizing the sum of production and transaction costs. Strategic behaviour posits that firms transact by the mode which maximizes profits through improving a firm's competitive position *vis-à-vis* rivals. These two theories are often complementary.

For small innovations a joint venture may be an effective mechanism for deterring the entry of other enterprises. More generally, joint ventures are a form of defensive investment, by means of which firms hedge against strategic uncertainties, especially in industries of moderate concentration where collusion is difficult to achieve despite the benefits of co-ordinating the interdependence among firms.

An organizational learning perspective of joint ventures views joint ventures as a means by which firms learn or seek to retain their capabilities. In this perspective a joint venture is encouraged if neither party owns each other's technology, nor understands each other's routines. Thus the form of joint venture is a vehicle by which organizational knowledge is exchanged and imitated.

Kogut goes on to suggest that transaction cost and organizational learning explanations involve microanalytical details which are difficult to acquire. For this reason, he implies, case studies will be the most appealing methodology to provide information and insight. Thus, it should be expected that the theories and their derived hypotheses will fare differently, depending on contextual factors and the type of research questions being pursued.

Ohmae (1989)

The equity share held by the foreign partners depends, Ohmae implies, on the strategic management orientation of the foreign partner. He advocates a 'shared management' approach, on the basis that having more direct control does not necessarily mean better management. One can buy a company's equity, but cannot buy the mind or the spirit or the initiative or the devotion of its people. Treat the collaboration as a personal commitment – it's people that make partnership work.

Horst (1972)

Horst suggests that in order to reflect the complexity and dynamic nature of the foreign investment processes, in-depth studies are needed. He also found that import barriers are an important enticement in effective FDI.

Dale (1988)

With the increased debt of the LDCs, with the disappearance of voluntary commercial bank lending in the early 1980s, and with the increased risk of excessive foreign borrowing, Horst emphasizes the changed situation of the developing countries, which are now more interested in attracting direct investment. In many cases the use of joint ventures is a response to governmental regulations.

Borensztein (1989)

Borensztein describes the unfavourable effect of huge external debt on investment in the debtor country and suggests that under these circumstances the probability of seeking joint foreign direct investment by the domestic firms in the debtor country is substantially increased.

Mintzberg (1979)

This author advocates using the strategy of 'direct research' for phenomena that are complex and dynamic in nature (e.g. the functioning of organizations, including decision making). 'Direct research' is the gathering of data on description and induction by relying on simple methodologies. Measurements are taken of many elements in real organizational terms. Induction is used to synthesize many diverse elements into configurations of ideal or pure types.

Bonoma (1985)

Bonoma also asserts that 'many interesting phenomena cannot be understood if removed from their social context.' There are identifiable sets of research situations where qualitative, in-depth inductive approaches are desirable, even if accompanied by some risks to data integrity. In particular, they are useful when a phenomenon is broad, complex, where the existing body of knowledge is insufficient to permit the posing of detailed questions, and when a phenomenon cannot be studied outside its natural context. The problem/opportunity recognition, design, and implementation of joint ventures exemplify such natural context phenomena.

Decision system analysis (DSA) (cf. Howard, Hulbert and Farley 1972) was used to collect the data for the study. The DSA research procedure is a means of systematically developing flow-charted descriptions of the decision processes in designing and implementing the joint venture. After initial contact, three waves of interviewing are used to develop, verify and validate the flow-charts. The decision processes reported to be used by the participants in the joint venture are also verified by an analysis of available documents related directly to the design and implementation of the joint venture. The initial interviews included a detailed questionnaire.

In using DSA, after the open-ended semi-structured initial interviews, protocols and individual flow-charts of decision processes are prepared. In follow-up interviews these flow diagrams are shown to the managers initially interviewed to learn additional details and make corrections. After completing the suggested revisions, the flow-charts are shown again to the managers in a third round of interviews, as well as being shown to new respondents who occupy positions equivalent to those respondents in the original sample.

This third round of validating interviews was done and the results are reported in this chapter. The third round involves interviewing two additional managers (one of whom did not participate in the first two rounds, but who was involved in the creation of the Hungarian–Japanese joint venture and who is the representative of the Japanese partner). This interview was to be conducted by telephone and based on the flow-chart of decision-making process previously sent by mail to the interviewee.

Survey Instrument

The survey form included the following question:

1. When was the first contact made to discuss the idea of the joint venture?
2. When was the first joint venture agreement signed by the participating organizations?
3. When was the joint venture registered with the Hungarian government?
4. When did production start-up occur?
5. When did the first domestic and export sales occur?
6. When, if ever, did the joint venture first result in a profitable return to the joint venture partners?

Questions concerning the phases in the decision-making process and the activities and interactions of persons included the following topics:

1. Who first brought up the idea of forming the joint venture?
2. What were the events and reasons that led to the idea of forming an IJV?
3. What was decided at the time of the initial contact by the different organizations participating in the meeting?

4. What information was sought, if any, before and after the first meeting among participants?
5. Who specifically was involved in the first contact and meetings?
6. What information was learned, if any, while considering the idea of the IJV among the participating organizations?
7. What additional meetings were held during discussions about forming the IJV, who attended each of these meetings, and what were the outcomes of each of these meetings?
8. What other IJVs or other forms of international business relationships were considered, if any, before or during the discussions about the specific joint venture;
9. Was some type of process used to compare IJV alternatives? If yes, describe the process;
10. What equity share goal was sought by each participant in the IJV, and why did each participant seek this particular equity share?
11. How, why, and what specific equity shares were agreed among the participants?
12. What facilitating organizations (e.g. legal, banking, trading companies, transportation, and government) assisted in the design and creation of the IJV?
13. What organizations design was desired by each organization participating in the IJV?
14. What organization design was decided upon for the IJV, and how was the decision made?
15. What surprise or unplanned events occurred during the discussions leading to the IJV, and how did these events affect the design of the IJV?
16. What products, target markets and marketing strategies were discussed for the IJV, and what decisions were made about these issues?

Implementation questions in the survey included the following topics:

1. What suppliers are being used and what supply problems are being experienced, if any?
2. What products are being manufactured and what manufacturing problems are being experienced, if any?
3. What domestic and export marketing channels are being used?
4. Who are the senior managers, what organizations forming the IJV are represented by the senior managers, and how are the senior managers compensated?
5. How are the employees in the IJV organized and compensated?
6. What sales and profit levels are being achieved by the IJV in domestic export markets?

Results

PoliFoam was the first Japanese–Hungarian joint venture to operate in Hungary. The company's activity involves the manufacturing and marketing of polyethylene foam products, which are used as insulation materials in construction, as packaging material, shoe accessories, and as leisure and sports goods such as camping mats and swimming boards. PoliFoam was established in 1984 and started production in 1986.

Phase 1: Solution-opportunity identification

The steps in the first phase of the decision-making process are depicted in Figs 8.1 and 8.2, and summarized below. The two enterprises most involved in the decision process were Pannonplast in Hungary and Furukawa in Japan. Answers to the questions, who first brought up the idea of forming the joint venture, and what were the events and reasons that led to the idea of forming an IJV, are summarized below.

In 1981 the CEO of Pannonplast made a business trip to Japan and saw the polyethylene foam product, which she thought was a suitable product for her company's product development strategy.

After returning to Hungary she assigned a young engineer in the R&D department to research the possibilities of manufacturing and marketing polyethylene foam products in Hungary, giving a deadline of December 1982.

The following steps were taken. Because of the lack of technical knowledge about polyethylene foam, an intensive literature research was started regarding the product features and its application. An intensive patent search was conducted to get information about the technology and to develop the list of potential licensors among which was the Japanese firm visited in 1981. Based upon the product feature, market research for defining rough demand and potential field of application was conducted.

Based upon product feature and patent research, requests for quotations for supplying the technology and related machinery were solicited. Quotations were received from the USA (1), Japan (3), and Italy (1) and were evaluated using conjunctive and weighted compensatory heuristics. Criteria chosen included the level of technology, including environmental pollution aspects, range of product size, completeness of technology and machinery, willingness to offer technical assistance in starting up production and product application, technical level of equipment (automation), price, extent of applicability of the product, and willingness to test Hungarian raw materials before signature of any contract.

After the first round of evaluation the US, Italian, and one Japanese firm remained on the roster. (The other two Japanese firms failed to qualify because one did not want to test Hungarian raw materials and the second was not ready to deliver technical assistance.) Both of these factors were crucial, given that the product and technology were brand new in Hungary, and Pannonplast did not have any experience in producing and marketing them.

Number one in the ranking was Furukawa. The offered technologies were diverse, and the price range was wide – from $0.5 million to $5 million.

The first meetings with the Italian and the Japanese representatives were in Hungary, in the autumn of 1982. The CEO of Pannonplast and engineers also visited the US company in 1982. During the meetings with the three companies, technical negotiations were carried out and the willingness to form a joint venture was solicited from the US and the Italian firms. Both were interested.

The Hungarian partner (Pannonplast) mentioned several obvious reasons for the joint venture: because Hungary's hard currency deficit ($10 billion at that time) was enormous, it would have been practically impossible to get an import licence for the machinery and the production licence. Although joint ventures had been allowed since 1972, only a handful of them existed in 1981. Nor was 100 per cent foreign ownership possible.

To establish a joint venture could represent a kind of niche, providing a great opportunity for PR exposure. There were no other Japanese–Hungarian joint ventures at that time, although joint ventures with American and Italian partners already existed. The opportunities for organizational knowledge and learning greatly reduced the risk of failure of the product in the Hungarian market.

In January 1983 representatives of Pannonplast (after extensive telex and mail contacts, and visits by Japanese executives to Pannonplast) approached Furukawa with a very cautious suggestion for a joint venture. They outlined several options for potential Hungarian participants, including commercial banks. The negotiations from the Japanese side were led by the export department manager of the Plastic Division. The Japanese were non-committal, but expressed a willingness to study the proposals.

Meanwhile the US and the Italian contacts were also developed. However, the Japanese were the favoured partner, having submitted a more competitive quotation, and because of the Pannonplast CEO's personal commitment to the idea of establishing the first Japanese–Hungarian joint venture in Eastern and Central Europe. (The CEO, who was a woman, saw it as something of a personal challenge to bring the conservative Japanese company into a joint venture agreement.)

After daily discussions about arrangements for establishing joint ventures in Hungary, the next meeting took place in June 1983. The Japanese export manager visited Pannonplast and the outcome of the meeting was a declaration of intent to formally evaluate the joint venture proposal, if the joint feasibility study provided favourable.

Summarizing the reasons for a joint venture, on the Hungarian side:

1. Technical manufacturing know-how paried with ongoing follow-up learning of managerial skill and systems (e.g. production control, management planning system, management information system, incentive system).
2. The necessity of considering a form of international co-operation other than simple export-import transaction, because of Hungary's large BOP deficit and the country's restrictive foreign trade policy, which would have thwarted the import of a $2.3 million manufacturing facility.
3. The personal values and ambitions of the Hungarian CEO.
4. Taking advantage of the emerging fashion in Hungary for FDI in the form of joint ventures.

For the Japanese side (revealed by the third round of interviews) the advantages of the arrangement were as follows:

1. Joint venture was practically the only way of exporting the machinery and technology to Hungary (Furukawa, the joint venture partner, was the machine supplier).
2. The opportunity of entering the European market with the foam product, which otherwise would have had a high transportation cost.

3. Access to new markets.
4. Another motivation stemming from strategic consideration for Furukawa to enter a joint venture agreement was the fact that at the time the JV agreement was being negotiated, another license agreement for the same technology was expiring. This agreement had prevented production and sales of products in Europe under license. Thus the new license agreement with the Hungarian firm would end the absence of Furukawa products in Europe.

Although there are certain elements in the decision process which imply pressure to move towards a joint venture agreement, the depicted decision process implies that from the standpoint of stimuli, the Japanese–Hungarian joint venture is rather a problem decision closer to opportunity decision than a crisis decision. The presence of multiple stimuli suggested by Mintzberg, Raisighani and Theoret (1976) also underpins the problem decision, for which only one solution emerged from the design process. Although Pannonplast solicited and evaluated a number of offers, judgement seems to have been a favoured mode of selection.

Phase 2: Evaluation

The evaluation phase is summarized in Fig. 8.3. Furukawa and C.Itoh have a total of 14 per cent equity in the joint venture. One of the explanations of this small ratio is given by Ohmae (1989) as a theoretical comment on the dangers of equity. Furukawa's low share ratio is also to be explained by the company's original intention to export directly. Although this intention was thwarted by the Hungarian foreign trade policy regulations, Furukawa was anxious to reduce their exposure to risk in the joint venture. In 1984 Hungary had not yet started its policy of political and economic reform. Furukawa was the first Japanese company to enter into a joint venture agreement in Hungary, a socialist CPE. The perceived risk was obviously high.

The Hungarian partner wanted the Japanese to have higher equity share originally, but because the Japanese tied this decision to other criteria (test run performance, guarantees) which were also important to the Hungarian partner, Pannonplast accepted the low equity ratio.

The commercial banks were included because, unlike Pannonplast, they had experience in designing joint ventures and in getting through the approval procedure.

The evaluation of the IJV proposal by Furukawa took place before the 1989 IJV law. Thus, Furukawa sought and gained assurance from the Hungarian government in 1984 that Furukawa's profit could be repatriated in hard currency.

At one point (March 1984) during the discussions, when the price of the machinery and know-how supplied by Furukawa was being negotiated, the idea of a joint venture was almost abandoned. The Hungarian partner pushed so hard and argued vehemently against the technical level of the machinery that the Japanese stood up and left. The process was interrupted.

The negotiations after two months returned to a previous phase at which the content of the know-how and the equipment were discussed. The Japanese were ready to add more in content, rather than reducing the price. They also relaxed earlier export restrictions.

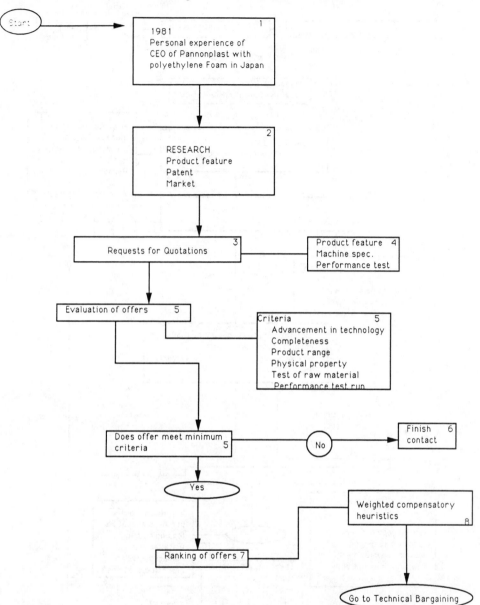

Fig. 8.1. Solution-opportunity identification.

Mintzberg (1979) implies that solutions may be rejected in evaluation choice as having too low a pay-off; they may encounter constraints they cannot satisfy; they may simply not appeal to those expected to authorize them. Organizations faced with failure in finding or designing an acceptable solution may return to an earlier point in the development phase. In some cases a previously rejected alternative is reintroduced under new conditions. If resources will not permit a new solution, or if a decision maker meets with continued failure, a previously unacceptable solution may be accepted.

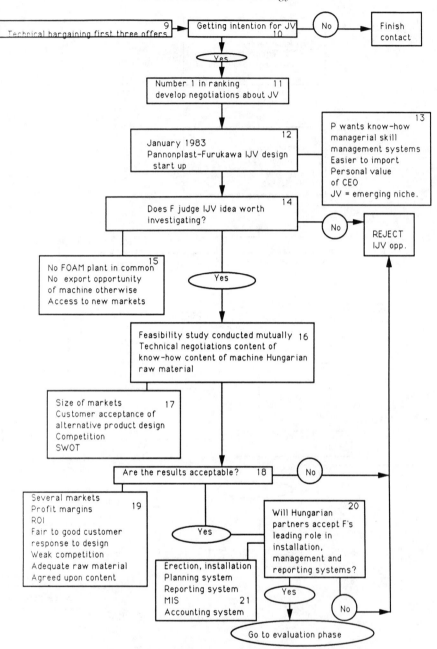

Fig. 8.2. Technical bargaining and feasibility study.

Phase 3: Design and implementation

Details of the design and implementation are summarized in Fig. 8.4. In designing the new IJV the partners sought and were granted start-up tax concessions from the government. The board of directors meets once a year, and the supervisory

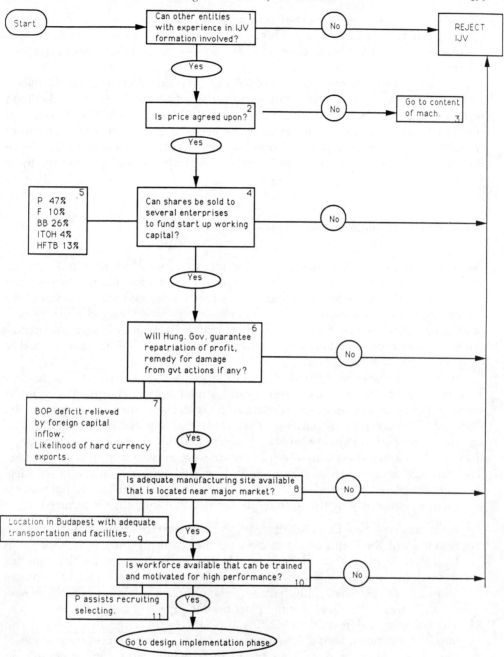

Fig. 8.3. Evaluation phase.

board meets four times a year to review performance and approve budgets and strategic decisions.

The incentive system relies on bonuses for managers, which are related to the profit performance. All managers, including the CEO, are paid in Hungarian currency. Factory workers receive 90 per cent of their compensation as salary, but

annual bonuses are also given related to profits of the enterprise. A new manufacturing plant was built before production started in July 1986. Legal work was
completed in January 1990 to enable the JV to meet the requirements of the new
Hungarian IJV Law.

The results of the IJV include sales of 159 million forints and profits of 28 million
forints in the first calendar year of operation (1987). Sales in 1988 were 233 million
forints and profits 74 million forints. Sales in 1989 were 290 million forints and
profits 76 million forints. Approximately 84 per cent of sales in 1989 came from
domestic markets and 16 per cent from Western European customers. Extensive
product innovation took place, the number of products doubling during three
years.

Strategic Implications and Conclusions

Because of changing circumstances, the importance of joint ventures and strategic
alliances has grown dramatically. Thus, there is considerable interest in knowing
what makes effective corporate relationships work. Understanding intercompany
relationships involves microanalytical detail (Kogut 1988). Thus, the use of case
studies of industries of a few joint ventures may be helpful in learning intercompany relationships and building theoretical propositions grounded in reality
(Woodside and Kandiko 1990).

The present paper is intended to describe why and how the Japanese–
Hungarian joint venture was designed and implemented. The process of interviews led to numerous findings in relation to the decision-making processes. The
depicted decision process implies, that from the standpoint of stimuli, the
Japanese–Hungarian joint venture is a problem decision, closer to an opportunity
decision than a crisis decision. Multiple stimuli were present during the processes.
The partners (more especially Pannonplast) started with the image of an ideal
solution, solicited offers, and finally one solution emerged from the design process
(Furukawa). Reasons why the solution-driven decision might have occurred:

1. From the cost benefit point of view, Pannonplast clearly did not have the
    resources or the skill needed to develop the foam production technology in
    Hungary. Even if it could have bought the know-how, given the complex
    technology and the brand-new product, the application of which requires
    education of customers, the chances of Pannonplast solving this problem suc-
    cessfully were low. Thus, Pannonplast needed Japanese co-operation.
2. The solution was related to existing problems – the large BOP deficit, and
    import restrictions, would have thwarted a direct export-import transaction.
3. Joint ventures as a new form of organizational action were emerging in
    Hungary; the government favoured joint ventures and it was easier to get the
    import licence for the machinery in this way.
4. The CEO of Pannonplast was likely to adopt this new form of organizational
    action in order to gain environmental legitimacy for herself (Bjorkman 1989).
5. Given the political and economic set-up in Hungary in 1983, the joint venture
    as a solution to the problem of producing and marketing polyethylene foam in
    Hungary was a ready one to be attached to this issue.

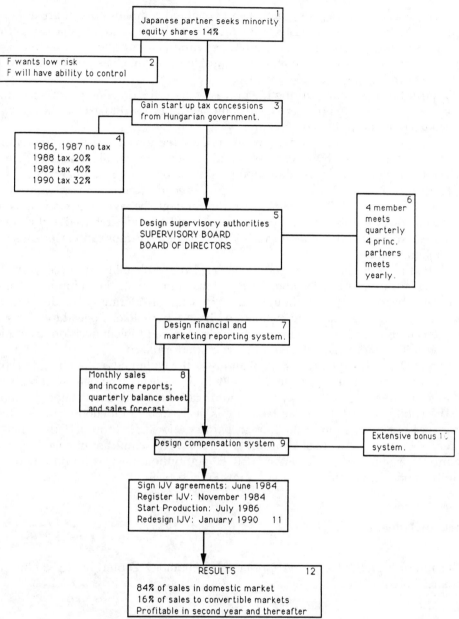

Fig. 8.4. Design and implementation of IJV.

Although offers were solicited and evaluated by applying conjunctive and weighted compensatory heuristics, judgement and bargaining seem to have been favoured modes of selection as the process matured towards an evaluation and design phase.

Perhaps because judgement is the fastest, most convenient, and least stressful choice routine, it is especially suited to the kinds of data found in strategic decision making (Mintzberg, Raisighani and Theoret 1976).

In the selection phase, conjunctive and weighted compensatory heuristics were applied. As the theory suggested, the decision makers sought satisfactory performance on some criteria (product variety, environmental protection, technology). On other criteria, the decision makers sought to get as much as possible (performance test run, image of joint venture).

Interruptions occurring during the process caused the decision process to return to earlier phases. Often the garbage-can model can be used to explain how certain problems influenced decision making.

As expected, the three waves of interviews reinforced the three motivating perspectives proposed by Kogut (1988) and disclose the specific motive of gaining access to new markets in less developed countries with large external debts.

The organizational learning rationale proposed by Kogut for motivating joint ventures is observed. Transaction cost and strategic behaviour explanations are complementary to this reason. Representatives of both sides referred to the organization's expertise of the other firm in different spheres as motivations for considering a joint venture.

Mutual respect between partners increased the probability of success. As the partners got to know each other better, developing trust, the solution of minor problems became faster. A thoughtful approach, considering every detail in the opportunity identification and evaluation phase is more likely to lead to successful implementation and performance afterwards. Also, a problem decision, a solution opportunity is more likely to result in a good performance.

In an LDC with large external debt and risk, the willingness of a foreign partner to enter a joint venture agreement is likely to be reduced. The perceived high risk of investment made the Japanese reluctant to take on a high equity share position.

The equity share held by the Japanese is likely to be a function of the strategic management orientation of the foreign partner. No single form of equity share is likely to be always the most appropriate for IJVs. No significant impact on performance of a minority share versus a 50–50 equity holding was found among US multinationals involved in joint ventures (Franko 1989).

Acknowledgements

The author is grateful to the MTC, Market Technology Center, in Stockholm, that financed the project.

References

Bjorkman, I. (1989) *Foreign Direct Investments: An Empirical Analysis of Decision Making in Seven Finnish Firms*, Helsinki: The Swedish School of Economics and Business Administration.
Bonoma, T. V. (1985) 'Case Research in Marketing: Opportunities, Problems, and a Process', *Journal of Marketing Research* 22, May: 199–208.
Borensztein, E. (1989) 'The Effect of External Debt on Investment', *Finance and Development* 26, September: 17–19.
Dale, W. (1988) 'Investment in LDCs: The Debate Continues', *The Columbia Journal of World Business* 23, Spring: 5–9.

Franko, L. G. (1989) 'Use of minority and 50–50 joint ventures by United States multi-nationals during the 1970s: the interaction of host country policies and corporate strategies', *Journal of Business Studies* 20, Spring: 19–40.

Horst, J. (1972) 'Firm and Industry Determinants of the Decision to Invest Abroad', *Review of Economics and Statistics* 54, August: 256–66.

Howard, J. A., Hulbert, J. M. and Farley, J. U. (1972) 'Information Processing and Decision Making in Marketing Organizations', *Journal of Marketing Research*: 75–7.

Kogut, B. (1988) 'Joint ventures: theoretical and empirical perspectives', *Strategic Management Journal* 9: 319–32.

Mintzberg, H. (1979) 'An emerging strategy of "direct" research', *Administrative Science Quarterly* 24, December: 582–90.

Mintzberg, H., Raisighani, D. and Theoret, A. (1976) 'The structure of "unstructured" decision processes', *Administrative Science Quarterly* 21, June: 246–75.

Ohmae, K. (1989) 'The Global Logic of Strategic Alliances', *Harvard Business Review* 67, March–April: 143–54.

Woodside, A. and Kandiko, J., (1991) 'Decision-Processes in Strategic Alliances: Designing and Implementing International Joint Ventures in Eastern Europe', *Journal of European Marketing* 1: 151–187.

9

Facing Both Ways: Baltic Economies After Independence

John Hiden and Thomas Lane

Patterns past and present

A brief examination of the longer perspective on the Baltic countries is essential to a full understanding of current economic developments there. There are two reasons for this. First, there are underlying trade patterns which have existed for centuries and which are likely to be repeated in some form or another. The second, more practical reason, is that current Baltic policy makers are reverting to the period of independence enjoyed by those countries between the wars for models, as well as to contemporary European examples.

The entrepreneurial tradition of the Baltic peoples stretches back to the Hanseatic League and beyond. After their incorporation into the Tsarist Russian Empire in the eighteenth century, the Baltic provinces (future Estonia and Latvia) eventually became major centres of Russian industry. Before the First World War they were also entrepôts for almost a third of European Russia's trade.[1]

Lithuania was not as important to Russian industry as the Baltic provinces. This is merely one example of many differences between the three republics, which are too often seen as identical triplets by the West. For example, Lithuania has an earlier and more developed history of independence; it is largely Catholic, whereas Estonia is mainly Protestant and Latvia is a mixture of both; each republic has its own distinctive language.

As fully independent countries after the First World War, all three Baltic states hoped to profit from an expected surge of trade between West Europe and the new but unknown Soviet markets. However, this trade did not reach the levels expected. Nevertheless, between the wars the independent Baltic states faced and overcame the enormous challenge of restructuring their commerce and industry, carving out their own small sectors of the world economy in the process. Their economies followed similar lines, however, and therefore business between them was slight.[2]

Today, this broad pattern still applies, but their combined prospects in international trade are much brighter. The pressure for East–West trade has intensified in the wake of Perestroika in the former Soviet Union and there has been greatly increased activity in the Eastern Baltic by the Scandinavian countries. The potential for increasing north–south commerce is also self-evident. The Baltic states will be key players as intermediaries in business conducted between Western Europe and the newly independent republics of the Commonwealth of Independent States (CIS). Estonia, Latvia and Lithuania will therefore offer greater opportunities for foreign enterprise and investment than their relatively small size might suggest.

To attract Western participation, the Baltic countries are working hard to make major adjustments to their economic and political systems. The Baltic states must break away from the legacy of sovietization.

Breaking the mould?

Superficially, there appeared to be some advantages to being part of the Soviet 'empire', with its potentially rich economic opportunities. In industrial terms the Baltic republics experienced a rapid growth in productivity as a result of Soviet investment in new and large-scale industry on Baltic soil after the Second World War and Baltic levels of per capita income remained substantially higher than elsewhere in the former Soviet Union – in 1987 the per capita national product of the Baltic states was 32 per cent higher than the Soviet average. In general, the living standards of both Latvia and Estonia surpassed the average for the USSR as a whole by a margin of 35 per cent to 40 per cent. Moreover, Baltic industries were relatively modern, in comparison with those of other Soviet republics.[3]

Under sovietization the Baltic republics developed important areas of specialization. Examples include the manufacture of radio and television sets, electric trains and telephone exchanges. In comparative terms, the Baltic republics were over-represented in Soviet production of other consumer durables, such as tape recorders, motor bikes, sewing machines, refrigerators, textiles and shoes. The diversity of consumer goods produced by the Baltic republics was and is a major source of their economic strength (although their total production by the 1980s was only about 3.5 per cent of that of the Soviet Union as a whole).[4]

In agriculture, too, increased productivity figures were notable, after an initial decline following the Second World War. The intensively farmed acres of the Baltic republics provided a basis for extensive stock breeding and expanding food production. Over 12 per cent of the meat produced in the USSR came from the Baltic republics, which also exported surplus milk, fish, fruit and vegetables to Russia and the other republics of the USSR. The outside world was reminded of the Baltics' capacity to feed themselves during the Soviet blockade of Lithuania in the first part of 1990.[5]

The Baltic republics enjoyed the benefits of cheap raw materials and energy from elsewhere in the Soviet Union. The shutdown of oil and gas supplies to Lithuania during the Soviet blockade of 1990 made it all too clear how much Baltic industry depended on the central authorities for cheap energy. Lithuania also received coal and gas at below world prices for domestic heating.

These 'advantages' were underlined by Gorbachev's repeated claim that the Baltic states could not prosper outside the Soviet Union. Western opinion tended to accept this argument, amid scepticism about the economic prospects for Baltic independence. However, the central authorities of the former Soviet Union con-cealed the costs to the Baltic republics and other drawbacks of being locked into the Soviet command economy.

The first of these relates to the basic management structure. For most of the period of Soviet rule, successive Soviet governments pursued the goal of central management. The disadvantages were all too obvious. The rate of growth of real per capita incomes in Estonia (although still high in comparison with elsewhere in the Soviet Union) halved between 1971 and 1985. What growth there was resulted from increasing the supply of labour and resources in Estonia, rather than from intensive investment or rationalization.

The indigenous labour force in the Baltics had been depleted by mass executions and deportations during and after the War. After 1945 the shortage of labour was dealt with by immigration of ethnic Russians to the Baltic republics.[6] This process increased Moscow's political control and provides the background to the recent ethnic conflicts in the Baltic republics. It accounts for the fear of the native Baltic peoples that unless they became independent and checked immigration, they would become minorities in their own lands. (It must be remembered that for many of the Russian immigrants, even after independence, the Baltic republics remain attractive places in which to live and work.)

Additional factors of production also came from the old Soviet Union. Many of the huge industrial plants built in the Baltics after 1945 received their raw materials from remote parts of the USSR and produced specialized products for the other Soviet republics. Gradually, Baltic industries became dependent on intra-union deliveries. Extreme levels of dependence were thus generated between the various parts of the industrial structure of the Soviet Union. The deliberate enmeshing of the Soviet and Baltic economies under Stalin and his successors after 1945 created a formidable obstacle to independence. By the early 1980s, for example, almost 90 per cent of industrial concerns in the Baltic were run solely or jointly by All-Union authorities.

Sovietization also brought with it a worsening environmental situation in Estonia and Latvia. Environmental concern (particularly in the heavily polluted north-eastern part of Estonia, Virumaa) played a major role in reinforcing the determi-nation of Baltic leaders to speed up their plans for economic self-management.[7]

On economic and political grounds, therefore, the three Baltic republics share the drive to mitigate the legacy of Soviet over-investment in heavy industry since the Second World War. A movement towards developing small-scale and medium industry is inevitable in the independent Baltic countries (as it was after 1918, when they left Russia).

Occupation, over-dependence on Soviet markets, pollution and its effects – all these are factors which Baltic leaders insist outweighed the benefits of life within the Soviet Union. Moreover, they argue that Sovietization destroyed the function-ing economies which the Baltic nations had managed to build in the period before the outbreak of the Second World War.

The Baltic governments are robustly asserting their ability to flourish as indepen-dent states, as they undoubtedly did between 1918 and 1940. At the same time, they recognize that continuing links with the East are both necessary and desirable. It might be more accurate, therefore, to talk about recasting, rather than entirely destroying the mould. Current Baltic economic reforms strongly suggest this.

Economic reform – Baltic style

Even before full independence in 1991, the Baltic governments had amply demon-strated their commitment to economic reform. All three republics had been wrestling to prepare legislation for this eventuality for almost two years. Briefly, the Baltic peoples made more use than the other Soviet republics of the limited practical opportunities to implement regional economic self-management which Gorbachev accepted in principle in November 1989. (Regional self-management formally came into effect in January 1990, although in reality the central authorities continued to place endless obstacles in the way of its practical implementation.)[8]

From this intensive 'battle' (little remarked by Western media coverage) between new Baltic legislation and the then still operative laws of the Soviet Union, orig-inated some of the current plans for the full-scale economic restructuring of the Baltic countries. In short, the Baltic states did not have to start the process of liberalization and privatization entirely from scratch on becoming independent.

The pace of reform has, of course, accelerated with independence. The con-straints exercised by the former Soviet Union have gone and additional impulses to reform have been applied by Western agencies, which include the IMF, the World Bank, the European Community and the European Bank for Reconstruction and Development. In general, the likely pattern of macroeconomic reform will resemble the Polish model. Foreign trade will be seen as an essential element in the process of economic reconstruction. However, Baltic exports cannot expect to succeed in competitive world markets unless their economies rest on solid foundations. Achieving the right base will involve adopting most of the following policies:

1. Establishing new Baltic currencies as soon as possible and detaching them from the rouble. These currencies will be convertible at least internally at a realistic rate of exchange, ensuring that there is a closer alignment of domestic and world prices.
2. Permitting steadily increasing import competition in order to weaken mon-opolies, bring costs under control, improve quality of products, and lower input costs for export industries. Increased trade will assist the flow of exper-tise, improve access to new technology and enhance the supply of know-how.
3. Controlling imports by means of tariffs rather than quotas. It would be un-realistic, however, to expect producers in the Baltic states to bear the full weight of world competition immediately. Hence the aim of the governments should be to reduce tariff protection in stages.
4. Offering direct trading rights to enterprises and permitting them to retain most of their foreign currency earnings. Significant progress has already been made in this direction.
5. Balancing government budgets as a condition of controlling inflation. This will involve the phasing out of producer subsidies, the freeing of prices (already largely achieved), and the establishment of market-determined rates of interest.
6. Enacting fiscal and other policies to provide attractive opportunities for foreign investors. Yet these policies alone, without economic and political stabiliz-ation, cannot achieve optimal results.

7. Consolidating market reforms and achieving substantial privatization to introduce dynamism into entrepreneurial decision-making.

This entire programme has been summed up in the words: stabilization, liberalization and privatization. It is worth looking at several aspects of this programme in turn.[9]

Budgetary and monetary policy

In order to balance budgets, determined efforts have been made to curb government spending, which in itself contributed towards squeezing inflation out of the economy. In early 1992 it was accurate to speak of hyperinflation in the Baltic economies. The Polish example indicated that matters would get worse before they got better. Freeing prices initially increased inflation, but since at the same time it reduced the large amount of rouble savings (monetary overhang), prices eventually began to fall. Freeing prices was, in any case, a vital element in reducing price subsidies, themselves a major factor in high government expenditure.

The need to establish convertible currencies was firmly grasped in the Baltic countries. They urgently needed to break away from the catastrophic rouble zone, but for this to be achieved fully, borders had to be firmly controlled. Independence brought the achievement of this goal much nearer. The Baltic governments succeeded in transferring to their own currencies during 1992 and 1993.

Economic stabilization was a vital element for a successful currency issue. As well as balanced budgets, a minimal institutional structure oriented towards a market economy was indispensable. Confidence in the new currencies both at home and abroad was also a prerequisite for their successful introduction. In this connection the advantages of a currency board outside the countries concerned were canvassed. Although this would have ensured that monetary policy was free of political interference, and that no more currency would be created than reserves or resources permitted, this proposal was politically controversial in newly-independent states.[11]

Conversely, the necessity for the creation of stabilization funds prior to the introduction of new currencies was widely accepted both at home and abroad. The decision of Britain, France and the United States, along with other Western countries, to credit the newly independent Baltic countries with the gold and other assets held on Baltic accounts in Western central banks since 1940 contributed significantly towards the creation of stabilization funds. At today's values the Baltic gold in the Bank of England is worth, for example, about £90 million. Siim Kallas, President of the Bank of Estonia, stated that Estonia's share would be used as backing for the new Estonian currency, the kroon. However, much more would be needed. The Bank of Estonia estimated that $250 million would be required as a stabilization fund to secure the kroon's convertibility. Echoing the practice of the inter-war period, the Vice-President of the Bank argued that convertibility might also be guaranteed by including Estonia's forests in the balance of the Bank. A mere 2 per cent of these would cover about $150 million of the required stabilization. A similar judicious mixture between gold, natural assets and hard currency through foreign loans could be used to set up stabilization funds in Latvia and Lithuania.[12]

Although attention was fixed mainly on currency issue and state banking, the commercial banking sector developed rapidly, particularly since independence. According to Rein Kaarepare, former Chair of the Tartu Commercial Bank in Estonia, twenty-five commercial banks were in existence in Estonia by the beginning of 1992. Some of these were new foundations, like his own bank, while others were former branches of the old Soviet system, under new names and management.[13]

The Tartu Bank was founded in September 1988 with a share capital of 3 million roubles, which increased to 90 million roubles. It had some 5,000 shareholders, including 400 companies and over 4,500 private shareholders, many from abroad (the United States, Canada, Germany, Sweden, the United Kingdom, etc.). The Tartu Bank was, in turn, a shareholder in other Estonian companies – for example hotels, printing concerns, property companies and other banks.

The January 1992 balances of the Tartu Bank were 1.2 billion roubles and 200 million Swedish kroner. With some 6,000 hard currency clients, the bank also offered all the old services on the rouble side formerly available in the Soviet Union, including loans. The bank's hard currency transactions began two years previously, when it opened an account with the Svenska Handelsbank. Prior to that its foreign transactions had to be via the Soviet Union's Foreign State Bank, which occasioned huge delays. The rate of development of the commercial banking system in the Baltic states suggests that many of the companies will not be viable in the long run.[14]

Questions about the exact relationship between the Baltic State banks and the private banks have yet to be resolved. The law on banking passed in Estonia in the autumn of 1989 was, in the then Soviet conditions, illegal. Hence, only with the restoration of independence could the central bank operate openly and fully to carry out the brief of elaborating an overall framework of banking legislation by preparing draft laws on, for example, the granting of credit and mortgages. The absence of detailed legislation was the biggest obstacle to the restoration of a normal credit system. The Bank of Estonia was in effect, therefore, reduced to regulating 'banking' in its widest sense by collaborating with the emergent commercial sector. It will be recognized that this is an unsophisticated means of control and direction. At the time of writing the ultimate relationship between State banks and commercial banks remains to be determined.[15] Clearly, banking training and the transmission of know-how are absolutely vital to the sound development of banking in the Baltic states.

Marketization

Subsidies for producers were a major feature of economic management in the command economy. Reducing subsidies naturally helped to balance budgets, but at the same time caused producers to increase their prices. The phasing out of loans at artificially low rates of interest forced producers to borrow at market rates and increased awareness of the real costs of investment.

Even before independence, when the centrally controlled allocative mechanism had begun to break down, enterprises were making informal arrangements with each other to safeguard supplies of raw materials of semi-finished products. Since independence the imperative of increasing direct contact between enterprises in the Baltic states and the former Soviet Union has strengthened. The new arrangements provided either for payment in hard currency or for barter deals, in both cases at world prices. Increasingly producers had recourse to the new commodity exchanges which sprang up in the three Baltic capitals and in the CIS.

Replacing the former command system by market mechanisms was an essential first step in the modernization of the Baltic economies. However, it will not on its own lead to more dynamic enterprise. For this to happen, a dramatic shift in ownership is necessary. State-owned organizations in the Soviet style were not, to put it bluntly, noted for producing entrepreneurs. These are now urgently required in the Baltic countries, as their governments recognize. The inter-war experience of the Baltic states – not shared by the other former Soviet republics – has deepened their commitment to free enterprise.

Privatization and small business development

The Baltic governments have all emphasized the connection between economic modernization and privatization. During the Soviet period only 0.9 per cent of all industrial production in Lithuania originated in the private economy. Almost every enterprise was a huge monopolist in its field, and small and medium-sized firms were virtually non-existent. This homogeneous sector was infertile soil for the development of innovation, competition and efficiency. On the other hand, privatization without the introduction of competition would simply be to transform public monopolies into private ones – hence the importance of encouraging inward investment and weakening protection.

The first steps towards privatization involved introducing guarantees of individual property rights in law. According to Article 44 of the Provisional Basic Law of Lithuania, for example, the property of the republic consists of the private property of its citizens, the property of groups of citizens, and state property. The fundamental property law is the so-called Law on Enterprises, which upholds the right of all forms of enterprise to have equality in their legal rights and the conditions of their operation. This is an important symbolic break with the past; in stressing that all owners have equal rights, the idea is repudiated that private property is some form of inferior holding (by implication parasitic or exploitative). The law also allows for new types of business organizations, similar to those in developed free market economies.[16]

The next stage has been to develop a privatization programme for state properties. In Latvia this envisages the privatization of 25–30 per cent of state-owned property (excluding land) within the new few years. Priority will be given to small properties to be sold to individuals, to enterprises supplying the market with goods and services, and to properties enjoying a relatively rapid rate of return on capital. Privatization of industry will start with small enterprises (up to 300 workers). In the case of medium-sized and large enterprises, shares will be sold to both Latvian and foreign investors, transforming the firms into joint-stock companies.[17]

The problem of a savings shortage has had to be confronted. Lithuanian government estimates in 1991 put the total savings of Lithuanians at about 7 billion roubles, which amounted to only 15 per cent of the book value of the enterprise targeted for privatization. The introduction of the voucher system was designed to overcome this problem. Vouchers to the value of two-thirds of the value of the property subject to privatization were to be issued, the number of vouchers for each citizen being related to age. It was argued that the voucher system would speed up the pace of change and make privatization more attractive to the population, as well as helping to overcome the shortage of capital. Another possibility of encouraging privatization would be provision for the purchase of shares by instalments, at low rates of interest.[18]

Although the giant firms loom large in discussion of privatization, most rapid progress has been made in the establishment of small private businesses. This is due not only to privatization but to active encouragement by governments in the formation of new businesses, especially in the under-developed services sector. Furthermore, as big businesses decline under the impact of new political and economic conditions, small businesses will help to create jobs for the increased numbers of unemployed.

In Lithuania privatization, starting in September 1991, encouraged former owners of property to reclaim it. In addition, sales of existing companies and the creation of new small businesses have already changed the structure of ownership in the Lithuanian economy. Many privately-owned small businesses emerged in areas such as manufacturing, construction, retailing and catering, design, hotel services, communications and finance. According to data held on the register of enterprises of Lithuania, at the beginning of 1992 there were more than 40,000 small businesses, representing about 85 per cent of the total number of registered enterprises. Most of these were microfirms with one owner and two or three employees, usually members of the family. By contrast there were only 6,515 limited liability companies.[19]

It is expected that the rapid development of small businesses in Lithuania will continue. A Law on Small Enterprise was passed in December 1991, aimed at encouraging people to take the risk of starting up their own firms. This law conferred several advantages on small firms. For example, a tax benefit was given to enterprises with up to fifty employees – for the first two years after the formation of the company such enterprises were to be granted tax rebates on up to 70 per cent of their profits, falling to 50 per cent for the third and following years. This concession would only apply when two-thirds of the firm's income was derived from the sale of its own production. In addition, expenditure on research, innovation and investment could be set off against profits tax. Enterprises with between fifty and one hundred employees could acquire tax credits permitting them to postpone payment of profits tax for three years.[20]

The most rapid progress towards privatization has been in returning land to private ownership. In this sector foreigners have been denied the right to purchase, in order to protect the Baltic countries from 'dangerous' (presumably excessive) buy-outs and the possible depletion of national resources. Foreigners may therefore only rent land, though current proposals in Estonia would permit purchase.

Baltic citizens have been given the legal right to acquire agricultural land. In Latvia, for example, the law on agrarian reform of November 21, 1990 permitted them to obtain land for rent in the first instance. Former owners (before July 21,

1940) or their descendants were to be permitted to reclaim possession in 1993 without making payment. Other tenants wishing to become proprietors after 1993 will be required to pay.

Progress has also been made in the privatization of collective and state farms. These farms will either be reorganized into associations with limited liability or, alternatively, they may be divided into individual family farms. In Latvia, as elsewhere, the private sector has already taken hold, as exemplified in the tremendous current and projected growth in the number of private farms since the advent of agricultural reforms. Prior to the end of 1991 there were over 10,000 new private farm start-ups. According to the Latvian Ministry of Agriculture there were to be an additional 35,000 new farms in 1992, and by 1996 there will be approximately 60,000 private farms, accounting for 70 per cent of arable land in Latvia.[21]

Foreign Trade

The achievement of political independence has not untied the numerous knots binding the Baltic republics to the former Soviet republics in the East. The aims of the Baltic governments, are, it is true, to diversify foreign trade patterns, to encourage trade with the rest of Europe, North America and Asia, and to provide favourable conditions for foreign investment. So far, however, the growing contacts between Western companies and Baltic enterprises are still too few in number and too small in scale to replace the dominant trade relationships with Russia, Ukraine, Belorussia and the rest, though they are beginning to challenge them.

Geography, familiarity, and established trading connections should ensure that the former Soviet Union will continue to play a major role in Baltic imports and exports for some time to come. The Soviet economy dictated that even in the immediate pre-independence period, after several years of Perestroika, over 85 per cent of Baltic trade was conducted with other Soviet republics. About half of the remainder was with Comecon countries and the rest with Scandinavia and Western Europe.

Exports from the Baltic republics to the former Soviet Union were dominated by a handful of industries, the largest shares coming from machinery, light industry products, foodstuffs and chemicals. However, Lithuania and Estonia also exported electricity, the former from its nuclear power station at Ignalina, the latter from its shale oil-fired thermal stations in the North East. In addition, Lithuania exported oil products from its Mazeikiai refinery. Imports from the Soviet republics consisted mainly of energy supplies, chemicals, machinery, processed foods and animal foodstuffs.

Overseas trading partners were found in Scandinavia and Eastern and Western Europe. For example, Latvia's exports of machinery such as electric railway coaches, vans, and diesel engines, along with pharmaceuticals, and building materials, went mainly to Poland, Germany and Sweden. Estonia stood out for the quite high proportion of foodstuffs, light industrial products and wood, paper and pulp sold in foreign markets.[22]

Data on the balance of trade (including trade with the former Soviet republics) have, until recently, been unreliable. At the time of writing available figures suggest that the Baltic states ran a balance of trade deficit with their trading partners. The deficit widened substantially if trade is valued at world prices, since the substantial imports of gas and oil from Russia were, until 1991, priced in roubles at well below world market prices. Siim Kallas, President of the Bank of Estonia, disclosed that Estonian hard currency earnings from foreign trade totalled around $300 million per annum, whereas indispensable imports amounted to $500 million. The substantial projected deficit in overall trade for the three republics combined suggested an imminent balance of payments crisis. If this were not covered by foreign credits, domestic output would fall dramatically, leading to unemployment and an exacerbation of social tensions. Fortunately, full membership of the IMF in 1992 created drawing rights and credits which in turn increased confidence among foreign investors.[23]

Trade with the former Soviet Union

From 1990 the Baltic states began to negotiate a series of economic agreements with the former Soviet republics. Their purpose was to safeguard supplies of food, raw materials and industrial inputs in the face of the economic collapse of the centre. The most important of these arrangements were concluded with the Russian Federation, their biggest trading partner. However, the agreements have not been free of problems. For example, the Latvian–Russian treaty signed by President Yeltsin in January, 1991 had not come into operation more than a year later.[24]

Other agreements were undermined by Russia's introduction in late 1991 of a system of licenses for exports to the Baltic states. As a result, partly by design, partly as a result of bureaucratic tardiness, Russian suppliers were unable to send the agreed products to their trading partners in the Baltic, or simply delayed delivery. Talks at the highest level, for instance between President Yeltsin and former President Landsbergis of Lithuania, failed to overcome these problems.[25]

The IMF delegation which visited Latvia in February 1992 is reported to have promised to put pressure on Russian officials to relax their policy on export licensing. This approach seemed to produce results. The Latvian–Russian trade agreement of March 1992 identified a range of products for import and export during the rest of 1992. Whether this would prove more effective than previous agreements remained to be seen. Until the Russians are able to fulfil their agreements they will continue to be criticized by those who see entirely sinister motives behind Moscow's actions. In reality, the problems of its own reconstruction and reform with which Russia is grappling are the most likely cause of the disruption of agreements with the Baltic states.

The impact of licensing

Licensing exacerbated already existing shortages of food, raw materials, energy and manufactured goods. It was known in January 1992, even before licensing, that Lithuania would only receive 30 per cent of its cattle feed requirements from the former Soviet Union in 1992. Russia had already failed to meet its contractual obligations to supply flour and cereals to Estonia in 1991, only 44 per cent of contracts being fulfilled. It later confirmed that no cereals would be delivered in 1992. The shortfall in energy supplies also became acute in January. Hence, the prohibition of unlicensed exports of raw materials and other goods from Russia in January 1992 had a devastating impact on the Baltic economies. The ban affected up to 1,100 commodities and raw materials traded with Latvia, and brought commerce to a virtual standstill.[26]

Shortages of raw materials from Russia and other CIS members compelled Baltic industry to reduce production. Owing to a shortage of certain metals, the Latvian and Lithuanian radio-electronic industries and the machinery industry of Estonia were particularly badly affected. In late February three large enterprises were reported as being at a complete standstill in Lithuania and unemployment was predicted to rise substantially. Estimates suggested that industrial output in 1992 would not exceed 60 per cent of the previous year's figures and there were almost frenzied attempts to obtain supplies from any available source in Russia and the other republics. Reports suggested that about half of all purchases of raw materials on CIS commodity exchanges were being made by Baltic firms. Baltic enterprises were also active in trying to establish joint ventures with Russian firms to overcome supply shortages.

The reorientation of Baltic external trade will not be helped by the current fragility in Russo–Baltic trade relations. The Baltic countries obviously need the assurance of regular trade with Russia and the other republics in the East if they are to expand their embryonic commercial relations with the rest of the world. Fortunately, the Baltic states have some useful bargaining counters. Russia needs Baltic products as inputs for its own industry. The Baltic countries are also monopoly suppliers of certain commodities to the Russian market and of course they command Baltic ports through which Russian trade routes pass.

Diversification of trade is one of the keys to economic development in the Baltic states. The Baltic governments' policy is to attract foreign investment in order to modernize their manufacturing sectors and infrastructures. Greater efficiency will provide the opportunity to expand exports to the West, repay earlier loans, and purchase additional capital equipment and consumer goods. The cycle will, with luck, become self-sustaining.

The achievement of independence and the difficulties of trading with the Commonwealth states have, however, increased the pace of Baltic integration into Western markets. Latvia, for example, signed agreements with Denmark and the Netherlands in 1991 and emphasized the importance it placed on strengthening commercial ties with the Scandinavian countries. Estonia, too, signed a trade agreement with Sweden outlawing trade discrimination and envisaging the establishment of free trade under GATT rules. Estonia has also conducted trade discussions with its neighbour and close trading partner Finland, and with the Netherlands and Austria. There have been numerous contacts between representatives of Western companies and Baltic enterprises. Prominent in this respect are Finnish, Swedish, Danish, German and US firms. Baltic enterprises have also participated in trade fairs, both in their own region and in Scandinavia.[27]

The Baltic governments have taken determined action to improve the prospects for foreign trade. Taxes have been reduced – for example, only 15 per cent of Latvian hard currency earnings from foreign trade are deducted by the Latvian government. Similarly encouraging was the partial abolition of export licences and quotas for goods exported from Estonia for hard currency. Although some licences are still required, this is balanced by the abolition of all export and import taxes on foreign economic activity.

Prospects for Baltic exports

Improvements in quality, marketing and packaging will be required if exports of Estonian, Latvian and Lithuanian goods are to compete in Western markets. In this respect the much-publicized joint ventures, coupled with direct investments by foreign companies, are of considerable significance. They can have a major impact in the field of technology transfer, management and skills training, distribution and retailing, quality control and customer relations. Improvements in these fields can also be achieved by know-how training abroad. The dominant ethos of old Soviet-style management has to be undermined if Baltic exporters are to succeed. The experience of the past few years, particularly Estonia's close economic ties with Finland, suggests that some Baltic entrepreneurs are alive to economic opportunities and will adjust to new conditions, particularly now that they are free of the Soviet incubus.

In the inter-war period a major contribution to export earnings came from agriculture.[28] Even assuming improvements in productivity, however, it is now unlikely that farm products will lead an export boom – the amount of land devoted to agriculture has fallen by one-third, compared with the inter-war period. Moreover, the CAP is a major obstacle in the way of increased agricultural exports to the West, as it is unlikely that the French and German farm lobbies will be sympathetic to increased access for Baltic products.

Opportunities for Baltic traders in the markets of Central and Eastern Europe cannot be discounted. A shared historical experience under communism serves to strengthen understanding and to reinforce the economic advantages of forging links with this part of Europe. These states are also experiencing the same problems of adjusting to the market and casting off their communist heritage. Closer association will provide a counter-balance to increased dependence on the developed West and to existing ties with Russia.

The Baltic interface

The Baltic states are well placed to exploit their intermediary role between Russia and the West. There are indications that Russia is planning to become less dependent on these traditional routes in future, but it is difficult to see how they can be dispensed with, even in the medium term. For the foreseeable future much East–West trade will be carried through Baltic ports, a number of which, like Klaipeda, Ventspils, and Liepaja, are ice-free throughout the year. The opportunity for substantial hard currency earnings from the provision of port, warehousing and transport facilities is considerable. Latvian calculations suggest earnings in hard currency from the railways of $2 million and from the ports $700 million annually.[29]

Tallinn is not an ice-free port, but its depth of water is a considerable advantage for international shipping and it is well placed to benefit from transit traffic to and from Russia. Tallinn New Port handles almost exclusively transit trade, mostly imports of refrigerated food and grain. In 1990 it handled 3.9 million tonnes of grain, which made it the biggest grain port in the former Soviet Union. Total tonnage passing through the port is in the order of 7 million tonnes, composed mainly of imports. Stif Lofberg, a Danish transport expert, recently suggested that to take full advantage of these transit opportunities, there would have to be substantial new investment in modernizing the port facilities, railways and roads.[30] The intermediary role will be increasingly important in the growing transit traffic from Scandinavia, especially Finland, to Eastern and Southern Europe and the Middle East. Taking full advantage of this opportunity will involve substantial investment in the North–South motorway, the so-called Via Baltica, from Tallin to the Lithuanian–Polish border.

The first steps in setting charges for transit traffic from Russia were taken in an agreement between Latvia and Russia in early 1992. The Russian government conceded that the use of Latvian railways and port facilities for Russian exports of oil and imports of grain would be paid for in kind, up to 6 per cent of these commodities being allocated to Latvia in payment.

The closeness of Tallinn and other Baltic ports to Scandinavia and Western Europe offers the prospects of increased hard currency earnings from tourism. In recent years some 140,000 tourists have visited Estonia each year, about 80 per cent of them from the West. In an era of so-called 'tourist fatigue', the novelty and attractiveness of the eastern Baltic shore will draw many more Westerners to this region. Latvia is also engaged in the promotion of tourism, particularly through its national association of travel agents. Tourism was expected to have grown by some 30 per cent in 1992 compared with 1990. Foreign and domestic investment in tourist facilities has been encouraged by favourable tax measures. It is clear that many opportunities still exist to improve hotel provision, develop road and motorway facilities and provide more restaurants and cafés.

The Baltic states are correct to go for growth by diversifying their foreign trade. By this means they have a reasonable expectation of increasing their hard currency earnings to pay off loans and support essential imports. Unlike the inter-war period they will, commercially speaking, be able to look both ways, to their considerable advantage.

Foreign Investment

The Baltic governments have made great efforts to attract inward investment. Legislation offering inducements as well as guarantees to foreign lenders and trading partners has been passed in all three parliaments. Negotiations with representatives of the International Monetary Fund, the European Bank for Reconstruction and Development, the World Bank and the European Community have aimed at creating a stable monetary environment as a precondition for receiving

development funding. Many discussions have taken place with foreign companies to attract investment from abroad. Although many of these have been
successful, probably the larger number have been only exploratory. Membership
of the IMF acted as a catalyst for substantial foreign investment from both public
and private organizations.

Both the governments and the funding bodies have agreed on priority areas for
investment when funds become available. The Estonian government in 1991 outlined a list of projects where international economic assistance was urgently
sought. The projects were divided into three categories: the most urgent included
food aid, the provision of medicines and fuel, agricultural inputs, and the maintenance of municipal services. Of slightly lower priority were credits for Estonian
banks, the establishment of a stabilization fund for the new Estonian currency
and the creation of a development fund for small business. Over the longer
period of three years the priorities in Estonia, as in the other Baltic republics,
were transport, telecommunications, environmental protection, computerization,
energy, and the restructuring and privatization of industry and agriculture.[31] By
comparison, the Nordic Investment Bank, whose analysis related to all three Baltic republics, concluded that most of the investment should go into ecology, the
timber and fishing industries, and telecommunications and roads.[32]

The governments have acted quickly to provide a secure legal framework for
foreign investment. A Latvian law, for example, guarantees foreign investments
in the republic and provides equal treatment under local laws. Expropriation of
foreign investment by the government is prohibited, except in extraordinary
cases, where there will be full compensation in hard currency. Each of the
republics provides tax incentives for foreign investors. In Estonia companies
whose founding capital is at least 30 per cent foreign-owned will obtain a two-
year tax exemption, increased to three years where foreign capital accounts for
half the total investment. In Latvia too there are a variety of tax breaks, including
tax holidays for up to five years based on the size of the investment or the sector
of the economy. For example, tax concessions are granted to investments which
will reduce dependence on imports of raw materials.[33]

A major concern of foreign investors, the right to repatriate hard currency
profits, has been fully recognized in Baltic legislation, subject only to the payment
of profits tax, where appropriate. In addition, companies in Estonia with a minimum of 30 per cent foreign investment are permitted to export their products
without an export licence. Baltic governments have also shown an awareness that
an uninhibited flow of foreign investment depends on a number of other factors,
including bilateral and multilateral international agreements covering mutual protection of investments, double taxation and trade and co-operation. Latvia has
started to prepare such agreements with a number of Western countries, and has
already signed a trade agreement with Sweden, an investment incentive agreement with the United States, and a declaration with the European Free Trade
Association.

Conclusions – Life after the Soviet Empire

In conclusion, the Baltic states face a massive practical task in restructuring their economies and adapting to the demands of the market system. An awareness of the negative impact of sovietization should not, however, blind us to the necessity for the Baltic countries to have a continuing, but greatly transformed, economic relationship with the former Soviet republics. These traditional economic links offer the most immediately practical way forward for Estonia, Latvia and Lithuania, because they will find it exceedingly difficult in the short term either to replace sources of raw materials and energy, or to create extensive enough alternative markets. This was confirmed by the response of the Baltic states in negotiating bilateral trading agreements with individual republics of the old USSR as the old central authority of the Soviet Union broke down in 1990–1. The agreements were designed, as we have seen, at least to ensure continuing inputs of raw materials into the Baltic economies.

Continuing trade with Russia and other CIS members is also vital until Baltic exports reach the sort of standard which would enable them to compete more effectively and consistently in world markets. Western investment (like the transmission of management know-how) is vital in this context, to modernize Baltic factories. Baltic consumer goods production could then be increased in quantity as well as quality to meet the enormous demand in Russia and the other republics. All plans for the near to medium-term economic development being considered in the Baltic republics therefore stress the need for Western inputs of investment and know-how on the one hand, CIS raw materials and markets on the other. The latter include markets for Baltic agriculture, but on a sound economic basis.

As part of the transformed relationship, the Baltic states plan to capitalize on their position as access points for European business to the vast markets beyond their borders. They are small (though still significant) markets in themselves; in addition they can continue to profit from their long experience of doing business with their eastern neighbours, notably by acting as intermediaries for West European entrepreneurs anxious to secure agents and facilities for East–West commerce.

There are marked advantages for foreign investment in the Baltic republics, when compared with other parts of the former Soviet empire. The standard of education of the Baltic peoples is generally higher, the knowledge of foreign languages (especially English, German and Swedish) is greater and the traditional Western work ethic has not been wholly erased by Sovietization. The higher living standards of the Baltic peoples also make them potentially more interesting as consumers to Western exporters. The Baltic republics have already had experience of foreign investment. Notwithstanding the rather poor record for joint ventures in the Soviet Union as a whole over the past few years, some of the most successful of these have been in the Baltic republics.

Clearly the Baltic states must still work hard to convince Western investors that they are more worth investing in than some other parts of the world. They have, however, taken many of the appropriate economic measures at a time when they have suffered acutely from the dislocation emanating from the east. Western observers, not least in the IMF and the World Bank, will be watching carefully the legislation and economic policy-making of the three governments in the future. However, the skilful and courageous manner in which the Baltic republics are trying to manage the transition to independence, as well as the commitment of the native population to abandoning the command economy, offer grounds for optimism in the long term.

Notes

1. Hiden, J. and Salmon, P. (1991) *The Baltic Nations and Europe: Estonia, Latvia and Lithuania in the Twentieth Century*, London: 76–7; cf. Crohn-Wolfgang, H. F. (1922) 'Die Republik Lettland and ihre wirtschaftliche Zukunft', *Jahrbücher für Nationalöconomie und Statistik* 1(118): 44.
2. In general see Romas, I. (1934) *Die wirtschaftliche Struktur der baltischen Staaten und die Idee einer Zollunion*, Rytas.
3. Cf. Vincentz, V. (1990) 'Ohne prallen Geldbeutel keine Eigenverantwortung, *Die Welt*, April 20.
4. Van Arkadie, B. *et al.* (1991) 'Economic Survey of the Baltic Republics', unpublished study for the Swedish Ministry of Foreign Affairs, June: 1–11.
5. *Idem*: 1–11, 315–20.
6. Cf. Hiden and Salmon, op. cit.
7. *Report on the USSR* 22(25), June 22, 1990; *Atmoda*, October 7/8, 1989; Nahaylo, B. and Swoboda, V. (1990) *Soviet Disunion: A History of the Nationalities Problem in the USSR*, London: Hamish Hamilton: 267.
8. Lloyd, J. (1989) 'Estonians test the limits of liberalisation in the Soviet Union', *Financial Times*, May 7.
9. The phrase is Mats Karlsson's in a paper to the conference 'The Reintegration of the Baltic States into the World Community', The Royal Institute of International Affairs, London, January 23 and 24, 1992 (hereafter RIIA).
10. *Baltic Independent*, February 14–20, 1992.
11. Michael Foot, 'Currency Issues: A Western Perspective', RIIA.
12. *Baltic Independent*, January 9–15, January 31–February 6, 1992.
13. Kaarepere, R., 'Current State and Development Plans for the Banking System', RIIA.
14. *Idem*.
15. Cf. address by Bank of Estonia President, Siim Kallas, RIIA.
16. Zambaite, N. (1992) 'Small Businesses in Lithuania: Reality and Prospects', in Hiden, J., Lane, T. and Heywood, T. (eds), *Baltic Briefing* 1(2), May.
17. Gailis, M. (1992) 'The Current Economic Situation and Investment Opportunities in Latvia', *Baltic Briefing* 1(2), May.
18. *Baltic Independent*, November 8–14, November 22–8, 1991.
19. Zambaite, op. cit.
20. *Idem*. The Tartu Commercial Bank has now gone into liquidation.
21. Gailis, op. cit.
22. Van Arkadie, op. cit.: 191ff.
23. Kallas, J. 'The Current Economic Situation and the Transformation Process' and Hanson, P. 'Trade and Economic Cooperation: The Baltic States and their neighbours', RIIA.
24. *Financial Times*, November 7, 1991; *Pravda*, January 4, 1991; *Baltic Independent*, December 27–January 8, March 6–12, 1991–2; *Baltic Observer*, February 16–24, 1992; *Ekonomicheskaia Gazeta*, No. 10, March 1992.
25. *Baltic Independent*, January 24–30, 1992; *Literaturnaia Gazeta*, February 12, 1992.
26. Sekmokas, A., Deputy Minister of Economics, Lithuania, 'The Current Economic Situation and the Transformation Process', RIIA; *Baltic Independent*, January 9–15, January 24–30, 1992.
27. *Izvestiia*, November 22, 1991; *Baltic Observer*, February 16–24, 1992; *Baltic Independent*, February 21–7, March 13–20, 1992.
28. PRO FO371 32742 N1740/1740/59 and N2802/1740/59, May 29, 1942.
29. 'The Transport Systems of the Baltic States', *Baltic Briefing* 1(2), May 1992.

30. *Baltic Independent*, November 1–7, 1991.
31. See *A Summary of the Estonian Government's 3 × 3 Program*, September 1991, and the *Law on Tax Concessions for Foreign Capital Enterprises*, Supreme Council, Republic of Estonia, September 10, 1991.
32. Cf. also Ora, A. (1991) 'Baltic states agree to customs union', *Baltic Independent*, October 3.
33. Gailis, op. cit.; Republic of Estonia, *Law on Tax Concessions for Foreign Capital Enterprises*, September 10, 1991.

10

Japanese MNCs as Potential Partners in Eastern Europe's Economic Reconstruction

Terutomo Ozawa

Prior to the very recent change in the politico-economic system of East European countries and the former Soviet Union, Japan's commercial contact with them through trade, not to speak of investment, had been quite limited. The Soviet Union occasionally did attract Japanese interest, mainly as a potential supplier of minerals and energy, particularly in barter exchange for capital goods. A principal reason why there was no substantial programme of Japanese economic co-operation concerned the territorial dispute over the Kurile Islands captured by the Soviet Union at the end of the Second World War. Eastern European economies such as Hungary, Czechoslovakia, Poland, and others which until recently were members of Comecon had no significant commercial relations with Japan. What little trade and investment they managed to develop outside the communist bloc was mostly with Western Europe, with which they have close historical, cultural, and ethnic ties. Hence Japanese industry's commercial knowledge about – and interest in – East European countries and the former Soviet Union (hereafter both identified collectively as Eastern Europe) is, on the whole, rather lacking.

Nevertheless, the current revolutionary shift of these economies toward the democratic market system – their eagerness to learn the ropes about improving industrial strength under capitalism – have quite suddenly raised interest in those countries in attracting Japanese capital, technology, and managerial skills – perhaps more so than Japanese industry itself is prepared for at the moment. Yet, as this chapter intends to show, once the preparatory phase of involvement is over, Japanese industry will deepen its commercial ties with Eastern Europe, both more swiftly and more deeply than generally expected for a variety of reasons which are to be analysed below.

An unexplored territory

Table 10.1 summarizes Japan's commercial relations (trade and investment) with Eastern Europe. The value of Japan's trade (exports and imports combined) with the region comprises only a small fraction of the latter's total trade, indicating that Japan is at present a minor player. In 1990, for example, Japan accounted for only 1.2 per cent of Czechoslovakia's trade, 2.2 per cent of Hungary's, 2.5 per cent of Poland's, 1.4 per cent of Yugoslavia's, 2.9 per cent of Romania's, and 2.7 per cent of the former Soviet Union's.

Interestingly, the pattern of trade between Japan and Eastern Europe has been of the 'classical' type, in the sense that Japan, the more advanced and industrialized, exports manufactures (such as industrial goods and high value-added consumer goods), while the latter sells mostly raw materials, fuels, marine and forest products, and some semi-processed goods, a pattern of trade which ironically matches what the Marxists would certainly look upon as 'colonial' trade and 'unequal exchange'.

Trade has thus been based intrinsically on absolute availability advantage, since most of the goods which Japan buys from Eastern Europe are not available in Japan, the same applying to the goods the latter buys from Japan. Hence there is near-perfect complementarity and no structural conflict of trade (imports) with domestic interests as seen in purely comparative advantage-based trade, in which comparatively disadvantaged industries at home are necessarily 'injured' by cheaper imports. Comparative advantage-based trade is all but non-existent, so far as the pattern of trade between Japan and Eastern Europe is concerned. Yet the volume of trade has so far been limited largely because of political/ideological barriers. As will be detailed below, now that the entire former Soviet bloc has cast off communism and embraced the open-market capitalist ideology, the potential for commercial exchange between Japan and Eastern Europe is greater than ever before.

Similarly, Japan's share so far in the number of joint ventures in Eastern Europe is negligible because of the existing high transaction costs, both actual and perceived, for Japanese multinationals – much higher than for their Western counterparts. As of the end of 1990, Japanese industry had entered into only forty-eight joint ventures, a mere 0.4 per cent of the estimated total of 11,234 registered joint ventures in Eastern Europe. Thirty-three Japanese joint ventures, the largest concentration, are organized in the former Soviet Union, followed by eight in Hungary, three in Bulgaria, and two in Yugoslavia. Many of these, however, are not in actual operation yet, unlike the other ventures organized by Western multinationals.

Japan's minuscule presence as a joint venture partner, compared to that of the Western, especially European, countries, closely parallels its relative insignificant current position as a trade partner, and reflects its lack of knowledge and interest. Indeed, this fact is clearly mirrored in the findings of a recent survey taken by the Japanese government at the end of 1990 (Table 10.2). In assessing the attractiveness of East European economies either as potential manufacturing sites or as potential sales (marketing) outposts, Japanese firms in the manufacturing sector are far less optimistic and far less enthusiastic than their Western counterparts (Table 10.2A). A similar survey on the attractiveness of the Soviet Union as a potential market showed the same result (Table 10.2B).

Unfamiliarity with the local economic conditions in Eastern Europe (largely because of historically limited opportunities to interact with those countries) obviously raises the costs of international business, particularly the costs of direct

Table 10.1: Trade and investment relations between Eastern Europe and Japan, 1990.

	Total value of trade (exports + imports)	Value of trade with Japan (%)	Major exports to Japan	Major imports from Japan	Total number of joint ventures (with Japan)
Czechoslovakia	Kc455,651 million	Kc179 million (1.2%)	Aluminium, metal products, glass products, malt	Machinery, cars, VCRs	699 (1)
Hungary	$13,182 million	$289 million (2.2%)	Iron, metal products, alkaloids, chemicals	Diesel engines, VCRs, cars, synthetic fibres	abt 2,600 (8)
Poland	$19,986 million	$492 million (2.5%)	Alumina, metals, milk products	Machinery, cars, VCRs	2,185 (1)
Yugoslavia	$33,179 million	$464 million (1.4%)	Ferro-silicon, organic chemicals, wood (for skis), marble, wine, crystal products	TVs, telephones, office equipment	3,021 (2)
Romania	$8,599 million	$180 million (2.9%)	Alumina, coking coal	TVs, VCRs	570 (0)
Bulgaria	n.a.	n.a.	Ethylene, alumina	Machinery	107 (3)
Former USSR	R131,629	R3,436 (2.7%)	Gold, diamonds, pig iron, coal, cotton, timber, fish	Steel, chemicals, metals, machinery, plant, TVs, VCRs, transportation equipment	2,051 (33)

Source: Compiled from JETRO, *1991 Hakusho: Sekai to Nihon no Boeki* (1991 White Paper: Japan's Trade with the Rest of the World), Tokyo, and *1991 Hakusho: Sekai to Nihon no Kaigai Chokusetsu Toshi* (1991 White Paper: Japan's Foreign Direct Investment with the Rest of the World), Tokyo.

T. Ozawa

Table 10.2: Comparative assessments of the Eastern bloc by West European and Japanese manufacturers (end of 1990).

A: Eastern Europe as a potential production base (a) and a potential marketing outpost (b)

	West European firms		Japanese firms	
	(a)	(b)	(a)	(b)
Very attractive	15.3%	32.9%	1.1%	6.8%
Somewhat attractive	36.5	55.3	10.6	26.0
Not very attractive	32.9	9.4	51.3	46.4
Totally unattractive	9.4	2.4	35.5	19.2
No answer	5.9	0	1.5	1.5

B: The Soviet Union as a potential market

	West European firms	Japanese firms
Very attractive	37.6%	7.1%
Somewhat attractive	30.6	21.0
Not very attractive	22.4	44.6
Totally unattractive	9.4	25.5
No answer	0	1.8

Source: Ministry of International Trade and Industry, *1991 Tsusho Hakusho* (1991 White Paper on International Trade): 267, 287.

investment. It is well posited in the theory of international involvement that the marginal cost of operating directly in foreign markets is a declining function of the experiences (contacts) with those markets accumulated in the past (Aharoni 1966). Hence, the usual pattern of involvement is a sequential learning process, starting with exporting (or importing, as the case may be) and proceeding to the establishment of sales (or procurement) offices/warehouses/customer services, then to licensing agreements (or long-term purchase contracts – often with loans given to foreign suppliers), and finally to direct investment in local productions (equity acquisition). This process of reducing the incremental cost of foreign investment is usually one of muddling-through and groping (rather than being purely rational) composed of both 'investigations' and a series of 'market development' efforts at each different stage of involvement.

This type of cautious approach can be expected to occur when the market involved is previously unexplored territory that has all of a sudden opened up to the outside world. Japanese firms are following precisely this classical pattern of gradual involvement in Eastern Europe, and this process is expected to continue in the foreseeable future as they go through the initial learning phase.

Nevertheless, there are many good reasons, as analysed below, to expect that the marginal cost of operating directly in Eastern Europe on the part of Japanese multinationals, though currently much higher than for Western multinationals, will drop precipitously and converge, possibly even becoming lower, in the near future, a trend roughly depicted in Figure 10.1. It should be noted that the marginal cost functions shown are of a dynamic type, since the total cost functions themselves will shift downward over time as the former Soviet bloc begins to lay

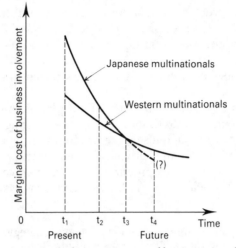

Fig. 10.1. Comparative marginal (dynamic) costs of business involvement, Japanese vs. Western multinationals.

out the foundations for market economies and as a variety of economic assistance and co-operation from the West already committed in substantial amounts help achieve political stability and improve the infrastructural facilities, both physical and intangible, necessary for the free-enterprise system.

Preparatory investigation and market development, Japanese style

Given the present uncertainties (political and commercial) about Eastern Europe and the high degree of hesitancy on the part of Japanese industry because of unfamiliarity, Japanese multinationals are still not quite prepared, either psychologically or strategically, to move in as decisively and set up direct local operations on as significant a scale as their Western counterparts. More information and many more measures of reducing business risks are needed before they make long-term commitments. Japanese multinationals are thus in the very early, water-testing phase of exploration. There are, however, underlying forces that are inexorably 'pushing' them into stepped-up direct involvement.

One strong undercurrent pushing Japanese multinationals towards Eastern Europe is the growing role of the Japanese government as a major donor of economic aid. For that matter, the Japanese government itself is being pushed towards the region by pressure from the West to make financial contributions commensurate to Japan's status as an economic superpower which has benefited greatly from the West's staunch and costly defence against communism; Japan now has an obligation to help secure stability in the region.

At the G-7 economic summit in July 1991, Japan pledged $2.5 billion in humanitarian aid and trade assistance for the then Soviet Union, in response to the initiative taken by EC to put together a $7 billion emergency aid package, with its own pledge of $1.54 billion. Prior to that, Japan had offered a $500 million loan from its Export-Import (Ex-Im) Bank to each East European country, including $200 million to Hungary for structural adjustment support as a co-financed loan with the World Bank. In addition, a series of grants of technical assistance and emergency food aid have been arranged. Thus Japan has emerged as a major – often the leading – financier in assisting economic reconstruction in many former communist countries. For example, Japan currently accounts for as much as 40 per cent of Hungary's foreign debt.

Small wonder, then, that as Japan's official aid plan is implemented, Japanese industry is about to be drawn into Eastern Europe's economic reconstruction. For it is a well-known policy of the Japanese government to implement economic assistance in close alliance with Japan's private sector, in order to apply the latter's capability to promote local development under what is called 'comprehensive economic assistance' (Ozawa 1989). As Japan's Overseas Economic Co-operation Fund (OECF) reports:

> In order to implement a comprehensive development strategy, it is critical to take advantage of the private sector's ability to transfer funds, its managerial know-how and the technical expertise it offers to developing countries. Accordingly, Japanese private corporations are encouraged to actively support Japan's economic co-operation programme.[1]

In reality, however, the reverse is true in most cases; Japanese private corporations are actively supported by Japan's economic co-operation programme. This is certainly the case with respect to Japan's aid to Eastern Europe at present.

Government assistance will sharply reduce the cost of business involvement, since it essentially subsidizes private operations, a subsidy justified for the sake of enhancing the social benefits (the maintenance of world peace by stabilizing Eastern Europe) by promoting the private sector's involvement as a wealth-generating mechanism. After all, what the region needs is privatization, and no one other than the private enterprises of the advanced market economies can demonstrate how it actually can be done.

Indeed, a large portion of Japan's economic aid so far offered is designed to reduce private risks – the private risks of Japanese industry associated with its commercial exchanges with Eastern Europe. When the $2.5 billion aid package was promised for the erstwhile Soviet Union, it included as much as $1.8 billion (no less than 72 per cent of the total) as a fund to cover the additional cost of Japan's government-run trade and investment insurance programme specifically allocated for the Soviet Union. Hungary also received $400 million coverage in trade and investment insurance on the occasion of the Hungarian prime minister's visit to Japan in September 1991.[2] The Japanese government regards the expanded insurance programme as an effective aid, since the local investment projects, among others, backed by such insurance could also secure more loans against their future profits.[3] In other words, such insurance serves as seed money for private funding.

No doubt, the Ex-Im Bank of Japan encourages Japanese exports of machinery and plant facilities, as well as Japanese direct investment. For instance, Suzuki Motor's joint venture in Hungary to produce passenger cars is supported by both Japan's Ex-Im Bank and the International Finance Corporation (IFC). The joint venture is 50 per cent owned by Autokonszern RT, a Hungarian holding company, 30 per cent by Suzuki, and 10 per cent each by IFC and C. Itoh & Co. The venture, initially capitalized at ¥20 billion ($138.7 million), will build 15,000 subcompact cars a year in 1992, 50,000 cars by the third year, and eventually 100,000 units – with engines of 1,000 cc and 1,300 cc.[4] Similarly, Daihatsu Motor's planned venture in Poland was supposed to be partly financed by Japan's Ex-Im Bank, although this project hit a snag when Poland defaulted and Japan's Ex-Im Bank suspended any further lending. However, it will most likely soon be revived (Nakamura, 1990).

Along with the Ex-Im Bank, OECF and the Japanese International Co-operation Agency (JICA) are actively involved in helping Japanese industry to organize joint ventures by providing funds for feasibility studies and for training local personnel.

Another 'get-acquainted' measure taken by Japanese industry in this early stage has been the dispatching of a large number of study missions organized by powerful business groups such as *Keidnaren* (Federation of Business Organizations), *Nikkeiren* (Federation of Employers' Associations), and the Japan Chamber of Commerce and Industry – usually in joint efforts with Japanese government officials (from the ministries and agencies such as the Ministry of International Trade and Industry (MITI) and Japan External Trade Organization (JETRO)). Academics and researchers from universities and research institutions are also frequent participants. For example, a special seven-day mission in January 1990 to help the Soviet Union's transportation and storage problems, included executives from East Japan Railway, Nippon Express, and Japan Airlines, researchers from private think-tanks (such as Nomura and Mitsubishi), and government officials from the Ministry of Transportation.[5]

For the time being, these semi-private study missions are organized largely on a 'non-partisan' basis, so to speak, since any major industrial group (*keiretsu*), if it chooses, is represented as a mission member, along with other groups. Yet once the incipient phase of information-gathering is over, different industrial groups (such as Mitsui, Mitsubishi, Sumitomo, and the like) are most likely to begin to pursue their own separate courses of action, especially as they organize specific development projects on a group-affiliation basis.

Closely related to the activities of industrial groups are Japan's unique transaction-facilitating organizations, general trading companies (*sogo shosha*). These are the trail-blazers of new overseas markets normally acting for their own closely affiliated industrial groups. These companies have already been active in rendering their information-gathering and business go-between services for possible joint ventures and trade opportunities. They themselves have begun to form strategic alliances with Key European firms, as will be discussed below. In addition, the general traders are skilful multinational negotiators and effective buyers of overseas natural resources such as oil, coal, minerals, timber, and marine products, which have traditionally been handled by them in the Japanese economy (Kojima and Ozawa 1984). Their role as direct investors in natural resource development is expected to rise in the resource-rich former Soviet bloc.

Since Japan is surely one of the world's largest importers of overseas resources, and the bulk of those resource imports are intermediated by a handful of general traders, Japan can often exercise considerable monopsony power, despite the keen inter-firm rivalry that exists among them. The breaking up of the Soviet empire into a large number of independent republics may further enhance Japan's bargaining power – thereby improving its terms of trade – as each republic has to deal separately with Japan's general trading firms.

All these developments, along with other factors examined below, that are likely to reduce the private costs of business involvement, point to the possibility of a rapid advance of Japanese industry into East European markets.

A 'pincer' approach and 'divided' integration

How will Japanese industry deal with the vast new market, composed of a large number of newly independent economies, extending from the Sea of Japan, through Siberia and the Urals to the Baltic Sea and to the Adriatic Sea? Japanese industry is again adopting an incremental 'get acquainted' approach in its geographical advance into Eastern Europe through direct business activities (direct investment as well as contractual agreements) and starting from two opposite sides of the region – from the Russian Far East and also from Western Europe, especially the new unified Germany – in a sort of pincer movement.

On the eastern front, there has recently been a great deal of trade and investment between Eastern Russia, especially Vladivostok, Nakhodka, and Khabarovsk, and Japan, notably Niigata as its major port. That Russian region is richly endowed with oil, natural gas, forest and marine products, and also tourist resources. The Sakhalin government, in particular, is eager to develop its natural resources in collaboration with foreign multinationals. Japan has already established the Sakhalin Oil Development Co-operation Co. (Sodeco), a consortium prepared to co-operate with the region in resource development. It is estimated that Sakhalin possesses more than 1.5 billion barrels of crude oil, and natural gas equivalent to 18 billion barrels of crude, and that it will cost more than $10 billion to explore and extract these resources, though such development is expected to proceed in a series of steps, initially requiring about $2.5 billion.[6] If fully developed, Japan would have an enormous energy supply right in its own backyard. The Japanese consortium is reportedly requesting a loan from Japan's Ex-Im Bank to cover close to half the initial cost.

The Japanese government itself is inclined to give a preferential treatment in its aid plans to the resource-rich but underdeveloped Eastern Russian region, which is considered politically more stable than its Western side. Besides, resource development in the Western region has already been initiated by Western multinationals, whereas the Eastern region is still largely untouched, thereby leaving a desirable territory for Japanese multinationals to develop, especially by linking its regional development to the Pacific Rim. A senior official at the Ex-Im Bank of Japan is quoted as saying that 'Far East' and 'energy resources' are key words in Japan's long-term aid policy towards Russia.[7] New hotels, communications, transportation, and other travel amenities are currently being built in Russia's coastal region facing the Sea of Japan, to accommodate the needs of businessmen and tourists.

In addition, the United Nations Industrial Development Organization (UNIDO) has formulated a blueprint to create a 'Greater Vladivostok Free Economic Zone', a zone including Nakhodka and bordered by China and North Korea to the south-west. UNIDO expects that the zone, with a radius of about 150 kilometres, will require $15–20 billion in total investment by 2010, and that the present population of 1.2 million will increase to 2.2–2.3 million over the same period.[8]

At the same time, on the far side of Eastern Europe, Japanese multinationals will advance eastward from Western Europe. In recent years Germany in particular has been attracting a large number of Japanese business operations – more rapidly than the UK, which had been the most attractive host country for Japanese multi-nationals until German reunification. In this regard, Japan's big general trading companies have been especially active in forging strategic alliances with German and Austrian firms, which have been the most active partners so far in the econ-omic reconstruction of their Eastern neighbours:[9]

- Mitsubishi Corporation is leading the Mitsubishi group in strengthening its ties with Daimler-Benz AG to develop joint programmes in R&D, production, and marketing in autos, electronics, and aerospace.
- Nissho Iwai Corporation has reached collaborative agreements with Metall Gesellschaft to develop markets in the former Soviet bloc in five key fields: non-ferrous metals, chemicals, machinery, steel and finance.
- C. Itoh & Co. has acquired a 5 per cent interest in German steelmaker Kloeckner-werks AG and has made agreements for co-operation in steel, machinery, and automotive parts.
- Marubeni Corporation has linked up with state-run Austrian Industries in product and market development for Eastern Europe, among others, in the area of plant exports and electronic home appliances.

In short, what Japanese multinationals on the western side of Eastern Europe are trying to do is to ride on the favourable easterly trade wind of Western Europe by aligning themselves with Western, notably German and Austrian, firms as busi-ness partners. Simultaneously, on the Pacific side, Japanese multinationals are promoting regional growth in Eastern Russia tied to the Japanese market and other East Asian economies. The erstwhile Soviet empire is thus about to be split and pulled towards two regional growth centres, the EC and the Pacific Rim.

Japan as a repository of policy and industrial experience

There is every indication that a tremendous potential exists for Japan's deeper involvement in Eastern Europe's reconstruction. Indeed, it may well be the case that ten years from now, Japan's presence will have risen swiftly, so swiftly as to cause some consternation for the West. As sketched out in Figure 10.1, the marginal cost of involvement for Japanese multinationals may indeed decline sharply, encouraging their direct business involvement. This is because, in addition to the complementary trade relations discussed above, Japan has accumu-lated what may be called policy know-how and experience, along with the neces-sary institutions, for industrial restructuring and upgrading, know-how and ex-perience that are relevant to and useful for Eastern Europe, where keen interest has already been expressed in learning from Japanese experience. Interestingly enough, Eastern Europe is currently confronted with many of the industrial re-structuring problems that Japan faced during the course of its own post-war catch-ing-up efforts.

Under Comecon, the Soviet empire established a highly centralized, intra-bloc division of labour in which relatively industrialized countries such as former East

Germany, Poland, Czechoslovakia, and Yugoslavia specialized in heavy and chemical 'smokestack' industries and a limited range of (light) consumer goods industries, while the Soviet Union provided industrial raw materials, semi-finished products, and energy resources, as well as markets for manufactures. Under communism, private consumption was kept to the bare minimum – and hence the consumer goods sector. This was in the interest of mobilizing resources for the extended supplies of military hardware and services. The first reform task required of the former communist bloc at the moment, then, is to move away from the lop-sided capital goods and military hardware sectors and to develop consumer-oriented independent market economies by dismantling the centralized command economy. It is also imperative for them to clean up the environmental damage caused by the unbridled expansion of smokestack industries. Economies which are at present fragmented also need to expand trade and direct investment in order not only to recapture but also to go beyond the benefits of one fully integrated former zone, the Soviet empire. Trade channels to facilitate access to Western markets, in particular, need to be established.

In sum, Eastern Europe must achieve:

1. price decontrol and marketization (introduction and expansion of the market system with the price mechanism as the main co-ordinator of economic activities);
2. resource reallocation away from the smokestack industries and toward consumer-goods and consumer-service industries;
3. pollution abatement and restoration of ecological balance;
4. expansion of trade and investment, not only with former Comecon members, but more importantly with the advanced West;
5. absorption of modern technology and stepped-up R&D, especially in the area of consumer goods manufacturing and exporting;
6. optimization of the role of the government in industrial upgrading.

Interestingly enough, these were mandates which confronted Japan in its recent history, albeit in varying degrees. The first task Japan had to tackle in its post-war reconstruction effort was price decontrol, a task Japan successfully accomplished while keeping inflation under control. No surprise, then, that the Soviet Union, immediately after the failed coup of 1991, asked Japan's Economic Planning Agency (EPA) to serve as an adviser for a joint study on a comprehensive reform plan for the Soviet economy, a study that would draw upon Japan's post-war reconstruction programme for transforming the war-time controlled economy into a market economy without any serious inflationary side-effects.[10] Although the Soviet Union is now a thing of the past, a similar programme – what EPA calls 'intellectual aid' – is likely to be retained in some of the newly independent republics, notably Russia. But Eastern Europe as a whole seems to have no choice but to endure cold turkey in its price decontrol programme.

As for the rest of the reform mandates for Eastern Europe listed above, Japan is equally suited to provide advice on policy formulation, since only in recent decades has Japan successfully transformed itself from an environmentally disastrous smokestack economy into a high-tech, 'cleaner' one by adopting, adapting and improving on, the latest Western technologies through its own R&D efforts. The government has been a skilled facilitator of Japan's industrial upgrading. Thus

Japan's experiences, in both the public and private sectors, are no doubt relevant and applicable in many ways for the tasks now facing Eastern Europe. What follows, therefore, is a brief review of Japan's post-war industrial upgrading and an examination of its relevancy and applicability for the current needs of the former Soviet bloc.

As presented elsewhere (Ozawa 1991a and 1991b), Japan has gone through four basic structural transformations since the end of the Second World War, a process greatly assisted by the Veblenian advantages of being a latecomer in industrial development, because Japan has been able to avail itself of opportunities to trade, interact with, and learn from the advanced West. In many respects, Eastern Europe is presently in a position similar to that of Japan at the end of the Second World War. The four phases of industrial upgrading Japan has experienced can be summarized as follows:

Phase I   'Heckscher-Ohlin' industries (1945–mid-1960s)
Expansion of labour-intensive manufacturing in textiles, toys, simple household electrical appliances, sundries, and other low-wage goods. Rising wages and labour shortages soon made these industries less competitive.

Phase II   'Non-differentiated Smithian' industries (late 1950s–early 1970s)
Scale economy-based modernization of heavy and chemical industries such as steel, shipbuilding, petrochemicals and synthetic fibres. Environmental costs of these pollution-prone, resource/energy-consuming industries became socially intolerable.

Phase III   'Differentiated Smithian' industries (late 1960s–present)
Assembly-based mass production of consumer durables, such as automobiles and electric/electronic goods. Its export dependency came to cause trade friction.

Phase IV   'Schumpeterian' industries (early 1980s onwards)
Mechatronics-based flexible manufacturing – small-lot, multi-variety production, along with innovations in HDTV, new materials, fine chemicals, advanced microchips, and opto-electronics.

It should be kept in mind that the above phases-based industrial metamorphosis has not been clear-cut in transition, but rather overlapping; while new industries come to dominate the whole structure, some declining industries still linger on. After all, the growth to dominance of a new type of industry in a previous period (t_1) needs to have been fostered as an infant industry in a previous period (t_n). This sequential progression of industrial upgrading from the crude to the more sophisticated is in line with what Adam Smith called 'the natural order of things' and 'the natural progress of opulence' (Smith 1776/1908: 290–924). Japan's stages-based transformation actually retraces, in a highly time-compressed fashion, the evolutionary changes experienced by the advanced Western countries over a much longer span of time.

Early on (Phase I), Japan thus repeated the strategy of exploiting the then most abundant factor, low-wage workers, to promote labour-driven industrialization as it had done in the pre-war period; it first rebuilt export competitiveness in labour-intensive light industries. Made-in-Japan manufactures in those days were synonymous with cheapness and shoddiness. But that was the best Japan could then do in order to create employment at home and earn precious foreign exchange overseas. This phase is probably irrelevant for most East European economies, since their wage rates are already fairly high and their labour force are quite human capital-based.

During the second thrust of development, Japan's industrial reorganization focused on heavy and chemical industries, such as steel, heavy machinery, and petrochemicals, despite the paucity at home of the natural resources needed by such industries (Phase II). Although these capital-intensive, higher value-added industries were considered consistent with the goal of raising productivity and increasing wage rates, they soon caused environmental havoc as they were extremely pollution-prone, especially in a geographically constrained country like Japan. Pollution and ecological destruction in Japan reached probably the worst level in the world at that time. This rising social cost compelled Japanese industry to restructure itself towards more knowledge-intensive, 'cleaner' industries. The outcome of Phase II industrialization thus presents a close parallel to the current economic conditions in Eastern Europe, and how Japan went about upgrading its industrial structure and cleaning up the environment is a highly relevant lesson for the latter.

It was against this background that at the start of the 1970s, the Japanese government announced a new economic policy, a proposal made by the Industrial Structure Council of the Ministry of International Trade and Industry (MITI). The new policy emphasized a reorientation of industry away from the resource-dependent, environmentally harmful heavy and chemical sector, towards R&D-based industries which could compete in the world market in terms of quality, variety, and sophisticated design and engineering, rather than price (which was a product largely of scale economies).

The Phase II industrialization, with the main focus on heavy machinery and chemicals which are energy- and material-intensive, came to be commonly known in Japan as the era of *ju-ko-cho-dai* ('heavy, thick, long, and big'). A new popular motto, *kei-haku-tan-sho* ('light, thin, short, and small') soon appeared as a consensual directive for Japanese industry to follow. Japanese industry, indeed, succeeded in translating these ideal characteristics into many innovative products that it brought to the market, one after another, starting in the early 1970s. There exists a great potential for Eastern Europe, especially the former Soviet Union, to learn from this industrial upgrading, since it is a region that suffers from industrial pollution and the crudeness (high material intensity) of its industrial products:

> A relative abundance of energy until recent years, low domestic energy prices, and the operation of the economic mechanism have combined to produce a profligate energy system. Energy-saving and conservation technologies have been neglected and resources extracted often with little regard to environmental consequences. . . .
>
> The Soviet economy is material-intensive or, more accurately, is characterized by relatively wasteful use of traditional materials. . . .
>
> The bulk of the inflated output of the Soviet steel industry is a product of low quality, its inadequate standards of hardness forcing users to build metal-intensive, overweight machines in order to compensate for its inherent lack of strength. It has been estimated that, on average, Soviet civilian machinery products are 15 to 20 per cent heavier than their foreign equivalents.
>
> (Cooper 1991: 42–43)

They are clearly still in the age of *ju-ko-cho-dai*, as Japan was in the late 1960s and early 1970s.

In Japan's next stage (Phase III) of industrial upgrading, environmentally com-patible, higher-quality, assembly-based industries – notably consumer electronics, office equipment, and automobiles – emerged as the dominant manufacturing industries. This stage of industrial upgrading proved to be compatible not only with the supply-side requirements (to move away from low value-added process-ing of imported natural resources and to capitalize on human capital at home) but also with the demand-side considerations (to meet the rising demands of now-affluent domestic consumers).

Indeed, up until the end of the second stage (until Japan's international pay-ments condition began to exhibit a favourable balance), the welfare of Japanese consumers had been secondary to the expansion of exports in order to earn pre-cious foreign exchange, although the age of mass consumption had its beginning in Japan, starting in the early 1960s with such slogans as 'the consumer is the king' and 'consumption is a virtue'. Yet it was not before the advent of the 1970s that Japan finally reached what W. W. Rostow calls a 'stage of mass consumption' in his stages theory of economic growth (Rostow 1960). For example, early on the govern-ment did not allow the import of Western technology or of 'brands' related to consumer goods; overseas travels for leisure were strictly prohibited in terms of foreign exchange allocation before the end of the 1960s. Indeed, it was only in the 1970s that an explosive rise in the demand for automobiles at home – the ultimate symbol of capitalist consumerism – materialized. In 1965, only 5.7 per cent of Japanese households owned cars, but the ratio had risen to 22 per cent by 1970 and to 40 per cent in 1975 (Oshima 1980: 139). Import restrictions in such consumer-oriented areas as packaging and distribution, furniture, cosmetics and sundries, dress designs, and leisure activities were liberalized only towards the end of the 1960s. Here, again, there is a close parallel between what the former Soviet bloc now needs to achieve and what Japan accomplished a couple of decades ago – namely, 'motorization' and 'consumerization'.

Viewed in the above light, and at some risk of over-simplification, Japan's tech-nological drive of the 1950s can be characterized basically as 'supply-push', since the major stimulus to technological progress came from the ready availability of advanced technologies already market-tested in the West, particularly in the capital goods sector, and from the policy emphasis of the government on building heavy industries; that of the 1970s, by contrast, may be distinguished as 'demand-pull', for it was domestic consumer demand that played a key role in encouraging manufacturers to introduce a succession of new products, many of which had some important innovative characteristics designed specifically to satisfy the grow-ing Japanese consumer markets. The prime example was the expanded output of subcompact cars, which were economical in petrol consumption and suitable for the narrow streets at home, by the Japanese automobile industry which had pre-viously produced mostly trucks and buses. The industrial sector thus began to be oriented more towards differentiated, higher value-added consumer durables. The future course of Eastern Europe now similarly lies in shifting from the supply-push to the demand-pull orientation, that is, to move away from the 'non-differentiated Smithian' industries (scale-based, energy/material-intensive) to the 'differentiated Smithian' industries (less resource-intensive and more consumer-oriented).

In particular, the present consumer goods sector in the former Soviet empire is in a dismal condition, reminiscent of that in Japan in the early 1950s:

> 'Until the recent period, which has seen a sharp policy turn in favor of consumption and welfare, most consumer-related sectors have been located near the base of the pyramidic economy. This applies to the light and food industries and the manufacture of a wide range of household goods. The overall technological level is low and the quality of many consumer goods leaves much to be desired. Household electrical and electronic goods at times exhibit quite remarkable backwardness. Most washing machines now in production are of a type dating from the 1950s, almost half the television output consists of black and white models of notoriously poor reliability, and to date there has been no manufacture of dishwashing machines.
>
> (Cooper 1991: 46)

Yet these consumer durables are probably the most promising growth industries, which will benefit enormously from the absorption of Western, particularly Japanese, manufacturing technologies as Eastern Europe becomes more consumer-oriented.

During Phase III restructuring, the emergence of mass consumption markets at home and Japan's effort to export consumer durables to high-income Western countries, notably the United States, in turn necessitated market-oriented R&D. It was against this backdrop that corporate research centres were set up one after another by leading Japanese manufacturers in the latter half of the 1960s and the early 1970s, emulating the activities of US corporations. This movement occurred *pari passu* with a rapid rise in R&D expenditure, especially in the latter half of the 1960s, when Japanese enterprises seriously stepped up research efforts and 'indigenous technological development' (*Jishu Gijutsu Kaihatsu*) became a catchphrase. R&D expenditures jumped from about ¥250 billion in 1965 to more than ¥800 billion in 1970, more than tripling over the five-year period.

Although Japan's R&D activities were then still mostly directed towards commercializing imported technologies, the groundwork was laid to upgrade Japan's industrial structure to the next phase of building 'Schumpterian' (R&D-based) industries, namely, Phase IV upgrading. Given the high level of human capital accumulation and technological sophistication in the former Soviet empire, though unevenly distributed both sectorally and geographically, the region has an excellent capacity to absorb advanced technology from the West and initiate commercial R&D, thereby fostering Phase IV structural transformation, as Japan earnestly strived to achieve in the 1970s.

In this connection it is worth noting that Japan's borrowing of industrial knowledge from the West was not confined to the realm of production alone: Japanese business managers were also eager learners of Western organization and management techniques, if not philosophies. In fact, such now familiar terms as automation, marketing, human relations, and productivity (*seisanse*) are all words which were introduced into the Japanese lexicon only in the post-war period. Eastern Europe will similarly be inundated with fresh capitalist concepts and practices.

In an effort to inculcate labour efficiency, the Japan Productivity Centre (JPC), a governmental organization established in 1959 with the help of the United States (which contributed ¥2.3 billion to the total fund of ¥10 billion) played a pivotal role in providing Japanese businessmen with the opportunities to visit US and European factories, business offices, and research centres in order to learn first-hand the secrets of Western management. Numerous seminars, lectures, and special guidance programmes were given to visiting Japanese managers, union leaders, and public officials.

In reciprocity, Japan is now actively transferring productivity know-how to the rest of the world and especially, to other Asian countries, through the Asian Productivity Organization (APO), the JPC's sister organization. A similar arrangement is likely soon to be made for Eastern Europe. Some preliminary contact was made between the JPC and the Soviet Union, which in fact, filed an application to become an observer of the APO in 1990.[11] Some former Soviet republics will probably reactivate the joint programme with the APO.

It was also during the 1960s that the now famed practice of quality control (QC) circles began to take root in Japan. The basics of control charts and sampling inspection with the use of statistical principles was introduced into Japan by W. E. Deming, of the United States, in 1950, and the first seminar on QC was given by J. M. Juron, also of the United States, in 1954. Although the techniques and concept of statistical quality control and total quality control, originally developed by academics in the United States, were thus imported, the practical QC techniques at the workshop level were developed to take advantage of Japan's special workplace environment by Japanese corporations themselves. Here, Japan has a unique advantage in transferring QC-related skills to Eastern Europe.[12]

In short, what Eastern Europe must undertake is essentially Phase III and Phase IV transformations; the development of consumer-oriented assembly-based industries, notably automobiles and electronics (that is, 'commercialization' of industrial activities, including 'motorization', as epitomized by the 'differentiated Smithian' industries which are less pollution-prone, higher value-added, and consumer-focused) and the growth of 'Schumpterian' innovation-based industries (that is, knowledge-intensification of industrial structure). And it is with respect to the industrial transformations of these two phases that Japan has an enormous potential to help Eastern Europe by way of direct involvement through investments (both direct foreign investment and a variety of contractual forms of knowledge transfers, but initially more via the latter route). Because of its great success of industrial upgrading in the recent past. Japan is a huge repository – perhaps larger than any other – of transferable skills, knowledge and experience.[13]

Sensing this potential relationship, in December 1991 MITI took the intiative to inaugurate a special organization to promote technical support to the Soviet Union, an organization comprised of eighteen groups from the government sector (such as the Japan Petroleum Development Association, the Japan Small Business Corporation, and the Japan External Trade Organization) and the private sector (such as the Japan Consulting Institute). This organization will continue to function as the major semi-public conduit to provide technical assistance to the Eastern bloc.[14] It is worth noting that Japan already ranks second, next to the former West Germany, as a supplier of technology to the Eastern bloc.[15]

Conclusions

Although Eastern Europe is pulled strongly towards Western Europe, particularly the EC, Japan's direct business involvement in the region is expected to increase quite rapidly. The relatively high level of economic aid directed by Japan to the Eastern bloc necessarily opens up many opportunities for Japanese multinationals, as the Japanese government stresses the private sector's role in promoting trade and investment as the major tools of economic co-operation. As a result, a substantial portion of Japan's official aid is channelled through its trade and investment insurance programme, loans from its Ex-Im Bank, and infrastructural services and funding by OECF and JICA. All this effectively reduces the private costs of advancing into Eastern Europe.

There is a significant complementary basis for trade between the former Soviet Union, which for the time being is most likely to depend on the exports of natural resources such as oil, natural gas, coal, timber, pulp and marine products as a way of earning hard currency, and Japan, which is in a suitable position to assist in the development of natural resources through direct investment and by importing such resources, and which can also supply consumer goods, especially cars and electronic goods, through trade and a variety of investment such as licensing and joint ventures.

Moreover, Japan's post-war experience with industrial restructuring and upgrading as a latecomer which has successfully caught up with the advanced West provides many valuable lessons. During the very process of catching up, Japan has developed and accumulated a huge stock of industrial technologies and skills which can be tapped by the Eastern bloc. Indeed, the Phases III and IV of structural upgrading which Japan accomplished in the 1970s and the 1980s are exactly the next stages of industrial catching-up required of Eastern Europe.

Japanese multinationals are advancing into the region from two opposite flanks: eastward, mostly in joint ventures with Western firms, from Western Europe where they have only recently begun to secure footholds through direct investment and strategic alliances and westward from the Russian Far East, notably Sakhalin, which can develop a highly complementary relationship in trade and investment with Japan and other emergent East Asian economies. The former Soviet empire will thus be linked up with two regional growth centres, the European Community and the Pacific Rim.

Notes

1. OECF (1984) *The Overseas Economic Co-operation Fund: Its role and activities:* 6, as quoted in Ozawa 1989.
2. 'Visit seen spurring Hungary projects,' *Nikkei Weekly*, September 21, 1991: 3.
3. *Japan Times Weekly*, International Edition, November 4–10, 1991: 18
4. Graven, K. (1990) 'Suzuki Reaches Accord to Build Cars in Hungary', *Wall Street Journal*, January 10, A10.
5. *Wall Street Journal*, December 4, 1990: 4.
6. Tamiya, A. (1991) 'Japan seen concentrating Soviet aid in far east', *Nikkei Weekly*, October 12: 1.
7. Ibid.: 1.
8. 'Free trade zone planned for Soviet Far East: UN organization coordinates efforts', *Nikkei Weekly*, November 9, 1991: 3.
9. Oishi, N. (1991) 'Strategic alliances set with EC giants', *Nikkei Weekly*, June 22: 15
10. Isaka, S. (1991) 'Japan – Soviet economic plan on way', *Nikkei Weekly*, September 21: 3.

11. 'Transferring Management Know-how to the USSR', *Tokyo Business Today*, July 1991: 64.
12. These post-war developments are discussed in Ozawa (1986).
13. In analyzing the possible strategies that can be pursued by Eastern Europe, John H. Dunning (1991) proposes three alternative models: the 'developing country' model, the 'reconstruction' model (patterned after Germany and Japan), and the 'systemic' model. My 'structural upgrading' model can be interpreted as an elaboration of the 'reconstruction' model. Dunning's reservations about the applicability of the model to the Eastern bloc equally apply: 'However, this model fails to take account of the enormous institutional impediments and the extent of the political and attitudinal change required by most East European nations (East Germany may be an exception) *before* private enterprise (which, after all, was stifled for only a decade or so in both Japan and Germany) is prepared to undertake the entrepreneurship, investment – including investment in R&D and manpower training – for economic reconstructing and growth' (p. 7).
14. 'Group forming to push technical support to Soviets', *Nikkei Weekly*, December 14, 1991: 3.
15. For example, in 1987 Japan ranked second among the six major technology exporters to the Eastern bloc; West Germany exported $447 million worth of technology, Japan $235 million, France $158 million, UK $141 million, Italy $75 million, and US $66 million. 'Hudson, R. (1990), 'East Awaits Flow of Western Technology', *Wall Street Journal*, May 30: A8.

References

Aharoni, Y. (1966) *The Foreign Investment Process*, Boston: Division of Research, Graduate School of Business, Harvard University.

Cooper, J. (1991) 'Soviet Technology and the Potential of Joint Ventures', in Alan Sherry *et al.* (eds), *International Joint Ventures: Soviet and Western Perspectives*, Westport, Conn.: Quorum Books.

Dunning, J. H. (1991) 'The Prospects for Foreign Direct Investment in Eastern Europe', *Discussion Papers in International Investment and Business Studies*, Series B Vo. IV (1991/92), Department of Economics, University of Reading.

Kojima, K. and Ozawa, T. (1984) *Japan's General Trading Companies: Merchants of Economic Development*, Paris: OECD.

Nakamura, Y. (1990) 'Veil o nugu To-oh' (Unveiling Eastern Europe) in T. Keizai, *1990 Kaigai Shinshutsu Kigyo Soran* (Listing of Japanese Firms Investing Abroad), Tokyo: Toyo Keizai: 9–15.

Oshima, T. (1980) *Jidosha Sangyo* (The Automobile Industry), Tokyo: Toyo Keizai Shimposha.

Ozawa, T. (1986) 'Japan', in J. H. Dunning (ed.), *Multinational Enterprises, Economic Structure, and International Competitiveness*, Chichester, John Wiley.

Ozawa, T. (1989) *Recycling Japan's Surpluses for Developing Countries*, Paris: OECD.

Ozawa, T. (1991a) 'Japan in a New Phase of Multinationalism and Industrial Upgrading: Functional Integration of Trade, Growth and FDI', *Journal of World Trade*, 25(1), February: 43–60.

Ozawa, T. (1991b) 'Japanese Multinationals and 1992', in B. Burgenmeier and J. Mucchielli (eds), *Multinationals and Europe 1992*, London: Routledge.

Rostow, W. W. (1960) *The Stages of Economic Growth: A Non-Communist Manifesto*, Cambridge: Cambridge University Press.

Smith, A. (1776/1908) *An Inquiry into the Nature and Causes of the Wealth of Nations*, London: Routledge; New York: E. P. Dutton.

11

Norwegian Companies in Eastern Europe: Past Involvement and Reaction to Recent Changes

Gabriel R. G. Benito and Lawrence S. Welch

Introduction

The recent dramatic political events in Eastern Europe[1] have resulted in major changes at all levels of the different national economies. The sheer extent of change and accompanying turmoil have made it difficult for outsiders to assess the eventual outcomes. With the ground shifting so rapidly, there is a high level of uncertainty about longer-term market possibilities and appropriate market responses. Assessment of the general situation is made even more difficult by the fact that the various countries in the area are dismantling their command economies and moving to market-based economies at different speeds and along different paths.

Nevertheless, Western companies are seeking to develop business in this uncomfortable environment. The prospect of many positive changes with emerging new opportunities has created a high level of interest amongst Western companies. As an early reaction, a survey of US chief executives found that 67 per cent saw Eastern Europe as a major new market which was expected to be comparable in importance to Western Europe within twenty years (Alpert 1990: 75).

Already there are many well-publicized examples of Western companies entering into a variety of arrangements to penetrate the newly-opened markets of Eastern Europe, as well as using them as a base from which to service Western markets, in some cases (Manasian 1991). The environmental protection equipment and services sector has been targeted by many Western companies as an area of particular marketing interest because of the severe pollution problems in Eastern Europe and in view of the likelihood of Western support, particularly from nearby European countries, to help deal with the sources of the pollution (Essaides 1991; Roos, Veie and Welch 1992).

In seeking to assess likely Western responses to developments in Eastern

This research has been financed by a grant from the Norwegian Council for Applied Social Research (NORAS).

Europe, those companies already involved in operations there, having been faced with the very real questions of whether and how to maintain activities through the turmoil, would appear to be uniquely placed to provide an indication of the nature and direction of reaction – at least in the early stages. For this purpose, Norwegian companies with operations in Eastern Europe were surveyed regarding their response to the changes taking place. The survey was undertaken during the summer of 1990, soon after the first major changes had taken place in Eastern Europe, when the ultimate course of events was still very unpredictable, and the subsequent developments in the Soviet Union in 1991 seemed inconceivable. As such the survey has to be regarded as historically time sensitive, although it can be argued that in one sense little has changed: there is still a strong sense of continued turbulence, of uncertainty about the ultimate form and state of the various economies in question, and about related prospects for interested Western companies. Clearly, though, the nature of past dealings is bound to affect perceptions about how business can be developed in the future. As a consequence, the investigation was set within the context of past relationships – at both the macro and micro levels.

Hence, the following section of this chapter gives a short overview of Norway's trade with Eastern Europe, with an emphasis on more recent patterns. There then follows a description of the company survey, presenting some characteristics of the companies surveyed and their operations in East European markets, and giving a brief summary of the findings with regard to the reasons for and mechanisms of doing business in these countries. Following this there is a section reporting the survey findings on how companies assessed the results that had been achieved so far from their operations in Eastern Europe, and on their plans and expectations for the future, both in the short and longer term. Finally, there is a concluding discussion of the results and their implications.

Norwegian Trade with Eastern Europe: General Overview

Historically, there have been significant and enduring trade links between Norway and the eastern parts of Europe. These date as far back as medieval time, when the western city of Bergen, being a member of the Hanseatic League, took part in the extensive and well-organized trade across Europe in that period. Somewhat later, the so-called Pomor trade between the northern regions of Norway and Russia took place for more than two centuries, but coming to an end with Russia's Bolshevik Revolution.

More recently, trade between Norway and the East European countries was substantial throughout the inter-war period and until the onset of the 'cold war' in the late 1940s. For example, in 1947 the eastern European markets – principally the Soviet Union, Poland and Czechoslovakia – accounted for nearly 10 per cent of total Norwegian exports (Ponte Ferreira 1990b). Due to several factors, perhaps most importantly the general deterioration of East–West relations, but also the self-sufficiency policies adopted by East European countries and the subsequent development of an internal socialist trade area through Comecon as well as the liberalization of intra-West trade, trade flows between Norway and the East European countries decreased steadily, reaching very modest levels in the 1960s and 1970s. This development corresponds quite closely to the broader picture of East–West trade relations throughout the post-war period (Ponte Ferreira 1990a).

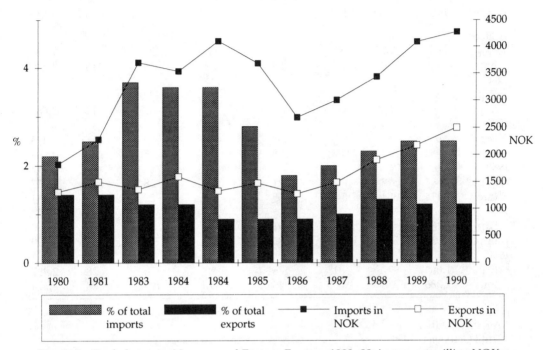

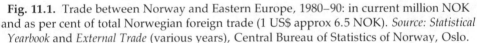

Fig. 11.1. Trade between Norway and Eastern Europe, 1980–90: in current million NOK and as per cent of total Norwegian foreign trade (1 US$ approx 6.5 NOK). *Source: Statistical Yearbook* and *External Trade* (various years), Central Bureau of Statistics of Norway, Oslo.

East European countries continued to be of minor importance as trading partners during the 1980s. They had in particular become almost negligible as export markets for Norwegian goods, representing only about 1 per cent of total Norwegian exports. However, imports from Eastern Europe have remained at a somewhat higher level, thus entailing, as shown in Fig. 11.1, an enduring, and in relative terms large, surplus of imports over exports.

A breakdown by country of the trade with Eastern Europe from 1980–90 (Table 11.1) shows that the Soviet Union is unquestionably Norway's most important trading partner in the area, consistently accounting for nearly half of Norway's trade with Eastern Europe. Other trade partners of some significance include Poland and the former GDR, and to a somewhat lesser extent Czechoslovakia and Hungary. On the whole, Poland emerges as Norway's second largest trade partner in the area, representing moreover a relatively large and seemingly growing market for Norwegian exports, whereas the former GDR was mainly a source of imports. In the case of Czechoslovakia and Hungary the trade figures indicate stable trade relations throughout the period, but at quite low volumes. Finally, the figures clearly show that the Norwegian trade with Romania has been highly irregular, with imports and exports varying considerably from year to year. Trade seems to have been virtually non-existent in the case of Bulgaria.

Table 11.1: Trade between Norway and Eastern Europe, 1980–90: breakdown by country, in million NOK (current values).

Year	Soviet Union	Poland	GDR	Czecho-slovakia	Hungary	Bulgaria	Romania	Total
1980–5[a]								
Exp	667	282	97	150	112	29	93	1,430
Imp	1,168	490	1,055	234	116	10	116	3,189
1986								
Exp	672	198	92	139	90	32	54	1,277
Imp	806	408	884	329	122	22	112	2,683
1987								
Exp	618	383	178	188	76	39	11	1,493
Imp	982	507	808	278	140	25	258	2,998
1988								
Exp	896	517	147	221	81	38	7	1,907
Imp	1,114	384	840	265	119	29	683	3,434
1989								
Exp	1,183	482	201	191	79	36	8	2,180
Imp	1,932	538	909	286	148	12	265	4,090
1990								
Exp	1,069	977	131[b]	176	88	28	28	2,497
Imp	2,386	558	506[b]	346	176	195	108	4,274

Notes:
[a] Average 1980–5.
[b] Until October 1, 1990.
Source: Statistical Yearbook and *External Trade* (various years), Central Bureau of Statistics of Norway, Oslo.

Table 11.2: Composition of trade between Norway and Eastern Europe in 1990: main commodity groups (SITC-Rev. 3), in million NOK.

	Imports	%	Exports	%
0. Food	292.3	6.8	236.5	9.5
1. Beverages and tobacco	8.2	0.2	1.7	–
2. Crude materials	1,074.0	25.1	304.1	12.2
3. Mineral fuels	752.4	17.6	678.3	27.2
4. Non-mineral oils and fat	20.2	0.5	27.1	1.1
5. Chemicals	409.1	9.6	186.1	7.5
6. Manufactured goods	675.5	15.8	298.9	12.0
7. Machinery and transport equipment	703.6	16.5	663.2	26.6
8. Miscellaneous manufactured articles	338.9	7.9	99.9	4.0
9. Other	–	–	1.1	–
Total	4,274.2	100.0	2,497.2	100.1

Source: External Trade 1990 Volume 1, Central Bureau of Statistics of Norway, Oslo.

Table 11.2 exhibits a breakdown by products of the trade between Norway and Eastern Europe in 1990. Although at a very aggregate level, the figures in Table 11.2 are nevertheless indicative of some basic patterns. First, the trade is strongly concentrated. For example, the extractive sectors, i.e. crude materials and mineral fuels, account for about 40 per cent of total imports as well as exports, while manufactured goods and machinery have a comparable share. Second, there is a high degree of correspondence, in terms of the main commodity groups, between imports and exports. For any given group of commodities, their share in exports is closely matched by their share in imports. Such a pattern is typical for the type of negotiated trade that usually takes place with centrally-planned economies.

While Eastern Europe has been of some significance in Norway's foreign trade in the past, it has clearly become a market area of relatively minor importance in the post-war period, especially during the 1980s. It would appear that the dramatic changes of recent times were probably a necessary prelude for any reawakening of interest on the part of Norwegian companies.

The Company Survey

Methodology

The principal aim of the survey was to provide an overview, at the micro level, of Norway's outward business relations with the Eastern European countries. Hence, we wanted to reach as many Norwegian firms involved in business operations in Eastern Europe as possible.

A major initial task was to compile a list of relevant firms. Several sources were consulted, including lists of participants in two conferences on Eastern Europe held in Oslo during the autumn of 1989, and inspection of two business-oriented daily newspapers as well as *Eksport-Aktuelt*, a magazine published twice a month by the Norwegian Export Council, during the second half of 1989 and the first half of 1990. A total of 182 companies were identified as probable exporters to Eastern Europe, or otherwise engaged in business operations in these countries.

A questionnaire was developed for the data collection. Personal interviews with managers from three Norwegian companies were conducted prior to the development of the survey instrument. The interviews gave a valuable insight into the problem areas and generated ideas for many items in the questionnaire. Later on, the interviewed managers also served as a pilot test group for a preliminary version of the questionnaire.

All companies sent the final version of the questionnaire were called up in advance in order to obtain the name of an appropriate respondent, usually the marketing director or the export manager.

The survey was undertaken during the summer of 1990. Replies were received from ninety-eight companies, a 54 per cent return rate. Of these, fifty-one companies had business experience from Eastern Europe and completed the questionnaire; ten companies returned only partly completed questionnaires, as they were planning to export to Eastern Europe but had not yet started exporting; thirty-three companies reported that they had no or insignificant business experience from Eastern Europe; finally, four companies refused to participate.

The survey appears to have given a quite satisfactory coverage of the target population. The value of exports to Eastern European countries by the fifty-one respondent companies totalled 1.5 billion NOK in 1989, representing almost 70 per cent of Norway's total exports to these countries in that year. A country breakdown of exports specified by the companies shows that coverage rates ranging from 100 per cent for Bulgaria to a low 19 per cent in the case of the former GDR, thus indicating some areas of bias in the sample. However, it should be noted that several companies failed to produce country-specific figures, stating instead their total exports to Eastern European countries.

The companies and their operations in Eastern Europe

The survey provided a basis for drawing a broad picture of Norwegian companies' involvement in Eastern European markets. In this section we will present some characteristics of the respondent companies and their operations in Eastern Europe.

A majority of the respondent companies (60 per cent) were in the industrial sector, most of these having, not surprisingly in the light of the pattern of trade between Norway and Eastern Europe, industrial and business markets as their main line of business. Only six companies regarded consumer goods as their principal line of business. Of the remaining companies, roughly half were trading companies, while the other half were in other parts of the services sector. The respondent companies were quite evenly distributed in terms of their size, about half of them being small and medium-sized, i.e. yearly sales of less than 200 million NOK. With respect to international involvement and experience, however, it appears that a clear majority of the companies must be characterized as being highly 'internationalized'. For example, 67 per cent of the companies reported that their export-to-sales ratio exceeded 0.5. Also, nearly two-thirds of the companies in the survey reported that they had fifteen or more years of export experience, and a similar fraction had established sales or manufacturing subsidiaries in foreign countries.

When asked about the nature of their involvement in the East European markets, most companies singled out exports as their principal activity. A majority of the companies also stated that their first business operation undertaken in these markets had been export operations. However, as reported in Table 11.3, a surprisingly large number of firms were, or had been, engaged in other types of operations as well. These ranged from ownership as well as contractual arrangements to a variety of other activities such as imports and brokerage of goods and raw materials. Perhaps most noteworthy is the considerable number of subsidiaries (twelve) established in Eastern Europe by Norwegian companies. It should be noted, however, that almost all were quite new and hence quite small. Only two subsidiaries had more than ten employees at the time of the survey, among them the oldest one (established in Hungary in 1979). Another interesting finding is that a majority of the companies in the survey had operated in more than one East European market. Many companies displayed a considerable breadth not only in the type of activities conducted, but also in the number of different markets they were involved in.

Contractual arrangements often serve as substitutes for ownership modes when foreign direct investment is prohibited or severely restricted (Kogut 1986), as was the case with most East European countries until the latter half of the 1980s. Therefore, as restrictions on foreign ownership have gradually been relaxed by the East European countries, one would expect a corresponding move from contractual modes to ownership modes. The survey data indicate that Norwegian companies have certainly responded in this direction: only two of the nine contractual arrangements reported by the companies were of a recent date (1989 and 1990), the other seven having been entered into prior to 1986. By contrast, eleven out of twelve subsidiaries established by the companies were less than four years old by the time of the survey.

Table 11.3. Types of operations in Eastern Europe undertaken by the companies up to the time of the survey.

| Country | Exports | No. of companies engaged in: | | |
		Subsidiaries[a]	Contractual arrangements[a]	Other activities[b]
Soviet Union	23	7	1	6
Poland	24	1	5	3
GDR	16	1	1	4
Czechoslovakia	17	–	–	2
Hungary	15	2	–	2
Bulgaria	16	1	1	3
Romania	9	–	1	5

Notes:
[a] When established:
    Contract operations – 1986: 7, 1987–90: 2.
    Subsidiaries – 1986: 1, 1987–90: 11.
[b] 'Other activities' include imports, brokerage etc.

Doing business in Eastern Europe: motives and experiences

In the questionnaire the companies were asked about a range of topics related to strategic as well as operational dimensions of conducting business in East European countries. Overall, the companies displayed a high degree of uniformity regarding their motives for entering East European markets. Although they were offered a total of ten different items in the questionnaire, three motives stood out as being particularly decisive: (1) the likely importance of these markets in the future; (2) the supply of products well-suited to these markets; and (3) the need for expansion into new markets. Unexpectedly, several factors commonly regarded as being of major importance for decisions of this kind, such as the proximity of markets, reaction to moves by competitors, and unsolicited export orders from abroad, received average ratings of only medium or even low importance. Taken overall, the results indicate that strategic long-term considerations were the main driving force behind the companies' entry into Eastern Europe.

One of the aims of the survey was to identify problem areas and obstacles to doing business in Eastern Europe, and to assess their magnitude. For this purpose the questionnaire contained a total of twenty-seven items pertaining to three broadly defined groups: (1) contact, interaction and co-operation; (2) operational/ functional issues; and (3) knowledge and competence. Moreover, the companies were asked to specify the extent to which problems were encountered, both in the initial and the more established phases of their business operations in Eastern Europe.

The results indicate that the most severe problems facing the companies were related to certain operational issues. The greatest difficulties were found to appear in connection with physical distribution, probably not unexpectedly, given the generally underdeveloped state of the infrastructure in the East European countries (von Amerongen 1990). Issues related to production, such as ensuring efficient production and reaching satisfactory levels of quality of products, also posed serious problems. However, experience of such problems was limited to a fairly small number of companies in the sample, principally those that in one way or another (mostly through various types of contractual arrangements) had been involved in production activities in these countries. Nevertheless, the findings are in line with the results reported in a number of previous studies of Western firms engaged in co-operative manufacturing ventures in Eastern Europe (Miller 1978; Högberg and Wahlbin 1984; Paliwoda and Liebrenz 1984). The seriousness of the problems associated with distribution and production activities is aggravated moreover by their apparent tendency to be of a quite enduring nature, in part reflecting the fact that they are to a large extent beyond the locus of control of the companies.

The second area that produced a number of high problem-ratings was contact and interaction with various actors in the East European countries. Identification of the relevant actors in the decision-making process was, on the whole, associated with some difficulty, especially with regard to discovering the identities of those actors that actually influenced and made the purchasing decisions, whereas 'gate-keepers' were identified somewhat more easily. However, as the average ratings were generally considerably lower for companies in the 'established' phase as compared to those in the 'initial' phase, it would seem that such problems are of a fairly transient nature, representing primarily an obstacle in the initial development of business. On the other hand, the ongoing dismantling of the centrally-planned economies has introduced new, but still very unsettled, contingencies that may well create obstacles for 'old-timers' as well as for new entrants. Because an 'un-learning' process will be required, it is even conceivable that companies with extensive prior involvement in East European markets may actually suffer a type of handicap vis-à-vis newcomers in certain situations (Roos, Veie and Welch 1992).

Perhaps as interesting as those issues that were assessed as being problematic, are the areas that were generally found to create fewer problems. The broadly defined group of issues related to knowledge and competence represent such an area. The survey findings indicate that issues like market knowledge, access to qualified personnel, and language barriers, did not represent severe problems for most of the companies. A similar picture was found in connection with the companies' assessment of how difficult it was to co-operate and interact with the foreign trade organizations and with other authorities in the East European countries. On the whole, these relations could be characterized as relatively trouble-free. Although the companies experienced difficulties in orienting themselves in the decision-making process as such, at least initially, the type of interaction that took place at the more personal and operational levels appears to have been less problematic.

Relatively few problems were reported either, about a range of economic and financial aspects of the operations, such as obtaining the same prices as in other markets, getting paid for deliveries, and gaining export guarantees, loans and credits. In the same vein there was surprisingly infrequent usage of countertrade among the companies in the survey. A majority of the companies (60 per cent) actually reported that they had never been engaged in countertrade. Only three companies in the survey stated that countertrade (in various forms) occurred frequently. In general, the companies did not regard the profitability of their operations as a major problem. The companies did, however, express concern about the period of time it took from initial contact being made to the achievement of positive results, on average rating this point towards the 'highly problematic' end of the scale. Other studies provide similar findings (Hecht and Oliver 1988). It seems that time-consuming, lengthy negotiations have been endemic to the centrally-planned systems of these countries.

Reactions to Changes in Eastern Europe

A key objective of the investigation of Norwegian companies' involvement in Eastern Europe was to obtain not only an assessment of their past experience but also, of particular importance, an outline of their plans for the future – in the context of the considerable changes taking place in June 1990. Of course, such plans have to be seen in the light of past experience, as noted already, even though the changes taking place in Eastern Europe have been unique in historical terms. In the light of heightened uncertainty and change there is a tendency for companies to lean even more strongly on those elements of the situation that are known from direct experience (Carlson 1975; Johanson and Vahlne 1977).

Table 11.4: Assessment by the companies of results achieved in East European markets up to the time of the survey – distribution of responses.

	Very poor (1)	(2)	(3)	(4)	Very good (5)	Total
No. of responses	–	12	18	10	8	48
Per cent	–	25.0%	37.5%	20.8%	16.7%	100.0%

Companies were asked to rate their business involvement in Eastern Europe up to the time of the survey on a five-point scale from 'very poor' (1) to 'very good' (5). The results are shown in Table 11.4. Of the forty-eight companies responding to this question, perhaps surprisingly, none considered their results to have been 'very poor', although 25 per cent classified their experience as 'poor'. This was in contrast to the 37.5 per cent of companies that considered their results to have been 'good' (20.8 per cent) or 'very good' (16.7 per cent), i.e. in general the balance was towards a relatively positive assessment of the results from their involvement in East European markets.

These results are actually surprisingly close to those obtained in an earlier study of Swedish industrial co-operation agreements with East European enterprises (mostly Polish and Hungarian). In this study, 30 per cent of outcomes were rated as unsuccessful or very unsuccessful, whereas 43 per cent of outcomes were regarded as successful or very successful (Högberg and Wahlbin 1984: 72). In both studies a wide range of types of problem was noted, some seemingly insoluble over time, because they were of a systemic character, but the companies concerned seem to have been able to cope with them, treating them as something to be expected and as part of the normal way of doing business in Eastern Europe, if not elsewhere.

For companies considering future prospects in Eastern Europe, the type of changes actually occurring in the different countries is clearly important. As a way of accessing the thinking in the Norwegian companies regarding this factor, they were asked an open-ended question regarding what politico-economic developments would be of greatest importance for their operations in Eastern Europe. In their replies, the most frequently noted developments were:

- liberalization of the economy – towards a market-based system;
- in line with above grouping, companies stressed financial and foreign currency issues – such as convertibility of the currency and making 'hard currency' available;
- political developments were also considered important – such as democratization, greater stability and the establishment of Western-style laws and rights.

The general impression gained from the responses was that such developments were seen as likely to occur as an inevitable part of the change process underway, and that they would have a beneficial effect on operations. When asked to assess political developments in the different East European countries, rated on a scale of 'very negative' (1) to 'very positive' (5), the (average) results were as follows:

Poland	3.93
Hungary	3.44
Eastern Germany	3.19
Soviet Union	3.19
Czechoslovakia	3.00
Bulgaria	2.67
Romania	2.63

Thus, although the overall position on East European political developments was positive, there was a quite substantial differentiation by country. In interviews with three companies conducted prior to the formal questionnaire survey, the managing director of a trading company with extensive experience in Eastern Europe stated that 'the Central European countries – Poland, Czechoslovakia and Hungary – are generally interesting because of low risk. In the case of the Soviet Union one should be careful. Smaller companies should stay away from the Soviet Union.' Another interviewee (the vice president of marketing with a large industrial group) also commented that 'the most difficult country is the Soviet Union. The political situation is very uncertain and unstable.'

Companies in the survey were also asked to indicate their plans for the future with regard to operations in Eastern Europe. Despite limitations on interpreting the answers to such a question, particularly in such turbulent times, it was nevertheless felt that they could at least provide some insights into the general mood and direction of their thinking. The results are shown in Table 11.5.

Table 11.5: Plans indicated by the companies for future presence in East European countries ($n = 51$).

	No. of responses[a]	Per cent
Increase exports to present markets in Eastern Europe	32	62.7
Expand into new East European markets	24	47.1
Establish own subsidiaries in Eastern Europe	13	25.5
Retain present level of involvement	11	21.6
Reduce the level of involvement	3	5.9

Note:
[a] Multiple responses were allowed for the first three items.

Of the fifty-one respondent companies, thirty-two (63 per cent) planned to increase exports in their existing Eastern European markets, presumably taking the view that their prospects could be expected to improve in these markets. Twenty-four companies – i.e. around half of the sample – planned to expand operations into new Eastern European markets. Perhaps even more significant, though, thirteen companies (25 per cent) indicated that they had plans to establish their own subsidiaries within Eastern European countries – an interesting result when seen in light of the limited number of Norwegian subsidiaries in Eastern Europe that actually existed at the time of the survey. Only three companies out of the total sample were planning to reduce their involvement in Eastern Europe. In general, therefore, the companies in the survey, when looking at future involvement in Eastern Europe, appear to have taken a relatively expansionist stance.

Table 11.6: Expectations held by the companies as to the outcome of future business operations in Eastern Europe – distribution of responses in per cent.

	Very poor (1)	(2)	(3)	(4)	Very good (5)	No. of responses
Short run	6.5%	10.9%	58.7%	19.6%	4.3%	46
Long run	2.2%	2.2%	22.2%	44.4%	28.9%	45

The basis for this preparedness to commit is perhaps revealed in answers to a further question on future involvement, in which companies were asked how they thought their operations would fare in the future – the short run and the long run – rated on a five-point scale from 'very poor' (1) to 'very good' (5). The answers are shown in Table 11.6. The results are much more positive for the long run than for the short run: for example, 73.3 per cent of the companies felt that in the long run, operations would be good or very good, whereas only 23.9 per cent of the companies had a similar view of the short run.

In interviews, some of the 'short-term' problems became readily apparent. It was clear that the changes already taking place had begun to disrupt existing lines of communication and that the marketing process had become more demanding. As the function of the foreign trade organizations gradually breaks down, their role as 'gate-keeper' and decision-maker is being dispersed, principally to end-users. As one respondent (a senior level employee of a large diversified industrial group) pointed out, 'sometimes it is a problem of figuring out who is actually deciding', and that there is now a lack of an 'institutionalized meeting place'. 'One has to arrange everything oneself. Identifying customers and dealing with them becomes important'. This concern was echoed by another interviewee, a vice president of a large industrial group, who stressed that the new 'fuzzy' situation which had been created was making the identification of trade partners/customers one of the 'biggest problems'. In principle, this customer search requirement is, of course, no different from that in normal Western markets, although it is difficult at present to access ready-made data sources in locating customers/partners and obtaining information about them (Manasian 1991).

Conclusion and Implications

The results of the survey of Norwegian firms operating in Eastern Europe paradoxically seem to reveal both expectations about problems in the business climate there, particularly in the short run, and an overall sense of optimism. Perhaps this partly reflects an emotional attachment and commitment, which is not evident among, for example, Japanese companies (Sasseen 1991). Admittedly the survey was undertaken at quite an early stage of the change process, but it was already clear that there would be significant disruption and uncertainty about the final outcomes. In general, though, in the first half of 1990 there was a broad feeling of optimism, even euphoria, which has since given way to a more sober assessment of prospects in Eastern Europe (Manasian 1991; Roos, Veie and Welch 1992). It could be argued, however, that those companies already involved in operations there, dealing with the day-to-day realities of such business, would be less affected by the general mood.

Among respondent companies there was, not surprisingly, a differentiated view of the various countries in Eastern Europe. A similar survey today would probably produce a changed relative assessment of the different countries' prospects. The perception of Romania and Bulgaria would probably even be worse, while the dramatic developments in the Soviet Union in 1991 would most likely have caused a major reassessment of that country – or rather, those countries. Direct experience does of course tend to sharpen the sense of the individuality of different foreign markets.

Overall, though, there is a certain consistency in the results, indicating a positive view of developments based on past experience and looking through the immediate disruption to longer-term prospects. The fact that such a high proportion of the survey participants (75 per cent) felt that past operations were acceptable or better – in the light of the obvious problems – seems to reveal a high level of realistic expectation about the business. The positive view is further reflected in the number of companies planning to expand into new East European markets. Twenty-five per cent of the companies planned to establish subsidiaries, whereas only three companies indicated that they would be reducing their involvement. The preparedness to commit, however, appears to have been related to a longer-term view of East European prospects, which were rated much more highly than in the short term.

Therein of course is one of the basic difficulties when considering involvement in Eastern Europe. Despite the tantalizing general appearance of newly-opening markets, with the disruption, economic problems and uncertainty of the moment there is a strong temptation to adopt a 'wait-and-see' attitude, which has been the approach of many outsiders. Japanese companies, in particular, have exhibited considerable reluctance to invest in Eastern Europe, even when backed by government-supported, low-priced credit lines. The London head of the Japanese government's Export-Import Bank has commented that 'Japanese firms continue to look at Eastern Europe with extreme caution. ... Most want to see the basic infrastructure in place and the economic climate improve before they will consider putting money into these countries' (Sasseen 1991: 48).

For many other companies, though, the concern is that by waiting too long the market will be ceded to other new entrants, who will be difficult to dislodge at a later stage. Companies already involved in business operations in Eastern Europe, such as those taking part in the survey, have certain insider advantages, for example contacts with key people and institutions, as well as access to necessary raw materials, which are often critical factors in a changing environment. At the same time, though, there is a danger of becoming locked into networks which will become irrelevant in the restructuring process. Interviews indicated that already in mid-1990 some Norwegian companies had experienced increased marketing problems with the decline of the role of the foreign trade organizations as centralized purchasers of foreign goods and services. Flexibility is obviously a critical requirement in the current environment, but the ability to be flexible depends on a clear understanding of the situation, and that is difficult for an outsider; a basic learning process has to be gone through. It is interesting to note that when the Soviet Union first allowed joint venture operations involving foreign companies, it was Finnish and West German companies which were most adept at establishing operative ventures, based on pre-existing activities (Holtbrugge 1989; Welch 1990). In this context it has been suggested in one Soviet review of joint ventures that:

> Even a small joint enterprise is a kind of window into our country for a number of foreign firms. If a firm finds out about our economic mechanisms through the setting-up of a small joint enterprise, it might decide to conclude larger agreements with the appropriate Soviet organizations and to develop mutually beneficial connections.
> (Aganbegyan 1989: 208)

The results presented here indicate that Norwegian companies have responded along similar lines to the ongoing changes in the Eastern European countries. However, in the rapidly changing environment of Eastern Europe, it remains an open question as to how substantial and permanent the insider advantages will be.

Note

1. For the purposes of this article Eastern Europe includes the former Soviet Union, Poland, Hungary, Czechoslovakia, Bulgaria, Romania and the former East Germany (GDR).

References

Aganbegyan, A. (1989) *Moving the Mountain: Inside the Perestroika Revolution*, London: Bantam Press.

Alpert, M. (1990) 'Wary Hope on Eastern Europe', *Fortune* (International) 121 (3) January 29: 75–6.

von Amerongen, O. W. (1990) 'Selling to the Soviets: A Pragmatic View', *European Affairs* 4(3): 51–3.

Carlson, S. (1975) 'How Foreign is Foreign Trade?' *Acta Universitatis Upsaliensis, Studia Economiae Negotiorum* No 15, Uppsala.

Essaides, G. A. (1991) 'Prospects for Profits: Czechoslovakia through 1993', *Business International* 38(8) February 25: 68–9.

Hecht, L. L. and Oliver, J. K. (1988) 'The Experience of US Firms with the Soviet Union: What Does the Past Tell Us To Do in the Future?', *Columbia Journal of World Business* 23(2): 91–8.

Holtbrugge, D. (1989) 'Managerial Problems of Joint Ventures in the Soviet Union', in Luostarinen, R. (ed.) *Dynamics of International Business*, Proceedings of the 15th EIBA Conference, Helsinki, Dec. 17–19: 189–214.

Högberg, B. and Wahlbin, C. (1984) 'East–West Co-operation: The Swedish Case', *Journal of International Business Studies* 15(1): 63–79.

Johanson, J. and Vahlne, J.-E. (1977) 'The Internationalization Process of the Firm – A Model of Knowledge Development and Increasing Commitments', *Journal of International Business Studies*, 8(1): 23–32.

Kogut, B. (1986) 'On Designing Contracts to Guarantee Enforceability: Theory and Evidence from East–West Trade', *Journal of International Business Studies* 17(1): 47–61.

Manasian, D. (1991) A Survey of Business in Eastern Europe, *The Economist* (Supplement) September 21.

Miller, J. C. (1978) 'Entry of US Companies into Eastern Europe and the USSR: Marketing Opportunities and Constraints', in Fisk, G. and Nason, R. W. (eds.), *Macro-Marketing: New Steps on the Learning Curve*, Proceedings of the Third Macro-Marketing Seminar, Rhode Island, August 13–16, 401–418.

Paliwoda, S. and Liebrenz, M. (1984) 'Expectations and Results of Contractual Joint Ventures by US and UK MNCs in Eastern Europe', *European Journal of Marketing* 18(3): 51–66.

Ponte Ferreira, M. (1990a) 'East–West Economic Relations: A Historical View', *NUPI-Paper* No 427, June, Norwegian Institute of International Affairs, Oslo.

Ponte Ferreira, M. (1990b) 'Norway's Exports to Eastern Europe and The Soviet Union: Past Trends and Prospects', *NUPI-Report* No 152, November, Norwegian Institute of International Affairs, Oslo.

Roos, J., Veie, E. and Welch. L. S. (1992) 'A Case Study of Equipment Purchasing in Czechoslovakia', *Industrial Marketing Management* 21(3), 257–264.

Sasseen, J. (1991) 'Japan takes it Gently', *International Management* 46 (9), November: 48–51.

Welch, L. S. (1990) 'The Implications of Perestroika for Developing Business with the Soviet Union, especially via Joint Ventures', *Management Paper* No 30, July, Graduate School of Management, Monash University, Melbourne.

12

Developing a Network Position in the Baltic States: The Case of Statoil in Estonia

Pervez N. Ghauri and Anne-Grethe Henriksen

Introduction

The dramatic changes in Europe in recent years have created a complexity of variables which have to be mastered by the companies. Apart from the changes initiated by the European Community and its programme for 1992, the liberalization of the Baltic states has been of particular interest for Nordic firms, which consider the Baltic states to be an extended and natural market for their products. The Nordic firms enjoy considerable advantages in these markets, as compared to firms from other regions. This new situation creates new challenges and opportunities both for these firms and also for researchers studying and analyzing new dimensions of international business which have never been experienced before.

A number of countries have worked together for the industrialization of Western Europe and the Baltic states have played a very important role in this process (Klinge 1984; Tilly 1990). Multinational and international companies, rather than states, are a common feature of today's industrial system. More recently it has also been observed that these companies and conglomerates are working more on a supranational level, with bigger integrated units spread over several countries or regions. Economic integration of nations is becoming the fashion of the day and is spreading to new areas and regions (Gerner 1990). Geographical, political, cultural and economic factors are working positively towards this process of integration and co-operation. GATT, EC, EFTA, ASEAN and the Pan-American Agreement are some examples of this development.

The liberalization of the Baltic states is fostering the development of co-operation, especially between the Baltic states and the Nordic countries (Mare Balticum 1990). There are numerous opportunities for Nordic firms for trade and investment in this region, provided they are able to develop new relationships and handle the new dimensions and problems involved in international business. This particular aspect demands a new perspective on international business operations.

It is not just a question of establishing business relationships with a foreign partner, but also of developing new industrial and market structures and a network of business relationships, beneficial not only for the firm but also for the local development and infrastructure (Mare Balticum 1990).

In the last decade, several studies have shown that firms develop and maintain long-term relationships with their suppliers, distributors and even with their competitors, using this network of relationships as part of their competitive strategy (Håkansson 1982, Ghauri 1989 and Johanson and Mattsson 1991). Studies in industrial marketing have also shown that this kind of networking can extend beyond the borders of countries and industries (Hägg and Johanson 1982). It has also been put forward that network relationships have played a major role in the internationalization and technological development of companies (Johanson and Mattsson 1988; Håkansson 1989; Hallén, Johanson and Seyed-Mohamed 1991).

Taking the above as its background, this study is part of a bigger research project entitled 'Nordic business relations in regional and international networks', co-ordinated by Uppsala University. Researchers from Sweden, Norway, Finland and Denmark are participating in this project, the main purpose of which is to investigate how Nordic firms are handling the changing situation in the Baltic states. There is a unique opportunity to study the development of networks in the process of dramatic market restructuring. Another purpose of the project is to create a common research forum around the network approach and international business studies through participants from different Nordic countries.

With the foregoing in mind as the overall purpose of the project, the study at hand has endeavoured to answer the following questions:

1. Which industries are represented from Norway and what types of structures exist in these industries in the Baltic states?
2. Which Norwegian companies are active in these states, and how have they entered these markets?
3. Which factors have been essential for these firms to develop a position in this new market?
4. Which problems are faced by Norwegian firms while entering these markets, and how are these problems solved?

In this particular report only one in-depth study is reported, however, it is anticipated that the project shall study all Norwegian firms active in the Baltic states in the coming three years. The results presented here and in the subsequent reports should be of great use for the Nordic business community, providing knowledge and insight into this important market. Each report and the final report will conclude with some managerial implications which could be used as guidelines for Nordic industry and businesses considering entering this market.

The report will also discuss the transfer of knowledge and technology from Norway and the implications of this on local industry structures, highlighting the problems faced in this process. It could therefore serve as a base for Norwegian government policy towards these countries as regards industrial support and trade relations.

Finally, as the project will discuss and analyze industry structures and how these are influenced by foreign trade and investments, it will be highly useful for the governments of Baltic states in promoting their industrial and trade relationships with Nordic and other foreign firms.

The network approach

As mentioned earlier, we are going to use the network approach as a theoretical base for our study. The network approach was developed through empirical studies in Scandinavia and there are several studies available using and advocating this particular approach in international business (Hägg and Johanson 1982; Thorelli 1986; Johanson and Mattsson 1988; Håkansson 1988; Ghauri 1989; Hallén, Johanson and Seyed-Mohamed 1991). According to this approach, the connection of firms to each other through relationships creates a network. Firms have to establish relationships with their suppliers, distributors, customers and even with their competitors to exchange information, technical knowledge, financial resources and marketing know-how. For an effective exchange of these resources the firms have to develop a trustworthy relationship with other actors in the same market (network). And, to develop trust among each other the actors/firms have to adjust and adapt to each other with regard to products, production systems and other routines. Moreover, they have to develop personal relationships with individuals/managers from each others' organizations. To develop a network of these bonds firms have to make investments in these relationships, which should be considered as any other asset of the firm (Johanson and Mattsson 1985).

The process of relationship development, the exchange process and factors influencing these relationships is reported in several studies (Ford 1980; Turnbull and Valla 1986; Cook and Emerson 1987; Blankenburg and Johanson 1992). Developing a network of relationships entails that the firms as well as other actors in the network have to adjust their already existing relationships. Consequently, the networks become rather stable structures, while being open for adaptations and adjustments. However, different networks may have different structures, tight or loose. In a 'tight' network, actors/firms would have very close and strong interdependence relationships with each other. In a 'loose' network, on the other hand, the firms/actors would have rather loose relationships, without strong interdependence. Some networks are 'tight' because of personal relationships between individuals from different firms and are prone to changes (restructuring), for example, when one or several individuals leave or change their position. Although, relationships between the firms is the most important factor in the structure of a network, some third-party relationships can also be crucial. For example, government authorities, banks or insurance companies may play the role of a crucial actor in a network.

According to this approach, the firms are striving to develop a position for themselves in a given network. The position of a firm, in a given network, is dependent on what relationships it has with other actors in the network and how strong these relationships are. It is in the interest of the firm to spend time and resources to nurture these relationships and to establish trust. Once a firm has established such a relationship it is an asset for the firm – in other words, the firm will have a competitive advantage. Moreover, the stronger (tighter) the network, the more difficult it is for a newcomer to enter that particular network and thereby the market. The network thus serves as a barrier to entry and is comparable to Japanese *keiretsu* and Korean *chaebols* (Prasad and Ghauri 1992).

Methodology

The overall project is based on the assumption that different actors in this process of relation development act according to perceived opportunity structure. It is not possible for actors to have perfect information on the consequences of their re-lationships, and to handle this uncertainty they strive to maintain and develop a position in a network, investing time and resources in these relationships. To understand factors influencing this position development process and why some actors succeed and others do not, a holistic case study method is most useful. The idea is not to study big establishments and success stories, but to understand the process.

The method used can be characterized as inductive and qualitative – inductive because the problem area, a position development in the Baltic states, entails new factors and dimensions of international business which cannot be studied with the help of existing entry strategy theories. Moreover, the market structure and factors in the above mentioned problem area have not already been described or analysed. Qualitative, because we have a longitudinal approach and the focus of study is on relationship development, which is difficult to quantify.

The case study method is considered most suitable for this type of study. As expressed by one author, case study is an empirical enquiry that 'Investigates a contemporary phenomenon within its real life context when the boundaries be-tween phenomenon and content are not clearly evident and in which multiple sources of evidence are used' (Yin 1984). It is also said that case study method is research strategy which focuses on understanding the dynamics present in a single setting (Eisenhardt 1989). Moreover, case studies can employ an embedded design, i.e. multiple levels of analysis in a single study. This strategy is recommended when 'how' and 'why' questions are asked about an event over which the re-searcher has little control. The method is often criticized for lack of rigour, its limitations for scientific generalization, and because it is often a very time-consuming method (Yin 1984). Hence, our ambition is not to generalize, but to understand, describe and analyse this process of position development in this market. Nevertheless, it is hoped that actors (and firms) facing the same type of situation (entering or developing a position in a particular market) would be able to benefit from the results of this study.

In Norway, we have gathered information on all firms which are in the process of entering the Baltic states, there being some twenty-five such firms. We intend to study all these firms, although in this paper only one case study is discussed, that of Statoil, a Norwegian oil and gas company. Statoil has come farthest, so far, in the process of establishing business in Estonia as compared to any other Nor-wegian company. We have interviewed the managers involved in this process at Statoil, collecting data in three phases: (1) case-study, going through the files and any other material available on the project e.g. discussions in the mass media etc.;

(2) situation analyses for the particular industry in Norway and in Estonia; (3) interviews with persons involved in this relationship development.

Statoil has been engaged in the process of establishing business in Tallinn, Estonia, since October 1990. In March 1991, a contract was signed to establish Eesti Statoil, a wholly owned subsidiary. This study covers Statoil's involvement from the beginning through the contract and the problems faced after the contract up to the present (December 1991). The data gathered concerns the above mentioned three phases; only Statoil managers have been interviewed. Hence, the study presents Statoil's perspective. By Statoil managers we mean executives involved in this deal from Statoil A/S Norway, from Statoil AB Sweden and the executive designated to manage Eesti Statoil in Tallinn, Estonia.

In this case the questions posed in the previous section and the model presented here are considered as propositions and the research is performed with the framework in mind. The model would, however, serve both as proposition and as a means for interpreting the findings. An analytical approach is used to draw conclusions using the model as a basis, instead of employing statistical methods which might be unsuitable for such a study. As explained by Yin (1984: 18), 'An essential feature is comparison of the emergent concept, theory or hypothesis with the existent literature. This involves asking what it is similar to, what it contradicts, and why?' According to Yin, the role of theory-building prior to the conduct of any data collection has been overlooked in the traditional way of doing case studies. Construction of a preliminary theory related to the topic of study should be included in order to create an understanding of what is being studied.

Statoil was selected for the study as it was the only firm in Norway which had come so far in the process of establishing business relationships in a Baltic state. Moreover, it was willing to provide access to the material and executives. The case is particularly interesting as the firm's head office in Stavanger (Norway) was entering a foreign market with the assistance from one of its subsidiaries, Statoil AB in Sweden. We therefore decided to interview the Swedish subsidiary as well, and also the executive designated to manage the subsidiary in Estonia, as in the later period he was responsible for the relationship development. Here the question arises, is it legitimate to alter and even add data collection methods during a study? The answer to this is 'yes', as the investigators are trying to understand each case individually and in as much depth as is feasible (Eisenhardt 1989).

Hence, the information was collected through multiple sources, including documentation in the mass media, formal studies, systematic literature search and administrative routines, archival records such as files on the project at the firm's office, and interviews with the head office in Norway, with the subsidiary in Sweden and with the manager responsible for the establishment in Estonia.

The Model

The model presented here illustrates the factors/variables involved in the process of position development in a foreign country using the network approach (Fig. 12.1). The shaded areas show the core of the network relationship process. These are the most dynamic parts of the process. The other parts are background factors influencing this process and the results of the process.

The model starts with an overall strategy of the firm including goals and objectives, which together with the environment leads to a choice of entry strategy. But it is the shaded and especially the circular part of the process which is most dynamic. Therefore, the continuous process leads to new relationships and different positions in the network. Hence, the position is always dynamic and is prone to changing over time.

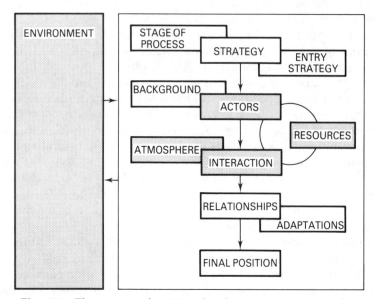

Fig. 12.1. The process of position development in a new market.

The environment
Each company operates within a larger social system, which determines and influences inter-company relations. In this case the environment includes political legal forces, economic forces, market structure, third parties involved and cultural differences. In this type of relationship we focus more on the organization and its relationship with the outside environment, than considering internal factors in an organization.

Strategy and stages of the process
By strategy we mean the process of adapting the pattern of activities and objectives of an organization to the external environment in which the organization operates. As the external environment is always changing, the strategy has to be a continuous process. (Håkansson and Snehota 1989). This also means that a company seeking to expand its activities into a new market has to reconsider its strategy. Establishing a new customer relationship requires a temporary commitment of considerable human and financial resources, often more than is required for maintaining existing relationships (Cunningham and Homse 1984).

The actors and the background factors
The process of relationship development depends not only on the elements of

strategy and interaction, but also on the characteristics of the parties, individuals as well as organizations, involved. Characteristics such as technology, organizational size and experience and the individuals involved are relevant.

Resources

In a network, each actor controls some resources directly and other resources indirectly through dependence relations with other actors. The dependence relations are an outcome of the bonds between the actors and their relative importance to each other (Cook and Emerson 1984). Resources such as goods, financial capital, technology, personnel and marketing know-how are important, but the importance of these resources varies at different times and situations. The most important resource, at all times, is perhaps the position a firm has developed in its network (Håkansson and Johanson 1988).

The interaction and the atmosphere

Interaction is inevitable in the process of relationship development as it allows the companies to make better use of each other's resources and know-how. Through this interaction firms exchange resources, products, information and services. Interaction and co-operation are used to demonstrate an intended presence in the counterpart's network. Firms with strong positions in their network will seek co-operation with prestigious actors considered important in networks (Håkansson and Johanson 1988). The atmosphere around an interaction involves the degree of co-operation/conflict, distance, power/dependence and expectations of the parties (Ghauri and Johanson 1983; Cavusgil and Ghauri 1990).

Relationships and adaptations

Relationships are complex, multi-level, dynamic and continuous over time. They consist of a web of interactive relations between individuals in both organizations, relating to both parties, entailing adaptations and the establishment of routines on both sides (Håkansson and Snehota 1989). There is a degree of co-ordination in the exchange activities and a change in one relation may affect changes in all the other activities of a firm. These relationships and adaptations are important for a firm, as they affect its productivity, control over the environment and development strength. Adaptation is an important aspect of relationships and social exchange processes between companies (Hallén, Johanson and Seyed-Mohamed 1991).

Position

The position of a firm in a network can be defined as the relative role and importance of the firm, and the strength of the relationships it has with the other firms in the network (Johanson and Mattsson 1985). According to Thorelli (1984), the position is based on the six areas concerning a firm and its relationships: the power, the economy base, the technology, the expertise, the trust and the legitimacy. It is, however, a relative concept as no two parties' positions are alike and it is evaluated and perceived by another party on the basis of previous experience and present expectations. As the evaluation and perception depends upon the interaction and relationship, it is considered to be an outcome of these two. This position is explained as macro and micro position. Micro position is the bargaining position of a party *vis-á-vis* one specific counterpart, while the macro position reflects the role and importance of a firm in the network as a whole (Johanson and Mattsson 1985).

The Case of Statoil in Estonia

Statoil is a Norwegian company in the global oil and gas business; as such it is always exploring new markets to enter. Sale of crude and refined oil is its main business, and North Western Europe and the Baltic region are considered its natural market.

Background factors

During the process of independence, the Estonian government approached Statoil and asked them to enter the country. Primarily, they wanted to have a guaranteed supply of oil in the event of conflict with the Soviet Union, as Estonia has no indigenous oil production. A ferry boat connection was established between Tallinn and Stockholm as a partnership project between Sweden and Estonia. Petrol storage was specifically planned on this ferry.

At this point, Statoil's head office in Norway started taking an interest in the market and in May 1990 the first meeting between the Statoil management and the Estonian government, represented by the Prime Minister, Edgar Savisaar, took place in Estonia. The initiative for this meeting also came from Estonia. As at that time Estonia was not yet independent, the laws of Soviet Union were to be followed, which was considered the main hindrance. At this stage, Statoil also tried to find a local partner for a joint venture, but failed to do so.

After a couple of weeks an information meeting was held at which the Estonian government and Statoil presented their plans. At this meeting, the Prime Minister, the Vice Prime Minister, the Minister for Economy, representatives from Tallinn City, mayors from other large cities, and some officials from the foreign office were present.

In June 1990 Norwegian Statoil authorized its Swedish subsidiary to handle this project, appointing Mr Sverker Liljefeldt as the person in charge. In January 1991 Statoil was the first foreign firm to have applied to the Estonian government to establish a wholly owned subsidiary for which approval was granted on March 18, 1991. After this approval Eesti Statoil Estonia was established in Tallinn and Statoil Sweden tried to enter into negotiations with Tallinn City for the establishment of an office and the first two petrol stations. The city officials were not interested in talking to the Swedish group, however, and demanded meetings with top management from the head office. According to Mr Liljefeldt:

> They wanted to talk to Mr Harald Norvik, the President and Chairman of the Statoil group, and not with the Swedish group. At that time we did not understand their attitude, but later we understood that there was something fishy. The people, sitting at important positions, wanted to meet top management so that they could do some private business.

Strategy

Statoil's overall strategy was very different in this market entry to normal internationalization process. Here the Baltic states were considered a good stepping stone to learn more about Eastern Europe. No market research or any other normal analysis was done. 'We decided that Estonia is not a major market and we should try without giving a very strong emphasis; if not successful, we should move on to another market in Eastern Europe' (Einer Slagstad, Statoil Norway).

The total investment was considered to be SEK 70 millions (SEK 6.5 = 1 US dollar). It is considered as a high-risk project, according to Mr Liljefeldt: 'This is not a short-term project, we know that we will not make any money for a long time, but we still want to be here. We do not think that it will be good enough to come here in five years' time'.

The interaction, relationships and the position

In May 1991 Statoil applied to rent sites in Tallinn to establish the first two petrol stations, although so far they have not received any answer from the authorities. Eesti Statoil has selected two lots of vacant land and obtained approval from the Architecture and City Planning Department, but they still need to have the permission of the local government. An office has, however, been opened and a managing director (Mr Sverker Liljefeldt) plus two other people have started working. It was planned to start with two petrol stations in Tallinn, with the long-term objective of establishing fifteen to twenty petrol stations in Estonia by 1996, selling primarily Western quality petrol (e.g. unleaded) to tourists and businesses for hard currency, and local quality to locals for local currency. The expected independence came earlier than planned and thereby the company expected to achieve its objective much earlier than originally thought. (At the outset it had been estimated that it would take at least five years before Estonia became formally independent.) One problem, however, was that the same people who were in power before independence remained in power, thinking in the same old-fashioned monopolistic way. There are great problems concerning convertibility of the currency, the legal system, property rights, democratically elected parliament and education. Evaluation of different products and services is almost impossible. 'Sometimes, it is very difficult to convince them that we are not cheating them as there is no mechanism to compare the prices and values of different things' (Liljefeldt).

Eesti Statoil, with Sverker Liljefeldt as managing director, is responsible for the whole process of negotiating, while Statoil's head office has the final authority. A number of third parties have been involved in the process, including the Swedish and Norwegian Ambassadors, the Swedish Export Council and even the Swedish Foreign Minister. Representing Estonia there have been the Director General of Foreign Economic Affairs and his office, the Foreign Minister, and the head of the Foreign Trade Department. On the other hand there is also a strong group of people who are creating problems in Estonia. While most people want Statoil to become established and can see the long-term benefits for the country, this small group wants to gain short-term personal benefits.

The competitor for Eesti Statoil is Eesti Kutus, a government-owned oil company with 100 petrol stations selling low-octane petrol. They also have a joint venture operations with Neste. Unleaded petrol is not available in the country. According to Liljefeldt, 'It is possible that another oil company is trying to enter this market, and they will be successful if they want to play with this group's rules'. As far as the resources of the parties are concerned, Statoil controls financial, technical and material resources, while Tallinn City controls the property rights.

During the last year Eesti Statoil was working intensively with Tallinn City and the Estonian government, but at present most of the interaction is with the third parties. The firm is also establishing lots of relationships and goodwill with other actors in the local network. Through these relations the company is getting the information it needs. According to Mr Liljefeldt:

> There is no planning ahead at all, we have given that up a long time ago, now we work each day to improve our position and relationships through collecting information and lobbying. These relationships and contacts are the only source of information as no other communication system is in function. The position of the particular group [the old gang] is weakened every day. People are beginning to realize what is going on and they are beginning to fear that Statoil might just leave the country while they want us to stay. Estonia needs us more than we need Estonia.

Eesti Statoil has been trying to find other solutions to this deadlock. For example, they have offered to calculate the present value of the rent for the entire period and invest that money in a project beneficial for the city, such as a water cleaning system which is highly needed. But this offer was also turned down; the demand from the city government is that a partnership should be established with Cartex, a company registered by the same group of people.

Statoil has suggested that it could rent the land in Tallinn for twenty-five years for one of the properties and for ten years for the second site, and is willing to pay a much higher rent than the local rate, comparable with rents in Swedish cities like Norrköping and Linköping. The city officials claim that there are no rules available which allow renting out government property to foreign companies (although if a partnership arrangement was offered to Cartex, presumably this could be arranged). Eesti Statoil is also trying to rent other property, not owned by Tallinn City but by the central government (Estonia), which is quite possible with the type of contacts Statoil has established. However, this has been kept secret from the Tallinn City officials.

Conclusions

On the surface, this case may seem unusual; however, it illustrates the kind of problems Western firms can expect to encounter while entering the Baltic states. We have seen in this case that Statoil has been dealing with several different parties, and that the counterpart, which in fact stands to benefit from the project, is creating obstacles for Statoil. Moreover, as the same people also control the political and legal forces, their motivation to introduce new legislation, and thereby an effective technology transfer, has been rather lacking.

The counterpart in Tallinn is demanding a partnership, while Statoil is not willing to give away ownership in the project purely to get the permission to rent the property:

> Yes we are willing to adapt to the local environment but it seems that the only adaptation we can make is to accept a joint venture with Cartex which we cannot accept. They have nothing to contribute except land, which by the way is not theirs. In our opinion, a joint venture partner should contribute with some resources.

In Estonia the Statoil case is openly discussed in the media – there is some degree of unhappiness that the internal forces in the country appear to be working against its development and that the state is blackmailing itself, which is very bad for Estonia's progress towards a market economy (*Eesti Express*, October 1991). According to Statoil, 'We are considered as a big fish and they do not want to let us off the hook. The Prime Minister, Edgar Savisaar, claims to understand Statoil's position and has promised to help, but … we have not seen any results' (Liljefeldt).

This case illustrates how crucial the characteristics of different actors involved in the process have been for the development of the relationship. Third parties have played an important role, and here the network approach has been quite useful. The Prime Minister of Estonia has been involved in the process and at the final stage, both the Swedish and the Norwegian Ambassadors, the Swedish Foreign Minister and the Export Council from Sweden have been helping Statoil. From the Estonian side, apart from the Prime Minister, the Foreign Minister, Director General of Foreign Economic Affairs and the Head of the Foreign Trade Department have all been involved. The fact that Statoil, with its head office in Norway, right from an early stage authorized its Swedish subsidiary to handle this internationalization process is also quite interesting. It was considered that the Swedish subsidiary had better networking capabilities than the head office. As illustrated by Fig. 12.2, the process was started by the head office, but was taken over by the Swedish subsidiary in later stages.

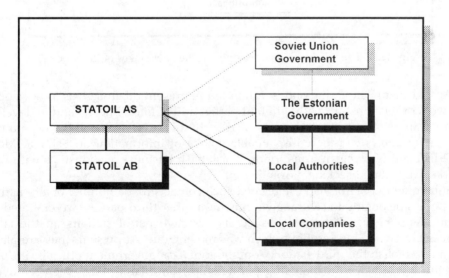

Fig. 12.2. The process of position development in Estonia – earlier stages.

Another important issue revealed by this case is that the political system in these states is still rather inefficient and corrupt. Moreover, the accusations about corruption and irregularities are openly discussed in the media both in Sweden and Estonia. For example, it has been publicized in several newspapers and magazines that Statoil has been refused to rent land because of the private interests of the city officials, and some Ministers and government representatives have been giving statements in favour of Statoil. The media have demanded more information on the Statoil case, so that the public could see the irregularities exercised by those in power (*Eesti Express*, October 1991; *Baltic Independent*, October 1991; *Kaubaleht*, November 1991; *Aktuell* Swedish Television Report and *Aftonposten*, September and November 1991). In the final stage Statoil was working more with other actors in the network than with the relevant party, influencing the media to mobilize public opinion and the other actors in the network. Statoil's networking is illustrated by Fig. 12.3.

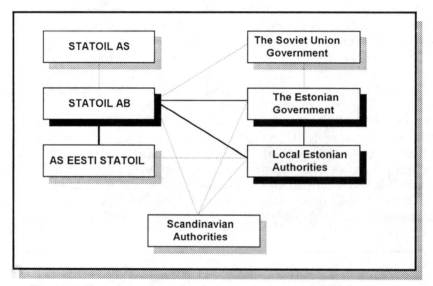

Fig. 12.3. The relationships developed in the later stages of the process.

According to Statoil, the only solution to the present dilemma was to develop a network of relationships with different parties and political interest and to develop support in Estonia through the mass media. In this respect, Statoil has been quite successful and is considered a valuable source of information on Estonia. Most Swedish and Norwegian firms trying to establish business relationships with this market contact and seek help from Statoil.

Subsequently, Statoil had established such contacts that a number of alternative properties belonging to central government or other third parties, were offered to them. As a result, Statoil established its first two petrol stations on the land previously owned by Aeroflot, which was moving out. At present, they are planning to establish the third station. A number of local government officials, including those which were demanding partnership from Statoil, have been removed from their positions and the new local government is being very co-operative with

Statoil. This new situation has provided them not only with other alternatives but also given them a stronger position against the city officials; this has only been possible due to network relationships developed during this process.

This case illustrates the typical problem a foreign firm can have while establishing in Estonia or other Baltic states. The problem with inefficient local government, bureaucracy and corruption, in one way or another, is highlighted. Moreover, the case reveals that by making use of effective networking with the government, mass media and other actors in the particular network, foreign firms can have a good chance of surviving and of establishing fruitful business relationships.

References

Blankenburg, D. and Johanson, J. (1992) 'Managing Network Connections in International Business', *Scandinavian International Business Review*, 1 (1): 5–19.

Cavusgil, S. T. and Ghauri, P. N. (1990) *Doing Business in Developing Countries – Entry and negotiation strategies*, London: Routledge.

Cook, K. M. and Emerson, R. M. (1984) 'Exchange Networks and the Analysis of Complex Organizations', *Research in the Sociology of Organizations*, Vol. 3, New York: JAI Press.

Cunningham, M. T. (1982) 'Barriers to Organizational Interaction', in Håkansson, H. (ed.), *International Marketing and Purchasing of Industrial Goods – an Interaction Approach*, Chichester: J. Wiley.

Cunningham, M. T. and Homse, E. (1982) 'An Interaction Approach to Marketing and Purchasing Strategy, in Håkansson, H. (ed.), *International Marketing and Purchasing of Industrial Goods – an Interaction Approach*, Chichester: J. Wiley.

Eisenhardt, K. M. (1989) 'Building Theories from Case Study Research' *Academy of Management Review*, 14 (4): 532–50.

Emerson, R. M. (1962) 'Power Dependence Relations', *American Sociological Review* 27 (February): 31–41.

Ford, D. (1980) 'The Development of Buyer–Seller Relationships in Industrial Markets', *European Journal of Marketing* 14 (5/6): 339–54.

Gerner, K. (1990) 'Två hundra års felutveckling – karakterisert av nationalisme, rasisme og territorialstaten – går mot sitt slut', *Nordrevy* 3: 11–16.

Ghauri, P. N. (1989) 'Global Marketing Strategies: Swedish Firms in South and East Asia', in Kaynak, E. and Lee, K. H., *Global Business: Asia Pacific Dimensions*, New York: Routledge.

Ghauri, P. N. and Johanson, J. (1979) 'International Package Deal Negotiations – The Role of the Atmosphere', in *Organization, Marknad och Samhelle* 16 (5): 335–64.

Hägg, I. and Johanson, J. (1982) *Företag i Nätverk*, Stockholm: SNS Förlag.

Håkansson, H. (ed.) (1982) *International Marketing and Purchasing of Industrial Goods – An Interaction Approach*, Chichester: J. Wiley.

Håkansson, H. (1989) *Corporate Technological Behaviour, Co-operation and Networks*, London: Routledge.

Håkansson, H. and Johanson, J. (1988) 'Formal and Informal Co-operation Strategies in International Industrial Networks'. In Contractor, F. J. and Lorange, P. (eds) *Co-operative Strategies in International Business* Lexington D.C.: Heath and Company.

Håkansson, H. and Snehota, I. (1989) 'No Business is an Island: The Network Concept of Business Strategy', *Scandinavian Journal of Management* 4 (3) 187–200.

Hallén, L. and Johanson, J. and Seyed-Mohamed, N. (1991) 'Interfirm Adaptation in Business Relationships', *Journal of Marketing* 55 (April): 29–37.

Johanson, J. and Mattsson, L.-G. (1985) 'Marketing Investments and Market Investments in Industrial Networks', *International Journal of Research in Marketing* 2: 185–95.

Johanson, J. and Mattsson, L.-G. (1988) 'Internationalism in Industrial Systems – A Network Approach', *Strategies in Global Competition*: 287–314.

Mare Balticum – Ekonomis og Kulturens hav (1990) Näringslivets delegation, Helsingfors.

Prasad, B. and Ghauri, P. N. (1992) 'On Keiretsu and other Business Networks', *Oslo Business School*, working paper 05/1992.
Sandström, P. (1991) *'Baltiskt Dilemma'*, Stockholm: SNS Förlag.
Thorelli, H. B. (1986) 'Networks: Between Markets and Hierarchies', *Strategic Management Journal* 7: 37–51.
Tilly, C. (1990) *Coercion, Capital and European States, AD–990–1990.*
Turnbull, P. W. and Valla, J. P. (eds) (1986) *Strategies for International Industrial Marketing*, London: Croom Helm.
Yin, R. K. (1984) *Case Study Research – Design and Methods*, Sage Publications Inc., USA.

Newspapers and Journals

Alatalu, E., November 1991, 'Who is directing the events on the Estonian gasoline market', *Kaubaleht, Trade Paper.*
Holte, E., September 1991, 'Statoil venter fortsatt på sine Estland-tomter', *Aftenposten*, Oslo.
Ignats, Ü., November 1991, 'Hard resistance to Statoil: The quarrel about a piece of land hinders investment into Estonia'.
Lillemets, M. and Luik, H. H., October 1991, 'Why not Statoil?', *Eesti Express*, Tallinn.
Legrain-Tombach, P., October 1991, 'Eesti Statoil start-up delayed', *Baltic Independent*, Tallinn.
Probert-Ehaver, K., November 1991, 'Baltic fuel crisis deepens', *Baltic Independent*, Tallinn.

Television Report

Aktuell, Swedish Television Report, Sveriges Radio, Stockholm, by Kent Wennstrøm.

Interviews

Einar Slagstad, Regional Manager, Statoil Stavanger, Norway.
Sverker Liljefeldt, Statoil Sweden, Project Manager Eesti Statoil, Estonia.
Kent Wennstrøm, Journalist, Sveriges Radio, Stockholm.

13

Investment in Eastern Europe: The Case of the Netherlands

Charles P. de Mortanges and Willem B. Caris

Introduction

The political and economic changes that continue to take place in Eastern Europe have resulted in a flurry of activity coming from the West, as organizations of various kinds have come to realize the considerable potential the transition economies of Eastern Europe may offer. This chapter offers a preliminary description and analysis of the experience of several Dutch manufacturing firms that entered the Eastern European market through investment. More specifically, it tries to provide answers to questions related to the decision-making process when making investments as an entry strategy into Eastern Europe.

The name 'Eastern Europe' is used in this chapter for the region consisting of nine (former) countries with various common characteristics: Albania, Bulgaria, the former Czechoslovakia, the former German Democratic Republic, Hungary, Poland, Romania, the former Soviet Union and former Yugoslavia. At the time of writing, the former German Democratic Republic has been reunified with West Germany, the Soviet Union has dissolved into fifteen different independent republics, and Yugoslavia is in a civil war that has divided the country into five different republics.

Most of the business activity of Western firms in Eastern Europe, beyond exporting, used to be labelled 'East–West industrial co-operation'. Cieslik (1983) defined East–West industrial co-operation as 'various forms of operations which:

- are extended over a number of years;
- go beyond the straightforward sale or purchase of goods and services;
- result in the complementary and/or reciprocally matching flows of goods and services'.

Included in this definition were co-operative agreements such as licensing arrangements, turnkey operations, management contracts, co-production agreements and joint ventures. It is important to be aware of the third part of this definition, which illustrated the goals of self-sufficiency and independence from the West.

Western direct investment in Eastern Europe has been relatively small. One indicator of Western direct investment in Eastern Europe is the total number of registered joint ventures. Because of the broader definition of the term 'joint venture' that is applied in Eastern Europe, the registered joint ventures also include cases of 100 per cent foreign investments. Bertrand (1990) estimated the total registered joint ventures in the region in April 1990 (six months after the fall of the Berlin Wall), to be over 5,000. A research project undertaken by Van Berendonk, Oosterveer and Associates (1992) mentions a total of 34,121 registered joint ventures in March 1992 in Eastern Europe, excluding Albania, East Germany and all former Soviet republics except Russia (see Table 13.1). Bearing in mind that, although Albania is not yet open for private investment, East Germany and the former Soviet republics are countries where there has been considerable private investment, our own estimate of the total registered joint ventures in the region is in the range of 40,000 to 50,000. Unfortunately, we are unable to give more precise information. However, it is clear from these figures that investment activity has increased dramatically over the past two years.

It should be noted that not all of the registered joint ventures include Western partners. Roughly three-quarters of the total number of joint ventures do. Furthermore, it is important to note that not all of these joint ventures are active. Some are registered, but have not turned out one single product or service. Van Berendonk, Oosterveer and Associates (1992) estimate the proportion of inactive joint ventures to be between 30 per cent and 40 per cent. Consequently, our estimate of the total number of active Western direct investments in Eastern Europe would be between 20,000 and 25,000 as of March 1992.

The major sectors of Western investment include electronics and related industries, tourism and transport of people, wholesale activities, construction and various services (Bodde 1990).

It is estimated that of all registered joint ventures in Eastern Europe, only two per cent to 3 per cent involve Dutch participants. This is a relatively small share compared to those of countries like West Germany (22 per cent), Austria (13 per cent) and the United States (12 per cent). Of these top three foreign investors, two countries, West Germany and Austria, have borders with one or more countries in Eastern Europe. An overview of the total number of joint ventures and the number of joint ventures involving a Dutch partner, for selected countries is presented in Table 13.1.

Table 13.1 shows a total of 733 registered Dutch joint ventures in the seven selected countries. However, as already mentioned, not all registered joint ventures are operational, and of these 733 registered joint ventures, only 394 could be traced. This means that the parent companies in the Netherlands as well as in the Eastern European country could be identified (Van Berendonk, Oosterveer and Associates 1992).

More information on the individual scale and nature of Dutch investment in Eastern Europe has proved to be difficult to obtain. Since companies in the Netherlands are not required to publicly register their investments in Eastern Europe, no complete list of investments is available. Companies often prefer to keep a low profile on this matter. Similarly, government institutions and Eastern European representatives in the Netherlands have been reluctant to provide information on these investments. The fact that so little is known about Dutch investment in

Table 13.1: Registered joint ventures in selected countries (March 1992).

Country	Registered JVs	Registered Dutch JVs	Dutch JVs' share (%)
Bulgaria	239	1	0.42
Czechoslovakia	3,000	31	1.03
Hungary	11,000	200	1.82
Poland	5,286	298	5.63
Romania	9,327	162	1.74
Russia	2,600	30	1.15
Yugoslavia (1990)	2,669	11	0.41
Total	34,121	733	2.15

Source: Van Berendonk, Oosterveer and Associates (1992)

Eastern Europe has inspired us to investigate particular aspects of these investments. The rest of this chapter is devoted to the research project we have undertaken to this end.

Objectives of the Research

The first question that comes to mind is why Dutch companies choose to invest in Eastern Europe. We have chosen to look at this question within the framework of international market entry strategy. International market entry strategy is the name of a whole set of decisions that are to be made with respect to the commitment of company resources to overseas markets.

Root (1987) discerns five main elements of an international market entry strategy:

1. choosing the target product/market;
2. setting objectives and goals in the target market;
3. choosing an appropriate entry mode;
4. designing the marketing plan for the foreign market;
5. monitoring operations and revising the entry strategy.

This is an iterative process, because the five areas of decision-making are highly interrelated.

The main focus of our research is on the third element: the choice of an appropriate entry mode. However, because of the interdependence of all elements of an international market entry strategy, some attention should be paid to other elements of the process as well. As a result the following three questions that define the scope of this study are:

1. Which people influenced the decision of the firm to invest in the Eastern European market?
2. Why did the firm decide on investment as the entry mode, instead of, for example, exporting or a contractual mode?
3. Which problems did the firm encounter, relative to its choice of investment as the entry mode?

Thus, in the first and the third question, parts of the first and the fifth element of the international market entry strategy decision-making process as described by Root (1987) appear. To get a preliminary insight into the three issues listed above, a survey was carried out among decision-makers of several Dutch companies that had recently invested in Eastern Europe.

Theoretical Background

In this section, relevant theories on the people that influence the decision to enter a foreign market are reviewed, followed by an explanation of relevant theories on the entry mode decision. Finally, the subject of problems with the investments is taken up. This section is not intended to give an overview of all existing theories. Rather, it attempts to clarify the theoretical foundation on which the questionnaire is based.

Influencing groups

Many textbooks acknowledge that very often a firm starts its international operations in response to an unsolicited order from an outside party, rather than as a result of carefully searching for international opportunities. It is our opinion that in the practice of management, the influence of different kinds of actors in a firm's environment on the decision to invest abroad is essential. Robinson (1978) identifies the following nine groups that influence the decision of a firm to invest abroad:

1. *Foreign governments*   In order to promote economic growth in their country, they try to attract foreign investors.
2. *Foreign licensees*   This group wants to expand the business it is doing with the firm.
3. *Foreign business groups*   These are groups that have identified an opportunity in their home market, but to exploit it they need assistance from foreign firms.
4. *Overseas representatives and customers*   These groups fear that exports cannot meet the demand from the foreign market.
5. *Important competitors*   If competitors make a move, the firm often has to follow that move in order to keep up.
6. *Other firms from the home country*   These firms desire an overseas source.
7. *Government of the home country*   The government often stimulates foreign investment in the framework of its foreign economic policy.
8. *Banks, legal firms, and the like*   These groups have establishments abroad and have an interest in developing a clientele for those establishments.
9. *Promoters*   These are people, usually within the firm, that promote foreign investment for profit reasons.

This list, which seems almost exhaustive, was used in that part of our questionnaire that attempts to identify specific groups that influenced the Dutch firms' decision-makers.

Entry mode decision

Over time, three different theoretical approaches regarding the entry mode decision have evolved. Young *et al.* (1989) label these:

- the economic approach;
- the stages of development approach;
- the business strategy approach.

The economic approach is not suitable in this particular case, since it is very theoretical and thus very difficult to test (Anderson and Gatignon 1986). Our focus will be on the other two approaches, which are more normative and, therefore, have better applied managerial orientation.

The stages of development approach is based on the internationalization process of the firm as described by Johanson and Vahlne (1977). According to this approach, the form of operations in a foreign market changes gradually over time, from low risk/low control modes (e.g. exporting or licensing) to high risk/high control modes (e.g. joint ventures or wholly-owned subsidiaries). The stages of development approach is useful for our research project, because it is very simple to check its validity.

The business strategy approach stresses that firms have to deal with external uncertainty and multiple objectives when making an entry mode decision. The complex nature of the decision-making process resulting from this makes rational decision-making extremely difficult. In this respect, the business strategy approach is clearly different from the other two approaches. An example of the business strategy approach can be found in Root (1987). He lists a set of external and internal factors that are regarded as influencing the entry mode decision. Root's set of external factors consists of:

- *Target country market factors*   This category includes size and competitive struc- ture of the target country market, as well as the quality of the marketing infrastructure.
- *Target country production factors*, including quality, quantity, and cost of pro- ductive agents, but also the quality and cost of the economic infrastructure in the target country.
- *Target country environmental factors*   This category consists of a list of political, economic and sociocultural factors, among which are government policies and regulations, geographical distance, several features of the economy, external economic relations, cultural distance and political risk.
- *Home country factors*   Under this label a set of market, production and economic factors in the home country is captured.

The set of internal factors consists of two groups:

1. *Product factors*   This group includes product differentiation, nature of the product, service and technology intensity and required level of product adaptation.
2. *Resource/commitment factors*   This category consists of two factors actually: the availability of resources to the firm and the firm's willingness to commit them to the overseas markets.

Table 13.2 provides an overview of the typical environmental conditions that generally favour the choice of investment as an entry mode.

Table 13.2: Environmental conditions generally favouring investment as an entry mode.

External factors (host country)	*External factors (home country)*
High sales potential	Large market
Oligopolistic competition	Oligopolistic competition
Low production costs	High production costs
Restrictive import policies	
Liberal investment policies	*Internal factors*
Great geographical distance	Standard products
Dynamic economy	Service-intensive products
Liberal exchange controls	Service products
Exchange rate depreciation	High product adaptation
Small cultural distance	Substantial resources
Low political risk	High commitment

Source: Root (1987: 16–17)

The business strategy approach is used in the research project because it is also simple to use and very comprehensive.

Problems

A lot of books contain accounts of problems that can arise in investments abroad. For our purpose, a comprehensive inventory of problems that are particularly relevant to Western investments in Eastern Europe was found in Bieszki and Rath (1989). Their work explores East–West joint ventures from the viewpoint of the Western, as well as of the Eastern partner. Our study is limited to the perspective of the Western partner. Bieszki and Rath specify several potential problems that could occur on the side of the Western partner:

- *Loss of control over technology* A primary motive of Eastern European governments is, usually, the acquisition of technology in order to be able to make the products themselves in the future. Therefore, they often try to seize, or copy, the technology to become independent of the Western firm.
- *A strong export orientation on the side of Eastern European partners* If the joint venture starts to export heavily, it can pose a threat to the parent company or another affiliated company in other markets.
- *Security of the invested capital* If there are no laws that guarantee Western partners' capital rights, the risk of expropriation might be an insurmountable problem to the Western investors.
- *Currency problems* The non-convertibility of almost all Eastern European currencies presents obvious problems, for example when repatriating profits.
- *Bureaucratic barriers* The Eastern European countries are still characterized by enormous bureaucracies, which clearly impedes doing business.
- *Internal problems of the economy* Economic instability in the countries of Eastern

Europe, which is exacerbated by economic reforms, obviously adds to the economic risk of investments in Eastern Europe.

All these problem areas have been included in our questionnaire.

In addition, two other types of problems are, we believe, important enough to be investigated. One of them is drawn from the general literature on joint ventures and includes all problems with partners which arise from differing strategic interests (Killing 1982). One such potential source of conflict was identified by Bieszki and Rath (1989), namely a strong export orientation on the part of the Eastern European partner. The other source of conflict is referred to in a more recent article, specifically on the managerial challenges in former communist countries. Por (1991) identifies several problems that a Western firm could have with its employees from Eastern Europe. These problems are believed to concern the working practices that evolved under communist rule. Examples of these difficulties are: deliberate falsification of information, bribery, making private information public, work avoidance, and lack of initiative and accountability.

Research Methodology

The survey method used for the research project was a postal survey. However, the responses of two of the sampled firms were obtained through personal interviews, to test the questionnaire. Since these personal interviews did not indicate any problems with the questionnaire, we felt confident of obtaining the responses through a mail survey.

The questionnaire of the research project consisted of four parts, coded (A) to (D). The (A) questions provided necessary background information on certain variables that were considered important in characterizing the sample population. The (B) questions dealt with the people that influenced the firm's decision to invest in Eastern Europe. The (C) questions investigated the environmental factors that influenced the decision to use investment as the entry mode. Finally, the (D) questions were concerned with the problems the companies faced in their investment in Eastern Europe.

The questions that were coded with an (A) were open-ended, whereas nearly all the others were closed. A five-point scale, ranging from 1 (= not important) to 5 (= extremely important), was used in order to provide clearly differentiated options to the respondent, without making the range of options too narrow. A 'don't know/ no opinion' option was omitted from the questionnaire, because in this case that option would have been the same as the 'not important' option. For all remaining questions, for which the structured form was not feasible, the open-ended form was used.

Earlier, we developed an estimate of 40,000 to 50,000 registered joint ventures in Eastern Europe. In the same section the percentage of joint ventures involving a Dutch partner was estimated at between 2 per cent and 3 per cent. Consequently, a very broad interval estimate of the total number of registered joint ventures involving a Dutch partner in Eastern Europe would range from 800 to 1,500. Considering that 30 per cent to 40 per cent of these joint ventures are not operational, we would estimate the population of operational Dutch joint ventures in Eastern Europe that is of interest for our research project to be between 500 and 1,000.

In the last part of 1991 the questionnaire was presented to executives of two Dutch firms with an investment in Eastern Europe, during a personal interview. In the first part of 1992 the questionnaire was mailed to another twelve Dutch companies that had invested in Eastern Europe. Most companies were identified through information that was sent to us, upon request, by the Treuhandanstalt in Berlin, Germany, and the Joint Venture Association in Budapest, Hungary. Additional companies were identified through the popular press. Since we obtained seven responses, the response rate was 50 per cent.

We are aware of the fact that the sample may not be representative of the whole population. Therefore generalizations of the results have to be treated with caution.

Analysis of the Results

Description of the responding companies

Regarding the size of the companies, a classification can be made into three groups:

1. *Small companies*, having annual sales of less than 10 million guilders and less than 100 employees;
2. *Medium-sized companies*, having annual turnover between 10 and 50 million guilders and/or between 100 and 500 employees;
3. *Large companies*, with annual sales of over 50 million guilders and over 500 employees.

According to this classification, five of the responding parent firms were large, one was medium-sized and one was small.

Using the same criteria for the subsidiaries, two could be considered large investments, three were of medium size, while the other two were small.

The geographical distribution of the subsidiaries of our respondents was as follows: Hungary accommodated four of them, East Germany two, and Poland one. This pattern is more representative than it looks at first sight. Hungary, East Germany and Poland are among the front-runners as host countries to Dutch investments.

Of the responding companies, four produced consumer goods, while the other three produced investment goods. Thus, all companies were manufacturers – there were no service firms among our respondents.

While the investment of one of our respondents was operational as of the beginning of 1992, three were established in 1991, two have existed since 1990, and one was started in 1989. In this respect it is important to see that only one investment had been concluded before the definitive breakdown of communism in Eastern Europe. However, in this respect the responding firms are also representative of the whole population, the majority of investments having been made after the breakthrough in 1989.

Regarding the type of investment, the subsidiaries of the respondents can be classified as follows: three were majority joint ventures, two were equity joint ventures, while the last two were minority joint ventures. This means that in less than half of the observed cases the Dutch firm was the dominant partner.

Of the responding firms five (71 per cent) had employed export activities in the host country before, while the other two (29 per cent) had made no earlier attempts in the market. It is striking to see that none of the responding firms had employed a contractual agreement prior to the investment. After all, contractual agreements are often regarded as the best substitute for an investment in countries, like the Eastern European countries were in the past, where foreign ownership is unwanted (Kogut 1986).

The aforementioned result also implies that for 71 per cent of the cases we observed, the 'stages of development' approach holds. Another research project that was published recently by Van Berendonk, Oosterveer and Associates (1992), found that 57 per cent of the firms they sampled had been active in some way in the Eastern European market prior to investment. Therefore, the conclusion seems justified that the stages of development approach holds for the majority of Dutch investments in Eastern Europe.

A summary of the results of this section is shown in Table 13.3.

Table 13.3: Profile of the responding companies.

Question	(7 respondents)	Responses
(A1/A2)	Parent company size	1 Small
		1 Medium
		5 Large
(A2/A4)	Subsidiary size	2 Small
		3 Medium
		2 Large
(A5)	Host country	4 Hungary
		1 Poland
		2 Germany
(A6)	Type of product	4 Consumer good
		3 Investment good
(A7)	Year of establishment subsidiary	1 1989
		2 1990
		3 1991
		1 1992
(A8/A9)	Type of investment	2 Minority JV
		2 Equity JV
		3 Majority JV
(A10)	Prior activities in host country	5 Export
		2 None

Influencing groups

The results on the influencing entities are summarized in Table 13.4. The groups of people are ranked, first, by median score, because this is the proper measure by which results on our five-point scale should be analysed. The results are ranked by mean in the second place, since this provides a higher level of differentiation.

Table 13.4: Research results on the importance of the influence of different groups on the foreign investment decision.

Question	(7 respondents)	Median	Mean	St. dev.
(B5)	Competitors	3	3.29	1.25
(B4)	Foreign repres./customers	3	3.14	0.90
(B9)	Internal promotors	3	3.00	1.41
(B3)	Foreign business groups	3	2.71	1.25
(B1)	Foreign governments	1	2.29	1.89
(B8)	Banks, legal firms, etc.	1	1.43	0.79
(B7)	Home government	1	1.29	0.49
(B2)	Foreign licensees	1	1.00	0.00
(B6)	Other home-country firms	1	1.00	0.00

Table 13.4 indicates that, according to our sample, the most important group influencing the investment decision-making process is competitors. There are numerous examples of the entry of Western firms into Eastern Europe in order to follow, or even beat, competitors in the market. One famous example is, of course, the automobile industry, where fierce battles were fought by Western European producers over stakes in Eastern European automobile manufacturers like Skoda in Czechoslovakia, or FSO in Poland (Schares and Templeman 1990). Dutch firms seem to be no exception to this rule.

A second group that was rated as important by the respondents in our sample, is that of overseas representatives and customers. These groups have often identified opportunities in the market that can no longer be served by means of exports. They demand a greater involvement and a transfer of technical and marketing skills to the host country in order to set up production there. These representatives and customers often become partners in the investment later. The results of the Van Berendonk, Oosterveer and Associates (1992) research report strongly support our own observations in this respect. They concluded that the conversion of an existing relationship with an Eastern European trade partner is the most common reason for Dutch companies to start a joint venture.

Internal promoters seem to be the third important group to influence the investment decision. The results indicate that it is important to have influential people within the company who personally make a case for the investment. These people can do this for several reasons. One reason can be that they have personal or other ties to a specific host country. Another can be that they aspire to a management position in the subsidiary themselves.

Foreign business groups are the last group that is regarded by the respondents as having an influence over the foreign investment decision-making process. These groups are often in the same situation as the overseas representatives and customers. They have identified a viable opportunity in the market, but lack the technical and marketing skills needed to exploit this opportunity. They too can become partners later.

Governments, whether Eastern European or Dutch, do not seem to be a significant factor influencing the investment decision process, and rated median scores of 1 in both cases, although the high standard deviation of 1.89 and the mean of 2.29 both indicate that there were several respondents that rated the influence of Eastern European governments to be substantial. This is an interesting observation, since all Eastern European governments claim to make considerable efforts to promote foreign investment, recognizing its importance as a stimulus for necessary economic growth. Similarly, the Dutch government, within the framework of European Community policy towards Eastern Europe, could also be expected to promote investment. Nevertheless, the conclusion seems to be that the respective policies of both groups are ineffective. 'German and European Community subsidy policies are ineffective and counterproductive', was the view of one respondent.

Banks, legal firms and different Dutch firms, other than competitors, are not important influencing groups according to our sample. The respondents seem to agree that the ties to these firms are too loose to be an important stimulus for them to invest in Eastern Europe.

Finally, there is a simple explanation for the fact that the median and mean scores on the importance of foreign licensees are so low. None of the firms had employed licensing activities in the market prior to investment. Consequently, none of the responding firms could rate the importance of foreign licensees higher than 1. However, the results concerning the importance of overseas representatives and customers, and foreign business groups, indicate that it is very likely that licensees, had they been present, would have been an important influencing group.

The open question on any additional influencing groups generated only negative responses. This is an encouraging result, since it seems to indicate that no important influencing groups were missing in our list.

Environmental factors

The results of the questions on the environmental factors influencing the decision to invest in Eastern Europe are presented in Table 13.5. The environmental factors are ranked according to the same principle as the influencing entities in Table 13.4.

Commitment to the Eastern European market is regarded as the most important single factor in the entry mode decision-making process. Recall in this respect the importance of promoters within the company as an influencing group. Synthesizing these two results one can conclude that it is the commitment of these promoters to the investment and the market that seems to be an essential force in the foreign investment decision process. An illustration of this is the process of West German investments in East Germany in general, and the investment of Volkswagen AG, based in Wolfsburg, West Germany, in the former Trabant factories in Zwickau, East Germany, in particular. This investment represents much more than just an economic decision. It also sets the stage for a co-operative relationship between the two cities of Wolfsburg and Zwickau (Thurow 1991b).

Table 13.5: Research results on the importance of environmental factors influencing the foreign investment decision.

Question	(6 respondents)	Median	Mean	St. dev.
(C20)	High commitment	3	3.50	0.55
(C1)	High sales potential (fc)	3	3.17	1.33
(C7)	Dynamic economy (fc)	3	3.17	1.17
(C19)	Substantial resources	3	3.00	0.63
(C5)	Liberal investm. policy (fc)	3	2.67	0.52
(C11)	Low political risk (fc)	3	2.50	0.84
(C2)	Oligopol. competition (fc)	2	2.67	1.21
(C4)	Restrict. import policy (fc)	2	2.50	1.38
(C8)	Liberal exch. controls (fc)	2	2.50	1.52
(C3)	Low production costs (fc)	2	2.00	1.10
(C10)	Small cultural distance (fc)	2	2.00	0.89
(C16)	Service-intensive products	1	1.83	1.33
(C6)	Great geograph. distance (fc)	1	1.50	0.84
(C9)	Exch. rate depreciation (fc)	1	1.50	0.84
(C18)	High product adaptation	1	1.50	0.55
(C14)	High production costs (hc)	1	1.33	0.82
(C15)	Standard products	1	1.33	0.82
(C17)	Service products	1	1.33	0.82
(C12)	Large market (hc)	1	1.17	0.41
(C13)	Oligopol. competition (hc)	1	1.17	0.41

Note: (fc) = foreign country, (hc) = home country

High sales potential is another important factor. Most respondents regarded this factor as a necessary prior condition for investment. The reason for this is that a high sales potential is the largest single quantifiable benefit in a cost/benefit analysis of an investment. Thus the impact of the sales potential on the outcome of a cost/benefit analysis of the investment is decisive. Supporting this finding is the fact that Van Berendonk, Oosterveer and Associates (1992) concluded that market expansion is the most common goal of Dutch joint venture in Eastern Europe.

The dynamics of the Eastern European economies are a third important factor in the decision of Dutch companies to invest. The economic systems are in transition and in the medium to long run an expansion of the economies is expected. All this calls for companies to enter the market with investments in order to be close and thus be able to react to the changes. Illustrative of this is the observation that so many companies investing in Eastern Europe explicitly indicate that they are in it for the long term (Allen *et al.* 1991).

Ample financial resources are also an important factor when a Dutch company wants to invest in Eastern Europe. The respondents indicated that it was essential to them that the resources needed to invest were present at the time the decision had to be taken. This means that no big debt burden needed to be incurred in order to be able to make the investment. Proof of the importance of this factor can be found in the fact that most firms investing in Eastern Europe can be considered large firms. Recall, for example, the fact that in our sample five out of the seven firms had sales of over Dfl 50 million and over 500 employees. These large firms are the most likely to have these ample financial resources to invest in Eastern Europe.

Foreign country government policies seem to be of moderate to substantial importance. Liberal investment policies score a median of 3, whereas restrictive import policies and liberal exchange controls have a median score of 2. This means that the prior conditions for investment are fulfilled by Eastern European governments. However, as the low median of Eastern European governments as influencing groups indicated, the actual stimulation of investment by these governments failed. A useful recommendation for the Eastern European governments would thus be to focus more towards the actual stimulation of inward investment by foreign companies, for example by giving them tax breaks. An example of the effectiveness of this instrument is the Avia Praha truck deal in Czechoslovakia, where Mercedes-Benz AG was offered a ten-year tax break (Aeppel 1992).

Low political risk is the last foreign country factor that respondents find clearly important. Of course, political risk in Eastern Europe is judged relative to political risk in countries in other regions. It is interesting to see, however, that managers judge the political risk to be relatively low. In this respect, of course, the sample bias can be important, since Hungary, East Germany and Poland are likely to be among the more stable of the East European countries. One can imagine that this score would have been lower if companies that invested in the Balkan states, the Soviet Union, or even more so in Yugoslavia, had been included in the sample. Van Berendonk, Oosterveer and Associates (1992) also support this finding.

Oligopolistic competition in the foreign country as a consideration is of moderate importance. In comparison, oligopolistic competition in the home country is regarded as being less important. The conclusion seems justified that the shape of competition neither in the foreign, nor in the home market seems to be a decisive factor. The most illustrative in this respect is that not only companies operating in oligopolistic markets, home and abroad, have invested in Eastern Europe, but also companies engaged in other types of competition.

Low production costs in the foreign country are of only moderate importance, and high production costs in the Netherlands are even less important. This observation contrasts with the widespread belief that considerable production cost advantages exist in Eastern Europe. Labour cost advantages are frequently offset by disadvantages in other production costs, like, for example, capital costs. Moreover, the labour cost advantages are likely to have a short-term nature and to disappear in the long run.

Large geographical distance and small cultural distance, with respective medians of 1 and 2, do not seem to be decisive influences on the foreign investment decision process. Again companies view these distances in relative terms. In that light it is understandable that the geographical distance to these countries, which are on the same continent, is judged as being relatively small, whereas the cultural distance is judged to be relatively large.

Product factors, whether these are service intensity, standardization, adaptation, or the fact that they are services *per se*, all score medians of 1. The low importance of the fact that products are services is perfectly normal, since all firms in the sample are manufacturers. Yet the low response of the other three questions is very striking, since product factors are often regarded as directly influencing the success or failure of any business enterprise. However, for this group of factors one can thus question its importance in the entry mode decision process.

Exchange rate depreciation was considered to be unimportant by the companies in the sample, again for the reason that investments in Eastern Europe are focused almost exclusively on the long term. Exchange depreciation is of too short or medium a term to be of significant influence.

Regarding the open-ended question on additional environmental factors, the results are encouraging. Only two additional environmental factors were mentioned by the respondents. The first one is a globalization of customer markets. In line with this, producers adopt a global view in choosing locations for production sites. One company mentioned their resulting strategy of global presence as being important in the decision to choose investment as an entry mode.

The second additional environmental factor that was suggested, is the change in ideas regarding the environment in the Netherlands. Building a plant that produces pollution in the Netherlands will encounter heavy objections from many organizations. However, Eastern European governments pursue a more liberal policy in this respect, as economic considerations have a higher priority for them.

Problems

This subsection is concerned with the questions on the problems Dutch companies encountered with their investments in Eastern Europe. The results are presented in Table 13.6.

Table 13.6: Research results on the importance of different problems with the foreign investment.

Question	(7 respondents)	Median	Mean	St. dev.
(D5)	Bureaucratic barriers	4	3.57	1.40
(D6)	Internal economic problems	3	3.00	1.00
(D7)	Problems with employees	3	3.29	1.38
(D1)	Conflicts with partners	3	2.29	0.95
(D3)	Security of invested capital	2	2.57	1.27
(D2)	Loss of control over technology	2	1.86	0.69
(D4)	Currency problems	1	1.29	0.49

The most important single problem to the investors in our sample is bureaucratic barriers. The median score of 4 indicates that this problem is very important. This problem still exists, because many of the institutions of the communist era are still in place, and they are probably staffed with the same people. It is interesting, however, to note that one of the respondents indicated that their investment had not experienced a problem in this respect, the simple reason for this being that its partner was a state-run enterprise, presumably having all the right connections with government officials. The importance of this problem is also witnessed by Van Berendonk, Oosterveer and Associates (1992), whose findings indicate that bureaucracy is the most common problem at the start of a joint venture. In later stages the problem is found to be less important, but still considerable.

Internal problems of the economy are an important problem too, although less important than bureaucratic barriers. It is interesting to compare this result to the median score of 3 of the question on the importance of the dynamic economy as an environmental factor. The result on that question indicated that firms found it important to invest, in order to be close to the market and be able to respond to economic changes.

Problems with employees are of substantial importance to Dutch investors. Although cultural differences do not seem to be an important factor in the decision to invest, with a median of 2 on the corresponding question in the preceding section, they nevertheless create major problems in respect of employees. It seems as though Dutch companies might have underestimated the cultural differences between the Netherlands and Eastern Europe. This is surprising, considering that the media provide numerous examples of problems with Eastern European employees. For example, one Dutch firm (not part of our study) discovered that many of their employees had several jobs on the side, as was completely normal under the old communist system. The problem that resulted from this was that the workers were not fresh and motivated when they came to their regular job in the morning (Jellinek 1990). The key word in solving the problems is patience; as Thurow (1991a) puts it: 'For here, where both work places and work forces have been warped by 40 years of communism, an acquisition involves taking over not only a failing company but also a failed way of life.' It is obvious that changing people's way of life takes time. In this respect too, the Van Berendonk, Oosterveer and Associates (1992) research supports our own findings. Cultural differences are named in their report as the second most common problem at the start of the joint venture. Similarly, problems with personnel rank third in importance in the daily course of business in the Dutch joint ventures in their sample.

Conflicts with partners are a fourth important problem. It is worth mentioning that the importance of conflicts with partners was related negatively to the level of control of the Dutch parent in the sample, i.e. firms having a higher level of control tended to rate the importance of this problem lower. This supports Killing's (1982) observations, which suggested a similar relationship. A further explanation of this result can be a strong export orientation on the side of the Eastern European partner, which was already suggested by Bieszki and Rath (1989). This explanation is likely to be more valid now than ever. The economic reforms in Eastern Europe have increased the importance of hard (Western) currencies in these countries' economic systems. Since they depend on their exports for the inflow of hard currencies, the joint venture partners are likely to have a strong export orientation.

Problems with protecting the invested capital are only moderately important. The reason is, of course, that Eastern European governments have recognized the need for laws on the security of foreign investors' interests, if they want to attract foreign investments.

Loss of control over technology is also of only moderate importance. The fear of many companies that Eastern European partners are only after their technological skills, with which to start a competing firm of their own, thus seems groundless too. It is possible, however, that before 1989, this problem was more important for Dutch investors.

Finally, currency problems are rated unimportant by the respondents in our study. There may be an explanation for this. The investments in Eastern Europe are focused almost exclusively on the long term. This implies that for at least the first years any profits will usually be reinvested within the host country. Consequently, they do not need to be converted to other currencies yet. Added to this, in East Germany the German Mark is the new currency, and in Poland and Hungary there is internal convertibility of their currencies.

The open-ended question on any problems that were not included in our list, generated more responses than the other two open questions. This indicates that this list of factors is less complete than the other two. Four additional problems were mentioned by our respondents. The first one is the inadequate infrastructure in Eastern Europe. The problem applies not only to the physical condition of roads and means of transport, but also to the energy supplies and the (lack of) facilities in the field of telecommunications, especially international ones. Bad quality of the lines and wrong connections are a part of the everyday reality of doing business in Eastern Europe (Hays 1991).

The second additional problem that was mentioned by one company official concerned the repatriation of profits. Controls on money flowing out of the country make it very difficult to repatriate profits that are made.

A third problem is the poor organization of existing distribution channels. This problem may actually influence firms to change from exporting to investment in Eastern Europe, because the investment gives them more possibilities to carry out part of the distribution themselves and to watch closely the activities of their distributors.

The fourth and last additional problem is the counter-productiveness and ineffectiveness of German and European Community subsidy policies, which has already been mentioned in relation to two questions on influencing people. Although one particular respondent, with an investment in East Germany, did not give an elaborate explanation, it seems that the company refers to the often-voiced concern that (West) German investors are generally given preferential treatment when it comes to investment subsidies in East Germany. Such preferential treatment most likely leads to a non-optimal division of subsidies and poses a problem for investors from other countries.

Conclusions

In this final section we will suggest answers to the questions that were the objectives of our research project. These suggested answers are not necessarily the ultimate answers to the questions. To get those a larger sample population would have been necessary.

Which people influenced the decision of the firm to invest in the Eastern European market?

Our study indicates that the following parties are most influential in this decision:

1. competitors;
2. Eastern European representatives and customers;

3. internal promoters;
4. Eastern European business groups.

Why did the firm decide on investment as the entry mode, instead of for example exporting or a contractual mode?
Our research finds that the choice for investment is influenced most by the following environmental factors:

1. a high commitment to the Eastern European market;
2. a high sales potential in the Eastern European country;
3. the dynamic economy in the Eastern European country;
4. the availability of substantial resources;
5. the liberal investment policies in the Eastern European country;
6. a low political risk in the Eastern European country.

Which problems did the firm encounter, relative to its choice of investment as the entry mode?
According to our findings the most important problems the firms are facing are:

1. bureaucratic barriers in Eastern Europe;
2. problems with Eastern European employees;
3. internal problems of the Eastern European economy;
4. problems with Eastern European partners.

This study analysed the experiences of Dutch investors in three countries of Eastern Europe. Our sample consisted of seven mostly large manufacturing firms headquartered in the Netherlands. As such, the results must be considered only preliminary. We believe that the number of questions relative to our research areas is sufficient. However, in order to draw more definite and meaningful conclusions, the sample size needs to be larger. It is our intention to continue to expand our research, as more data on companies entering Eastern Europe, involving joint ventures, becomes available.

References

Aeppel, T. (1992) 'Czech Official Raps Terms of Mercedes Truck Venture', *Wall Street Journal Europe* January 9: 3.
Allen, R. E. *et al.* (1991) 'We asked . . . What Is Your Greatest Concern About Expanding Into Eastern Europe?', *Columbia Journal of World Business*, Spring: 18–19.
Anderson, E. and Gatignon, H. A. (1986) 'Modes of Foreign Entry: A Transaction Cost Analysis and Propositions', *Journal of International Business Studies* Fall: 1–26.
Bertrand, K. (1990) 'Marketers Rush to Be First on the Bloc', *Business Marketing* October 20–23.
Bieszki, M. and Rath, H. (1989) 'Foreign Capital Investment in Poland: Emerging Prospects for German–Polish Joint Ventures under the New Law', *Management International Review* 4: 45–67.
Bodde, W. (ed.) (1990) *Zakendoen in Oost-Europa*, 's-Gravenhage Economische Voorlichtings Dienst/Stichting Economische Publikaties.

Cieslik, J. (1983) 'Western Firms Participating in the East–West Industrial Co-operation: The Case of Poland', *Management International Review* 1: 69–75.

Hays, L. (1991) 'Comstar Phone Venture in Soviet Union Is Slowed by Bureacracy, Currency Woes', *Wall Street Journal Europe* April 2: 70.

Jellinek, P. M. (ed.) (1990) *Zaken Doen in Midden- en Oost-Europa*, Schoonhoven: Academic Service.

Johanson, J. and Vahlne, J. E. (1977) 'The Internationalization Process of the Firm: A Model of Knowledge Development and Increasing Foreign Market Commitments', *Journal of International Business Studies*, Spring/Summer: 23–32.

Killing, J. P. (1982) 'How to Make a Global Joint Venture Work', *Harvard Business Review* May–June: 120–127.

Kogut, B. (1986) 'On Designing Contracts to Guarantee Enforceability: Theory and Evidence from East–West Trade', *Journal of International Business Studies* Spring: 47–61.

Por, J. T. (1991) 'Managing in Communism's Wake', *Wall Street Journal Europe*, May 14: 8.

Robinson, R. D. (1978) *International Business Management: A Guide to Decision-Making*, Second edn. Hinsdale: Dryden Press.

Root, F. R. (1987) *Entry Strategies for International Markets*, Second edn., Lexington, Mass.: Lexington Books.

Schares. G. E. and Templeman, J. (1990) 'Western Carmakers Are Racing For The East', *Business Week* October 22: 22–23.

Thurow, R. (1991a) 'Seeing the Light: In Hungarian Plant, GE Finds Biggest Job is Retooling of Minds', *Wall Street Journal Europe*, September 25: 1 and 8.

Thurow, R. (1991b) 'Jobs on Wheels: VW Investment Brings Hope to Eastern Area That Once Built Trabis', *Wall Street Journal Europe* December 16: 1 and 5.

Van Berendonk, Oosterveer and Associates (1992) *Nederlandse Joint Ventures in Midden- en Oost-Europa: Ervaringen en meningen uit de praktijk*, Eindhoven: Research Report, Van Berendonk, Oosterveer and Associates, International Management Consultants.

Young, S., Hamill, J., Wheeler, C. and Davies, J. R. (1989) *International Market Entry and Development: Strategies and Management*, Englewood Cliffs, NJ: Prentice-Hall.

14

Co-operative Ventures of Western Firms in Eastern Europe: the Case of German Companies

Refik Culpan and Nino Kumar

Recent political and economic changes taking place in Eastern Europe have increased the demand from these countries for Western capital and technology. Western companies have responded to such demands either eagerly, or with some reservations or mixed feelings. As a result, many Western firms have established business linkages with the former Soviet Union and other East European countries, despite the continuing political and economic uncertainty in these countries. The strategic behaviour of Western firms, although accompanied with ambiguity, in their business involvements in Eastern Europe markets warrant close attention.

Thus this chapter explores the strategic behaviour of Western firms in their business linkages with Eastern European organizations. In doing so, a conceptual model was constructed to reflect East–West business co-operations. The model deals with the motives concerning Western firms' forms of business alliances between East and West, and with the environmental uncertainties surrounding such business transactions. Furthermore the paper inquires into the forms of co-operations preferred by Western companies as they affect the operations of these ventures.

The chapter starts with the introduction of principal theories of strategic alliances and moves into the review of the past studies on East–West business ventures, then it presents the characteristics of Eastern European markets. Subsequently the chapter introduces a conceptual model on East–West business co-operations. Finally, it concludes with a discussion of and recommendations for East–West co-operative ventures.

Strategic alliances in general have become a centre of attention because of their increasing importance in international business (Auster 1987; Contractor and Lorange 1988; Morris and Hergert 1987). Most of the studies (Harrigan 1988; Hennart 1988; Killing 1983; Kogut 1988a and Stuckey 1983) focus on international joint ventures (IJVs), a major form of interfirm co-operation. Some develop research propositions (Borys and Jemison 1989) while others examine governance forms of alliances (Osborn and Baughn 1990). However, only a few studies are empirical investigations of East–West business co-operations.

For the purpose of this paper, we define strategic alliances as business linkages between two firms with or without equity participation. As this definition implies, strategic alliances may take two principal forms. One major category is equity participation, with or without creating a new legal entity. When a new entity is created by equity participation, this is called a joint venture (JV); otherwise they are referred to as portfolio investments or stock swaps. Another category of alliance includes non-equity (contractual) agreements such as licensing, franchising, research and development (R&D) collaborations, and marketing alliances. In East–West business deals, international joint ventures (IJVs) and contractual agreements seem to be the most relevant forms.

Theoretical Perspectives

Although there is no unified theory of strategic alliances, theories of IJVs can be extended to other forms of alliance. Theoretical explanations for joint ventures can be considered in three categories: transaction cost economics, organizational resource dependency, and competitive advantage (Culpan, forthcoming; Kogut 1988b). We briefly introduce each one as a theoretical background of our research.

Transaction cost economics

Transaction cost economics suggests that firms seek to minimize transaction costs in their dealings with other firms. 'Transaction costs refer to the expenses incurred for writing and enforcing contracts, for haggling over terms and contingent claims, for deviation from optimal kinds of investments in order to increase dependence on a party or stabilize a relationship, and for administering a transaction' (Kogut 1988b: 320). As a pioneer of transaction costs theory, Williamson (1975) suggested that firms choose alternative arrangements that minimize the sum of production and transaction costs.

Some scholars (Buckley and Casson 1976; Hennart 1982, 1991; Rugman 1981; Stuckey 1983) have applied transaction costs theory to joint ventures. Unlike Williamson, who concentrated on governance choice, they focused on international transactions. For example, Buckley and Casson (1988) posited that:

> Joint ventures are, first and foremost, a device for mitigating the worst consequences of mistrust. In the language of internationalization theory, they represent a compromise contractual agreement that minimizes transaction costs under certain environmental constraints. But some types of joint venture also provide a suitable context in which parties can demonstrate mutual forbearance and thereby build up trust. This may open up possibilities for coordination that could not otherwise be entertained. The prospect of this encourages partners to take an unusually open-ended view of JV partnership and gives JVs their political and cultural mystique.
>
> (Buckley and Casson 1988: 52)

Similarly, Hennart argues that 'all JVs can be explained as a device to bypass inefficient markets for intermediate inputs. The presence of inefficiencies in intermediate markets is then a necessary condition for JVs to emerge' (1989: 364). The high transaction costs involved in acquisition of raw materials and components, tacit knowledge, and loan capital, as well as managing a distribution of a product, entail JV arrangements.

Furthermore, Buckley and Casson pointed out that '[a]ll the parties involved in a venture have an inalienable *de facto* right to pursue their own interest at the expense of others. It is one of the hallmarks of institutional economics – and transaction cost economies in particular – that it recognizes the widespread application of this' (1988: 34). These scholars consider that mutual forbearance is the incentive for a co-operative venture, because it prevents the participating parties from cheating each other, which frequently occurs in non-cooperative ventures. Through such forbearance, the partners build commitment and trust.

The transaction cost perspective illuminates the search by firms for co-operative ventures as a device to avoid high transaction costs in inefficient markets. It is especially useful in explaining international R&D partnerships concerning large-scale or innovative projects. Kogut and Singh articulated on this phenomenon as follows: 'in growing industries where R&D investment is important, foreign entrants may create joint ventures with larger firms in order to acquire technology from incumbents for use in their home markets or gain marketing arms for their innovations' (1988: 241).

Nevertheless, transaction cost economics emphasizes only the minimizing of costs and assumes that firms only pursue reactive strategies, therefore the creation of a new market cannot be explained by this approach. Firms, however, may also take a proactive stand by entering new markets in order to increase their market shares even with higher costs in the short-run.

Resource dependency approach

The resource dependency approach suggests that organizations depend on other organizations within their environment to acquire needed resources. Pfeffer and Salancik (1978) described how organizations cope with the uncertainty (created by interdependence) by managing interdependence through interorganizational co-ordinations. In this regard, Pfeffer and Nowak (1976) believed that the formation of joint ventures is a means of stabilizing the flow of resources that the company needs and of reducing the uncertainty confronted by the firm. The authors contended that there are two types of interorganizational interdependence causing uncertainty. First, competitive interdependence means that while firms compete for markets and for financial and human resources, such competition also occurs among other organizations (Thomson and McEwen 1958). Second, symbiotic interdependence with other organizations refers to 'a mutual dependence between unlike organizations' (Hawley 1950: 36). Thus Pfeffer and Nowak (1976) considered that JVs are undertaken to cope with these two forms of interdependence. Although the resource dependency approach brings some clarifications for interorganizational linkages, it fails to explain why an organization with no resources or minimum resources co-operates with others. For instance, why does a multinational corporation (MNC) establish a joint venture with a firm from a developing country, although the MNC does not need any resources from that nation? There must be another explanation for the co-operative behaviour of firms. This lends itself to a third explanation, competition advantage.

Competitive advantage

The competitive advantage approach explains co-operative ventures as a firm's efforts in gaining or sustaining a competitive superiority over its competitors. In other words, a co-operative venture may provide such competitive advantages as relative cost advantage (Porter 1980, 1985). For example, an international joint venture may provide those competitive advantages, namely, relative cost advantages deriving from economies of scale, differentiated products because of superior technology or product quality, or segmenting markets and appealing to only a limited group of consumers or industrial buyers.

Porter and Fuller (1986) deem strategic alliance ('coalitions', in their terms) in the context of a firm's international strategy:

> two key dimensions of international strategy are the international configuration of a firm's activities (where and how many places they are located) and the extent to which activities located in different countries are coordinated (how do they relate). Coalitions are a means of performing one or more activities in combination with another firm instead of autonomously – they are thus a means of configuration. The choice of a coalition implies that it is perceived as a less costly or more effective way to configure than the alternatives of on the one hand developing the skills to perform the activity in-house or on the other hand of merger to gain the capability to perform the activity or to buy products or skills in arm's length transaction.
>
> (Porter and Fuller 1986: 321)

Thus, the expectations from strategic alliances in both configuration and co-ordination can become clear by relating coalitions to the activities on the value chain, which disaggregates a firm into the discrete activities performed in developing, producing, marketing, selling, servicing after sale of a product or service (Porter and Fuller 1986).

Competitive advantage theory probably is the most convincing argument on co-operative behaviour of participating firms. To a large extent, it embraces the cost minimization objective of transaction cost theory and sourcing aspect of resource dependency approach within a competitive advantage framework.

The general theories of co-operative ventures explained above provide insights into interfirm collaborations and the motives of participating firms usually between two Western firms. However, the business relationship between a Western firm and an Eastern European enterprise might present different characteristics, because of the Western partner's usually higher bargaining power *vis-à-vis* its Eastern European counterpart. Nevertheless, it is important to find out how valid these theories in explaining the co-operative behaviour of parties are in practice. This paper attempts to test the above mentioned theories in the case of Western firms' co-operations with Eastern European enterprises. Initially we assume that firms engage in co-operative ventures with all those motives as defined by the general theories of interfirm co-operation. Accordingly, a conceptual framework was designed, which is described below.

Since the focus of this paper is on East–West business co-operation, a brief review of the past studies on this subject is now introduced.

Past studies on East–West Business Ventures

Many researchers have examined the linkage of Western firms with the former Eastern bloc countries. The large body of literature examines joint ventures between MNCs and local state-owned enterprises (Bertrand 1990; Boukaouris 1989; Deutsches Institut 1990; Gibson 1990; Maggs 1988; Sheer 1988; Turner 1991). Sheer (1988) noted the increasing attention of the Soviet Union to the establishment of joint ventures with the West as a way of efficiently and continually transferring technology and material skills, and to earn needed capital. According to the US International Trade Administration, there were 140 joint ventures between the US and Hungary, and sixty between the US and Poland as of April 1990.

For Soviet–US joint ventures, Rosten (1991) identified 'the major issues that the US partners deem important and those issues that were difficult to resolve during the course of the negotiations' and also probed 'the major hurdles that the joint ventures had to overcome to commence operations'. The author (1991) claimed that Western companies can enhance the chance of success by observing the following eight fundamental rules: partner selection, alternative co-operative agreements, sound business strategy, structuring the agreement, Western role in operations, operation planning for shortages, repatriation of profits, and difference in culture.

Quelch, Joachimtaller and Nuemo (1991) pointed out that despite the recent liberalization movement in Eastern Europe, such obstacles concerning cultural, technological, and supply sources still remain. They addressed key strategic issues, such as which product markets to enter and when to enter them. The authors drew on the experience of ten Western executives for practical advice on negotiating joint ventures and marketing business in Eastern Europe.

By exploring joint ventures with the Soviet Union, Herzfeld asserted that through the turmoil, Western companies should grow and integrate vertically, on the basis that roubles will someday be worth owning:

> [n]o joint venture in the Soviet Union will prosper in today's environment unless it is actually a top-to-bottom chain of linked or integrated enterprises, more or less in command of supplies and with independent access to customers. A joint venture must remain independent both of world suppliers – who do require hard currency – and of those Soviet suppliers or distribution channels with standards for quality or responsiveness that are not likely to be acceptable right now.
>
> (Herzfeld 1991: 81)

Watson and Frazer (1991), after assessing Eastern European industries, discussed Western companies' possible links with Eastern European producers. The authors warned Western firms that they should not be misled by short-term market signals or get involved in business projects without a systematic analysis of the market opportunities.

Although earlier research has articulated on the motives of Western firms, it almost exclusively emphasizes market entry objective of Western firms in case studies. Usually the focus of these studies is the transfer of technology from a Western company to an Eastern European country. Despite the abundance of writings on East–West business relationships, most of them (Granick 1975, Wilczynski 1976) are outdated because of the recent changes in the political and economic structures in these countries. Others (Dickie 1991; Hertzfeld 1991;

Quelch, Joachimtaller and Nuemo 1991; Watson and Frazer 1991) offer only managerial guidelines for doing business in Eastern Europe.

The present study views co-operative agreements of Western firms as a part of
their overall international business strategy and attempts to place co-operative
ventures into an appropriate perspective. Unlike the earlier investigations, this
research inquires into the premises of three well-accepted theories of international
co-operative ventures mentioned above in the case of Western–East European
business co-operations.

Turbulent Markets of East Europe

Eastern Europe is going through radical changes so rapidly that any information or
fact about the countries becomes outdated very quickly (Heger 1989). Changes like
the political restructuring in the USSR and Czechoslovakia, and the ongoing civil
war in Yugoslavia, make very difficult to assess the present market conditions and
predict the future. Nevertheless, we can present some facts and figures to demonstrate the recent augmented interest by Western firms in Eastern European
markets. As Table 14.1 shows, major Western business firms have engaged in
Eastern Europe to take advantage of marketing opportunities in these countries.

Table 14.1: The biggest joint ventures of Western firms in Eastern Europe.

Investor	Country	Partner	Country	Industry	Investment in $ million
Volkswagen	Germany	Skoda, BAZ	Czechos.	Automobile	6,630
CBC	France	Tourinvest	Czechos.	Hotels	175
GE	USA	Tungsram	Hungary	Lights	150
GE	USA	Raba-Györ	Hungary	Autos, Engines	150
Pilkington	UK	HSO	Poland	Glass	140
Guardian	USA	Magyar Üveg	Hungary	Glass	120
Suzuki, C. Itoh	Japan	Ikarus	Hungary	Automobile	110
Linde	Germany	Technoplyn	Czechos.	Technical gases	106
Elektrolux	Sweden	Lehel	Hungary	Refrigerator	83
Hamburger	Austria	Dunapack	Hungary	Packing material	82
Ford	USA	Videoton	Hungary	Auto components	80
Sanofi	France	Chinoin	Hungary	Medicine	80
US West, Bell	USA	(State enter.)	Czechos.	Telephone	80
Sara Lee	USA	Compack	Hungary	Food	80
ABB	Switzerland	Zamech	Poland	Turbines	50

Source: Der Spiegel, July 8, 1991: 96

There has been a big surge in the number of joint ventures registered in the
Eastern European countries. According to the Economic Commission for Europe
(ECE), as a result of liberalization of their joint venture legislations, Hungary,
Poland, and the former USSR accounted for the bulk of the surge in the foreign
direct investment. For example:

in the USSR, since the registration of joint ventures began on 1 January 1987, the number has risen dramatically, with the major increase occurring in 1989. ... The increase can be attributed, at least in part, to the new regulations adopted in December 1988, authorizing co-operatives to participate in joint ventures.

(Industry and Development 1991: 5)

As Table 14.1 shows, the total amount of Western investment into Eastern Europe up to now has not been so significant; however, there is an increasing business interest in the region. Once these countries emerge from the period of political turmoil, more Western firms will enter these potential markets.

On January 1, 1991 around 16,000 JVs were registered in Eastern Europe with participation of Western firms (Handelsblatt 1991). Germany was the leading investor in Eastern Europe, followed by Austria with its 2,500 JVs (15 per cent of all JVs). Germany was the major foreign investor in Bulgaria and Czechoslovakia, while the Netherlands led in Romania. These JVs were mainly in services and trade.

Total German direct investments in Hungary and Poland, for example, increased to DM 110 million in 1986 from DM 34 million in 1983. Although the total amount is not so significant, there is evidence of a surge in investments in recent years.

Hungary has attracted about $1 billion capital investment (more than 30 per cent coming from Germany) in about 5,000 JVs with partners from the West (*Nachrichten fü Außenhandel* 1991). Poland has about 3,000 JVs, but a large number of them do not operate yet. Although the USSR has about 2,600 JVs, only one-third of them operate. Czechoslovakia presently has 1,700 JVs, despite its late start, and the trend is fast-increasing. Capital investments in Czechoslovakia have been usually small amounts, for example, two-thirds of the JVs are with capital under $30,000. Romania with 600 JVs attracted about $66 million capital, whereas Bulgaria has only seventy JVs, one-third of which do not operate.

Although there was a boom in the registration of JVs in Eastern Europe in 1990, these JVs must be judged cautiously because there is a big gap between registration and actual operation. According to a survey conducted by the Viennese Institute for International Economic Comparison, the capital transferred from the West to Eastern European countries is between $1.6 and $1.8 billions. This Austrian study concluded that special barriers to investment into these countries include information, motivation, sales and purchasing problems, uncertainty about the organizational capacities of the JVs, financial problems and property ownership issues. Small JVs are usually set up to take advantage of local market opportunities. Next to Hungary, Czechoslovakia seems to be an attractive market and then comes Poland. The former USSR is considered to be a risky market. For Bulgaria and Romania, it is riskier to establish JVs than to export to these countries.

A Conceptual Model for East–West Business Alliances

A conceptual framework has been constructed to demonstrate the business relationships between a Western firm and East European organizations/enterprises. The framework consists of firm characteristics, motives for co-operation, forms of co-operation, and environmental uncertainty. A Western firm's characteristics are defined in terms of its size and technological intensity. The assumption was that the size of a Western firm affects its decisions to enter Eastern Europe and also the form of its involvement (Kumar and Steinmann 1991). Additionally, technological intensity of firms measured as the ratio of its annual R&D expenses to its annual sales is taken into consideration. It is believed that firms with differing technological intensity might demonstrate different strategic responses to market conditions in Eastern Europe. Such a technological intensity variable is used in various areas of research, including early inquiries on strategic alliance (Osland and Baughn 1990).

Motivation for co-operation is defined in accordance with the principal theories of strategic alliances. Thus, the motives of Western firms are defined as minimizing transaction costs, acquiring needed resource, and gaining competitive advantage. Since these general motives are sufficiently discussed above, there is no need to provide further explanations for them here. The motivation of Western firms, however, are closely linked with the criteria of partner selection. For instance, choosing a partner on the basis of its market position or local connections reflects competitive advantage and transaction cost perspectives respectively. Thus partner selection implies motivation of parties, which needs to be examined. Indeed, it is not difficult to find several studies on partner typologies and selection (Geringer 1988 and 1991; Harrigan 1986).

Forms of co-operation are considered in two categories. The first includes equity participations such as joint ventures, which happen to be a major form of co-operation. The second category is non-equity co-operation, including licensing, franchising, and marketing agreements.

Environmental uncertainties refer to the existence of political instability, poor infrastructure, lack of foreign investment regulations, lack of skilled labour or of competent managers, currency convertibility problems, conflicts stemming from language, business mentality, and cultural differences, lack of foreign funds, and low purchasing power of local currency. Such uncertainties are characterized by low or high levels as they are perceived by Western managers. Additionally, competitiveness in Eastern European markets can be judged as being high, moderate, or low.

Overall, establishing co-operative linkages is considered as the strategic response of Western firms to Eastern European market opportunities.

Discussion and Conclusion

The motives of Western firms for co-operative ventures may vary according to the size of company. While the competitive advantage motives seem to be influential for the smaller Western firms, the transaction cost motives play a significant role on the decisions of the larger firms. For example, the reasons for JVs by large firms can be related to transaction cost theory. Indeed, the literature on JVs (Hennart 1988; Buckley and Casson 1988) confirms this argument. Although there is a discrepancy between the prevailing motives for non-equity agreements and those for JVs, this discrepancy seems to stem from differentials in the firm size. The larger firms might demonstrate a greater inclination toward equity participation (JVs) as compared to the smaller firms which preferred non-equity arrangements. We believe that this differentiation can be explained by the strengths and competence of bigger firms to control internal markets. On the other hand, since smaller firms lack such resources they tend to use firm-specific advantages such as proprietary technology and product niches (Kumar 1987; Porter 1990).

We believe that small- and medium-sized Western firms are active players in emerging Eastern European markets. We can find supporting arguments in the literature for small- and medium-sized firms' involvements in global markets. For example:

> Small companies, not just large ones, can compete globally. Small and medium-sized companies account for a substantial portion of international trade, especially in nations such as Germany, Italy, and Switzerland. They often focus on narrow segments or compete in relatively small industries. . . .
> With limited resources, smaller firms face challenges in gaining foreign market access, understanding foreign market needs, and providing after-sale support. These problems are solved in different ways in different industries.
>
> (Porter 1990: 62)

Thus, small- and medium-sized firms should not be inhibited from exploiting Eastern European markets because they may find a market segment or product niche appealing to the buyers in these countries.

The results of our review suggest that in spite of the present political and economic turmoil in Eastern Europe, Western companies have confidence in those markets and uncertainty does not discourage them from exploiting opportunities in these emerging economies. Nevertheless, most firms still perceived a high rate of environmental uncertainty in this region. Probably choosing the option of a co-operative venture is a kind of safeguard against this uncertainty while they seek competitive advantages.

Although there are still major obstacles to market entry to Eastern Europe, Western companies should not wait until all these obstacles are removed. They should play an active role in the Eastern European market. It appears that this mission will be carried out by technology-intensive companies in highly competitive industries, who have previous foreign business experience.

European firms in particular hold a competitive advantage in Eastern Europe, compared with US and Japanese firms. Reasons for this include their geographical proximity to the market, traditional ties with Eastern Europe, going back to before the Second World War, and the high level of interest of Western European companies in the region. For the short term, co-operative ventures seems to be favourable arrangements in comparison to wholly-owned subsidiaries. For the purpose of long-range strategic benefits, however, foreign firms should also consider developing wholly-owned subsidiaries for market entry and expansion.

Given the present economic structure in Eastern Europe, most of the partners happen to be state-owned enterprises and state agencies. However, as the market economy develops, more private initiatives will emerge. Western companies are recommended to develop partnerships with such private enterprises because they will be more suitable partners with compatible business values and competence. Most Western firms experience conflict with their state-owned partners as a result of their not understanding capitalist management philosophy. Western firms should look for partners who have footholds in the market (e.g., holding a good market share and channel control). Finding such an established private partner may seem an unrealistic ambition for the time being, but it is to be expected that the private initiatives with higher efficiencies will quickly emerge and will be potential candidates for co-operation. The different size of Western firms with different motives may engage in symmetrical local partners (Harrigan 1985).

The satisfaction of business partners with particular joint ventures may facilitate further collaboration between the partners. Furthermore, the promotional policies of home governments (e.g., Germany) will enhance additional co-operation between East and West.

Empirical evidence on the strategic behaviour of European and non-European companies is needed. It is hoped that the presentation in this chapter provides some understanding of Western firms' involvement in Eastern Europe; thereby the behaviour of other Western firms can be interpreted or compared with.

References

Auster, E. R. (1987), 'International corporate linkages: Dynamic forms in changing environments'. *Columbia Journal of World Business* 22(2): 3–6.

Bertrand, K. (1990) 'Marketers rush to be first on the bloc', *Business Marketing* 75(10): 20–23.

Borys, B. and Jemison, D. B. (1989) 'Hybrid arrangements as strategic alliances: Theoretical issues in organizational combinations', *Academy of Management Review* 14(20): 230–249.

Boukaouris, G. N. (1989) 'Joint ventures in the USSR, Czechoslovakia and Poland', *Case Western Journal of International Law* 21(1): 1–53.

Buckley, P. J. and Casson, M. (1988) 'A theory of co-operation in international business', In F. J. Contractor and P. Lorange (eds.), *Co-operative Strategies in International Business*, Lexington, Mass.: Lexington Books.

Buckley, P. J. and Casson, M. (1976) *The Future of the Multinational Enterprise*, New York: Holes & Meier.

Contractor, F. J. and Lorange, P. (1988) (eds.) *Co-operative Strategies in International Business*, Lexington, Mass.: Lexington Books.

Cuplan, R. (ed.) *Multinational Strategic Alliances*, Binghampton, NY: The Haworth Press, forthcoming.

Der Speigel, July 8, 1991.

Deutsches Institut für Wirtschaftsforschung (1990) (hrsg.) *Ost-West Kooperationen – Bestandsaufnehme und – Ergebnisse einer Umfrage*, Berlin: DIW.

Dickie, R. B. (1991) 'Western business should approach Eastern Europe mindful of experience in East Asia', *California Management Review* 33(4): 118–26.

Geringer, J. M. (1988) *Joint venture partner selection: Strategies for developed countries*, Westport, Conn.: Quorum Books.

Geringer, J. M. (1991) 'Strategic determinants of partner selection criteria in international joint ventures', *Journal of International Business Studies* 22(1): 41–62.

Gibson, S. J. (1990) 'Telecommunications and the Perestroika revolution', *Canadian Business Review* 17(2): 29–31.

Granick, D. (1990) *Enterprise Guidance in Eastern Europe, A Comparison of Four Socialist Economies*, Princeton, NJ: Princeton University Press.

Handelsblatt, Dusseldorf, February 12, 1991.

Harrigan, K. R. (1985) *Strategies for Joint Ventures*, Lexington, Mass.: Lexington Books.

Harrigan, K. R. (1986) *Managing for Joint Venture Success*, Lexington, Mass.: Lexington Books.

Harrigan, K. R. (1988) 'Strategic alliances and partner assymetries', In F. Contractor and P. Lorange (eds), *Cooperative Strategies in International Business*, Lexington, Mass.: Lexington Books.

Hawley, A. (1950) *Human Ecology*, New York: Ronald Press.

Heger, S. (1989) *Joint Ventures in der Sowjetunion – rechtliche – Voraussetzungen und wirtschaftliche Aspekte*, Wien.

Hennart, J. F. (1988) 'A transaction costs theory of equity joint ventures', *Strategic Management Journal* 9: 361–374.

Hennart, J. F. (1990) 'The transaction cost theory of joint ventures: An empirical study of Japanese subsidiaries in the United States', *Management Science* 37(4): 483–96.

Herzfeld, J. M. (1991) 'Joint ventures saving the Soviets from Perestroika', *Harvard Business Review*, January–February: 80–91.

Industry and Development, 29, Vienna: UNIDO, 1991.

Killing, P. K. (1983) *Strategies for Joint Venture Success*, Praeger Publishers.

Kogut, B. (1988a) 'A study of the life cycle of joint ventures', in F. J. Contractor and P. Lorange (eds.), *Cooperative Strategies in International Business*, Lexington, Mass.: Lexington Books.

Kogut, B. (1988b) 'Joint Ventures: Theoretical and empirical perspectives', *Strategic Management Journal*, 9, 319–332.

Kogut, B. and Singh, H. (1988) 'Entering the United States by joint venture: Competitive rivalry and industry structure', in F. Contractor and P. Lorange (eds.) *Cooperative strategies in international business*, Lexington, Mass.: Lexington Books.

Kumar, B. N. (1987) *Deutsche Unternehmen in der USA*, Wiesbaden: Gabler.

Kumar, B. N. and Steinmann, H. (1991) 'Technology transfer by Western small- and medium-sized enterprises to developing countries', in M. Trevor (ed.) *International Business and the Management of Change*, Aldershot: Avebury.

Maggs, P. B. (1988) 'Joint enterprises in relation to Soviet Banking and Finance Law', *Columbia Journal of World Business* 23(2): 13–23.

Morris, D. and Hegert, M. (1987) 'Trends in international cooperative agreements', *Columbia Journal of World Business* 22(2): 15–21.

Nachrichten für Außenhandel, (Eschborn), May 7, 1991.

Osborn, R. N. and Baughn, C. C. (1990) 'Forms of interorganizational governance for multinational alliances', *Academy of Management Journal* 33(3): 503–29.

Pfeffer, J. and Nowak, P. (1976) 'Joint ventures and interorganizational interdependence', *Administrative Science Quarterly* 21 (September): 398–418.

Pfeffer, J. and Salancik, G. R. (1978) *The External Control of Organizations*, New York: Harper & Row.

Porter, M. E. (1980) *Competitive Strategy*, New York: The Free Press.

Porter, M. E. (1985) *Competitive Advantage: Creating and Sustaining Superior Performance*, New York: The Free Press.

Porter, M. E. (1990) *The Competitive Advantage of Nations*, New York: The Free Press.

Porter, M. E. and Fuller, M. B. (1986) 'Coalitions and global strategy', in M. E. Porter (ed.) *Competition In Global Industries*, Boston, Mass.: Harvard Business School Press.

Quelch, J. A., Joachimthaler, E. and Neno, J. L. (1991) 'After the Wall: Marketing guidelines for Eastern Europe', *Sloan Management Review*, 32(3): 82–93.

Rosten, K. A. (1991) 'Soviet–U.S. Joint Ventures: Pioneers on new frontier', *California Management Review* 33(2): 88–108.

Rugman, A. (1981) *Inside the Multinationals*, New York: Columbia University Press.

Sheer, A. B. (1988) 'Joint ventures in the USSR: Soviet and Western interests with considerations for negotiations', *Columbia Journal of World Business* 23(2): 25–41.

Stuckey, A. (1983) *Vertical Integration and Joint Ventures in the Aluminum Industry*, Cambridge, Mass.: Harvard University Press.

Thomson, J. D. and McEwen, W. J. (1958) 'Organizational goals and environment', *American Sociological Review* 23, 23–31.

Tuner, J. N. (1991) 'Soviet–U.S. joint ventures: Pioneers on a new frontier', *California Management Review* 33(2): 88–108.

Watson, P-W and Frazer, S. (1991) 'Eastern Europe: Commercial opportunity or illusion?', *Long Range Planning* 24(4): 17–22.

Williamson, E. O. (1975) *Market and Hierarchies: Analysis and Antitrust Implications*, New York: The Free Press.

15

Understanding the Former Soviet Market: An Interaction Approach

Alexander de Wit and Eric Monami

Introduction

At a time when fundamental political, social and economic reforms are shaking the republics of the former Soviet Union, we have undertaken an investigation of foreign trade activities in that part of the world, starting from the situation which existed before Perestroika. Our aim is to analyse the consequences for Western firms of the decentralization and the opening up of the CIS markets.

One of the main concerns of the current economic situation is the lack of hard currencies that potential Eastern customers are facing nowadays. It seems reasonable to assume that this problem and its implications for Western firms marketing goods in the CIS are well known and are understood by most people.

In this chapter, we will focus on those aspects of the economic reforms that are connected, in various ways, to the reshaping of business networks and relationships, as well as on the different factors related to this ongoing phenomenon. This includes the disappearance or conversion of formerly existing actors, and the emergence of new partners bringing in new resources or managing existing ones differently.

Given the specificity and the rapidity of these processes, we have based our chapter mainly on empirical evidence drawn directly from our investigations in the CIS. These investigations consist largely of interviews with several managers of three Swedish companies involved in business activities in the CIS and with their business partners from the former Soviet republics. We are very grateful to all our interviewees for having given us all the information presented here and for their patience in doing so, sometimes during several hours of discussion.

The authors are very grateful to Nazeem Seyed Mohamed from the University of Uppsala. This chapter would never have been written without his support and constructive comments. The project was financed by Marketing Technical Centre (MTC).

Theoretical Frame

Analysis of this highly unstable environment required appropriate theoretical tools and methods of investigation. This section reviews the main propositions that we attempt to test in the framework of business interactions in the former Soviet Union. Our empirical work is presented in the next section.

Given the clear accordance between our goals and the basic ideas that constitute the Interaction Approach developed by the IMP Group, we based our work on the findings provided by this group of researchers. Industrial marketing and purchasing, they argue, often take place within the context of a relationship between the buying and selling firms, both of which are active components in the interaction process. Their relationship may be distant and impersonal, but is often close, complex and long-term (Håkansson and Östberg 1975; Ford 1984, 1990).

Consequently, both formal and informal changes are important in international business. The actors – organizations or individuals – have memories of their interaction, so that the success of their relationship depends on its history. The parties have to learn about each other's ways of doing and viewing things and how to interpret each other's acts. Generally, this can only be attained through business exchange (Håkansson and Johanson 1988). The parties involved not only need knowledge about prices, quality, but also about deliveries, services, reliability, development possibilities, etc. Much of that knowledge can only be gained after transactions have taken place (Johanson and Mattsson 1988).

Besides, they need knowledge about each other's resources, organization and development possibilities. The process of acquiring this knowledge goes far beyond the completion of formal exchanges between suppliers and buyers. Indeed, it is important that it continues for a considerable time without there being an exchange of product or money. Consequently, another important aspect of the relationship is the adaptations which the parties may make not only in the elements exchanged, but also in the process of exchange itself (IMP Group, 1982).

The different 'exchange episodes' that build up a relationship, when successfully executed, also play a critical role in reducing uncertainty between the two parties and in developing mutual trust between them. This social process, which often takes time, leads to the routinization of these exchange episodes and to some expectations regarding the partner's roles or responsibilities. Eventually, Ford argues, these expectations become institutionalized to such an extent that they may not be questioned by either party and may have more in common with the traditions of an industry or a market than rational decision-making by either of the parties. Consequently, social exchange episodes gradually interlock the two firms with each other (Håkansson and Östberg 1975; Ford 1978). This is particularly significant when a spatial or cultural distance exists between the two parties, which is obviously the case between Swedish businessmen and their Soviet partners – managers or bureaucrats.

Personal contacts play a major role in this framework. As Turnbull states, the need for information exchange, evaluation of product and service offerings, and negotiation, are usually best met through interaction on a person-to-person basis. Interpersonal contacts provide a means of reducing the risk surrounding the specification and selection of a product and a supplier. They may play an even greater role when a firm is acting in a foreign environment. In the early stage of internationalization, the primary role of these contacts, Turnbull argues, will be to reduce psychic distance[1] between the parties to a relationship, as well as the technical and economic characteristics of the foreign country (Turnbull 1979).

The next section explains how we attempted to understand the impact of the current economic reforms on the mentioned variables or groups of variables, and how we evaluated the role that social exchanges and personal contacts might play, under these circumstances, in sustaining and creating a competitive advantage.

Empirical Frame and Methodology

As already mentioned in the introduction, this paper is based on important empirical material collected over a two-year period, by means of face-to-face interviews, in three major Swedish companies. In such a fast-moving environment, where communication means are limited and where the parties are so distant in many senses, it seemed interesting to assess the opinions expressed on both sides of the negotiation table. This is why the list of interviews on which our case studies are based comprises not only Swedish managers, but also some of their ex-Soviet business partners – managers and state officials. Within the Swedish firms, the comments of the managers and planners based in Sweden were augmented by the views and anecdotes expressed by their representatives in the CIS market.

First we have sought to acquire a better understanding of the Soviet foreign trade system before Perestroika. This has helped us to compose the description of the organizational structure of Soviet foreign trade activities presented later in this chapter, which is intended to provide the necessary background of our research. We then introduce, in the same descriptive manner, the main changes that have affected this structure and its constituents in recent years, that is the decentralization of the decision-making. At this stage, this move is perceived only as a gradual and ongoing phenomenon.

We go on to concentrate on some of the consequences of this process on the general business environment and on the evolution of the Western firms' usual counterparts – organizations as well as individuals. This is where it becomes obvious that these changes are bound to affect Western companies' organizations, their activities and their competitive position. To assess this influence, we analysed, with the help of our interviewees, the impact of the decentralization on various variables such as uncertainty or instability, access to information, competence and experience of counterparts, and other elements which we perceived as important, given the fundings provided by the Interaction Approach. The business environment we examine here has undergone crucial changes that have radically modified the characteristics of these variables. Given their nature, we preferred to work by means of relatively open questions, in our attempt to sort out the relevant variables and to understand their evolution. Finally, the paper focuses on a few issues and factors that should be borne in mind by foreign firms having or willing to establish trade relationships in the CIS. The final section is devoted to the discussion of those aspects of our interviewees' activities which they perceive as competitive advantages, given the specific features of the environment in which they were performed.

The three companies referred to in our research and the executives we inter-viewed are briefly introduced in the appendix. The main Soviet organizations mentioned in this chapter are presented in the following section, devoted to their activities.

Background of the Study: The Soviet Foreign Trade System Before Perestroika

Presentation of the main participants

In the past, Soviet companies' activities were controlled by the ministry in charge of the industry to which they belonged. When it was decided, at ministry level, to purchase new equipment or machinery from abroad, the process would come under the responsibility of the appropriate FTO. The organization of exports was roughly the same. Initially, Foreign Trade Organizations were responsible for handling absolutely all foreign trade contracts. For instance, Michael Koïstinen reports, prior to the official break-up of the Soviet Union, the FTO responsible for foreign trade in the field of the automotive industry was a department of the Soviet Ministry of Automotive Industry.

The Ministry was divided into different departments: trucks, cars, etc., for each of which a vice-minister was responsible. NAMI was a research centre employing 5,000 engineers. The UVS department was responsible for contacts with Western companies. When a factory wanted to export part of its production (even when this consisted of goods produced surplus to the plan requirements) or when it needed a component or equipment from abroad, it had to apply to the UVS department within the Ministry of Automotive Industry. UVS officials would then order the Foreign Trade Department inside the same Ministry to handle the export or import operation.

Foreign companies could only have contacts with officials from the UVS and the Foreign Trade Department. They were not allowed to have contacts with other departments within the Ministry, or with the factories. The UVS department was run by KGB officials whose main objective was to ensure that foreign companies would not be able to obtain specific information concerning the industry. The next section explores how this monopoly has been abolished in recent years.

In most fields of activity, when there were several small plants producing the same category of goods, regional holdings or 'combinats' were responsible for a number of plants in their respective region. They belonged to the Ministry in charge of their industry.

When a Soviet company wanted to acquire new equipment, it had to apply to its Ministry, which would then decide whether or not to approve the investment. The Ministry could also take the initiative of setting up an investment programme without any request on the part of its companies. In both cases, it would then transfer the purchase order to the Ministry of Foreign Economic Relations which gave a Foreign Trade Organization the task of handling this purchase.

The FTOs were characterized by a complex hierarchical structure and a high degree of specialization, not only among them but also in the way they were functioning. They were divided into different specific product categories. Within each of these departments, different tasks or stages of the trading process were handled by different employees. Certain employees were specifically dealing with price negotiations, others with payment methods or shipping procedures, etc.

The usual foreign trade procedure

The whole process usually ran this way: in the first stage, an engineer from the FTO was appointed to deal with the purchase project. This person sent inquiries to several potential suppliers, who then provided the FTO with detailed information about their equipment or products, as well as a first quotation. His second task was to collect all the material and organize the first discussions with the potential suppliers. His role was to sort out the technical issues, to keep in touch with the ultimate user in order to make sure that the offers corresponded with the requirements, and to compare the different competing offers. But he never dealt with the pricing aspects.

As soon as technical discussions were finalized and it came to pricing negotiations, the vice-director or director was involved in the process. At this stage, people from several other departments could intervene in the negotiation process – for example, the pricing department came into action. It performed an in-depth analysis of price constituents, often based on statistical data about world markets. The pricing department reported these issues to the vice-director or director.

Depending on the size of the project, the contract would be signed by the director or the vice-president. Major contracts involved the president of the FTO. When the purchase involved technically complicated equipment, Ministry representatives were involved in negotiations concerning the characteristics of the equipment. In some cases, even the users could intervene in the process. However, this was not usual and, in any case, only the FTO's officials would determine prices and payment conditions.

Consequently, foreign companies were generally not allowed to have direct contacts with the end-users of their products or with their suppliers. A member of a foreign firm who wanted to meet a Soviet citizen would have to apply for a meeting at the Ministry of Foreign Economic Relations. Clearly, this used to be a fundamental issue for Western companies doing business in the Soviet Union.

A case of import: the experience of Alfa-Laval Fats and Oils before 1985

When a factory in the food industry wanted to acquire some equipment, it had to apply to the Ministry of Food. The Ministry could also decide to invest in one or several of the factories on its own initiative. Once the decision had been made, it gave the Foreign Trade Organization, Technopromimport, the task of handling the purchase of the equipment. Technopromimport started the process by sending inquiries to several potential suppliers.

After they had sent their quotations, potential suppliers were involved in the first stage of negotiation with representatives from the Ministry of Food. Indeed, when negotiating a contract, suppliers first had to reach an agreement with specialists from the Ministry of Food about the technical characteristics of the equipment. Alfa-Laval usually had to make lots of changes and adaptations until they came to a solution which suited everybody. It then started the commercial discussions about prices and financial issues with Technopromimport. Alfa-Laval was not allowed to have contacts with the final users of its equipment. This is illustrated in Fig. 15.2 below.

A case of export: the experience of IKEA

The same basic principles ruled export activities. This can be illustrated by IKEA's experience in handling export contacts with Russian partners. Since, as in import operations, Soviet factories were not allowed to do any direct business with foreign companies, IKEA had to sign a contract with the Foreign Trade Organization, Exportles, in order to enter the Soviet market. According to this contract, Exportles was in charge of finding suppliers for IKEA, and became its official partner for all its deals in the Soviet Union. At that time, Sevzapmebel, a huge state holding company controlled by the Ministry of Wood, still owned all furniture factories in the North-Western part of the Soviet Union and was therefore designated by Exportles to find the right suppliers for IKEA in that region and to take care of routine matters. However, Exportles remained responsible for the negotiation and signing of the contracts (though Sevzapmebel actively participated in the negotiation process).

Even though the factories, which belonged to the Ministry of Wood, were not allowed to do business directly, they had contacts with IKEA in order to discuss the technical aspects of the contract and to allow quality control. They were also allowed to take part in the negotiation of the contracts, but were not involved in the decision-making. This is illustrated in Fig. 15.3 below (dotted lines symbolize the former contract pattern).

Disintegration and Decentralization

A gradual process

The totally centralized structure of Soviet industry has undergone major changes over the last few years, starting from Michael Gorbachev's appointment as the head of the Soviet Union and the beginning of Perestroika in 1985.

The degree of centralization of the Soviet decision-making process and of the contact pattern of foreign companies in the Soviet Union has diminished dramatically through gradual decentralization steps. Consequently, some participants have lost their monopoly positions, while new actors have become involved in the decision-making process and have started to have access to totally new responsibilities.

First of all, Soviet ministries have started to lose their monopoly in their field of activity, to the advantage of republic ministries. Republic ministries started to bypass Soviet FTOs and to undertake trade negotiations on their own. Of course, in some cases, this created some confusion, as in the case of one of the companies involved in this research in a deal for packaging equipment in the Ukraine. The Swedish company received an inquiry from Soyuzpromimport, the FTO responsible for imports in that field. According to the official procedure, the organization had been asked by the Ukrainian Ministry of Food to organize this purchase. However, some time later, the same ministry decided, in an attempt to accelerate the whole procedure, to send their own inquiry to the Swedish company. It took some time for the Swedish businessmen to realize that the two inquiries concerned the same order. Finally, the Ukrainian Ministry of Food negotiated the contract itself and simply bypassed Soyuzpromimport to buy the equipment it needed. This would have been unthinkable in the past. Figure 15.1 illustrates this process.

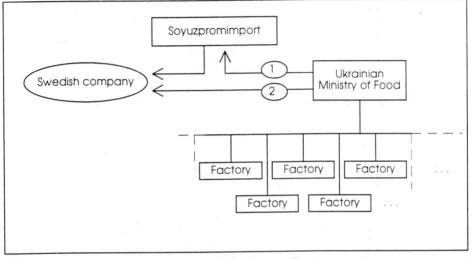

Fig. 15.1. Illustration of the decentralization process.

The situation today

In recent years, some companies have started to play an active role in foreign trade. Clearly, among the changes described in this section, this one is likely to have the greatest fundamental consequences for Western businessmen working in the CIS. Before reverting to this important aspect of our study in the next section, this ultimate move towards a decentralized decision-making process is illustrated by the case of Alfa-Laval in the field of fats and oils.

We have already introduced the usual contact pattern of Alfa-Laval Fats and Oils in the Soviet Union before 1985. We described the role played by the Ministry of Food and Technopromimport and stressed the fact that Alfa-Laval was not allowed to have contacts with the end users of their equipment. As a matter of fact, the latter started to play a role in the decision-making process in 1985, although the final decisions were still made at the level of the two central administrations. Starting from that moment, contacts were allowed between Alfa-Laval and the factories.

In 1988, a major reform was introduced which further decreased the degree of centralization of foreign trade. A 1988 decree allowed foreign firms to do business directly with Soviet producers without having to go through an FTO. As a consequence, foreign actors could deal with a large range of new business partners. This is illustrated in Fig. 15.2 (dotted lines symbolize the former contact pattern).

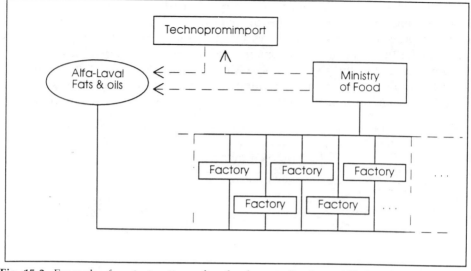

Fig. 15.2. Example of contact pattern after the decentralization – Alfa-Laval Fats and Oils.

In IKEA's case, the contact pattern has also evolved considerably. The Soviet Ministry of Wood no longer exists. Exportles has become a joint-stock company and has lost its monopoly on wooden furniture exports. Due to anti-trust laws established in the framework of the demonopolization process, Sevzapmebel has also lost its monopolistic position, and has been reorganized into small state enterprises. These enterprises are allowed to do business by themselves or to export through any authorized organization.

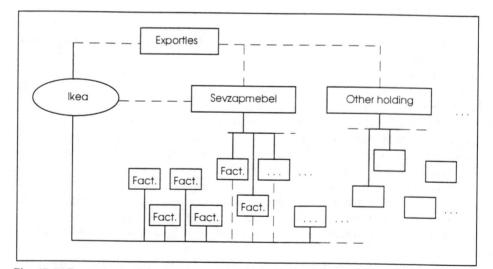

Fig. 15.3. Example of contact pattern after the decentralization – IKEA International A/S.

partition of the Soviet Union into fifteen independent states has accelerated the decentralization process and has consequently strongly modified the business environment. Structures and rules have been changing day after day, major actors have disappeared – notably the Soviet ministries – while new actors have progressively built a strong position.

In the next section, we will try to underline the main issues of this unstable and fast-moving environment.

A New Business Environment

Emergence of a class of new and inexperienced decision-makers

The decentralization process implies that decisions are nowadays generally taken at the companies' management level. New people have been involved in decision-making who are unaccustomed to assuming such responsibilities. The company manager used to be alone responsible for implementing at the company level decisions previously taken by the central planning authority, Gossplan. In that sense, he was a controller rather than a manager.

Nowadays, as economic structures are being shaken, managers are increasingly responsible for the decision-making, but a lot of them have no experience at all in many fields which they have to take care of. One of these is international trade. Indeed, as we described earlier on, Eastern bloc firms used to rely totally on Foreign Trade Organizations in the handling of trade transactions with foreign firms. As a consequence, their managers often perceive transactions with foreign partners as being a risky process.

This perception of risk can be illustrated by the attitude of IKEA's suppliers. During the first stages of the process that gave them the right to do business directly, the factories supplying IKEA did not start to do so. Most of the managers were aware of their lack of experience in international business and thus preferred to rely on the traditional state organizations. Furthermore, according to Christer Bauer, the manager of IKEA's St Petersburg office, when a factory wanted to do business directly, IKEA first had to make sure that the people from the factory were capable of doing business in this way.

This is confirmed by an Exportles official, who underlined the fact that no Soviet factory was able to do business with IKEA, due to their lack of experience. 'Exportles, on the contrary, had the required skills and information'.

Nevertheless, a lot of Eastern 'businessmen' want to take advantage of the restructuring process to set up trading companies. The fact that they are doing so does not imply that they are managing well. However, it is interesting to note that nowadays many of these companies as well as industrial firms employ former FTO officials to handle their business relations with the West.

Lack of market information

Another important factor that characterizes the current business environment is the relative absence of a market structure and information. Due to the anarchical decentralization process and the disappearance of the Soviet Union and its structured state organizations, no reliable market information system is available nowadays. Yet this is one of the cornerstones of an efficient market economy.

It is indeed extremely difficult today for a Western actor to find out who needs a given type of good, or who can produce it. As we have already mentioned, this lack of information, combined with the transition to a market economy, has generated the appearance of a new field of activities: the trading business. Consequently, whereas before Perestroika there were only seventy specialized Foreign Trade Organizations entitled to carry out foreign trade transactions, there were about 30,000 organizations, both state entities (former official FTOs, state firms, etc.) and private entities (co-operatives, joint-ventures, etc.), who had received this right just before the break-up of the Soviet Union.

It is obviously extremely difficult nowadays to make an assessment of the number of organizations involved in foreign trade. The role of certain FTOs and of some of their former officials remains crucial. They still benefit from their relatively extended knowledge of national and international markets and they often know best how to handle foreign trade activities.

An unstable business environment

Companies are also facing problems due to the absence of permanent structures, clear rules, stable authorities and local partners strong and financially sound enough to be reliable. This can be illustrated by Lenraumamebel's case. Lenraumamebel is a joint-venture founded in 1988 by the Russian Combinat Sevzapmebel and the Finnish company Rauma-Repola. This joint venture already had an agreement to supply IKEA at the time of its creation and is equipped with the most advanced machinery for computer-assisted manufacturing of high-quality flatpack furniture. This equipment was partly financed by IKEA and the factory was built for IKEA's production lines. Since its creation, Lenraumamebel has faced major difficulties. The actual deliveries have been totally different from what had been planned, due to an accumulation of problems related to the supply of energy and raw materials.

Furthermore, the new trading companies are generally not considered as being very reliable partners with whom it would be possible to build up a successful relationship. Many newly created 'trading companies' contacted IKEA in order to play a role as intermediary between the Swedish company and the Russian factories, or in order to involve IKEA in any other kind of business (such as the trading of caviar). IKEA has never done any business with those intermediaries. They are most of the time created to make a few deals and disappear. This implies that some of them might be helpful counterparts for Western or Eastern companies willing to get rid of occasional excess production in the former Soviet market, but on the contrary, companies wishing to establish long-term relationships in the CIS should be very cautious regarding this kind of potential partner.

Challenging Issues for Western Companies

In this section, we review some of the tactics that the executives involved in our research use and recommend to reinforce the competitive position of a firm, given the specific environment. It seems clear that social exchanges and personal contacts play a major role in this process. First of all, they obviously help business people to assess the reliability and the trustworthiness of a potential partner. They can also appear as a way of taking advantage of the changes by means of an appropriate commitment to local partners and better adaptations to users' needs. More than ever they are an incomparable means of bridging the socio-cultural distance.

Commitment

The current changes also have consequences for competition. Previously, each central organization was responsible for the purchases of all the companies operating in a given field. As a consequence, foreign suppliers active in the Soviet market were always dealing with the same counterpart, and the decision-makers of the FTO knew those Western firms as well.

Gunnar Stenström underlines that the long-term relationships which Axel Johnson had with individuals at the FTO and Ministry level, played a major role in the placing of orders. More than in any other part of the world, long-term relationships gave companies engaged in the Soviet Union for several years a competitive edge *vis-à-vis* potential new entrants.

This can be illustrated by the following statement from Michael Koïstinen, manager of AxSovjet:

> In the past, the persons who were responsible for centralized purchases did not really take time to consider all offers and opportunities properly. That is why it was a major competitive advantage to have good personal contacts at the FTO and Ministry level in order to be the first supplier to come to their mind. Indeed, FTOs had to handle many purchases at the same time. As a consequence, the 'Soviet way of buying' often consisted of contacting an old partner and having him supply the required product or equipment. That is why Axel Johnson's image and contacts were extremely important. They represented an efficient barrier to entry.

As the decentralization process has allowed people within Soviet companies to play a role in the purchasing decision, it is likely that those new actors will reconsider more exhaustively the offer and will give foreign companies trying to enter the market more opportunities to reach their goal. This partly explains why, despite the unstable environment, many Western companies are trying to enter the market nowadays.

Nevertheless, foreign companies that have been active in the Soviet market for some years will still have an advantage over their competitors due to their experience in this market and the knowledge Soviet customers have of their products or equipment (not to mention the importance of personal contacts, again).

Alfa-Laval, for instance, assumes that the hundred plants they sold to the Soviet Union give them an advantage over their competitors. Users of their equipment have been obliged to acquire a good understanding of it due to the absence of technical assistance (Western companies were not allowed to have contacts with their end-users and consequently could not provide them with any maintenance service or technical assistance).

The recent changes have other consequences on the competitive climate. Foreign firms now also have to cope with the development of Eastern competitors. Indeed, as a result of the decentralization and the opening up of the economic system, Soviet firms are getting increasingly involved in exchange processes with foreign countries, for instance through joint ventures. Clearly, this kind of agreement can also be used to implement co-operation and to demonstrate the commitment to local partners.

In 1991, for instance, Alfa-Laval created a joint venture responsible for service and spare parts distribution. Although the manager is a Swede, he is working with four Russian engineers. This joint venture might even start to produce equipment one day, but this will not be the case in the near future. The joint venture was created in order to involve Russians in the development of service activities. Even though most of the Swedes working in the former Soviet Union speak Russian, technicians coming over from Sweden to install and service the equipment do not. Recruiting Russian technicians is thus extremely convenient and facilitates contacts between Alfa-Laval and its customers. It is also cheaper.

The main advantage of the joint venture is that it allows Alfa-Laval to come closer to the end-users of its equipment. Morgan Kjellén, representative of Alfa-Laval in Moscow, underlines that 'it is a way of coming closer to the customer, of finding him, reaching him and sending people to him'.

Adaptation

The Foreign Trade Organizations were usually buying products and equipment for a large number of companies at the same time, in accordance with the objectives fixed by Gossplan, which mainly reflected political decisions. The Ministry of Food, for instance, bought twenty complete margarine plants in 1988, following a government decision to invest in the production of margarine. Alfa-Laval sold ten margarine plants to the Ministry of Food in the framework of this giant 1988 investment.

Since the bureaucrats of the Foreign Trade Organizations were basically buyers and their process expertise was rather limited, important mistakes were often made in the purchases. This led to appalling situations: sometimes the Soviet companies did not even need the equipment they received, sometimes they could not use it, as they never received a basic component or did not have any spare parts. A complete margarine production plant bought from Alfa-Laval in 1988 is still lying in its packing cases.

Today, as a consequence of the decentralization process, purchases are increasingly handled by each company individually. The development of direct interactions between Western suppliers and Eastern end-users has allowed customers to intervene directly in the purchase, while suppliers have been given a chance to adapt their products, services, or equipment and to assist their customers in the installation, the learning process, the exploitation and the maintenance of the equipment. (The considerably shorter life-cycle of Alfa-Laval's products in the Soviet Union certainly reflects the need for those interactions.) This process is bound to make the adaptation ability a key variable of trade relationships with the CIS. This arrangement would have been unthinkable a few years ago, when no direct contacts existed between suppliers and users.

As a consequence, foreign suppliers and Eastern customers have also started to develop more technical interaction and to negotiate joint-development programmes. This may enable foreign suppliers to better understand the Eastern companies' needs in order to start developing products and equipment adapted to the specific requirements and expectations of those customers. Besides, it is definitely likely to reinforce the company's position regarding its Eastern customers.

This is how Exportles officials themselves describe IKEA as a good partner that 'understands the Soviet market and the suppliers' problems, invests money in Soviet firms, and is helpful and patient.' On the other hand, since the marketing staffs of Western companies manufacturing technically advanced equipment very often consists of engineers, they prefer, from a marketing point of view, to have contacts and to negotiate with the people using the equipment, rather than bureaucrats with whom it is usually more difficult to examine highly technical issues.

Sociocultural distance

Doing business in the former Soviet Union means entering a totally different world. Companies dealing with Soviet partners should be aware of the cultural gap when making strategic decisions. The system in which Soviet managers and workers have been educated and have built up their experience was based on values which differ totally from those shared in market economies. A manager from a Soviet company could be defined as state representative whose function was to control the proper execution of the centrally defined objectives. The paternalistic role of the State inhibited ideas, productivity and a sense of responsibility on the part of companies' members, both at the management and workers level. Their approach regarding production, marketing and sales differ totally from that of the West.

This gap can be illustrated by the following anecdotes: IKEA once signed a contract with a Russian factory for the production of clear-varnished chairs. However, when the supplier delivered the chairs, IKEA discovered that they were white. Since it had not been possible to find the raw materials, the supplier had decided to produce white chairs instead. IKEA immediately returned the chairs. The supplier was furious and could not understand what the problem was, as in the Soviet Union demand did not play any role in the design of products; chairs are chairs, and whatever their colour, they are sold anyhow. Soviet companies usually did not even have any sales department: the planning system determined the customer of each unit produced by the factories. IKEA also faced major problems related to keeping to deadlines, quality requirements, production volumes, and other elements on the part of their Russian suppliers.

This fundamental gap between the two approaches is a key issue for Western firms trying to develop activities in the CIS. Successful co-operation requires the two partners to adapt to each other.

Conclusion

For some companies, the old bureaucratic command system was in fact relatively satisfactory to deal with. At the time nearly all transactions were handled centrally,

Western companies could negotiate large trade agreements with only a couple of individuals from one or two Ministries and Foreign Trade Organizations in Moscow. These contracts, which were valid for the whole of the Soviet Union, also enabled them to sell several plants or equipments of identical design.

The system has undergone major changes in recent years which have had a considerable impact on the business relationships Western companies develop in that part of the world. Fig. 15.4 attempts to summarize the main conclusions of our investigations in the CIS.

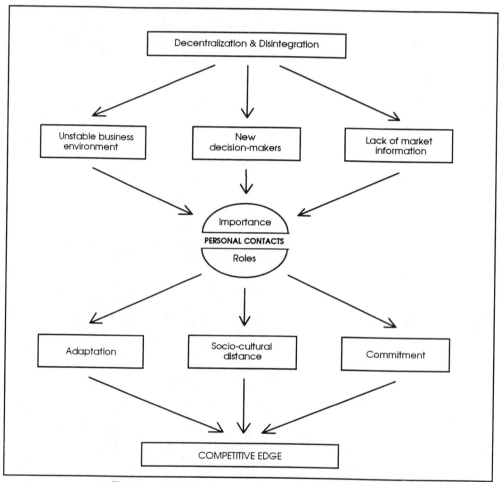

Fig. 15.4. Importance and roles of personal contacts.

In the framework of the recent decentralization and disintegration process, Soviet Ministries and FTOs have been replaced by similar organizations in individual republics. However, state organizations have lost their monopoly on business relationships with Western partners. These reforms, combined with the surrounding chaos, have had considerable consequences on certain variables that influence Western firms' positions in the former Soviet Union. These variables appeared to be classifiable into three categories, illustrated in Fig. 15.4.

As a consequence of these dynamic factors, Western companies are bound to reshape their contact patterns in the CIS. However, we have also stressed the fact that state organizations and their employees were bound to continue to play an important role in foreign trade due to their knowledge of the market, to their access to scarce financial resources and to the lack of experience of new potential counterparts.

The managers we have interviewed in the framework of this study all stressed the new possibilities offered by the direct involvement of users in business relationships. These opportunities or challenges, we argue, can be analysed in terms of ability to demonstrate commitment to local partners, to adapt to their specific characteristics and needs, and to manage the sociocultural distance.

Appendix 1: Presentation of the Companies Involved in Our Research

Alfa-Laval

Alfa-Laval, one of Sweden's oldest and largest engineering companies, is active in three areas: industry, food and agriculture. Alfa-Laval is the leading manufacturer of separators, compact heat exchangers and milking machines and is the market leader within the dairy and other food industries. In the field of fats and oils, the company covers every link in the chain from crude oil processing to refining and modification, including final margarine production. This allows the company to offer complete production lines.

Alfa-Laval was already active in pre-Revolution Russia. After the introduction of the Bolshevik regime, Alfa-Laval was one of the first Western companies to establish business contacts with the Soviet Union. However, it had to wait until 1976 before opening an office. The company has been entrusted with the delivery of many large projects. The Fats and Oils department sold its first plants to the Soviet Union in 1953. Alfa-Laval Fats and Oils' major project in the Soviet Union, when it sold ten margarine plants to the Ministry of Food, took place in 1988.

AxTrade

AxTrade is an international trading group focusing mainly on specific industrial goods, such as steel, pumps, valves, machine tools and forestry products as well as medical and healthcare equipment. The international operations acquired from the principal owner, Axel Johnson AB, form the core of AxTrade's activities.

Like Alfa-Laval, AxTrade was also active in pre-Revolution Russia. In 1972, the company was among the first Western firms to open an office in the country. AxSovjet is the organization covering the CIS market inside AxTrade. It often works with small and medium-sized companies, as it is extremely difficult for these companies to set up their own organizations in the former Soviet Union. AxSovjet has also signed agreements with large companies, such as Texas Instruments, Electrolux CR, Saab-Scania and Perstorp, to name a few examples. In order to remain competitive in the dramatically changing environment, AxTrade reconsidered its activities in the Soviet Union in 1989. As a result, the company focuses its activities in the CIS on four main areas: food and packaging, raw materials, automotive and medical products.

IKEA

IKEA was created in 1943 as a mail-order firm. Furniture and other home furnishing products were introduced to the range in 1950. After having been conceived by IKEA's designers, the furniture is produced by subcontractors who deliver their production to IKEA's warehouses. The furniture is then distributed and sold through IKEA's shops.

In 1974, IKEA established contact for the first time with the Soviet FTO Exportles, which was under the control of the Ministry of Foreign Trade. In 1976, IKEA signed its first contract with the Ministry of Wood, concerning the production of furniture by a Russian factory, Priozersk. It was only in 1988 that IKEA really made headway in the Soviet market when, after a visit by the Prime Minister of the Soviet Union, Mr Ryzkov, to the IKEA store in Göteborg, Mr Kamprad, IKEA's founder was invited to sign a letter of intent containing guidelines for co-operation.

The company opened an office in Moscow in 1988 and in Leningrad (now St Petersburg) in 1989. IKEA also has a small technical office in Tallinn. The establishment of a permanent representation has enabled the company to develop its activities in the Soviet Union.

Appendix 2: List of Interviewees

Martin Johansson, Researcher at the Department of Business Studies, Uppsala University
Vitaly Zinovchuk, Lecturer, Department of Management, Zhitomir University of Agriculture
Douglas Wilson, Marketing Manager, Alfa-Laval Fats and Oils
Lennart Klasson, Regional Manager, Alfa-Laval Fats and Oils
Gunnar Stenström, Director, USSR Department, AxEast
Bernt Malm, Marketing Manager, Scanditronix
Michael Koïstinen, Manager USSR Department, AxEast
Claes Lundeman, Director, Axel Johnson Moscow Office
Göran Tideström, Director, Alfa-Laval International Engineering
Morgan Kjellén, Representative, Alfa-Laval Moscow office
Helena Alström, Marketing Manager, Alfa-Laval International Engineering
Harry Ranta Eskola, Project Leader, Scanditronix
Galina Gratcheva, Scientist at the Institute of the Human Brain
Christer Bauer, Deputy Chairman IKEA St Petersburg
Bo Delarvé, Deputy Chairman IKEA Moscow
Eligij Dementiev, Technical Service-Raw materials IKEA St Petersburg
Representative, Lenraumamebel
Representative, Ladoga
Representative, Ladoga

Representative, Exportles
German Alekseev, Deputy Chairman, Sevzapmebel
B. Panfil, Trade Representative at the Soviet Consulate
Professor Yastremsky, Department of Economics, State University of Kiev

Note

1. Beckerman (1956) defines psychic distance as factors preventing or disturbing the flows of information between firms and markets

References

Cunningham, M. T. and Culligan, K. (1988) 'Competitiveness through network or relationships in information technology product markets', *Proceedings of 4th IMP Conference*, Manchester.

Ford, D. (1980) 'The development of buyer–seller relationships in industrial markets', *European Journal of Marketing* 14.

Ford, D. (ed.) (1990) *Understanding Business Markets: Interaction, Relationships, Networks*, London: Academic Press.

Håkansson and Johanson, J. (1988) 'Formal and informal cooperation strategies in international industrial networks', in F. J. Contractor and P. Lorange (eds) *Cooperative Strategies in International Business*, Lexington, Mass.: Lexington Books.

Håkansson, H. and Östberg, C. (1975) 'Industrial marketing – an organizational problem?', *Industrial Marketing Management* 4: 113–23.

Håkansson, H., Johanson, J. and Wootz, B. (1976) 'Influence tactics in buyer-seller processes', *Industrial Marketing Management*, 319–32.

IMP Group (1982) in Håkansson, H. (ed.) *International Marketing and Purchasing of Industrial Goods: an Interactive Approach*, Chichester, John Wiley.

Johansson, J. and Mattsson, L-G. (1986) 'International marketing and internationalization processes – a network approach' in S. Paliwoda and P. N. Turnbull (eds) *Research in International Marketing*, London: Croom Helm.

Johansson, J. K. and Mattson, L-G. (1988) 'Internationalization in industrial systems – a network approach', in N. Hood and J-E. Vahlne (eds) (1988) *Strategies in Global Competition*, New York: Croom Helm.

Johansson, J. and Vahlne, J-E. (1977) 'The internationalization of the firm: a model of knowledge development and increasing foreign commitments', *Journal of International Business Studies*, Spring–Summer: 23–32.

Turnbull, P. W. (1979) 'Roles of personal contacts in industrial export marketing', *Scandinavian Journal of Management*, 325–37.

16

From Centrally Planned to Market Economy – the Road from CPE to PCPE

Guillermo A. Calvo and Jacob A. Frenkel

This chapter deals with key issues arising during the early stages of transformation of centrally planned economies (CPEs) into functioning market economies (MEs). The analysis is motivated by the recent experience with economic transformation and restructuring in Eastern Europe and USSR.

The economic system in CPEs launching such a transformation is highly distorted. Prices do not represent real social costs, incentives systems are absent, losses of unprofitable state-owned enterprises are automatically financed, legislation vital for the functioning of markets is not in place, private ownership and property rights are underdeveloped, markets are missing, shortages prevail and, occasionally, inflation is high.

In analysing this transformation, it is relatively simple to characterize the initial conditions of CPEs, as well as to specify the features of MEs. It is more difficult, however, to provide an analytical framework that highlights the process of transition. During the transition period the old central planning system is dismantled (or is collapsing), while the new market system (and its associated institutions and policies) is still not in place. This transition period, during which the economy is no longer centrally planned, but has not yet achieved the status of a market economy, may be quite long. The economy during that period is referred to as a 'previously centrally planned economy' (PCPE). On its way to reform, a centrally planned economy is likely to spend a significant period as a PCPE before becoming an ME.

There are many ways to transform a CPE into an ME. Since neither history nor

Reprinted from IMF *Staff Papers* **38**, 268–299.

Guillermo A. Calvo is Senior Advisor in the Research Department of the IMF.

Jacob A. Frenkel, Economic Counsellor and Director of the Research Department, is a graduate of Hebrew University and the University of Chicago. Before joining the Fund, he was David Rockefeller Professor of International Economics at the University of Chicago.

The authors wish to acknowledge helpful comments from Joshua Aizenman, Mario Blejer, Robert Flood, Sara Guerschanik-Calvo, Pablo Guidotti, Elhanan Helpman, Leonardo Leiderman, J. Saúl Lizondo, Kent Osband, Lars Svensson, and Carlos Végh.

economic theory provides a clear guide to the optimal pace and sequence of reform measures, it is unlikely that a 'master blueprint' for economic transformation could be found. Rather, the solution for the optimal pace and sequence of reform measures is likely to depend on the special circumstances prevailing in each of these economies.[1]

The process of economic transformation and restructuring is bound to be long and complex. Typically, there is also a lengthy delay between the time of political decision to launch a transformation programme and the time of its actual implementation. During this transitional pre-reform period, economic policies are negotiated and designed, political consensus is cemented, and key features of the institutional infrastructure are developed. In the pre-reform period actual policy reform measures are not yet implemented, and many of the basic features of the economic system are still of the centrally planned variety. However, the private sector, being clearly aware that fundamental changes are planned, begins to modify its patterns of consumption and asset holdings. Such anticipatory behavioural changes are reflected in prices, exchange rates, and rates of interest, among other important economic variables.

The purpose of this chapter is to highlight some of the main forces set into motion during the pre-reform period. During that period – as illustrated by the recent experience in Czechoslovakia and, to some extent, in the USSR – economic actions on the part of the private sector are governed by *expectations* of the reform, rather than by the policy measures themselves. To examine this feature of the transformation process, we analyse in some detail the implications of an anticipated price reform.

Most economic reform programmes designed to transform CPEs into MEs place great emphasis on the removal of subsidies that distort the prevailing price structure. It is reasonable to assume, therefore, that the private sector in anticipating the removal of subsidies expects a rise in the price level – the experience in Poland in early 1990 is a case in point. There are various reasons for such expectations. First, with lower subsidies, retail prices – typically set according to mark-up pricing rules – will rise so as to reflect the higher cost. Second, even with a more competitive determination of prices, it is likely that prices are somewhat less flexible downwards than upwards. Therefore, the changes in relative prices consequent on the removal of subsidies will result in a higher price level. Third, policy makers might be expected to react to the unemployment associated with the reallocation of resources by adopting expansionary measures, thereby fuelling inflation.

In the following section we develop a simple model of the CPE designed to clarify the key mechanisms and effects of anticipatory behaviour induced by expected price reform. This model is then used to illustrate the dynamic behaviour of the economy during the pre-reform period. Many of the changes occurring on the way to reform may have disruptive effects and, unless these are fully understood, may provide confusing signals to both the private sector and to policy makers. Our analysis identifies the key forces set in motion and thereby sheds light on the evolution of the economy on the road to reform.

Armed with this information, the model is then used to analyse the effects of *expected* price reform. We study in detail the anticipatory responses taking place during the pre-reform period and focus on the evolution of exchange rates, asset holdings, and aggregate demand. In this context, we pay special attention to the consequences of wage indexation, an issue that has figured prominently in recent reform programmes. It is shown that a high degree of wage indexation carries with it the danger of transforming microeconomic distortions into macroeconomic difficulties. This consideration must be taken into account in the design of domestic safety nets supporting the transformation efforts.

One of the central pillars of economic policy during the process of transformation is credit policy. This chapter contains an analysis of the implications of credit policies in CPEs, in which, typically, credit and financial markets are poorly developed. We highlight the various channels through which such policies exert their influence, and identify key factors responsible for the vulnerability of these economies to excessively tight credit policies.

We then examine alternative policies designed to offset some of the disruptive effects of anticipatory behaviour. Special attention is given to reactive wage and interest rate policies. We show that such reactive policies require a high degree of fine-tuning, and may themselves be extremely disruptive.

There then follows a study of the relation between excess liquidity ('liquidity overhang') and the budget. The analysis, which is motivated by recent experience in the USSR and, to some extent, in Romania and Bulgaria, examines alternative means of eliminating excess liquidity and argues that all means involve a tax policy of one form or another. In this regard, the choice of policies depends on the 'incidence of the tax', and on efficiency considerations. We pay special attention to the interdependence between privatization, tax policies, and credibility. The final section contains concluding remarks.

A Simple Model of the CPE

In this section we develop a simple model embodying pertinent features of the CPE, especially those related to imperfections in domestic financial markets. The formal model, which is designed to highlight key mechanisms of anticipatory dynamics, abstracts from many potentially important factors. Therefore, it is not intended to be fully applicable to concrete cases without some modifications. Its main conclusions, however, are likely to prevail in more realistic formulations. The model consists of two basic building blocks: the assets market and the goods market. In what follows we discuss the characteristics of these markets.[2]

Assets market

In the absence of well-functioning capital markets and a fully developed system of property rights and private ownership, asset holders are assumed to hold liquid assets. These assets can be denominated in domestic currency (for example, savings accounts or cash), or in foreign currency. The latter may consist of foreign exchange or other liquid assets whose value depends directly on the exchange rate (for example, foreign cigarettes). The desired composition of this somewhat restricted portfolio of liquid assets is governed by the difference between the rates of return on these assets. Specifically, the desired ratio of domestic- to foreign-currency-denominated assets is assumed to depend on the difference between the domestic rate of interest and the expected percentage change in the nominal exchange rate. Formally, equilibrium in the asset market is represented by equation (1):

$$L(\epsilon - i_m) = M/EF,$$ (1)

where E denotes the nominal exchange rate, defined as the price of foreign exchange in terms of domestic currency; M denotes assets denominated in domestic currency; F denotes assets denominated in foreign currency (which, in what follows, are occasionally referred to as foreign exchange); ϵ denotes the expected percentage change in the exchange rate; and i_m denotes the rate of interest earned by holders of domestic currency deposits. A rise in ϵ reduces the desired ratio of domestic- to foreign-currency-denominated assets, while a rise in i_m raises that ratio. Assuming equality between expected and actual exchange rate changes, equation (1) can be rewritten as

$$\dot{E}/E = l(M/EF) + i_m,$$ (2)

where the function l depends negatively on the ratio M/EF. As indicated by equation (2), asset holders are willing to absorb a higher ratio of domestic- to foreign-currency-denominated assets only if the rate of return on domestic saving accounts, i_m rises, or if the expected (equal to actual) rate of depreciation, $\dot{E}/E$, falls.

Goods market

The second key building block of the model is the goods market. The economy is assumed to produce internationally tradable goods as well as non-tradable goods. We consider, first, the market for tradable goods. To set the stage for the subsequent analysis in which credit market conditions play a central role, we postulate that the level of production of tradable goods depends positively (at least for some range) on the availability of official credit. This is because credit enables firms to acquire working capital that facilitates supply, while the dependence of supply on official credit reflects the segmentation of the underdeveloped domestic credit market. Accordingly, we denote the supply of tradable goods by θy_T, where y_T denotes the supply of tradable goods obtained under conditions of full availability of credit, and θ denotes a coefficient, whose value ranges between zero and unity, indicating the degree of tightness in the credit market. Accordingly, a tighter control over credit policy lowers the coefficient θ, reflecting the limited ability of firms to offset the reduction in official credit through a greater reliance on alternative sources of finance. This inability, in turn, stems from the segmentation of credit markets and from the reluctance of lenders to extend credit to economic entities information about whose creditworthiness is limited. The lack of information may be particularly acute in situations where the government, prior to assuming a tighter control of credit policy, permitted enterprises to enjoy 'soft' budget constraints by providing unprofitable enterprises with automatic access to credit. Where enterprise losses are automatically financed, the government is viewed as the lender of last resort and as the provider of implicit credit insurance without charging competitive risk premia; in such circumstances, information about creditworthiness is unlikely to be available, since with 'free' government insurance the private sector has no incentive to collect such information.

The demand for tradable goods is assumed to depend negatively on their relative price – that is, the real exchange rate – and positively on real wages. The specification of the demand function as depending on real wages rather than on total income (including profits) reflects another key structural feature of the CPE; that is, the behaviour of state enterprises as demanders is largely unrelated to profits and economic performance. Furthermore, the absence of private ownership and the lack of a developed stock market imply that the economic performance of state enterprises, as measured by profits, is not fully capitalized into private sector wealth and therefore does not exert a direct impact on demand. Reflecting these considerations, the demand for tradable goods can be written as $D_T(E/P, W/P)$, where W denotes the nominal wage; P denotes the price of the domestic (non-tradable) good; and, hence, with the price of the tradable good in terms of foreign currency defined to be identically equal to unity, E/P is the real exchange rate, and W/P is the real wage (in terms of domestic goods).[3]

The excess supply of tradable goods represents the accumulation of foreign exchange by the private sector and the government. To simplify, we abstract from the official holdings of foreign exchange and focus on the behaviour of the private sector. In doing so, we assume that currency transactions are carried out at the free (or black market) exchange rate. Formally, the rate of accumulation of foreign exchange (foreign-currency-denominated assets), F is specified by equation (3):

$$\dot{F} = \theta y_T - D_T(E/P, W/P). \tag{3}$$

Thus far, we have examined the equilibrium condition in the market for internationally tradable goods, which governs the dynamics of foreign currency holdings. We consider next the market for non-tradable goods and assume that the demand, D_N, depends positively on the real exchange rate and on the real wage. Formally, let the demand function be $D_N(E/P, W/P)$.

The conditions governing the supply of non-tradable goods depend on more detailed specific circumstances. In some cases, where productive resources are under-utilized, supply adjusts to meet demand. In these 'Keynesian' circumstances, demand fluctuations induced by changes in the real exchange rate and real wages result in corresponding supply responses, and are reflected in the degree of capacity utilization and unemployment. In other cases, where capacity is fully utilized, but inventories are ample, demand fluctuations are reflected in accumulation or decumulation of inventories. In yet other cases, where capacity is fully utilized and inventories do not adjust, demand fluctuations are reflected in shorter or longer delivery lags and queues.[4]

Which of these three patterns of adjustment in the market for non-tradable goods prevails depends on structural considerations, as well as the policy stance. Relevant factors include the degree of flexibility of labour markets, labour hoarding practices, credit policies governing the holding cost of inventories of intermediate and final goods, credit availability, and the like. In practice – as demonstrated by experience in Poland during 1990 – the three patterns can coexist. Accordingly, a rise in demand consequent on a rise of the real exchange rate or of the real wage results in lower unemployment and inventories, and possibly, in longer delivery lags and queues.

Dynamics and Expected Price Reform

In this section we analyse the dynamics of the model. Our focus on dynamics aims at illuminating economic processes set in motion during the *early* phases of the economic transformation programme by the expectations of future policy actions. We start with a diagrammatic exposition of the model that serves to highlight its dynamic characteristics, and then examine in detail the dynamic consequences of expected price reform.

Dynamics of the model

In analysing the dynamics of the model, we recall that during the pre-reform phase, prices and wages are determined administratively, while official currency convertibility is absent. We assume that during that phase the rate of return on savings accounts, nominal wages, the price of domestic goods, and the money supply are determined by the central authorities. Thus, in equations (2) and (3) – which constitute the dynamic building blocks of the model – we treat i_m, W, P, and M as exogenously given.

As indicated by equations (2) and (3), the dynamics of the model are governed by the evolution of the nominal exchange rate, E, and the stock of foreign exchange rate, F. Figure 16.1 is used to describe the model. The $\dot{E} = 0$ schedule shows combinations of exchange rates and foreign exchange holdings that are consistent with portfolio equilibrium as specified in equation (2). Along that schedule the rate of change of the nominal exchange rate is expected to be zero, and the prevailing ratio of domestic- to foreign-currency-denominated assets, M/EF, is willingly held. Since the nominal money supply, M, and the rate of interest paid on domestic deposits, i_m, are constant, the domestic currency value of foreign exchange EF, is also constant along with the $\dot{E} = 0$ schedule. This schedule is negatively sloped, with an elasticity of unity, since a rise in F must be offset by an equiproportional fall in E in order to hold EF constant. A rise in foreign currency assets will be willingly held only if asset holders expect a depreciation of the domestic currency in terms of foreign exchange. Thus, as indicated by the vertical arrows in Fig. 16.1, all points to the right of the $\dot{E} = 0$ locus correspond to situations in which $\dot{E} > 0$, and vice versa.

The $\dot{F} = 0$ schedule shows the unique value of the nominal exchange rate that is consistent with no accumulation or decumulation of foreign exchange holdings by the private sector, as specified by equation (3). Since the price of domestic goods and the nominal wage rate are assumed to be given, changes in the nominal exchange rate result in equivalent changes in the real exchange rate, while the real wage (in terms of domestic goods) is unchanged. In such circumstances, there is a unique value of the nominal exchange rate that generates a demand for tradable good that equals the domestic supply, θy_T. The latter is also assumed to be given, since, for the time being, the domestic credit conditions governed by θ are unchanged. A rise in the nominal exchange rate lowers the demand for tradable goods and results in accumulation of foreign exchange. Thus, as indicated by the horizontal arrows in Fig. 16.1, all points above the $\dot{F} = 0$ schedule correspond to situations in which $\dot{F} > 0$, and vice versa.

The steady state of the model is shown by point A, at which both the nominal

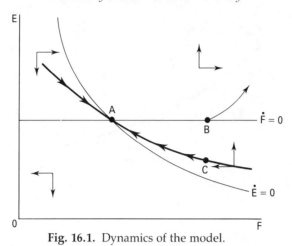

Fig. 16.1. Dynamics of the model.

exchange rate and the stock of foreign assets remain constant. Any other combination of E and F would trigger dynamic changes in the directions indicated by the arrows in Fig. 16.1. As is evident from the figure, there exists a unique path that yields a motion of these variables converging to the steady state of the system. Given the parameters of the model, any combination of E and F other than those along the boldface schedule will set in motion dynamic forces that move the economy away from the steady state. For example, if the economy were at point B, then the dynamic forces set in motion would call for a depreciation of the currency and a further accumulation of foreign exchange. The path would never converge to the steady state and would not be governed by the 'fundamentals' of the model. The only path that is not explosive is the one that leads toward the steady state of the system. This path is consistent with the fundamentals: since the latter are assumed to be stationary over time, the former should not be explosive. This path is represented by the boldface schedule in Fig. 16.1. To ensure that the economy does not follow an ever-diverging path, given its foreign currency holdings converging to point B, the exchange rate E will need to fall instantaneously to point C along the converging path. We restrict our analysis to such paths.

In order to gain insight into the working of the model and lay the foundations for the subsequent analysis, we consider an initial equilibrium at point A, and suppose that both nominal wages and prices rise by the same proportion. Since these changes do not affect the portfolio of assets, they do not alter the position of the $\dot{E} = 0$ schedule. The rise in P, however, lowers the real exchange rate, E/P, and raises the demand for tradable goods. As a result, the private sector decumulates foreign exchange. To maintain equilibrium in the tradable goods market with constant holdings of foreign exchange, the nominal exchange rate must rise in the same proportion as the price level so as to restore the initial value of the real exchange rate. It follows that the $\dot{F} = 0$ schedule shifts upwards to the position indicated by the $\dot{F}' = 0$ schedule in Fig. 16.2. The new steady-state equilibrium is obtained at point C, and the instantaneous equilibrium is shown by point B along the boldface locus.

The percentage depreciation of the domestic currency required by the satisfaction of initial conditions along the converging path is smaller than the

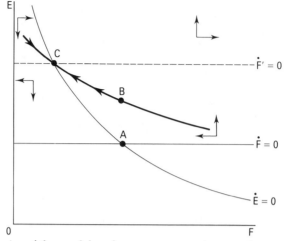

Fig. 16.2. Dynamics of the model under an exogenous increase in wages and prices.

percentage rise in wages and prices. The resultant decline in the real exchange rate stimulates demand for tradable goods and induces a decumulation of foreign exchange. At the same time, the initial depreciation of the currency raises the domestic currency value of foreign exchange holdings and alters portfolio composition. The new ratio of assets is willingly held only if it is accompanied by a further expected depreciation of the currency. Accordingly, along the path toward the new steady-state equilibrium, $\dot{F} < 0$ and $\dot{E} > 0$. Along the path, the percentage depreciation of the currency is smaller than the percentage decumulation of foreign exchange, and thus the domestic currency value of foreign exchange, EF, falls. It follows that in order to maintain portfolio equilibrium along the path, the expected percentage depreciation of the currency declines, reaching zero as the economy reaches the new steady-state equilibrium at point C. In the new steady-state equilibrium the real exchange rate and the ratio M/EF return to their initial values, while the holdings of foreign exchange fall by the same proportion as the initial rise in wages and prices.

The preceding analysis illustrates the working of the model by considering the dynamic consequences of an exogenous rise in wages and prices. We build on this analysis below.

Expected price reform

One important feature of the transformation from a CPE to an ME is the replacement of the centrally administered prices, which are governed by large subsidies, with market-determined prices, which reflect the true production cost. The removal of subsidies is likely to result in a significant rise in the nominal prices of the subsidized goods. In what follows, we analyse the implications of an expected rise in the price level consequent on the removal of the subsidies. As noted earlier, during the first phase of the transformation process the economic actions of the private sector are governed by the expectations of such price changes, since the actual changes in prices take place only later when the price liberalization plan is implemented.

To capture key elements of the economic response to the expected price reform, we can use the simple model developed above. As an expository benchmark we assume that wage earners expect to be compensated fully for the rise in domestic prices; this assumption serves to highlight the role of wage indexation in the analysis. Accordingly, we examine the effects of an expected future rise in domestic prices accompanied by an equiproportional rise in wages.

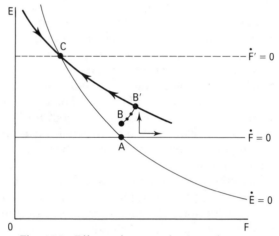

Fig. 16.3. Effects of expected price reform.

In Fig. 16.3 the initial pre-reform steady-state equilibrium is shown by point A, indicated by the intersection of the $\dot{E} = 0$ and the $\dot{F} = 0$ schedules. As indicated in the previous analysis, once prices and wages have risen equiproportionally, the new steady-state equilibrium is shown by point C, indicated by the intersection of the (unchanged) $\dot{E} = 0$ and the $\dot{F}' = 0$ schedules. The converging path associated with the *new* equilibrium is indicated by the boldface schedule. Of course, as long as prices and wages have not changed, the dynamic forces governing the economic system are those prevailing in the pre-reform period, indicated by the arrows in Fig. 16.3.

In determining the economic response to the anticipated price liberalization, we first note that any abrupt change in the exchange rate results in correspondingly abrupt capital gains or losses. Consequently, asset holders attempting to benefit (or mitigate the losses) from expected sharp exchange rate changes will attempt to modify *in advance* the composition of their portfolios. It follows that *expected abrupt changes in the exchange rate cannot occur along an equilibrium path.* If, on the basis of new information, asset holders conclude that at some future date abrupt change rate changes will be necessary, then the anticipatory response of asset holders will result in an immediate change in the exchange rate. The immediate change will be of a magnitude that precludes any further expected abrupt change.

Applying this principle to the analysis in Fig. 16.3, we note that upon receipt of the information that the price reform is expected, the domestic currency depreciates immediately, as the exchange rate jumps from point A to point B. At point B the domestic currency value of foreign exchange, EF, has risen, as has the real exchange rate, E/P. The new portfolio composition is willingly held only if the currency is expected to depreciate further, as implied by the arbitrage condition in equation (2). Likewise, the reduced demand for tradable goods consequent on the rise in the real exchange rate implies an accumulation of foreign exchange, as implied by equation (3). Accordingly, the dynamic forces operating on the economic system move the equilibrium toward point B'; the precise configuration of the dynamic path is determined by the arrows that are governed by the pre-reform situation. As is evident, in the transition between the equilibria indicated by points B and B', the holdings of foreign exchange, as well as the nominal and real exchange rates, rise. Throughout that period the expected percentage depreciation of the currency also rises. These are the general characteristics of the period up to the actual implementation of the price reform programme. Once the reform is implemented, the economic system is governed by the dynamic forces corresponding to the new situation (not drawn), and the equilibrium path becomes the boldface schedule passing through point C in Fig. 16.3. The previous argument implies that when the price reform is implemented as expected, further abrupt changes in the nominal exchange rate are ruled out. It follows that the economy reaches point B' precisely at the time of the initial jump in the exchange rate, and is reflected in the precise position of point B.

Once the economy reaches the equilibrium at point B', domestic prices and the wage rate rise abruptly, thereby resulting in a sharp fall in the real exchange rate. The rise in the demand for tradable goods induces a decumulation of foreign exchange. Furthermore, since at point B' the domestic currency value of foreign exchange exceeds its corresponding steady-state equilibrium level (at points A and C), it follows that the currency is expected to depreciate further. The resulting path of foreign currency holdings and the exchange rate is portrayed by the boldface schedule. Along this path the real exchange rate rises, foreign currency holdings fall, and the domestic currency value thereof also declines. This dynamic process ends once the economy arrives at its new steady-state equilibrium. In that equilibrium, the real exchange rate, the composition of assets, and the domestic currency value of foreign exchange are the same as in the pre-reform steady-state equilibrium (point A). However, foreign currency holdings have fallen while the domestic currency has depreciated. The proportional change in both equals (in absolute value) the proportional rise in prices and wages.

So far, we have assumed that nominal wages, W, are fully indexed to the domestic price, P. Consequently, the demand for tradable goods (and thereby changes in the holdings of foreign exchange) was influenced only by changes in the real exchange rate. To examine the sensitivity of the analysis to the degree of wage indexation, it is useful to explore the implication of the opposite extreme case in which nominal wages are completely unindexed. Our interest in wage indexation stems from the fact that recent economic reform programmes have paid much attention to the appropriate degree of wage indexation, reflecting interest in the macroeconomic and income distribution consequences of the price reform.

Under circumstances in which nominal wages are fixed (and, hence, unindexed), the expected rise in domestic prices lowers post-reform expected real wages. This, in turn, lowers the post-reform demand for tradable goods, D_T. To stimulate the demand for tradable goods to the level prevailing before the fall in real wages, the real exchange rate would need to fall. It follows that the displaced $\dot{F} = 0$ schedule in Fig. 16.3 must lie below the $\dot{F}' = 0$ schedule (along which the real exchange rate equals its pre-reform level). However, since the post-reform $\dot{F} = 0$ schedule is displaced upward, the qualitative characteristics of the previous analysis remain intact.[5]

As is evident, the dynamics of the system depend critically on the degree of wage indexation. In particular, the evolution of the nominal exchange rate during the transition period may have profound implications for the inflationary consequences of the price reform. The higher the degree of wage indexation, the larger the depreciation of the currency, and the greater are the inflationary pressures. As argued in subsequent sections, these pressures may result in a credit crunch, reducing working capital and negatively affecting the supply of output. It follows that a high degree of wage indexation carries with it the danger of transforming a *microeconomic* problem (associated with the subsidized prices) into a *macroeconomic* problem (associated with a flare-up of inflation). Thus, the more effective is the domestic safety net designed to protect wage earners, the more likely it is that macroeconomic problems will ensue. There is, therefore, a trade-off between the degree of domestic political support for the economic transformation programme (a support that is enhanced by high wage indexation) and the degree of price and output stability during the transition period.

Our analysis of the effects of an expected price reform can now be extended to examine the effects on the market for non-tradable goods. We first recall from the analysis in Fig. 16.3 that with wages fully indexed to domestic prices, the real exchange rate rises throughout the period of transition toward price reform. It then drops sharply once the reform is implemented, and subsequently it rises back toward its initial pre-reform level. These changes in the real exchange rate result in an initial rise in the demand for non-tradable goods, followed by a sharp decline occurring at the time the price reform is implemented. During the subsequent period the demand recovers gradually until it reaches its pre-reform level. Depending on the pattern of adjustment in the market for non-tradable goods, these demand changes induce corresponding fluctuations in employment, capacity utilization, and so on. To simplify matters, consider the situation in which the supply of non-tradable goods (and thereby the level of employment and capacity utilization) adjusts to satisfy the demand. Under these circumstances, employment rises during the initial phase; it then suffers a sharp decline once the price reform is implemented. Subsequently, employment recovers gradually until it returns to its initial pre-reform level.

If the degree of wage indexation is less than complete, then it can be verified that the initial rise in the real exchange rate and the increase in the level of employment are less pronounced, their subsequent fall upon implementation of the price reform is more pronounced, and their recovery during the subsequent period is incomplete. It follows that the levels of employment and capacity utilization obtained with a low degree of wage indexation are lower than the corresponding levels obtained with a high degree of wage indexation. A parallel analysis applies to the evolution of inventories and queues if, in the face of fluctuating demand, these are the dominant forms of adjustment in the market for non-tradable goods.

The foregoing analysis of price reform presumed that the rise in prices consequent on the removal of subsidies is determined by the free operation of market forces. In practice, as illustrated by experience in Poland and Romania, especially in the area of energy pricing, governments have attempted to avoid an excessively large price shock by adopting a strategy of administered pricing. This strategy permits the spreading of what otherwise would have been a once-and-for-all price rise over a lengthy period of time. However, our previous analysis of anticipatory behaviour suggests that some of the benefits from administratively spreading the price rise over time may be illusory. The private sector, being familiar with the administered pricing strategy, is likely to modify its behaviour in anticipation of future price rises. The resulting pattern of adjustment may be much less smooth than the one envisaged by the designers of the strategy. The possible disruptions stemming from such anticipatory behaviour point to the benefits of an early replacement of administered pricing by market-determined pricing. Such a replacement, which could be followed by an eventual dismantling of the adminis-tered-pricing apparatus, would provide a useful signal of the commitment of the government to the programme of economic transformation and restructuring.[6]

Credit Policy

The analysis in the previous section focused on the implications of an anticipated future price reform. To simplify matters, we examined the 'pure' case in which prices are expected to rise, owing, for example, to a removal of subsidies. We have not incorporated into the analysis anticipatory responses to other policy measures that are likely to be an integral part of the policy reform package. Specifically, the restoration of credit control is viewed as one of the central pillars of economic policy programmes aimed at transforming CPEs into PCPEs. Indeed, tight credit control is seen as one of the most important measures necessary to combat inflation and establish credibility. Therefore, in anticipating future price reform, the private sector is likely to assume that the removal of subsidies is accompanied by a tight credit policy. In this section we analyse the mechanisms through which credit policy influences the economy.[7] To gain insight, we first examine another pure case in which credit policy is taken in isolation, rather than in conjunction with the expected removal of subsidies.

The main rationale behind the use of restrictive credit policy to combat inflation is well known; it is grounded in theory and is substantiated by experience. The conventional channel through which credit contraction influences the economic system is its restraining effect on aggregate demand. However, as was indicated earlier, in economies that are not yet fully developed MEs, official credit may have strong effects on aggregate supply.

Consider the effect of a contractionary credit policy. This policy influences the economy through three channels: the supply of output, the demand for output, and portfolio choice. Starting with the supply side, we note that the credit crunch reduces working capital and provokes a decline in output. The reduced supply of tradable goods results in a depreciation of the currency, upward pressures on the prices of tradable goods, and, thereby, on the general price level.[8] These pressures are more pronounced the higher the degree of wage indexation. Moreover, higher wages and prices increase the need for working capital and aggravate the credit crunch. It follows that the severity of the credit crunch increases with the degree of wage indexation. In this example, credit contraction (in particular, under conditions of wage indexation) results in stagflation: it reduces output and exerts inflationary pressures.

The negative supply-side effects may be of special relevance for PCPEs. As emphasized earlier, with segmented and underdeveloped financial markets, the reduction in working capital induced by an official credit contraction has adverse implications for the enterprise sector. Firms whose access to other sources of finance is limited will attempt to mitigate the shortage of working capital by relying on inter-enterprise credit. An expansion of the inter-enterprise credit network may reduce the severity of the credit crunch on output in the short run, but is unlikely to offset it completely. Furthermore, as discussed below, an excessive reliance on an inter-enterprise credit network has profound macroeconomic consequences for both the effectiveness of monetary policy and the efficiency of resource allocation.

We consider next the mechanisms through which the credit crunch affects demand. First, firms whose access to the credit market is limited attempt to build up working capital both by running down inventories of inputs and final goods and by reducing demand for the products of other firms. Second, to the extent that the credit crunch raises interest rates, it contributes further to the reduction in demand.

The combined effect of the changes in supply and demand depends on their relative magnitudes. If the net effect of the credit crunch is dominated by the fall in supply, then the qualitative results of our earlier analysis of the negative supply-side effects hold. If, however, the reduction in demand more than offsets the fall in supply (with proper allowance given to inventory change), then the contraction in official credit induces an instantaneous appreciation of the currency.[9]

The analysis, thus far, has focused on the effects of credit policy on the market for internationally tradable goods. As a result, the economic consequences for that policy depended entirely on whether it generated excess demand or supply. Parallel to its effect on the market for internationally tradable goods, the credit crunch also influences the market for non-tradable goods through its effect on the demand and supply of these goods. As in the previous analysis, the supply effects may be distributed among changes in output and capacity utilization, changes in inventories, and changes in queues.

The third mechanism through which credit policy affects the economy is through its effect on portfolio choice, especially if the credit contraction is associated with a rise in the deposit interest rate. It can be verified that, in and of itself, this factor provokes an instantaneous appreciation of the domestic currency.[10]

The foregoing discussion highlighted the three main factors that need to be taken into account in the analysis of the economic consequences of credit policy: the supply effects, the demand effects, and the portfolio effects. Which of the three effects dominates depends, of course, on the specific circumstances. Furthermore, the relative importance of these three effects will vary over time. Specifically, effects associated with changes in inventory holdings are by their nature more pronounced in the short run; they play, therefore, a more important role immediately after the implementation of the credit crunch. Other effects, such as those associated with changes in financial portfolios, may prevail for a longer period. Since the effects of credit policy on the economy may change significantly over time, close attention should be given to its dynamic consequences.

From the discussion of the evolution of the economy following the credit squeeze, it should be evident that a similar analysis applies to the effects of an expected future credit crunch. In that case, market participants will respond immediately to the anticipated future change in credit policy. As a result, the exchange rate, foreign currency holdings, and other key economic variables will change, even though no policy action has yet taken place. The model can be readily used to illustrate the dynamics induced by these anticipatory phenomena. Such dynamic considerations are of special relevance for PCPEs, in which the depth and breadth of financial markets, as well as the volume and nature of inter-enterprise credit, change over time.

A credit crunch resulting in a sharp rise in both deposit and loan rates of interest may be especially damaging under the institutional environment prevailing in PCPEs. In such an environment, the increased fragility of the banking system (induced by the rise in deposit rates) superimposed on the financial vulnerability of enterprises (induced by the rise in loan rates) puts significant strains on the economic system. These strains may be especially severe in these economies due to the elaborate network of interfirm credit and the underdeveloped financial system. In such circumstances, financial difficulties of one firm may spread to other firms through the credit network.

This interdependence of firms linked through the network of interfirm credit impedes the effectiveness of the signals provided by the price system for an efficient allocation of resources. In MEs with well-functioning markets, the price mechanism helps to distinguish between firms that should go out of business and those that should survive. This important allocative function of the price mechanism is impaired in PCPEs, since interdependence among enterprises makes it difficult to distinguish between 'good' and 'bad' firms. Thus, a credit crunch designed to reduce *macroeconomic* distortions may give rise to further *microeconomic* distortions.[11]

The Dangers of Fine-Tuning

The previous sections examined the implications of anticipatory reactions to price reform and the implications of credit policies. The two analyses have been conducted separately so as to highlight the dynamic processes set in motion in each of the pure cases. In practice, the expected rise in prices consequent on the removal of subsidies – designed to reduce *microeconomic* distortions – is likely to be accompanied by current or expected future credit policies – designed to prevent a flare-up of *macroeconomic* distortions. The two pure cases provide the ingredients relevant for the analysis of the more complex case in which both phenomena appear simultaneously.

Rather than going through the tedious procedure of combining the two pure cases, we turn next to an examination of some specific policy responses that can be used to mitigate, or even offset, some of the undesirable dynamic consequences that were illustrated by the pure cases. In this context, we focus on wage and interest rate policies. The results of this examination demonstrate the difficulties associated with fine-tuning.

Consider, for example, the effect of a rise in the price of non-tradable goods. As shown in the previous analysis, such a price rise induces an immediate depreciation of the domestic currency, followed by a transition period during which the currency continues to depreciate, while foreign currency holdings decline (see Fig. 16.2). Is there a wage policy that would prevent this adjustment while keeping the system at the initial equilibrium? In principle, the rise in demand for tradable goods induced by the real appreciation of the currency can be offset by an appropriate fall in the real wage. Thus, if the real wage were to fall in this fashion, the system would remain at its initial equilibrium, and the cost of adjustment could be avoided.[12] However, such a decline in the real wage aggravates the reduction in demand for non-tradable goods induced by the real appreciation of the currency. As a result, the output of non-tradable goods falls, inventories of unsold goods accumulate, and a recession ensues.

The same principles apply with greater force to the case in which the rise in prices has not yet taken place but is expected to occur in the future (see Fig. 16.3). In that case, the real wage policy necessary to maintain external balance will need to change continuously so as to offset the dynamics of the system. However, as with the previous analysis, the maintenance of external balances induces a recession in the market for non-tradable goods.

The complexity of the policy attempting to offset the dynamic evolution of the system – and the extraordinary degree of fine-tuning that such a policy necessitates – is not specific to the above example in which the burden of adjustment falls on real wages. Rather, it is a general characteristic of policy responses designed to offset anticipatory dynamics. For example, the monetary authorities may attempt to offset the effects of the anticipated price rise by altering the interest rate paid on deposits and, thereby, affecting portfolio balance. As in the previous analysis, it can be verified that, to be successful in offsetting the undesirable consequences of anticipatory dynamics, the monetary authorities need to adopt an extremely complex fine-tuning interest rate strategy.[13]

Using an interest rate policy to offset the dynamics of anticipatory adjustment may be especially tempting, since, in principle, the rate of interest can be modified in short intervals. It can be shown, however, that such a policy cannot be sustainable and, in fact, is likely to be explosive. The maintenance of initial equilibrium requires ever-rising deposit rates, which ultimately will put in question the viability of the banking system. In addition, the rise in deposit rates may exert upward pressures on loan rates and thereby put in question the viability of enterprises. Both of these developments may undermine the credibility of policy makers as market participants lose confidence in the viability of the entire policy strategy. Indeed, one of the main difficulties faced by policy makers in PCPEs is the possible lack of credibility of announced policy attentions. In such circumstances, a policy strategy that relies on continuously changing policy actions and, as in this particular example, on continuously tightening credit, is unlikely to contribute to the build-up of credibility.

This last conclusion is of special relevance, since it limits somewhat the force of the argument that a tight credit policy contributes to the build-up of credibility through demonstrating the resolve of policy makers. While, as a general guide, especially when implemented in the context of a comprehensive economic programme, this argument makes a lot of sense, the drawbacks associated with an excessive reliance on tight credit may, in fact, erode credibility. The negative supply-side effects of a credit crunch in PCPEs reflect the infancy of credit markets in such economies. A key implication is that to restore the conventional potency of credit policy, efforts should be directed at financial market reform, aimed at the development of domestic credit markets, coupled with the development of appropriate regulatory and supervisory systems.

Liquidity Overhang and the Budget

Our analysis of the process of transformation from CPE to PCPE focused on the early phases of the transition during which the expected removal of subsidies to consumer and intermediate goods entails expectations of future price rises. These expectations may arise from the observation that the removal of subsidies often results in sizable price jumps, as illustrated by recent experience in Poland. They may also be grounded in the belief that the economy has a liquidity overhang. For our purposes, a liquidity overhang can be defined as a situation in which price liberalization and the removal of subsidies bring about a rise in the *measured* average price level. In addition to the direct effects of the removal of subsidies, the measured price level rises because elements of cost (reflected in queues and delivery lags), which were not included in measured prices before the reform, become explicit afterwards.

There are essentially three mechanisms to reduce a liquidity overhang: first, by increasing the attractiveness of domestic liquid assets through a rise in the rate of interest paid on domestic currency deposits; second, through a rise in prices associated with the price liberalization; and, third, through a reduction in liquidity. The first mechanism raises the demand for real liquid assets, while the second and third both lower the real supply of such assets. These three mechanisms have been emphasized, in varying degrees, in connection with the debate on the various means of reducing the liquidity overhang in the USSR, and, to some extent, in Romania and Bulgaria.

In analysing the first of these three mechanisms, we note that a rise in the deposit rate, especially in circumstances prevailing in PCPEs, may have adverse implications for the government budget. In such economies the banking system is 'owned' to a large extent by the government. Therefore, a rise in the rate of interest paid by banks is a drain on the budget. In fact, in many respects, bank deposits may be regarded as public debt service. From this perspective, credit and budget policies are closely linked to each other, and the rise in the deposit rate will need to be financed through new taxes. The budgetary drain induced by the higher deposit rate will be greater, the lower is the interest elasticity of the demand for real liquid assets. The effectiveness of this mechanism of alleviating the liquidity overhang will depend on the capacity of the tax system to generate the necessary tax revenue, and on the distributive and efficiency implications of the associated 'incidence of the tax'. Furthermore, an assessment of the desirability of this mechanism will need to take into account the effects of the deteriorated budget on credibility.

The second mechanism for eliminating the liquidity overhang – through a rise in the measured price level – was analysed implicitly in previous sections. There, the anticipatory behaviour of the private sector was based on the assumption that the price reform results in a price rise. For concreteness, in terms of our notation, we identify the measured price level with P. Although we will not elaborate further on this mechanism, it is worth noting that the price rise is a tax on the real value of domestic liquid assets. Therefore, an evaluation of this mechanism also depends on the specific incidence of the tax and on its effects on political support, on the efficiency of resource allocation, and on policy credibility. These effects depend, in turn, on the capacity of the government to avoid the transformation of what in principle should be a once-and-for-all price rise into an inflation spiral.

Consider next the third possible mechanism for the elimination of the liquidity overhang – a reduction in liquidity. In principle, the excess liquidity could be reduced either through direct confiscation (a monetary reform), or through open market sales of assets. The adoption of a monetary reform may be highly effective in bringing about a rapid elimination of the overhang. Indeed, there have been several historical episodes in which monetary reforms were implemented successfully, especially in the context of a comprehensive programme dealing with hyperinflation. Since, however, the incidence of the tax associated with a monetary reform is not distributed evenly across the population, it may erode the political support necessary for a successful implementation, and may require appropriate incomes policies designed to provide social safety nets and to secure political support. Furthermore, the direction of the effects of this confiscatory policy (along with the accompanying incomes policies) on economic efficiency and on credibility is not unambiguous.

The elimination of liquidity overhang through open market sales is also subject to some limitations. In PCPEs the possibility of conducting open market sales is limited by the absence of conventional financial instruments and by the underdevelopment of capital markets. However, in such economies, the government owns a large portion of existing assets and, in many cases, wishes to undertake a privatization programme. In such circumstances, the excess liquidity can be absorbed through open market sales of the housing sector and of state enterprises. In addition, the increased size of the market economy resulting from the privatization process may increase the demand for liquidity and reduce the size of the overhang as transactions shift from the barter to the monetized sector.

The difficulties in designing an effective privatization programme are well known.[14] They include the problems of establishing a fair market price for an enterprise without the help of a well-functioning market-place, developing the legal infrastructure necessary for the effective use of entrepreneurial drive, developing domestic credit and financial markets necessary for intermediation, and establishing mechanisms dealing with the redistribution of rents and the potential for corruption. In addition to these and other difficulties associated with the incidence of the tax, privatization has profound implications for the budget. On the one hand, sales of state enterprises generate (no-recurring) revenue (which, however, cannot be spent, because, otherwise, a new liquidity overhang would result); on the other hand, the transfer of income-producing assets to the private sector results in a (recurring) loss of future revenue. To make up for this lost revenue, the government needs to find a new source of recurring income.[15]

In searching for a new source of recurring income, the government will be tempted to levy new (previously unannounced) taxes on the enterprises just sold to the private sector. Such a strategy would, however, be counterproductive. In setting their bids for state enterprises, potential buyers will take into account the possibility that the government will be tempted to raise taxes. Such anticipations tend to lower the market price of state enterprises, reducing the proceeds from privatization, and leaving the liquidity overhang problem unsolved. To prevent the erosion of privatization proceeds, the government must provide reliable and believable signals that such 'surprise' taxes will not be levied. To produce such credible signals, the government must demonstrate its capacity and unequivocal commitment to tap new sources of tax revenue. These new sources of tax revenue must cover the *entire* loss of recurrent revenue resulting from the privatization programme. Thus, for a privatization programme to be implemented effectively, the government must levy new taxes on entities other than the newly privatized enterprises.

The foregoing analysis of the various means to eliminate liquidity overhang through a reduction in *real* liquidity reveals that in all cases the private sector ends up being taxed by the *full amount* of the overhang. In deciding on the policy response for the liquidity overhang, the government must recognize that the various solutions differ in the incidence of the taxes that they entail.[16]

Additional important factors that should be taken into account in choosing among the various solutions to the liquidity overhang problem include their differential effects on the efficiency of resource allocation and on the reputation and credibility of the government. The beneficial effects of privatization on the efficiency of resource allocation can be significant if the privatization of state enterprises and the housing sector provides incentives for higher productivity and better maintenance of the capital stock. Such benefits are especially pronounced in circumstances where domestic capital markets are in their infancy. Indeed, in most CPEs and PCPEs these markets are underdeveloped, segmented, and lack the know-how necessary for their effectiveness. In this regard, the opening of the economy to foreign investment can be highly beneficial. In addition to providing financial and managerial capital, privatization programmes that encourage direct foreign participation can be useful in providing access to international capital markets. Foreign investors bring with them know-how, contacts, and information. Their presence and active participation yield the added benefit of improving the functioning of domestic capital markets.

The preceding discussion suggests that the government could announce its intention to accompany the price reform with one of the three types of mechanisms discussed above. If fully credible, the announcement of such a policy package would eliminate the anticipatory dynamics and make it unnecessary to resort to costly policies of fine-tuning during the transition period. Full credibility is the *sine qua non* for the success of this strategy. It must be recognized, however, that as a general rule governments finding themselves on the road from CPE to PCPE do not possess the full details of their future economic programmes. Furthermore, the private sector will lack experience with the operation of markets in transition. In addition, policy makers and the private sector alike will be keenly aware that other experiences of economic transformation (especially during the early phases) have occasionally been associated with a rise in prices and departures from previously planned policies. Against this background, it is very likely that government pronouncements are not fully credible. Thus, it is improbable that the government can prevent the anticipatory dynamics during the transition period unless it resorts to costly fine-tuning. Furthermore, to achieve credibility, the government may need to adopt front-loaded measures. Therefore, in practice, the government may not be able to delay adoption of the accompanying measures until the date of the price liberalization. These considerations suggest that the transitional pre-reform period characterizing the early stages of the transformation from CPE to PCPE should be as short as possible.

Concluding Remarks

The transformation of CPEs into MEs is a long and complex process. Invariably, the early phases of the transformation involve a great degree of uncertainty and vulnerability. During the early phases, the old system has collapsed, but the new system is not yet in place. The 'rules of the game' are still vague, and the detailed policy course unknown. While the policy strategy is debated, the economic behaviour of households and investors is governed by expectations. This paper deals with issues arising during the early stages of the transformation of CPEs, and identifies key factors governing its evolution.

An important theme in the analysis is that observed patterns of exchange rates, asset holdings, and economic activity in general reflect both economic policies already in place and policy measures that are expected to be implemented in the future. The anticipatory character of economic behaviour is of special relevance in the early stages of the transformation process. During these stages there are expectations of comprehensive future policy actions, while policy measures actually taken are few and limited in scope. To highlight this anticipatory feature, we developed a simple model in which the behaviour of asset holders plays a critical role. The model was used to analyse the consequences of expected price liberalization. We demonstrated how the expectations of future price reform induce a depreciation of the currency, sharp changes in the current account of the balance of payments (driven by defensive actions on the part of the asset holders), and corresponding changes in economic activity. In this context, we paid special attention to the role of wage indexation and showed that a high degree of wage indexation carries with it the danger of transforming a microeconomic problem (associated with subsidized prices) into a macroeconomic problem (associated with a flare-up of inflation).

A major focus of our analysis was the role of credit markets and the effects of credit policies. In this regard, we noted that the special circumstances prevailing in these economies include lack of depth and breadth of financial markets and a complex network of inter-enterprise debt. The critical dependence of firms on working capital and the lack of an information system necessary to assess risk and creditworthiness and, more generally, to distinguish between good and bad firms complicates the conduct and effectiveness of credit policy. The analysis illustrates the pitfalls of transplanting policies appropriate for market economies into an environment lacking the basic institutional infrastructure – including regulatory and supervisory systems – necessary for the operation of credit and financial markets. This consideration underscores the benefits of an early development of domestic credit and financial markets, as well as the desirability of finding ways to 'clean' the balance sheets of enterprises and banks by expunging bad debts.

The benefits from trade liberalization also depend on the quality of capital markets. Trade liberalization provides the economy with the right price signals. Exposure to world prices helps to demonopolize the economy, enhance competition, and improve the allocation of resources. However, in adjusting to the removal of protection, even good and economically viable firms may require credit. The adoption of hard budget constraints eliminates the automatic financing of enterprises' deficits by the government. Without sufficient access to capital markets, such good firms may be forced out of business, thereby reducing the benefits from trade liberalization. Moreover, in attempting to protect themselves, the good but endangered enterprises may be tempted to join the bad and economically non-viable enterprises in lobbying against trade liberalization, thereby reducing the likelihood that liberalization will be adopted. These considerations imply that the benefits from, and support for, trade liberalization can be significantly enhanced by an early development of domestic capital markets.

The dynamic evolution of the economy during the early stages of transformation is complicated, costly, and disruptive. The profound changes in the rules of the game and in the policy regime may result in fundamental changes in the behavioural patterns of market participants. Policy-makers may be tempted to use an arsenal of policy instruments in attempts to offset disruptive changes in key economic variables. To examine the consequences of such efforts, we analysed the implications of wage policies as well as interest rate policies designed to offset the anticipatory changes. We showed that, to be successful, the authorities must adopt an extremely complex fine-tuning strategy of policy response. The lack of full credibility of announced policies, superimposed on instant credit markets, increases the likelihood and costs of policy mistakes. We therefore rejected the fine-tuning strategy and emphasized the desirability of a quick implementation of price reform.

In circumstances of a liquidity overhang, the removal of subsidies associated with price reform induces a significant jump in the price level. We examined alternative means by which such a liquidity overhang can be alleviated. In addition to a rise in prices, such means include a rise in interest rates and a fall in the nominal money stock. We showed that all of these measures involve taxation of one form or another. The choice among the various alternatives depends on (1) the capacity of the tax system to generate revenue, (2) the distributive and efficiency implications of the incidence of the tax, (3) its effects on political support, and (4) policy credibility. In this context, our analysis examined the consequences of privatization as a means to absorb excess liquidity. Aside, of course, from the obvious efficiency benefits that private ownership entails, we showed that to be fully effective, privatization must be accompanied by increased taxes in the amount of the liquidity overhang. In the absence of such increased tax revenue, privatization results in medium-term budget deficits and a rise in public debt. This consideration underscores the benefits from an early development of an effective tax system.

Our analysis illustrated the interdependence among price reform, trade liberalization, reform of financial and capital markets, economic stabilization, and budget and tax reform. Obviously, the adoption of a comprehensive reform programme encompassing the entire economic system is desirable. Indeed, macroeconomic and structural reform measures introduced simultaneously are likely to reinforce each other, provide confidence and momentum, and reduce the risk that the process will be reversed. The enhanced confidence would lengthen the planning horizon of savers, investors, and enterprises, stimulate domestic and foreign investment, and contribute to the credibility of the transformation process.

In practice, however, it is unlikely that the prevailing socioeconomic conditions can always generate the political support necessary for the adoption of a rapid, comprehensive, and all-inclusive reform. Frequently, choices need to be made as to the appropriate pace and sequence of reform measures. In this regard, there is no blueprint. Indeed, as indicated at the beginning of this chapter, the optimal pace and sequence of reform measures depend on circumstances that differ across countries. These circumstances reflect diversities of historical backgrounds, economic, legal, and political institutions, entrepreneurial traditions, as well as attitudes toward the role of markets and incentives. Such disparate circumstances imply that the economic reform programmes of different countries may differ in their areas of vulnerability. For example, one society may be highly sensitive to the effects of reform on the level of employment, while another may be especially susceptible to the prices of foodstuffs. Likewise, one society may be highly sensitive to the effects of reform on the level of employment, while another may wish to protect the real value of private sector savings. Such differences in sensitivities may be reflected in the choice of the sequencing of reform measures, as well as in the characteristics of safety nets.

In choosing among alternative safety nets, one should be aware that there is no way to protect all segments of society. A comprehensive reform programme must involve sacrifices by a substantial share of the population. Furthermore, in designing the mechanism through which the safety net is effected, one should avoid as much as possible the introduction of new distortions. In this regard, the safety nets should not interfere with the incentives to work, save, and invest, nor should they tamper with monetary and exchange rate policies. Rather, they should be allowed for in the budget and effected through income transfers.

Although different countries may wish to choose different sequences of reform measures, in many cases such a choice may not be available if policy options are overtaken by events. In view of the fast-changing circumstances in these economies, it may well be preferable to adopt a timely, albeit somewhat imperfect, comprehensive reform programme than to search for the perfect programme, encompassing a fine-tuned sequence of policy measures. The danger of a lengthy probe for the perfect sequence under conditions of fast-changing circumstances is that, once implemented, the programme may turn out to be outdated and irrelevant.

Whatever the choice of sequence, the early steps must reflect the notion that a necessary condition for a successful transformation is its credibility. A well-designed economic programme will not be effective if it is not credible. In this regard, a crucial early step must be a fundamental change in the mentality and attitude of the policy-maker. The policy-maker should recognize the limitations of discretionary policies, the virtues of transparent and simple rules that encourage entrepreneurial pursuits, and, above all, should be cognizant of the fact that policy actions (and inaction) convey powerful signals to the market-place. In this regard, the early steps must be meaningful and bold. They must convey the credible message that the government's support for the economic reform process is absolute, that the government is aware that some setbacks along the part are inevitable, but, at the same time, that postponements and reversals of policy commitments would entail a very high political cost. Such a message is likely to reduce the degree of uncertainty, increase the confidence of consumers, lengthen the time horizon over which economic plans are made, stimulate domestic and foreign investment, and contribute to the success of the economic transformation process.

Notes

1. Recently, there has been a flurry of interest in issues related to transformation of centrally planned economies. Examples of recent, relevant literature are Calvo (1990), Dornbusch (1990), Fischer and Gelb (1990), Klaus (1991), Kornai (1990), Lipton and Sachs (1990a), Marer (1990), McKinnon (1991), Portes (1990) and Wolf (1990).
2. The structure of the model is related to the one developed in Calvo and Rodriguez (1977) and Frenkel and Rodriguez (1982).
3. It would be more appropriate to specify the demand function as depending on the wage *bill* rather than the wage *rate*. The latter is used for the sake of simplicity. For the present purposes, however, this simplification does not alter the main thrust of the analysis. Similar reasoning applies to the exclusion of other relevant variables like interest rates, real balances, and other assets.
4. The difference between the patterns of adjustment in the markets for tradable and nontradable goods is introduced to highlight the diversity of adjustment mechanisms that are called for in the absence of full price flexibility. In our specification the flexibility of the (black) market exchange rate captures the anticipatory feature of the pre-reform period. Thereby, this flexibility introduces a mechanism of adjustment in the market for tradable goods that is absent in the domestic goods market, and underlies the assumption that output in the tradable good sector is not governed by domestic demand.
5. To verify this result, we note that, using the homogeneity postulate, the demand for tradable goods (see equation (3)) can equivalently be specified as a function of P/W and E/W. Without wage indexation, the excess demand for tradable goods induced by the expected rise in the domestic price can be eliminated by an appropriate rise in E. Thus, in that case, once the domestic price rises, the $\dot{F} = 0$ schedule is displaced upwards. This upward displacement reflects the implicit gross substitution assumption. A similar analysis applies for partial wage indexation. The higher the degree of wage indexation, the larger the upward displacement of the $\dot{F} = 0$ schedule.
6. In addition to these considerations, it is noteworthy that administered price changes are unlikely to deal effectively with the huge distortions in relative prices that are so prevalent in CPEs and PCPEs. Identification and correction of such relative price distortions will need to rely on market forces.
7. For a related discussion on the role of credit policy, see Calvo (1990). For a broader analysis on the role that credit markets play in the economic transformation process, see Calvo and Frenkel (1991).
8. In terms of the model, the credit contraction reduces the credit coefficient, θ, and results in lower output of tradable goods. The reduced supply of tradable goods, in and of itself, results in an upward displacement of the $\dot{F} = 0$ schedule in Fig. 16.2 to the position indicated by the $\dot{F}' = 0$ schedule. Consequently, the domestic currency depreciates instantaneously, and the initial equilibrium shifts from point A to point B in Fig. 16.2. Thereafter, the nominal exchange rate and the holdings of foreign exchange move along the boldface schedule toward point C. During the transition, the currency continues to depreciate in nominal and real terms, while the private holdings of foreign exchange decline, in terms of both foreign and domestic currency.

9. In terms of the model, if the fall in supply dominates the reduced demand, then the $\dot{F} = 0$ schedule shifts upwards, and the dynamic analysis follows along the lines indicated in the previous footnote. If, however, the fall in demand exceeds the reduction in supply, then the $\dot{F} = 0$ schedule shifts downwards, and the currency appreciates instantaneously. This is followed by a transition period during which the currency continues to appreciate, thereby exerting downward pressures on prices. Throughout, the holdings of foreign exchange (whether measured in terms of domestic or foreign currency) rise.

10. In terms of the model, a rise in i_m raises the desired ratio of domestic to foreign currency in private sector portfolios and induces a downward displacement of the $\dot{E} = 0$ schedule. It can be verified that the instantaneous appreciation of the domestic currency is followed by a transition during which the currency depreciates to its original level, while foreign currency holdings decline.

11. For a detailed analysis of the role that credit markets play in distinguishing between 'good' and 'bad' firms in the context of economic transformation, see Calvo and Frenkel (1991).

12. In terms of the analysis in Fig. 16.2, a fall in the real wage, W/P, compensating for the real appreciation of the currency (that is, the fall in E/P), keeps the $\dot{F} = 0$ schedule in Fig. 16.2 intact. Hence, the initial values of the nominal exchange rate and of foreign currency holdings do not change, and the initial equilibrium prevails.

13. In terms of our model, the fine-tuning policy of a rise in the deposit rate, i_m, induces a downward displacement of the $\dot{E} = 0$ schedule in Fig. 16.3, and sets in motion a new equilibrium path. The complexity of a fine-tuning policy would be enhanced once one allows for the possibility that the sharp change in the economic regime associated with the economic transformation process induces changes in the behavioural patterns of economic agents.

14. Examples of recent analysis of issues arising in privatization efforts in PCPEs are Frydman and Rapaczynski (1990) and Lipton and Sachs (1990b). For an examination of these and other privatization schemes, see Borensztein and Kumar (1991).

15. In calculating the full budgetary implications of absorbing liquidity through asset sales, allowance should also be made for the saving on the interest payments on the savings accounts in which the liquid assets were held.

16. Similar considerations apply to proposals to absorb the liquidity overhang by sales of housing. Unless the government reduces significantly the rent control provisions (representing thereby a specific incidence of the tax), there will not be much incentive for tenants who pay ridiculously low rents to purchase high-price housing.

References

Borensztein, E. and Kumar, M. S. (1991) 'Proposals for Privatization in Eastern Europe', *Staff Papers*, International Monetary Fund, June: 300–26.

Calvo, G. A. (1990) 'Financial Aspects of Socialist Economies: From Inflation to Reform', paper presented at the Conference on Adjustment and Growth: Lessons for Eastern Europe, October (Pultusk, Poland: World Bank, 1990); forthcoming in *Adjustment and Growth: Lessons for Eastern Europe*, eds V. Corbo, F. Coricelli and J. Bossak (Washington: World Bank, 1991).

Calvo, G. A. and Frenkel, J. A. (1991) 'Obstacles to Transforming Centrally Planned Economies: The Role of Capital Markets'. In *The Transition to a Market Economy in Central and Eastern Europe*, by P. Marer and S. Zecchini (eds) (Paris: Organization for Economic Cooperation and Development, forthcoming, 1991).

Calvo, G. A. and Rodriguez, C. A. 'A Model of Exchange Rate Determination Under Currency Substitution and Rational Expectations', *Journal of Political Economy*, 85: 617–25.

Dornbusch, R. (1990) 'Economic Reform in Eastern Europe and the Soviet Union: Priorities and Strategy', paper presented at the Conference on the Transition to a Market Economy in Central and Eastern Europe, November (Paris: Organization for Economic Cooperation and Development and World Bank).

Fischer, S. and Gelb, A. (1990) 'Issues in Socialist Economy Reform', paper presented at the Conference on the Transition to a Market Economy in Central and Eastern Europe, November (Paris: Organization for Economic Cooperation and Development and World Bank).

Frenkel, J. A. and Rodriguez, C. A. (1990) 'Exchange Rate Dynamics and the Overshooting Hypothesis', *Staff Papers*, International Monetary Fund, 29: 1–30.

Frydman, R. and Rapaczynski, A. (1990) 'Markets and Institutions in Large-Scale Privatizations', paper presented at the Conference on Adjustment and Growth: Lessons for Eastern Europe, October (Pultusk, Poland: World Bank; forthcoming in *Adjustment and Growth: Lessons for Eastern Europe* by V. Corbo, F. Coricelli, and J. Bossak (eds) (Washington: World Bank).

Klaus, V. (1991) 'A Perspective on Economic Transition in Czechoslovakia and Eastern Europe', Keynote Address, *Proceedings of the World Bank Conference on Development Economics, 1990*: Washington: World Bank: 13–18; also in *A Road to Market Economy (Selected articles, speeches and lectures held abroad)* Prague: Top Agency: 18–23.

Kornai, J. (1990) *The Road to a Free Economy, Shifting from a Socialist System: The Example of Hungary* (New York: W. W. Norton and Company).

Lipton, D. and Sachs, J. (1990a), 'Creating a Market Economy in Eastern Europe: The Case of Poland', *Brookings Papers on Economic Activity: 1* (Washington: The Brookings Institution).

Lipton, D. and Sachs, J. (1990b), 'Privatization in Eastern Europe: The Case of Poland', *Brookings Papers on Economic Activity: 2* (Washington: The Brookings Institution).

Marer, P. (1990), 'Pitfalls in Transferring Market-Economy Experiences to the European Economies in Transition', paper presented at the Conference on the Transition to a Market Economy in Central and Eastern Europe, November (Paris: Organization for Economic Cooperation and Development and World Bank).

McKinnon, R. I. (1991), *The Order of Economic Liberalization: Financial Control in the Transition to a Market Economy* (forthcoming).

Portes, R. (ed.) (1990), 'Economic Transformation of Hungary and Poland', reports prepared by a group of independent experts, *European Economy*, No. 43 (March) 2–218.

Wolf, T. A. (1990), 'Macroeconomic Adjustment and Reform in Planned Economies', IMF Working Paper 90/27, Washington: International Monetary Fund, April.

17

The Internationalization of Business and the Challenge of East European Development

Neil Hood and Stephen Young

Introduction

This chapter sets out to examine the characteristics of the foreign direct investment which has been beginning to flow to Czechoslovakia, Hungary and Poland since the commencement of the economic reforms over the past few years. It also relates these investment trends to the underlying theory of international production and to the decision processes which determine international market entry and development modes. The three countries cited have been chosen since progress towards reforms has been most substantial in these cases, but many of the principles which emerge are likely to apply in other parts of Eastern Europe.

It would be possible to regard the accelerating pace of the internationalization of business and the opening up of the Eastern European economies as not being directly related. This perspective would see Eastern Europe being slowly absorbed into international trade with no particular degree of urgency. However, there is a high level of expectation that the resources of international corporations will require to make a vital and early contribution to the economic restructuring of these countries, particularly since it involves the privatization of existing industries and the transition to the market system. Moreover, at the geopolitical level, there is a recognition that it is in the wider European (and global) interest to integrate the Eastern European economies, primarily through the processes of the internationalization of business rather than through extensive aid transfers, given the scale and severity of the transformation required.[1] This set of considerations has as much to do with both potential social and political unrest and population migration, as it does with emerging markets. Expressed another way, there are particularly pressing reasons for the reconciliation of the company-specific and the country-specific interests, as the former responds to an emerging market opportunity and the latter seeks to sustain a radical process of transformation.

It is towards a tentative assessment of the way these two processes are beginning to be related, that this chapter is addressed. The first section briefly sets out the country-specific characteristics of Eastern Europe, while the second moves on to the company-specific considerations initially through an examination of some of the conceptual issues underlying foreign direct investment; then by considering the choice of market entry modes, before subsequently examining the evidence of corporate strategies currently being applied in Eastern Europe. The third examines the question of reconciling country and corporate requirements, recognizing that both are undergoing different but equally profound changes. The nature of these changes is then briefly linked to EC integration and the integration of Eastern Europe through foreign investment, before drawing some overall conclusions.

Country-Specific Characteristics

While it is not the purpose of this paper to examine the Eastern European econo- mies in detail, there are some essential country-specific features which must be underlined, not least because of the influence which they bring to bear on the strategies of foreign investors. Four of the most critical are examined in this section.[2]

The first is to recall that the dissolution of the former central planning systems and their replacement by new structures, economic institutions and appropriate policy instruments, pose very complex problems of transition. This complexity has to be superimposed on the political risks associated with these changes. Together they create formidable obstacles to the early emergence of an environment which remotely relates to the experience of many Western or Eastern businesses.[3] While it is relatively easy to conceptualize the phasing of reform (Fig. 17.1), the reality is much more complex, not least because of the high degree of interdependence between the three aspects of reform shown. Even if the company-specific aspects of this alone are considered and the macroeconomic dimensions are left aside, transition has many dimensions and uncertainties. Many of these have a direct bearing on the decision-making processes of a potential foreign investor who invariably has much experience of operating in different economic climates, but who also has options as to where to invest. These uncertainties include the abol- ition of controls over the marketing of an enterprise's output, the relaxation or removal of controls over prices, granting enterprises the right to make their own investment decisions, liberalization of imports, legal reform on issues regarding company creation, property rights, contract, and so on. Self-evidently all these changes cannot happen overnight and in several instances, especially in Czecho- slovakia, Hungary and Poland, major steps have been taken with a recognition of the need for systematic, sustained and radical reform – although there are often serious implementation lags. Clearly all these issues apply to business enterprise of any kind, independent of size or nationality of ownership. But there is scope for arguing that the greater need is that of emerging indigenous business, given the scale of the change required and the experience of major international companies in different environments together with their ability to negotiate their own entry conditions, provided the basic framework is in place. However, the evidence

PHASING OF REFORM

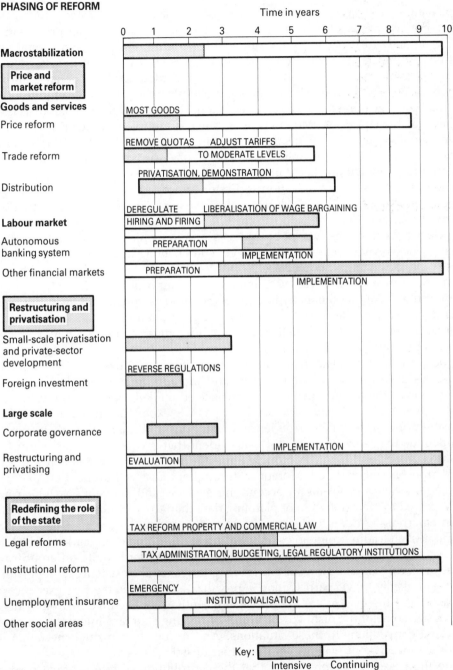

Fig. 17.1. Phasing of reform.

Source: World Bank

already suggests that the differential is in favour of the foreign rather than the indigenous.

The second issue which must be considered is the role which privatization appears destined to play in most of these economies as a pivotal means of

implementing transition. Given the paucity of reliable inward investment data, and
the recent occurrence of these events, it is impossible to say whether privatization
will eventually turn out to be the dominant mode by which foreign capital and
technology impacts upon Eastern Europe. What is clear is that at this stage, and
from the point of view of the host country, it is regarded as a basic policy platform
largely because of the profound economic, political and social change required and
the total package of resource which international businesses can transfer in as they
implement their projects. Moreover it is being strongly encouraged by Western
governments and financial institutions such as the IMF and the World Bank,
because it is probably the only possible way of ensuring the quantum change
which is required within state enterprises.

The possibilities for privatization in Eastern Europe on a significant scale will
depend on many variables, not least on the establishment of the ownership of the
assets concerned. Related to this is the shape of legislation regarding business,
especially as regards the type of business association which is permitted. Privatization agencies have been set up under general enabling legislation to implement
these processes while working closely with Western merchant banking companies,
but the processes themselves were initiated without a financial infrastructure to
support them. Among the many imponderables in these privatizations is the issue
of taxation. To some degree this is because the programme is often associated with
general tax reform, but it is also the case that different tax conditions might emerge
for privatized and other firms.

One of the most fundamental privatization issues is the question of valuation of
the assets of businesses offered for sale and the appropriate capital structure to
bring them to the market. Even in a sophisticated market economy, the valuation
of state assets can be a controversial issue, as UK experience has demonstrated.
The absence of appropriate experience, institutions and financial markets merely
compounds the problem. Indeed it was evident that several of the early privatizations in Poland and Hungary brought almost no revenue to the state budgets and
were probably undervalued. Moreover, throughout Eastern Europe there are profound underlying problems of accounting systems and conventions which are
more geared to the generation of planning data than to determining the real profit
of an enterprise. Added to this are the valuation difficulties arising from the fact
that almost all leading companies only existed to serve Comecon markets which in
themselves were artificial, with prices and quality standards quite different from
those of world markets. None of this is to argue against the existence of opportunities for market entry via participation in privatization – indeed the very existence of
the asset and the market are the principal incentives for the investor. But it does
emphasize some of the distinctive features of relating standard international practices and conventions to these situations. And it does herald the expectation of
continued public controversy over the values of state assets.

The third issue to emphasize is that the contribution of international corporations is being made within an economic environment which has been largely
bypassed by most internationalization processes for some forty years. Moreover,
any modest internationalization which did occur was not initiated by enterprise
level decisions, but within the state bureaucracy at the macro level. This in turn has
led to a marked lack of ability to deliver change in international commercial relations at either level, as experience over the last decade has shown. Poland

provides a salutory example of this in the implementation lag for the economic reform programme announced in 1981. In spite of the major underlying pressures of hard currency debts of around $40 billion (much of which is gradually being written off), the dependence of enterprises on imports from the West and the need to accelerate private inward capital flows, international business relations are still largely determined through the hierarchic, centrally organized system, and success in changing this has been very limited.[4] Of course there have been examples of contractual co-operation. One study[5] identified ninety-nine of these in the mid-1980s, a third of which involved transnational corporations, with these accounting for some 80 per cent of turnover, although in total their overall contribution to the economy was not large. More recently, since 1986, equity co-operation has been encouraged and this may well accelerate the technological development of companies and their overseas orientation.

The fourth issue is particularly fundamental to the subject of this chapter. Many companies in Eastern Europe are readily categorized as 'value subtractors', in that at world prices the value of the resources which they consume is worth more than what they produce. For manufacturing industries, both artificial energy prices and captive customers have combined to create this position, from which many companies are unlikely to recover irrespective of efficiency gains. One study[6] has estimated that between 20 and 25 per cent of manufacturing industries in Poland, Czechoslovakia and Hungary could be value subtractors. In specific terms it concluded, for example, that the food, tobacco and leather industries of Czechoslovakia, the Hungarian iron and steel industry, and the Polish basic chemical, cement and non-ferrous metallurgy industries could be so regarded. Clearly the lack of accounting data mentioned previously makes such estimates difficult and merely compounds the valuation challenge for a potential foreign investor. But the value added question does point strongly to the view that many basic businesses in these three economies will not find buyers from any source. From the perspective of the foreign enterprise, this will in turn create opportunities either for exports to these markets, or, in some cases, for greenfield investments – unless the governments concerned restrict imports and refuse to permit direct investment. For the respective governments, the outcome will be business closures and rising unemployment.

Against the background outlined in this section, it is important to stress the recent, and in some cases tentative, nature of the reforms which are now underway in Eastern Europe. Foreign investment can clearly only be part of any given set of solutions, and may be most important as a catalyst. If parallels are to be drawn from other countries, the bulk of investment in Eastern Europe will be financed by domestic savings. This remains the case in industrialized countries which have both easy access to international capital markets and a long history of direct foreign investment. Moreover, in many developing economies inflows of foreign capital are equivalent to less than 10 per cent of domestic savings. Even under rapid reforms and optimistic assumptions, estimates[7] would suggest that Eastern Europe as a whole might attract some $7 billion direct foreign investment per annum by 1995, as against some $1 billion of actual spend in 1991. In short, the processes of internationalization even in this particular situation can only be regarded as a contributor to the transition and reform programmes, and as a result the expectations of all parties have to be appropriately tempered.

Company-specific Considerations

Concepts

From the perspective of the company, there are two basic questions to address: namely why would international enterprises consider entering into investment in Eastern Europe at this stage? and second, what investment strategies and priorities would they be expected to display? While the first of these can readily be considered in terms of existing theoretical work, the second can only be tentatively examined on the basis of the early evidence. There are simply no historical precedents for what these three countries are endeavouring to do as they plan to privatize 40–50 per cent of their economies within a five-year period.[8]

The eclectic paradigm[9] is one of most widely accepted frameworks to explain the internationalization of business. It sets out to explain the extent, form and pattern of international production, which it views as relying on three distinct sets of advantages. The first set is ownership-specific advantages (O). While these could take many forms and there could be many characteristics of a firm which enable it to develop international production, they are often seen as falling into two categories, viewed respectively as having their origin in structural and transactional market imperfections. In Eastern Europe, both may be uniquely important in stressing the role which multinational corporations will play in transformation. On the structural side, the advantages of simply being multinational, with all that entails in terms of capital, technology, management and networks, are powerful, especially where there are indigenous businesses with low cost, skilled workforces and good technology, to be joint venture partners. As regards transaction costs, these are artificially high by world standards, given the regulatory regime in which business has existed and the presence of severe market distortions, including artificial prices, raw material allocation systems, arbitrary investment criteria and so on. The internalization of these as between parts of a multinational business network is likely to yield significantly lower transaction costs, although some of these distortions are at the macro level and not readily internalized. The presumption here of course, is, that the international company can either negotiate with the government concerned to be able to minimize the costs associated with inefficiencies and blockages in its business environment, or so transfer its own corporate culture as to offset these to some degree. Clearly both of these remain open questions.

This leads to the second set of advantages which are associated specifically with internalization (I), namely the international company's ability to transfer the O advantages across national boundaries within its own organization, rather than exploiting these advantages by selling them in the market. Clearly many international businesses have experience both of achieving these transfers within very different environments and of using quite different business modes of operation. At the moment, the predominant relationship in Eastern Europe is the joint venture (or some other form of partnership) or acquisition of a state-owned company. Joint ventures tend to predominate where they are enforced by host country regulations, and are not ideal ways of transferring O advantages. In East Europe the preference of both parties lies in this direction, but for different reasons. For the company, opportunity dominates, while for the country, reform and transition are leading variables. From the perspective of the foreign enterprise, some of the principal risks to be evaluated are associated with the ability to internalize an East European operation and make it subject to the same business disciplines and culture which underpin its competitive position elsewhere. Of course, it much depends on whether the product is designed for internal consumption or for export markets, given the gross undersupply in many product areas. Such situations could readily lead to a level of inefficiency being tolerated, at least for a period until the full internationalization effects can be realized – as they must be from the recipient economies' perspective, given the chronic need for hard currency and foreign trade to offset the losses in Comecon markets.

The third and final set of advantages within the eclectic paradigm are locational (L) and can favour a home or a host country. These are often viewed as both structural and transactional. As far as structural locational advantages are concerned, these cover all factor costs. In the East European context, lower labour costs would appear to be attracting certain types of business, but this could readily be offset by the continuance of lower levels of productivity which have character-ized these economies. In this case the O, I and L advantages will need to be carefully balanced. Moreover, other factor costs offer little benefit, with capital costs being high (around 25–40 per cent interest rates) and supply low. There has been much debate not so much about land costs, as about land tenure and hence availability. The factor cost situation is further compounded by spiralling levels of inflation in all three countries. Taking all of this together, there is little doubt that factor costs alone will not be sufficient to enhance the investment flows to Eastern Europe. However, the transactional dimension of locational advantages gives every evidence of being a dominant consideration. In this category are advantages of specific locations which offer the firm enhanced leverage opportunities and lead to early strategic investments in such markets. For example, there have been substantial opportunities to buy into companies with very high market shares in basic commodities, as part of privatization – as in the case of Proctor and Gamble purchasing Rakona in Czechoslovakia, a company with 60 per cent of the deter-gents market. Again, the seller's market in consumer products such as domestic appliances has led to intense competition to purchase market access.

One important aspect of location-specific variables should be stressed. Within the EC it is widely recognized that much inward investment from international companies is the subject of extensive (though regulated), competitive bidding through the use of investment incentives employed as instruments of regional policy. Clearly such incentives or disincentives can change the relative attractive-ness of different host countries for certain projects. In Eastern Europe there will be very few financial inducements available, beyond tax holidays. The competition to attract investment is therefore likely to remain largely based on the market oppor-tunities available, the existence of suitable partners at an acceptable purchase price, and the overall medium-term attractiveness of the business environment, includ-ing input prices, quality and productivity. In essence this places Eastern European countries in a more reactive and less proactive mode than has been normal in other disadvantaged areas in Europe, and interest is likely for some time to remain on a privatization-led strategy rather than that of targeting greenfield projects in the manner adopted by, for example, Ireland or Spain. Progressively, however, it is to be expected that when the privatization phase is over, there will be intense competition for new prestige projects in Eastern Europe and the former USSR. Already some areas are promoting export-processing zones and special economic development areas.

The foregoing paragraphs have suggested that the eclectic paradigm, in spite of some of the operational limitations which it has given the growing complexity of the variables in the OLI format, provides some pointers towards forming an understanding of the internationalization processes as they might apply to Eastern Europe. But there are other concepts which are equally useful. One of these is the internationalization model initially associated with the Uppsala School in Sweden.[10] This regards internationalization as a gradual process involving an interplay between the development of knowledge about foreign markets and operations on the one hand and an increasing commitment of resources to foreign markets on the other. In the light of the Eastern European environment it might well be expected that the preponderance of projects from international interests would reflect this iterative approach. The model implies that this will generally be a 'small step' process, except where the firm has large resources or related market experience which enables it to evaluate the true risks involved. Moreover, it presumes that firms progressively enter new markets with successively greater psychic distance – defined in terms of differences in language, culture, environment, and so on. In the context of the three countries in Eastern Europe which are being considered here, this model might predict that a large volume of small projects would, other things being equal, come from adjacent countries and cultures where investors already have experience of both the markets and the general environment. The Uppsala model, while useful, is clearly very partial and excludes many relevant explanatory factors which may underlie internationalization processes. This has led to others[11] relating these processes to the concept of industrial networks, emphasizing the uniqueness of these in different sectoral, technological and market environments. Again this is a crucial dimension of the East European situation, where Comecon networks have been the principal (or sole) experience of many enterprises and where foreign investment often appears to offer the only possible opportunity to enter new networks within the required timescale.

It must be acknowledged, however, that the circumstances in Eastern Europe which have recently confounded expectations in so many respects, also pose a considerable challenge to the theories of foreign direct investment. There are two principal reasons for this. First, such theories have only recently addressed the role of international mergers and acquisitions in the light of the changing patterns of international involvement and the lesser emphasis placed on greenfield investments. As market entry strategies have changed and become much more diverse, so the theoretical framework has been (belatedly) revisited. Second, in the East European environment at this stage, the acquisition/partnership route is almost the only one available to foreign investors and it is the outcome of a privatization process. Looked at from a traditional theoretical standpoint, there is therefore a bounded choice of market entry strategy and hence the trade-offs between costs, risks and control have to be measured within a relatively narrow band of options. In many cases the decision is simple, in that there is no practical alternative but to acquire.

In this context, much of the theoretical work undertaken elsewhere is not particularly helpful. For example, it has been suggested that companies which internationalize as latecomers within their industry have a greater propensity to acquire than those which are more experienced in international business.[12] Although it is too early to draw definite conclusions, the opposite may be true in Eastern Europe, in that many major international companies have acquired early strategic positions in these markets. Other theoretical work[13] has sought to explain international acquisitions in terms of the existence of a 'valuation gap', whether expressed in financial or information terms. There is a case for perhaps arguing that this concept has something to say about the Eastern European situation, in that such is the size of the gap in many industries that no other mode of market transaction with the local business would be possible other than acquisition, given the necessity to gain I advantages – even if that were not the government's preferred (or required) method of involvement. Of course, there are other reasons for this being the case, namely where acquisition is regarded as a pre-emptive strike, simply because it allows the internalization of markets for the acquiring firm and precludes this for others.[14]

Although this discussion has been focused on international acquisitions, it should be recalled that there is a wealth of literature on success and failure of acquisitions, irrespective of the environment and business conditions, and much empirical work on their performance.[15] There is every reason to think that the balance of probability points to many major problems arising as an acquisition/partnership approach is implemented in Eastern Europe, especially when the evidence on the strategic, organizational and managerial fit of successful acquisitions is borne in mind. It will inevitably be difficult to determine fully the potential correctness of fit in many privatization cases, in spite of processes of due diligence being undertaken in the conventional manner.

This section has been exclusively concerned with the motivation which might underlie international business investment in Eastern Europe, based on a number of accepted concepts. While these do offer some insights and aid in certain aspects of interpreting trends, they are inevitably partial and invariably do not provide strong predictors of the market entry modes or specific corporate strategies which might emerge in this particular situation. The next two sections are therefore directed to these two issues.

Market entry modes

When examining some of the choices which have been made by foreign investors in Eastern Europe to date, it is particularly useful to distinguish between market servicing methods in terms of risk and control, especially in the light of many aspects of the previous section. Table 17.1 provides one of many ways of classifying international business arrangements with these parameters in view. The progression is from export modes through the range of contractual modes to direct investment. To a degree, the final grouping, namely coalitions and strategic alliances, is difficult to categorize in terms of risk and control, since much will depend on the nature of the agreement as to what is actually involved for each party. Moreover, it could involve any of the first three categories in the table, but particularly licensing and contractual and equity joint ventures.

Table 17.1: Foreign market entry modes.

1. *Export entry modes*
    (a) indirect
    (b) direct agent/distributor
    (c) direct branch/subsidiary

2. *Contractual entry modes*
    (a) licensing
    (b) franchising
    (c) management contracts
    (d) turnkey contracts
    (e) contract manufacturing/international subcontracting
    (f) collaboration agreements

3. *Investment entry modes*
    (a) wholly-owned/majority-owned: new establishment
    (b) wholly-owned/majority-owned: acquisition
    (c) joint venture: new establishment/acquisition

4. *Corporate coalitions and strategic alliances*

Source: Young, S., et al. (1989) *International Market Entry and Development: Strategies and Management*, Hemel Hempstead: Harvester Wheatsheaf.

It is evident that all of the modes of involvement in Table 17.1 can be found in Eastern Europe. For example, until the mid-1980s, exports and the sale of licences constituted the dominant form of foreign involvement. Meanwhile exports remain the predominant mode of entry. Historically, however, many of the more substantial arrangements between foreign investors and governments or enterprises were variants within category 2f. These industrial co-operation agreements (ICAs) have taken many forms and involve several dimensions of categories 1 and 2. They frequently were linked to either counter-trade or counter-purchase agreements, and to co-production, where the foreign investor supplied technology, components and other inputs in return for a share of the output. At the present time it is not easy to fit the new emerging relationships with foreign investors into any one category. While many of them are in categories 3b and 3c, some appear to also have dimensions of 2f, in that there are undertakings of various types to invest in the acquisition, develop the business in certain directions, remain in partnership with the government, and so on. In reality many of the joint ventures involving foreign partners operate as wholly-owned subsidiaries. As has been already observed, much of this is opportunity-led and, while it may appear to be a constrained choice from among the options in Table 17.1, this conclusion should not be too hastily drawn. What is clear is that at present there are few investments in category 3a, but as has been noted, this is likely to emerge in due course. Neither is category 4 much in evidence, although many of the acquiring investors bring a network of alliances with them, and their full impact on East European ventures will become clear only when the new operations develop a solid record of performance.

As was suggested in the previous section on the internalization concept, there are some open questions about how I advantages are gained in joint ventures and collaborative arrangements. The theory has conventionally assumed that these are a less efficient means of operating internationally than wholly-owned subsidiaries. One of the arguments in support of that view is that, while the foreign enterprise would gain local knowledge through such an arrangement, it might also lose because of the danger of its proprietary knowledge being exploited elsewhere. In East Europe, it could be argued that the indigenous base is so weak and the inherited systems so ineffective, that such potential diffusion is likely to be limited. Moreover, the potential loss on the part of the foreign enterprise in these early stages is less likely to be through technology diffusion than through underestimating the need for change in the acquired company, the development of markets, and so on. It should, in addition, be noted that in the East European case, the equity interest of the foreign enterprise are invariably dominant, thus further offering the positive gains from internalization in due course.

Investment trends

It will be evident from the previous sections that the strategies of foreign enterprises in these three economies will be determined by the interaction of both company-specific and country-specific variables. At this stage it is often difficult to determine the relative importance of these two sets of variables, since this will be dependent to a large degree on factors such as the prior experience of the partners in joint operations, the risks involved in particular projects, the terms on which the assets are made available for investment, and so on. In many cases the two sets of interests are finely balanced. In order to begin to analyse how these might shape the nature of foreign investment, Table 17.2 advances a series of propositions and sets out some overall judgement as to whether company or country issues appear to dominate at this early developmental stage. Clearly many of the country-specific variables have to be taken by the companies as a point of departure on a transition route, the end of which is uncertain. The company on the other hand has more choice. The propositions which emerge are based on the partial evidence of the principal characteristics of the investment to date.

Before looking at the strategies which are emerging in detail, several issues should be borne in mind. First, the terms and conditions for foreign investment have only recently been established – in Poland in 1989, Hungary in 1990 and Czechoslovakia in 1991 – and even now there remain considerable numbers of unresolved issues, as case evidence accumulates. Second, there is no comprehensive data source on what is actually happening on the ground. In this context there is a need, for example, to distinguish between the announcement of an agreement, its date of operational commencement, and the declared value of the deal, since it invariably involves foreign equity purchase plus a commitment of some kind to refinancing and redeveloping the acquired company or partner. It is currently very difficult to make these distinctions in practice and hence the actual impact of foreign investment is less clear than the declared intention behind it. Third, there is inevitably a considerable level of caution on the part of many of the investing business to be too precise about their plans, not least because of their inexperience in operating in Eastern European environments.

Bearing these considerations in mind, Table 17.2 introduces five sets of related

Table 17.2: Propositions regarding international business investment in Eastern Europe.

	Company factor	Country factor
1. *Commitment*		
• Average level of investment per project would be low	×	×
• Large volume of small projects, directed to local services	×	×
2. *Country of origin*		
• Predominant sources for small projects would be adjacent Western economies	×	
• All major fdi source countries for large projects	×	
3. *Industry sector*		
• Limited number of large scale investments		
– in basic industries, often where large market shares possible (food, glass, cement, detergents, chemicals)		×
– in strategic industries (telecomms, utilities, automobiles, hotels)		×
– in expectation of emerging consumer markets (electronic products, appliances)		×
• Few investments in heavy and defence related industries	×	×
• Significant numbers of projects attracted by low wage costs	×	×
• Large numbers of industries will attract no foreign investment interest		×
4. *Mode of entry*		
• Predominantly through privatization schemes as government preferred entry mode		×
• Mainly joint venture partnerships		×
• Relatively few greenfield operations	×	
5. *Market orientation*		
• Largely for domestic consumption in initial years in most projects	×	
• Emergence as export platform for former Comecon markets in selected sectors		×

propositions which would appear to hold at this early stage in the transition process, and each of these are now considered in turn.

Commitment

Two distinct processes have to be considered under this heading, namely small and large privatizations. Although the former comprise very large numbers of local shops, restaurants, garages and so on, they have been directed primarily to smaller-scale local investors or returning nationals. The large privatizations only began to gain any momentum in 1991, although, as shall be noted later, a number of strategic foreign investors cut through the preparation stages at an early date. However, when the data are examined, there are large numbers of registered companies in Hungry (some 5,000) and Poland (some 3,000) with foreign share-holders, most of which are very small, many being little more than shell companies. In terms of published data associated with the early stages of reform, it would appear that as a result, the average foreign capital contribution is modest. For example, in Poland, between January 1989 and December 1990, the average was $134,000 against a legal minimum commitment of $50,000. This tends to suggest a considerable level of risk aversion on the part of foreign investors, but the vast majority of these investors are not international companies in any event. Where relevant, in this area the company and the country factors are almost of equal importance.

Country of origin

It would appear that the small foreign projects mentioned in the previous section are largely from relatively local businesses in adjacent countries, who already have detailed market knowledge. For example, by January 1991 some 1,600 small-scale foreign joint ventures had been registered in Czechoslovakia, over 50 per cent of which were of Austrian or German origin. Similarly, in Poland some 32 per cent of the 4,300 registered foreign joint ventures up to June 1991 were from Germany. It is quite probable that this rapidly growing number of small-scale investments from surrounding countries will prove to be both a critical capital source and a catalyst to encourage individual entrepreneurial effort in these economies. As such its role should not be underestimated.

At the level of the major investments, as evidenced in Table 17.3 for projects where the commitment is $80 million or above, the range of countries of origin is much wider. These reflect investment decisions by large multinational companies and are in the mainstream of internationalization processes. A similarly wide range of countries of origin emerges in Table 17.4 in the case of the food industry.

Whether in the large or small investments, the dominance of company-specific assessment and risk evaluation skills is acknowledged in both these propositions.

Industry sector

The evidence seems to point to three principal groups of industries attracting foreign direct investment from major companies. First there is the basic industries group, where there is much opportunity to address immediate needs in response both to consumer preference and the needs of industrial reconstruction. For example, in the food and drink industry (Table 17.4) opportunities have been taken to acquire market share, since production has been highly concentrated, with single local companies having as much as two-thirds of the sales of products such as confectionery and beverages. Moreover, early entry by Western companies allows brand loyalty to be established in markets which have largely been cut off from traditional marketing techniques and where there are many possibilities for new products to be introduced. In this basic industries category, but much less visible, are industries such as glass, cement, detergents and chemicals, all of which have been actively pursued. The second group are classified as strategic largely

Table 17.3: Large international business investments in Czechoslovakia, Hungary and Poland, 1989–91.

Home country	Investor	Partner	Industry	Commitment[a] ($ m)
Germany	Volkswagen	Skoda, Baz (C)	Cars	6,630
US	Dow Europe	Sokolov (C)	Chemicals	200
France	CBS	Tourinvest (C)	Hotels	175
US	Gen. Electric	Tungsram (H)	Lighting	150
US	Gen. Motors	Raba (H)	Engines, Cars	150
		BAZ (C)	Engines, Cars	150
UK	Pilkington	HSO Sandomierz (P)	Glass	140
US	Guardian	Hungarian Glass (H)	Glass	120
Japan	Suzuki	Autokonzem (H)	Cars	110
Germany	Linde	Technoplyn (C)	Gases	106
Sweden	Electrolux	Lehel (H)	Appliances	83
Austria	Hamburger	Dunapack (H)	Packaging	82
US	Ford	New plant (H)	Car components	80
France	Sanofi	Chinoin (H)	Pharmaceuticals	80
US	US West	Czech govt. (C)	Telephones, Switches	80

Note:
[a] The figures here (and in Tables 17.4 and 17.5) should be interpreted with considerable caution as declarations of intended investment at the time the deal was stuck. The final outcome will be dependent on many variables which can only be more closely specified as the project develops. For this reason commitment figures have not been declared in many projects

because of the implications which they have for the infrastructure or the industrial structure and earning power of the economies concerned. They include telecommunications, utilities, hotels and, most notably, automobiles. In the latter case, this was the earliest industry to attract strong foreign interest, with Volkswagen taking majority control of Skoda in Czechoslovakia, committing itself to using the name as its fourth marque and planning a large-scale development programme for the company. Both Ford and GM, meanwhile, are building new factories in Hungary as some of the few examples of agreed greenfield investments to date. In this industry the local and export market potential, together with the engineering base and low labour costs, are clearly major incentives for strategic investment which, as Table 17.5 shows, have already taken quite different forms across the three economies.

One of the most active areas of foreign interest has undoubtedly been hotels, with all the larger cities being overwhelmed by project enquiries due to the shortage of supply and poor quality of existing provision. Equally, hotel privatizations have attracted much attention, not least because of very public disputes about the difference between asset and business valuations. This strategic group extends to most aspects of the infrastructure, as evidenced, for example, by Hungary's invitation for tenders for foreign capital for private toll roads and the Czechoslovakian plans to privatize Transgas, the main trunk gas pipeline which runs through the country from the former Soviet Union to Western Europe. Moreover, there is growing evidence of 'follow the leader' investments. For example, in the media

Table 17.4: Food and drink industry investments in Eastern Europe, 1989–91.

Investor	Partner	Sector	Purpose[a] of deal	Commitment[b] ($m)
BSN (France)	Benesov Dairy (Czech)	Dairy	Joint venture to produce Danone yogurt	N.A.
BSN/Nestlé (Switzerland)	Cokoladovny (Czech)	Chocs, Biscuits	Planned acquisition of joint stake	N.A.
Jacobs/Suchard (US/Switz)	Budapest Edespiari Vallalat (Hungary)	Coffee, Confectionery	Joint venture	N.A.
Nestlé (Switzerland)	Intescsokolade (Hungary)	Chocs	Acquisition of 97%	N.A.
PepsiCo (US)	Wedel (Poland)	Chocs	Acquisition of 40%	$25 m
Sara Lee (US)	Compack Trading & Packing (Hungary)	Beverages, Household products	Acquisition of 40%	$60 m
Tate & Lyle (UK)	Hajdusai Cukorgyar (Hungary)	Sugar, foods	Acquisition of 34.4%	£10 m
United Biscuits (UK)	Gyori Keksz	Biscuits	Acquisition of 84%	N.A.

Notes:
[a] It should be explained that irrespective of the quoted equity proportions, many of these deals are structured in a way which gives the foreign investor effective control.
[b] See Note to Table 17.3.

Table 17.5: Automobile investments in Czechoslovakia, Poland and Hungary, 1989–91.

Investor	Partner	Project	Commitment[a] ($m)
General Motors	BAZ (C)	Opel Kadetts for local market and transmissions for export	150
	RABA (H)	Opel Kadetts and engines (67% stake)	150
	Villszov (H)	Auto wiring parts (60% stake)	N/A
Volkswagen	Skoda (C)	Modernise and increase production from 180,000 to 400,000 units (70% stake)	6,000
Fiat	FSM (P)	Car production in exchange for parts and equipment (estimated to be worth $650 m)	N/A
Renault	BAZ (C)	Production of up to 30,000 Trafic vans	N/A
Ford	(H)	Ignition and fuel system parts (new subsidiary)	80
Suzuki	Autokonszem (H)	Production of 105,000 Swift sub-components (30% stake)	46

Note:
[a] See Note on Table 17.3.
Source: Morawetz, R. (1991) *Recent foreign direct investment in Eastern Europe*, Working Paper No. 71, Geneva: ILO.

and newsprint area, the early investments in Hungary by News Corporation and Maxwell Communications have led to the subsequent involvement of Robert Hersant, Axel Springer, Bertelsmann and others in these industries.

There is little doubt, in view of the need to channel savings to productive uses, that one of the greatest infrastructural needs is for financial institutions. In the short term, in the absence of an effective stock exchange, this requires foreign banking methodology and participation. For example, the Poles have been pursuing a 'twinning' system between many of their banks and Western banks, aided by the international Finance Corporation (World Bank). This involves the taking of small equity stakes in Polish banks. However, while all three countries have allowed private banks to invest, and the numbers having offices have grown, the investments remain small. Equally, although there have been several capital funds raised for East European investment, most have found it difficult to identify viable investments.[16]

There are fewer examples of the third category in Table 17.2, where substantial investments have been made in consumer products, especially durables. Clearly there is a considerable latent demand for these products, but relatively few quality companies available for acquisition. This is a widespread problem and even at this early stage, selective investments by foreign partners have already picked up most of the prime candidates where profitability and short- to medium-term potential have been readily identified. Within this particular industry grouping, few companies have featured in the largest deals in Table 17.3. It is suggested in Table 17.2 that country factors dominate in determining the specific areas for investment choice, largely because the industry structure and performance, plus the early market opportunities, are overriding considerations.

The final three industry-related propositions in Table 17.2 require only brief comment. There is little sign of foreign interest in any real scale in either the heavy industrial sectors (excluding certain chemical and glass projects) or those which are defence-related. Many of the former are seriously run down, in sectors where there is overcapacity elsewhere or in which the value-subtracting problem is particularly severe. As to the latter, the requirement for rationalization, diversification or reorientation clearly comes at a time when major defence contractors worldwide are reassessing their strategies in the light of radically different prospects for defence spending. Neither of these areas are likely, therefore, to be attractive to foreign investors in the early rounds, and this is generally recognized in the lists of companies which have been put on offer in all three countries. As for the attractiveness of low wage costs, this is clearly only a meaningful incentive if productivity can be increased substantially and its net effect will much depend on the individual project and sector. However, it does have the potential in principle to form a base for lower-cost supply to the EC. Finally, and of particular concern, there is the likelihood that there will be no foreign investment interest in very large tracts of East European industry for country-specific reasons, and the State in various forms will require to continue to be closely involved with them.

While it is possible to cite some evidence of flows of foreign direct investment in many of the industrial sectors set out in Table 17.2, the nature of the inherited problems and the scale of change within these invested companies should be stressed. Moreover, the actual achievements of privatization via capital from multinational enterprises has been slow, not least because of the faltering process of transition to a market economy and the inherent instabilities of prices, exchange rates and government finances.

Mode of entry

All three of the propositions in Table 17.2 would seem to be consistently borne out in the three economies, with the first two being shaped principally by local country conditions. While several of the largest foreign projects predated the finalization of privatization procedures, they were negotiated in anticipation of their existence. While the end product is largely joint venture, the approach now being pursued by the three countries to achieve this is different. Both Poland and Czechoslovakia have mass privatization programmes, albeit of different types. When Poland announced the first major wave of privatization in June 1991, this involved some 25 per cent of the industrial sales and 12 per cent of total employment in the economy. It is anticipated that 60 per cent of the equity in companies will go into between five and twenty National Wealth Management Funds, with the state retaining 30 per cent and employees being given 10 per cent stakes. Although these funds will be chaired locally, the day-to-day management will be by Western banks and fund managers – thus raising some interesting new local dimensions of investor relations for the acquiring international company. In contrast, the Czechoslovakian programme, equally concerned about local ownership and equity, involves selling vouchers to the population at large and using these to buy shares in companies of their choosing as these are privatized.

The Hungarian approach has been quite different, in that it was the first of the East European economies to move into reforms via 'spontaneous privatization' which allowed the state managers to initiate the conversion and sale of their own factories from 1989. This is turn led to a considerable volume of privatization and associated foreign investment. However, this system was widely criticized and was open to abuse, hence the government took direct control of the State Property Agency (SPA) and moved ahead in a more deliberate and transparent manner, but with less interest in mass equity participation.

It is not easy to be accurate about the net effect of these methods on foreign investor sentiment. Of the three countries, for environmental, political and historical reasons, Hungary has attracted the most foreign direct investment. This is estimated at over $1.5 billion in 1991, which probably doubled the stock at the end of 1990. Various estimates suggest that investment in Poland and Czechoslovakia may now be running at a rate of some $0.5 billion per annum. The total for all of Eastern Europe in 1990 probably did not exceed $1.2 billion, and so while there is evidence of growth, it is not yet dramatic. However, for reasons noted previously, all these figures must be treated with considerable caution. What is clear is that they primarily constitute joint venture partnerships and involve few greenfield operations. The latter may be expected to emerge with increasing frequency, and it is evident that the foreign investment agencies in the three countries are handling growing volumes of inquiries for this mode of entry, often associated with existing acquisitions or partnerships. Several factors are likely to influence the timing of this phase, including the performance of existing acquisitions, both the stability and the liberalization of markets, and the economic performance of both the individual country and the region as a whole. Here the company-specific perspective on these events as they unfold will be critical in placing these economies on the agenda of greenfield investors.

Market orientation

This is a particularly difficult issue to evaluate at this stage, since most foreign companies have been cautious about publicly committing themselves to market strategies. Many of the indigenous partners selected have either mainly produced for domestic markets or for Comecon. It is evident that all three governments are particularly anxious to see international companies play a major role in export-led growth to offset the Comecon losses, but many of the major industry acquisitions do not have substantial short-term export potential. In this regard, corporate opinion is a key issue. At the same time there has been much market skimming by foreign investors and, by entering into partnerships with the best performers in each sector and country, it is clear that some strong export performances will emerge if productivity and competitiveness can be enhanced at an early date. In this instance the general stability and management of the economies will be an important country-specific consideration in leading to the establishment of export platforms.

While it is clearly not yet possible to make any judgement on the outcome of these investment decisions, it is worth considering some of the evidence which does exist from elsewhere on the performance of foreign direct investment involving joint ventures and acquisitions. As has been observed, there are reasons for contending that the East European situation is unique in many regards, but not totally so. For example, the evidence elsewhere suggests that there are two particular considerations which frequently impact on joint venture performance, namely partner symmetry and management arrangements. As regards the former, partner size or resource complementarity have been shown to be important, with similar asset size having a positive impact on joint venture performance,[17] although other evidence has failed to relate joint venture stability to size differences.[18] On the subject of types of management arrangement, the evidence does not suggest that any one type of control is exclusively associated with success, whether in developed or developing countries;[19] nor is there any clear evidence that joint ventures are more or less successful if they emerge from a previous history of co-operation. To some extent this type of evidence of corporate interaction offers encouragement to Eastern Europe, although the specific circumstances of partnership may well lead to particular instabilities in relationships in this case.

Finally, there are perhaps three matters associated with foreign acquisitions which should be noted. First, there is a considerable volume of evidence from Western economies that there is a positive relationship between the market share of the acquisition target firms and profitability. Some of this is of long standing[20] but has been regularly confirmed and again supports market share strategies such as are being applied in Eastern Europe. However, on the second issue to be touched upon, namely the financial state of the target firm, the evidence is less hopeful. In a Western context, poor financial health has frequently been a reason for companies being open to acquisition and hence liable to significant change at all levels when acquired. Moreover, there are grounds for believing that pre-acquisition profitability and performance after foreign acquisition are positively correlated. There is no reason to believe that this would not hold in Eastern

Europe, and this is reflected, as has already been observed, in the 'skimming' strategies which are being applied. The last issue is that of whether performance is enhanced by integration. Clearly there is no optimal degree of integration, and practice will depend entirely on the motivation of the foreign investor. While some recent evidence[21] has regarded the most effective approach to be one of partial integration (in areas such as finance and sales) and one which happens immediately following the foreign acquisition, practice varies widely. This is, however, a fundamental issue in East Europe where the requirement for integration in all respects is probably compelling in most cases, from both the company and country viewpoint. Some wider aspects of this are examined in the next section.

Companies, countries and European integration

In determining the net contribution which foreign direct investment will play in the economic development in Eastern Europe, it is evident that this will depend on the outcome of many project-specific decisions. However, at the aggregate level, it will also be dependent on the reconciliation of company and country-specific interests, not all of which will be compatible. In a distinctive sense, the transformation which is underway in Eastern Europe means that governments have a crucial role to play both in shaping country-specific advantages and in ensuring that every possible step is taken to improve the competitiveness of their economies. Without direct and sustained action to improve both, it may prove impossible to reduce the barriers which many international companies find in the transfer of their competitive advantage to Eastern Europe and hence reduce the benefits which could flow from substantial volumes of direct investment.

Against this background, there are two particular sets of forces whose outworkings are crucial to internationalization in Eastern Europe. These are respectively the current dominant forces shaping international corporate strategies and the relationship between EC integration and potential enlargement to include, in whole or part, the countries of Eastern Europe. Each of these is now considered in turn.

Foreign direct investment is not occurring in Eastern Europe within a corporate vacuum. It is taking place within a much wider context, some aspects of which are particularly relevant to the contribution which it might make to these economies. For example, international business now takes place in greater variety of forms than ever before and firms require to be flexible enough and to have the capabilities to operate in a range of methods of foreign operations.[22] As a result, trade in the conventional sense has changed dramatically, with contractual relationships between links in the value added chain overtaking arm's-length transactions between independent firms. This is reflected in the fact of some three-quarters of world trade taking place directly or indirectly between the subsidiaries of international companies. The strength of this integrating force is critical for Eastern Europe, not least because it poses the question as to how rapidly these new investments can become part of international networks, making their contribution in supplying and sourcing for the corporate entity. One crucial unknown in this is how consumers in the West will evaluate products made in Eastern Europe as a result of foreign direct investment. There are, for example, some interesting trade-offs between global brand images and country images.[23] In the immediate future, as has been noted, the demands of country-specific markets may well dominate, with the more probable prospects thereafter being supply points for either Eastern Europe and the former USSR, or for EC markets. Clearly the consequences for hard currency earnings in these alternative scenarios are a crucial matter of government interest and priority, but the outcome in individual cases will be driven largely by the short- to medium-term performance of the new joint ventures. It would be reasonable to assume that, with few exceptions, the strategic focus will only gradually move from being country-centred to fully participating in multinational integration.

Closely allied to this corporate interest in Eastern Europe are the forces shaping EC integration and enlargement. The last few years have witnessed a dramatic growth in acquisitions, mergers, rationalization schemes, and collaborative ventures of all types in preparation for the completion of the EC internal market. Until the recent opening up of Eastern Europe, this process had largely passed these economies by – even now it is difficult to claim that many of the investments considered are in any direct way part of that phenomenon. In the EC context, moreover, there has been some debate on the ways in which corporate integration might best be encouraged to promote the objectives of regional integration.[24] Among the issues to emerge, for example, is whether regional integration in Europe helps to reduce the impediments to corporate integration by European firms – rather than on the part of foreign direct investors. Indeed cross-border mergers, joint ventures, emergence of country groupings within sectors and so on have been evidence of this.

It has to be recognized that Eastern Europe is very distant from most of these processes, because of the more immediate and more fundamental tasks at hand. By no means the least of these are the employment effects of restructuring[25] and the strength of the political consensus about the role of foreign capital in that process. This in turn poses the question as to what stage EC-led corporate integration will have reached when Eastern Europe gains full membership, and how it could possibly catch up without a major growth in the internationalization processes considered in this paper. The early discussions on potential EC membership during 1990 and 1991 have already highlighted sensitivities in some member states about low-cost imports in chemicals, steel, textiles, agricultural produce and automobiles, although some progress has been made towards the relaxing of trade constraints. It is evident that low-cost sourcing strategies from foreign-owned plants in Eastern Europe will be the subject of careful scrutiny and will require consistent and delicate political handling, if the necessary gains from trade are to be realized. This may be particularly the case if, as is possible, there was to be a growing volume of acquisition or greenfield investment from Japan or other Far Eastern sources, designed to gain privileged access to the EC market.

Conclusions

The tentative evidence produced here suggests that there are already many reasons for regarding the internationalization of business and East European development as closely linked, although not yet inextricably. Investment volumes are modest and have been slow to develop. For example, the European Bank for Reconstruction and Development estimates that direct private investment in the whole of Eastern Europe in 1991 was only about $3 billion, largely because of the slow progress of large-scale privatization plans. Meanwhile progress towards freer trade with Eastern Europe, which would be essential to unlock more investment, has been slow. In addition, there are large sectors of the three economies concerned where there is little sign of interest on the part of foreign investors, and where alternative solutions which may involve foreign capital and technology in other forms, have yet to be found. The scale and method of reform, with its heavy dependence on privatization, serve only to emphasize the experimental nature of these changes and the dependence on Western know-how to implement them. There are powerful reasons for regarding Eastern Europe as a testing ground for international business, given the principles upon which it is largely founded; and given that it is being called upon to address both system failure and market failure. It remains to be seen whether the country interests and the corporate interests can be harmonized across a sufficiently broad front to make a vitally needed contribution towards East European reform.

Notes

1. The full extent of this is almost impossible to estimate. One recent attempt (Collins, S. and Rodvik, D. (1991) *Eastern Europe and the Soviet Union in the World Economy*, Washington DC: Institute for International Economics, 76-80) has suggested that to catch up with average incomes in the EC in the next decade, the six countries of Eastern Europe would require $420 billion investment per annum, some two-thirds of their current output.
2. For a full discussion of these issues see, for example, Kornai, J. (1990) *The road to a free economy*, New York: Norton; Blommestein, H. and Marrese, M. (eds) (1991) *Transformation of Planned Economies: Property Rights Reform and Macroeconomic Stability*, Paris: OECD.
3. It should be recalled that estimates of the state-owned sector's share of value added in these economies pre reforms have been put at 97 per cent for Czechoslovakia, 86 per cent for Hungry and 82 per cent for Poland. The estimates are from Milanovic, B. (1989) *Liberalization and Entrepreneurship: Dynamics of Reforms in Socialism and Capitalism*, New York.
4. Fonfara, K. and Collins, M. (1990) 'The Internationalisation of Business in Poland', *International Marketing Review* (4).
5. Cieslik, J. (1985) 'Forging inter-firm Relationships in East–West Trade through Contractual Arrangements – the Case of Poland', Second Open International Marketing and Purchasing Research Seminar on International Marketing, Uppsala, Sweden.
6. Bulter, W. H. and Kletzer, K. M. (1991) *Competitiveness and Industrial Restructuring in Czechoslovakia, Hungary and Poland*, London: Centre for Economic Policy Research, Discussion Paper 543, July.
7. Debs, R., Shapiro, H. and Taylor, C. (1991) *Financing Eastern Europe*, Washington DC: Group of Thirty.
8. The largest privatization effort to date has been that of Chile, where some 470 enterprises (producing 24 per cent of the country's value added and employing 5 per cent of its labour force) were sold between 1973 and 1989. This was largely accomplished by returning these businesses to their previous owners. The scale of the Eastern European ambition is further highlighted when it is considered that the World Bank estimates that under 1,000 firms were privatized throughout the world between 1980 and 1987.

9. Among his extensive writings on this subject, see Dunning, J. H. (1988) 'The Eclectic Paradigm of International Production: A Restatement and Some Possible Extensions', *Journal of International Business Studies* (1), Spring.

10. Initially developed in the Swedish context, this has been widely applied elsewhere – see, for example, Davidson, W. H. (1983) 'Market Similarity and Market Selection: Implications of International Marketing Strategy', *Journal of Business Research* 11.

11. Johnson, J. and Mattsson, L.-G. (1988) 'Internationalisation in Industrial Systems – A Network Approach', in N. Hood, and J. E. Vahene, (eds), *Strategies in Global Competition*, London: Croom Helm.

12. Vernon, R. (1979) 'The Product Cycle Hypothesis in a New International Environment', *Oxford Bulletin of Economics and Statistics* 41.

13. Calvet, A. L. (1982) 'Mergers and the Theory of Foreign Direct Investment', in A. M. Rugman (ed.) *New Theories of the Multinational Enterprise*, London: Croom Helm.

14. This approach is developed in Casson, M. (1990) *Enterprise and Competitiveness: A System View of International Business*, Oxford: Clarendon Press.

15. Love, J. H. and Scouller, J. (1990) 'Successful Growth by Acquisition', *Journal of General Management* 15(3).

16. Around thirty-five or forty investment funds were set up between 1989 and 1990 in Western capital markets with interests or potential interests in investment in Eastern Europe, almost all of which were less than 50 per cent invested by mid-1991. In most cases they planned to be fully invested within twelve to eighteen months. However, the delays in establishing the regulatory framework within which such funds could operate, the shortage of appropriate deals and the complexities associated with proper accounting procedures are invariably cited by fund managers as a major obstacle to action. In effect, these factors have thus restricted the flow of international portfolio investment into East Europe.

17. Harrigan, K. R. (1988) 'Strategic Alliances and Partner Asymmetries', in F. Contractor, and P. Lorange (eds), *Co-operative Strategies in International Business*, Lexington, Mass.: Lexington Books.

18. Kogut, B. (1988) 'Joint Ventures: Theoretical and Empirical Perspectives', *Strategic Management Journal* 9(4).

19. Beamish, P. W. (1988) *Multinational joint ventures in developing countries*, London: Routledge.

20. Kitching, J. (1973) 'Acquisitions in Europe – Causes of Corporate Successes and Failures', *Business International*, Geneva.

21. 'Making Acquisitions Work – Lessons from Companies' Successes and Mistakes', *Business International*, Geneva, 1988.

22. As considered, for example, in Young, S. *et al.* (1989) *International Market Entry and Development: Strategies and Management*, Hemel Hempstead: Harvester Wheatsheaf; Gomes-Casseres, B. (1989) 'Ownership Structures of Foreign Subsidiaries: Theory and Evidence', *Journal of Economic Behaviour and Organisation*, 11.

23. For a consideration of this issue, see Nebenzahl, I. D. and Jaffe, E. D. (1991) 'Shifting Production to East European Countries: Effect on Brand Value', paper presented to 17th Annual Conference of the European International Business Association, Copenhagen, December.

24. Dunning, J. H. and Robson, P. (1988) 'Multinational Corporate Integration and Regional Economic Integration', in J. H. Dunning, and P. Robson, (eds), *Multinationals and the European Community*, Oxford: Basil Blackwell.

25. Samoradov, A. (1991) 'Coping with the employment effects of restructuring in Eastern Europe', *International Labour Review* 128(3); Welge, M. K. and Holtbrugge, D. (1989) 'Employment Effects of Foreign Direct Investment in the Former Centrally Planned Economics', paper presented to 17th Annual Conference of the European International Business Association, Copenhagen, December.

18

Marketing under Newly-emerging East European and Soviet Conditions – Some Thoughts on What Needs to be Done

Jacob Naor

Recent upheavals in the Eastern bloc and continuing upheavals in the former USSR suggest the need for a re-examination of some long-standing beliefs concerning these countries. Systems that had in the past been considered economically and ideologically stable, have proved not to be so. Indeed the rapidity of change has caught both Western observers and domestic opposition leaders wholly unprepared, grasping for ways to move from bureaucratically controlled central planning to some form of market system. As yet, there are unresolved basic issues such as the degree to which state property should be converted to co-operative ownership or privatized in order to increase efficiency, and what restriction to retain on market operations and prices in order to maintain equity. While these and similar issues are frequently the subject of controversy in non-socialist countries as well, they are of immediate concern to decision makers in the East who face the daunting task of having to restructure their systems under socioeconomic emergency conditions.

This paper will focus on the problems facing the emergence of marketing under conditions of economic restructuring, and on some of the steps needed, both short-term and long-term, to enable incipient marketing activities to take place. While recognizing the disparity between Eastern bloc and Soviet conditions, and conditions within these various countries regarding issues such as the level of economic development, degree of central control, bureaucratization, and infrastructure development, to mention but a few, the chapter will nevertheless attempt to focus on some major issues that appear to be common to all. In addition, occasional

College of Business Administration, 323 Donald P. Corbett Hall, University of Maine, Orono, Maine 04469.

The author has done extensive research in the area of East European and Soviet reform efforts and marketing practices. In the Summer of 1990 and 1991 he conducted a series of marketing seminars in the Soviet Union.

references will be made indicating the degree of applicability of an issue to a particular country. This approach appears justified, since all of the countries under consideration are currently becoming mixed economies, retaining large state-owned manufacturing and service sectors. The aim will thus be to indicate what needs to be done to enable marketing to function in systems that are undergoing major structural changes.

Newly Emerging Conditions

As is well known, sellers' markets and monopolistic production and distribution conditions characterized Eastern bloc and Soviet markets since the inception of centralized planning. Under such conditions there was little need for marketing. Indeed, perennial shortages and customer dissatisfaction with available goods and services were widespread, and are well documented in the popular press.[1] Despite periodic efforts to put greater emphasis on the production of consumer goods, industrial production continued until recently to enjoy priority status, contributing in large measure to consumer discontent, which no doubt fed and stimulated political discontent.

Table 18.1: General constraints on Eastern bloc and Soviet economic activities.

Category	Prior to recent changes	Current
Political	Soviet-bloc allegiance	Varying moves to non-aligned status
Economic – macro	Centralized planning, command economy	Move to decentralized planning, indicative planning
– micro (enterprise)	Operational planning, limited decision-making	Move to strategic planning, extensive decision-making
– structural	Monopolization, bureaucratization	Move to demonopolization, greater enterprise independence
Ideological	State as predominant owner of means of production	Mixed economy, with declining proportion of state ownership
Market conditions	Predominantly sellers' markets	Movement towards partial buyers' markets

Table 18.1 presents a framework of constraints to economic activities in the Eastern bloc and the former Soviet Union, indicating conditions within which economic activities took place in the past, as well as current conditions. As indicated in the table, the current transitional period appears to be characterized by moves towards economic decentralization, some demonopolization, and reduced control from the centre in all socioeconomic spheres, accompanied by a devolution of decision-making power to the enterprise level. Such manifestations appear cur-

rently to be more pronounced in certain countries such as Hungary, Czecho-slovakia, and Poland, but may be seen to pertain to the others as well. Mixed economy conditions, with varying proportions of public ownership of the means of production, are emerging. Most importantly for marketing, market conditions appear to be changing across the spectrum. Traditional sellers' markets (with such accompanying features as shortages and heavily subsidized prices) are gradually being replaced by sectoral buyers' markets as market-determined prices become more widespread. Clearly, to the extent that such trends continue and intensify, so will the need for the utilization of marketing grow. Indeed, as the case of the former Soviet Union indicates, the traditional emphasis on production is rapidly yielding to the realization that distribution, and pricing, as well as product devel-opment and promotion (particularly in foreign trade) may well be indispensible tools for overcoming the economic impasse that has accompanied the recent up-heavals.

What Needs to be Done

Given the rapidly changing environments, deteriorating economic conditions, and the desire to move to some form of 'market economy', Eastern decision-makers are confronted by a host of new dilemmas. While urgent needs are apparent in some functional marketing areas, much of the needed infrastructure required for efficient market operations is not in place.

The existing distribution and pricing systems had been based primarily on state orders which, on the basis of central plans, specified what needed to be produced and by whom, as well as how the goods were to be distributed. Prices were set either by fiat or by agreement between producers and pricing authorities, with no reference to demand and supply conditions. Resource scarcities were thus not reflected in costs, while distribution was designed primarily to maximize econo-mies of scale, disregarding consumer need satisfaction in the process. The existing infrastructure, while adequate for earlier periods of the industrialization process, proved wholly inadequate for satisfying ever-growing consumer needs and desires with regard to such things as quality, assortment, style, packaging, and purchase conditions of goods.

Due to the generally deteriorating economic conditions in the region under consideration here, it appears necessary to stress the crucial importance of time, regarding steps that need to be taken to remedy infrastructure deficiencies as well as those which are needed to enable marketing activities to take place. Some urgent steps are needed almost immediately, while others could wait, in line with the pace and nature of economic restructuring, much of which is as yet uncertain. One thing is clear: priorities need to be established for meeting both infrastructure and marketing needs, in order to use resources effectively while avoiding catastrophic breakdowns.

Major need categories that are seen to require attention in this context are as follows: marketing infrastructure needs, needs related to the practice of marketing, and needs related to marketing education. Each of these includes some needs requiring immediate attention and longer-term needs. The rest of the chapter will deal with some details concerning these categories and suggestions as to what appears to need doing.

Restructuring the Marketing Infrastructure

A variety of specific infrastructure-related needs appear to require attention. It would seem to make sense to assign priorities to the handling of infrastructure-related needs on the basis of at least three criteria: (1) avoiding system breakdown (i.e., the need for the restructuring of distribution in the former Soviet Union); (2) providing essential conditions needed for marketing operations; (3) aiding sectors that are, or could be, potential hard currency earners (such as the gas and oil sector in the USSR). Since the focus here is on the domestic industry, we will deal with the first two points only.

Socialist systems, as suggested, have in the past undergone varying reform processes, ranging from highly advanced efforts (as in the case of Hungary – Berend 1990) to those that, while paying lip service to reforms, until recently did little to bring about effective changes (as, for example, in the case of Romania and the former USSR). In all cases, however, the following infrastructure areas saw neglect to one degree or another: industrial structure, financial services, insurance services, transportation and distributional facilities, communication facilities and informational services.[2]

The previous industrial structure or organization is considered here a fundamental marketing infrastructure impediment, since the effectively monopolized and competition-free economy permitted or required little marketing. While large-scale demonopolization would require time, some short-term efforts to permit and aid the establishment of small and medium-sized enterprises, whether private, co-operatively or state-owned, and entrepreneurially or professionally run, are urgently needed. Competitive pressures between such entities, and on large existing state enterprises, would tend to result. Such pressures should provide the basic impulse or stimulus for the introduction of marketing activities at the micro level, and should be watched for carefully.

The availability of credit (and insurance), as well as the legal framework for such activities appear to be crucial. Decentralization tendencies involving previously centrally run financial institutions may aid this process, in addition to making business or market performance major lending criteria for credit-granting institutions. And some legal reforms regarding small and medium-sized businesses, already under way for some time in Hungry, are urgently needed elsewhere as well.

Transportation and distributional needs appear pressing, as stated. Much could be done in the short run, presumably, to upgrade and rationalize existing facilities. In the case of the former Soviet Union, some emergency measures to avoid system breakdown may be unavoidable. However, even there, in the case of retailing, existing facilities could in many cases be upgraded relatively easily (more shelf space, better displays) and rationalized (in terms of traffic patterns, paying procedures, introduction of devices to reduce queuing, better ventilation and the like). Some training of sales personnel could also be initiated in the short term, reducing customer dissatisfaction at the retail level. Many wholesaling needs, particularly in the former Soviet Union again, neglected until now, would presumably have to be addressed over the longer term, while most retailing needs could be more rapidly addressed. Meeting physical distribution needs is crucial however. Beyond emergency measures, steps to rationalize the operation of existing facilities (warehouses, trucking, and rail facilities) appears to be urgently required. Some computerization and mechanization of goods-handling operations could presumably be introduced relatively quickly. Well-targeted Western technical help in these areas could be highly effective, pending longer-term needs assessment and restructuring efforts.

The sorry state of communications facilities in most East European countries and the former Soviet Union (telephone, fax facilities, and the like) is clearly a major constraining factor. Little can be done if marketing information cannot be collected and disseminated in a timely fashion. Technical help, targeted to those institutions or centres having marketing capabilities or potential for such activities, would appear useful.

Similar comments may be made regarding information or communication-providing service organizations (such as advertising agencies and marketing research services). There is an urgent need to establish at least some agencies of this kind, since expertise in these areas appears to be practically non-existent at the enterprise level. Initiating at least some consumer-centred research efforts is essential in the short run, in order to avoid wasteful marketing efforts. While some centrally-run institutions conducting market research have been in existence under centralized planning (Naor 1991), much more is needed now under increasingly decentralized conditions. Here, too, initial steps could build on available domestic expertise, and technical assistance could be targeted to permit the collection of some urgently needed marketing data. Some of the most glaring infrastructure deficiencies could thus be addressed. However, restructuring after years of neglect will clearly require time. Initial marketing operations will thus most likely continue to be plagued by severe ongoing infrastructure failings.

Marketing Needs of Practitioners

Practitioners attempting to operate under such underdeveloped environmental conditions clearly face enormous difficulties. And yet, the need for some 'essential' marketing activities is growing in the short term and will increase with emerging sectoral buyers' market conditions. In the Soviet case this is evident in the rapid emergence of so-called 'free' or 'open' markets, which have become major alternatives to the official, subsidized, and shortage-plagued distribution system. A brief discussion of some of the areas that require marketing activities, in both the short run and in the long run, follows.

Pricing

The pricing area, as the example of Poland indicates, requires immediate attention across the spectrum of countries under consideration, cognizant with the desire expressed by all to move to some form of market economy. Enterprises are, or will be shortly, entrusted with price-setting authority regarding existing and new products, a function that had previously been exercised by the central authorities.

Several options appear open to decision makers, both with regard to scope and speed of price liberalization. Poland, opting for a so-called 'shock therapy' option, moved most rapidly and in a broad scope, despite attendant risks of massive social and political destabilization. In Hungary, on the other hand, despite the fact that reforms had been most highly advanced, the government moved more cautiously. Thus while in 1989 63 per cent of all prices reflected market conditions, this figure was expected to increase to only 70 per cent by the end of 1990 (Kadar 1990). Other East European countries may be expected to follow a cautious price liberalization pattern as well. Still, the need for price-setting expertise at the enterprise level will undoubtedly grow.

A major short-term obstacle facing price-setting in most cases is the absence of reliable and meaningful data on costs and demand. The costs of industrial inputs do not, as a rule, as yet reflect market conditions, thus do not measure 'true' costs, and cost accounting at the enterprise level is underdeveloped. Data on demand is even less available. Little is thus known on the price elasticities of various goods, which, under previous monopolistic conditions, tended to be highly inelastic. Similarly little had been done in the area of segmentation in this regard. Pricing under such conditions appears difficult at best.

In the short run, there is an urgent need to collect and obtain at least rudimentary data on costs and demand. Some cost accounting procedures needed to ascertain fixed and variable production costs could presumably be introduced fairly rapidly. Some crucial demand data regarding price sensitivity (particularly of items involving discretionary expenditures) could similarly be obtained. As competition, both domestic and that of imports, is seen to grow, data on the prices of direct and potential substitutes and complements would be needed as well. Instituting price and cost-related data collection procedures at the enterprise level thus seems imperative in the short run, to permit a more rational allocation of resources. With scarcities reflecting prices, product shortages may then be expected to decline.

In the long run, one would hope for increased segmentation efforts, leading to greater availability of demand and price elasticity data by segment, and improved cost data at the enterprise level that would increasingly reflect the 'true' costs of inputs. Notions such as the development of strategic pricing policies by product or product lines would clearly be needed then to permit the proper utilization of pricing towards achieving strategic enterprise goals.

Distribution

As stated, it appears reasonable in the short run to rationalize and improve existing physical distribution facilities and activities. Increasing the efficiency and effectiveness of existing distributional networks appear to be important initial goals. Wastage and spoilage in transportation and warehousing must clearly be reduced. Introducing a more customer-friendly retailing environment must be high on the agenda of priorities, and some measures in that regard could be introduced rapidly. The expected intensification of competitive retail pressures (through decentralization, diversification of ownership forms, and the entry of subsidiaries of foreign retail organizations) would clearly hasten such developments. Efforts of marketing practitioners should thus be directed to the introduction of practices that enhance customer satisfaction or that would reduce existing customer dissatisfaction. As to the logistics of distribution, such notions as profit centres, and the need for functional integration and co-ordination between the various levels within channels of distribution would, in addition, appear to be particularly useful in the short run.

In the longer run, issues such as proper channel design and the operational evaluation of feasible channel options should receive attention. This could lead to efforts to overhaul facilities and operations, as well as to the training of management and staff that would be needed at various channel levels. Wholesaling, much neglected until now, or entirely absent as in the Soviet case, would require major and continuing attention. At all channel levels, mechanization and computerization efforts would appear central to efforts to satisfy ever-growing and expanding customer needs. Both in the short and long run, clear priorities may need to be established to avoid developmental bottlenecks. An early introduction of price liberalization measures would, in any event, reduce existing pressures on the distribution system and provide more time for the introduction of needed changes.

Product

In the area of product development and management, some basic 'upgrading' efforts are needed in the short run in areas such as packaging, labelling, and branding. Foreign technical assistance could be targeted to such areas that have seen neglect. The expected increase in competitive pressures in domestic markets should motivate marketing practitioners to consider product differentiating efforts along these lines. Similarly more product innovation may be forthcoming, particularly under pressure of foreign imports. This in turn will require knowledge and expertise in the area of new product development. Specialized agencies, such as branches of foreign companies in the initial stages, dealing with product development on a contractual basis, may be an efficient way of providing needed expertise to domestic enterprises in the short run. In the longer run, domestic experts, operating at the enterprise level, would have to be trained to permit manufacturers to engage in product innovation on a continuing basis. The expected radical decentralization of decision-making from the centre to the enterprise level would clearly be an essential prerequisite for such activities. Under increasingly competitive conditions, the need for the strategic management of products over their life cycle would intensify.

Expertise and experience in brand management would now be needed at the enterprise level. Training of such managers would clearly require time, as would a desired reorientation of top managements from production concerns to marketing concerns. In the short run, as suggested, upgrading efforts directed at glaring deficiencies in such areas as packaging, labelling, and branding would appear to deserve high priority.

Promotion

It appears that even small-scale improvements in advertising and personal selling practices may, in the short run, yield effective results. Pressures towards greater utilization of advertising and selling efforts will presumably grow as the phenomenon of surplus goods becomes more widespread. Improved targeting of advertising, and greater attention to message design and impact may become more pressing concerns. Efforts at training existing sales forces, away from passive order-taking to more customer-pleasing behaviour may, even in the short run, be highly effective. The opening up of domestic markets to foreign competition will undoubtedly hasten such developments.

In the long run, more extensive training and retooling efforts will clearly be needed. Data on media habits by demographic population segments will be required, as well as expertise in such areas as advertising campaign design, message design, and testing of commercials. Here too, subsidiaries of foreign advertising agencies could initially fill the breach.

In the short run, advertising and personal selling upgrading efforts should result in alleviating short-run surpluses and a gradual reduction of consumer discontent at the retail level. Upgrading the effectiveness of sales efforts in the longer run would appear to require changes in the status of the selling function, which in the past had traditionally been dismissed as economically unproductive. Providing increased remuneration and incentives to sales personnel would lead to increased prestige, and bring forth improved performance in an area that has contributed much to consumer discontent in the past.

Market and marketing research

The preceding sections have pointed to areas where data needs are apparent, both in the short run and long run. In the absence of meaningful data, effective marketing efforts will clearly not be forthcoming. Here, too, foreign technical assistance, effectively targeted, may be needed at least initially, to provide essential data needs. The training of domestic experts should urgently be initiated, but will require time. Regional domestic instabilities, so flagrant in the Soviet case, will be added obstacles to research efforts, compounding the difficulties in researching the various culturally, ethnically, and socially diverse population entities found in most East European nations. Marketing and market research efforts will thus have to be conducted under most trying and challenging conditions. But some efforts are clearly urgently needed, and for the reasons cited, will often have to be subculture-specific. And early efforts to obtain market data would clearly have to precede efforts to obtain marketing data. Here, too, priorities appear to be needed, tied to the functional priorities discussed previously. In all cases, pressing market needs pertaining to basic need categories, will have to be addressed ahead of areas involving discretionary decision-making.

Needs in Marketing Education

An urgent need clearly exists to introduce or strengthen the teaching of marketing, as well as that of other business topics at the undergraduate and graduate levels at East European and Soviet higher institutes of learning. Much already has been done, particularly in Hungary, but there exists a clear need to institutionalize the teaching and dissemination of business knowledge in a comprehensive and culturally appropriate way.

Lacking here, too, are 'infrastructure' conditions, such as suitable teaching materials that apply specifically to the Eastern environment. Environmental conditions emerging in the East appear to require differing managerial approaches and differing applications of principles and concepts, whether in marketing or in other business disciplines. Such differences would have to be reflected in new texts and materials, both for managerial training as well as basic education. Simple translations of existing Western texts, intended and suitable for conditions prevailing in highly developed economies, would clearly not do. Yet this appears to be the approach resorted to widely, particularly in the former Soviet Union.[3]

In the short run there appears to be a need urgently to address the most pressing requirements of practitioners first, in line with what has been presented so far. A variety of seminars, to be conducted initially by Western experts familiar with local conditions, stressing simple and basic marketing practices, would appear to be required. The author has been involved in such efforts, as stated.

Such training would have to involve 'hands-on' work, to permit the rapid acquisition of some badly needed experience, and should use examples and exercises appropriate to local conditions. Otherwise, little in the way of practical results would be achieved. Simple, basic operations, suitable to underdeveloped or just developing infrastructure conditions, would have to be stressed. Initially, this would involve little computer work, since few computers are available as yet at the enterprise level. As environmental conditions change and develop, so the approaches and materials would need upgrading. Competitive pressures would then exist for applications requiring more advanced skills and knowledge.

Similar thinking appears applicable to the introduction of marketing courses at the university or institute level, albeit with a longer time horizon. The training of competent local marketing instructors would have to be accorded high priority, similar to that accorded to the development of original teaching materials. Such 'retooling' of instructors could presumably take place locally, as it should involve practical work with local enterprise executives. Indigenous marketing approaches tailored to local conditions could thus emerge that would subsequently be transmitted to students in a culturally appropriate way. Great care should be taken not to impose knowledge available elsewhere 'as is'. While easy to implement, such knowledge or skills, indiscriminately applied, may often be inappropriate and ineffective.

The transitional period involved here appears to require careful monitoring and the gradual and ongoing upgrading of contents and approaches to be used in the teaching of marketing. While this is clearly not unique to this situation, the difference here lies in the magnitude of the task involved and in its urgency. Failure to take steps such as were suggested here could lead to wasted efforts and could retard the pace of economic development.

Training of faculty and students, at both the undergraduate as well as the graduate level, may focus initially on such core courses in marketing as a principles course and marketing research, consumer behaviour, and marketing management courses. The graduate exposure would provide greater depth, scope, and research opportunities. Decision-makers in the East, under growing environmental pressures, will increasingly realize that all organizations, regardless of purpose and ownership, will require marketing in order to survive and prosper. For educational efforts to be effective, an 'ideology-free' approach to marketing, targeted to the specific needs of mixed economies such as those emerging currently in the East, should be utilized.

Summary

Recent upheavals in the former Soviet Union and East European countries have underscored the vital importance of marketing for the economic development of the region. While major concerns pertaining to the private, co-operative, or state ownership of means of production, or the degree to which market activities should be constrained, are still unresolved, the importance of marketing is increasingly recognized as these economies continue to decentralize and devolve more decision-making power to the enterprise level.

Some major problems inhibiting effective marketing operations under existing conditions in the East have been examined here. Despite a wide disparity in the socioeconomic conditions of the countries involved, common problems include a variety of infrastructure deficiencies as well as common problems facing emerging marketing practitioners and marketing educators. An attempt was made to analyse these problem areas from short-term and long-term perspectives. Recommendations as to what should be done urgently and what needed to be done over the longer term were provided. This could be useful in attempts to set priorities in those areas. Some recommendations in this regard for marketing practitioners, which may initially require some targeted foreign assistance, include the collection and dissemination of some basic cost and demand data needed in the area of pricing, the upgrading and rationalization of existing distribution facilities and activities, improvements in the areas of product packaging, labelling and branding, and efforts to upgrade sales force and advertising activities.

In addition, the necessity of searching for environment-specific and environment-appropriate marketing approaches, applications, and educational resources was stressed. Quick fixes, in the form of translated foreign text, or transplanted activities of all kinds 'as is', would surely be ineffective. Some appropriate adaptations, in an ideologically neutral manner, of standard marketing techniques and activities intended for practitioners appear to be urgently required. The above steps, in addition to some early steps regarding the upgrading of the marketing infrastructure, as were suggested here, may be the most urgent tasks requiring attention. It is hoped that the suggestions provided here will stimulate further efforts that will assist the emergence of socially useful marketing activities in the East.

Notes

1. For an in-depth analysis for some of the reasons for shortages in a highly developed socialist system, see Naor (1991).

2. For an example of one of the more developed infrastructure conditions, that of Hungary, see Gehrt, Naor and Strausz (1989).
3. The author, in collaborating with some Soviet colleagues, is currently engaged in developing a series of educational marketing materials that are 'environment specific' and that attempt to address the most pressing needs of Soviet executives.

References

Berend, I. (1990) *The Hungarian Economic Reforms 1953–1988*, New York: Cambridge University Press.

Gehrt, K. C., Naor, J. and Strausz, G. (1989) 'Exploring the Suitability of Direct Marketing to East-bloc Distributional Systems: The Case of Hungry', *Journal of Global Marketing* 3(1).

Kadar, B. (1990) 'Liberalization – The Hungarian Way', *Hungarian Business Herald* 2: 8–12.

Naor, J. (1991) 'Demand Research and the Planning of Consumer Good's Supplies in a Centralized Socialist System – The Case of the Former German Democratic Republic', *European Journal of Marketing* 25(8).

19

The Impact of Eastern Liberalization on East–West Countertrade

C. W. Neale, C. L. Pass and D. D. Shipley

Introduction

Countertrade (CT) has become a generic term applied to any set of cross-border contracts linking a seller's exports to imports from the buyer, and covers practices ranging from direct exchange (barter) to long-term buyback contracts. Barter and its modern CT variants appear to some 'like some disease-causing microbe once thought safely eradicated by modern science' which has 'made a startling come-back in the past few years' (Cohen and Zysman 1986: 41). Initially reported as a highly undesirable, even quasi-illegal practice, it is now regarded, if not with equanimity, then as a fact of business life. Meanwhile, understanding of the internal mechanics of CT deals and of the motivations of CT partners has escalated.

During the post-war period, a major proportion of trade between former Comecon countries and a significant proportion of East–West trade was conducted in this way. As the Eastern bloc economies expanded, albeit at rates slower than those experienced in Western Europe, their needs for factors of production incorporating advanced technology outstripped their capacity to finance the required imports by conventional means. As a result, Western suppliers increasingly were subjected to demands to deal via CT, with the implied threat that the sale would otherwise be lost to a competitor.

Several official reports (e.g. UN 1979; OECD 1981; Ford 1986) recorded the growing incidence of CT, often in less than enthusiastic terms. Some Western nations were 'flatly opposed' to CT, while others, although regretting the necessity to trade in this way, were prepared to give it qualified approval. However, it should not be assumed that all Eastern bloc nations were CT enthusiasts. According to one official source:

> The Hungarian government has never in the past (and obviously not in the present) advocated the idea of trading with any country, and specifically with the West, on a countertrade basis. In Hungary, we never had any compulsory, legislatory directive or incentive to counter-trade with the West.

The recent developments in Eastern Europe, a traditional stronghold of CT, have led to suggestions that demands for CT will decline (van Hoof 1991). There are several reasons for this. At a general level, the sheer freedom from the bureaucratic interference required by a centrally planned regime, will probably promote more enterprising attitudes and require speedier and more efficient business trans-actions, whereas CT is slow and cumbersome, often subject to protracted negotiations.

More specifically, recognition at official as well as business levels of the develop-ment gap between Western and Eastern Europe will lead to greater demands for technology-based imports from the West. Freedom from controls over the pattern of import and export trade may lead to a greater ability on the part of Eastern exporters to supply goods which Western firms really require, for which they are prepared to offer hard currency. The arrival of Western banking, accountancy and consultancy resources in Eastern Europe will sharpen local expertise, and enhance the likelihood of additional loan facilities being granted to finance such imports. Finally, the very fact that tied trade was associated with the old regimes is likely to lead local enterprises to seek alternative trading media.

CT with the former GDR has already virtually ceased since German reunifi-cation, and recent events threaten the continuation of CT in several other states. As with Hungary, Romanian CT is now insignificant since the country, according to a Romanian official, now 'acts for free trade, [we offer] no encouragement for CT, and we press for hard currency'. In general, the historical motives for CT in the region are disappearing. It is no longer mandatory in any Eastern country, and conventional modes of trade financing are increasingly available.

Although many of these countries remain highly indebted and suffer chronic domestic and foreign currency shortages, this financial stringency is likely to ease in the long term through internal development and injections of Western aid, possibly including substantial debt remissions. The German government is already reported to have spent £60 billion on reunification. However, perhaps the greatest threat to CT in Eastern Europe stems from the dismantling of the bureaucratic apparatus which formerly administered CT transactions (Jasch 1989).

This chapter is organized as follows. In the next section, we briefly examine the characteristics of the main types of CT; we then analyse the reasons for its recent growth, especially in trade with pre-liberalized Eastern Europe, before going on to present findings from a recent survey among leading exporters. In the light of this evidence, the final section considers the future prospects for CT as a motive force in East–West trade.

Anatomy of Countertrade

All CT deals have a common characteristic – reciprocity. In each case, a seller provides a buyer with goods (or services) and undertakes in return to purchase goods (or services) from the buyer. To some, tying sales to purchases represents a throwback to a darker, moneyless age, when a hungry carpenter had to find a farmer whose barn-door needed repairs. The invention of money and the evolution of markets were a direct response to the double coincidence of wants problem. CT is thus often presented merely as an inefficient alternative to trading via cash or credit, although this assessment is simplistic.

Another common feature of CT deals is their complexity, as the following examples indicate. ICL, the British computer manufacturer, provided components to Poland for building portable televisions to Western European standards and then acted as sales agent for the assembled TVs in the West. The Poles then purchased ICL personal computers in kit form with the hard currency received for the TV sets. These machines were customized for the Polish market and sold locally for zlotys, which were then used to subsidize production of yet more televisions which ICL sold in the West. 3M Corporation set up a Swiss subsidiary to negotiate deals with Eastern Bloc countries. The proceeds from selling $1 million of Polish nails were deposited in a European bank and the Polish government drew on the account to buy 3M healthcare products.

Schuster (1978) quotes the Soviet gas pipeline deal, where several different forms of CT were mixed together in a complex deal involving German pipe producers, a separate firm of gas suppliers and the Soviet Union as supplier of natural gas and initiator of the deal. Essentially, the Western firms were to be paid for their respective construction and distribution services in the form of natural gas throughput.

Types of countertrade

Barter
As noted, the simplest type of CT is barter, or direct goods-for-goods exchange – exports are traded for goods (or services) from the importing market, without a cash transfer. Recently, Greece exchanged 200,000 tonnes of wheat for 600,000 tonnes of Algerian crude oil. The British computer manufacturer, ICL, has accepted eggs, furniture, jewellery and plastic in exchange for computers in Eastern Europe.

Compensation
This is a derivative of barter, and more prevalent. Compensation also involves direct exchange of goods, but each leg of the transaction is valued in monetary units and reflected in a counterflow of finance. Figure 19.1 illustrates a compensation deal between a Western exporting firm and the sort of state import agency which operated in pre-liberalization days.

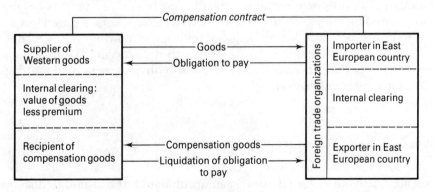

Fig. 19.1. Compensation with assignment. *Source:* Raemy-Dirks (1986).

'Financial flows' may consist of the clearing of claims, and do not necessarily require foreign exchange transfers. Indeed, most such deals are arranged to avoid currency transfers. Payment for the primary delivery is allowed on credit by the supplier, whose claim for payment is registered in a clearing account and is liquidated by the counter-delivery.

Counter-purchase

This is the commonest form of CT. As a condition of securing a sale, the exporter undertakes to purchase goods and services selected from a 'shopping list' of available goods. For example, Iran once purchased $24.5 million of Indonesian tea, plywood, rubber and other goods in return for Indonesian purchases of Iranian crude oil. Counter-purchase differs from barter and compensation by the existence of an option to take delivery of the counter-traded goods at any time within a specified period. In this respect, it resembles a futures contract.

Switch-Trading

Imbalances in long-term bilateral trade, often between Eastern European countries and developing nations, may lead to the accumulation of uncleared credit surpluses. For example, Brazil once had a large credit surplus with Poland. Such surpluses can be tapped by third countries, so that UK exports to Brazil might be financed from the sale of Polish goods to the UK or elsewhere. Switch deals typically involve swapping the documentation (and destination) of goods in transit, thus making the forward contract and delivery option transferable.

Buyback

In a buyback, suppliers of plant or equipment agree to take payment in the form of the future output of the investment. For example, Italy sold a $90 million synthetic fibre plant to the former Soviet Union in return for deliveries of acrylic fibre. In effect, a single forward deal is replaced by a long-term subcontracting arrangement, essentially a series of forward contracts.

Sercu (1990) argues that all CT techniques involve combinations of standard contracts (import, import-financing, and forward export). A CT contract is not merely a device for trading without cash – it is a deal in which imports, secured loans, and exports form part of a 'bundled package' of trade and financing contracts. But this bundling is costly and complex, so why do such deals occur? We must look for specific advantages of packages to explain the incentive to tie several interlocking contracts into one complex deal.

Motives for Countertrade Involvement

Various specific motives for CT have been documented. It is useful to distinguish 'Eastern' motives from the 'Western' motives.

The Eastern perspective

From the Eastern perspective, incentives to CT can be classified as economic, political and developmental, although these categories inevitably overlap.

Economic motives
Eastern European countries have often used CT to bypass hard currency shortages and deep debt crises and to augment import volumes (OECD 1981; Roosa 1985). Moreover, as in the case of buybacks, CT may enable both Western firms and Eastern countries to predetermine the terms of trade by setting the implied values of goods, thus reducing foreign currency risk. CT enables countries to concede, or even initiate, secret price-cuts to stimulate exports during periods of flat demand, without causing long-term damage to world prices. Similarly, Eastern European countries have imposed CT terms on Western exporters beset by excess capacity during recession (Nykryn 1985), to overcome Western import barriers, such as anti-dumping restrictions, and to redress trade balances (Gonzalez 1985).

Political motives
The pervasive influence of political motives was a powerful impetus for Eastern European demands for CT. Under the former tight state control of trade and industry, CT was used to promote political ideals. The Foreign Trade Organizations (FTOs) which formerly administered CT in Eastern countries used their powers to deter low-priority imports by imposing deleterious obligations on importers, and to surmount Western import barriers (Nykryn 1985). The clandestine nature of CT enabled it to be used as a mask to regulate the types and volumes of imports and to administer internally unpopular austerity regimes. Moreover, the FTOs used CT to mask imports of strategically important products, at the expense of more socially desirable, popular and urgently-needed consumer goods.

Developmental motives
The third group of CT motivators is linked with internal industrial development ambitions, although these are not exclusively associated with Eastern Europe (Okoroafo 1988; Jones 1990). Common incentives for demanding buyback or offset terms are to enhance a country's technology stock, its infrastructure, labour skills and employment levels (Kaikati 1976; Wills, Jacobs and Palia 1986; Griffin and Rouse 1986). By allocating additional CT credits to exporters in favoured industries, it is possible to stimulate the diversification of a nation's industrial base. This is further facilitated when CT is used to penetrate new markets by accessing the marketing channels of Western firms (Zurawicki 1988) to overcome adverse country-of-origin stereotypes and the costs of distribution (Yoffie, 1984).

The Western perspective

Western exporters generally prefer hard currency or letters of credit to payment in goods, since currency is more liquid, more certain and less troublesome, despite greater exchange rate volatility in recent times. If, however, Western exporters face problems like general spare capacity and strongly competitive rivals, they may accept customer demands for CT to meet their own volume objectives and achieve contributions to fixed costs.

CT is often regarded as a 'second-best' alternative, reluctantly adopted only when orthodox approaches appear unworkable. However, experience breeds expertise, a 'global counter-trade service industry' (Palia 1990) has arisen to handle CT risks, and many firms now operate specialist units to manage their CT operations. Why do they use CT rather than orthodox trading channels?

Zurawicki (1988) stresses the desire by 'weak' Eastern marketers to tap into Western marketing channels. The needs of 'inefficient' marketers can be exploited by the Western exporter to enter and develop a new market. CT can also be more efficient than orthodox trade if access to a ready-made customer reduces search and transactions costs, such as agents' commission. It may avoid the bureaucratic delays in a currency rationing process operated by an importer's government, advancing the receipt of traded goods and hence, income from selling them. CT thus resembles selling accounts receivable (Mirus and Yeung 1986). Parsons (1985) sees counter-purchase as a means of selling commodities forward where no formal forward or futures market exists.

CT may be an internalizing device whereby large diversified multinationals can source new materials, components and supplies if offered on terms superior to the regular offers from current vendors (Kogut 1986). This form of 'company-oriented' CT satisfies the needs of the counter-delivery recipient and can reduce distribution costs, thus achieving better terms of trade than by paying market prices.

A CT arrangement may be a response to imperfections in centrally planned and other less developed economies, with only embryonic market systems, unreliable legal systems and paucity of information (Mirus and Yeung 1991). In some transactions, the quality of goods and services is often only fully observable to suppliers, encouraging sellers to under-supply the unobservable characteristics. Conversely, property rights over information-based goods and services are difficult to protect. CT may be a useful device for dealing with such principal–agent and property rights problems. The exporter finds that the value of the contract depends on his own efforts to identify and sell exportable local goods, while his own property rights are not easily appropriated. CT terms, despite serious drafting and implementation costs, may thus be preferable, under certain conditions, to sets of independent contracts.

CT thus occurs in response to market imperfections and, in the case of trade with command economies, official restrictions on conventional trade and currency dealings. However, from the Western perspectives, involvement in CT may be interpreted in two ways. On the one hand, it may be merely opportunistic, representing an *ad hoc* and essentially short-term means of boosting sales and achieving a contribution to fixed costs at a time of particularly awkward trading conditions. On the other hand, it could be seen as a way of obtaining an initial toehold in the market, serving as a forerunner to a longer-term market presence when conditions permit.

Recent liberalization programmes introduced in a number of Eastern European countries have several possible implications for East–West CT. The establishment of more conventional trading relationships could well obviate the need for some forms of CT or reduce reliance on them. This would apply particularly to 'opportunistic' CT.

The opening-up of hitherto restricted markets, and more positive official attitudes towards conventional trade deals and inward investment, can be expected to encourage established traders to increase their involvement in these markets, as well as encouraging new traders and investors. Already there has been a considerable activity in this direction, particularly in regard to direct investment. The need to strengthen their economies through technology transfer has led Eastern authorities to give particular attention to joint ventures.

Joint ventures

Recent joint-venture initiatives include Fiat's purchase of a 51 per cent stake in its long-standing associate FSM in the first stage of the privatization of Poland's car industry. In this context, it is possible that some counter-trading will be displaced by firms preferring to develop a long-term presence in Eastern European markets through equity-based joint ventures and contractual forms of strategic alliances such as co-production and co-marketing agreements. Fiat also plans to buy into Russia's VAZ motor manufacturing company which produces Ladas, offering a mixture of cash, technology transfer, and licence deals. Fiat is likely to export existing designs for production at VAZ's Togliatti plant, which it helped to set up over twenty years ago. It plans to build up its presence in Russia as a 'second leg' within Eastern Europe to complement the much larger car interest in Poland, eventually producing 300,000 cars p.a. To date, this is the largest expansion by a Western company anywhere in Eastern Europe.

Fiat will not be alone in Russia. British Aerospace, manufacturer of Rover cars, is planning to invest 'tens of millions of pounds' in building 150,000 units of its Montego model in order to capitalize on low Russian labour costs and to get into position for building up market share in Eastern Europe. Finance will be provided via an equity stake in its partner, NAMI, the state-controlled organization responsible for motor vehicle technology and design in Russia and the other states of the former USSR.

In the air transport sector, Air France is leading a consortium to buy 40 per cent of Czechoslovakian Airlines (CSA) in a deal valuing the group at $150 million. The state government and local financial institutions will retain the remainder of the shares. Meanwhile, British Airways will set up a Moscow-based airline, Air Russia, in partnership with Aeroflot. BA will take a 30 per cent holding, with Aeroflot splitting the rest of the majority stake with Moscow's domestic airport. The new airline will use Russian airspace to shorten trans-Asian flights, slicing hours off long-haul services.

In the tobacco industry, BAT Industries has purchased a majority shareholding in Pecsi Tobacco Factory, Hungary's largest cigarette manufacturer with 45 per cent of the local market. BAT also plans to improve the quality of the country's tobacco crop. This purchase came only a month after Philip Morris's acquisition of the Egri Tobacco Factory. Both multinationals clearly believe that expansion in demand in Eastern Europe for Western brands is likely to offset the sales decline in the more health-conscious Western markets.

As these examples illustrate, strategic alliances between businesses (each of which continues to retain its own individual identity), enable them to obtain access to technologies, know-how, capital and markets to augment their own resources and capabilities. Pairing resources and capabilities in this way allows strategic partners to achieve synergistic effects otherwise unobtainable on an individual basis, while allowing each partner to focus and concentrate its efforts on its core business strengths.

Strategic alliances can be particularly effective ways of expanding internationally. Partners can contribute established marketing and distribution systems, production and R&D facilities and local knowledge of the markets they serve. They can ensure that products get to market more quickly and more effectively, particularly where they need to be modified to meet local regulations covering product standards and packaging, and the preferences of local customers. Alternatively, firms may choose to service foreign markets through wholly owned manufacturing and sales subsidiaries so as to exercise full control over their operations.

Empirical Insights

Investigations into CT have usually been conducted via detailed questionnaire methods (e.g. Huszagh and Barksdale 1986; Shipley and Neale 1988; Rabino and Shah 1989) but these have often generated low response rates. This is largely due to the semi-clandestine nature of CT and the understandable reluctance of many executives to allow it to be known that their firms are prepared to enter into CT deals. The value of an extensive mailed survey, especially in these early days of liberalization, is thus open to question.

Allowing for these arguments, and in order to undertake an exploratory study of the impact of liberalization, efforts were made in late 1991 to contact a small group of leading exporters (twenty of the *Financial Times* 'Top 100' exporters) which had co-operated in an earlier study (Shipley and Neale 1988). Companies were asked whether they had engaged in counter-trade with East European businesses, and if so, whether this form of trade had increased, remained the same, or decreased in the period since 1985, the date of the earlier study.

Four companies reported increased CT, one company no change and five companies reported either sharp decreases in, or a total cessation of, CT. Ten companies with no past or current CT involvement in Eastern Europe were currently exporters to, or investors in, this region. All companies were invited to comment on their mix of trading and investment positions in the area. Profiles of these companies are displayed in Tables 19.1, 19.2, 19.3 and 19.4, according to the behaviour of their CT in recent years.

Companies with increased countertrade

Of the four companies (designated companies A, B, C, and D) which reported an increase in counter-trading, company A produces chemicals, company B oil, company C cigarettes, and company D non-alcoholic beverages.

For companies A and B, exports to Eastern Europe accounted for less than 10 per

Table 19.1: Companies with increased countertrade.

Companies reporting an increase in counter-trading	E. European exports as % of total exports	Countertrading as % of E. European exports	Main forms of countertrading	Main E. European export market	Countertrading as % of main E. European export market	Other involvements
A (chemicals)	1–9	1–9	*barter *counter-purchase buyback switch trade *increase others no change	USSR	1–9	'Significant' joint venture
B (Oil)	1–9	1–9	barter	USSR	10–24	'Minor' joint venture
C (tobacco)	10–24	1–9	barter counter-purchase	Poland	0	'Significant' joint venture licensing
D (beverages)	1–9	25–49	*barter *counter-purchase buyback switch trade *increase others no change	Hungary	50–100	'Significant' franchising licensing

cent of their total world-wide exports, and, despite a modest increase in CT, this medium continued to account for under 10 per cent of total East European exports.

For company A, the USSR represented its main East European market, and barter and counter-purchase the main forms of counter-trading. Company B's main Eastern European customer was also the USSR, with barter accounting for around 18 per cent of its exports to this market. For company C, exports to Eastern Europe accounted for 10–24 per cent of its world-wide exports, although like Companies A and B, counter-trading accounted for under 10 per cent of its exports to Eastern Europe. The company was not involved in CT in its single largest Eastern European market, Poland, but conducted CT in most of the other countries making up the former East European bloc. Its barter and counter-purchases had both increased since 1985.

In the case of company D, exports to Eastern Europe were also under 10 per cent of its total world-wide exports, but compared to other companies a much higher proportion of its exports to Eastern Europe were counter-traded – over 25 per cent of its exports to the area as a whole, and over 50 per cent of its exports to its main market, Hungary. The company engaged in all forms of CT, but only barter had shown a significant increase since 1985.

Companies A, B, and C cited their customers' reduced access to foreign currency and credit as the most important factors accounting for an increase in their CT involvement. Increased in-house counter-trading expertise was also considered important by companies A, C and D. Company D also claimed 'greater awareness of counter-trade opportunities', and enhancement of its competitive advantage in the market, as equally important factors favouring CT. The difficult access to foreign currency/credit remained a dominant influence. This supports the view that in many sectors, financing problems will continue into the foreseeable future, despite the advent of more open trading conditions. Although the pressure to CT may be relaxing, it seems that continued Western readiness to accept CT terms may still be a valuable competitive weapon in some markets.

In addition to its CT interests, company A had a direct presence in a number of Eastern European markets through joint ventures. These joint venture initiatives arose largely as a result of the company's 'own strategic analysis' of the opportunities offered by the development of the Eastern European economies, but other significant factors were various approaches to the company from Eastern European businesses and the official preference for joint ventures, by East European governments, rather than wholly-owned foreign direct investment (FDI). Interestingly, the joint ventures were seen as a natural progression from counter-trade, indicating the superiority of a direct market presence to establish a long-term sales base.

Company B also had a limited joint venture presence in Eastern Europe. Factors stimulating this involvement included both approaches from Eastern European governments and businesses and the company's own strategic analysis. Joint ventures were viewed as 'better than counter-trade as they allow greater control over input and output quality', but were not considered to be a natural extension of counter-trade. That is, CT was seen as a response to restrictive market circumstances, rather than as a 'normal' strategic option.

Company C had established a 'significant' joint venture and wholly owned FDI presence in Eastern European markets, and also used licensing arrangements. Joint ventures were viewed as a natural progression from exporting/counter-trading, but an amalgam of factors involving the company's own strategic evaluation and approaches from the Eastern European authorities/enterprises underscored the company's long-term commitment of resources.

Company D augmented its substantial counter-trading presence in Eastern Europe by 'significant' franchising and licensing arrangements; it also had a 'minor' FDI interest in the area. Generally, however, strategic alliances were not considered to be decisively superior to counter-trading, although this view might well change as Eastern European markets became more liberalized.

Companies with decreased countertrade

Five companies (E, F, G, H, I) reported a decline or cessation of countertrading in Eastern Europe (E produces engines, F pharmaceuticals, G textiles, H steel and I oil). In all cases, exports to Eastern Europe accounted for under 10 per cent of their world-wide exports. Moreover, only one of the five continued to countertrade in Eastern Europe.

Company E's counter-purchase dealings in the area had declined by over 25 per cent since 1985, and accounted for 10–24 per cent of its East European exports. Company F was formerly involved in barter and counter-purchase, G in counter-purchase, buyback and switch trading, H in counter-purchase, and I in barter, counter-purchase, buyback and switch trading.

Of the possible reasons for reduction or cessation of countertrading, 'customers' greater access to foreign currency' and 'customers' greater access to credit' merit careful attention. We have already noted that restrictions on the availability of foreign currency and credit are two of the most important motivators for CT. *A priori*, then, the removal of these restrictions should lead to a reduction in the necessity to resort to CT. However, the harsh reality is that access to foreign currency and credit still remains a problem for many companies operating in this area and the attempt to move to more market-driven economies will take many years to accomplish.

Those companies which had withdrawn from CT in Eastern Europe cited a number of reasons. For company F, for instance, negotiations had become 'more time consuming/complex', but more importantly, the company had replaced counter-trading by licensing and a small direct investment presence. Negotiation complexity probably reflects the abolition of the FTOs and the need to bargain with individual smaller enterprises.

Company G had found it 'more difficult to resell the goods offered'. This company had no other involvement in the area, apart from direct exports.

Company H cited a combination of factors: 'higher costs', 'more difficult to resell the goods offered', 'greater uncertainty involved', 'negotiations more time consuming/complex'. This company however, was contemplating entering into strategic alliances with Eastern European concerns to develop a longer-term involvement in the area.

Company I described itself as an 'opportunistic' counter-trader, preferring to service foreign markets through licensing, conventional exporting and direct investment, including joint ventures where appropriate. It had a 'significant' direct investment involvement in Eastern Europe. Its position on counter-trading was described thus:

Table 19.2: Companies with decreased countertrade.

Companies reporting a decrease/cessation in countertrading	E. European exports as % of total exports	Countertrading as % of E. European exports	Main forms of countertrading	Main E. European export market	Countertrading as % of main E. European export market	Other involvements
E (engines)	1–9	10–24	counter-purchase	N/A	N/A	'Minor' joint venture licensing
F (pharmaceuticals)	1–9	Cessation	barter counter-purchase	Poland	–	'Significant' licensing, 'minor' wholly-owned FDI
G (textiles)	1–9	Cessation	Counter-purchase buyback switch trade	Poland	–	None
H (steel)	1–9	Cessation	Counter-purchase	Poland	–	None
I (oil)	1–9	Cessation	barter counter-purchase buyback switch trade	N/A	–	'Significant' joint venture, wholly owned FDI, licensing

You will note that current counter-trade activity is nil. This is true today, but will not necessarily be true tomorrow, as we are always alert to profitable counter-trade opportunities. Experience has shown us that the time and effort required to set-up a counter-trade deal is rarely worthwhile. Therefore we are (in general) not actively seeking counter-trade opportunities, although we are always receptive to proposals from other parties.

Company E remained involved in counter-purchase activity in Eastern Europe. Again, a combination of factors were cited for reduced counter-trading: 'negotiations more time consuming/complex', 'higher costs' and 'greater uncertainty'. The company had a 'minor' licensing and joint venture presence in the area. Although joint ventures were not seen as a 'natural progression from counter-trading' the company intended to strengthen its joint venture presence in the area, as this would allow the company to both control its technology and develop its customer base more effectively than exporting.

Companies with unchanged countertrade

Company J (engineering products) reported 'no change' in its CT. It had a 'minor' licensing involvement in the area, but had no immediate plans to establish a direct investment presence. Exports to Eastern Europe accounted for under 10 per cent of its world-wide exports, with counter-trading accounting for under 10 per cent of Eastern European exports (main market – Poland). The company intended to continue all forms of counter-trading as appropriate in the present economic circumstances, in particular, customers' continuing problems of obtaining foreign currency and credit.

Nine companies, while exporting to Eastern Europe, had not actively sought to engage in counter-trading. In eight cases, exports to Eastern Europe accounted for under 10 per cent of their total exports. Five of the nine companies (K, L, M, N and P) had established strategic alliances in Eastern Europe.

Both companies K and N had established a 'minor' joint-venture presence in the area, driven both by their own strategic analysis, and an 'approach from East European authorities/enterprises'; company N was also involved in licensing.

Company L reported a 'significant' joint venture in the area, together with licensing. Joint ventures were considered to be superior to counter-trading as they allowed 'greater control of operations', 'avoided releasing control of technology' and provided 'greater in-house marketing expertise'. This suggests better-targeted marketing strategy, based on enhanced market knowledge and cultural empathy.

Companies M and P were currently involved in various minor licensing and franchising arrangements, and company M indicated that a joint venture might be sought to strengthen its market presence for strategic reasons. Similarly, companies O and R reported that they were examining the possibility of establishing joint ventures in the near future.

Companies Q and S had no immediate plans to move beyond conventional exporting.

Finally, one company (T) had entered the Eastern European market by establishing a joint venture in Hungary without previous exporting contact with any Eastern European market, following an approach by an Eastern European enterprise.

Table 19.3: Companies with unchanged countertrade.

Company reporting 'no change' in countertrading position	E. European exports as % of total exports	Countertrading as % of E. European exports	Main forms of countertrading	Main E. European export market	Countertrading as % of main E. European export market	Other involvements
J (engineering products)	1–9	1–9	barter counter-purchase buyback switch trade	Poland	1–9	'Minor' licensing

Table 19.4: Companies with no countertrade.

Companies reporting exporting (but no countertrading)	E. European exports as % of total exports	Main E. European export market	Other involvements
K (chemicals)	1–9	Czechoslovakia	'Minor' joint venture
L (engines)	1–9	Yugoslavia	'Significant' joint venture, 'minor' licensing
M (trucks)	1–9	Hungary	'Minor' franchising, licensing
N (lifts)	1–9	Poland	'Minor' joint venture, licensing
O (tyres)	1–9	Yugoslavia	None (but joint venture a possibility)
P (chemicals)	1–9	USSR	'Minor' franchising, licensing
Q (engineering)	1–9	Poland	None
R (steel products)	1–9	Hungary	None (but various deals in hand)
S (engineering)	10–24	USSR	None
Company reporting no exporting T (food products)	0	Hungary	'Significant' joint venture

Assessment

Like Mark Twain's death, reports of the imminent demise of CT appear greatly exaggerated. There is little question that Western firms, eager to avoid the often substantial transaction costs of CT, would prefer to receive hard currency for their exports, but until currencies like the koruna and the zloty achieve full convertibility and Western banks and aid agencies significantly expand their lending to Eastern European *enterprises*, as distinct from governments, it is difficult to see how East–West trade can expand without CT. Insistence on hard currency by Eastern agencies may often be counter-productive and contribute to industrial dislocation.

In this respect, a most important development is the establishment of Western-backed banking agencies within Eastern European countries to provide small-scale venture capital to assist industrial reconstruction.

At issue is not simply the rise and possible fall of East–West CT, but whether it will give way to more permanent forms of industrial co-operation, and on what scale. While currency problems continue, CT will persist, but it is likely to be augmented by an acceleration of more formal types of strategic alliance, like joint ventures.

It is tempting to suggest that CT is merely a staging post *en route* to such alliances, which are 'a natural progression from CT'. For a firm with an established market bridgehead via CT involvement, the dismantling of many of the legal and institutional impediments, thus alleviating the property rights and agency problems, will encourage the consolidation of a more secure presence in markets deemed to be of strategic importance.

Among our small sample of exporters, there was support for this gradual progression, indicated most strikingly by the case of the pharmaceutical company which had ceased to take part in CT, having set up a joint venture in Poland – i.e. it no longer counter-traded because 'it now has no need to'.

However, this gradualistic argument should not be overstressed. Some companies have set up JVs without having prior experience of CT, or indeed, any other contact, with the host country. These companies have clearly 'jumped' the CT phase of building up trading relationships. Also, there is the case of the reactive 'opportunistic' counter-trader, which appeared to regard CT as an inconvenience to be exploited only when short-term profit opportunities were revealed.

The prospects for CT largely hinge on the future availability of Western funding to lubricate trade. Without this, CT is likely to persist, at least in the medium term, as existing counter-traders continue or possibly increase their activities, and as other companies, newly aware of the strategic importance of the more open Eastern markets, 'test the water', initially via CT involvement. Other companies will 'leapfrog' this stage and take full or partial equity stakes in local enterprises.

Summary

In this paper, we have considered the implications for counter-trade of the recent liberalization of political and economic structures in the countries of the former Eastern bloc. CT is often regarded as a response to market imperfections, such as the difficulty of enforcing property rights in economies with less-developed legal systems, so that removal of institutional restrictions and greater availability of information is likely to remove the need to counter-trade. However, orthodox trade requires mutual currency convertibility or reliable access to trade finance. Until these are established, CT activity is likely to feature in trading relationships with many former CMEA countries. Meanwhile, continuing removal of institutional barriers will encourage the formation of increasing numbers of more formal strategic alliances between Western and non-governmental Eastern partners.

References

Cohen, S. S. and Zysman, J. (1986) 'Countertrade, Offsets, Barter, and Buybacks', *California Management Review* XXVIII(2): 41–56.

Ford, J. G. (1986) 'Report on Countertrade', presented to the *Commission on External Relations of the European Parliament*, PE Doc. A 2-117/86.

Gonzalez, J. (1985) 'Countertrade in Developing Country Policy', *11th World Banking Conference*, Paris.

Griffin, J. C. and Rouse, W. (1986) 'Countertrade: A Third World Development Strategy', *Third World Quarterly* January: 177–204.

van Hoof, L. (1991) 'The Transformation of Eastern Europe and its Influence on Countertrade', *International Trade and Finance Association Conference*, Marseilles.

Huszagh, S. M. and Barksdale, H. (1986) 'International Barter and Countertrade: An Exploratory Study' *Journal of the Academy of Marketing Science* 14(1): 21–8.

Jasch, R. (1989) 'Countertrade Questions', *Countertrade and Barter Quarterly* Feb–March: 22.

Jones, S. F. (1990) 'North–South Countertrade, Barter and Reciprocal Trade with Developing Countries', *Economist Intelligence Unit Special Report* No 174, London.

Kaikati, J. (1976) 'The Reincarnation of Barter as a Marketing Tool', *Journal of Marketing* 40(2): 17–24.

Kaikati, J. (1981) 'The International Barter Boom: Perspective and Challenges', *Journal of International Marketing* 1 (8).

Kogut, B. (1986) 'On Designing Contracts to Guarantee Enforcibility: Theory and Evidence from East–West Trade', *Journal of International Business Studies* 7(2): 47–62.

Mirus, R. and Yeung, B. (1986) 'Economic Incentives for Countertrade', *Journal of International Business Studies* 27(3), Fall: 27–39.

Mirus, R. and Yeung, B. (1991) 'Countertrade: What Have We Learned?', *International Trade and Finance Association Conference*, Marseilles.

Neale, C. W. and Shipley, D. D. (1990) 'Empirical Insights into British Countertrade with Eastern Bloc Countries', *International Marketing Review* 7(1): 15–31.

Nykryn, J. (1985) 'Combining Import Deals with Export Activities', in Saunders, C. T. (ed.) *East–West Trade and Finance in the World Economy*, London: Macmillan.

Okoroafo, S. C. (1988) 'Determinants of LDC-Mandated Countertrade', *International Marketing Review* 5(1): 17–24.

Organization for Economic Cooperation and Development (1981) *East–West Trade: Some Recent Developments*, Paris: OECD.

Palia, A. P. (1990) 'Worldwide Network of Countertrade Services', *Industrial Marketing Management* 19(1): 69–76.

Parsons, J. E. (1985) 'A Theory of Countertrade Financing of International Business', *Sloan School of Management Working Paper* WP1632-85.

Rabino, S. and Shah, K. (1989) 'Countertrade and Penetration of LDC Markets', *Columbia Journal of World Business* 22(4), Winter: 31–7.

Raemy-Dirks, C. (1986) 'Countertrade: Linked Purchases in International Trade', in Gmur, C. J. (ed.) *Trade Financing*, London: Euromoney Publications.

Roosa, R. V. (1985) 'Countertrade in the World Economy', in R. Pringle (ed.) *Countertrade in the World Economy*, New York: Group of Thirty.

Schuster, F. (1978) 'Bartering Processes in Industrial Buying and Selling', *Industrial Marketing Management* 7: 119–27.

Sercu, P. (1990) 'Pros and Cons of Countertrade: A Critical Note', *European Institute for Advanced Studies in Management Working Paper* 90–07.

Shipley, D. D. and Neale, C. W. (1987) 'Industrial Barter and Countertrade', *Industrial Marketing Management* 16(1): 1–8.

Wills, J., Jacobs, L. and Palia, A. (1986) 'Countertrade: The Asia–Pacific Dimension', *International Marketing Review* 3(3): 20–7.

United Nations Economic Commission for Europe (1979), *Countertrade Practices in the Region*, TRADE/R385, November 9.

Yoffie, D. B. (1984) Profiting from Countertrade', *Harvard Business Review*, May–June: 8–16.

Zurawicki, L. (1988) 'Marketing Rationale for Countertrade', *European Management Journal* 6(3) Autumn: 299–308.

20

The Prospects for Foreign Direct Investment in Central and Eastern Europe

John H. Dunning

Introduction

Much has already been said, written and speculated about the subject of foreign direct investment (FDI) in Central and Eastern Europe.[1] Almost daily, we read about new joint equity ventures being set up in Eastern Germany, Russia, Poland or Hungary; or of a strategic alliance being concluded between a Central European and a Western or Japanese firm; and, scarcely less frequently, about the efforts of one or other of the East European governments to revamp its foreign investment rules and regulations, or to offer new tax concessions to make its country more attractive to foreign investors.

Some Facts and Figures

Yet substantive and reliable data on the full extent of the participation by foreign firms in East European countries, or even the flows of investment into these countries, is hard to come by. Moreover, what data we do have are rarely comparable across countries or industrial sectors. This, is a way, should come as no surprise, as for so long, because of the absence of any proper financial or accounting procedures in Central and Eastern Europe, most domestically produced economic statistics have been of dubious value.

Perhaps the best, and certainly the most publicized data we have, concerns the number of joint ventures involving foreign (by which we mean non-East European) registered firms. As shown in Table 20.1, these reveal a rapid growth of the

An earlier version of this chapter first appeared in the June 1991 issue of *Development and International Cooperation*. Readers interested in the subject of FDI in Central and Eastern European countries will find the contents of that issue especially interesting.

intentions of foreign firms to invest in Eastern Europe. At the beginning of 1988, 165 ventures involving foreign partners had been established. A year later, this figure had risen to 562; by March 1990 to 3,595, by December 1990 to 14,640 and by July 1991 to 25,845. More particularly, in the first half of 1991, there was a dramatic increase in new joint ventures registered in Romania and Bulgaria.

Table 20.1: Joint ventures registered in Central and Eastern Europe 1988–91.

	Investment stake July 1, 1991 (estimated billion)	Population mid-1989 (million)	Jan. 1 1988	Jan. 1 1989	Jan. 1 1990	Jan. 1 1991	July 1 1991
Soviet Union	$3.2	288.0	23	191	1,275	2,905	3,700
Hungary	$1.1	10.6	102	270	1,000	5,695	9,100
Poland	$0.4	37.9	13	55	918	2,800	4,350
Czechoslovakia	$0.4	15.6	7	16	60	1,600	3,700
Bulgaria	n/a	9.0	15	25	30	140	800
Romania	$0.2	23.2	5	5	5	1,500	4,195
Total	$4–5	384.3	165	562	3,274	14,640	25,845

Source: ECE Data Bank on East–West joint ventures.

However, as yet, only a small percentage – probably about 10 per cent – of these ventures, are currently operational. The great majority of registered ventures – particularly in high technology sectors in the former USSR – have come to naught. We do, however, know that, as of mid-1991, the highest proportion of joint venture start-ups had occurred in Poland and Hungary and in the service, rather than the manufacturing sector.[2]

The table also shows that the rate of growth of joint ventures is currently concentrated in three countries, viz. the former Soviet Union, Hungary and Poland. In the Soviet Union, where the growth potential of a large market is the main attraction, the estimated foreign capital invested in July 1991 was $3.2 billion; an amount about the same as the stock of inward investment in Sweden, Nigeria or Singapore. In Hungary, which is, perhaps, furthest along the road towards a market economy, it was $1.1 billion, about the same as the FDI stock in Pakistan, Uruguay or Cameroon; whereas, in Poland, in spite of a larger population and longer experience with joint venture capital,[3] the less stable political and social regime has limited inward direct investment to around $340 million.

Who are the major foreign players in Eastern Europe? According to the ECE data bank on East–West joint ventures, of the 1,721 joint ventures reported as having been established in Czechoslovakia, Hungary and Poland in the early 1990s,[4] 533 or 31.1 per cent involved Western German partners, 308 or 17.8 per cent other EC partners, 304 or 17.7 per cent Austrian partners, and 98 or 5.7 per cent US partners. As Table 20.2 shows, the distribution of foreign investors in the former USSR is rather more dispersed, although, in October 1990, Western European firms still accounted for 60.8 per cent of the 1,884 joint ventures which had then been registered, and US or Canadian firms for 14.0 per cent.

Table 20.2: Registered or Operational Foreign Investment Projects in Selected Countries in Central and Eastern Europe by Origin of Foreign Partner.

	Czechoslovakia[a] (March 1991)		*Hungary[a]* (Jan. 1990)		*Poland[b]* (Jan. 1990)		*USSR[b]* (Oct. 1990)	
Western European	88.6		77.7		81.2		60.8	
(of which EC)		(39.5)		(34.5)		(60.3)		(34.2)
North America	1.8		7.0		8.4		13.4	
(of which US)		(1.8)		(6.5)		(6.1)		(11.4)
Japan	0.0		0.3		0.1		1.8	
CMEA Economies	5.2		NSA		1.5		7.7	
Developing countries	1.3		1.5		2.0		9.9	
Unclassified or multiparty	3.1		13.4		6.8		6.4	
Totals	100.0		100.0		100.0		100.0	
Total number of projects	228		582		911		1,884	

Notes:
[a] Registered.
[b] Operational.
Source: ECE Data Bank on East–West joint ventures.

There is some evidence to suggest that physical distance and cultural affinities are important determinants in the choice of foreign partners. Thus Austrian firms are the leading investors (by number of joint ventures) in Hungary, while Swiss firms are unusually active in Czechoslovakia, and US and Finnish foreign investors in the USSR. There is also some intra-central and East European FDI. For example, in 1990, the erstwhile CMEA countries accounted for 9.8 per cent of the registered foreign investment projects in Czechoslovakia and 7.7 per cent of those in the USSR. There has also been a considerable upsurge of interest shown by developing country investors in the larger East European countries. By October 1990, there were 116 joint ventures involving developing country partners registered in the USSR, of which twenty-eight were Indian and twenty-four Chinese.

Finally, according to Ozawa (1992), as of the end of 1990, Japanese firms had concluded only forty-eight joint ventures with Central or Eastern European firms, thirty-three of which were within the former Soviet Union.[5]

Which sectors tend to attract the most inward investment? An analysis of the sectoral distribution on the investment intentions by foreign firms, set out in Table 20.3, reveals some noticeable differences. Within manufacturing industry which is currently attracting the most interest of Western capitalists in the Soviet Union and Poland, the former country seems to offer the best prospects in most branches of the mechanical engineering sector (and especially in office equipment and computers), whereas in Poland, the favoured sectors include food processing, clothing and wood products. In Hungary, business services, trade and transport undertakings account for 33 per cent of all approved applications by inward direct investment. In the Soviet Union, fast food chains and construction and business services (including computer-related activities) attract the largest share of

Table 20.3: Sectoral Registered or Operational Distribution of Joint Ventures in Selected Central and Eastern Europe Involving Foreign Partners.

	Czechoslovakia[a]		Hungary[a]		Poland[b]		USSR[b]	
Primary activities	3.9		1.5		4.3		2.0	
Agriculture, forestry and fishing		3.5		1.5		4.0		1.8
Other		0.4		–		0.3		0.2
Secondary activities	32.0		46.0		74.6		49.6	
Technology intensive[c]		15.7		19.3		19.0		23.0
Other		16.3		26.7		55.6		26.6
Tertiary activities	64.1		52.5		21.2		48.4	
Trade		19.7		15.8		3.2		3.3
Hotels & restaurants		2.1		0.9		3.2		6.8
Business-related activities		19.7		20.6		5.2		21.5
Infrastructure[d]		14.4		13.2		7.6		11.6
Other		8.2		2.0		1.9		5.4
Totals	100.0	100.0	100.0	100.0	100.0	100.0	100.0	100.0
Total number of projects	228		582		911		1,884	

Notes:
[a] Registered.
[b] Operational.
[c] Defined as chemicals, engineering and precision instruments, motor vehicles and rubber and plastics.
[d] Transport and communications includes construction, education, health, social work and sewage disposal.
Source: ECE Data Bank on East–West joint ventures.

operational investments. In Poland, construction, trade and hotels, and in Czechoslovakia, trade and business activities stand out as the service sectors with the largest number of joint ventures. Although some Central and East European countries have extensive mining and other natural resources, apart from some oil and agrichemicals investments in the former USSR, there has been very little foreign participation in these sectors.

Of the more noteworthy individual investments (or investment intentions) by MNEs in Central and Eastern Europe, mention might be made of several investments by MNEs, e.g. Siemens (Germany), Alcatel (France), ABB (Sweden/Switzerland) and General Electric (USA), in the telecommunications and energy sectors; a $3 billion capital stake by Volkswagen in the Skoda motor car plant in Czechoslovakia; a $1.5 billion investment by the same company in a new production facility in East Germany to produce the Golf and Polo ranges of cars; a $200 million investment by General Motors in a railway carriage and machine factory in Hungary; a $150 million participation by General Electric in Tungsram, Eastern

Europe's leading light-bulb manufacturer; Suzuki and Itoh's 40 per cent stake in a $10 billion venture to manufacture motor cars in Hungary; Gillette's joint venture in the former Soviet Union to produce razor blades; ASEA Brown Boveri's acquisition of a majority stake in a leading Polish turbine and generator producer; and MacDonald's multi-million dollar stake in a chain of fast food restaurants in the former Soviet Union, East Germany and Hungary. Several leading Western accounting and management consultancy MNEs have also set up offices in the former Soviet Union, Hungry and Poland.[6] In addition, there are several instances of MNEs – especially from Japan and the US – forging alliances with Austrian or German firms from the Western länder, to penetrate Central and Eastern markets.[7]

Most foreign-owned joint ventures are set up either to serve the domestic market of the host country or to serve foreign (and mostly other European) countries with goods and services which require resources and capabilities in which that country is comparatively well endowed (or is expected to be endowed). It is the prospect of Hungary, Poland and Czechoslovakia – not to mention the Eastern länder of Germany – syphoning away manufacturing activity which might otherwise have been created in their territories that is causing some European and Far Eastern countries concern. There have been several well-publicized cases of both Japanese and Western manufacturers switching the location of their new investments from the Iberian Peninsula and Greece to Central and Eastern Europe[8] in order to take advantage of lower wage and transport costs,[9] and, in some sectors, a well-trained and skilled labour force.

As might be expected, the relative importance of foreign-owned enterprises in most Central and East European economies is still extremely small. In Poland, it was estimated that in 1989 they accounted for only 1.9 per cent of all enterprises, 3.1 per cent of exports and 1.6 per cent of all employment. In other East European countries the proportions were considerably less, although Hungarian statistics suggest that in some manufacturing sectors, foreign joint ventures now account for 25 per cent or more of the country's exports. However, when one recalls that, prior to 1987, joint ventures were not permissible at all in the Soviet Union, the opening up of the economy to both international trade and investment has been quite remarkable.

The Prospects for More MNE Activity

So much for a thumbnail sketch of the present state of foreign direct investment in Central and Eastern Europe. What now of the prospects for the future?

Most commentators agree that, taking a long-run perspective, the economies of Central and Eastern Europe offer a tremendous challenge and opportunity to foreign direct investors. Yet, at the end of 1990, the countries comprising this area, which had a combined population of over 400 million, received about the same amount of investment as did Ireland and Norway, each of which had populations of less than five million. Even industrial market-oriented countries, with the same average income per head as the most prosperous of the East European economies, attracted forty times more investment per head of population.

Assuming just a doubling of living standards and a completion of the major privatization schemes planned by the major East European economies by the year 2000,[10] it would not be unreasonable to expect foreign and intra-Eastern European investment to rise from its 1990 figure of $2–3 billion to around $100 billion – or about two-fifths of its current level in Western Europe.

These, however, are just orders of magnitude of what *could* be achieved. The human capabilities and natural resources of most Central and East European countries are impressive. What is lacking is the right institutional structure, managerial access to foreign markets, entrepreneurial and work culture, organizational capabilities and monetary incentives to efficiently utilize and upgrade these resources and capabilities.

While foreign MNEs are uniquely able to supply many of the necessary ingredients for economic growth, a reshaping of attitudes to work and wealth-creation, the redesigning of the way economic activity is organized and the supporting legal framework, especially with respect to property rights and contracts, the costs of establishing and running a market system, and the introduction of macroeconomic policies which encourage domestic savings, but accept the discipline of currency convertibility and an open trading system, are too substantial for individual companies – and, sometimes, for individual countries – to bear. These are the *real* costs of restructuring the economies of Central and Eastern Europe; and, at least some progress on this front must be made, and be seen to be made, prior to any substantial commitment of direct investment funds by foreign MNEs.

Alternative Models of Development

What then, is the most likely course or path of development in Eastern Europe?

Let us consider three possible models, or scenarios – accepting that the pattern and pace of restructuring is likely to vary, for example, between Hungary and Albania, or between Czechoslovakia and Bulgaria or between Romania and Poland. The first is the *developing country* model. This hypothesis that, currently, the economies of the leading erstwhile communist countries can be likened to that of the industrializing developing countries, and that just as these, notably Brazil, Mexico, Korea, Thailand, Taiwan and Singapore, have moved along a particular development path or trajectory – from attracting little to attracting substantial inflows of foreign capital – so, as they develop, Central and East European countries will do the same. The model also seems appropriate insofar as the new regimes are in a similar position to many in the third world, in that the organizational and institutional capacities for capitalist development are currently inadequate and frequently distorted (Radice 1991).

While at first sight this seems an attractive scenario, the assumptions on which it is based are questionable. World Bank statistics suggest that, in the mid-1980s, the population of most East European economies (Albania is the main exception) were considerably better educated, medically cared for, and housed, than those of even the most prosperous developing countries (Singapore and Hong Kong are exceptions). They also consumed more energy, and their R&D expenditure as a percentage of gross national product even approached that of some Western economies.[11] On the other hand, the industrial performance of these countries, and their commercial, transportation and communications infrastructures were generally no better than those of many middle-income developing countries, and considerably inferior to those of the fastest-growing newly industrialized countries. And, the proportion of the gross national product absorbed by central government was two to three times that of the developing countries of the same income levels. Table 20.4 sets out some details of health and educational standards of a group of eight Central and East European countries, including Yugoslavia.

The second model is to compare the present situation of East European economies with that of West Germany and Japan after the Second World War. Let us call this the *reconstruction model*. This model has intuitive appeal, in that it might be supposed that the resource potential of the larger East European countries is comparable to that of the two most war-devastated countries, but that to exploit these resources requires a fund of technological, organizational and management capabilities no less than that demanded by Japan and Germany in 1945. At the same time, this model fails to take account of the enormous institutional impedimenta and the extent of the political and attitudinal and cultural changes required by most Central and Eastern European nations before private enterprise (which, after all, was stifled for only a decade or so in both Japan and Germany) is prepared to undertake the entrepreneurship and investment – including investment in R&D and manpower training – for economic restructuring and growth.

The third model is one which combines the more appropriate ingredients of the developing country and reconstruction models, but also takes account of the macro and micro-organizational and attitudinal changes necessary for economic progress. This might be called the *systemic model* – the word 'systemic' being chosen because it suggests that the willingness and ability of foreign (or, for that matter, domestic) investors, rests mainly on the speed and extent to which East European economies can reorganize both their economic and legal systems, and the ethos of their people towards entrepreneurship and wealth-creating activities.

The three scenarios suggest different roles for FDI. For example, depending on whether Central and East European governments adopt a German or Japanese strategy towards inward investment – and we think the former is much more likely – the reconstruction model points to the most speedy and widespread involvement of foreign-owned firms. The likely contribution of inward direct investment in the developing country model will depend on the momentum and pattern of economic development, how this integrates into the world economy, and the kind of foreign participation it is likely to induce. Like the first scenario, the extent of foreign investment predicted by the systemic model depends on the nature of the systemic changes required and the rate and efficiency with which they are introduced; but the model does suggest a much slower initial participation of foreign firms, due to the substantial establishment and learning costs they might have to incur in setting up production units and in marketing their products.

Because of the current differences in the economic development, political systems and institutional frameworks of the individual Central and East European countries, it is likely that each country will follow a somewhat different path of integrating itself into the world economy. The former GDR is, in fact, already following the course of the reconstruction model, with Hungary and Czechoslovakia two or three steps behind. By contrast, Albania, Romania, and Bulgaria are more likely to fit into the developing country model. But much will depend on

Table 20.4: Education and Health Facilities in Central and Eastern European Countries.

	Education			Health			
	Primary	Secondary	Tertiary	Population per physician (1984)	Daily calorie supply (1989)	Infant mortality (per 1000 of births) (1990)	Life expectancy (1990)
	(% of population in appropriate age group)						
	(1989)	(1989)	(1989)				
Central and East European Countries							
USSR	106	na	na	270	3,386	24	71
Hungary	94	76	15	310	3,644	15	71
Poland	99	81	20	490	3,505	15	71
Romania	95	88	9	570	3,155	27	70
Czechoslovakia	92	87	18	280	3,632	12	72
Bulgaria	97	75	26	280	3,707	14	73
GDR	106	na	na	440	3,814	8	77
Albania	99	80	9	na	2,761	28	72
Yugoslavia	95	80	19	550	3,634	20	72
Developing Countries							
Upper middle income Countries	104	56	17	940	2,987	45	68
Middle income Countries	102	55	17	2,250	2,860	48	66

Source: World Bank: World Development Report 1992.

the speed and extent to which each country proceeds with its privatization process; the extent to which governments are able to rid themselves of their centralized and bureaucratic control and instead become more mission-oriented and supportive of an emerging private sector to help produce the wealth required in the most cost-effective manner;[12] and how far it is able to stimulate both the entrepreneurial ethos of its people, and the upgrading of the expectations of industrial and domestic consumers for better produced and superior quality products.

In any event, the role of FDI is likely to fluctuate according both to the form and stage of economic development. This idea has been explored by the author in other publications (Dunning 1988, 1993).[13] In two recently published papers, Teretumo Ozawa (1991b, 1992) has suggested that, in her economic development, Japan passed through four stages of industrial restructuring. The first was in the 1950s and was marked by the production and exports of labour-intensive, and fairly low skill products. As Japanese wage rates rose, and her human and technological capacity became more sophisticated, her comparative advantage shifted into scale-intensive, non-differentiated products, e.g. heavy chemicals, steel, shipbuilding, etc. The third phase, which lasted from the mid-1960s to the early 1980s, was that in which Japan made considerable inroads into the international markets for mass production durable goods, e.g. motor vehicles and consumer electronics. The fourth stage, in which the Japanese economy is now entering, is that in which production and exports are highly innovatory and skill-intensive or, as Ozawa puts it, are Schumpeterian-type products. Depending on the policies of host governments, inward FDI may play an important role in fashioning each of these development phases; but outward direct investment is not likely to materialize to any major extent until Stages 3 and 4 are reached.

The application of the Japanese model to the development and restructuring of the Eastern European economies and the role which MNEs might play in the process, will depend very much on location-specific assets which the individual countries can accumulate, and the policies pursued by their governments to advance their 'diamond of competitive advantages'.

As to the existing technological assets, some hints may be gained from an examination of the kind of patents, registered by the world's leading enterprises, in the US, which they attribute to their innovatory activities in Eastern Europe. In an exercise conducted over the period 1969 to 1986, John Cantwell (1990) identified the industrial sectors in which the Warsaw Pact countries recorded an above-average share of registered patents. The chemical (excluding pharmaceutical) and mechanical engineering sectors both stood out, with both high research-intensive and labour-intensive sectors recording well below the average share of patents. Of the foreign firms which carried out the most technological activity in Eastern Europe, those of West European – and especially of German origin – scored the highest, with those of US and Japanese origin well behind in second and third places.

The Role of MNEs

What then of the likely role of MNEs in this restructuring process? In the mid-1980s, the authors of some twelve country profiles concluded that inbound and outbound MNE activity had a generally beneficial affect on trade, productivity and economic restructuring (Dunning 1985). It may, then, be reasonably expected that the opening of Central and Eastern Europe to market forces will, by encouraging inward direct investment, markedly improve the economic lot of its citizens. If the experience of most countries in Western Europe and the more market-oriented developing countries is anything to go by, then foreign technology, management expertise and the access to foreign markets can, providing the conditions are right, play a critical role in Central and Eastern European economic development.[14]

At the same time, we would contend that such a role is likely to be different than that experienced by Western European countries in the past, or developing countries today, in at least three ways. First, the form of foreign participation is likely to be more pluralistic. It may well be that, as in Western Europe, the 100 per cent owned affiliate will eventually become the dominant form of participation by foreign firms. But, we would also expect a multitude of collaborative agreements, subcontracting and networking arrangements, crossing many different lines of economic activity, both along and between value chains, to be concluded. An example of such pluralism is shown in the motor industry, where Volkswagen and Fiat are both substantially involved in a number of Central and East European economies but in very different ways.

Second, we would anticipate that at least the larger MNEs will respond to the challenges and opportunities of Eastern Europe in terms of the likely affect on their *global* marketing and production strategies. This is what is already largely happening in Western Europe and, to some extent, in the US and Canada as well. If current trends are anything to go by, Western and Japanese MNEs are unlikely to treat their East European affiliates as stand-alone ventures, but to treat them as part and parcel of a Pan-European or even an international network of activities. This would suggest that from the start, the managerial strategies and organizational systems of European joint ventures, will, in so far as they are endorsed by the local partners, be locked into those currently pursued by the foreign firms. Western European firms, in particular, look forward to new and enlarged markets for their products, over which they may spread escalating costs of R&D and marketing; and by so doing, enabling them to compete more effectively with Japanese and US MNEs. In some sectors in which there is currently surplus production capacity in the Western world, both US and European firms are hoping that increased demand opportunities, especially in the former Soviet Union, Poland and East Germany, will help absorb some of this slack.

Third, there is every suggestion that, to some extent at least, the international community, and especially the EC – has an enormous stake in the success of the political and economic restructuring of the erstwhile communist bloc countries. By such means as direct grants, aid or loans; by the encouragement of private direct investment, e.g. by tax incentives and investment insurance schemes; by the provision of information about production and marketing conditions, laws and regulations in different East European countries; by action taken to improve economic transparency and to promote a better understanding on the part of Western investors of the business environment in Eastern Europe (e.g. the PHARE programme); by assisting the education and training of East European technicians, scientists, accountants, and the like; by the encouragement of industrial co-operation agreements between EC and East European firms; by technical advice on the appropriate macroeconomic and structural adjustment policies for East European governments to pursue, individual Western governments, the European Commission, the EBRD[15] and various international agencies such as the World Bank, are likely to exert an even more critical influence on the shape of an enlarged Europe in the 1990s, than did (US) Marshall aid and similar schemes play in the design of Western Europe in the 1950s.[16]

Certainly there is no shortage of ideas for the kind of multilateral aid programme which might be given to Central and East European countries. One particularly interesting suggestion, called the Strasbourg Plan for Central and Eastern Europe, was put forward in 1991 by Michael Palmer, former Director General of the European Parliament (Palmer 1991). Palmer argued that an aid package of around $16.7 billion a year is needed from the advanced industrial nations, if economic restructuring in the seven Central and East European countries (including the former GDR) is to be completed in the next two decades or so. This equates with between 0.1 per cent and 0.5 per cent of the GDPs of the leading Triad countries in 1990.

However, as a *quid pro quo* for such financial aid, it is proposed that each of the recipient governments should work out an overall plan for economic growth, and within the plan, a 'shopping list' of priorities. The governments should then launch a joint appeal to the international community. It is envisaged that priority should be given to radical improvement in transport and communication networks, a rapid reduction of environmental pollution, establishing an efficient market system, and encouraging currency stabilization and balance of payments support. As with the earlier Marshall Plan, the basic goal would be to establish the necessary conditions for private investment, including FDI, to be profitably undertaken.

We do not need to identify, in any detail, the ingredients of these necessary conditions. Suffice to assert that both the productive and institutional infrastructure of most Central and East European countries is two or even three generations behind that of Western Europe. In a recently published assessment of the market-building strategies in Hungary, Poland and Czechoslovakia, the OECD concluded that the only real progress that had been made was in the area of restoring property rights to private owners, removing some market imperfections, e.g. consumer subsidies, and trade flow distortions, and increasing investment in education and labour skills.[17] But such are the prizes offered to foreign firms by their resources and markets, and to Western democratic governments by the prospects of a free and thriving market of 400 million inhabitants, that the incentive to overcome the huge barriers to restructuring is very great indeed. To this extent, we believe that a parallel can legitimately be drawn between the US interest in the economic and political recovery of West Germany and Japan, and that of the OECD nations, in the future of Central and Eastern Europe.

Again, at the risk of generalizing, we would submit that the extent and pace at which East European economies will become fully integrated with the rest of Europe, will largely depend on the outcome of three factors. The first is the ability of governments to efficiently promote restructuring *and* to convince their own people that, in spite of additional economic hardships they will inevitably have to endure, there is light at the end of the tunnel, and the democratization of markets will release a treasure of talents and entrepreneurship. The second is the likely future course of the economy of the Commonwealth of Independent States (CIS).

The potential market of this economy is three times greater than the rest of Eastern Europe combined. If the CIS flourishes, this is likely to create demand for products from the more advanced Central and East European economies, and hence, encourage further foreign investment into them. The third determinant is the extent to which the necessary finance capital for long-term development can be found in a global economy in which the claims for international savings are so much greater than the supply. At the end of the day, capital constraints could well limit the pace and pattern of the economic regeneration of Eastern Europe.

We conclude this section with a review of two recent surveys of the opinions of business executives about the investment opportunities offered by different countries in Eastern Europe. The first is that conducted by *Financial Executive* and published in its September/October 1990 issue. The former GDR was perceived to offer the most attractive business environment to foreign investors, while Hungary was thought to afford the best indigenous assets for undertaking business. Some further details are set out in Table 20.5. Yugoslavia (which was included in the survey) and Czechoslovakia were ranked third or fourth – although, interestingly, Yugoslavia was believed to have the best history of entrepreneurship, yet the worst but one record of the speed or stability in economic reform. Currently, Romania and Bulgaria would not appear to be serious contenders for inward direct investment.

In another field study conducted by three US business school analysts in August 1990 (Michail, Nandola and Prasad 1990), and based upon questionnaires completed by a sample of seventy-nine US business executives, it was found that of some eight possible modalities for exploiting East European markets, joint ventures with US minority equity interest were listed as the fifth most likely, following exporting from a West European subsidiary (ranked first), exporting from the US, licensing, bartering and counter-trade. Joint ventures with a US majority interest were ranked seventh after management contracts; while the least likely form of entry was thought to be the wholly owned subsidiary.

Concerning the perceived ability of East European countries to adapt to the changes required of them if they were to attract more investment, the respondents considered the progress made by East Germany the most significant, followed by that of Poland, Czechoslovakia, and Hungary. Of the seven categories of change identified, the most progress had been made with political reform and the host country attitude towards foreign direct investment; and the least progress in the upgrading of infrastructure. Finally, it was the opinion of the US executive that West German MNEs from Germany were likely to be the most likely future investors in Eastern Europe, with those from the USA and Japan following some way behind.

Conclusions

The resources and markets of Central and Eastern Europe offer huge and exciting challenges to Western and Japanese firms; and also to fledgling indigenous entrepreneurs. These opportunities are likely to be exploited in a variety of ways, notably through trade, joint ventures and strategic alliances between Central and

Table 20.5: Indicators of attractiveness to foreign direct investors.

(a) Business environment

	Standing with Western banks	Speed/stability of economic reform	Reliability of infrastructure	Extent of currency convertibility	Extent of profit repatriation	Extent of government bureaucracy	Average score
East Germany	1	1	4	1	1	2	1.8
Hungary	4	2	2	2	2	1	2.2
Czechoslovakia	2	3	1	4	4	3	2.8
Yugoslavia	6	7	3	3	3	4	4.3
Poland	7	5	5	5	4	5	5.2
Bulgaria	3	4	7	6	7	7	5.8
Soviet Union	5	6	6	6	6	8	6.1
Romania	8	8	8	6	8	6	7.3

(b) Business asset attractiveness

	Existence of export-oriented business	History of entrepreneurship	Average score
Hungary	1	2	1.5
East Germany	2	3	2.5
Yugoslavia	4	1	2.5
Czechoslovakia	3	3	3
Poland	5	5	5
Soviet Union	6	6	6
Bulgaria	7	7	7
Romania	8	8	8

Source: Financial Executive Sept/October 1990.

Eastern European and foreign firms. Because of their specific advantages and their operating presence in many different countries, MNEs are ideal vehicles for spearheading industrial restructuring. Through their ability to transfer technology and management skills; through their introduction of up-to-date industrial practices and quality control techniques; through their example and their spill-over affects on local entrepreneurship, suppliers and competitors; and through their network of international linkages – with both large and small firms – they can provide much of the competences and initiatives for economic growth.

However, such investment will only occur if it advances the global strategies of companies. In a scenario of increasing shortages of capital but widening opportunities for growth, this places considerable burdens on the authorities of East European economies to offer the most favourable environment for value added activities – be these to produce goods and services for the domestic or international market. This is emphatically not simply a question of liberalization of investment policies or of offering foreign investors generous fiscal incentives. Equally, if not more important, there is a need for governments to both create and sustain an economic and social environment in which both domestic and foreign firms can compete effectively and foster the right attitudes on the part of labour and management alike towards productivity improvements and competing in a global environment. While, as we have said, MNEs can supply some of these initiatives, particularly in so far as they can link the recipient countries into the world economy, at the end of the day, it is the responsibility of governments as custodians of the welfare of their citizens to set the commercial, institutional and attitudinal framework in which private enterprise can both flourish and provide the much-needed engine for economic development.

While the long-term future for FDI in Central and East Europe is highly promising, the next decade or so is likely to be a particularly taxing time for both foreign investors and the governments of host countries. The current recession, the collapse of intra-regional trade, brought about *inter alia* by the worsening economic situation in the CIS, and the Middle East crisis, have each added to the already daunting restructuring problems facing most of Central and Eastern Europe. Indeed, economists are agreed that, economically speaking, things must get worse before they can get better. In addition, uncertainties about legal instability, ownership restrictions, currency non-convertibility and supply constraints, and the absence of the required legal accounting and financial infrastructure, are causing Western firms to reappraise the optimistic scenario on which they had earlier based their investment intentions. In the words of Carl McMillan (1991), 'The initial euphoria and the favorable business climate it engendered has now begun to wear off. The new mood is reinforced by greater awareness of the practical difficulties posed by investment in the area'.

These are sensible words. At the same time, it would be unfortunate if the pendulum of business attitudes and expectations should swing too much towards the pessimistic. One very recent encouraging sign is the commitment of the heads of government of the seven leading industrial nations, to assist the former Soviet Union in its efforts to move away from a command-dominated to a market-oriented economic system.[18] Should this commitment be translated into action, the medium-term future of FDI in Central and Eastern Europe is, indeed, a promising one.

Notes

1. For the purposes of this paper, we shall not consider Yugoslavia as part of East Europe, although there are many similarities between that country and those dealt within this article. In fact, of course, Yugoslavia has many institutional advantages over the rest of East Europe; and, since the mid-1960s, has made considerable progress in the introduction of market-oriented economic reforms and the development of a cadre of managers and entrepreneurs. For further details, see Rojac (1991).
2. About one half of operative joint ventures involving foreign firms in the former USSR are also in the service sector.
3. For example, in the decade before the political reforms, some 700 foreign enterprises were set up in Poland (June 1990).
4. The precise date varies between January 1990 for Hungary and Poland to March 1991 for the Czech and Slovak Republics.
5. Ozawa asserts that this miniscule presence of Japan as an investor in Central and Eastern Europe closely parallels its relatively insignificant position as a trade partner. He quoted a survey undertaken by the Japanese government in 1990 (MITI 1991) in which, while 51.8 per cent of European-owned firms assessed Central and Eastern Europe as a very or somewhat attractive potential production base, only 11.6 per cent of Japanese firms so opined. Unfamiliarity with local economic conditions, language difficulties and greater investment attractions in other parts of the world were the main reasons given for the lack of investment by potential Japanese investors.
6. Further details of recent acquisitions and newly established joint ventures are given in McMillan (1990) and in Samuelsson (1992).
7. Examples quoted by Ozawa (1992) include an agreement between Nissho Iwai Corporation and Metall Gesselschaft to develop markets in the former Soviet bloc countries in five key fields: non-ferrous metals, chemicals, machinery, steel and finance; and that between the Murebeni Corporation and Austrian Industries in product and market development in the area of plant exports and electronic home products to Eastern Europe. It may also be worth observing that some of the investment classified as German has in fact been undertaken by foreign-owned subsidiaries located in that country.
8. These include the decision of the Mitsubishi group to switch a new manufacturing plant from Spain to Eastern Europe, Suzuki, which initially planned to set up an assembly plant for motor cycles in Portugal and subsequently opted for Eastern Europe, and Foundation Publishing which decided to expand its typesetting operations by establishing a joint venture in Budapest rather than in Greece.
9. In early 1991, for example, monthly wages were $140 in Hungary and $45 in Poland, as compared with $235 in Portugal and $400 in Spain.
10. These include the sale of over 8,000 state-owned companies in Poland (in which foreign firms may acquire up to a 10 per cent equity stake), and the public auctioning of up to 100,000 small and medium-size trading and service firms in Czechoslovakia.
11. Although much of this expenditure was directed to defence and space-related activities.
12. For an interesting critique of the economic role of the US government which could well be applied to the Central and Eastern European situations, see Osborne and Gaebler (1992).
13. See, for example, Chapter 5 of Dunning (1988). The investment development cycle suggests that as countries develop, their propensities to be invested in, or to engage in outward investment, proceeds through various phases with the inward/outward ratio being at its highest as countries approach full industrialization.
14. For a more critical view of the role of MNEs in economic development – particularly in nations newly exposed to international competition – see O'Hearn (1990).
15. The European Bank for Reconstruction and Development, which has been set up with a capital of ECU 10 billion to help finance market-oriented projects in Central and East Europe.
16. For a review of these programmes, see Commission of the European Communities,

Industrial Cooperation with Central and Eastern Europe: Ways to Strengthen Cooperation, Brussels (Communication from the Commission to the Council and European Parliament) SEC (90) 1213, July 1990.

17.   As summarized in *International Economic Insights* (2), March/April, 1991.
18.   As put forward in a six-point plan designed primarily to promote the trade of, and provide technical assistance to, the Soviet Union, agreed at the G7 Summit of Heads of Governments, held in London in July 1991. For details of this plan, see *Financial Times*, July 18, 1991.

References

Bornschier, V. (1980) 'Multinational corporations and economic growth: A cross-national test of the decapitalization thesis, *Journal of Development Economies* 7: 191–210.

Cantwell, J. C. (1990) *East–West Business Links and the Economic Development of Poland and Eastern Europe*, Reading: University of Reading, mimeo.

Commission of the European Communities (1990) *Industrial Cooperation with Central and Eastern Europe: Ways to Strengthen Cooperation*, Brussels (Communication from the Commission to the Council and European Parliament) SEC (90) 1213, July 1990.

Dunning, J. H. (ed.) (1985) *Multinational Enterprises, Economic Structure and International Competitiveness*, Chichester and New York: John Wiley.

Dunning, J. H. (1988) *Explaining International Production* London: Unwin Hyman.

Dunning, J. H. (1993) *Multinational Enterprises and the Global Economy*, Wokingham, Berkshire, Reading, Mass.: Addison Wesley.

Gutman, P. (1990) *From Joint Ventures to Foreign Direct Investment: New Perspectives in Eastern Europe and the Soviet Union*, Revised version of paper presented at a Conference on Opportunities and Contracts for East West Soviet Ventures, Moscow, December 7–16.

McMillan, C. (1991) *Foreign Direct Investment Flows to Eastern Europe and the Implications for Developing Countries*, paper prepared for Department of Economic and Social Affairs, UN, April.

Mikhail, A. D., Nandosa, K. N. and Prahad, S. B. (1990) *Perceptions of US Executives in Doing Business in Eastern Europe and the USSR: Testing the International Exchange Framework*, Paper presented at the 16th Annual Conference of *European International Business Studies Association*, Madrid, December.

O'Hearn, D. (1990) 'TNCs intervening mechanisms and economic growth in Ireland: A longitudinal test and extension of the Bornschier model', *World Development* 18: 417–29.

Osborne, D. and Gaebler, E. (1992) *Reinventing Government: How the Entrepreneurial Spirit is Transforming the Public Sector*, Reading, Mass.: Addison Wesley.

Ozawa, T. (1991a) 'Europe 1992 and Japanese multinationals transplanting a subcontracting system in the expanded market', in Bürgenmeier, B. and Mucchielli, J. (eds) *Multinationals and Europe 1992*, London and New York: Routledge.

Ozawa, T. (1991b) 'Japan in a new phase of multinationalization and industrial upgrading: Functional integration of trade growth and FDI', *Journal of World Trade* 25: 43–60.

Ozawa, T. (1992) 'Japanese MNCs as potential partners in East Europe's economic reconstruction', in Buckley, P. J. and Ghauri, P. N. (eds) *The Liberalization of Eastern Europe and the Impact of International Business*, London: Edward Elgar.

Palmer, M. (1991) *A Plan for Economic Growth in Central and Eastern Europe*, Luxembourg: mimeo.

Radice, H. (1991) *Transnational Corporations and Eastern Europe*, University of Leeds School of Business and Economics Discussion Paper G91/108.

Rojac, M. (1991) 'Liberalization of foreign investment legislation in Yugoslavia', *Development and International Corporations* 12: 69–83.

Samuelsson, H. F. (1992) *Foreign Direct Investments in Eastern Europe: Current Situation and Potential*, Geneva: ECE/UNCTC.

UNCTC (1989) *CTC Reporter* 28, Autumn.

World Bank (1990) *World Development Report 1990*, Oxford: Oxford University Press.

21

Market Opportunities in Eastern Europe: MNCs' Response

Subhash C. Jain and Lewis R. Tucker

Following the overthrow of their communist regimes in 1989, the Eastern European countries entered a new era. Although political freedoms were quickly achieved, the tasks of reconstruction, modernization and stability are still in their early stages. Each country confronts the challenge of trying to promote democratic integration and economic growth, while striving to preserve national stability.

The political change in the region has created an economic climate full of both opportunity and great risk. Identifying risk and assessing the merits of investing capital into the region is one of the most important tasks facing Western corporations today. Are the potential profits sufficient to justify the myriad risks involved?

The above question can only be answered after considerable scrutiny of the firm's priorities and resources, which will vary from industry to industry. The corporate culture is also quite important in arriving at the decision. Only companies which are both equipped and willing to enter into a long-term campaign in a politically and economically volatile market will find doing business in the region attractive.

In this chapter an effort has been made to analyse what kind of companies may be interested in Eastern Europe, and what they might do to successfully conduct business there. The paper is split into two sections. The first section empirically examines the investment intentions of MNCs, using innovation theory and cross-cultural differences among companies as the underlying concepts. The second section provides practical guidelines to companies interested in entering Eastern Europe.

Corporate Interest in Eastern Europe

Market attractiveness

The collapse of the Eastern bloc economic system was not simply one of the great news stories of 1989; it may prove to have been one of the most important economic developments of the century.[1] The economic and political developments in Eastern Europe have unleashed new opportunities for MNCs; the significance of the events in Eastern Europe is further underscored when viewed in the context of the precursive role they played in the demise of communism in the USSR. Long held back by an economic system that guaranteed a job and the necessities of life, but little more, the citizenry of Eastern Europe have engaged in a highly visible effort to establish free market economies. Eastern European nations are eagerly seeking Western capital and technology to improve their domestic economies, the eventual hope being that quality improvements and increased competitiveness provided by Western management techniques and resources will enhance the ability of these nations to attract investment capital and export manufactured goods in world markets.[2]

There are fundamental drivers that encourage multinationals to look to Eastern Europe for trade and investment. First, Eastern Europe is a big and relatively prosperous market, with a population of 100 million people that is 70 per cent literate. It is a region of tremendous natural and economic resources. Second, Eastern Europe represents a virtually untapped market for private enterprise. Third, and perhaps most importantly, Eastern European officials recognize and acknowledge the need for an economic transfusion. Since January 1987, more than 10,000 joint ventures between Eastern Europe and foreign businesses have been founded.[3] Moreover, the governments of the world's free market economies are making it easier to do business with the Eastern bloc countries. The United States, for example, has extended 'most favoured nation' trade status to all these countries, except Romania, thereby reducing tariff duties on their goods coming into the United States.

While potential opportunities in Eastern Europe apparently abound, not everyone in the industrialized world is equally sanguine about them. The United States, for instance, is more sceptical than its European allies about the ability of Eastern European nations to maintain, enhance, and sustain their new economic and political perspectives. The US government is concerned about such matters as how much assistance, how much financing, and how much new technology the West should turn over to countries that for forty years were considered a major threat to world peace.[4] On the other hand, the Western European nations and Japan are more optimistic about events in Eastern Europe and are pledging both financial and technical assistance to the development efforts in that region.[5]

As with nations, companies vary in their outlook towards the opportunities in Eastern Europe. General Electric Company, for example, has completed a $150 million contract to acquire a 50 per cent stake in Tungsram, Hungary's state-owned maker of light bulbs. Volkswagen plans to spend $6.1 billion to rebuild the Czech car plant, Skoda, over the next ten years.[6] Yet, many companies are concerned about the conditions in Eastern Europe and are not ready to take the risk of entering these markets.

Hindrances

The differing attitudes of companies toward Eastern Europe is presumably attributable to the numerous obstacles identified through a market opportunity assessment of these nations.[7] Unlike the situation found in the stable industrialized markets, it is not simply a matter of selecting from among a number of alternative market entry strategies. The company venturing into Eastern Europe confronts a variety of difficulties as these nations experience the traumatic shocks of moving from a command-oriented to a market-oriented economy.

These difficulties represent barriers to the realization of market opportunities, since they influence the perception of the investment climate and market potential in the Eastern European countries. Kraljic characterizes these difficulties as 'gaps' that exist between Eastern and Western economies:[8]

1. *Technology gap* – both in 'hardware' (the technical standards of existing plants and the efficiency of their processes) and in 'software' (the rate of improvement in technology and in operating efficiency).
2. *Productivity gap* – estimated to be at least 30–50 per cent below Western levels.
3. *Marketing gap* – concepts of markets and consumers and their central importance to business decisions are largely unknown; goods are distributed, not marketed.
4. *Capital gap* – profitability and investment capability of their enterprises are much lower than in the West.
5. *Environment gap* – in contrast to the growing environmental consciousness in the West, the catastrophic pollution in Eastern Europe has so far received only limited attention.
6. *Infrastructure gap* – most of these countries are weak in road, rail, and air transportation networks and in communication networks and services.
7. *Motivation gap* – years of 'equalizing' the working population has discouraged private initiative and willingness to take responsibility, and has led to an erosion of the work ethic.
8. *Management gap* – there is a serious absence of leadership ability and advanced business know-how among managers.
9. *Legislative gap* – constitutional issues and legislative actions have been focused on securing the dominant position of the party and driven by central planning mechanisms, as opposed to relying on serving the needs of constituents.
10. *Democratic gap* – all of the gaps aforementioned have been made worse for decades by the suppression of a democratic mindset caused by the Communist Party's dominance and claim to sole leadership.

Although there are country-specific variations, the weaknesses that Eastern Europe shows are essentially systemic and result not from specific choices or actions, but from long entrenched patterns of social, economic and political dynamics.

The dynamic challenges of Eastern Europe have been chronicled from a variety of perspectives. A large body of research has emerged that falls within the descriptive purview of comparative economic analysis. More specifically, studies focusing on this region have analysed such market opportunity assessment factors as political stability, economic development, infrastructure, market and cultural conditions. Countries have been profiled in depth on these factors and compared to one another, as well as to their Western European counterparts. These comparative market opportunity profiles have then been linked to either a number of generic management strategies or to strategies developed in a specific case context. These approaches provide valuable insights for multinational strategists exploring new market opportunities,[9] and for public policy-makers attempting to attract foreign investment. However, one perspective that has not been empirically explored concerns the perceptions of multinational strategists of the market opportunity factors underlying the viability of investments in Eastern Europe: it would be interesting to know how this region is viewed by multinational decision-makers from different parts of the world. The research described here attempts to assess the perceptions of Eastern Europe market opportunity factors held by the top executives of multinational corporations headquartered in North America, Europe and Japan.

Our research on Eastern Europe shows that MNCs' interest in Eastern Europe is significantly determined by two corporate factors: their innovativeness and culture. More innovative firms, as opposed to their less innovative counterparts, are more receptive to capitalizing on opportunities in Eastern Europe. Similarly, companies affiliated to certain regions may show greater interest in Eastern Europe than others, due to different cultural influences. Research on these two determinants of investment propensity is reviewed below.

More innovative versus less innovative firms

Innovation is a widely used concept and has been defined in a variety of ways to reflect the particular requirements and characteristics of a specific study. For example, Zaltman, Duncan and Holbeck (1973) define innovation as any idea, practice or object which is perceived as 'new' by a person, organization or group that might potentially adopt it.[10] Organizations essentially engage in innovative behaviour in order to cope with environmental changes. Innovative coping strategies include the application of new technology, entry into new markets, or administrative changes that facilitate organizational goal realization.[11]

It is posited here that a positive response to environmental changes – i.e. the emerging market opportunities in Eastern Europe – falls within the conceptual framework of innovative administrative behaviour. This conceptualization is similar to that utilized by Lee and Brasch (1976) in their research on the adoption of exporting as an innovation strategy.[12] An innovation perspective is also found in the work of Aharoni[13] who referenced the research of Burns and Stalker,[14] and Carter and Williams[15] in his treatise on foreign investment decision processes.

Using data (consisting of 128 completed responses) from a joint research project undertaken by Booz Allen & Hamilton, Inc., Nihon Keizai Shimbun and the *Wall Street Journal*, Tucker, Jain and Failer found significant differences between more and less innovative firms in their planned investment into Eastern Europe.[16] They measured innovativeness based on two variables: organizational attributes, and innovation attributes. The organizational attributes comprised size (measured by sales revenue and number of employees), profitability (measured by return on assets), centralization vs. decentralization (measured in terms of an MNC's propensity to 'consolidate/reduce/centralize' or 'add/decentralize' as a part of its globalization process), and organizational commitment to internationalization (measured by the percentage of sales derived from the domestic business).

The innovation attributes included performance uncertainty (degree of resistance to entering Eastern Europe because of the uncertainty of obtaining positive results), negative consequences (degree of resistance to entering Eastern Europe because of the perceived downside risk), complexity (referring to perceived difficulties in entering Eastern Europe), compatibility (organizational resistance to entering Eastern Europe due to incompatibility with current policies), modification (perceived difficulty in modifying an organization's operational capabilities to enter Eastern Europe). These innovation attributes were incorporated into a 'deterrent' index explaining the propensity of organizations to be innovative. Firms with significantly smaller deterrent indices were hypothesized to be more likely to enter Eastern Europe than those with higher indices. In summary, innovative behaviour – i.e., entry into Eastern Europe, is influenced by both organizational and innovation attributes.

Using innovativeness as the underlying factor for identifying companies interested in Eastern Europe, policy-makers in these nations can take appropriate measures to stimulate their interest in opportunities in the area. For example, US and host government agencies can identify innovative firms and provide them with incentives for making investments in Eastern Europe. Moreover, the deterrents that prevent MNCs from considering investments in Eastern Europe are in many cases more perceived than real. The Eastern European governments can take steps to mollify the apprehensions that foreign companies have about investing in their countries. They can prioritize the kind of information they should provide or the kind of promotional campaign that they might sponsor to dispel misconceptions among the potential investors.

Cross-cultural management styles

There exist among companies striking and significant differences of style which affect their operations.[17] Such differences, among other factors, are based on cultural characteristics of the society in which the company is headquartered.[18] For example, it has often been said that culturally Japanese companies look to the long term, while American companies are more interested in short-term results.[19] Whitehill noted that Asian and European managers consistently prefer to attach more weight to the exercising of authority. American managers, on the other hand, have a deep and constant need to be liked, and above all want to be friendly.[20] While American firms score high on the use of return on investment (ROI), portfolio and management consultants, Europeans score moderate, and the Japanese score very low in the use of all these concepts.[21] A number of studies shed light on cross-cultural managerial differences in such diverse areas as values, attitudes and decision-making.[22] Arnold notes that the cultural background of a firm has a tremendous impact on organizational behaviour which, in turn, affects its process of globalization.[23] The implication is that, influenced by their culture, companies from different parts of the globe will show different levels of interest in making investments in Eastern Europe.

Analysis of Booz Allen & Hamilton data, mentioned above, showed significant differences in a number of factors *vis-à-vis* Eastern Europe among companies from North America, Western Europe, and Japan. The significance of culture is attested to by the fact that while multinationals did not differ significantly in their assessment of opportunities in Eastern Europe, companies from Europe showed greater interest in the region. Almost two-thirds of the European companies indicated plans for making investments in Eastern Europe, compared to 35 per cent of the North American companies, and only 8 per cent of the companies from Japan. Similarly, European companies were more optimistic about opportunities in Eastern Europe than either the North Americans or Japanese. Only 47 per cent of European respondents perceived any new problems emerging in Eastern Europe, but as many as 87 per cent of Japanese and 67 per cent of US executives foresaw such a possibility.

Interestingly, companies from different parts of the world varied little in their perceptions of the investment barriers in Eastern Europe. Of the nine barriers noted in Table 21.1, MNCs from North America, Europe and Japan differed significantly only on three – financing, extraction of hard currency, and availability of reliable suppliers. Yet, as noted above, European companies have shown greater interest in Eastern Europe than their counterparts in North America and Japan. The Eastern European perspectives of the European MNCs can most likely be attributed to their cultural closeness to Eastern Europe. However, in several cases European respondents were more sensitive to barriers than companies elsewhere. For example, 45 per cent of European companies considered adequacy of management resources as a barrier, but only 32 per cent of North American and 23 per cent of Japanese firms found it a barrier. Despite that, European companies, dictated by cultural affinity, find opportunities in Eastern Europe worth pursuing. Presumably, the European firms believe they can effectively overcome the barriers that lie in the path of realizing these opportunities. Interestingly, Japanese MNCs tend to discount the effect of these barriers, yet exhibit the lowest level of investment intentions among the three MNC groups.

Conclusion

Investment in Eastern Europe is a long-term process that will test the creativity and staying power of corporations and governments from Western Europe, Japan and North America. Now that the initial euphoria over economic and political reform has run its course, the scale of the challenge ahead is coming into clearer focus. While the scope of future business opportunities in Eastern Europe justifies MNCs' attention, they will prudently weigh the consequences before moving in.

By any standard, major investment in these countries carries high levels of risk. However, a key factor is the high level of education of the population, well developed technical skills, and a great desire for Western products and lifestyles. If this wellspring of talent and aptitude can be supplied with needed equipment, materials, and management expertise, then over the long term there is reason to believe that healthy profitable business can be sustained.

Companies in Europe are likely to be much more adept at taking advantage of opportunities in Eastern Europe than Japanese and Americans. This may be attributed to the cultural closeness that Europeans maintain with Eastern Europe. Further, companies willing to postpone returns from operations in Eastern Europe for several years are more likely to venture into the region. The operative phrase is 'long-term'. Eastern Europe ventures demand commitment, patience and flexibility.

Table 21.1: MNCs' perceptions of barriers to entry in Eastern Europe.

MNC headquarters	Financing[a] Hard currency[a]	Government legislation	Political instability	Barriers Management resources	Distribution network	Energy and communications	Reliable suppliers[a]	Intermediate goods
North America	30% 47%	35%	21%	32%	24%	16%	10%	6%
Europe	28% 42%	36%	36%	45%	22%	13%	16%	11%
Japan	6% 24%	22%	38%	23%	14%	8%	2%	5%

[a] Differences are significant at the 0.0001, 0.0067, and 0.0132 level, respectively.

Strategic Guidelines

Entry strategy

There are three generic entry strategies for conducting business with Eastern Europe.[24] These are (1) making it here and selling it there; (2) making it there and selling it there; and (3) making it there and selling it here (see Table 21.2).

Table 21.2: Entry strategy alternatives in Eastern Europe.

Manufacturing location	Markets	
	West	East
West		Make it here and sell it there
East	Make it there and sell it there	Make it there and sell it here

Making it here and selling it there

Manufacturing goods in the West and selling them in Eastern Europe is a trading opportunity. This strategy makes sense, since Eastern European consumers are hungry for Western consumer goods. In addition, there is tremendous demand for modern industrial technology and the sophisticated capital equipment needed to transform the inefficient and unproductive industries in the region. However, in the short run, this type of opportunity is limited by three factors: size of the market, lack of wealth, and lack of hard currency.

Individually, the nations of Eastern Europe are quite small. Poland, the largest country in the region, is only slightly larger than the combined economies of the New England states. Czechoslovakia is about the same size as the Netherlands, and Hungary is smaller than Belgium and Taiwan. While it is true that currently their industrial and consumer markets are still quite small, they have the potential to grow. The second factor that limits trading opportunities is the lack of wealth. First, in terms of GNP per capita, the gap in wealth between, on the one hand, Western nations and Japan, and on the other hand, the nations of Eastern Europe, is significant, and it is widening because of the growth rate differentials. Second, the average industrial wage paid in these countries is quite low. This adversely affects the purchasing power. The third factor is the lack of hard currency, which limits the market potential for industrial products.

Attempts to overcome this problem have not yet met with great success. For example, barter is complicated, time-consuming and costly. Moreover, goods which are readily marketable in the West are normally sold directly by the producing enterprise or their foreign trade organization. The technique, used by some Western companies which have set up retail operations in Eastern Europe, of offering products for sale in local currency some days and in hard currency on others has backfired on those who have tried it. The consortium approach tried by some did not work, either.[25] The trade consortia (for example, American Trade Consortium) were set up in part to share hard currency earnings among the members. But this approach had two problems: one partner subsidizes another, and one partner's return may depend on another partner's performance.

Making it there and selling it there

In Eastern Europe, opportunities to pursue this strategy are limited for two reasons examined above: general lack of wealth and the problem of currency convertibility. It can be argued that for this strategy, the currency convertibility issue may not be of immediate concern if two conditions can be met. First, if there is cause to believe that one day the cash flows earned in local currency will be convertible, and second, if there are attractive opportunities to re-invest local currency cash flows in the interim period. As long as these two conditions are in doubt, it makes no sense to invest hard currency to earn paper money.

Making it there and selling it here

Perhaps this strategy offers the best opportunity for Western businessmen to participate in these economies in any meaningful way. Making goods in these countries which can be exported to the West, particularly Western Europe, is the key not only to earning a real profit on one's investment, but also in creating wealth in the Eastern European economies. Simply put, in the short run, the best opportunity for Eastern European nations and multinational corporations is to help these nations in making things which can be sold in industrialized countries. For many companies, facilities for component or product manufacturing in Eastern Europe could become an important element in their global competitive strategy.[26] The key to evaluating the potential represented by this type of opportunity will be found in understanding what type of products can be sourced competitively from these countries.

If investment in export-oriented ventures is the major short-term opportunity open to Western business people, they should be careful, because many of the rules of thumb one would apply to investing in the West do not apply with equal strength in Eastern Europe. Essentially, there are four pitfalls which MNCs may encounter in Eastern Europe.[27]

1. *Investing to supply pockets of pent-up demand* Investing in market segments where demand and growth in demand are strong makes good sense in most situations. In economies moving away from central planning, however, the logic may not hold up. Market pricing mechanisms work efficiently only when there is over-capacity. There are very few sectors of these economies where conditions of over-capacity exist. Not considering imports, investment in new capacity will be required to fill the gap between demand and capacity. The bigger the gap, the longer it may take. In the mean time, governments will be pressured to control prices (and hence, profit potential) in these sectors. If MNCs compete best in situations where rational pricing prevails, they might want to look first for sectors in which the time to 'over-capacity' is not too far in the future.

2. *Investing in projects where the only source of competitive advantage is low-cost labour*

Many Western business people will be convinced to invest in Eastern European manufacturing solely on the basis of low labour costs. While the lack of wealth may inhibit trade opportunities, the low cost of labour is clearly an advantage for investors in these countries. But companies must be careful of investing where the only competitive advantage is low-cost labour. Labour will not be low-cost forever, and the speed with which the value and, hence, cost of labour will rise could be extraordinary.

3. *Building a plant designed for 'low-cost labour' in Eastern Europe*   When investing in this low labour-cost area, companies need to be careful how they design the plant. The technology and capital-to-labour ratios used in plants which a company might situate in Sri Lanka or Indonesia are probably not appropriate for Eastern Europe. The likely velocity of real wage increases and their ultimate equilibrium point seem to argue that Eastern European plants should not be all that different from facilities one would design for Western European wage and labour productivity levels.

4. *Investing in sectors which will not survive in the long run*   Companies must be careful to invest in sectors of these economies which will survive the shake-out which will come in the long term. While it would seem obvious to an economist, individual business people may not fully appreciate that sectors of these economies will ultimately disappear. One of the reasons these countries have had low overall productivity is that they have been forced to produce too broad a range of goods. As their national wealth begins to build and they are able to trade for goods which can be produced more cheaply abroad, some sectors of their economy will move 'offshore'. The Poles may ultimately buy their shoes from the same countries where Americans buy theirs. That, of course, will be unfortunate for a company which invested ten years' of time and tens of millions of dollars in improving the productivity of a Polish shoe manufacturing joint venture.

Investing in Eastern Europe involves a grand human experiment of both political and economic dimensions. What Western companies are willing to do with their capital and know-how will have considerable impact on how things turn out there. Investing today is the only way we can create trading opportunities tomorrow. There are both economic and political rationalizations for this statement. Lest they underestimate the seriousness of the message, companies should remember the success enjoyed by those who have taken the long view in the former Soviet Union. Occidental Petroleum, Fiat and Pepsi have all done well, and will continue to profit from their relationships with the country. They were there long before it was thought fashionable, or even possible, to do deals in the USSR. And, so while the American business community needs to be careful and they need to do their homework well, they also need to be encouraged to get moving, lest they lose the opportunity to the Europeans and Japanese.

Country-by-country differences

Not all Eastern European countries offer the same opportunity for export-oriented investments. Many factors will determine which country is best for what kind of industry. In addition, conditions change from one time period to another. Basically, the country selection should be based on the following factors.[28]

1. Investment opportunity available in the country – both the quantity and quality of the opportunities.
2. Foreign government's attitude toward Western investment – the flexibility of a nation's laws and the government's overall encouragement of direct foreign investment.
3. Investment practices, including repatriation of profits – investment protection provided by the foreign government and how easily profits can be removed.
4. Capability of the labour force. 'Cheap' labour is available in all the countries in the region, but how well individuals work in these countries is a more telling factor.
5. General economic prospects – will a country's poor economic performance adversely affect a Westerner's investment?

Below is a partial list of potential areas for investment in different countries. Sectors like consumer goods production are priorities in every country in the region.[29]

- *Hungary* Telecommunications, commercial and residential real estate, transportation, pharmaceuticals, and computer hardware and software.
- *Czechoslovakia* Tourism, vehicles, food storage facilities, textiles, chemicals, and polymer.
- *Poland* Food processing (particularly meat), small agricultural machinery, medical equipment, medicine, chemicals, polymer, energy (pumps for crude oil), textiles, steel.
- *Bulgaria* Consumer goods, electronics, machine-building, biotechnology, energy, pollution control technology, minerals, metallurgy.
- *Romania* Energy, chemicals, textiles, agricultural equipment, medical infrastructure, furniture, heavy machinery, food processing, agriculture (in general), and tourism.

In conclusion, the following are the suggestions for getting started in Eastern Europe.

- Understand the nature of the opportunities you seek. Be realistic as to the size and timing of the opportunity.
- Rather than looking for opportunities, seek to create them.
- Understand the strategic significance of these opportunities for you and your competitors.
- Know what you want to do before you pick a partner.
- Do not rely on your partner to be totally objective in evaluating the requirements for the venture's success.
- Do not be inhibited by current instability and uncertainty. In the short term, use 'options' to limit your downside.

The framework, logic and thought process one would use investing in the West may not fully apply in Eastern Europe.[30] It is important for interested companies to first think through the situations where they are uniquely able to add value, and then to attempt to create the opportunity, rather than merely respond to one uncovered. Business people need to know what the opportunity to invest in Eastern Europe means to their competitors. Presumably, the rush by the automotive companies to invest in Eastern Europe stems from the realization that there are a limited number of good deals to be done and that those who are first will be advantaged. Such a perspective could lead a firm into bad investment. Furthermore companies should first know what they want to do before picking a partner. A large number of companies sign letters of intent first and then do feasibility studies. This is like putting the cart before the horse. This is one of the reasons why many deals in these nations have not proceeded beyond the company registration stage.

At the same time, a Western company cannot rely on the local partner to be driven by the same motivations that it has. For the partner there is little downside, since so far no one in these countries has been rewarded or punished for taking economic risk. Finally, in Eastern Europe today the risk to investment is very high relative to the returns one seems likely to earn in the short term. There are ways to manage this risk and to reduce the magnitude of the potential loss while retaining the potential for gain. Companies should view the investment process as a series of 'options' purchases, where at each stage they invest in the opportunity to take the next step.[31] With each 'option' a company buys, it acquires more time and information, and with adequate information the level of risk may be reduced.

Notes

1. Sasseen, J. (1989) 'Breaking the Frontiers of Eastern Europe', *International Management* March: 18–22.
2. Quelch, J., Joachimsthaler, E. and Nueno, J. L. (1991) After the Wall: Marketing Guidelines for Eastern Europe', *Sloan Management Review* Winter: 24–31.
3. 'Eastward Ho! The Pioneers Plunge In', *Business Week* April 15, 1991: 51.
4. *Idem.*
5. Cutts, R. L. (1991) 'Eastern Europe's Troubles Open Door for Japanese Expansion', *California Management Review* Spring: 58–68.
6. Tully, S. (1990) 'G.E. in Hungary: Let There Be Light', *Fortune* October 22: 137.
7. Stertz, B. and Roth, R. (1990) 'To Western Industry Eastern Bloc Auto Market Is Losing Some Luster', *The Wall Street Journal* November 14: 1.
8. Kraljic, A. P. (1990) 'The Economic Gap Separating East and West', *Columbia Journal of World Business* Winter: 14–19.
9. One such approach is discussed in the second section of this paper.
10. Zaltman, G., Duncan, R. and Holbeck, J. (1973) *Innovations and Organizations*, New York: John Wiley & Sons.
11. Capon, N. and Glazer, R. (1987) 'Marketing and Technology: A Strategic Coalignment', *Journal of Marketing* July: 1–14.
12. Lee, W-Y. and Brasch, J. J. (1976) 'The Adoption of Exports as an Innovation Strategy', *Journal of International Business Studies* Spring–Summer: 85–93.
13. Aharoni, Y. (1966) *The Foreign Investment Decision Process*, Boston, Mass.: Harvard Business School.
14. Burns, T. and Stalker, G. M. (1961) *The Management of Innovations*, Chicago, Il.: Quadrangle Books.
15. Carter, C. and Williams, B. (1959) 'The Characteristics of Technically Progressive Firms', *Journal of Industrial Economics* March: 87–104.
16. Tucker, L. R., Jain, S. C. and Failer, B. (1994) 'MNC Market Opportunity Analysis of

Eastern Europe: An Innovation Perspective', forthcoming in *Journal of EuroMarketing* (1/2).

17. See Uttal, B. (1983) 'The Corporate Culture Vultures', *Fortune* October 17: 66.
18. Campbell, N. C. G., Graham, J. L., Jolibert, A. and Meissner, H. G. (1988) 'Marketing Negotiation in France, Germany, the United Kingdom and the United States', *Journal of Marketing* April: 49–62.
19. Wilcox, J. (1990) 'East/West Culture Clash', *Training and Development Journal* June: 1–12. See also 'Japanese Corporate Culture', *The Economist* August 25, 1990: 58.
20. Whitehill, A. (1989) 'American Executives Through Foreign Eyes', *Business Horizons* May–June: 42–8.
21. *Idem*.
22. Tse, D. K., Lee, K-H., Vertinsky, I. and Wehrung, D. A. (1988) 'Does Culture Matter? A Cross-Cultural Study of Executives' Choice, Decisiveness, and Risk Adjustment in International Marketing', *Journal of Marketing* October: 81–95.
23. Arnold, M. R. (1990) 'European and US Managers: Breaking Down the Wall', *The Journal of Business Strategy* July/August: 28–31.
24. Morais, R. C. (1990) 'Forward to the Past' *Forbes* May 28: 86–96.
25. Elicker, P. (1990) 'Privatization in Eastern Europe: What the Potential Foreign Investor Needs to Know', *Business Economics* October: 17–23.
26. Hertzfeld, J. M. (1991) 'Joint Ventures: Saving the Soviets from Perestroika', *Harvard Business Review* January–February: 80–91.
27. 'Profile: One Company's Business Experience in Poland', *Eastern Europe Business Bulletin* June/July 1991: 2.
28. Kempe, F. (1991) 'East Europe Offers Investors Big Profits and Big Perils', *The Wall Street Journal* January 11: A6.
29. Anderson, S. (1990) 'The Eastern Bloc Investment Report Card', *Bloc* April/May: 10–13.
30. Naor, J. (1990) 'Research on Eastern Europe and Soviet Marketing: Constraints, Challenges and Opportunities', *International Marketing Review* (1): 7–14.
31. Hertzfeld, J. M. (1991) *op. cit.*

22

Synthesis – the Economics of Change in Eastern and Central Europe

Peter J. Buckley and Pervez N. Ghauri

This collection of writings on the economics of change in Eastern and Central Europe has served to focus minds on the difficulties of managing change. Business practitioners require new modes of operation. Academics and analysts require different types of explanation and prediction, and policy-makers need new approaches to create conditions for growth.

An Approach to Change

The papers in this volume make it clear that a structured, long-termist approach to change is essential in Eastern and Central Europe. This approach needs to take account of improvements in infrastructure, in training, in business culture and business methods. The capital requirements necessary to effect change are enormous and the need to find areas of comparative advantage is pressing.

Infrastructure

It is clear that the basic physical infrastructure required for successful development is not in place in much of Eastern and Central Europe. Deficiencies in communications, transport networks, power and water supplies are inhibitors of the basic processes of production and service provision. The capital requirements here are huge and lumpy.

Privatization

The process of privatization in Eastern and Central Europe is crucial to the attainment of a market-based economy. The institutions of private ownership have been peripheral in periods of central planning and state ownership, and now need to be created or revived. However, this is not a straightforward, uncontroversial issue. The speed at which privatization is to take place, its organization (by auction, or by giving away the assets, or by issuing vouchers to citizens), post-privatization management and the competitive structure which is to be attained are all controversial issues (see Bolton and Roland (1992) and discussion). Moreover, as Carlin and Mayer (1992) argue, there are widespread imperfections in the market for corporate control in post-centrally planned economies. Transfer of ownership may be ineffective in improving performance, because those individuals currently endowed with wealth may not be best qualified to manage the resources in the future. There is a case for government restructuring before sale, and for interference in the selling itself, in the presence of widespread market failure. Unfortunately, many governments in the region have lost the belief that they can adequately manage their economies and have lost the trust of their citizens.

Training

Training requirements are of great urgency for both management and workers.

Management training is of vital importance in achieving successful change. East and Central Europe suffers from a profound shortage of managers who can take decisions in a decentralized, price-driven economy. Managers in the former Soviet Union are unused to dealing with prices other than those given as fiats by a higher authority. As all property was state-owned, managers have not been required to concern themselves with the value of factory assets (Hill 1992). Little or no attention has been paid to management development in East and Central Europe, and much previous training has been outdated by events. In Chapter 2, Casson pointed out the difficulties of transplanting off-the-shelf solutions from Western economies, and selectivity among Western management development models is crucial. But who is to do the selecting?

The responsibility for worker training is, by default, falling upon the enterprises which employ the workers. Foreign firms in particular are seen as exemplars and implementers of training schemes. However, training represents both an up-front cost of entry and a continuing burden on the enterprise. Much of the cost involves unlearning of previous practice by workers. If productivity is to be raised and real wages with it, training represents an essential plank in any scheme of revitalization.

Business culture

The people of Eastern and Central Europe have been faced with a massive discontinuity. The protective cultures which they have evolved are based on continuity. Major, long-term disruptions can therefore be predicted in socioeconomic and political structures. The chief concern of this volume has been economic change, and it is clear that major discontinuities will occur in the future role of the firm in society.

In the former Soviet Union in particular, the worker had a high degree of dependence on the firm which employed him. Access to consumer goods and even housing was through the firm. Loss of employment therefore meant loss of access to these services and often to health and recreational facilities. The assumption of these non-direct activities by other bodies, notably the new republics, will be extremely difficult, not least because of the expense. Social disruption is bound to follow.

Firms under former regimes were also excessively vertically integrated. The move from such an industrial base to a less vertically integrated structure linking externalized facilities by markets and contracts represents a profound change in structure and in attitudes. The old, heavily vertically integrated structure was a reaction to risk. As suppliers were unreliable, or non-existent, the risk-reducing alternative was to perform all feasible operations in house. The response to such a change must involve the creation (or in some cases revival) of business networks. Crucial elements in successful business networks are beliefs in the market mechanism and in reciprocity in business relationships. Fundamental to both is trust between individuals. Such a culture cannot be built overnight – it depends on repeated reinforcing interactions (Casson 1991).

A further profound change is the requirement to legitimize entrepreneurial activity. It is vital to recovery that individuals are empowered to take decisions and to change the way the economy works. However, early experiences in moving to market systems are often discouraging. The apparent success of 'get rich quick' merchants, black marketeers and formerly marginalized individuals is discouraging for solid citizens. The activities of new entrepreneurs in shady (if not illicit) areas of the economy are dispiriting for those trying to create a spirit of enterprise. This may be a phase through which liberalizing economies must pass, but it is unpleasant and may provoke hostile and damaging (if understandable) reactions. The problem of how to encourage entrepreneurship while discouraging shady profiteering is a major policy issue.

Respect for the customer is generally lacking in the societies under discussion. The emergence from a society where producer interests were paramount to a more consumer-orientated society requires new priorities. Vestiges of the barter system remain. Many companies in the CIS have no service data, after-sales services are non-existent, and there are no data on how products actually perform in practice (Hill 1992).

Capital Requirements

Restructuring the economies of Eastern and Central Europe requires vast amounts of capital. Domestic savings have been eroded by inflation and by lack of suitable savings instruments – hoarding has often been the order of the day. Germany is only gradually discovering the immense cost of restructuring and upgrading the economy of the former GDR, one of the most 'successful' former socialist states. Difficulties in raising domestic capital thus arise from the twofold bind of an unwillingness to lend and a low taxable surplus from earnings. This creates a vicious circle, for without investment in infrastructure, training and institution-building, market reforms cannot hope to work. Foreign capital requirements are thus enormous. However, there is a marked reluctance of capitalist companies to commit scarce investment funds to the former Eastern bloc because of their evaluation of the risks. Many companies are holding off, following a 'wait and see' policy. There are worrying signs that many foreign joint venture partners are waiting for company values to fall before committing themselves to buying into or taking over their partners or other related companies. Foreign capital is not just desired for its own sake. In the form of foreign direct investment it brings with it a package of resources – not only capital but also technology, management, skills and the hope that it will transfer cultural values of entrepreneurship, risk-taking and the work ethic.

A dual strategy could thus be envisaged with public funding (aid) being used to revitalize infrastructure, institution building and training, while foreign direct investment creates new private opportunities. The evidence so far is that both these flows are well below expectations and are likely to continue to be so.

The Search for Comparative Advantage

In order to generate incomes and to achieve growth, the economies of Eastern and Central Europe have to find a niche, or a set of niches, in world markets. This search for comparative advantage will not be easy and it may not be rapid. In many cases there has been an erosion of an uncompetitive industrial base because of the exigencies of cost reduction. Defence-linked research may have provided some niches for the CIS, but linkages with non-defence outlets are virtually non-existent. The Cocom ban on computers, visual display units and other high technology inputs has destroyed CAD and CAM systems. Little or no R&D activity is being undertaken across whole swathes of the economy.

Some temporary relief has been obtained by some countries in unloading stock on to less developed countries. However, the necessity is to penetrate the advanced countries and to earn hard currency. A basic difficulty here is that of addressing aspects of the marketing mix other than price – most notably quality. Many goods are cheaper in Eastern and Central Europe than in the EC, but the quality is not comparable. Agricultural produce, for instance is not of the quality required by sophisticated consumers. Protectionist barriers are also a great hurdle in the areas where low cost may be a factor – basic foodstuffs, textiles, commodity metals. Distribution issues pose a further problem; physical distribution is inadequate and the sophisticated networks necessary to place a product in an advanced market are not available.

Protectionism

The problems of East and Central Europe are taking place against a widespread, deep and prolonged recession in Western economies. In such circumstances, the danger of protectionism is always present. While the West has not sunk into all-out beggar-my-neighbour protectionist policies, many nations are unwilling to allow the sphere of free (or freer) trade to expand. The difficulties in completing the Uruguay Round of GATT negotiations are evidence of this tendency. Access to

Western markets is a primary condition for the success of emergency economies; this access is only grudgingly granted. It is clear that much of the output of Central and Eastern Europe is not of the quality, reliability or general acceptability required in sophisticated consumer markets. This is one further reason why foreign direct investment from Western countries is so much desired by host nations – it provides access to distribution channels in the advanced countries. 'Trade not aid' is an inappropriate slogan for East and Central Europe, but 'aid with trade' is crucial.

A further unfortunate aspect of the creation of so many new states in East and Central Europe – from the debris of the Soviet Union and Yugoslavia, and from the separation of Czech and Slovak lands – is the need to nation-build. Nation-building includes gaining control over the domestic economy. This means expulsion of non-nationals however defined, often brutally, and it often means protectionism. This had led to the fragmentation of markets, the separation of industries from their hinterlands of supply and former outlets, and to the creation of new bureaucracies. Thus the Baltic states miss out on being seen as a gateway to Russia, economies of scale are lost and access to large, unified markets is denied. This represents a new barrier to growth and a further disincentive to inward foreign investment.

The Environment

The extent of the damage to the environment wrought by the former regimes in East and Central Europe is only now beginning to be appreciated. This environmental damage is not an 'add on' cost of regenerating the economies, it is a root problem. The costs of operating to anything approaching Western norms are massive, and this makes take-overs of existing plants prohibitively expensive. In effect much of the fixed assets in place must be written off. Restructuring existing enterprise is often a more expensive proposition than starting anew. There is a further disincentive effect with particular impact on inward investment. This is the cost of persuading executives and advisers from the West to reside, albeit temporarily, in degraded environments. This, at the very least, raises the costs to the host country of attracting skilled managers from abroad.

Long-run damage is also being inflicted on local residents from environmental pollution. Many areas are effectively no-go regions for investors, tourists or anyone mobile with any choice in the matter. Clean-up costs are often prohibitive, even in the medium term. Thus resources are wasted.

Conclusion

Eastern and Central European economies are caught in a vicious circle of low productivity, inadequate investment, inferior institutions, declining markets and political dangers. Citizens of these countries are naturally impatient for change. There are no quick and easy solutions, but time is pressing. The danger of military coups, authoritarian regimes and incipient fascism provide powerful arguments for quick fixes. The market solution seems to rest on real wages being allowed for (or being forced to) find a lower equilibrium level. The political pressure to inflate is strong, but such pressure has a deleterious effect on workers' motivation, a key to increasing productivity.

The creation of new institutions is a long and difficult process, particularly if the models of the past are inadequate. External aid in all its forms seems tiny in relation to the need to buy time until stable, consensual institutions are in place. Despite the need for a long-termist approach, short-term palliatives are vital if East and Central Europe is not to fall into an abyss of chaos.

References

Bolton, P. and Roland, G. (1992) 'Privatization Policies in Central and Eastern Europe', *Economic Policy* 15, October: 275–303 (followed by a discussion).
Carlin, W. and Mayer, C. (1992) 'Restructuring Enterprises in Eastern Europe', *Economic Policy* 15, October: 311–46 (followed by a discussion).
Casson, M. (1991) *The Economics of Business Culture*, Oxford: Clarendon Press.
Hill, M. R. (1992) 'Management in the Commonwealth of Independent States', paper given to British Academy of Management Conference, Bradford, September.

Index